Richard Frederick Littledale

The Priest's Prayer Book

With a Brief Pontifical. Sixth Edition

Richard Frederick Littledale

The Priest's Prayer Book
With a Brief Pontifical. Sixth Edition

ISBN/EAN: 9783744747653

Printed in Europe, USA, Canada, Australia, Japan

Cover: Foto ©Lupo / pixelio.de

More available books at **www.hansebooks.com**

THE

PRIEST'S PRAYER BOOK.

WITH

A BRIEF PONTIFICAL.

Sixth Edition, enlarged.

LONDON:

J. MASTERS AND CO., 78, NEW BOND STREET.

MDCCCLXXXIV.

15TH THOUSAND.

LONDON:
PRINTED BY J. MASTERS AND CO.,
ALBION BUILDINGS, BARTHOLOMEW CLOSE, E.C.

PREFACE.

THIS Volume is designed as an Appendix to the Book of Common Prayer, and to provide the parochial Clergy with Offices and Collects for those occasional ministrations for which no formal or authorized provision has been made. Nearly all matter which may be found in the Prayer Book itself has consequently been omitted, but by a simple method of cross references the Officiant is enabled to utilize such portions of the Book of Common Prayer as are available for the case in hand.

The Offices, and particularly those for the Visitation of the Sick, are based on ancient models, and are constructed so as to allow of the greatest plasticity in their use. In structure these forms consist of two parts: one invariable, designed as a framework; the other, changeable within certain limits, to admit of diversity. A rigid and invariable form, even if appropriate, either causes wearisome repetition, or compels the substitution of one that is inappropriate, for the sake of change; and this inconvenience makes itself especially felt when the Priest has to pay constant visits to a single case, or else to many cases of the same type.

As all the Offices of the Sick are identical in construction, an analysis of one of them will serve to indicate the method of using each of the others. That for a Blind Person (p. 64) is selected because of its necessarily special character, which might seem to preclude variety of treatment, and either to enforce the use of a stereotyped formula, or else to require the substitution of matter having but little direct bearing on the case.

It begins with the Invocation of the Holy Trinity, the Our FATHER, and the Creed. Then follow three pairs of versicles, the first of which marks the character of the whole Office as especially suitable for the Blind. "℣. Thou also shalt light my candle. ℟. The LORD my GOD shall make my darkness to be light." The same idea is contained in the Antiphon, which strikes the key-note, and indicates the spirit in which the Psalms which follow are to be understood. This Antiphon is, "I believe verily to see the goodness of the LORD." Four Psalms are then given; any one or more of which may be used, and each of which has some special reference suitable to the Blind. Thus Ps. 17 in the 3rd verse says, "Thou hast proved and visited my heart in the night-season." In the 5th verse, "O hold Thou up my goings in Thy paths, that my footsteps slip not." And in the 16th verse, "But as for me, I will behold Thy presence in righteousness, and when I awake up after Thy likeness I shall be satisfied with it." The other Psalms, upon examination, will be found to be similarly appropriate. At the close of the Psalms the Antiphon in its fuller form is repeated, and thus serves to fix in the mind of the Patient the special meaning which the Psalms should have for *him*. Next comes the Scripture Reading, selected upon the same principle. In brackets, at the close of each Reading, are references to several other Scriptures which may be substituted for it, first from the Epistles and Gospels in the Book of Common Prayer, and then from an Appendix of Readings in the Priest's Prayer Book itself. Thus the Epistle for S. Stephen's Day speaks of the foretaste of the Beatific Vision as granted to the martyr in his time of trial: that for the 3rd Sunday in Lent teaches that Christians are "children of light;" the Gospel for Quinquagesima Sunday records the miracle of healing the blind, and so of the others. When the Lection is ended, the Officiant says, "But Thou, O LORD, have mercy upon us," to which answer is made, "Thanks be to GOD," and then follow versicles intended to bring home the full teaching of the Lection to the mind of the sufferer, and to point its special application to his own case. Thus the first pair runs, "℣. Thine eyes shall see the King in His beauty. ℟. They shall behold the land that is very far off." Then come the Gloria and its response, followed by another pair of versicles running thus: "℣. Blessed are the pure in heart. ℟. For they shall see GOD." With this the hortatory and didactic portion of the Office closes, and it is followed by the precatory part, beginning with—"℣. The LORD be with you. ℟. And with thy spirit." Next in order come the Kyrie and the Our FATHER, to which is subjoined a group of appropriate versicles from the Psalms, in which petitions for light, guidance, and protection are offered up. At the close of these Versicles comes a Collect. Bracketed after this are references to suitable Collects in the Common Prayer Book, and also to others in the Priest's Prayer Book, denoted by black numerals, any of which may be added to or substituted for the one given in the Office. The entire Service closes with an appropriate Benediction. It will be seen that while the fixed portion of the Office prevents any departure from the spirit which pervades it, yet that great diversity is obtainable in the moveable portions. Thus the Psalm can be varied in four ways; the Chapter in ten; the Collect in five: so allowing in this, one of the least changeable of the forms given, $4 \times 10 \times 5 = 200$ different combinations. Some of the other Offices can be varied more than ten times as often, and still further variety can be obtained by the employment of one or more Hymns, which may either be used as independent Lections, or be incorporated in the Office. In the latter case, the Hymn should be inserted either just before the Antiphon to the Psalms, or just after the Responses to the Scripture Reading.

Versicles and Responses have been largely employed, instead of a mere unbroken sequence of Psalms and Collects: (1) Because the Church never contemplates the use of an Office, however private, in which the people have no audible part: (2) Because a more fervent and ejaculatory character is thus given to the service: (3) Because they serve to keep the specific character of each Office unchanged, however much its variable portions may be shifted.

Where there is no person present able to make the Responses, the Officiant should recite them together with his own part, exactly as in the private recitation of Matins and Evensong.

It is unnecessary to speak in detail of the other portions of the volume. It may, however, be well to remark that, although some of the Benedictions are properly Episcopal, they are so as a matter of order, and not of essential right, and therefore may be pronounced by a Priest, when the ministration of a Bishop cannot be obtained.

It will be perceived, even upon a cursory examination, that the object of the Priest's Prayer Book is not to supersede the use of the Book of Common Prayer, but to be merely ancillary and subordinate to it, and by Tables and References to assist the Clergy in applying to their more private parochial ministrations the materials already provided for their use in the public ordinances of the Church.

For the sake of brevity, the full Collect endings have not been given in the text, but catch-words have always been introduced, to indicate the proper form with which each Collect should conclude. In reciting its termination, it should be carefully observed to Whom the Collect is addressed. The following examples will, it is hoped, be a sufficient guide. The usual catch-words are printed in Roman type, the words to be added by the Officiant are annexed in italics, though some slight modifications are occasionally required.

Through (the same) *Jesus Christ our Lord.*

Who liveth *and reigneth with Thee and the Holy Ghost, One God, world without end.*

Who with Thee *and the Holy Ghost, liveth and reigneth, ever One God, world without end.*

. Who livest *and reignest with the Father and the Holy Ghost, One God, world without end.*

Where Thou, with the FATHER, *and the Holy Ghost, livest and reignest One God, world without end.*

Where, with the FATHER and the SON, Thou livest *and reignest ever One God, world without end.*

Through Thy mercy, *O our God, Who art blessed, and livest and reignest for ever and ever.*

Grant this for the sake *of Jesus Christ, Thy Son, our Lord.*

NOTE TO THE FOURTH EDITION.

This fresh issue of the Priest's Prayer Book has been thoroughly revised and widely expanded, in accordance with much valuable counsel given to the Editors, and with the increasing needs of the Church in the present day. Many Offices, Collects, and Hymns have been added, and no pains have been spared to bring the work fairly abreast of the requirements of the clergy.

But whereas former revisions of the volume merely aimed at filling up with greater completeness the voids in the private ministrations of the Parish Priest, it has been thought expedient to go somewhat further in this one, and to provide for certain public occasions, for which no authorized formularies exist. The Office for the Burial of Children is the most salient example of the kind.

Two reasons have induced the Editors to adopt this change of plan. On the one hand, the Priest's Prayer Book has obtained a recognized position in many parts of the Anglican Communion where the Act of Uniformity is not binding, and it seems reasonable to provide for such places. On the other, the recent revision of the Lectionary shows that further changes in the Common Prayer Book are by no means distant or improbable, and the new Offices here presented may perhaps serve in some degree to indicate the direction in which an increasing number of practical men, both amongst the Clergy and Laity, are desiring addition and improvement in our authorized formularies.

By far the most important feature, however, in this Fourth Edition, is the brief Pontifical which has been added for the use of the Episcopate. It has been most carefully drawn up, like the earlier portion, from a great variety of old Service-Books of the Syriac, Greek, French, Spanish, Italian, German, and English Churches, with such modifications, as appear to be called for by the peculiar circumstances of our Communion and time.

There has been, in truth, till the appearance of this purely tentative issue, no provision made amongst us during three centuries for the ministrations of Bishops, except the Ordinal and the Confirmation Office in the Book of Common Prayer, and, outside of it, the meagre and undignified form in general use for the Consecration of Churches and Cemeteries, by no means adequate for its proposed object, and drawn up in an age unfamiliar with liturgical studies.

Some few Offices in this Pontifical are superfluous in England, as, for example, those for the Confirmation and Enthroning of Bishops, as there is a fixed legal form for the one ceremony amongst us, and a traditional use for the other in every Cathedral. But America and the Colonies have no authoritative services for the purpose, and it is hoped that those here given, based on ancient examples, may prove useful.

To the Bishops and theologians who have been good enough to examine and revise the proofs of the Pontifical, and to other Prelates and Divines who in various ways have given their assistance, more particularly in the compilation of the list of theological works which will be found at the close of the Volume, the Editors proffer their sincere and grateful acknowledgments.

The List, though drawn up with much care and after consultation with many learned persons, makes no claim to exhaustiveness either in its categories or in the books classified under each head, but aims at giving in a compendious and eclectic fashion the ablest and most useful books on each subject, without regard to their origin or to the special bias of their authors; and it is hoped that in this wise it will not merely facilitate the studies of individual Clergymen, but will serve in some measure as a guide in the formation of Diocesan Libraries at a distance from England, where bibliographical information is difficult to obtain. It appears at present unavoidably in a somewhat rough and tentative state, but the Editors trust that they may be enabled to present it in an improved and corrected form at some future time.

LONDON, *Feast of the Transfiguration*, 1870.

NOTE TO THE FIFTH EDITION.

In this revised issue of the Priest's Prayer Book the following additions and improvements have been made. The order of the matter has been rearranged to allow of the book being divided, so as to group all the Offices in most frequent demand in the first part; seventy more Collects, twenty more Scripture Readings, Offices for the Installation of Deans and Canons, and for the delegation of a Missionary, have been introduced; a table of Collects, Epistles, Gospels, and Post-Communions for special occasions has been drawn up; and the *Bibliotheca Sacerdotalis* has been doubled in extent, as well as arranged more conveniently for reference, so as to serve better than before its primary object of guiding the choice of books for diocesan libraries in the Colonial Churches.

LONDON, *August*, 1876.

NOTE TO THE SIXTH EDITION.

In the present reissue of the Priest's Prayer Book, besides careful revision in several places, the following additions have been made; Office for Admitting a Server; Benediction of a Parish or Mission Room; Benediction of a Civil Marriage; Benediction of a single Grave; Benediction of an Organ; and Admission of a Deaconess. The *Bibliotheca Sacerdotalis* has been largely expanded, and some further rearrangement of the volume, to admit of its being conveniently divided into two parts, has been adopted.

LONDON, *Conversion of S. Paul*, 1884.

ADMONITIO SUMMI SACERDOTIS CHRISTI JESU,

Piscatores hominum, Sacerdotes Dei,
Præcones veridici, lucernæ diei,
Charitatis radio fulgentes, et spei,
Auribus percipite verba oris Mei.

Vos in sanctuario Mihi deservitis :
Cavete, ne steriles aut inanes sitis,
Si Mecum perpetuo vivere velitis,
Vos vocavi palmites; Ego, vera vitis.

Vos estis Catholicæ Legis protectores,
Sal terræ, lux hominum, ovium pastores,
Muri domus Israel, morum correctores,
Vigiles Ecclesiæ, gentium doctores.

Si Legis protectio cadat, lex labetur;
Si sal evanuerit, in quo salietur ?
Nisi lux appareat, via nescietur :
Et ni pastor vigilet, ovile frangetur.

Vos cœpistis vineam Meam procurare,
Hanc doctrinæ rivulis debetis rigare,
Spinas atque tribulos prorsus extirpare,
Ut radices Fidei possint germinare.

Vos estis in areâ boves triturantes,
Prudenter a paleâ grana separantes ;
Vos habent pro speculo legem igno-
rantes,
Populi qui fragiles sunt et inconstantes :

Quidquid vident Laici vobis displicere,
Dicent procul dubio sibi non licere;
Quidquid vos in opere vident adimplere,
Credunt esse licitum, et culpâ carere.

Cum pastores ovium sitis constituti,
Non estote desides, sicut canes muti ;
Vobis non deficiant latratus arguti;
Lupus rapax invidet ovium saluti.

Grex fidelis triplici modo sustinetur,
Meo sacro Corpore, quo salus augetur ;

Sermonis compendio, quod discrete detur;
Ciboque corporeo, ne periclitetur.

Omnibus tenemini vestris prædicare ;
Sed quid, quibus, qualiter, ubi, quando
     quare,
Debetis sollicite præconsiderare,
Ne quis in officio dicat vos errare.

Spectat ad officium vestræ dignitatis,
Omnibus petentibus Mea dare gratis ;
Ne cujusquam hominum munera pendatis,
Ne cum Giezi pariter lepram incurratis.

Gratis Eucharistiam plebi ministrate,
Gratis et absolvite, gratis baptizate,
Vobis gratis cœlitus data gratis date,
Salutemque omnium sedulo curate.

Vestra conversatio sit religiosa,
Munda conscientia, vita virtuosa,
Regularis habitus, mensque gratiosa :
Nulla vos coinquinet labes criminosa :

Nullus fastus elevet ad id quod non estis,
Gravis in intuitu habitus sit testis;
Nihil vos illaqueet curis inhonestis,
Quibus claves traditæ sunt regni cœlestis.

Estote breviloqui, ne vos ad reatum
Pertrahat loquacitas, nutrix vanitatum :
Verbum quod loquimini, sit abbreviatum :
Nam in multiloquio non deest peccatum.

Estote benevoli, sobrii, prudentes,
Justi, casti, simplices, pii, patientes,
Hospitales, humiles, subditos docentes,
Consolantes miseros, pravos corrigentes.

Nam si sic gesseritis curam pastoralem,
Vereque vixeritis vitam spiritalem,
Postquam exueritis chlamydem carnalem,
IPSE vobis conferam stolam immortalem.

CONTENTS.

Gloria in Excelsis Deo

THE PRIEST'S PRAYER BOOK.

Private Offices.

PRIME.

In the Name of the FATHER, and of the SON, and of the HOLY GHOST. Amen.

Our FATHER, &c.

℣. O LORD, open Thou our lips. ℟. And our mouth shall show forth Thy praise. ℣. O GOD, make speed to save us. ℟. O LORD, make haste to help us. ℣. Glory be to the FATHER, &c. ℟. As it was, &c. Alleluia.

Hymn.

Now that the daylight fills the sky,
We lift our hearts to GOD on high,
That He, in all we do or say,
Would keep us free from harm to-day:

Would guard our hearts and tongues
　from strife:
From anger's din would shield our life:
From all ill sights would turn our eyes:
Would close our ears from vanities.

Would keep our inmost conscience pure:
Our souls from folly would secure:
Would bid us check the pride of sense
With due and holy abstinence.

So we, when this new day is gone,
And night in turn is drawing on,
With conscience by the world unstained,
Shall praise His Name for victory gained.

All laud to GOD the FATHER be;
All laud, Eternal SON, to Thee;
All laud, as is for ever meet,
To GOD the Holy Paraclete. Amen.

Antiphon. I laid me down and slept.

Ps. 54. Save me, O GOD, &c.

119 (1—32.) Blessed are those that are undefiled, &c.

Ant. I laid me down and slept, and rose up again, for the LORD sustained me.

The Chapter. 1 S. John i.

If we walk in the light, as He is in the light, we have fellowship one with another, and the Blood of JESUS CHRIST His SON cleanseth us from all sin.

℣. But Thou, O LORD, have mercy upon us. ℟. Thanks be to GOD. ℣. O CHRIST, SON of the living GOD. ℟. Have mercy upon us. ℣. Thou Who sittest at the right hand of the FATHER. ℟. Have mercy upon us. ℣. Glory, &c. ℟. O CHRIST, SON of the living GOD, have mercy upon us. ℣. O CHRIST, arise, help us. ℟. And deliver us, for Thy Name's sake. ℣. The LORD be with you. ℟. And with thy spirit. ℣. Let us pray.

LORD, have mercy, &c.

Our FATHER, &c. I believe, &c.

℣. Unto Thee have I cried, O LORD. ℟. And early shall my prayer come before Thee. ℣. O let my mouth be filled with Thy praise. ℟. That I may sing of Thy glory and honour all the day long. ℣. LORD, turn Thy Face from my sins. ℟. And put out all my misdeeds. ℣. Make me a clean heart, O GOD. ℟. And renew a right spirit within me. ℣. Cast me not away from Thy presence. Ᵽ. And take not Thy HOLY SPIRIT from me. Ᵽ. O give me the comfort of Thy help again. Ᵽ. And stablish me with Thy free Spirit. Ᵽ. Then shall I teach Thy ways unto the wicked. Ᵽ. And sinners shall be converted unto Thee. Ᵽ. Our help is in the Name of the LORD. Ᵽ. Who hath made heaven and earth.

The Confession.

I confess to GOD the FATHER Almighty, to His Only-Begotten SON JESUS CHRIST our LORD, and to GOD the HOLY GHOST, and before the whole company of heaven, that I have sinned exceedingly in thought, word, and deed, through my fault, through my own fault, through my own most grievous fault [especially . . . .] Wherefore I beseech GOD the FATHER, His Only-Begotten SON JESUS CHRIST our LORD, and GOD the HOLY GHOST

to have mercy upon me, and to bring me to everlasting life.

Ᵽ. Wilt Thou not turn again and quicken us, O LORD? Ᵽ. That Thy people may rejoice in Thee. Ᵽ. Show us Thy mercy, O LORD. Ᵽ. And grant us Thy salvation. Ᵽ. Vouchsafe, O LORD. Ᵽ. To keep us this day without sin. Ᵽ. O LORD, have mercy upon us. Ᵽ. Have mercy upon us. Ᵽ. O LORD, let Thy mercy lighten upon us. Ᵽ. As our trust is in Thee. Ᵽ. Turn Thee again, O LORD, at the last. Ᵽ. And be gracious unto Thy servants. Ᵽ. LORD, hear our prayer. Ᵽ. And let our cry come unto Thee. Ᵽ. Let us pray.

Third Coll. for Matins. O LORD, our heavenly FATHER, &c.

[*Here may be added,* **26—34**, **36—38, 108—113**. *See pages* 20—22, 30, 31.]

TERCE.

In the Name, &c.
Our FATHER, &c.

Ᵽ. O GOD, make speed, &c. Ᵽ. O LORD, make haste, &c. Ᵽ. Glory, &c. Ᵽ. As it was, &c. Alleluia.

Hymn.

Come, HOLY GHOST, our souls inspire, &c.

Ant. O learn me.

Ps. 119 (33—80.) Teach me, O LORD, &c.

Ant. O learn me true understanding and knowledge.

The Chapter. Rev. xxii. 17.

The Spirit and the Bride say, Come; and let him that heareth say, Come, and let him that is athirst come; and whosoever will, let him take the water of life freely.

Ᵽ. But Thou, &c. Ᵽ. Thanks, &c. Ᵽ. Now the LORD is that Spirit. Ᵽ. And where the Spirit

of the LORD is, there is liberty. Ᵽ. Glory, &c. Ᵽ. As it was, &c. Ᵽ. The Spirit itself beareth witness with our spirit. Ᵽ. That we are the children of GOD. Ᵽ. The LORD, &c. Ᵽ. And with, &c. Ᵽ. Let us pray.

LORD, have mercy, &c.
Our FATHER, &c.

Ᵽ. Send out Thy light and Thy truth, that they may lead me. Ᵽ. And bring me unto Thy holy hill, and to Thy dwelling. Ᵽ. O let us live. Ᵽ. And we shall call upon Thy Name. Ᵽ. Turn us again, O LORD GOD of Hosts. Ᵽ. Show the light of Thy countenance, and we shall be whole.

1. Grant, we beseech Thee, Almighty and Merciful GOD, that Thy HOLY SPIRIT may come unto us, and dwell in us, and make us to be a worthy temple of His glory. Through.

SEXT.

In the Name, &c.
Our FATHER, &c.

℣. O GOD, make speed, &c. ℟. O LORD, make haste, &c. ℣. Glory, &c. ℟. As it was, &c.

Hymn.

O GOD of truth, O LORD of might,
Who ord'rest time and change aright,
And send'st the early morning ray,
And light'st the glow of perfect day:

Extinguish Thou each sinful fire,
And banish every ill desire;
And while Thou keep'st the body whole,
Shed forth Thy peace upon the soul.

O FATHER, that we ask be done,
Through JESUS CHRIST, Thine only SON;
Who, with the HOLY GHOST and Thee,
Shall live and reign eternally. Amen.

Ant. The ungodly laid wait for me to destroy me.

Ps. 119 (81—128.) My soul hath longed, &c.
Ps. 22. My GOD, my GOD, &c.

Ant. The ungodly laid wait for me to destroy me, but I will consider Thy testimonies.

The Chapter. Isa. iv. 6.

There shall be a tabernacle for a shadow in the daytime from the heat, and for a place of refuge, and for a covert from storm and from rain.

℣. But Thou, &c. ℟. Thanks, &c. ℣. I said, I will go up to the palm-tree. ℟. I will take hold of the boughs thereof. ℣. Glory, &c. ℟. As it was, &c. ℣. Therefore shall He lift up mine head. ℟. Above mine enemies round about me. ℣. The LORD be with you. ℟. And with thy spirit. ℣. Let us pray.

LORD, have mercy, &c.
Our FATHER, &c.

℣. Hide not Thy face from Thy servant, for I am in trouble. ℟. O haste Thee and hear me. ℣. Draw nigh unto my soul and save it. ℟. O deliver me, because of mine enemies. ℣. LORD, hear, &c. ℟. And let, &c. ℣. Let us pray.

2. O LORD JESU CHRIST, Who at the sixth hour of the day didst ascend the Cross for the redemption of the world, and didst shed Thy precious Blood for the remission of our sins; grant, we humbly beseech Thee, that by the merits of Thy Passion and Wounds, we may, after our death, enter into the gates of Paradise with joy. Who.

3. O LORD JESU CHRIST, Who wast lifted up upon the Wood of the Cross that all the world, which was in darkness, might be enlightened; pour forth, we beseech Thee, that light upon our souls and bodies, through which we may attain unto life everlasting. Who.

NONE.

In the Name, &c.
Our FATHER, &c.

℣. O GOD, make, &c. ℟. O LORD, make, &c. ℣. Glory, &c. ℟. As it was, &c.

Hymn.

O GOD, Creation's secret Force,
Thyself unmoved, all motion's source,
Who from the morn till evening's ray,
Through all its changes guid'st the day:

Grant us, when this short life is past,
The glorious Evening that shall last:
That by a holy death attained,
Eternal glory may be gained.

O FATHER, that we ask be done,
Through JESUS CHRIST, Thine only SON;
Who, with the HOLY GHOST and Thee,
Shall live and reign eternally. Amen.

Ant. Mine eyes prevent the night watches.

Ps. 119 (129—176.) Thy testimonies, &c.

Ant. Mine eyes prevent the night watches, that I might be occupied in Thy words.

The Chapter. 1 Thess. iv. 14.

If we believe that JESUS died, and rose again, even so them also that sleep in JESUS shall GOD bring with Him.

℣. But Thou, &c. ℟. Thanks, &c. ℣. I will ransom them from the power of the grave. ℟. I will redeem them from death. ℣. Glory, &c. ℟. As it was, &c. ℣. O death, I will be thy plagues. ℟. O grave, I will be thy destruction. ℣. The LORD, &c. ℟. And with, &c. ℣. Let us pray.

LORD, have mercy, &c.

Our FATHER, &c.

℣. Cast me not away in the time of age. ℟. Forsake me not when my strength faileth me. ℣. Hide not Thy face from me. ℟. Lest I be like unto them that go down into the pit. ℣. Quicken me, O LORD, for Thy Name's sake. ℟. And for Thy righteousness' sake bring my soul out of trouble. ℣. LORD, hear, &c. ℟. And let, &c. ℣. Let us pray.

4. O LORD JESU CHRIST, Who for our sakes didst tread the paths of death; make known to us the way of life, that as Thou wast reckoned with the transgressors in Thy death, and with the rich in Thy burial, so we, who are dead in trespasses and sins, may be raised up by Thee to the land of true riches. Who.

COMPLINE.

In the Name, &c.

The LORD Almighty grant us a quiet night and a perfect end.

The Chapter. 1 S. Pet. v. 8.

Brethren, be sober, be vigilant, because your adversary the devil, as a roaring lion, walketh about, seeking whom he may devour, whom resist, steadfast in the faith.

℣. But Thou, O LORD, have mercy upon us. ℟. Thanks be to GOD. ℣. Our help standeth in the Name of the LORD. ℟. Who hath made heaven and earth.

Our FATHER, &c.

I confess to GOD the FATHER Almighty, to His Only-Begotten SON JESUS CHRIST our LORD, and to GOD the HOLY GHOST, and before the whole company of heaven, that I have sinned exceedingly, in thought, word, and deed, through my fault, through my own fault, through my own most grievous fault, [especially . . . .]

Wherefore I beseech GOD the FATHER Almighty, His Only-Begotten SON JESUS CHRIST our LORD, and GOD the HOLY GHOST, to pity me, and to have mercy upon me.

The Almighty and merciful GOD grant to us pardon, absolution, and remission of all our sins.

℣. Turn Thou us, O GOD our SAVIOUR. ℟. And let Thine anger cease from us. ℣. O GOD, make speed to save us. ℟. O LORD, make haste to help us.

Ant. I will lay me down in peace.

Ps. 4. Hear me when I call, &c. 31 (to ver. 6.) In Thee, O LORD, have I put, &c. 91. Whoso dwelleth under, &c. 134. Behold now, praise the LORD, &c.

Ant. I will lay me down in peace, and take my rest; for it is Thou, LORD, only that makest me dwell in safety.

Hymn.

The day is past and over :
  All thanks, O LORD, to Thee !
I pray Thee that offenceless
  The hours of dark may be.
O JESU ! keep me in Thy sight,
And save me through the coming night !

The joys of day are over :
  I lift my heart to Thee ;
And call on Thee that sinless
  The hours of sin may be.
O JESU ! keep me in Thy sight,
And save me through the coming night !

The toils of day are over :
  I raise the hymn to Thee ;
And ask that free from peril
  The hours of fear may be.
O JESU ! keep me in Thy sight,
And guard me through the coming night !

Lighten mine eyes, O SAVIOUR,
  Or sleep in death shall I ;
And he, my wakeful tempter,
  Triumphantly shall cry :
" He could not make their darkness light,
Nor guard them through the hours of night !"

Be Thou my soul's preserver,
  O GOD ! for Thou dost know
How many are the perils
  Through which I have to go :
Lover of men ! O hear my call ;
And guard and save me from them all !

The Chapter. Jer. xiv.

Thou, O LORD, art in the midst of us, and we are called by Thy Name. Leave us not, O LORD our GOD.

℣. But Thou, O LORD, have mercy upon us. ℞. Thanks be to GOD. ℣. Into Thy hands, O LORD, I commend my spirit. ℞. For Thou hast redeemed me, O LORD, Thou GOD of truth. ℣. Keep us, O LORD, as the apple of an eye. ℞. Hide us under the shadow of Thy wings.

Ant. Save us, O LORD.

Nunc dimittis. LORD, now lettest Thou Thy servant, &c.

Ant. Save us, O LORD, watching, guard us sleeping, that we may watch with CHRIST, and rest in peace.

LORD, have mercy upon us, &c.
Our FATHER, &c. I believe, &c.

℣. Blessed art Thou, O LORD GOD of our fathers. ℞. And greatly to be praised and glorified for ever. ℣. Let us bless the FATHER, and the SON, and the HOLY GHOST. ℞. Let us praise and exalt Him for ever. ℣. Blessed be Thou, O LORD, in the firmament of heaven. ℞. And greatly to be praised and glorified, and highly exalted for ever. ℣. The Almighty and merciful LORD bless and protect us. ℞. Amen. ℣. Vouchsafe, O LORD. ℞. To keep us this night without sin. ℣. O LORD, have mercy upon us. ℞. Have mercy upon us. ℣. O LORD, let Thy mercy lighten upon us. ℞. As our trust is in Thee. ℣. LORD, hear our prayer. ℞. And let our cry come unto Thee. ℣. Let us pray.

5. Visit, we beseech Thee, O LORD, this habitation, and drive far from it all the snares of the enemy. Let Thy holy angels abide ·in it to preserve us in peace, and let Thy blessing be ever upon us, through JESUS CHRIST our LORD.

[*Here may be added,* **45, 52—55, 64, 92, 93, 102—104.** *See pages* 23—25, 28—30.]

The Almighty and merciful GOD, the FATHER, the SON, and the HOLY GHOST, bless and preserve us, now and for evermore. Amen.

THE ANGELUS.

℣. The Angel of the LORD announced to Mary. ℞. And she conceived of the HOLY GHOST.

Hail, Mary, full of grace, the LORD is. with thee, blessed art thou among women, and blessed is the fruit of thy womb, JESUS.
℣. Behold the handmaid of the LORD. ℞. Be it unto me according to thy word.
Hail, Mary, &c.
℣. The WORD was made flesh. ℞. And dwelt among us.
Hail, Mary, &c.

Collect for Annunciation.

SELF-EXAMINATION.

Prayer before Self-Examination.

6. Open, Lord, mine eyes, that I may see my sins: Examine me, and prove me: Try out my reins and my heart: Look well if there be any way of wickedness in me; and lead me in the way everlasting, for Jesus Christ's sake. Amen.

Questions for Daily Use.

Did I last night say all my prayers carefully, and go to bed with a good conscience and trust in God?

Did I refrain from evil thoughts during wakefulness?

Did I rise in good time? think first of God? make all my accustomed acts of devotion? say them as really speaking to God? In church, did I join in the Service with my whole heart?

Have I tried in everything to do God's will? Have I truly loved Him?

Have I given way at all to evil thoughts? against God? against my neighbour? against myself?

Have I said anything wrong? to the injury of religion? of my neighbour?

Have I knowingly done what God would not have me do?

Have I been idle, doing slightly, or leaving undone, the work which God has given me to do?

Have I wasted time in light or frivolous reading, conversation, or employment?

Have I been thoroughly patient, contented, and trustful? not been self-satisfied?

Have I been temperate and pure in all things?

Have I been quite honest and sincere in all that I have said and done?

Have I made the life of Jesus my pattern in all things?

The following questions should be asked every night as to the Besetting sin.

How often have I committed it to-day? Is this more or less than before?

How often have I overcome when tempted?

How often have I resisted before being overcome? with what resolution?

Questions bearing directly on the Clerical Life.

Have I omitted saying my daily office? Matins? Evensong?

Have I been inattentive, hurried, or wandering in public or private prayer?

Have I made due preparation before celebrating Holy Communion, and offered thanksgiving afterwards?

Have I broken my fast before celebrating, without positive necessity, as e.g. a sudden call to administer the Viaticum to a dying person?

Have I omitted celebrating, or being present at the celebration of Holy Communion on any Sunday or greater Festival? When positively prevented, have I made an Act of Spiritual Communion?

Have I shown any want of care or reverence, external or internal, in the ministry of Public Worship?

Have I been careful to recite the Service, and read the Lessons, in a clear and intelligible manner?

Have I taken due care that the church and all things belonging to it are kept in such order as becomes the House of God?

Have I joined in the public worship of Schismatics, or co-operated in the working of religious societies directed by them?

Have I been diligent in study, especially of Holy Scripture, remembering that without it I cannot perform my primary duty to my flock?

Have I been diligent in the instruction of my flock, and in the preparation of my sermons?

Have I striven to make my sermons clear and simple, remembering that I have to preach the Gospel to the poor?

Have I ever compromised the truth—kept back important doctrines of the Church—or paltered with my plain duty for fear of giving offence?

Have I ever put forward my own private opinions as being of equal authority with the teaching of the Church?

Have I ever insisted on matters of trifling importance, to the scandal of the weaker brethren?

Have I endeavoured to give frequent opportunities of Public Worship to my flock, and striven to make it attractive to them?

Have I, through fear of men, acquiesced in the appropriation of my church by the more wealthy parishioners, to the exclusion of the poor?

Have I shown obedience to my ecclesiastical superiors in all things lawful?

Have I ever disobeyed the law itself in obedience to the unlawful command of a superior?

Have I been diligent in the supervision of schools and charities?

Have I been prompt in attending to sick calls?

Have I ever refused to attend the sick through fear of infection to myself or household?

Have I shown diligence and care in the bestowal of alms, so as not to neglect the destitute, nor indolently to encourage mendicancy?

Have I ever repelled, put off, or received coldly those who sought me for ghostly counsel or advice?

Have I ever disclosed or hinted at what was told me in Confession?

Have I allowed personal feeling or pique to influence my parochial visitation and intercourse?

Have I allowed my personal convenience to interfere with my parochial duties?

Have I been ready to warn sinners in private, and to abstain from all personalities in the pulpit or other public places?

Have I been sedulous to magnify my office without magnifying myself?

Have I been courteous and considerate to all, especially to the poor and to servants?

Have I been ready to rise early so as to give the beginning of the day to prayer? Have I been punctual at Divine Service?

Have I been fervent in intercessory prayer?

Have I shown fitting reverence in speaking of holy persons, places, and things?

Have I abstained from habits and amusements inconsistent with my calling, and tending to weaken my influence?

Have I refrained from non-residence, or from frequent and unnecessary absences from my parish?

Have I been careful to provide for the due celebration of Divine Service, &c., during my absence?

Have I always dressed and comported myself as a Clergyman, and refrained from adopting lay attire when from home?

Have I been careful to devote a large portion of my income to pious and charitable purposes?

Have I checked all secular display and luxury in my household?

Have I incurred unnecessary expenses, allowed myself to run in debt, or delayed payment of what I owed?

Have I incurred expenses, which I could not at the time meet, for church building, for schools, charitable purposes, or for the adjuncts of Public Worship?

Have I steadily put a stop to gossip, and especially religious gossip, when carried on in my presence?

Have I endeavoured to act as a peacemaker, and resolutely refused to be drawn into quarrels myself?

Have I avoided taking information touching my parishioners at second-hand, or delegating authority to unfit persons?

Have I been circumspect in my dealings with my flock, especially with the female portion of it?

Have I avoided undue interference with others, especially the private affairs of families?

Have I been strictly temperate in my diet, and regular in observing the fasts of the Church?

Have I been careful to inquire into the antecedents of persons seeking to be married, so as not to join those together who are within the forbidden degrees, or have been divorced?

Have I abstained from ascribing bad motives, especially to my theological opponents?

Have I been eager for popularity, or set myself to obtain promotion?

Have I bought a living, or allowed one to be bought for me? If so, what amends have I made?

Have I ever taken a fee either for administering Holy Baptism, or for registering it? Have I connived at this offence in others?

Have I ever quitted a parish where I was of use, merely for the sake of increased income?

Have I been fickle in moving from place to place? In altering my plans of parochial work?

Have I ever accepted incompatible duties?

As Incumbent. Have I taken my fair share of work—treated my Assistant Curates with due courtesy—avoided slighting or rebuking them in the presence of others—given them a fair stipend—upheld them in disputes arising out of the conscientious discharge of their office?

As Assistant Curate. Have I remembered that I am only the deputy of the Incumbent, and am bound either to obey his directions, or to leave his parish? Have I censured his conduct, or complained of him to the parishioners—contradicted his teaching in the pulpit—tried to make a party for myself in the parish—held aloof from forwarding his plans?

———

Prayer after Self-Examination.

7. O Lord, Thou knowest all my sins, and my faults are not hid from Thee. Give me ever true penitence and faith, that with a holy disposition of mind, I may make my confession and obtain pardon of Thee, the just and merciful God, through the atoning blood of Thy dear Son, Jesus Christ. Amen.

Act of Contrition.

8. O Eternal Father, Just and Righteous Judge, Who art of purer eyes than to behold iniquity; in deep contrition I offer unto Thee with fullest confidence the precious Blood of Thy dear Son as the perfect atonement for all my numberless offences. I beseech Thee that Thou wouldst apply It both now and ever to my heart, that It may give me deep contrition, may purify me yet more and more from my iniquities, and cleanse me from all my sins, through the same Thy Son Jesus Christ our Lord. Amen.

EJACULATIONS.

On first awaking.
Lighten mine eyes, O LORD, that I sleep not in death.

O GOD, Who hast given me another day of life, behold, I devote it and myself to Thee. Amen.

On rising.
In the Name, &c.

I laid me down and slept, and rose up again, for the LORD sustained me.

While washing.
O LORD JESU, Who didst wash us from our sins in Thine Own Blood, wash away all the stains of my soul, and I shall be whiter than snow.

While dressing.
Clothe me, O LORD, with Thy heavenly grace, and cover me with the robe of righteousness.

Before reading Holy Scripture.
My delight shall be in the Law of the LORD, and in Thy law will I exercise myself day and night.

When the clock strikes.
Watch ye therefore, for ye know not when the Master of the house cometh, at evening, or at midnight, or at cockcrowing, or in the morning.

On leaving the house.
The LORD preserve my going out and coming in, from this time forth for evermore.

Before a walk.
Show me Thy ways, O LORD, and teach me Thy paths.

For custody of the eyes.
Turn away mine eyes, lest they behold vanity, and quicken Thou me in Thy way.

On going into a Church.
LORD, I have loved the habitation of Thy House, and the place where Thy honour dwelleth.

On beginning any work.
A. M. D. G.

Or,
LORD JESU, grant that I may accomplish this work to Thy glory and my salvation, as may be pleasing unto Thee.

On completing any work.
O LORD JESU, I commend unto Thee this work of mine, to be perfected and finished by Thee, and I offer it unto Thee in union with Thine own works.

Before conversation.
Set a watch, O LORD, before my mouth, and keep the door of my lips.

Before taking medicine.
Heal me, O LORD, and I shall be healed; save me, and I shall be saved, for Thou art my praise.

In sudden pain.
O LORD, by Thy Cross and Passion strengthen me: LORD, let this cup pass from me; nevertheless, not my will, but Thine be done.

Grace before Meat.
[℣. The eyes of all wait upon Thee, O LORD. ℟. And Thou givest them their meat in due season. ℣. Thou openest Thine hand. ℟. And fillest all things living with plenteousness. ℣. Glory, &c. ℟. As it was, &c.]

Bless, O LORD, these Thy gifts which we are about to receive of Thy great bounty. Through.

Grace after Meat.
[℣. All Thy works praise Thee, O LORD. ℟. And Thy saints give thanks unto Thee. ℣. They show the glory of Thy kingdom. ℟. And talk of Thy power. ℣. Glory, &c. ℟. As it was, &c.]

Thanks be to GOD for these and all His bounties bestowed on us. Through.

On lying down in bed.
In the Name, &c.

I will lay me down in peace and take my rest, for it is Thou, LORD, only that makest me dwell in safety.

OFFICE BEFORE CELEBRATING.

Ant. Remember not, LORD, our offences.

Ps. 84. O how amiable, &c.
85. LORD, Thou art become, &c.
86. Bow down Thine ear, &c.
116 (v. 10—16.) I believed, &c.
130. Out of the deep, &c.

Ant. Remember not, LORD, our offences, nor the offences of our forefathers, neither take Thou vengeance of our sins.

LORD, have mercy upon us.
Our FATHER, &c.

℣. I said, LORD, be merciful unto me. ℟. Heal my soul, for I have sinned against Thee. ℣. Turn Thee again, O LORD, at the last. ℟. And be gracious unto Thy servants. ℣. O LORD, let Thy mercy be showed upon us. ℟. As we do put our trust in Thee. ℣. Let Thy Priests be clothed with righteousness. ℟. And let Thy Saints sing with joyfulness. ℣. Cleanse me, O LORD, from my secret faults. ℟. And keep Thy servant from presumptuous sins. ℣. LORD, hear my prayer. ℟. And let my cry come unto Thee. ℣. Let us pray.

9. O merciful LORD, incline Thine ears to our prayers, and enlighten our souls by the grace of Thy HOLY SPIRIT, that we may worthily celebrate Thy Holy Mysteries, and may love Thee with an everlasting love.

10. Inflame our hearts, O LORD, we beseech Thee, with the fire of Thy HOLY SPIRIT, that we may serve Thee with chaste bodies, and please Thee with pure souls.

11. We pray Thee, O LORD, that Thy Holy Comforter may enlighten our minds, and, as Thy SON hath promised, may lead us into all truth.

12. Let the virtue of Thy HOLY SPIRIT, O LORD, be present with us, to purge us from all evil, and to keep us from all harm.

13. GOD, Who didst teach the hearts of Thy faithful people by the sending to them the light of Thy HOLY SPIRIT; grant us by the same SPIRIT to have a right judgment in all things and evermore to rejoice in His holy comfort.

14. Visit, we pray Thee, O LORD, and cleanse our consciences, that when Thy SON, our LORD JESUS CHRIST, cometh to us, He may find in us a mansion fitted for His abode.

15. O GOD, Who in this wonderful Sacrament hast left unto us a perpetual memorial of Thy Passion; grant to us, we beseech Thee, so to venerate the Sacred Mysteries of Thy Body and Blood, that we may always perceive in ourselves the fruit of Thy Redemption. Who livest.

PRAYERS BEFORE HOLY COMMUNION.

To be said as opportunity offers.

SUNDAY.

O Supreme High Priest and true Chief Bishop, JESUS CHRIST, Who didst offer Thyself to GOD the FATHER, a pure and spotless Victim upon the Altar of the Cross for us miserable sinners, and Who didst give us Thy Flesh to eat, and Thy Blood to drink, and didst ordain that Mystery in the might of the HOLY SPIRIT, saying, "This do, in remembrance of Me;" I entreat Thee by the same Blood, the great price of our salvation; I entreat Thee by that wonderful and unspeakable love wherewith Thou didst vouchsafe so to love us, miserable and unworthy, as to wash us from our sins in Thy Blood, teach me, Thy unworthy servant, whom, among Thine other gifts, not for any merit of mine, but of the condescension of Thy mercy alone, Thou hast vouchsafed also to call to the dignity of

Priesthood, teach me, I pray Thee, by Thy HOLY SPIRIT to handle so great a Mystery with such reverence and honour, with such devotion and fear as I ought and as it becometh me. Make me through Thy grace, always so to believe and understand, to conceive, and firmly to hold, to think and to speak of this wondrous Mystery, as shall please Thee, and benefit my soul. Let Thy good SPIRIT enter my heart, there to be heard without utterance, and without the sound of words speak all truth. For these things are exceeding deep and covered with a sacred veil. Of Thy great mercy, grant me to celebrate this solemnity with a clean heart and pure mind. Free my heart from all defiling and unholy, from all vain and hurtful thoughts. Fence me with the holy and faithful guard and mighty protection of Thy blessed Angels, that the enemies of all good may fly away ashamed. By the virtue of this vast Mystery, and by the hand of Thy holy Angels, repel from me and all Thy servants the hard spirit of pride and vainglory, of impurity and uncleanness, of doubting and mistrust. Let them be confounded that seek after my soul to destroy it; let them perish that seek my hurt.

MONDAY.

King of Virgins, and Lover of chastity and innocence, extinguish in my frame, by the dew of Thy heavenly blessing, the fuel of evil concupiscence, that so one even purity of soul and body may abide in me. Mortify in my members the lusts of the flesh, and all hurtful emotions, and give me true and persevering chastity, with Thine other gifts which please Thee in truth; so that I may with chaste body and pure heart offer unto Thee the sacrifice of praise. For with what mighty contrition of heart and fountain of tears, with what reverence and awe, with what chastity of body and purity of soul, should that Divine and Heavenly Sacrifice

be celebrated, wherein Thy Flesh is indeed taken, where Thy Blood is indeed drunk, wherein things lowest and highest, earthly and divine, are united, where is the presence of the holy Angels, where Thou art in a wonderful and unspeakable way both Sacrifice and Priest.

TUESDAY.

Who can worthily celebrate this Sacrifice unless Thou, O GOD, makest him worthy? I know, O LORD, yea, truly do I know and this do I confess to Thy lovingkindness, that I am not worthy to approach so high a Mystery, by reason of my very many sins and numberless negligences; but I know, and truly with my own heart do I believe, and with my mouth confess, that Thou canst make me worthy, Who alone canst make that clean which cometh from that which is unclean, and sinners to be righteous and holy. By this Thine Almighty power I beseech Thee, O my GOD, to grant that I, a sinner, may celebrate this Sacrifice with fear and trembling, with purity of heart and streams of tears, with spiritual gladness, and celestial joy; let my mind feel the sweetness of Thy most blessed presence, and the guardianship of the holy Angels round about me.

WEDNESDAY.

For now, O LORD, mindful of Thy venerable Passion, I approach Thine Altar, to offer Thee that Sacrifice which Thou hast instituted, and commanded to be offered in remembrance of Thee for our wellbeing. Receive it, we beseech Thee, O GOD Most High, for Thy holy Church, and for the people whom Thou hast purchased with Thy Blood. And since Thou hast willed that I, a sinner, should stand between Thee and this Thy people, although Thou canst discern no good work in me, yet at least reject not the office of the dispensation intrusted to me; let not through my unworthiness the price of their salvation be wasted, for whom Thou didst vouchsafe to be a saving Victim and Redemption. We bring before Thee, O LORD, if Thou wilt graciously vouchsafe to behold, the tribulations of the poor, the perils of the people, the groans of prisoners, the miseries of orphans, the necessities of strangers, the helplessness of the weak, the depressions of the languishing, the infirmities of the aged, the aspirations of the young, the vows of virgins, the wailing of widows.

THURSDAY.

For Thou, O LORD, hast mercy upon all, and hatest nothing that Thou hast made. Remember what is our substance, because Thou art our FATHER, because Thou art our GOD. Be not angry with us for ever, nor restrain the multitude of Thy mercies upon us, for it is not in our righteousness that we pour forth our prayers before Thy Face, but of Thy great mercies. Take from us our iniquities, and graciously kindle the fire of Thy HOLY SPIRIT within us. Take away the heart of stone from our flesh, and give us a heart of flesh, to love Thee, choose Thee, please Thee, follow Thee, enjoy Thee. We pray Thy mercy, O LORD, that Thou wouldst vouchsafe graciously to look upon Thy family attending on the ministry of Thy holy Name; and that the prayers of none may be in vain, the supplication of none empty, do Thou put into our minds those prayers which Thou art graciously pleased to hear and accomplish.

'FRIDAY.

We entreat Thee also, O LORD, Holy FATHER, for the souls of the faithful departed . . . . that this great Sacrament of Thy love may be unto them salvation and health, joy and refreshment. O LORD my GOD, grant them this day a great and abundant feast of Thee, the living GOD, Who camest down from heaven, and gavest life unto the world, even of Thy holy and blessed Flesh, the Lamb without spot, Who takest away the sins of the world; even of that Flesh which was taken of the holy and glorious Virgin Mary, and conceived of the HOLY GHOST, and of that Fountain of mercy which from the soldier's spear flowed from Thy most sacred Side, that therewith enlarged and sated, refreshed and comforted, they may rejoice in Thy praise and glory.

I pray Thy clemency, O LORD, that on the bread to be offered unto Thee may descend the fulness of Thy benediction, and the sanctification of Thy Divinity. May there descend also the invisible and incomprehensible Majesty of Thy HOLY SPIRIT, as it descended of old on the sacrifices of the fathers, Which may make our oblations Thy Body and Blood. And teach me, an unworthy Priest, to handle so great a Mystery with purity of heart and the devotion of tears, with reverence and trembling, so that Thou mayest graciously and favourably receive the sacrifice of my hands for the good of all, living and departed.

SATURDAY.

I beseech Thee also, O LORD, by this most sacred mystery of Thy Body and Blood, wherewith we are daily fed, washed, and sanctified in Thy Church, and are made partakers of the One Supreme Divinity, give unto me Thy holy virtues, that fulfilled therewith I may approach with a good conscience unto Thy holy Altar, so that these holy Sacraments may be made unto me salvation and life; for Thou hast said with Thy holy and blessed mouth, "The Bread which I will give is My Flesh, which I will give for the life of the world. I am the Living Bread Which came down from heaven. If any man shall eat of this Bread, he shall live for ever."

O most sweet Bread, heal the palate of my heart, that I may taste the sweetness of Thy love. Heal it of all infirmities, that I may find sweetness in nothing out of Thee. O most pure Bread, having all delight and all savour, Which dost ever refresh us, and never failest, let my heart feed on Thee, and may my inmost soul be fulfilled with the sweetness of Thy savour. The Angels feed on Thee fully. Let pilgrim man feed on Thee after his measure, refreshed by this sustenance on his way.

Holy Bread! Living Bread! Pure Bread! Who camest down from heaven, and givest life unto the world; come into my heart, and cleanse me from all defilement of flesh and spirit. Enter into my soul, heal and cleanse me within and without; be the protection and continual health of my soul and body, so that I may by a straight way arrive at Thy kingdom; where not as now in mysteries, but face to face, we shall behold Thee; when Thou shalt have delivered up the kingdom to GOD Thy FATHER, and shalt be GOD All in all, then shalt Thou satisfy me with Thyself by a marvellous fulness, so that I shall never hunger nor thirst any more, Who with the same GOD the FATHER and the HOLY GHOST livest.

PRAYERS WHILE VESTING FOR THE HOLY COMMUNION.

At washing the hands.

Cleanse my hands, O LORD, from all stain, that pure in mind and body, I may be worthy to serve Thee.

The Amice.

Place, O LORD, the helmet of salvation upon my head, to repel the assaults of the devil.

The Alb.

Cleanse me, O LORD, and purify my heart, that, washed in the Blood of the Lamb, I may attain everlasting joy.

The Girdle.

Gird me, O LORD, with the girdle of purity, and quench in me the fire of concupiscence, that the grace of temperance and chastity may abide in me.

The Maniple.

Grant me, O LORD, to bear the light burden of grief and sorrow, that I may with gladness receive the reward of my labour.

The Stole.

Give me again, O LORD, the robe of immortality which I lost by the sin of my first parent, and although I am unworthy to come unto Thy Holy Sacrament, grant that I may attain everlasting felicity.

The Chasuble.

O LORD, Who hast said, My yoke is easy, and My burden is light, grant that I may so bear it, as to attain Thy grace. Amen.

The Dalmatic or Tunicle.

The LORD clothe me with the garment of Salvation, and cover me with the robe of righteousness.

Direction of Intention before Celebrating.

[A.] O GOD of heaven and earth, incomprehensible and merciful, I, an unworthy sinner, and most lowly minister of Thy Church, offer to Thy Divine Majesty this most august sacrifice of the Body and Blood of Thy SON in token of the honour and love which are Thy due; for Thy boundless praise and glory, in acknowledgment of Thy supreme excellence and majesty, of Thy rule over all creation, and of our subjection and dependence on Thee. In memory and reverence of the blessed Incarnation, Life, Passion, Death, Resurrection, and Ascension of the same Thy SON, and in obedience to His command that we should make remembrance of Him. In thanksgiving for all the blessings which Thou hast vouchsafed to bestow on me, an unworthy sinner, and on all Thy creatures. In honour and for the increase of the bliss and glory of the Blessed Virgin Mary, of all Thine Angels and Saints, [especially of S. *N.* whose feast is celebrated to-day.] In propitiation and satisfaction for my sins and those of all the world. For my present and future needs of body and soul, and for those of my parents, brethren, sisters, kindred, connections, neighbours, benefactors, and friends; for those of all Priests and Ministers of the Church, of all committed to my charge, of all mine enemies, of all to whom I have been an offence and a cause of sin, and of all to whom I am in any wise bound. For the exaltation of the Holy Catholic Church. For the uprooting of heresies. For the harmony and concord of Christian Princes. For the consolation, help, healing, patience, and deliverance of the afflicted, the poor, the captives, the tempted, the sick, and the dying. For the conversion of unbelievers. For the rising again of them that fall. For the perseverance of the righteous. For the refreshment, rest, and peace of all the faithful departed. But chiefly I offer it for the intention of . . . . .

Receive, O LORD, this my oblation in union with that love wherewith Thy SON our LORD JESUS CHRIST loved us and gave Himself for us, Who liveth and reigneth with Thee and the HOLY GHOST, GOD, for ever and ever. Amen.

[B.] I desire to celebrate the Holy Eucharist, and to consecrate the Body and Blood of our LORD JESUS CHRIST, to the praise of Almighty GOD, and in honour of all the Church Triumphant, for my profit and that of all the Church Militant, for all those who have commended themselves to my prayers, and for the prosperity of the Holy Catholic Church. Amen.

The Almighty and merciful LORD grant us joy and peace, amendment of life, time for true repentance, the grace and comfort of the HOLY SPIRIT, and perseverance in all good works. Amen.

To be said privately by the Celebrant on leaving the Sacristy to go to the Altar.

In the multitude of Thy mercies, O LORD, I go unto Thine Altar. O save and deliver me for Thy tender mercies' sake. Amen.

PRIVATE PRAYERS AT THE CELEBRATION.

When the Priest goes up to the Altar.

In the Name, &c.

Ant. I will go unto the Altar of GOD.

Ps. 43. Give sentence with me, O GOD, &c.

Ant. I will go unto the Altar of GOD, even unto the GOD of my joy and gladness.

When he takes his place at the north side.

Take away from us, O LORD, we beseech Thee, our iniquities, that we may enter with pure hearts into Thy most holy place.

On presenting the Alms.

Receive, O Holy Trinity, the offerings of Thy people, as Thou didst receive the gifts of Abel, the sacrifice of our father Abraham, the incense of Zacharias, the alms of Cornelius, and the widow's mites, and accept them through JESUS CHRIST our LORD.

On offering the Bread.

Receive, O Holy Trinity, this

Oblation which I, an unworthy sinner, offer before Thy Divine Majesty, in honour of Thine All holy Name, for mine own sins, and for the salvation of the whole Mystical Body of CHRIST, in the Name, &c.

On mixing Water with the Wine.

From the Side of our LORD JESUS CHRIST flowed Blood and Water; we therefore likewise mingle them, that the merciful GOD may vouchsafe to hallow both for the healing of our souls. Through the Same.

On Offering the Chalice.

We offer unto Thee, O LORD, the Cup of Salvation, beseeching Thy clemency that it may ascend before Thy Divine Majesty as a sweet odour, for our salvation, and for that of the whole world. Through.

To be pronounced over the Paten and Chalice.

Come, HOLY GHOST, Almighty, Everlasting GOD, and bless this Sacrifice prepared for Thy Holy Name.

[Benediction of the Incense at a solemn service.

O LORD, vouchsafe to bless this Incense, and accept it as a sweet smelling savour, and kindle in our hearts the fire of Thy love. Through.]

Receive, O Holy Trinity, this Oblation which we offer unto Thee, in memory of the Passion, Resurrection, and Ascension of JESUS CHRIST our LORD, that it may avail for His honour and our salvation; and may He vouchsafe to intercede for us in heaven, Whose memorial we celebrate on earth.

Before the Church Militant Prayer, the Priest washing his hands shall say:

I will wash my hands in innocency, O LORD : and so will I go to Thine Altar; that I may show the voice of thanksgiving : and tell of all Thy wondrous works. LORD, I have loved the habitation of Thy house : and the place where Thine honour dwelleth. O shut not up my soul with the sinners : nor my life with the blood-thirsty; in whose hands is wickedness : and their right hand is full of gifts. But as for me, I will walk innocently : O deliver me, and be merciful unto me. My foot standeth right : I will praise the LORD in the congregations.

Glory be to the FATHER, &c.

Before the Consecration Prayer.

Most merciful GOD, look graciously upon the Gifts now lying before Thee, and send down Thy HOLY SPIRIT upon this Sacrifice : that He may make this Bread the Body of Thy CHRIST, and this Cup the Blood of Thy CHRIST. Amen.

Immediately after the Consecration Prayer.

Wherefore, O LORD, we Thy servants and holy people, mindful of the blessed Passion, glorious Resurrection, and wonderful Ascension of the same JESUS CHRIST, our LORD and GOD, offer to Thy glorious Majesty of Thine own gifts a pure, holy, and Spotless Sacrifice, the Bread of eternal life, and the Cup of everlasting salvation. We humbly beseech Thee, Almighty GOD, cause our prayers and supplications to be borne by the ministry of Thy holy Angel to Thine Altar on high, in the sight of Thy Divine Majesty, that so many as are partakers of the precious Body and Blood of Thy SON at the Altar may be fulfilled with all heavenly grace and benediction.

Remember also, O LORD, the souls of Thy servants, who have departed before us with the sign of faith, and rest in the sleep of peace. We pray Thee, O LORD, that Thou wilt grant unto them, and to all who sleep in CHRIST, refreshment, light and peace. Through the Same.

To us also, Thy sinful servants, who hope in the multitude of Thy mercies, grant some portion and fellowship with Thy holy Apostles and Martyrs, and all Thy Saints, into whose company we beseech Thee to admit us, not for our merits, but of Thy mercy, through CHRIST our LORD, by Whom, O LORD, Thou dost always create, hallow, quicken, bless, and bestow upon us all these good things, through Whom, and with Whom, and in Whom, in the unity of the HOLY SPIRIT, all honour and glory be unto Thee, O FATHER Almighty, for ever and ever. Amen.

Before Communicating.

Lamb of GOD, That takest away the sins of the world, Have mercy, &c. Lamb of GOD, ... world, Have mercy, &c. Lamb of GOD, ... world, Grant us Thy peace.

Placing a particle of the Species of Bread in the Chalice, the Priest says :

Let this ho✝ly mixture of the Body and Blood of our LORD JESUS CHRIST be to me and to all who partake thereof salvation of body and soul, and a wholesome preparation for gaining and taking hold of everlasting life. Through.

LORD JESU CHRIST, SON of the Living GOD, Who by the Will of the FATHER, and the co-operation of the HOLY GHOST, hast given life unto the world by Thy death, deliver me, by this Thy Sacred Body and Blood, from all my sins, and keep me from all evil. Make me to abide always in Thy commandments, and suffer me not to be ever separated from Thee. Who livest.

LORD, I am not worthy that Thou shouldest come under my roof, but speak the word only, and my soul shall be healed.

To be said before Communicating in either kind.

What reward shall I give unto the LORD for all the benefits that He hath done unto me? I will receive { the Bread of Heaven, the Cup of Salvation, } and call upon the Name of the LORD.

After Reception.

Blessed be Thou, O LORD, Who hast vouchsafed to feed me with Thine own most precious Body and Blood.

Ant. I have found Him Whom my soul loveth.

Nunc dimittis.

Ant. I have found Him Whom my soul loveth : I will hold Him, and not let Him go.

On taking the Ablutions.

Grant, O LORD, that what we have received with our mouths we may retain with pure minds, and that Thy temporal gifts may be unto us for everlasting salvation.

Let Thy Body, O LORD, which I have received, and Thy Blood which I have drunk, abide within me ; and grant that no stain of sin may remain in me, whom Thy pure and holy Sacraments have refreshed. Who livest.

After the Ablutions.

May this Act of my homage, O Holy Trinity, be pleasing unto Thee, and grant that the Sacrifice, which I, a miserable sinner, have offered before Thy Divine Majesty, may be acceptable unto Thee, and through Thy mercy may be a propitiation for me, and all for whom I have offered It. Through.

While returning to the Sacristy.

Gospel for Christmas Day.

OFFICE AFTER CELEBRATING.

Ant. O how sweet is Thy Spirit, O LORD.

Ps. 23. The LORD is my Shepherd, &c.
34. I will alway give thanks, &c.
103. Praise the LORD, &c.

Ant. O how sweet is Thy Spirit, O LORD, Who, that Thou mightest show Thy kindness unto Thy children, giving them most sweet Bread from heaven, fillest the hungry with good things, and sendest the rich empty away.

LORD, have mercy, &c.
Our FATHER, &c.

℣. The merciful and gracious LORD hath so done His marvellous works, that they ought to be had in remembrance. ℞. He hath given Meat unto them that fear Him. ℣. What is man that Thou art mindful of him ? ℞. And the son of man that Thou visitest him ? ℣. My soul shall be satisfied even as it were with marrow and fatness. ℞. When my mouth praiseth Thee with joyful lips. ℣. Not unto us, O LORD, not unto us. ℞. But unto Thy Name give the praise. ℣. LORD, now lettest Thou Thy servant depart in peace. ℞. For mine eyes have seen Thy salvation. ℣. LORD, hear my prayer. ℞. And let my cry come unto Thee. ℣. Let us pray.

16. We beseech Thee, O LORD, visit Thy family, and with Thy watchful lovingkindness protect the hearts of those who are vowed to Thy holy Mysteries, that by Thine aid they may preserve the medicine of eternal life which they receive of Thy mercy.

17. We pray Thee, O LORD our GOD, that Thou wilt not suffer those whom Thou grantest to rejoice in Divine Communion to be subject to human perils.

18. We know, O LORD, the abundance of Thy mercy, and we therefore more confidently beseech Thee that Thou wouldest cause those sinners whom Thou dost feed unceasingly, to serve Thee worthily, and that Thou wouldest endow them with more abundant gifts.

19. We humbly entreat Thy Majesty, O LORD, that Thou wilt not suffer those to perish for whom Thou hast provided such remedies, but cause that the work of our salvation may increase with our attendance on the Divine Mysteries.

Prevent us, O LORD, in all our doings with Thy most gracious favour, and further us with Thy continual help ; that in all our works begun, continued, and ended in Thee, we may glorify Thy holy Name, and finally by Thy mercy obtain everlasting life.

20. Almighty GOD, let Thy grace help us, that we who have undertaken the priestly office may worthily and devoutly serve Thee in all purity and good conscience ; and if we cannot abide in such innocency of life as we ought, grant us at least to mourn duly for the evil which we have done, and that in the spirit of humility, and the resolution of a good will, we may serve Thee more faithfully for the time to come.

21. O LORD JESU CHRIST, Who for our sake didst in Thy bitter Passion suffer shame, and blows, and spitting, at the hands of sinners, yet in the fulness of Thy love dost still expose Thyself to the profaneness of ungodly men rather than withdraw Thy Sacred Body from our churches ; accept our thanksgivings for this Thy mercy, and grant us grace to bewail with true sorrow of heart the irreverence shown to Thee, and to repair, as far as in us lies, with heartfelt devotion, the many insults which Thou hast received and art daily receiving in this wondrous Mystery. Who livest.

THANKSGIVING AFTER HOLY COMMUNION.

To be said as opportunity offers.

Almighty and everlasting GOD, Preserver of souls and Redeemer of the world; very favourably regard me Thy servant humbled before Thy Majesty, and most graciously accept this Sacrifice which in honour of Thy Name I have offered for the saving health of the faithful, living and departed, as also for all our sins and offences. Take away Thine anger from me, stretch out Thine hand unto me; open unto me the gates of Paradise; deliver me in Thy might from all evils: and whatever guilt I have in mine own person incurred, do Thou forgive; and make me so to persevere in Thy precepts in this world, that I may be rendered worthy to be joined to the company of Thine elect; of Thine only gift, O my GOD, Whose blessed Name, Honour, and Dominion endureth for ever and ever. Amen.

I render thanks to Thee, O LORD, Holy FATHER, Almighty, Everlasting GOD, Who hast vouchsafed, not for any merits of mine, but of Thy great mercy alone, to feed me, a sinner, Thine unworthy servant, with the Body and Blood of Thy SON our LORD JESUS CHRIST; and I pray that this Holy Communion may not be for my judgment or condemnation, but for my pardon and salvation. May it be unto me an armour of faith, and a shield of good purpose, a riddance of all vices, and a rooting out of all evil desires: an increase of love and patience, of humility and obedience, and of all virtues, a firm defence against the wiles of all mine enemies, visible and invisible; a perfect quieting of all my impulses, fleshly and spiritual, a clinging unto Thee, the one True GOD, and a peaceful departure when Thou dost call. And I pray that Thou wouldest vouchsafe to bring me, a sinner, to that unspeakable Feast, where Thou, with Thy SON, and Thy HOLY SPIRIT, art to Thy holy ones true Light, complete Fulness, everlasting Joy, and perfect Bliss. Through the same.

PRAYERS WITH THE CHOIR IN THE VESTRY.

On putting on the Surplice.

Cleanse us, O LORD, and keep us undefiled, that we may be numbered amongst those blessed ones, who, having washed their robes, and made them white in the Blood of the Lamb, stand before Thy throne, and serve Thee day and night in Thy temple.

[*On putting on the Stole.*

O LORD, put upon my neck the yoke of righteousness, and cleanse my soul from all pollution of sin.

On putting on the Hood or the Tippet.

Arm me, O LORD, with the breastplate of faith, and the helmet of salvation, and the sword of the HOLY GHOST.

On putting on the Cope.

Of Thy mercy, O LORD, cover me with a shining garment, and strengthen me against the assaults of the evil one, that I may be worthy to praise Thy glorious Name, through the grace.

My soul shall be joyful in the LORD, for He hath clothed me with the garments of salvation, He hath covered me with a robe of righteousness, as a bridegroom decketh himself with ornaments, and as a bride adorneth herself with her jewels. Isa. lxi. 10.]

On preparing to enter Church.

O LORD, open Thou our lips and purify our hearts, that we may worthily magnify Thy glorious Name. Through.

Before a Celebration of the Holy Communion.

Come, HOLY GHOST, and inspire our hearts, that our LORD JESUS CHRIST at His coming may find in us a mansion prepared for Himself. Who liveth.

After a Celebration of the Holy Communion.

O GOD, Who in this wonderful Sacrament hast left unto us a memorial of Thy Passion ; grant unto us so to venerate the sacred Mysteries of Thy Body and Blood, that we may always perceive in ourselves the fruit of Thy redemption. Who livest.

On returning from an Ordinary Office.

Grant, O LORD, that what we have sung with our lips we may believe in our hearts, and may always steadfastly fulfil. Through.

ITINERARY.

The parts in [ ] may be added with a family when any of the members are going to foreign parts.

[Dearly beloved brethren, let us beseech with earnest prayer our LORD JESUS CHRIST, Who is the straight path of them that journey, and the unwearying salvation of them that sojourn, that He may bless *this* His servant in the way in which *he is* setting out, make *him* strong in bodily vigour, and still mightier in spiritual counsels, that *he* may be obedient to the Divine will, and prosperously finish the journey which *he is* about to begin.]

Ant. May the Almighty and merciful LORD direct us in the way of peace.

Benedictus. Blessed be the LORD.

[Ps. 77, (ver. 11—20.) I will remember the works, &c., or

107. O give thanks unto the LORD, &c.]

Ant. May the Almighty and merciful LORD direct us in the way of peace and prosperity, and may His holy Angels accompany us on our journey, that in peace, joy, and safety we may return to our homes.

Let us pray.

LORD, have mercy, &c. Our FATHER, &c.

℣. O LORD, save Thy servants. ℟. Which put their trust in Thee. ℣. Send us help from Thy sanctuary. ℟. And strengthen us out of Sion. ℣. Be unto us, O LORD, a tower of strength. ℟. From the face of our enemy. ℣. Let no evil happen unto us. ℟. Nor the son of wickedness approach to hurt us. ℣. Blessed be the LORD daily. ℟. And may the GOD of our salvation make our journey prosperous. ℣. Show us Thy ways, O LORD. ℟. And teach us Thy paths. ℣. O that our ways were made so direct.

℞. That we might keep Thy statutes. ℣. Let the crooked ways be made straight. ℞. And the rough places plain. ℣. The LORD shall give His Angels charge over thee. ℞. To keep thee in all thy ways. ℣. LORD, hear, &c. ℞. And let, &c. ℣. Let us pray.

22. O GOD, Who madest the children of Israel to go on dry land through the midst of the sea, and Who showedst the way to the Wise Men by the leading of a star; grant unto *us*, we beseech Thee, a prosperous journey and a quiet time, that with Thy Angel as *our* companion, *our* guardian, and *our* guide, *we* may reach the place whither *we* would go, and at length attain unto the gate of everlasting life.

23. O GOD, Who leddest Abraham Thy servant out of Ur of the Chaldees, and preservedst him unhurt throughout the days of his pilgrimage; we beseech Thee to take *us* Thy servants under Thy protection; be unto *us*, O LORD, *our* Helper in *our* setting out, *our* Solace by the way, *our* Shadow in the heat, *our* Covering in the storm, *our* Comfort in the cold, *our* Support in weariness, *our* Guardian in danger, *our* Staff in slippery places, and *our* Haven in shipwreck, that Thou being *our* Ruler and Guide, *we* may safely reach *our* journey's end, and at length return in safety to *our* own home.

First Collect at end of Communion Office : Assist us mercifully, &c.

24. Grant, we beseech Thee, Almighty GOD, that Thy family may walk in the way of salvation, and, by following the counsels of S. John the Forerunner, may come in safety unto Him Whom he preached, Thy SON JESUS CHRIST our LORD. Who.

For those about to Emigrate.

25. O GOD, Who didst send Thy servant Joseph into Egypt to prepare food for his father and his brethren against the day of famine and necessity, and bringing them into the land of Goshen didst nourish them there; mercifully guard and guide *this* Thy *servant* who *is* leaving this *his* native country to seek employment and sustenance in a foreign land. Prosper *his* undertaking, and keep *him* in all Thy ways, and so nourish *him*, of Thy goodness, in things spiritual and temporal, that *he*, knowing *himself* to be a *stranger* and *pilgrim* upon earth, may at length attain unto the pleasant land wherein is the heavenly Jerusalem, and there be filled with Thy bounty. Through.

℣. Let us depart in peace.
℞. In the Name + of the LORD. Amen.

COLLECTS AND INTERCESSIONS.

FOR THE USE OF THE CLERGY.

A General Intercession.

26. O LORD, Whose mercies are over all Thy works, Who wouldest not that any should perish, but that all should come to repentance; Thou Who hast suffered death for all, and hast left Thyself to us in the Sacrament of Thy love ; vouchsafe, I beseech Thee, Thy blessings upon Thy Church ; to Thy Priests concord and innocence ; to kings and rulers wisdom and justice ; to virgins chastity ; and steadfastness and continuance to those whose lives are dedicated to Thee. To my parents, relations, benefactors, and friends, give all such blessings as they need. To my enemies, persecutors, and slanderers, forgiveness for the wrongs which they have done. Vouchsafe to the married, purity; to penitents, forgiveness; to the just, perseverance; and pardon to sinners, of whom, alas, I am chief. Bring back all heretics and schismatics, enlighten the ignorant, restore the backsliding, give to widows and orphans sustenance, to the poor protection, to mourners consolation, to the sick and afflicted, comfort and relief, and lastly, to all the faithful, living and departed, grace, peace, and everlasting life. Through.

For the Church.

27. Almighty and everlasting GOD, Who hast in CHRIST revealed Thy glory unto all nations; protect the works of Thy mercy, that the Church spread throughout the world may abide with steadfast faith in the confession of Thy Name. Through the same.

28. O GOD, Who hast vouchsafed to raise up in every age defenders of Thy Church, to put down her enemies, and to restore the solemnities of Thy holy service; grant that we, following their footsteps, may so abide in Thy service, that overcoming all the snares of our enemies, we may rejoice in perpetual peace. Through.

29. O GOD, the might of them that hope in Thee, Who hast strengthened Thy Saints with the gift of constancy to defend the liberties of Thy Church; grant that we may valiantly strive against and overcome all obstacles. Through.

30. O LORD JESU CHRIST, LORD mighty in battle, make, I pray Thee, Thy Church militant mighty also in battle. Give her courage to attack all strongholds of infidelity and sin; arm her with patience under apparent failure, and perseverance against ever-renewed opposition. Above all, kindle in her such love of souls for Thy most blessed sake, that she may toil and travail for the salvation of all men, and may always and everywhere reflect Thine Image, and impart Thy consolations. Who.

31. O LORD JESU CHRIST, Strength of Israel, keep, I entreat Thee, Thy holy Church militant from backslidings and errors, from laxity and superstition, from coldness and lukewarmness, from dead faith and dead works, from the gates of hell, and from the bottomless pit. Who.

32. O LORD JESU CHRIST, Who standest for an Ensign of the people, rally around Thee Thy people, and bid them stand up, an exceeding great army, to do battle against the hosts of darkness. Let no traitor be in the camp, no deserter weaken the hands of his brethren, no panic turn to shameful flight, no fear make feeble, no rashness court ruin: but where Thou leadest, give us grace and courage to follow; that where Thou abidest, we also may abide with Thee. Who.

33. O LORD JESU CHRIST, Builder and Maker of the City which hath foundations, preserve Thy Church, I entreat Thee, evermore by Thine almighty power. Let her walls be salvation, and her gates praise; let her be all-glorious within, by the indwelling of the HOLY GHOST; let her raiment be of wrought gold, even of the alms, precious, self-denying gifts, and free-will offerings of Thy ransomed people. Through Thy mercy.

For the Peace and Unity of the Church.

34. O LORD JESU CHRIST, Who saidst unto Thine Apostles, Peace I leave with you, My peace I give unto you; regard not my sins, but the faith of Thy Church, and grant her that Peace and Unity which is agreeable to Thy will. Who livest.

For Church Synods.

35. O Almighty and Everlasting God, Who hast given the Comforter to Thy Church, that He should abide with it for ever; pour forth the blessing of Thy Spirit on our Prelates and Pastors now assembled in Thy Name: defend their hearts from all hindrances of this world, and from all earthly feeling. Grant them abundantly steadfastness of faith, purity of love, sincere desire for peace, and firmness of authority, that they, by the help of Thy Son Jesus Christ our Lord, may both rule Thy flock committed to their care, according to Thy will, and may also, together with their people, receive from the great Shepherd and Bishop of us all the rewards which are promised to Thy Saints, and be united to the number of Thine Elect. Through the same.

For the Holiness of the Priesthood.

36. O Lord God Almighty, Who hast separated us Thy servants from the people, that we may discharge the office of Priests unto Thee; mercifully separate us from sinners, that according to our calling we may be made a chosen generation, a royal priesthood, a holy nation, a peculiar people before Thee. Through.

37. O Lord Jesu Christ, Whose is the unchangeable Priesthood; grant, I pray Thee, that all who on earth are called to be Thy priests may daily follow in Thy blessed footsteps; may show forth in their lives and preaching Thy love and severity, Thy hatred of sin and love of sinners; may be patient toward all men, and for Thy sake may make themselves servants to all. Who.

38. O Lord Jesu Christ, a Minister of the Sanctuary and of the true Tabernacle; give Thine abundant grace, I beseech Thee, to all priests and deacons who minister in Thy Church on earth. Make them holy, blameless, righteous, temperate, meek, pure, zealous, loving: make them for Thy sake willing servants of Thy flock, diligently feeding Thy sheep and Thy lambs. Let all priests delight to celebrate Thy Blessed Sacrament, and all deacons rejoice to serve at Thine Altar. Who.

For all Priests.

39. O God, Who hast given us Thine Only-Begotten Son to be our High Priest, and hast joined unto Him other Priests to be His Ministers to make a pure Sacrifice unto Thee; grant that all who · have been counted worthy of this holy calling, may devoutly serve at Thine Altar, and present themselves as a pure and living offering. Through the same.

For Candidates for Holy Orders.

40. O God, Who dost ever hallow and protect Thy Church; raise up in it through Thy Spirit good and faithful stewards of the Mysteries of Christ, that by their ministry and example the Christian people may, under Thy defence, be guided in the way of truth. Through the same.

For one about to be Ordained or Consecrated.

41. Hear us, we beseech Thee, O Lord, our God, and pour forth upon Thy servant [N.] the blessing of Thy Holy Ghost, and grace to strengthen him for the Office of a Deacon, [*or* Priest, *or* Bishop,] that the beauty of all righteousness may shine forth in him, and also that he may render a good account of the stewardship intrusted to him, and may attain the reward of everlasting blessedness. Through.

For the Increase of Clergy.

42. O Almighty God, look mercifully upon the world, redeemed by the Blood of Thy dear Son, and send forth many more to do the work of the ministry, that perishing souls may be rescued, and Thy glorious triumph may be hastened by the perfecting of Thine elect. Through the same.

For the Superior Clergy.

43. O LORD GOD Almighty, graciously hear our prayers, and hallow the pastors and overseers of Thy flock, that our adversary the devil, overcome by their faith and holiness, may not dare to approach or injure the fold of the LORD. Through.

44. O LORD JESU CHRIST, the SON, consecrated for evermore, call and seal all souls for evermore unto Thy willing service. I pray for all Bishops consecrated to Thee after Thy likeness : help them in every point to copy Thee, their perfect Example. Make them holy, pure, full of good works and hospitality, meek, zealous, poor in spirit, fearless in defence of Thy Church, which is the pillar and ground of the truth. Remember them, O my GOD, for good. Who.

For the Bishop of the Diocese.

45. Grant, O LORD, to Thy servant N . . ., whom Thou hast set over Thy flock in this Diocese, the spirit of counsel and might, the spirit of wisdom and piety, that through the holy conversation of their Bishop the devotion of the faithful may increase, and that the salvation of the flock may be the joy and crown of the shepherd. Through.

During the Vacancy of a See.

46. May Thy boundless loving-kindness, O LORD, grant to Thy Church a Bishop who shall be pleasing to Thee in holiness of life, and profitable to us in watchfulness and zeal. Through.

For divers Orders in the Church.

47. O LORD JESU CHRIST, LORD of Glory, Who didst empty Thyself of glory for our sakes ; give us grace, I beseech Thee, with willing hearts to offer ourselves to Thee, all we are and all we have. Raise up, according to Thy will and for Thy glory, saintly priests, heroic missionaries, self-denying rich and poor, men and women devoted to Thy service, virgins espoused to Thee, married persons loving Thee above all, and each other as Thy precious and cherished gift. Guide us by that wisdom which is pure, peaceable, gentle, easily entreated, merciful, fruitful, without partiality or hypocrisy. And prosper, O LORD, Thy work in our hands. Who.

For Religious Orders.

48. O GOD, Who inspirest and bringest to perfection every good resolve, direct Thy servants in the way of everlasting salvation, and cause them who have left all, and have vowed themselves entirely to Thee, to meditate on heavenly things, and to serve Thee in the toil of penitence, in the spirit of poverty, and in lowliness of heart. Through.

For Sisterhoods.

49. O GOD, Who inhabitest and keepest pure hearts, grant to Christian virgins to know the excellence of virginity, to love that which they know, to preserve faithfully that which they love, that going forth to meet the Bridegroom with kindled lamps, they may be admitted to His heavenly marriage. Through the same.

For those engaged in Works of Mercy.

50. Bless, O LORD, we beseech Thee, all those who are devoted to serve Thee in works of charity, as well for the training of the young as for the reclaiming of the fallen [especially . . . .] Also those who are occupied in visiting the sick, the poor, and the ignorant [especially . . . .] Accept their labours, and grant that while they sympathise with others in their necessity and sorrow, they may bring them to share the joy of the Divine life wherein they live, and may with them attain to that fulness of spiritual perfection which they desire. Through.

For Church Workers.

51. O LORD, we beseech Thee to pour Thy heavenly blessing on all those who are engaged in doing and furthering good works in Thy holy Church; prosper their undertakings, grant them perseverance therein, and stimulate others by their example to like zeal in Thy service. Through.

For the Flock.

52. O LORD JESU CHRIST, look down from heaven, we beseech Thee, upon both the old and the young of Thy flock; bless them in their bodies, and bless them in their souls, and grant that those who have received Thy sign, O CHRIST, upon their foreheads, may, at the day of judgment, be acknowledged by Thee as Thy true children. Who livest.

53. Direct the flock, O LORD, over which Thou hast appointed me, in the way of everlasting salvation, and grant that we, following the example of Thy saints in life and doctrine, may together with them obtain a crown that fadeth not away. Through.

54. O LORD, plant in us all true belief, root out the thorns of false doctrine, and bring to perfection in us the seed of faith, by the overshadowing of the HOLY SPIRIT. Through.

55. O GOD the HOLY GHOST, Sanctifier of the faithful, visit, I pray Thee, the congregation of this parish with Thy love and favour; enlighten their minds more and more with the light of the everlasting Gospel; graft in their hearts a love of the truth; increase in them true religion; nourish them with all goodness, and of Thy great mercy keep them in the same, O blessed SPIRIT, Whom with the FATHER and the SON together we worship and glorify as one GOD, world without end.

For a Mission.

56. O LORD JESU CHRIST, the Great Shepherd of the sheep, Who seekest those that are gone astray, bindest up those that are broken, and healest those that are sick; bless, we beseech Thee, the efforts which Thy servants [are about to] make to convert souls unto Thee. Loosen the tongues of those who [shall] speak in Thy Name; open the deaf ears of the wanderers, that they may hear the words which belong unto salvation, and grant that those whom Thou dost raise to newness of life may, through Thy grace, persevere unto the end; of Thy mercy, O our GOD, Who art blessed, and livest and reignest for ever and ever.

For a Poor Parish.

57. O GOD, Who of Thy goodness preparest for the poor; mercifully look upon this parish, help it in its need, and so move the hearts of Thy faithful people to aid it from their substance, that the destitute may be succoured, the ignorant be taught, and the service of Thy House be worthily performed to Thy honour and glory. Through.

For the Poor of a Parish.

58. O LORD, the Helper of the needy, look in mercy, we beseech Thee, on the sorrows of Thy poor in this parish, and, tempering Thy judgments with mercy, relieve their distress, minister to their necessity, grant them patience in tribulations, and bring them at length unto that wealthy place where they shall hunger no more, neither know any more sickness, but be filled with the abundance of Thy house. Through.

For a Parish in want of Helpers.

59. O LORD, Who didst send the seventy disciples before Thy face into every city and place whither Thou Thyself wouldst come; mercifully regard our labours in this parish, multiply unto us fellow-helpers in the same, and so prosper the work of our hands upon us, that when Thou comest again Thou mayest find all things ready for Thee. Who livest.

For the Building or Restoration of a Church.

60. O GOD, Who didst put into the hearts of Thy servants David and Solomon to build a House to the glory of Thy Name [*or* the heart of Thy Prophet Ezra to rebuild Thy Temple ;] mercifully grant that we who desire to raise [*or* restore] a Church in Thine honour, may be blessed in our endeavour, and enabled to bring it to perfection. Through.

For the Peace of a Parish.

61. Almighty and merciful GOD, Builder and Keeper of the heavenly Jerusalem; build up and keep our dwellings and their inhabitants, that the home of peace and quiet may be in them. Through.

For one's Spiritual Children.

62. Almighty GOD, look mercifully, I beseech Thee, on all my spiritual children; grant them to grow in grace and the knowledge of Thee, guide them in all doubt, comfort them in all trouble, strengthen them in all weakness, and vouchsafe that my ministrations may be profitable to their souls. Through.

For School Children.

63. Pour down Thy blessing, O heavenly FATHER, upon those children whom Thou hast committed to my charge, and give me grace to train them in Thy faith, fear, and love, that as they grow in years they may grow in grace, and may

hereafter be found in the number of Thine elect children. Through.

For Sick Parishioners.

64. O GOD, Who art the Author of love, and Who delightest in true peace and affection; receive the prayers of Thy servants, and heal the sickness of all the faithful in this parish who are diseased [. . .], that with Thee as their Physician they may recover fulness of health, and when whole may alway obey Thy commandments. Through.

On the Recovery of one who has been sick.

65. O GOD, Who art the Giver of life, of health, and of safety, we bless Thy holy Name that Thou hast been pleased to deliver [. . .] from *his* bodily sickness. Gracious art Thou, O LORD, and full of compassion to the children of men. Teach *him* to praise Thee for Thy goodness, and to serve Thee in holiness and righteousness all the days of *his* life.

For Confirmation Candidates.

66. O GOD, the Giver of Heavenly might and increase, Who by the power of Thy HOLY SPIRIT dost confirm the first efforts of feeble souls; grant, we beseech Thee, through His anointing, cleansing of body and soul to Thy servants, who come to Confirmation, that through it all pollution of their ghostly enemies may depart from them. Let there be no room in them for spiritual wickednesses, no failure of ghostly strength, no lurking place for secret sins, but, as they come unto Thee in faith, confirm them by the operation of the HOLY GHOST. Through.

For the Newly Confirmed.

67. Pour, we beseech Thee, O LORD, Thy heavenly blessing upon Thy servants, to whom Thou hast given Thy sevenfold SPIRIT, vouchsafe unto them His grace and gifts, that they may be ever strengthened by Thy protection, that Thy love may be shed abroad in their hearts to cover and vanquish the multitude of their sins, that they may flee from all wickedness, ever striving to fulfil Thy statutes, and that He may graciously rest upon them Who once rested in glory on the Apostles. Through.

For the Unbaptized.

68. Almighty and merciful GOD, Who ever increasest Thy Church with fresh offspring; grant faith and understanding to our Catechumens [. . . . .], that born again in the baptismal font, they may be numbered with Thy children by adoption. Through.

69. O LORD GOD, open the inward ears of the unbaptized [. . . .], and make them enter through the gate of mercy, that by the laver of regeneration, obtaining remission of all their sins, they may be found in CHRIST JESUS our LORD.   Who.

For Schismatics.

70. Almighty GOD, Who willest not that any should perish; send down Thy HOLY SPIRIT, we beseech Thee, upon those who have been deceived by the fraud and malice of the devil, that they may cast away every false opinion, and with hearts enlightened to the knowledge of their end, may return once more into the unity of Thy truth. Through.

For the Jews.

71. O LORD JESU CHRIST, Who art the Temple of the New Jerusalem; guide, I pray Thee, wandering souls into that earthly Jerusalem which is Thy Holy Catholic Church. Let Thy compassions overflow all bounds, and gather into the sanctuary of Thy love every soul which can be made capable of loving Thee. And at last give us, O LORD, part in the worship of that blessed company to whom Thou, in the unity of the Adorable Trinity, shalt be All in all.

72. O LORD JESU CHRIST, Rod of Jesse, I beseech Thee, give us who are now Thy people a holy hope in Thy promises, and a holy fear of Thy threatenings. Receive again into the arms of Thy compassion Thine ancient nation, which Thou hast dispersed to the ends of the earth. Be not angry with them for ever; but whom Thou hast scattered, gather: bless them with us, and show us all Thy salvation.

For Unbelievers.

73. O LORD, Holy FATHER, Almighty and Everlasting GOD, we pray Thee that Thou wouldest make the path of Thy truth and wisdom plain before those who wander uncertainly and doubtfully in the darkness of this world, that when the eyes of their hearts are opened, they may acknowledge Thee One GOD, the FATHER in the SON, and the SON in the FATHER and the HOLY GHOST, and may attain the reward of this confession in the world to come. Through.

For Missions to the Heathen.

74. O LORD JESU CHRIST, Whose will it is that the multitude of the Gentiles should come to the knowledge of the truth through the preaching of Thy Gospel; be present, we beseech Thee, with those who make known Thy Name in heathen lands, and grant that those who have lived in the darkness of error may, by their ministry, be brought to the knowledge of Thee, Who art the true Light, to lighten every man that cometh into the world. And Who.

75. O most glorious LORD, magnify the joys of all the earth, to the end that faith, being spread abroad, may fill the whole world, and that according to the glory of Thy Name, Thou mayest enable us to glorify Thy praise. Through Thy mercy.

76. O Thou Who art great and highly to be praised, spread abroad the faith of Thy Church into all realms; to the end that as, in all her degrees, Thou art acknowledged to be GOD, Thou mayest also be praised in the united devotion of her people: receive of Thy mercy her prayers, and, in the midst of the tempests of this world, be Thou her diligent pilot: so that we may by Thy mercy enter that City which Thou hast founded for ever and ever, and may be received therein, and may tell within its towers Thy marvellous works. Through Thy mercy.

For the Propagation of the Faith.

77. Behold, O GOD our Defender, and look upon the face of Thine Anointed, Who gave Himself a ransom for all, and grant that from the rising up of the sun unto the going down thereof, Thy Name may be great among the heathen, and that in every place a pure oblation may be sacrificed and offered to that Thy holy Name. Through the same.

For unworthy Priests.

78. O most merciful LORD JESU, delivered up by priests and ungodly men to be mocked and scourged and crucified; look down and behold the reproach of Thy Church, which Thou hast loved, and for which Thou didst give Thyself, that Thou mightest hallow and glorify her. Deliver her from the hands of sinful priests who, despising Thy law, turn away men from Thy service, are a cause of stumbling to many, and through whom Thy holy Name is constantly blasphemed. Lay Thine hand upon them, O LORD, and convert them; restore Thy ministers as they were before, and Thine anointed as of old time. Purify the sons of Levi, and purge them as silver. Grant that they may offer unto Thee sacrifice in righteousness, and that as they have hitherto been to Thy sheep a savour of death unto death, they may henceforth be to them a savour of life unto life, so that all who behold them may know that they are a seed whom the LORD hath blessed. Grant this for Thy mercies' sake. Who livest.

Against Persecutors of the Church.

79. Almighty and most merciful GOD, with Whom is no unrighteousness; we beseech Thee in Thy pity to correct those whom the adversary, by his persuasion, hath stirred up to assail the possessions of Thy sanctuary. Through.

80. O LORD GOD of hosts, Who makest Thy Church ever unconquered; check the pride of her persecutors with the might of Thy right hand, that, put to shame for their amendment, they may through Thy mercy repent, and open their eyes to the light of Thy truth. Through.

For any who have asked our Prayers.

81. Stretch forth, O LORD, the right hand of Thy mercy upon Thy servants, that seeking Thee with their whole heart, they may have their needs supplied both in body and soul. Through.

For the Advancement and Perseverance of the Faithful.

82. Vouchsafe, we beseech Thee, O LORD, to strengthen and confirm all Thy faithful [especially . . . .], and to lift them up more continually to heavenly desires. Through.

For Benefactors.

83. Hear us, O merciful and gracious GOD, beseeching Thee for all Thy faithful who have bestowed their alms upon us: regard not our sins, but their faith, who in the faith of Thy Name have given to us of their temporal goods. Thou, O GOD, Who requitest all good works, repay them much for little, and eternal promises for earthly gifts, O Saviour of the world. Who livest.

For Friends.

84. O God, Who hast poured the gift of charity into the hearts of Thy faithful people through the grace of the Holy Spirit; grant unto Thy servants [. . . .], for whom we entreat Thy mercy, health of soul and body, that they may love Thee with all their strength, and with all their love accomplish Thy will. Through.

For those exposed to Temptations.

85. O God, Who willest not the death of a sinner, protect with Thy heavenly aid those who are exposed to special temptations [. . . . .]; and grant that, in the fulfilment of Thy commandments, they may be strengthened by the assistance of Thy grace. Through.

86. O God, Who justifiest the wicked, and desirest not the death of a sinner; we humbly beseech Thy Majesty mercifully to defend with Thy Divine protection Thy servants who put their trust in Thee, and keep them ever under Thy safeguard, that they may alway serve Thee, and not be separated from Thee by any temptations. Through.

For those in Trouble.

87. O merciful God and Heavenly Father, Who hast taught us in Thy Holy Word that Thou dost not afflict willingly, nor grieve the children of men ; look with pity, we beseech Thee, upon the sorrows of [. . . .], remember *him*, O Lord, in mercy ; sanctify Thy fatherly correction to *him;* endue *his* soul with patience under *his* afflictions, and with resignation to Thy blessed will : comfort *him* with a sense of Thy goodness ; lift up Thy countenance upon *him*, and give *him* peace. Through.

88. O Lord, hearken unto our humble petitions, and graciously vouchsafe the help of Thy most merciful pity to those on whom Thou inflictest the severity of Thy righteous chastisement. Through.

89. O Lord Jesu Christ, Who wast forgotten as a dead man out of mind ; show forth Thy loving kindness, I entreat Thee, to all persons who in this world feel themselves neglected, or little loved, or forgotten. Be Thou their beloved Companion, and let communion with Thee be to them more dear than tenderest earthly intercourse. Teach them to seek Thee in prayer, and to find Thee in Thy Blessed Sacrament : teach them to discern Thee in all with whom they come in contact, and to love and serve Thee in them. On earth grant them comfort by the repentance of any who have wronged them, and in Heaven comfort them in the communion of all Saints with each other and with Thee. Where.

90. O Lord Jesu Christ, Whose Visage was so marred more than any man, and Whose Form more than the sons of men ; conform unto Thy Will, I entreat Thee, in loving resignation, all persons on whom Thou hast not bestowed those natural gifts which attract human love. Adorn them with the spiritual graces which are lovely in Thine Eyes, and also in the eyes of men : and make them beautiful in body and soul when Thou comest in Thy kingdom. Where.

91. O Lord Jesu Christ, in Whom the fatherless find mercy, make all orphans, I beseech Thee, loving and dutiful unto Thee, their true Father. Be Thy Will their law, Thy House their home, Thy Love their inheritance. Through Thy mercy.

For those at Sea.

92. O God, Who didst bring our fathers through the Red Sea, and bear them through great waters ; we praise Thy Name, and humbly beseech Thee to vouchsafe to turn away all adversities from Thy servants at sea, and so to protect them from perils by the wood of the Holy Cross as to bring them with a calm voyage unto the haven where they would be. Through.

For the Conversion of Sinners.

93. Almighty GOD, we beseech Thee to hear our prayers for such as sin against Thee, or neglect to serve Thee [especially . . . .], that Thou wouldest vouchsafe to bestow upon them true repentance and earnest longing for Thy service. Through.

For the Lapsed.

94. O GOD of mercy, pity and pardon, GOD of love and peace, Who of Thy tenderness for mankind didst stretch forth Thy hands upon the Cross, Who didst call the Canaanitish woman and the publican to repentance; vouchsafe to convert Thy sinful servants, grant that they may confess their guilt before Thy holy Altar, and humbly seek remission of their sins. Mercifully grant them time for repentance, fruits meet thereof, and a profitable end in true contrition. Who.

95. Grant, we beseech Thee, O LORD, true fruit of repentance to those who have wandered out of the way through sin, that they may obtain pardon for their offences, and be restored cleansed to Thy holy Church. Through.

96. O GOD, merciful and gracious, hear our prayers which we offer in sorrow before Thee for our perishing *brother*, that, turned from the error of *his* ways, *he* may be delivered from death, and that where sin abounds grace may much more abound. Through.

97. O LORD JESU CHRIST, the Good Shepherd, Who feedest with Thine Own Body those sheep which Thou hast purchased with Thine Own Blood; mercifully seek out Thy lost sheep, and bringing it back to the fold, make it fit for the eternal pastures. Who livest.

98. O LORD JESU CHRIST, Who wast numbered with the transgressors, and hast vouchsafed to place on record Thy human descent through Tamar, Rahab, and Bathsheba; show mercy, I beseech Thee, on all fallen women; and give to them and to those who have sinned with them, repentance and amendment of life unto salvation. Through Thy mercy.

For Penitents.

99. Pour, we beseech Thee, O LORD, the spirit of grace and prayer upon Thy servants [especially . . .], that looking upon JESUS lifted up upon the Cross where they have nailed Him by their sins, they may feel true sorrow, may be healed quickly, and live. Through the same.

100. O LORD JESU CHRIST, Who desirest not the death of a sinner, but rather that he should be converted and live; despise not the sacrifice of a troubled spirit, of a broken and contrite heart, which these penitents offer unto Thee. Stablish that which Thou hast wrought in us, and loose Thou in Heaven that which I have loosed in Thy Name on earth. Hallow those ever more and more in Thy fear and love, whom Thou didst seek as their Shepherd when they were astray, and broughtest back on Thy shoulders. Keep them by Thy grace, lest their latter end be worse than the first. Look, O LORD, upon the sorrow of their hearts; be moved with compassion towards them; quickly bring forth the best robe and put it on them, that they may feast at Thy table, and eat with Thee. Who livest.

For returning Penitents.

101. O GOD, Who by the Blood of Thine only SON didst redeem mankind from the power of death;

quicken, we beseech Thee, the souls of all returning penitents, [especially . . . .], and receive upon their return those whom Thou didst recall when they were wandering. Hear their sighs, heal their wounds, strengthen their weakness. Grant them with such contrition to confess their sins, that in the day of judgment they may be found worthy of Thy glory, never more to be lost, as they have been restored by Thy love to the grace which they had forfeited. Hear us, we beseech Thee, for JESUS CHRIST'S sake, our LORD.

For the Faithful Departed.

102. O LORD our Redeemer, Who hast purchased mankind with Thine own Blood, ransoming us by Thy death from the sting of death, and giving us everlasting life through Thy Resurrection; grant rest unto all who have fallen asleep in holiness, in the desert or in the cities, at sea or on land, and in all places, to kings and priests and bishops, to the solitary and the wedded, to all ages and generations, and fit them for Thy heavenly kingdom. Where Thou.

103. O LORD, Fountain of Life, Who by Thy Divine Manhood dost set free the captives; mercifully grant unto Thy servants who pass hence to Thee in faith a dwelling-place in the joy of Paradise. Where.

104. O LORD our SAVIOUR, Who dost feed Thy faithful people in a green pasture, and leadest them to the waters of comfort; turn not away Thy servants from that pleasant land of rest. Where.

General Collects.

105. Almighty GOD, Who didst accept the service and oblation of Thy SON, our LORD JESUS CHRIST; mercifully look upon the devotion and service which I, an unworthy sinner, offer unto Thee in His Name, and grant that they may be acceptable in Thy sight, through His merits. Who liveth.

106. O LORD JESU CHRIST, the Good Shepherd, Who didst lay down Thy life for Thy sheep, and dost quicken them with the food of Thy Body and Blood; fill me, whom Thou hast appointed to keep Thy flock, with the spirit of Thy love, that I may freely spend and be spent for the salvation of Thy sheep. Who livest.

107. O GOD the HOLY GHOST, Who art the Giver of all good gifts; grant unto me the Spirit of Wisdom, that I may instruct Thy flock with the words of eternal truth, and the Spirit of Holiness, that I may go before them, and lead them into those heavenly pastures, where with the FATHER and the SON, Thou livest.

For the Fulfilment of Ordination Vows.

108. O GOD, Who hast turned us from the vanities of this world, and dost kindle in us the love of our high calling; inspire our hearts, and pour into us grace to persevere in Thee, that assisted by Thy power we may fulfil the solemn vows which we have made, and abiding faithfully in our calling may arrive at those blessings which Thou hast vouchsafed to promise to those who persevere unto the end. Through.

That the Grace of Ordination may be preserved.

109. Grant, we beseech, O LORD, that as Thou hast chosen us to stand before Thee, and to serve in Thy mysteries, so we may never fall from the grace of Holy Orders which we have received of Thy bounty. Through.

A Prayer for a Priest.

110. I give Thee thanks, O merciful GOD, that Thou hast chosen me, an unworthy sinner, to the priestly office, that I may beseech Thy mercy for myself a sinner, and for Thy people. Help me, O Almighty GOD, that I may discharge this mine office to the glory of Thy Name, and for the good of Thy people. Grant me the purity and life of angels, seeing that at my hands the Body and Blood of Thy dear Son has to be consecrated for the setting forth of Thy heavenly glory, and for the feeding of Thy flock. Let my thoughts and intentions be alway pleasing to Thee; let my light shine before men in life and example; let me further Thine honour, and the profit of souls, so far as in me lies; let me give myself watchfully unto prayer; and serve Thee, my GOD, fervently and gladly, and make provision for the spirit rather than for the flesh. Grant that I may be pure and chaste in body and soul at all times, lowly in heart, holy in conversation, that I may think little of worldly riches and be freed from earthly cares, that I may wait on Thee, my GOD, without distraction, and be more worthy to partake of Thy holy Sacrament, so that in all my doings Thou mayest be glorified. Through.

For Harmony with Fellow-workers.

111. O GOD, Who art Love, grant to Thy children who eat of Thy bread to bear one another's burdens in perfect goodwill, that Thy peace which passeth all understanding may keep our hearts and minds in CHRIST JESUS our LORD. Who.

112. O GOD, Who makest men to be of one mind in an house; take away from us all cause of dissension, that we may keep the unity of the Spirit in the bond of peace. Through.

113. O LORD, grant that Thy servants who are gathered together in Thy Name, and who eat of the same bread, may with one mind endeavour to provoke one another to love and to good works, that by their holy conversation the sweet savour of CHRIST may be shed abroad. Through the same.

For a good Assistant.

114. O LORD JESU CHRIST, Who sentest Thy seventy disciples two and two together for mutual aid and comfort in preaching the Gospel; grant me, I beseech Thee, the assistance of a wise, devout, and helpful colleague in the spiritual charge of this parish, that, bearing one another's burdens, we may fulfil Thy law. Through Thy mercy.

For a trustworthy Priest to take Sole Charge.

115. Grant, O LORD, that he to whom I shall commit the care of this parish may be a good minister of JESUS CHRIST, nourished up in the words of faith and of good doctrine, and an example to believers in word, in conversation, in charity, in spirit, in faith, in purity, that after my departing no grievous wolves may enter in among my flock, but that when I come again I may find them as I would, and rejoice greatly in their walking in truth, as we have received commandment from Thee. Through.

Against Temptations of the Flesh.

116. O LORD GOD, our Helper and Defender, help, by the power of the HOLY GHOST, us who receive Thy Holy Sacrament; let the strength of chastity and newness of holiness be revived in our flesh, that it, being snatched out of the hand of hell, may be presented by Thy command in the joy of the Resurrection. Through.

For Continence.

117. Vouchsafe us, O LORD, the gift of holy continence, and purifying our souls, hallow also our bodies, which are the members of CHRIST and the temples of the HOLY GHOST, through the merits of the pure Oblation of the Same CHRIST our LORD. Who liveth.

For true Contrition. (*Before Celebration.*)

118. O God, Father Almighty, Who art the Maker of all things, I humbly implore Thee, that whilst I confess before Thine Almighty Majesty that I, Thy servant, have grievously offended, Thou wouldest stretch out unto me the right hand of Thy compassion; to the end that, while I present to Thy loving-kindness this offering for my sins, Thou, O most Merciful, wilt be pleased to absolve me from the wickedness which I have committed. Through.

119. O God of mercy, compassion, and pardon, forgive, I beseech Thee, and pity me Thy servant; graciously be pleased to accept the offering which I present for my sins; of Thy favourable pity and tender mercy pardon whatsoever defilements I have contracted by carnal will and frailty; and grant unto me space for repentance and plenteous sorrow, that I may be counted worthy to receive of Thee forgiveness of my offences. Through.

120. O God, Who art the Saviour of all that live, Who desirest not the death of sinners, neither hast pleasure in the death of those that die; I humbly implore Thee to grant me pardon of my offences, that I may grieve over my trespasses, and hereafter sin no more; that whensoever the last day and end of my life shall come, the holy Angel may receive me cleansed from all sin. Through.

For Charity in Work.

121. O God, Who by Thy holy Apostle hast taught us to be made all things to all men for the salvation of souls; mercifully grant that we, endued with the Spirit of Thy love, may win souls unto Thee, and attain eternal life. Through.

For Steadfastness in Work.

122. O God, Who hast sent Thy servants to preach Thy Word, and to labour for the salvation of others; graciously pour Thy Spirit upon us, and endue us with Thy grace, that we may abide steadfastly in that holy calling. Through.

For Earnestness in Work.

123. Grant us, O Lord, spotless purity of life, and ardent zeal for the salvation of souls, that in all good works and steadfast faith we may preach Thee, and through Thy mercy at length come unto Thee, Who art the Author and Giver of everlasting blessedness. Through.

For Boldness of Preaching.

124. O God, Who for the increase of faith hast made us preachers of Thy Word; grant that what we believe in our hearts unto righteousness we may confess with our mouths unto salvation. Through.

For Manliness.

125. Grant us, O Lord, that being not like children, weak and unstable, we may come to the measure of the stature of a perfect man, and discharge with vigour the work which Thou givest us to do. Through.

For Moral Courage.

126. Grant us, O Lord, such boldness in Thee that we may set our faces as a flint, and not be ashamed, but, contending valiantly for the truth, may out of weakness be made strong, and conquer in Thy might. Through.

Against Self-deception.

127. O God, Who hast warned us that the heart is deceitful above all things; give us wisdom to know our shortcomings, errors, and secret faults, and mercifully cleansing us therefrom, keep us from the temptations of spiritual pride. Through.

Against Unreality.

128. O LORD JESU CHRIST, Who didst rebuke the barren fig-tree, bearing leaves but not fruit; vouchsafe unto us perfect sincerity in thought and deed, and grant that we may carry out in our lives what we have learnt in Thy holy Word. Through.

129. O LORD JESU CHRIST, the LORD Whose ways are right, keep us in Thy mercy from lip-service and empty forms; from having a name that we live, but being dead. Help us to worship Thee by righteous deeds and lives of holiness; that our prayer also may be set forth in Thy sight as the incense, and the lifting up of our hands be as an evening sacrifice. Through Thy mercy.

For Practical Wisdom.

130. O LORD JESU CHRIST, Who hast said that every scribe instructed unto the Kingdom of Heaven is like unto a man that is an householder, which bringeth forth out of his treasure things new and old; grant me such judgment and discretion that I may both steadfastly uphold the ancient laws and usages of Thy Church, and also may be ready to avail myself of new means to meet the fresh wants of this time, so that we may not only be rooted and grounded in Thee, but may continue to grow up unto Thee in all things. Who livest.

131. O LORD JESU CHRIST, Whose Name is called Wonderful, give us grace, I beseech Thee, with all prostration of heart and intellect to adore Thee, Who art with the FATHER and the HOLY GHOST One only LORD GOD. Suffer us not to be seduced from the faith by miscalled reason, or apparent facts of science, or wit and learning of misbelievers, or subtilties of Satan. Have compassion on those who err; and give us all faith to discern Thee, hope to 'reach after Thee, love to cleave unto Thee the Truth: Who, with the FATHER and the HOLY GHOST, livest and reignest one GOD blessed for ever.

When tempted to neglect Duty.

132. O LORD JESU CHRIST, Who by the mouth of Thine Apostle hast said that to him that knoweth to do good, and doeth it not, to him it is sin; grant that I may never cause Thy flock to suffer through my sloth or self-indulgence, but that, watching unceasingly for souls as one that must give an account, I may at length hear the joyful words, Well done, good and faithful servant, enter thou into the joy of thy LORD. Through Thy mercy.

133. O LORD JESU CHRIST, Who wentest about doing good, by Thy most merciful example lead us also, I pray Thee, to show mercy and to do good. Fill us with charity, that we may, as Thou callest us, minister to Thy poor, or pray for all men. Though we be weary, keep us from weariness in well doing; as we have freely received, grant us grace freely to give, and to believe Thy Word that it is more blessed to give than to receive. So in the day of Thy good pleasure may we rest from our labours, and our works follow us. Through Thy mercy.

For the Ministry of Truth and Peace.

134. O GOD, Who dost manifest Thy power by leading the enemies of the Faith out of the darkness of error into the light of truth, and by restoring truth and concord unto the nations; we beseech Thee that we may so labour for these ends, that Thy peace, which passeth all understanding, may keep our hearts and minds in CHRIST JESUS our LORD. Who with Thee.

For the Ministry of Love.

135. O GOD, Who raisest up in the hearts of faithful Pastors the

Spirit of Thy Son, to preach the Gospel to the poor, and to relieve the distresses of the sick and sorrowful; grant unto me, I beseech Thee, a full portion of the same spirit, that in humility and love I may so minister unto their necessities, as with them to be a partaker of everlasting consolation. Through.

For Ministerial Success.

136. O GOD, Who employest men to plant and water Thy Vineyard, whilst Thou alone givest the increase; grant Thy grace unto Thy fellow-workers, that, going on unto perfection in holiness and good works, they may not only save themselves but those who hear them. Through.

137. O LORD JESU CHRIST, LORD GOD of Elijah, as Thou didst put a word in his mouth which a king could neither gainsay nor resist; so now, I beseech Thee, endue Thy priests and preachers with power to convince the world of sin, and to set forth righteousness. Give them grace to wait on their preaching with earnest prayer, devout study, humble painstaking: strengthen them to plant and water, and do Thou, O LORD, give the increase. Who livest.

Before Officiating.

138. O LORD, our Heavenly FATHER, Almighty and Everlasting GOD, graciously look upon Thy servant, whom Thou hast appointed to minister at Thy holy Altar by .... Pour Thy grace and blessing into my soul, that I may be enabled rightly to perform the office of divine worship in Thy holy Temple. Kindle my heart with the love of Thy grace; turn away mine eyes lest they behold vanity; grant me the continual savour of Thy Divine Presence, and grant that I may so follow the example of Thy dearly beloved SON, that all may in me behold Thee, and so be-

holding adore an
Through the same.

Before the

139. O LORD, o｜
to praise Thy holy
my heart from al
and wandering the
my understanding
affections, that I
ently, and devoutl｜
so as to be heard
Thy Divine Majes

After &

140. O LORD
mercifully accept
and grant that w
Thy will on earth
heaven, may there
angels ever prai
Name. Through.

Before workin

141. O GOD, ↑
safed to raise up
teachers to train
the spirit of un
holiness; grant, ↑
that we, following
amples, may so a
that with them
eternal rewards.

Before visiti

142. Almighty
Who dost vouchsa
nistry of Priests t
Thee; we beseec
mercy that wha
visit Thou woulde
soever we bless
bless, and that ↑
mility draw nigh
put to flight, an
peace enter in. ↑
143. Grant, O
our words and c
through Thy mer
erring into the ↑
ness; and rule o↑
may ourselves eve
of Thy command

Before visiting the Sick.

144. O LORD our SAVIOUR, Who didst pass through this world comforting and doing good, and hast willed that we should rejoice with them that rejoice, and weep with them that weep; behold I, in obedience to Thy command, am about to visit and comfort Thy sick and suffering *servant*. Regard not my sins, O merciful LORD, but the task which I am discharging, and so endue me by Thine abundant grace that the sick *man*, lifted up in answer to my prayer, may be established in faith, hope, and charity, or if *he* have gone astray in *his* life, may be brought back to Thee and serve Thee, that *his* sickness may avail to *his* salvation. Through Thy mercy.

After visiting the Sick.

145. O LORD of mercy and Bestower of all good things, graciously vouchsafe that Thy servant whom I have now left may not be left by Thee, but be refreshed by that inward consolation, which surpasseth all the comforting of man. Forgive whatever errors I have committed from lukewarmness or weakness, and increase whatever good I have done. Suffer not the sick *man* to die in *his* sins, but rather that *he* may be converted and live, and that *he* may in all things gladly accept Thy will, whether life or death be appointed for *him*, and leave *him* not, O LORD, without Thy help until Thou seest *him* amongst Thy blessed ones. Through.

Before hearing Confession.

146. O LORD GOD Almighty, be merciful unto me a sinner, that I may fitly execute the priestly office to which Thou hast been pleased to call me, an unworthy sinner, appointing me to pray to Thy SON, our LORD JESUS CHRIST, in behalf of those sinners who turn to Thee in penitence. O GOD, Who wouldest have all men to be saved, and to come to the knowledge of the truth;

Who wouldest not the death of a sinner, but rather that he should be converted and live; receive my prayers for all Thy servants who shall come to Thee in penitence. Give unto them the spirit of compunction; deliver them from the snares of the devil, that, loosed from his chains, they may turn unto Thee in hearty and true repentance. Through.

147. Grant me, O LORD, wisdom which sitteth by Thy throne, that I may know how to judge Thy people in righteousness and Thy poor in equity. Make me so to handle the keys of the Kingdom of Heaven that I may open to none to whom it should be shut, and shut to none to whom it should be open. Let my intention be pure, my zeal sincere, my charity patient, my labour fruitful. Let me have gentleness without laxity, and severity without harshness. Let me not despise the poor, nor flatter the rich. Make me loving in drawing sinners, wise in questioning, skilful in teaching. Bestow on me, I beseech Thee, aptness in withdrawing sinners from evil, perseverance in establishing them in good, diligence in urging them to improvement, discretion in answers, straightforwardness in advice, light in obscurity, judgment in perplexity, persuasiveness over obstinacy. Let me waste no time in useless speech, nor be defiled by evil things. Let me lead others to salvation, and not be myself a castaway. Through.

148. O LORD JESU CHRIST, the Great Physician, Who didst sit at meat with publicans and sinners; mercifully keep me clean from all stain of sinful thought when ministering to guilty souls, that Thy grace, which is present to heal their diseases, may guard me from all contagion. Through Thy mercy, O our GOD, Who art blessed, and livest.

After hearing Confession.

149. O LORD JESU CHRIST, SON

of the living GOD, accept this my bounden duty and service, and in mercy accomplish that which Thou hast wrought by my means. And whercinsoever I have failed in my duty through negligence or imperfection, do Thou vouchsafe to supply all my defects. Unto Thy love I commend *each one of those* who *have* now confessed *their* sins unto Thee, beseeching Thee to keep *them* for evermore, to preserve *them* from falling back again into sin, and after this miserable life to bring *them* to Thine everlasting joy. Amen.

150. Shut the door of my mind, O LORD, against the images of evil things, that my soul may not henceforth be allured by any delight of sin. Grant me to serve Thee purely here, and to reign with Thee for ever. Through Thy mercy and merit, Who without spot of sin didst bear the sins of many, O blessed LORD JESU. Who.

Before any Office.

151. O merciful GOD, let that which is performed by our humble ministration be fulfilled by Thine effectual power. Through.

After any Office.

152. Be present, O merciful GOD, that what has been done by our office and ministry, may be confirmed by Thy blessing. Through.

Before a Baptism.

153. O GOD, Who art pleased to admit every age and sex to serve Thy Divine Majesty; we beseech Thee for *him* who is to be dedicated to Thee in Holy Baptism, grant that the sign of the holy Cross of Thine Only-begotten SON may protect *him*, that *he* may be Thine, may grow up unto Thee, fear Thee, love Thee, always know Thee for *his* Creator, and come by Thy guidance through the holy laver of Regeneration to the land of everlasting life. Grant this for the sake.

After a Baptism.

154. O GOD, Who hast granted unto Thy servant, through Holy Baptism, remission of sins and the life of Regeneration; let the light of Thy Countenance ever shine on *his* heart. Guard *his* faith safe from the assaults of *his* enemies, keep clean and unstained the garment of incorruption which *he* has now put on, and preserve in *him* unbroken the spiritual seal of grace, in Thy mercy to *him* and us. Through.

Before a Marriage.

155. We beseech Thee, Almighty GOD, to bless the institution of Thy Providence with Thy loving kindness, that Thou mayest keep in lengthened peace those whom Thou dost join in lawful union. Through.

After a Marriage.

156. Almighty and everlasting GOD, Who hast united Thy servants in the covenant of marriage, fulfil in them Thy blessing, that agreeing in unbroken affection they may please Thee by their holy conversation, and may be joined together in eternal fellowship in heaven. Through.

Before a Funeral.

157. O LORD, we beseech Thee, grant unto this Thy servant that the sins which *he* hath committed in this world may not be imputed unto *him*, but that *he*, escaping the gates of hell, and the pains of eternal darkness, may ever dwell in the region of light with Abraham, Isaac, and Jacob in the place where is no weeping, sorrow, nor heaviness; and when that dreadful day of the general resurrection shall come, make *him* to rise also with the just and righteous, and receive *his* body again to glory, then made pure and incorruptible. Set *him* on the right hand of Thy SON JESUS CHRIST, among Thy holy and elect, that then *he* may hear with them those most sweet and comfortable words, "Come, ye blessed of My FATHER, inherit the kingdom prepared for you from the beginning of the world." Grant this, we beseech Thee, O merciful FATHER. Through.

After a Funeral.

158. O LORD, incline Thine ears unto our prayers, wherein we call upon Thy mercy, that Thou wilt bestow the soul of Thy servant which Thou hast commanded to depart from this world, in the land of peace and rest, and cause it to be made a partner with Thy holy servants. Through.

[Also Collect for First Sunday in Advent.]

Before Study.

159. O LORD GOD, the Fountain of Wisdom, Who by Thy well-beloved SON hast taught us that every scribe instructed unto the kingdom of heaven should bring forth from his treasures things new and old; vouchsafe unto me diligence and foresight. Grant me the spirit of judgment that I may discern between good and evil; the spirit of understanding that I may fully know the purport of that which I read; the gift of memory that I may retain it; and readiness with fluency that I may use it in Thy service for the profit of souls committed to my teaching. Through.

160. Almighty GOD, Who hast created man in Thine own image, and made him a living soul, that he might seek after Thee, and have dominion over Thy creatures; teach us to study the works of Thy hands, that we may subdue the earth to our use, and strengthen our reason for Thy service; and so to receive Thy blessed Word, that we may believe on Him Whom Thou hast sent, to give us the knowledge of salvation and the remission of our sins. All which we ask in the Name of the same.

Before preparing a Sermon.

161. O GOD the HOLY GHOST, Who enlightenest the minds of Thy children; send down upon me, I pray Thee, the Spirit of wisdom and understanding, to lead me into all truth, that I may so feed the flock committed unto me with the words of eternal life, as with them to attain unto that place where Thou livest.

Before Preaching.

162. O LORD JESU CHRIST, Who hast done all things well, Who makest both the deaf to hear and the dumb to speak; put, I beseech Thee, Thy hands upon me; loose the string of my tongue, that I may speak plain. Open the deaf ears of Thy people, that they may hear the words which belong unto eternal life; through Thy mercy, Who livest.

After Preaching.

163. Almighty and everlasting GOD, the source and perfection of all goodness, grant us, we pray Thee, ever to do what is right, and to preach what is true, that by our acts and teaching we may give instruction to Thy faithful people. Through.

For a Clergyman unemployed.

164. Here am I, O LORD, send me as a messenger of Thy kingdom, as a labourer into Thy harvest, whithersoever Thou wilt, and if it be Thy good pleasure to set me aside for a time, grant me to serve Thee by patient waiting and purity of life. Through.

For Retired Clergy.

165. O LORD JESU CHRIST, our Great High Priest, eternal in the heavens, Who art Thyself the caller and sender of all Priests who minister in Thy holy Gospel on the earth; mercifully vouchsafe unto all who from any cause are withdrawn from active labour in that holy calling, that they may ever bear in mind the solemn vows that they have made unto Thee; may abstain from all worldly and sinful acts, words, and deeds; and may still do Thee true and laudable service in their several conditions, that they finally lose not the reward which Thou hast promised to Thy true and faithful servants. Who livest.

Occasional Offices.

OFFICE FOR CONFESSION.

BEFORE CONFESSION.

The Priest and Penitent kneel down.

In the Name, &c.
Our FATHER, &c.

℣. There is a shame that bringeth sin. ℟. And there is a shame that bringeth glory and grace. ℣. The LORD be with you. ℟. And with thy spirit. ℣. Let us pray.

Coll. for Ash Wednesday. Almighty and everlasting GOD, &c.
Coll. for Purity. Almighty GOD, unto Whom, &c.

THE FORM OF CONFESSION.

According to the use of Sarum.

The Priest seats himself. The Penitent remains kneeling, and says,

"Sir, pray for a blessing."
Priest. "The LORD be in thy heart and in thy lips, that thou mayest rightly confess thy sins."
Penitent. "I confess to GOD Almighty, FATHER, SON, and HOLY GHOST, and before the whole company of heaven, and to you, that I have sinned grievously, through my fault, through my own fault, through my own most grievous fault."

Then he proceeds with his Confession, saying,

"Since my last Confession, which was (at such a time,) I have," &c., &c.

The Priest hears the Confession without interruption, unless it be necessary, as where the Penitent is afraid to confess, or does not sufficiently explain the number, and kind, and circumstances of his sins.

He observes what is necessary, and enjoins a penance, varying as to state, condition, age, sex, disposition, &c.

The Penitent promises to perform it.

THE FORM OF ABSOLUTION.

Almighty GOD have mercy upon thee, and forgive thee thy sins, and bring thee to life everlasting.

He raises his right hand.

The Almighty and merciful LORD grant thee absolution and remission of all thy sins.

Our LORD JESUS CHRIST, Who hath left power to His Church to absolve all sinners who truly repent and believe in Him, of His great mercy forgive thee thine offences: And by His authority committed to me, I absolve thee from all thy sins, In the Name, &c.

The Passion of our LORD JESUS CHRIST, and His infinite merits, make whatever good thou hast done, or evil thou hast endured, be to thee for the remission of sins, and the increase of grace, and the reward of eternal life. Amen.

OFFICE FOR THE VISITATION OF A PRISONER.

In the Name, &c.

Remember not, LORD, our iniquities, nor the iniquities of our forefathers ; neither take Thou vengeance of our sins : Spare us, good LORD, spare Thy people, whom Thou hast redeemed with Thy most precious blood, and be not angry with us for ever.

Ans. Spare us, good LORD.

Let us pray.
LORD, have mercy, &c.
Our FATHER, &c.

℣. O LORD, show Thy mercy upon us. ℞. And grant us Thy salvation. ℣. Turn Thy face from our sins. ℞. And blot out all our iniquities. ℣. Send us help from Thy holy place. ℞. For Thine indignation lieth hard upon us. ℣. O LORD, hear our prayer. ℞. And let the sighing of the prisoners come before Thee.

Let us pray.

Grant, we beseech Thee, Almighty GOD, that we, who for our evil deeds do worthily deserve to be punished, by the comfort of Thy grace may mercifully be relieved ; through our LORD and SAVIOUR JESUS CHRIST. Amen.

166. O GOD, Who sparest when we deserve punishment, and in Thy wrath rememberest mercy ; we humbly beseech Thee, of Thy goodness, to comfort and succour all those who are under reproach and misery in the house of bondage ; correct them not in Thine anger, neither chasten them in Thy sore displeasure. Give them a right understanding of themselves, and of Thy threats and promises ; that they may neither cast away their confidence in Thee, nor place it anywhere but in Thee. Relieve the distressed, protect the innocent, and awaken the guilty ; and forasmuch as Thou alone bringest light out of darkness, and good out of evil, grant that the pains and punishments which these Thy servants endure, through their bodily confinement, may tend to setting free their souls from the chains of sin ; through JESUS CHRIST our LORD. Amen.

Here the Priest shall examine him concerning his faith, and rehearse the Articles of the Creed, Dost thou believe in GOD, *&c. And the prisoner shall answer,*

All this I steadfastly believe.

Then shall the Priest examine whether he repent him truly of his sins, and be in charity with all the world, and further admonish him particularly concerning the crimes wherewith he is charged ; and exhort him to prepare himself for the Holy Communion, against the time that it may be proper to administer it to him.
Then all kneeling, the Priest shall say the 51st Psalm.

Have mercy upon me, &c.

Let us pray.

O LORD, we beseech Thee, mercifully hear our prayers, and spare all those who confess their sins unto Thee ; that they, whose consciences by sin are accused, by Thy merciful pardon may be absolved ; through CHRIST our LORD. Amen.

167. O GOD, Whose mercy is everlasting and power infinite ; look down with pity and compassion upon the sufferings of *this* Thy *servant ;* and whether Thou visitest for trial of *his* patience, or punishment of *his* offences, enable *him* by Thy grace cheerfully to submit *himself* to Thy holy will and pleasure. Go not far from those, O LORD, whom Thou hast laid in a place of darkness, and in the deep; and forasmuch as Thou hast not cut *him* off suddenly, but chastenest *him* as a father, grant that *he*, duly considering Thy great mercies, may be unfeignedly thankful, and turn unto Thee with true repentance and sincerity of heart; through JESUS CHRIST our LORD. Amen.

Prayers for persons under sentence of Death.

When a criminal is under sentence of Death, the Priest shall examine whether he repent him truly of his sins, exhorting him to a particular confession of the sin for which he is condemned; and upon Confession, he shall instruct him what satisfaction ought to be made to those whom he hath offended thereby: and if he knoweth any combinations in wickedness, or any evil practices designed against others, let him be admonished to the utmost of his power to discover and prevent them.
After his Confession the Priest shall pronounce Absolution, if fitting.
After which shall be said the Collect following.

168. O Holy JESU, Who of Thine infinite goodness didst accept the conversion of a sinner on the cross; open Thine eye of mercy upon this Thy servant, who desireth pardon and forgiveness, now that in *his* latest hour *he* turneth unto Thee. Renew in *him* whatsoever hath been decayed by the fraud and malice of the devil, or by *his* own carnal will and frailness. Consider *his* contrition; accept *his* repentance; and forasmuch as *he* putteth *his* full trust only in Thy mercy, impute not unto *him his* former sins, but strengthen *him* with Thy blessed Spirit; and when Thou art pleased to take *him* hence, take *him* unto

Thy favour: this we beg through Thy merits, O LORD, our SAVIOUR and our Redeemer. Amen.

169. O FATHER of mercies and GOD of all comfort, we fly unto Thee for succour in behalf of this Thy servant, who is now under the sentence of condemnation. The day of *his* calamity is at hand, and *he* is accounted as one of those who go down into the pit. Blessed LORD, remember Thy mercies; look upon *his* infirmities; hear the voice of *his* complaint; give *him*, we beseech Thee, patience in this *his* time of adversity, and support under the terrors which encompass *him*; set before *his* eyes the things *he* hath done in the body, which have justly provoked Thee to anger; and forasmuch as *his* continuance appeareth to be short amongst us, quicken *him* so much the more by Thy grace and HOLY SPIRIT; that *he*, being converted and reconciled unto Thee before Thy judgments have cut *him* off from the earth, may at the hour of *his* death depart in peace, and be received into Thine everlasting kingdom; through JESUS CHRIST our LORD. Amen.

O SAVIOUR of the world, Who by Thy Cross and precious Blood hast redeemed us, save us and help us, we humbly beseech Thee, O LORD.

Then the Priest standing, shall say,

In the midst of life we are in death: of whom may we seek for succour, but of Thee, O LORD, Who for our sins art justly displeased?

Yet, O LORD GOD most holy, O LORD most mighty, O holy and most merciful SAVIOUR, deliver us not into the bitter pains of eternal death.

Thou knowest, LORD, the secrets of our hearts: shut not Thy merciful ears to our prayers; but spare us, LORD most holy, O GOD most mighty, O holy and merciful SAVIOUR, Thou most worthy Judge eternal, suffer us not at our last hour, for any pains of death to fall from Thee.

Benediction. The Almighty GOD, Who is a most strong tower to all those who put their trust in Him; to Whom all things in heaven, in earth, and under the earth, do bow and obey; be now and evermore thy defence; and make thee know and feel that there is none other name under heaven given to man, in Whom and through Whom thou mayest receive salvation, but only the Name of our LORD JESUS CHRIST. Amen.

And after that shall say,

Unto GOD'S gracious mercy and protection we commit thee: The LORD bless thee and keep thee: the LORD make His face to shine upon thee, and be gracious unto thee: the LORD lift up His countenance upon thee, and give thee peace both now and evermore.

At the time of Execution, besides all, or such parts of the foregoing Office as the Minister shall judge proper, shall be said the Commendatory Prayer for a person at the point of departure, *as it is in the Visitation of the Sick.*

The Collect for the Communion Service.

170. O GOD, Who declarest Thy Almighty power chiefly in showing mercy and pity; we beseech Thee to have mercy upon this Thy servant, who for *his* transgressions is appointed to die. Grant that *he* may take Thy judgments patiently, and repent *him* truly of *his* sins; that *he* recovering Thy favour, the fearful reward of *his* actions may end with this life; and whensoever *his* soul shall depart from the body, it may be without spot presented unto Thee; through JESUS CHRIST our LORD. Amen.

The Epistle. Heb. xii. 11.

No chastening for the present seemeth to be joyous, but grievous; nevertheless, afterwards it yieldeth the peaceable fruit of righteousness, unto them which are exercised thereby.

The Gospel. S. John v. 24.

Verily, verily, I say unto you, He that heareth My word, and believeth on Him that sent Me, hath everlasting life, and shall not come into condemnation; but is passed from death unto life.

For one imprisoned for the first time.

171. O GOD, Who, in mercy for the souls of Thy children, dost suffer temporal judgments to overtake them, that they may by penitence escape the sentence of condemnation at the last day; make Thy servant so to profit by this punishment, that *he* may be brought thereby to newness of life, and fulfilling henceforth *his* duties both towards GOD and man may be able to say at the last, It is good for me that I have been in trouble. Grant this.

For an old Offender.

172. Almighty GOD, Who mightest justly have cut off Thy servant in the midst of *his* many sins, but Who hast yet been pleased to spare *him*, that *he* may repent and return to Thee; grant this grace unto *him*, O LORD, and deliver *him* from the power of temptation, that *he* may go forth to return hither no more. And as Thou didst write Thy law on tables of stone, so imprint it upon the heart of Thy servant, that steadfastly walking in the path of Thy Commandments, *he* may henceforth by Thy help do those things which are well-pleasing in Thy sight. Through.

OFFICE WITH THE FRIENDS OF A PRISONER.

In the Name, &c.

Our FATHER, &c.   I believe, &c.

℣. Despise not the chastening of the LORD. ℟. Neither be weary of His correction. ℣. O GOD, make speed, &c. ℟. O LORD, make haste, &c. ℣. Glory, &c. ℟. As it was, &c.

Ant. GOD is a righteous Judge, strong and patient.

Ps. 25. Unto Thee, O LORD, will I lift up, &c.

50. The LORD, even the most mighty GOD, &c.

53. The foolish body hath said, &c.

60. O GOD, Thou hast cast us out, &c.

107, (1—23.) O give thanks unto the LORD, &c.

Ant. GOD is a righteous Judge, strong and patient, and GOD is provoked every day.

The Chapter.   2 Chron. vi.

If they sin against Thee (for there is no man that sinneth not,) and Thou be angry with them, and deliver them over before their enemies, and they carry them away captives unto a land far off or near : yet if they bethink themselves in the land whither they are carried captive, and turn and pray unto Thee in the land of their captivity, saying, We have sinned, we have done amiss, and have dealt wickedly : if they return to Thee with all their heart, and with all their soul, in the land of their captivity, whither they have carried them captives, and pray toward their land, which Thou gavest unto their fathers, and toward the city which Thou hast chosen, and toward the house which I have built for Thy Name : then hear Thou from the heavens, even from Thy dwelling-place, their prayer and their supplications, and maintain their cause, and forgive Thy people which have sinned against Thee.

[Ep. 4th S. a. Epiph. ; 3rd S. a. East. ; Gosp. 3rd and 6th S. a. T. App. 2, 13, 20.]

℣. But Thou, &c. ℟. Thanks, &c. ℣. If they be bound in fetters, and holden in cords of affliction. ℟. Then He showeth them their work, and their transgressions that they have exceeded. ℣. Glory, &c. ℟. As it was, &c. ℣. He openeth also their ear to discipline. ℟. And commandeth that they return from iniquity. ℣. The LORD, &c. ℟. And with, &c. ℣. Let us pray.

LORD, have mercy, &c.

Our FATHER, &c.

℣. O LORD, correct me, but with judgment. ℟. Not in Thine anger, lest Thou bring me to nothing. ℣. Turn our captivity, O LORD. ℟. As the rivers in the south. ℣. Wash us throughly from our wickedness. ℟. And cleanse us from our sin. ℣. LORD, hear, &c. ℟. And let, &c. ℣. Let us pray.

Then shall follow the Collect, O GOD, Who sparest, *in previous Office.*

[Colls. : O GOD, Whose nature and property. Sept. ; 4th S. in L.]

Benediction. The LORD JESUS CHRIST, SON of GOD, Who, bearing the marks of the Cross, broke the gates of brass and smote the bars of iron in sunder, shine on your darkness with His wonderful light.

VARIOUS BENEDICTIONS.

Each Benediction should begin as follows:

℣. Our help is in the Name of the LORD. ℟. Who hath made heaven and earth. ℣. The LORD be with you. ℟. And with thy spirit. ℣. Let us pray.

Of Gifts to the Church.

173. O LORD GOD, Who hast commanded every man to offer unto Thee of Thine own gifts, according to the purpose of his heart, and Who dost abundantly requite them from Thine eternal bounty; Who didst graciously receive the widow's mites; accept the offerings now made unto Thee by Thy *servant*, and grant that they may be stored up in Thine eternal treasures. Who.

Of Altar Vessels, &c.

174. O LORD GOD Almighty, Who didst during forty days instruct Thy servant Moses to make ornaments and fine linen for the use of Thy ministry and the Tabernacle of the Covenant; vouchsafe to bl+ess, hallow, and consecrate this [. . . . .] for the service of the Altar of Thy most glorious SON our LORD JESUS CHRIST. Who liveth.

Of Surplices, &c.

175. O GOD, Whose power is Almighty, Who art the Creator and hallower of all things; graciously hear our prayers, and vouchsafe Thyself to bl+ess and hallow these garments for the use of Thy ministers, and grant that all those that use them, attending in Thy Temple, and serving Thee devoutly and reverently in them, may become well-pleasing unto Thee. Through.

Of Service Books.

176. O LORD, cause the might of Thy HOLY SPIRIT to descend on these books, to cleanse, purify, bl+ess, and hallow them; and may He mercifully enlighten our hearts, and give us understanding to keep Thy commandments, and to fulfil them in good works according to Thy will. Through.

Of a Thurible.

177. O LORD GOD, Who when the plague raged amongst the children of Israel, murmuring in the wilderness, by reason of their rebellious obstinacy, didst vouchsafe to hear Aaron Thy Priest as he took a censer and put fire therein from off the altar and put on incense, and didst deliver them from the plague; bl+ess, we pray Thee, O LORD, this censer, and grant that so often as incense is burned therein Thou mayest make the prayer of Thy people ascend as a sweet savour unto Thee. Through.

Of Incense.

178. O LORD GOD Almighty, in Whose Presence the Heavenly Host, whose ministrations are of spirit and fire, standeth trembling; vouchsafe to behold, bl+ess, and sanc+tify this creature of incense, that all weakness, and all the wiles of the enemy may, as its perfume ascends, be put to flight, and be driven away from us, the work of Thy hand, whom Thou hast redeemed with the precious Blood of Thy SON, that we may at no time be hurt by the bite of the old Serpent. Hear us, O LORD, for the sake.

Of Tapers.

179. O LORD JESU CHRIST, SON

of the living God, bl+ess, we beseech Thee, this taper; pour upon it, by the power of the Holy Cross, Thy heavenly blessing, to dispel the darkness of mankind, that in whatsoever place it be kindled or set up, the princes of darkness may depart, tremble, and be put to flight with all their ministers from these habitations, and no more venture to disquiet or molest Thy servants, O Almighty God. Who livest.

Of a Crucifix.

180. Almighty and everlasting God, we humbly beseech Thy Majesty to bl+ess and hal+low this [crucifix *or* picture] in which is represented the most glorious Form of Thy Son our Lord Jesus Christ, and to vouchsafe that whoso looks upon it with true devotion towards Him may be granted health of body and mind, be delivered from all perils, and obtain whatever *he* asks for fitly. Through the same.

Of a Cross.

181. O Lord Jesu Christ, Almighty and everlasting God, Who by the will of Thy Father didst save the world by shedding Thy Blood in Thy Passion on the Cross; bl+ess and hal+low, we beseech Thee, as a sign of Thy Triumph and the banner of our salvation, this Cross, which we conse+crate in love and honour of Thy victorious Name, and grant that whosoever bears it or looks upon it may be ever mindful of Thy saving Passion, and bear about in his body Thy dying. Who livest.

Of a Tabernacle or Ciborium.

182. Almighty and Everliving God, Who by the hand of Moses didst command Thy servant Aaron to take of the manna which Thou didst send down from Heaven for the food of Thy people Israel, and to lay up the same to be kept continually before Thee; Who hast declared by Thy well-beloved Son that Thou givest unto those who believe to eat of the True and Living Bread which cometh down from Heaven, and giveth life unto the world; vouchsafe to accept, con+secrate, and bl+ess this receptacle, that therein the most holy Sacrament of the Body and Blood of Christ may be continually preserved for the honour of Thy Name, and for the spiritual food and nourishment of our souls. Through the same.

Of a Grave.

183. O God, through Whose mercy the souls of the faithful departed are at rest, vouchsafe to bl+ess this grave, and appoint Thine holy Angel to keep it, and deliver from all the bonds of sin the souls of such as shall be buried here, that they may ever rejoice in Thee, together with Thy Saints, in everlasting gladness. Through.

Of a Well.

184. O Lord God Almighty, Who makest and fashionest all things by Thy holy Will, and didst cause streams of water to flow out of the stony rock to fill Thy thirsting people; hearken now likewise to the prayers of us Thy servants, and grant us water in this place, clear and fit for drinking, sufficient for our need, and wholesome for our use, that we may give thanks unto Thy holy Name. Through.

Of a Medal or Badge.

185. O God, Who didst will that two cherubim should be set upon either side of the Mercy-seat; vouchsafe, we beseech Thee, of Thy Fatherly goodness to bl+ess and hal+low this medal (*or* badge) of . . . ., and grant that whosoever wears it, mindful of the mystery which it represents, may be kindled with devout affections and increase in holiness of life. Through.

Of a Church Banner.

186. O LORD GOD Almighty, bl+ess, we beseech Thee, this Banner, as Thou didst bless the brazen serpent lifted up upon a spear in the wilderness, prefiguring the lifting up of Thine Only-begotten SON upon the Cross in later time ; and bl+ess it, as Thou didst bless Thy chosen servant David, when he went forth against the Philistine with a sling and with a stone, foreshowing in the battle the might of Thine Only-begotten SON, Which was to come into the world. Look down upon us from above, and in mercy grant unto us those things which we neither dare to ask, nor hope to attain, but through the same.

Of a Wedding Ring.

187. Bl+ess, O LORD, this Ring which we bl+ess in Thy Name, that she who wears it may abide in Thy peace, continue in Thy favour, live, go on, and grow old in Thy love, and may be increased with length of days. Through.

Of a Military Flag.

188. O LORD JESU, SAVIOUR and Redeemer of all, bow down the ears of Thy loving-kindness to our humble petitions, and grant us the aid of Thy Right Hand, that as Thou didst bless Abraham vanquishing the five kings, and David the king holding his assembly of triumph in honour of Thy Name, so vouchsafe to bl+ess and hal+low this standard which is borne in our defence against the fierceness of our enemies, that Thy faithful servants and defenders of Thy people, marching beneath it, may rejoice in winning triumph and victory over their enemies by the power of the Holy Cross. Through Thee, O JESU CHRIST. Who livest.

Of a Good Work.

189. O GOD, from Whom every good thing hath its beginning, and receiveth its increase as it goeth on towards perfection ; grant, we humbly beseech Thee, that the work which we undertake for the glory of Thy Name, may be brought to completion by the eternal gift of Thy fatherly wisdom. Through.

Of Remedies.

190. Bl+ess, O LORD, this creature [N.], that it may be a remedy profitable to mankind, and grant, through the invocation of Thy most holy Name, that whosoever useth [*or* tasteth of] it may obtain health for *his* body, and salvation for *his* soul. Through.

Of a House or Place.

191. O LORD, bl+ess this house [*or* place], that in it there may be health, charity, peace, lowliness, kindness, gentleness, fulfilling of the Law, and thanksgiving to the FATHER, SON, and HOLY GHOST ; and let this bless+ing abide on this house [*or* place], and on those who dwell in it. Through.

Of a Ship.

192. We beseech Thee, O LORD, to keep Thy servants who trust in Thy Name with Thine unconquered Right Hand, which saved Noah in the ark during the flood, which rescued Peter trembling in the waters that came upon him, and the ship beset with a storm in the sea of Tiberias, and that in like manner Thou wouldst grant to this ship favourable winds and prosperous voyages, that they who rejoice in Thy Name may come in safety unto the haven where they would be, O CHRIST, Thou SAVIOUR of the world. Who.

193. May this ship speed over the waters as upon the wings of an eagle, the SON of GOD be its Pilot, and the Angels its helpers ; may favourable breezes be sent from heaven to fill its sails, and may its voyages be prosperous. Through Thy mercy, O SON of GOD, Ruler of the world. Who livest.

Of Fishing Nets.

194. O LORD JESU CHRIST, Who chosest fishers for Thine Apostles, and didst twice grant them a miraculous draught, bl+ess, we beseech Thee, these nets for the service of mankind, and vouchsafe that those who use them may labour diligently and prosperously in their calling in this world, and that when the net of the kingdom of heaven is drawn to the shore they may in no wise be cast away, but may be gathered into Thy vessels. Through Thy mercy, O our GOD, Who art blessed and livest.

A General Benediction.

195. O GOD, by Whose word all things that we do, or by which we are influenced, are hallowed; pour, we beseech Thee, Thy blessing upon us, and upon this Thy creature, that by the invocation of Thy holy Name we may, through Thy mercy, thankfully receive whatsoever the needs of this present life require. Through.

PERSONAL BENEDICTIONS.

A General Form.

The Power of the FATHER, the Wisdom of the SON, the Love of the HOLY GHOST, the Grace of the blessed and undivided Trinity, be with you and preserve you, now, henceforth, and for evermore.

On beginning a Good Work.

GOD, Who is the Alpha and Omega, and Who worketh in you both to will and to do of His good pleasure, be Himself the beginning and the end of your work.

Before a Journey.

The LORD thy GOD send His Angel before thee to keep thee in the way, and to bring thee into the place which He hath prepared.

Before a First Confession.

GOD, Who bringeth to light the hidden things of darkness, and maketh manifest the counsels of the hearts, give unto thee knowledge of thyself in the face of CHRIST JESUS our LORD.

Before Confirmation.

GOD, the GOD of all grace, Who hath called you unto His eternal glory by CHRIST JESUS, enlighten your soul with His sevenfold ray, and stablish you with His free Spirit.

Before First Communion.

The LORD so feed you with the Bread of Angels here on earth that you may at last sit down to eat Bread in the kingdom of heaven.

In Serious Trouble.

GOD, the SON of GOD, Who hath suffered you to be cast into the furnace of affliction, Himself walk with you in the fire, and deliver you out of your trouble.

In Ordinary Trouble.

CHRIST, Who comforteth us in all our tribulation, support you in your trial and bring you peace.

For Mourners.

JESUS CHRIST, Who wept at the grave of Lazarus, Himself be your comforter, and wipe away all tears from your eyes.

For Children.

JESUS, Who called little children unto Him, take you into His arms,

u to grow up unto Him
.

For Advent.

Son of God, Who came
s to restore you, free
e chains of your sins,
ay await His Second
out fear.

or Christmas.

Child of Mary, Who
d unto you a new birth
increase you in spiritual
stature until you attain
easure of the perfect

or Epiphany.

he Salvation of God,
ccept your service, and
your hearts with His
lory.

For Lent.

Who for you fasted forty
wilderness, preserve you
tation, and so sustain
iritual food that in the
that meat you may at
the Mount of God.

r Passiontide.

Who suffered for you,
o to bear with Him the

Cross that you may at length attain
unto the Crown.

For Easter.

Jesus, Who rose again from the
dead by the glory of the Father,
make you henceforth to walk with
Himself in newness of life.

For Ascension.

Christ, the Son of God, our
Great High Priest, Who is passed
into the heavens, pour down upon
you from thence His everlasting
benediction.

For Trinity Sunday.

(See the General Benediction.)

*For Feasts of the Blessed Virgin
Mary.*

God, the Son of Mary, at Whose
right hand stands the Queen in a
vesture of gold, bring you with joy
and gladness to bear her company
in the King's palace.

For Saints' Days.

Christ, the King of Saints, grant
you so to follow their example here
on earth, that you may hereafter
be partaker of their inheritance in
light.

BENEDICTION OF A CIVIL MARRIAGE.

*tanding before the Altar,
shall say to the Man,*

thou acknowledge this
hy wedded wife, to live
er God's ordinance in
ate of Matrimony ?
.

thou love her, comfort
, and keep her in sick-
health ; and, forsaking

all other, keep thee only unto her,
so long as ye both shall live ?
Ans. I will.

*Then shall the Priest say unto the
Woman,*

N., Dost thou acknowledge this
Man as thy wedded husband, to live
together after God's ordinance in
the holy estate of Matrimony ?
Ans. I do.

Wilt thou obey him, and serve him, love, honour, and keep him in sickness and in health; and, forsaking all other, keep thee only unto him, so long as ye both shall live?

Ans. I will.

Then shall they give their troth to each other in this manner.
The Minister shall cause the Man with his right hand to take the Woman by her right hand, and to say after him as followeth,

I, *M.*, acknowledge thee, *N.*, as my wedded wife, to have and to hold from this day forward, for better for worse, for richer for poorer, in sickness and in health, to love and to cherish, till death us do part, according to GOD's holy ordinance; and thereto I plight thee my troth.

Then shall they loose their hands; and the Woman, with her right hand taking the Man by his right hand, shall likewise say after the Minister,

I, *N.*, acknowledge thee, *M.*, as my wedded husband, to have and to hold from this day forward, for better for worse, for richer for poorer, in sickness and in health, to love, cherish, and to obey, till death us do part, according to GOD's holy ordinance; and thereto I give thee my troth.

Then shall the Priest join their right hands together, and say,

Those whom GOD hath joined together let no man put asunder.

Then shall the Minister say,

Forasmuch as *M.* and *N.* have consented together in holy wedlock, and have witnessed the same before GOD [and this company] and thereto have given and pledged their troth either to other, I pronounce that they be Man and Wife together, In the Name of the FATHER, and of the SON, and of the HOLY GHOST: Amen.

LORD, have mercy, &c.
Our FATHER, &c.

℣. O LORD, save Thy servant and Thine handmaid. ℟. Who put their trust in Thee. ℣. O LORD, send them help from Thy holy place. ℟. And evermore defend them. ℣. Be unto them a tower of strength. ℟. From the face of their enemy. ℣. O LORD, hear our prayer. ℟. And let our cry come unto Thee.

Let us pray.

O Eternal GOD, Creator and Preserver of all mankind, Giver of all spiritual grace, the Author of everlasting life; send Thy blessing upon these Thy servants, this man and this woman, whom we bless in Thy Name; that, as Isaac and Rebecca lived faithfully together, so these persons may surely perform and keep the vow and covenant betwixt them made, and may ever remain in perfect love and peace together, and live according to Thy laws. Through JESUS CHRIST our LORD. Amen.

And the Minister shall add this Blessing.

GOD the FATHER, GOD the SON, GOD the HOLY GHOST, bless, preserve, and keep you; the LORD mercifully with His favour look upon you; and so fill you with all spiritual benediction and grace, that ye may so live together in this life, that in the world to come ye may have life everlasting. Amen.

School Offices.

OFFICE FOR A DAY SCHOOL.

MORNING.

In the Name, &c.
Our FATHER, &c.   I believe, &c.

℣. O LORD, open Thou our lips.
℞. And our mouth shall show
forth Thy praise.   ℣. O GOD,
make speed, &c. ℞. O LORD, make
haste, &c.   ℣. Glory, &c.   ℞. As it
was, &c.

Alleluia.

HYMN.

Ant. Open Thou mine eyes.

Ps. 119 (33—40.)   Teach me, O
LORD, &c.

Ant. Open Thou mine eyes, that
I may see the wondrous things of
Thy law.

The Chapter.   Prov. ii.

My son, if thou wilt receive my
words, and hide my commandments
with thee; so that thou incline
thine ear unto wisdom, and apply
thine heart to understanding; yea,
if thou criest after knowledge, and
liftest up thy voice for understanding; if thou seekest her as silver,
and searchest for her as for hid
treasures; then shalt thou understand the fear of the LORD, and
find the knowledge of GOD.   For
the LORD giveth wisdom; out of
His mouth cometh knowledge and
understanding.

℣. But Thou, O LORD, &c.   ℞.
Thanks be to GOD.   ℣. The knowledge of wickedness is not wisdom.
℞. Nor the counsel of sinners prudence.   ℣. Glory, &c.   ℞. As it
was, &c.   ℣. The fear of the LORD
is the beginning of wisdom.   ℞.
And the knowledge of the Holy is
understanding.   ℣. The LORD, &c.

℞. And with, &c.   ℣. Let us
pray.

LORD, have mercy, &c.
Our FATHER, &c.

196. Almighty and everlasting
GOD, Who makest us both to will
and to do those things that be good
and acceptable unto Thy Divine
Majesty; we make our humble supplications unto Thee for these Thy
children.   Let Thy fatherly hand,
we beseech Thee, ever be over them;
let Thy HOLY SPIRIT ever be with
them; and so lead them in the
knowledge and obedience of Thy
Word, that in the end they may
obtain everlasting life.   Through.

3rd Coll. at Matins. O LORD, our
heavenly FATHER, &c.

The grace of our LORD, &c.

DISMISSAL AT NOON.

In the Name, &c.
Our FATHER, &c.

℣. Our help is in the Name of
the LORD.   ℞. Who hath made
heaven and earth.   ℣. Blessed be
the Name of the LORD.   ℞. From
this time forth for evermore.   ℣.
O GOD, make speed, &c.   ℞. O
LORD, make haste, &c.   ℣. Glory,
&c.   ℞. As it was, &c.

Alleluia.

HYMN.

℣. The LORD, &c.   ℞. And
with, &c.   ℣. Let us pray.

197. O LORD JESU CHRIST, Who
didst hang upon the Cross at this
hour for our sins; may it please
Thee to enlighten our hearts and

bodies, Thou SAVIOUR of the world. Who livest.

Prevent us, O LORD, &c.

The grace of our LORD, &c.

DISMISSAL AT NIGHT.

In the Name, &c.

Our FATHER, &c.   I believe, &c.

℣. Abide with us, O LORD, for it is towards evening. ℞. And the day is far spent. ℣. O GOD, make speed, &c. ℞. O LORD, make haste, &c. ℣. Glory, &c. ℞. As it was, &c. Alleluia.

HYMN.

The Chapter.   S. John viii.

Then spake JESUS again unto them, saying, I am the Light of the world: he that followeth Me, shall not walk in darkness, but shall have the light of life.

℣. But Thou, O LORD, &c. ℞. Thanks be to GOD. ℣. The LORD is my light and my salvation, whom then shall I fear? ℞. The LORD is the strength of my life, of whom then shall I be afraid? ℣. Glory, &c. ℞. As it was, &c. ℣. He will not suffer thy foot to be moved. ℞. And He that keepeth thee will not sleep. ℣. The LORD, &c. ℞. And with, &c. ℣. Let us pray.

LORD, have mercy, &c.
Our FATHER, &c.

Lighten our darkness, &c.

℣. Let us depart in peace. ℞. In the Name of the LORD.   Amen.

OFFICE FOR A NIGHT SCHOOL.

In the Name, &c.
Our FATHER, &c.   I believe, &c.

℣. The LORD's Name be praised. ℞. From the rising up of the sun unto the going down of the same. ℣. O GOD, make speed, &c. ℞. O LORD, make haste, &c. ℣. Glory, &c. ℞. As it was, &c. Alleluia.

HYMN.

Ant. Make me to understand the way of Thy commandments.

Ps. 119 (9—16). Wherewithal shall a young man, &c.

Ant. Make me to understand the way of Thy commandments, and so shall I talk of Thy wondrous works.

The Chapter.   1 Thess. v.

Let us not sleep, as do others; but let us watch and be sober. For they that sleep, sleep in the night; and they that be drunken, are drunken in the night. But let us, who are of the day, be sober, putting on the breastplate of faith and love: and for an helmet the hope of salvation.   For GOD hath not appointed us to wrath, but to obtain salvation by our LORD JESUS CHRIST, Who died for us, that, whether we wake or sleep, we should live together with Him.

℣. But Thou, O LORD, &c. ℞. Thanks be to GOD. ℣. I must work the works of Him that sent me while it is day. ℞. The night cometh when no man can work. ℣. Glory, &c. ℞. As it was, &c. ℣. Walk while ye have the light, lest darkness come upon you. ℞. For he that walketh in darkness knoweth not whither he goeth. ℣. The LORD, &c. ℞. And with, &c. ℣. Let us pray.

LORD, have mercy, &c.
Our FATHER, &c.

198. Defend, O LORD, us Thy servants with Thy heavenly grace, and grant that we may continue

Thine for ever, and daily increase in Thy HOLY SPIRIT more and more, until we come to Thine everlasting kingdom. Through.

DISMISSAL.

In the Name, &c.
Our FATHER, &c.

℣. O GOD, make speed, &c. ℟. O LORD, make haste, &c. ℣. Glory, &c. ℟. As it was, &c.

HYMN.

℣. Vouchsafe, O LORD. ℟. To keep us this night without sin. ℣. The LORD, &c. ℟. And with, &c. ℣. Let us pray.

Lighten our darkness, &c.

Benediction. GOD be gracious unto you, and give you all a heart to serve Him, and to do His will with a good courage and a willing mind.

OFFICE FOR A SUNDAY SCHOOL.

MORNING.

In the Name, &c.

Our FATHER, &c.   I believe, &c.

℣. My voice shalt Thou hear betimes, O LORD. ℟. Early in the morning will I direct my prayer unto Thee. ℣. O GOD, make speed, &c. ℟. O LORD, make haste, &c. ℣. Glory, &c. ℟. As it was, &c.

HYMN.

Ant. Hear my prayer, O GOD.

Ps. 54. Save me, O GOD.

Ant. Hear my prayer, O GOD, and hearken unto the words of my mouth.

The Chapter. Eph. iv.
Let all bitterness, and wrath, and anger, and clamour, and evil-speaking, be put away from you, with all malice : and be ye kind one to another, tender-hearted, forgiving one another, even as GOD for CHRIST's sake hath forgiven you. Be ye therefore followers of GOD, as dear children ; and walk in love, as CHRIST also hath loved us, and hath given Himself for us, an offering and a sacrifice to GOD for a sweet-smelling savour.

℣. But Thou, O LORD, &c. ℟.

Thanks be to GOD. ℣. All thy children shall be taught of GOD. ℟. And great shall be the peace of thy children. ℣. Glory, &c. ℟. As it was, &c. ℣. Like as a father pitieth his own children. ℟. Even so is the LORD merciful unto them that fear Him. ℣. The LORD, &c. ℟. And with, &c. ℣. Let us pray.

Collect for Whitsun Day. GOD, Who didst teach, &c.

Prevent us, O LORD, &c.

199. O GOD, Who didst reveal Thyself to Thy Prophet Samuel while he was yet a child ; grant unto us, Thy children, the knowledge of Thy Will, that we may ever walk in Thy commandments. Through.

The grace of our LORD, &c.

BEFORE GOING TO CHURCH.

In the Name, &c.

Ant. O go your way into His gates with thanksgiving.

Ps. 122. I was glad, &c.

Ant. O go your way into His

gates with thanksgiving, and into His courts with praise.

℣. Hear the voice of my humble petitions when I cry unto Thee. ℟. When I lift up my hands towards the mercy-seat of Thy holy Temple. ℣. O GOD, make speed, &c. ℟. O LORD, make haste, &c. ℣. The LORD, &c. ℟. And with, &c. ℣. Let us pray.

LORD, have mercy, &c.
Our FATHER, &c.

200. O LORD, we beseech Thee, keep our feet when we go into Thy house, that we may be ready to hear, and to offer the sacrifice of praise. Guard us from all wandering thoughts and heedless gestures, and make our service acceptable unto Thee. Through.

Benediction. The Only-Begotten SON of GOD vouchsafe to bless and succour us.

℟. Amen.

EVENING.

In the Name, &c.
Our FATHER, &c. I believe, &c.

℣. Let our prayer be set forth in Thy sight as the incense. ℟. And let the lifting up of our hands be an evening sacrifice. ℣. O GOD, make speed, &c. ℟. O LORD, make haste, &c. ℣. Glory, &c. ℟. As it was, &c.

HYMN.

Ant. Turn Thee again, O LORD GOD of Hosts.

Ps. 121. I will lift up, &c.

Ant. Turn Thee again, O LORD GOD of Hosts: show the light of Thy countenance, and we shall be whole.

The Chapter. Isa. lx.

The sun shall be no more thy light by day: neither for brightness shall the moon give light unto thee: but the LORD shall be unto thee an everlasting light, and thy GOD thy glory. Thy sun shall no more go down: neither shall thy moon withdraw itself: for the LORD shall be thine everlasting light, and the days of thy mourning shall be ended.

℣. But Thou, O LORD, &c. ℟. Thanks be to GOD. ℣. Abide with us, O LORD, for it is towards evening. ℟. And the day is far spent. ℣. Glory, &c. ℟. As it was, &c. ℣. Lighten our eyes, O LORD. ℟. That we sleep not in death. ℣. The LORD, &c. ℟. And with, &c. ℣. Let us pray.

201. O GOD of Abraham, GOD of Isaac, GOD of Jacob; bless these Thy children, and sow the seed of eternal life in their hearts; that whatsoever in Thy holy Word they shall profitably learn, they may in deed fulfil the same. Look, O LORD, mercifully upon them from heaven, and bless them, that they obeying Thy will, and alway being in safety under Thy protection, may abide in Thy love unto their lives' end. Through.

202. O LORD JESU CHRIST, Who didst sit lowly in the midst of the doctors, both hearing them and asking them questions; grant unto us, Thy servants, both aptness to teach, and willingness to learn, Thy blessed will. Who livest.

The grace of our LORD, &c.

BEFORE GOING TO CHURCH.

In the Name, &c.

Ant. Glory and worship are before Him.

Ps. 134. Behold now, praise, &c.

Ant. Glory and worship are before Him, power and honour are in His sanctuary.

℣. Thou also shalt light my candle. ℟. The LORD my GOD shall make my darkness to be light. ℣. O GOD, make speed, &c. ℟. O LORD, make haste, &c. ℣. Glory, &c. ℟. As it was, &c. ℣. The LORD, &c. ℟. And with, &c. ℣. Let us pray.

(Collect as in the morning.)

Benediction. The King of Angels bring us unto the fellowship of the heavenly citizens.

℟. Amen.

Parochial Offices.

OFFICE FOR A BIBLE CLASS.

In the Name, &c.
Our FATHER, &c. I believe, &c.

℣. Thy Word is a lantern unto my feet. ℟. And a light unto my paths. ℣. O GOD, make speed, &c. ℟. O LORD, make haste, &c. ℣. Glory, &c. ℟. As it was, &c.

HYMN.

Ant. Order my steps in Thy word.

Ps. 119 (97—105). LORD, what love, &c.

Ant. Order my steps in Thy word, and so shall no wickedness have dominion over me.

The Chapter. 2 Tim. iii.

Continue thou in the things which thou hast learned, and hast been assured of, knowing of whom thou hast learned them; and that from a child thou hast known the Holy Scriptures, which are able to make thee wise unto salvation, through faith which is in CHRIST JESUS. All Scripture is given by Inspiration of GOD, and is profitable for doctrine, for reproof, for correction, for instruction in righteousness; that the man of GOD may be perfect, throughly furnished unto all good works.

℣. But Thou, &c. ℟. Thanks be to GOD. ℣. Give me understanding, and I shall keep Thy law. ℟. Yea, I shall keep it with my whole heart. ℣. Glory, &c. ℟. As it was, &c. ℣. Show me Thy ways, O LORD. ℟. And teach me Thy paths. ℣. The LORD, &c. ℟. And with, &c. ℣. Let us pray.

LORD, have mercy, &c.
Our FATHER, &c.

℣. Teach me Thy way, O LORD. ℟. And I will walk in Thy truth. ℣. O knit my heart unto Thee. ℟. That I may fear Thy Name. ℣. So teach us to number our days. ℟. That we may apply our hearts unto wisdom. ℣. LORD, hear, &c. ℟. And let, &c. ℣. Let us pray.

Coll. 2nd S. in Adv.; Post-Comm. Colls.: O Almighty GOD, &c.; Prevent us, &c.

AFTER CLASS.

In the Name, &c.

℣. The LORD, &c. ℟. And with, &c. ℣. Let us pray.

Post-Comm. Coll. Grant, we beseech Thee, &c.

Benediction. GOD be gracious unto you, and open your hearts in His law and commandments, and send you peace.

OFFICE FOR A CONFIRMATION CLASS.

In the Name, &c.
Our FATHER, &c.   I believe, &c.

℣. They shall go from strength to strength. ℟. And unto the GOD of gods appeareth every one of them in Sion. ℣. O GOD, make speed, &c. ℟. O LORD, make haste, &c. ℣. Glory, &c. ℟. As it was, &c.

Alleluia.

HYMN.

" Come, HOLY GHOST," &c.

Ant. When Thou lettest Thy Breath go forth, they shall be made.

Ps. 43. Give sentence, &c.

Ant. When Thou lettest Thy Breath go forth, they shall be made, and Thou shalt renew the face of the earth.

The Chapter. Gal. v.

This I say then, Walk in the Spirit, and ye shall not fulfil the lust of the flesh. For the flesh lusteth against the Spirit, and the Spirit against the flesh : and these are contrary the one to the other : so that ye cannot do the things that ye would. But if ye be led by the Spirit, ye are not under the law. Now the works of the flesh are manifest, which are these; Adultery, fornication, uncleanness, lasciviousness, idolatry, witchcraft, hatred, variance, emulations, wrath, strife, seditions, heresies, envyings, murders, drunkenness, revellings, and such like : of the which I tell you before, as I have also told you in time past, that they which do such things shall not inherit the kingdom of GOD. But the fruit of the Spirit is love, joy, peace, long-suffering, gentleness, goodness, faith, meekness, temperance ; against such there is no law. And they that are CHRIST'S have crucified the flesh, with the affections and lusts. If we live in the Spirit, let us also walk in the Spirit.

℣. But Thou, &c. ℟. Thanks, &c. ℣. The SPIRIT and the Bride say, Come. ℟. And let him that heareth say, Come. ℣. Glory, &c. ℟. As it was, &c. ℣. As many as are led by the SPIRIT of GOD. ℟. They are the sons of GOD. ℣. The LORD, &c. ℟. And with, &c. ℣. Let us pray.

LORD, have mercy, &c.
Our FATHER, &c.

℣. Make me a clean heart, O GOD. ℟. And renew a right spirit within me. ℣. Cast me not away from Thy Presence. ℟. And take not Thy HOLY SPIRIT from me. ℣. Give me the comfort of Thy help again. ℟. And stablish me with Thy free SPIRIT. ℣. LORD, hear, &c. ℟. And let, &c. ℣. Let us pray.

Collects for Whitsun Day and 25th Sunday after Trinity.

———

Dismissal as in Bible Class, except this Benediction:

Benediction. The grace of the HOLY SPIRIT enlighten your hearts and understandings. Amen.

OFFICE FOR A COMMUNION CLASS.

See Office before Receiving Holy Communion, or the Litany of the Blessed Sacrament.

SCHEME FOR CONDUCTING A COTTAGE LECTURE.

In the Name, &c.

HYMN,

According to the Season.

Our FATHER, &c.

℣. He showed His Word unto Jacob. ℟. His statutes and ordinances unto Israel. ℣. O GOD, make speed, &c. ℟. O LORD, make haste, &c. ℣. Glory, &c. ℟. As it was, &c.

Ant. Thy Word is a lantern unto my foot.

Then shall follow one or more of the following Psalms :

8, 15, 19, 23, 46, 67, 91, 110 (1—8 ; 33—40), 125.

Ant. Thy Word is a lantern unto my feet, and a light unto my paths.

Here shall follow a short Scripture Reading and Lecture.

HYMN.

℣. The LORD, &c. ℟. And with, &c. ℣. Let us pray.

LORD, have mercy, &c.
Our FATHER, &c.

℣. LORD, I call upon Thee; haste Thee unto me. ℟. And consider my voice when I cry unto Thee. ℣. Let my prayer be set forth in Thy sight as the incense. ℟. And let the lifting up of my hands be an evening sacrifice. ℣. Set a watch, O LORD, before my mouth. ℟. And keep the door of my lips. ℣. O LORD, hear, &c. ℟. And let, &c. ℣. Let us pray.

The Collect for the day.
Prevent us, O LORD, &c.
Lighten our darkness, &c.

Benediction. Unto GOD's gracious mercy and protection, &c.

OFFICE FOR A MISSIONARY MEETING.

In the Name, &c.
Our FATHER, &c.

℣. The heathen shall fear Thy Name, O LORD. ℟. And all the kings of the earth Thy Majesty. ℣. O GOD, make speed, &c. ℟. O LORD, make haste, &c. ℣. Glory, &c. ℟. As it was, &c.
Alleluia.

Hymn.

Jesus shall reign where'er the sun
Doth his successive journeys run,
His kingdom stretch from shore to shore,
Till suns shall rise and set no more.

To Him shall fervent prayer be made,
And princes throng to crown His head :
To His blest Name shall incense rise
With every morning sacrifice.

People and realms of every tongue
Shall hail His love with sweetest song;
And infant voices shall proclaim
Their early blessings on His Name.

Blessings abound where'er He reigns,
With joy the captive bursts his chains,
The weary find eternal rest,
And all the sons of want are blest.

Be everlasting glory Thine,
O Worn made Flesh! O Word Divine!
To God the Father glory be,
And Holy Ghost, eternally. Amen.

Ant. The Lord shall increase you more and more.

Ps. 115. Not unto us, &c.
126. When the Lord, &c.

Ant. The Lord shall increase you more and more, you and your children.

The Chapter. S. Matth. xxviii.

And Jesus came and spake unto them, saying, All power is given unto Me in heaven and in earth. Go ye therefore, and teach all nations, baptizing them in the Name of the Father, and of the Son, and of the Holy Ghost: teaching them to observe all things whatsoever I have commanded you: and lo, I am with you alway, even unto the end of the world. Amen.

℣. But Thou, O Lord, &c. ℟. Thanks be to God. ℣. I will give Thee the heathen for Thine inheritance. ℟. And the utmost parts of the earth for Thy possession. ℣. Glory, &c. ℟. As it was, &c. ℣. Declare His honour unto the heathen. ℟. And His wonders unto all people. ℣. The Lord be with you. ℟. And with thy spirit. ℣. Let us pray.

LORD, have mercy, &c.
Our FATHER, &c.

℣. Call to remembrance, O Lord, Thy tender mercies. ℟. And Thy lovingkindnesses which have been ever of old. ℣. Let the Gentiles come to Thy light. ℟. And kings to the brightness of Thy rising. ℣. O Lord, look down from heaven. ℟. Behold, and visit this vine. ℣. Lord, hear our prayer. ℟. And let our cry come unto Thee. ℣. Let us pray.

Third Collect for Good Friday.

O merciful God, &c.

203. O God of all the nations of the earth, remember the multitudes of the heathen who, though created in Thine image, are perishing in their ignorance, and according to the propitiation of Thy Son Jesus Christ, grant that by the prayers and labours of Thy holy Church they may be delivered from all superstition and unbelief, and brought to worship Thee; through Him Whom Thou hast sent to be our salvation, the Resurrection and the Life of all the faithful, the same Thy Son Jesus Christ our Lord.

Also **68, 69, 74, 134.** (*See pages* 26, 33.)

At the conclusion of the Meeting.

℣. Stablish the thing, O Lord, that Thou hast wrought in us. ℟. For Thy Temple's sake at Jerusalem. ℣. Let us depart in peace. ℟. In the Name of the Lord. Amen.

OFFICE FOR A MEETING OF DISTRICT VISITORS.

In the Name, &c.
Our FATHER, &c.

℣. I will declare Thy Name unto my brethren. ℟. In the midst of the congregation will I praise Thee. ℣. Glory, &c. ℟. As it was, &c.

Ant. Prosper Thou the work of our hands upon us.

Ps. 67. God be merciful unto us, &c.

Ant. Prosper Thou the work of

our hands upon us, O prosper Thou our handywork.

The Chapter. S. Matt. xxv.

Then shall the King say unto them on His right hand, Come, ye blessed of My FATHER, inherit the kingdom prepared for you from the foundation of the world : for I was an hungered, and ye gave Me meat; I was thirsty, and ye gave Me drink: I was a stranger, and ye took Me in : naked, and ye clothed Me : I was sick, and ye visited Me : I was in prison, and ye came unto Me. Then shall the righteous answer Him, saying, LORD, when saw we Thee an hungered, and fed Thee? or thirsty, and gave Thee drink? when saw we Thee a stranger, and took Thee in? or naked, and clothed Thee? or when saw we Thee sick, or in prison, and came unto Thee? And the King shall answer and say unto them, Verily, I say unto you, Inasmuch as ye have done it unto one of the least of these My brethren, ye have done it unto Me.

℣. But Thou, O LORD, have mercy upon us. ℟. Thanks be to GOD. ℣. Deal thy bread to the hungry, and bring the poor that are cast out to thy house. ℟. When thou seest the naked, cover him, and hide not thyself from thine own flesh. ℣. Glory, &c. ℟. As it was, &c. ℣. Pure religion and undefiled before GOD and the FATHER is this. ℟. To visit the fatherless and widows in their affliction, and to keep himself unspotted from the world. ℣. The LORD, &c. ℟. And with, &c. ℣. Let us pray.

LORD, have mercy upon us, &c.
Our FATHER, &c.

℣. Show Thy servants Thy work. ℟. And their children Thy glory. ℣. Let Thy merciful kindness, O LORD, be upon us. ℟. As we do put our trust in Thee. ℣. Not unto us, O LORD, not unto us. ℟. But unto Thy Name give the praise. ℣. O LORD, hear, &c. ℟. And let, &c. ℣. The LORD, &c. ℟. And with, &c. ℣. Let us pray.

204. Almighty GOD, we humbly beseech Thee to bless this Church and parish, and to further with Thy continual help those who labour in it in Thy fear and for Thy glory; grant them lowliness of spirit, steadfastness of faith, perseverance in all good works, and bring them at last to Thy heavenly kingdom. Through. [Also **57, 59, 61.**]

At the conclusion of the Meeting.

℣. Blessed is he that considereth the poor and needy. ℟. The LORD shall deliver him in the time of trouble.

Benediction. GOD, the SON of GOD, grant that you may increase by the exercise of good works that joy which you have received by faith in Him.

℟. Amen.

OFFICE FOR A PAROCHIAL GUILD OR SOCIETY.

In the Name, &c.
Our FATHER, &c.

℣. Blessed are all they that fear the LORD. ℟. And walk in His ways. ℣. O GOD, make speed, &c. ℟. O LORD, make haste, &c. ℣. Glory, &c. ℟. As it was, &c.

Ant. Ye that fear the LORD, put your trust in the LORD.

Ps. 1. Blessed is the man, &c.
15. LORD, who shall dwell, &c.
101. My song shall be, &c.
112. Blessed is the man, &c.

Ant. Ye that fear the LORD, put your trust in the LORD, He is their Helper and Defender.

The Chapter. Rev. xxii.

Behold, I come quickly; and My

reward is with Me, to give every man according as his work shall be. I am Alpha and Omega, the beginning and the end, the first and the last. Blessed are they that do His commandments, that they may have right to the tree of life, and may enter in through the gates into the city. For without are dogs, and sorcerers, and whoremongers, and murderers, and idolaters, and whosoever loveth and maketh a lie. I JESUS have sent Mine angel to testify unto you these things in the churches. I am the root and the offspring of David, and the bright and morning star. . . . . He which testifieth these things saith, Surely I come quickly. Amen. Even so, come, LORD JESUS.

[Ep. 2nd S. a. Epiph.; 17th S. a. T. Gosp. 4th S. a. T.]

℣. But Thou, O LORD, have mercy upon us. ℟. Thanks be to GOD. ℣. All the paths of the LORD are mercy and truth. ℟. Unto such as keep His covenant and His testimonies. ℣. Glory, &c. ℟. As it was, &c. ℣. Them that are meek shall He guide in judgment. ℟. And such as are gentle, them shall He learn His way. ℣. The LORD be with you. ℟. And with thy spirit. ℣. Let us pray.

LORD, have mercy, &c.
Our FATHER, &c.

℣. O pray for the peace of Jerusalem. ℟. Peace be within thy walls, and plenteousness within thy palaces. ℣. Think upon the tribe of Thine inheritance, O LORD. ℟. And Mount Sion wherein Thou hast dwelt. ℣. O be favourable and gracious unto Sion. ℟. Build Thou the walls of Jerusalem. ℣. Help us now, O LORD. ℟. O LORD, send us now prosperity. ℣. LORD, hear, &c. ℟. And let, &c. ℣. Let us pray.

205. O LORD, defend this [guild] from all adversity, and of Thy gracious mercy deliver from the snares of the enemy those who seek Thee with their whole heart. Through.

[*Here may follow special Prayers according to the object of the Guild.*]

℣. The LORD, &c. ℟. And with, &c. ℣. Bless we the LORD. ℟. Thanks be to GOD. Amen.

At the conclusion of the Meeting.

In the Name, &c.

℣. LORD, Thou wilt ordain peace for us. ℟. For Thou also hast wrought all our works in us. ℣. The LORD, &c. ℟. And with, &c. ℣. Let us pray.

Post-Comm. Coll. Almighty GOD, the fountain, &c.

Benediction. The Almighty LORD, in Whom is the fulness of our salvation, ever have you in His keeping.

℟. Amen.

OFFICE OF ADMISSION INTO A PAROCHIAL GUILD.

In the Name, &c.

℣. We wait for Thy lovingkindness, O GOD. ℟. In the midst of Thy temple. ℣. Glory, &c. ℟. As it was, &c. ℣. O GOD, according to Thy Name, so is Thy praise unto the world's end. ℟. Thy right hand is full of righteousness.

Then the Priest, turning to the Candidate, shall say,

My *son*, what is thy desire? —
Ans. I desire admission into the

Guild of —————— and a share in the devotions and good works of its members.

Priest. Dost thou promise to conform to the rules of the Guild so long as thou shalt continue a member of it?

Ans. I do.

℣. The LORD, &c. ℟. And with, &c. ℣. Let us pray.

LORD, have mercy, &c.
Our FATHER, &c.

℣. O LORD, save Thy servant. ℟. Who putteth *his* trust in Thee. ℣. Send *him* help from Thy holy place. ℟. And evermore mightily defend *him*. ℣. Let the enemy have no advantage over *him*. ℟. Nor the wicked approach to hurt *him*. ℣. LORD, hear, &c. ℟. And let, &c. ℣. The LORD, &c. ℟. And with, &c. ℣. Let us pray.

206. Give ear, O LORD, to our prayers, and vouchsafe to bless this Thy servant, whom we design to receive in Thy holy Name, to a share in all spiritual blessings, and to the companionship of the Guild of —————— and grant .that by Thy grace *he* may lead a godly life in Thy Church, advancing in holiness, and, assisted by the prayers of this Guild, may obtain everlasting life. Through.

Then shall the Priest, turning to the Altar, on which the badge of the Guild is laid, say,

℣. Our help, &c. ℟. Who hath made, &c. ℣. The LORD, &c. ℟. And with, &c. ℣. Let us pray.

207. O GOD, Creator, Preserver, and Saviour of mankind, Bestower of Salvation, and Giver of spiritual grace, send down Thy bless+ing upon this badge, that whoso wears it, fortified with heavenly might, may preserve unblemished faith, steadfast hope, and fervent charity, and never be parted from Thee. Who livest.

I receive and admit thee [N.] into the fellowship of this Guild —————— and to a share in all its privileges and duties, in the Name.

Receive this Badge of —————— Guild [in token of ——————] making thy prayer to our LORD JESUS CHRIST, that by His merits thou mayest bear it without reproach, that He may guard thee from all adversity, and bring thee to everlasting life.

Then the Priest signs the new member with the sign of the Cross, saying,

Almighty GOD, the Creator of heaven and earth, Who hath vouchsafed to lead thee unto this company and fellowship, bl+ess thee, and in the hour of thy departure tread under foot the head of the Serpent, thine enemy, that thou mayest at length victoriously attain the palm and crown of thine everlasting inheritance. Through.

Offices for the Visitation of the Sick.

GENERAL OFFICE FOR THE SICK.

In the Name, &c.

Our FATHER, &c. I believe, &c.

℣. We must through much tribulation. ℟. Enter into the kingdom of GOD. ℣. O GOD, make speed, &c. ℟. O LORD, make haste, &c. ℣. Glory, &c. ℟. As it was, &c.

Ant. Give ear, LORD, unto my prayer.

Ps. 6. O LORD, rebuke me not, &c.
13. How long wilt Thou, &c.
57. Be merciful unto me, &c.
71. In Thee, O LORD, &c.
77. I will cry unto GOD, &c.
88. O LORD GOD of my salvation, &c.
90. LORD, Thou hast been, &c.
142. I cried unto the LORD, &c.

Ant. Give ear, LORD, unto my prayer, and ponder the voice of my humble desires.

The Chapter. Lam. iii., &c.

Let us search and try our ways, and turn again to the LORD; let us lift our heart with our hands unto GOD in the heavens. . . . Surely it is meet to be said unto GOD, I have borne chastisement, I will not offend any more. That which I see not teach Thou me; if I have done iniquity, I will do so no more.

[Ep. 1st S. in Adv.; 1st S. in L.; 4th S. a. T. Gosp. 3rd S. a. Epiph.; 2nd S. in L.; 3rd S. a. T. App. 50, 52, 61, 63.]

℣. But Thou, O LORD, have mercy upon us. ℟. Thanks be to GOD. ℣. I know, O LORD, that Thy judgments are right. ℟. And that Thou of very faithfulness hast caused me to be troubled. ℣. Though He cause grief, yet will He have compassion. ℟. For He doth not afflict willingly, nor grieve the children of men. ℣. The LORD, &c. ℟. And with, &c. ℣. Let us pray.

LORD, have mercy, &c.

Our FATHER, &c.

℣. Hear me, O LORD, and have mercy upon me. ℟. LORD, be Thou my helper. ℣. Make me a clean heart, O GOD. ℟. And renew a right spirit within me. ℣. So teach us to number our days. ℟. That we may apply our hearts unto wisdom. ℣. O let my soul live, and it shall praise Thee. ℟. And Thy judgments shall help me. ℣. LORD, hear my prayer. ℟. And let my cry come unto Thee. ℣. Let us pray.

208. O just and merciful GOD, deliver our soul from death, our eyes from tears, and our feet from falling, and show Thy loving kindness unto us, that as we are chastened by Thy justice we may be guarded by Thy mercy. Through.

[Coll. Septuag.; Ash-W.; Palm S.; 3rd and 4th S. a. East.; 1st, 4th, 10th, 12th, 17th, 18th S. a. Trin. **257—269, 281, 283, 300.**]

Benediction. The LORD JESUS CHRIST, Who vouchsafed to save the world by His coming, cleanse your soul and body from all sin.

FOR ONE TROUBLED IN MIND.

In the Name, &c.
Our FATHER, &c.   I believe, &c.

℣. Turn Thou us, O GOD, our SAVIOUR. ℟. And let Thine anger cease from us. ℣. O GOD, make speed to save us. ℟. O LORD, make haste to help us. ℣. Glory, &c. ℟. As it was, &c.

Ant. O put thy trust in GOD.

General Trouble.

Ps. 31. In Thee, O LORD, &c.
42. Like as the hart desireth, &c.
43. Give sentence with me, &c.
46. GOD is our hope, &c.

Remembrance of Sin.

25. Unto Thee, O LORD, &c.
119 (v. 169.) Let my complaint, &c.

Evil Thoughts.

13. How long wilt Thou forget, &c.
22. My GOD, . . . look upon me, &c.
86. Bow down Thine ear, &c.
88. O LORD GOD, &c.
119 (v. 25.) My soul cleaveth, &c.

When evil spoken of.

17. Hear the right, O LORD, &c.
27. The LORD is my light, &c.
41. Blessed is he, &c.
55. Hear my prayer, O GOD, &c.
56. Be merciful unto me, &c.

Despair.

23. The LORD is my shepherd, &c.
77. I will cry unto GOD, &c.

Ant. O put thy trust in GOD, for I will yet give Him thanks, which is the help of my countenance, and my GOD.

The Chapter. S. Matt. xi.

Come unto Me, all ye that labour and are heavy laden, and I will give you rest. Take My yoke upon you, and learn of Me ; for I am meek and lowly in heart : and ye shall find rest unto your souls. For My yoke is easy, and My burden is light.

[Ep. 4th S. in A.; 1st S. a. T. Gosp. Whits. M.; SS. Ph. and Jas.; All SS. App. 1, 2, 3, 63, 64.]

℣. But Thou, O LORD, have mercy upon us. ℟. Thanks be to GOD. ℣. O cast thy burthen upon the LORD. ℟. And He shall nourish thee. ℣. Glory, &c. ℟. As it was, &c. ℣. The LORD will not fail His people. ℟. Neither will He forsake His inheritance. ℣. The LORD be with you. ℟. And with thy spirit. ℣. Let us pray.

LORD, have mercy, &c.
Our FATHER, &c.

℣. From our enemies defend us, O CHRIST. ℟. Graciously look upon our afflictions. ℣. Pitifully behold the sorrows of our hearts. ℟. Mercifully forgive the sins of Thy people. ℣. Favourably with mercy hear our prayers. ℟. O Son of David, have mercy upon us. ℣. Both now and ever vouchsafe to hear us, O CHRIST. ℟. Graciously hear us, O CHRIST; graciously hear us, O LORD CHRIST. ℣. O LORD, let Thy mercy be showed upon us. ℟. As we do put our trust in Thee. ℣. Let us pray.

209. O most merciful GOD, grant us, we pray Thee, Thy grace by which we may trustfully cling unto Thee in joy or in sorrow. Let us love Thee, and fear Thee, and praise Thee, and adore Thee. O FATHER, Thy will be done in us, for Thy judgments are right, and Thou of very faithfulness hast caused us to be troubled. Blessed be Thy Name for evermore, and since Thou alone knowest what is good for us, do with us whatever may be for our salvation, and Thy glory. Through.

[Coll. Septuag.; 3rd S. a. T.; S.

a. Asc.; Colls. in Lit. **272—278, 284, 290—292, 299, 302, 373 —380.**]

Benediction. The LORD increase upon you the abundance of His blessing, and strengthen you with the hope of His heavenly kingdom.

IN A LINGERING ILLNESS.

In the Name, &c.
Our FATHER, &c. I believe, &c.

℣. It is of the LORD's mercies we are not consumed. ℞. Because His compassions fail not. ℣. O GOD, make speed, &c. ℞. O LORD, make haste, &c. ℣. Glory, &c. ℞. As it was, &c.

Ant. O hide not Thou Thy face from me.

General Cases.

Ps. 13. How long, &c.
16. Preserve me, O GOD, &c.
22. My GOD, . . . look upon me, &c.
23. The LORD is my shepherd, &c.
31. In Thee, O LORD, &c.
39. I said, I will take heed, &c.
57. Be merciful unto me, &c.
90. LORD, Thou hast been, &c.
119 (ver. 121 to end.) I deal with the thing, &c.
143. Hear my prayer, &c.

When disappointed at not recovering.

28. Unto Thee will I cry, &c.
70. Haste Thee, O GOD, &c.

When very feeble.

77. I will cry, &c.
88. O LORD GOD, &c.
102. Hear my prayer, &c.

Ant. O hide not Thou Thy face from me, nor cast Thy servant away in displeasure.

The Chapter. Ecclus. ii.

My son, if thou come to serve the LORD, prepare thy soul for temptation. Set thy heart aright, and constantly endure, and make not haste in time of trouble. Cleave unto Him, and depart not away, that thou mayest be increased at thy last end. Whatsoever is brought upon thee take cheerfully, and be patient when thou art changed to a low estate. For gold is tried in the fire, and acceptable men in the furnace of adversity. Believe in Him, and He will help thee; order thy way aright, and trust in Him. Ye that fear the LORD, wait for His mercy; and go not aside, lest ye fall. Ye that fear the LORD, believe Him, and your reward shall not fail. Ye that fear the LORD, hope for good, and for everlasting joy and mercy. Look at the generations of old, and see; did ever any trust in the LORD and was confounded? or did any abide in His fear and was forsaken? or whom did He ever despise, that called upon Him? For the LORD is full of compassion and mercy, longsuffering, and very pitiful, and forgiveth sins, and saveth in time of affliction.

[Ep. 4th S. in Adv.; 1st S. in L.; Tues. bef. East.; 3rd and 21st S. a. T.; S. Jno. Bapt. Gosp. 5th S. a. East.; S. Mark. App. 4, 5, 6, 50, 52, 53.]

℣. But Thou, &c. ℞. Thanks, &c. ℣. It is good for me that I

have been in trouble. R̹. That I may learn Thy statutes. ℣. Glory, &c. R̹. As it was, &c. ℣. I know, O Lord, that Thy judgments are right. R̹. And that Thou of very faithfulness hast caused me to be troubled. ℣. The Lord be with you. R̹. And with thy spirit. ℣. Let us pray.

Lord, have mercy, &c.
Our Father, &c.

℣. O Lord, save Thy servant. R̹. Who putteth *his* trust in Thee. ℣. Send *him* help from Thy holy place. R̹. And evermore mightily defend *him*. ℣. O Lord, comfort *him* when *he* lieth sick upon *his* bed. R̹. Make Thou all *his* bed in *his* sickness. ℣. Lord, hear our prayer.

R̹. And let our cry come unto Thee. ℣. Let us pray.

210. O God of heavenly might, Who by the power of Thy command drivest away every weakness and every infirmity from the bodies of men; mercifully help Thy servant, that freed from *his* sickness and restored to health, *he* may with renewed strength bless Thy holy Name. Through.

[Coll. 1st and 4th S. in Adv.; 3rd S. a. Epiph.; 4th S. a. East.; 1st and 4th S. a. T. **280, 282, 307, 326, 330.**]

Benediction. God Almighty bless you from heaven, Who by the Cross and Blood of His Passion vouchsafed to redeem us on earth.

FOR THE AGED AND INFIRM.

In the Name, &c.
Our Father, &c. I believe, &c.

℣. Seek ye the Lord and His strength. R̹. Seek His Face evermore. ℣. O God, &c. R̹. O Lord, &c. ℣. Glory, &c. R̹. As it was, &c.

Ant. Cast me not away in the time of age.

Ps. 15. Lord, who shall dwell, &c.
16. Preserve me, O God, &c.
24. The earth is the Lord's, &c.
31. In Thee, O Lord, &c.
37. Fret not thyself, &c.
71. In Thee, O Lord, &c.
84. O how amiable, &c.

Ant. Cast me not away in the time of age, forsake me not when my strength faileth me.

The Chapter. S. Luke xii.

Let your loins be girded about, and your lights burning; and ye yourselves like unto men that wait for their Lord, when He will return from the wedding; that when He cometh and knocketh, they may open unto Him immediately. Blessed are those servants whom the Lord when He cometh shall find watching: verily I say unto you, that He shall gird Himself, and make them to sit down to meat, and will come forth and serve them. And if He shall come in the second watch, or come in the third watch, and find them so, blessed are those servants. And this know, that if the goodman of the house had known what hour the thief would come, he would have watched, and not have suffered his house to be broken through. Be ye therefore ready also: for the Son of Man cometh at an hour when ye think not.

[Ep. 1st and 4th S. in Adv.; S. Jno. Ev.; 5th S. a. Epiph.; S. a. Asc.; 20th S. a. T.; S. Jno. Bapt. Gosp. 2nd S. in Adv.; 15th S. a. T.; Conv. of S. P. App. 7, 8, 9, 56, 60, 64.]

℣. But Thou, &c. ℟. Thanks, &c. ℣. A hoary head is a crown of glory. ℟. If it be found in the way of righteousness. ℣. Glory, &c. ℟. As it was, &c. ℣. The righteous LORD loveth righteousness. ℟. His countenance will behold the thing that is just. ℣. The LORD, &c. ℟. And with, &c. ℣. Let us pray.

LORD, have mercy, &c.
Our FATHER, &c.

℣. O LORD, show Thy mercy upon us. ℟. And grant us Thy salvation. ℣. Bow down Thine ear, O LORD, and hear me. ℟. For I am poor and in misery. ℣. Comfort Thou the soul of Thy servant. ℟. For unto Thee, O LORD, will I lift up my soul. ℣. Give ear, O LORD, unto my prayer. ℟. And ponder the voice of my humble desires. ℣. Let us pray.

211. O GOD, Who hast taught us that we have here no continuing city, but that we are strangers and pilgrims upon earth; mercifully grant unto Thy servant, who hath long and wearily travelled in the wilderness of this world, gladly to hear Thy voice when Thou callest *him*, and grace to attain unto *his* true home, where Thou livest.

[Coll. 1st S. in Adv.; 3rd and 6th S. a. Epiph.; 2nd S. in L. **350—352, 355.**]

Benediction. Almighty GOD, Who knoweth your weakness, vouchsafe unto you the gift of His blessing.

FOR A BLIND PERSON.

In the Name, &c.
Our FATHER, &c.   I believe, &c.

℣. Thou also shalt light my candle. ℟. The LORD my GOD shall make my darkness to be light. ℣. O GOD, &c. ℟. O LORD, &c. ℣. Glory, &c. ℟. As it was, &c.

Ant. I believe verily to see the goodness of the LORD.

Ps. 17. Hear, &c.
19. The heavens declare, &c.
27. The LORD is my light, &c.
146. Praise the LORD, &c.

Ant. I believe verily to see the goodness of the LORD in the land of the living.

The Chapter. 1 S. John iii.
Behold what manner of love the FATHER hath bestowed upon us, that we should be called the sons of GOD: therefore the world knoweth us not, because it knew Him not. Beloved, now are we the sons of GOD; and it doth not yet appear what we shall be: but we know that when He shall appear, we shall be like Him; for we shall see Him as He is. And every man that hath this hope in him purifieth himself, even as He is pure.

[Ep. S. Steph.; S. Jno. Ev.; 3rd S. in L.; S. Matt. Gospel Xmas D.; Quinquag. App. 10, 61, 70.]

℣. But Thou, &c. ℟. Thanks, &c. ℣. Thine eyes shall see the King in His beauty. ℟. They shall behold the land that is very far off. ℣. Glory, &c. ℟. As it was, &c. ℣. Blessed are the pure in heart. ℟. For they shall see GOD. ℣. The LORD, &c. ℟. And with, &c. ℣. Let us pray.

LORD, have mercy, &c.
Our FATHER, &c.

℣. Lead me, O LORD, in Thy righteousness. ℟. Make Thy way plain before my face. ℣. Lighten mine eyes, O LORD. R⁊. That I sleep not in death. ℣. Give Thine Angels charge over me. R⁊. To keep me in all my ways. ℣. Let them bear me in their hands. R⁊. That I hurt not my foot against a stone. ℣. Let light spring up for the righteous. R⁊. And joyful gladness for such as are true-hearted. ℣. LORD, hear, &c. R⁊. And let, &c. ℣. Let us pray.

212. O LORD JESU CHRIST, Who didst open the eyes of the blind who prayed unto Thee; mercifully grant that we, trusting in Thy love, may so pass through the darkness of this present world, as at length to behold Thy Face in glory. Who livest.

[Coll. 5th S. a. Epiph.; 3rd at Even. Pr. **354, 385.**]

Benediction. CHRIST, the SON of GOD, mercifully look upon your trouble, and by His light take away the darkness of your heart.

FOR A SICK WOMAN IN CHILDBED.

In the Name, &c.
Our FATHER, &c. I believe, &c.

℣. Lo, children and the fruit of the womb. R⁊. Are an heritage and gift that cometh of the LORD. ℣. O GOD, &c. R⁊. O LORD, &c. ℣. Glory, &c. R⁊. As it was, &c.

Ant. Hide not Thy face from me.

Ps. 20. The LORD hear thee, &c.
67. GOD be merciful, &c.
70. Haste Thee, O GOD, &c.
102. Hear my prayer, O LORD, &c.
121. I will lift up mine eyes, &c.

Ant. Hide not Thy face from me in the time of my trouble.

The Chapter. 1 Tim. ii., &c.

Adam was first formed, then Eve, and Adam was not deceived, but the woman being deceived was in the transgression. Notwithstanding she shall be saved in childbearing, if they continue in faith and charity and holiness with sobriety. . . . . A woman when she is in travail hath sorrow, because her hour is come; but as soon as she is delivered of the child she remembereth no more the anguish, for joy that a man is born into the world.

[Ep. 4th S. a. T. App. **11.**]

℣. But Thou, &c. R⁊. Thanks, &c. ℣. In my trouble I will call upon the LORD. R⁊. And complain unto my GOD. ℣. Glory, &c. R⁊. As it was, &c. ℣. Ye shall be sorrowful. R⁊. But your sorrow shall be turned into joy. ℣. The LORD, &c. R⁊. And with, &c. ℣. Let us pray.

LORD, have mercy, &c.
Our FATHER, &c.

℣. O LORD, save this woman Thy servant. R⁊. Who putteth her trust in Thee. ℣. Send her help from Thy holy place. R⁊. And evermore mightily defend her. ℣. O LORD, comfort her when she lieth sick upon her bed. R⁊. Make Thou all her bed in her sickness. ℣. LORD, hear, &c. R⁊. And let, &c. ℣. Let us pray.

213. O LORD, we beseech Thee to look mercifully upon Thy servant; lighten her pains, increase her strength, and grant her safe deliverance. Through.

[Coll. Septuag. **366—368.**]

Benediction. The LORD save your soul from death, and satisfy your desire with good things.

AFTER A MISCARRIAGE.

In the Name, &c.
Our Father, &c.   I believe, &c.

℣. As for our God, He is in heaven. ℟. He hath done whatsoever pleased Him. ℣. O God, &c. ℟. O Lord, &c. ℣. Glory, &c. ℟. As it was, &c.

Ant. The Lord gave, and the Lord hath taken away.

Ps. 77. I will cry unto God, &c.
88. O Lord God of my salvation, &c.
90. Lord, Thou hast been, &c.

Ant. The Lord gave, and the Lord hath taken away; blessed be the Name of the Lord.

The Chapter. 2 Sam. xii.

But when David saw that his servants whispered, David perceived that the child was dead: therefore David said unto his servants, Is the child dead? And they said, He is dead. Then David arose from the earth, and washed, and anointed himself, and changed his apparel, and came into the house of the Lord, and worshipped: then he came to his own house; and when he required, they set bread before him, and he did eat. Then said his servants unto him, What thing is this that thou hast done? Thou didst fast and weep for the child, while it was alive; but when the child was dead, thou didst rise and eat bread. And he said, While the child was yet alive, I fasted and wept: for I said, Who can tell whether God will be gracious to me, that the child may live? But now he is dead, wherefore should I fast? can I bring him back again? I shall go to him, but he shall not return to me.

[Ep. H. Inn.   Gosp. SS. Ph. and James.]

℣. But Thou, &c. ℟. Thanks, &c. ℣. Blessed are they that mourn. ℟. For they shall be comforted. ℣. Glory, &c. ℟. As it was, &c. ℣. Take heed that ye despise not one of these little ones. ℟. For in heaven their angels do always behold the face of My Father Which is in heaven. ℣. The Lord, &c. ℟. And with, &c. ℣. Let us pray.

Lord, have mercy, &c.
Our Father, &c.

℣. Out of the deep have I called unto Thee, O Lord. ℟. Lord, hear my voice. ℣. O let Thine ears consider well. ℟. The voice of my complaint. ℣. Comfort us now again after the time that Thou hast plagued us. ℟. And for the years wherein we have suffered adversity. ℣. O Lord, hear, &c. ℟. And let, &c. ℣. Let us pray.

214. O Lord Jesu Christ, Who wast conceived by the Holy Ghost, born of the Virgin Mary, and laid when an infant in the manger; have mercy upon this Thy servant, whom Thou hast been pleased to afflict with the loss of her offspring; grant her comfort in her sorrow, remission of her sins, and restoration to bodily health, and vouchsafe that her light affliction may work for her an exceeding and eternal weight of glory, through Thy loving-kindness. Who livest.

[Coll. East. Eve. **431.**]

Benediction. The Lord Jesus Christ, Who underwent our death and thereby overcame it, make you partakers of His everlasting life.

FOR A SICK CHILD.

In the Name, &c.
Our FATHER, &c.   I believe, &c.

℣. Fear not, little flock. ℟. For it is your FATHER'S good pleasure to give you the kingdom. ℣. O GOD, &c.   ℟. O LORD, &c.   ℣. Glory, &c.   ℟. As it was, &c.

Ant. The LORD preserveth the simple.

Ps. 8. O LORD our Governor, &c.
17 (1—8.) Hear the right, &c.
20. The LORD hear thee, &c.
23. The LORD is my Shepherd, &c.
34. I will always give thanks, &c.

Ant. The LORD preserveth the simple : I was in misery and He helped me.

The Chapter.   S. Luke viii.

And they brought unto Him also infants, that He would touch them : but when His disciples saw it, they rebuked them.   But JESUS called them unto Him, and said, Suffer little children to come unto Me, and forbid them not : for of such is the kingdom of GOD. Verily I say unto you, Whosoever shall not receive the kingdom of GOD as a little child shall in no wise enter therein.

[Ep. H. Inn. ; S. a. Christmas ; 6th S. a. Ep. ; Trin. S. Gosp. H. Inn. ; S. Matthias. App. 70.]

℣. But Thou, &c.   ℟. Thanks, &c.   ℣. Take heed that ye despise not one of these little ones.   ℟. For in heaven their Angels do always behold the face of My FATHER Which is in heaven.   ℣. Glory, &c.   ℟. As it was, &c.   ℣. In their mouth was found no guile.   ℟. And they are without fault before the throne of GOD.   ℣. The LORD, &c.   ℟. And with, &c.   ℣. Let us pray.

LORD, have mercy, &c.
Our FATHER, &c.

℣. I am small and of no reputation.   ℟. Yet do I not forget Thy commandments.   ℣. O look Thou upon me, and be merciful unto me. ℟. As Thou usest to do unto those that love Thy Name.   ℣. Call to remembrance, O LORD, Thy tender mercies.   ℟. And Thy loving kindnesses which have been ever of old. ℣. LORD, hear, &c.   ℟. And let, &c.   ℣. Let us pray.

215. O LORD JESU CHRIST, Who camest into this world as a little Child, in cold, and want, and suffering ; look mercifully, we beseech Thee, upon this infant, and in Thy great love grant *him* relief from *his* pain, Who livest.

[Coll. H. Inn. ; 2nd S. a. Tr. ; S. Mich. **370, 371.**]

Benediction. CHRIST, Who in His mercy took human Childhood upon Him, guard and defend you in all things.

BENEDICTION OF A SICK CHILD.

℣. Peace to this house.
℟. And all that dwell therein.

[℣. Thou shalt purge me with hyssop, O LORD, and I shall be clean.   ℟. Thou shalt wash me, and I shall be whiter than snow. ℣. Show us Thy mercy, O LORD. ℟. And grant us Thy salvation.

℣. O Lord, hear my prayer. ℟. And let my cry come unto Thee. ℣. The Lord, &c. ℟. And with, &c. ℣. Let us pray.

Hear us, O Lord, Holy Father, Almighty, everlasting God, and vouchsafe to send Thy holy Angel from heaven, to guard, cherish, protect, visit, and defend all that abide in this dwelling.   Through.]

Ps. 113. Praise the Lord, &c.

[*The Child shall then say, if able, the* Our Father, *and* Creed.]

℣. Out of the mouths of babes and sucklings. ℟. Thou hast perfected Thy praise, O Lord.   ℣.

Lord, hear, &c. ℟. And let, &c. ℣. The Lord, &c. ℟. And with, &c. ℣. Let us pray.

216. O God, unto Whom all things grow, and by Whom they are strengthened when grown; stretch forth Thy right hand on this Thy child, sick in *his* tender age, that restored to the vigour of health *he* may attain to fulness of years, and serve Thee faithfully and gratefully. Through.

Benediction. The blessing of God Almighty, Father, Son, and Holy Ghost, descend upon thee, and abide with thee.   Amen.

FOR A DYING CHILD.

In the Name, &c.
Our Father, &c.   I believe, &c.

℣. Jesus called a little child unto Him. ℟. And set him in the midst of them. ℣. O God, &c. ℟. O Lord, &c. ℣. Glory, &c. ℟. As it was, &c.

Ant. Suffer little children to come unto Me.

Ps. 8. O Lord our Governor, &c.
24. The earth is the Lord's, &c.
84. O how amiable, &c.
113. Praise the Lord, ye servants, &c.
138. I will give thanks unto Thee, &c.

Ant. Suffer little children to come unto Me, for of such is the kingdom of God.

The Chapter. Ecclus. xxxix., &c.
Hearken unto me, ye holy children, and bud forth as a rose growing by the brook of the field : and give ye a sweet savour as frankincense, and flourish as a lily, send forth a smell, and sing a song of praise, bless the Lord in all His works. Magnify His Name, and show forth His praise with the songs of your lips, and with harps, and in praising Him ye shall say after this manner : All the works of the Lord are exceeding good, and whatsoever He commandeth shall be accomplished in due season . . . . He that scattered Israel will gather him, and keep him, as a shepherd doth his flock. For the Lord hath redeemed Jacob, and ransomed him from the hand of him that was stronger than he . . . . He shall feed His flock like a shepherd ; He shall gather the lambs with His arm, and carry them in His bosom, and shall gently lead those that are with young.

[Ep. H. Inn.; 18th S. a. T.; S. Thos. Gosp. 2nd S. a. East.; S. Mich. App. 15, 66, 70.]

℣. But Thou, &c. ℟. Thanks, &c. ℣. God Himself shall be with them. ℟. And be their God. ℣. Glory, &c. ℟. As it was, &c. ℣. With joy and gladness shall they be brought. R/. And shall enter into the King's palace. V/. The Lord, &c. R/. And with, &c. V/. Let us pray.

Lord, have mercy, &c.
Our Father, &c.

V/. Bring Thy children to their own border, O Lord. R/. And let the children of Zion be joyful in their King. V/. Make them to be numbered with Thy saints. R/. In glory everlasting. V/. Then shall the lambs feed after their manner. R/. David shall feed them and be their shepherd. V/. They shall walk with Him in white. R/. For they are worthy. V/. Lord, hear, &c. R/. And let, &c. V/. Let us pray.

217. O Christ, Son of God, Who callest little children unto Thee by Thy heavenly teaching; grant that we may be ever children in guile, and perfect in keeping Thy commandments. Thou Who hast

said that of such is the kingdom of heaven, unite us for evermore to the company of them that are pleasing unto Thee. Through Thy mercy, O.

When in pain.

218. O Christ, unspeakable Light of the world, Who, as yet in Thy cradle and before Thou wast a Martyr, didst hallow infants with the palm of martyrdom, and madest them to suffer pain from the swords of cruel men; hear our prayer for this child, that *he* may triumph over *his* sufferings, and be joined with those who follow Thee, the Lamb, with hymns and songs whithersoever Thou goest. Who.

[Coll. H. Inn. ; S. Mich. **372**.]

Benediction. The Only-begotten Son of God, Who made infants to shed their blood for Him in Bethlehem, grant you a desire to do His will and a reward like unto theirs.

AFTER AN ACCIDENT.

In the Name, &c.
Our Father, &c. I believe, &c.

V/. Though he fall, he shall not be cast away. R/. For the Lord upholdeth him with His Hand. V/. O God, &c. R/. O Lord, &c. V/. Glory, &c. R/. As it was, &c.

Ant. O hold Thou up my goings in Thy paths.

Ps. 6. O Lord, rebuke me not, &c.

13. How long wilt Thou, &c.

102. Hear my prayer, O Lord, &c.

121. I will lift up mine eyes, &c.

142. I cried unto the Lord, &c.

Ant. O hold Thou up my goings in Thy paths, that my footsteps slip not.

The Chapter. Deut. xxxi., &c.

See now that I, even I, am He,

and there is no God with Me: I kill, and I make alive; I wound, and I heal; neither is there any that can deliver out of My hand. . . . . The Lord killeth and maketh alive; He bringeth down to the grave and bringeth up; He maketh sore and bindeth up; He woundeth, and His Hands make whole.

[Ep. Tues. bef. East. ; 3rd S. a. T. Gosp. 3rd S. a. Epiph. App. 13.]

V/. But Thou, &c. R/. Thanks, &c. V/. If the Lord had not helped me. R/. It had not failed but my soul had been put to silence. V/. Glory, &c. R/. As it was, &c. V/. The Lord upholdeth all such as fall. R/. And lifteth up all those that are down. V/. The Lord, &c. R/. And with, &c. V/. Let us pray.

LORD, have mercy, &c.
Our FATHER, &c.

℣. O LORD, save Thy servant.
℟. Who putteth *his* trust in Thee.
℣. Send *him* help from Thy holy
place. ℟. And evermore mightily
defend *him*. ℣. O LORD, comfort
him when *he* lieth sick upon *his* bed.
℟. Make Thou all *his* bed in *his*
sickness. ℣. Look upon *his* adversity and misery. ℟. And forgive
him all *his* sin. ℣. LORD, hear, &c.
℟. And let, &c. ℣. Let us pray.

219. O LORD JESU CHRIST,
Who didst stretch out Thine hand

to save Thine Apostle S. Peter
when sinking in the water; mercifully grant Thy help unto this Thy
servant whom Thou hast suffered
to fall into affliction, and vouchsafe
that *he*, calling upon Thee in faith,
may be restored by Thy loving-
kindness. Who livest.

[Coll. 3rd and 4th S. a. Ep.; 2nd
S. in L.; 4th, 8th, 15th, and 20th
S. a. T. **334—338, 360**.]

Benediction. Almighty GOD put
away from you all hurtful things,
and mercifully pour down upon you
the abundance of His blessing.

BEFORE AN OPERATION.

In the Name, &c.
Our FATHER, &c.

℣. Into Thy hands, O LORD, I
commend my spirit. ℟. For Thou
hast redeemed me, O LORD, Thou
GOD of truth. ℣. O GOD, &c. ℟.
O LORD, &c. ℣. Glory, &c. ℟.
As it was, &c.

Ant. Have mercy upon me, O
LORD.

Ps. 6. O LORD, rebuke me not,
&c.
20. The LORD hear thee in the
day, &c.
57. Be merciful unto me, &c.
91. Whoso dwelleth, &c.
121. I will lift up mine eyes, &c.

Ant. Have mercy upon me, O
LORD, for I am weak : O LORD,
heal me, for my bones are vexed.

The Chapter. 1 S. Pet. iv.

Beloved, think it not strange
concerning the fiery trial which is
to try you, as though some strange
thing happened unto you : but rejoice, inasmuch as ye are partakers
of CHRIST's sufferings ; that, when
His glory shall be revealed, ye may
be glad also with exceeding joy.

. . . . Wherefore let them that suffer according to the will of GOD
commit the keeping of their souls
to Him in well doing, as unto a
faithful Creator.

[Ep. Sex.; 4th S. a. T. Gosp. G.
Frid. App. 12.]

℣. But Thou, &c. ℟. Thanks,
&c. ℣. My soul is sore troubled.
℟. But, LORD, how long wilt Thou
punish me. ℣. Glory, &c. ℟.
As it was, &c. ℣. Heal me, O
LORD, and I shall be healed. ℟.
Save me, and I shall be saved, for
Thou art my praise. ℣. The LORD,
&c. ℟. And with, &c. ℣. Let us
pray.

LORD, have mercy, &c.
Our FATHER, &c.

℣. Keep us, O LORD, as the apple
of an eye. ℟. Hide us under the
shadow of Thy wings. ℣. Send us
help from Thy holy place. ℟. And
evermore mightily defend us. ℣.
Look upon our adversity and misery. ℟. And forgive us all our
sin. ℣. LORD, hear, &c. ℟. And
let, &c. ℣. Let us pray.

220. O LORD JESU CHRIST,

Who didst patiently endure the scourging and wounding of Thy holy Flesh, that Thou mightest save the souls and bodies of Thy people; strengthen Thy servant, we beseech Thee, to bear patiently whatsoever Thou shalt see fit to lay upon *him*, and grant that it may avail for the healing of *his* body and the correction of *his* soul. Who livest.

[Coll. 3rd S. a. Epiph.; Palm S.; Prayer in Lit., "We humbly beseech Thee." **332—337, 365.**]

Benediction. The grace of Almighty GOD protect you, that bruised in flesh, but quickened in spirit, you may be blessed by Him with His Heavenly Gift.

THANKSGIVING FOR RELIEF THROUGH AN OPERATION.

In the Name, &c.
Our FATHER, &c.   I believe, &c.

℣. I will restore health unto thee. ℞. And I will heal thee of thy wounds. ℣. O GOD, &c. ℞. O LORD, &c. ℣. Glory, &c. ℞. As it was, &c.

Ant. If the LORD had not helped me.

Ps. 16. Preserve me, &c.
71. In Thee, O LORD, &c.
77. I will cry unto GOD, &c.
86. Bow down Thine ear, &c.
129. Many a time, &c.

Ant. If the LORD had not helped me, it had not failed but my soul had been put to silence.

The Chapter.   Hosea vi.

Come, and let us return unto the LORD; for He hath torn, and He will heal us; He hath smitten, and He will bind us up. After two days will He revive us: in the third day He will raise us up, and we shall live in His sight. Then shall we know, if we follow on to know the LORD: His going forth is prepared as the morning; and He shall come unto us as the rain, as the latter and former rain unto the earth.

[Epist. 1st S. in L.; Palm S.; Tues. b. East.; East. D.; 4th S. a.

T. Gosp. S. Mark; Michaelmas. App. 4, 13, 42, 50.]

℣. But Thou, &c. ℞. Thanks, &c. ℣. The LORD hath chastened me and corrected me. ℞. But He hath not given me over unto death. ℣. Glory, &c. ℞. As it was, &c. ℣. The LORD preserveth the simple. ℞. I was in misery, and He helped me. ℣. The LORD, &c. ℞. And with, &c. ℣. Let us pray.

LORD, have mercy, &c.
Our FATHER, &c.

℣. Have mercy upon me, O LORD, consider the trouble which I suffer. ℞. Thou that liftest me up from the gates of death. ℣. Thou shalt make me hear of joy and gladness. ℞. That the bones which Thou hast broken may rejoice. ℣. O send out Thy light and Thy truth, that they may lead me. ℞. And that I may go to the Altar of GOD. ℣. LORD, hear, &c. ℞. And let, &c. ℣. Let us pray.

221. O LORD, Who castest down that Thou mayest lift up, and woundest unto healing; mercifully receive our praise and thanksgiving on behalf of this Thy servant, to whom Thou hast granted ease and relief, and vouchsafe that the chastisement of *his* body may avail for the purifying of *his* soul. Through.

[Coll. 3rd S. a. Epiph.; Sept.; 2nd S. in L.; 20th S. a. T. **259, 264, 277, 327, 329, 391.**]

Benediction. GOD, the SON of GOD, Who hath begun a good work in you, fulfil it in His good pleasure, and bring you to everlasting life.

IN GREAT BODILY PAIN.

In the Name, &c.

Our FATHER, &c. I believe, &c.

℣. Turn us again, O LORD GOD of Hosts. ℟. Show the Light of Thy Countenance, and we shall be whole. ℣. O GOD, &c. ℟. O LORD, &c. ℣. Glory, &c. ℟. As it was, &c.

Ant. Forsake me not, O LORD my GOD.

Ps. 6. O LORD, rebuke me not, &c.

27. The LORD is my light, &c.

38. Put me not to rebuke, &c.

42. Like as the hart, &c.

142. I cried unto the LORD, &c.

Ant. Forsake me not, O LORD my GOD: be not Thou far from me.

The Chapter. 2 Cor. iv.

We are troubled on every side, yet not distressed; we are perplexed, but not in despair; persecuted, but not forsaken; cast down, but not destroyed; always bearing about in the body the dying of the LORD JESUS, that the life also of JESUS might be made manifest in our body. For we which live are alway delivered unto death for JESUS' sake, that the life also of JESUS might be made manifest in our mortal flesh.

[Ep. Sex.; 4th S. a T. Gosps. for Holy Week. App. 13—16, 50, 52.]

℣. But Thou, &c. ℟. Thanks, &c. ℣. As for me, I will patiently abide alway. ℟. And will praise Thee more and more. ℣. Glory, &c. ℟. As it was, &c. ℣. GOD is our hope and strength. ℟. A very present help in trouble. ℣. The LORD, &c. ℟. And with, &c. ℣. Let us pray.

LORD, have mercy, &c.

Our FATHER, &c.

℣. Hear me, O LORD, and that soon. ℟. For my spirit waxeth faint. ℣. Let not the water-floods drown me. ℟. Neither let the deep swallow me up. ℣. O LORD, let it be Thy pleasure to deliver me. ℟. Make haste, O LORD, to help me. ℣. LORD, hear, &c. ℟. And let, &c. ℣. Let us pray.

222. O Almighty GOD, and heavenly FATHER, we beseech Thy gracious goodness, that as Thine Only-begotten SON, our SAVIOUR JESUS CHRIST, knowingly and willingly went forth to meet His bitter Passion and Death, so when Thou layest the Cross of grievous pain and sorrow upon us, we may, in like manner, bear it patiently and with willing minds, as the trial of our faith against the latter day and to Thine everlasting glory. Hear us, O merciful FATHER, for our LORD JESUS CHRIST's sake. Amen.

[Colls. 3rd S. a. Ep.; Septuag.; 4th S. in L.; Palm S.; Annun. **333—337, 404, 424.**]

Benediction. CHRIST, the SON of GOD, Who bore the shame of the Cross in our mortal body, deliver you from every hurtful suffering of pain.

IN FEVER.

In the Name, &c.
Our FATHER, &c.

℣. From above hath He sent fire into my bones, and it prevaileth against them. ℟. He hath made me desolate and faint all the day. ℣. O GOD, &c. ℟. O LORD, &c. ℣. Glory, &c. ℟. As it was, &c.

Ant. If any man thirst, let him come unto Me.

Ps. 6. O LORD, rebuke me not, &c.
13. How long wilt Thou, &c.
22. My GOD, look, &c.
39. I said, I will take heed, &c.
42. Like as the hart, &c.
57. Be merciful, &c.
63. O GOD, Thou art my GOD, &c.
102. Hear my prayer, &c.

Ant. If any man thirst, let him come unto Me, and drink.

The Chapter. Isa. xliv., &c.

Thus saith the LORD that made thee, and formed thee from the womb, which will help thee ; Fear not, O Jacob, My servant; and thou, Jesurun, whom I have chosen. For I will pour water upon him that is thirsty, and floods upon the dry ground : I will pour My spirit upon thy seed, and My blessing upon thine offspring . . . And the parched ground shall become a pool, and the thirsty land springs of water : in the habitation of dragons, where each lay, shall be grass with reeds and rushes . . . . Behold, I will do a new thing, now it shall spring forth, shall ye not know it ? I will even make a way in the wilderness, and rivers in the desert. The beast of the field shall honour Me, the dragons and the owls, because I give waters in the wilderness, and rivers in the desert, to give drink to My people, My chosen.

[Ep. 1st S. in L. ; 4th S. a. T. Gosp. 3rd S. a. Epiph. ; 21st S. a. T. ; SS. Ph. and Jas. App. 1, 13, 17, 52—55.]

℣. But Thou, &c. ℟. Thanks, &c. ℣. The LORD shall guide thee continually. ℟. And satisfy thy soul in drought. ℣. Glory, &c. ℟. As it was, &c. ℣. And thou shalt be like a watered garden. ℟. And a spring of waters whose waters fail not. ℣. The LORD, &c. ℟. And with, &c. ℣. Let us pray.

LORD, have mercy, &c.
Our FATHER, &c.

℣. Have mercy upon me, O LORD, for I am in trouble. ℟. And mine eye is consumed for very heaviness. ℣. Thou hast been my succour, leave me not. ℟. Neither forsake me, O GOD of my salvation. ℣. Deal Thou with me according to Thy Name. ℟. For sweet is Thy mercy. ℣. LORD, hear, &c. ℟. And let, &c. ℣. Let us pray.

223. O LORD JESU CHRIST, SON of GOD, Who didst walk in the midst of the burning fiery furnace with Thy three holy children; mercifully grant unto this Thy servant refuge with Thee from the heat and pain of *his* sickness. Through Thy mercy, O our GOD, Who art blessed, and livest.

[Coll. 3rd S. a. Epiph. ; 2nd S. in L. ; 8th S. a. T. **331, 332, 357.**]

Benediction. CHRIST the LORD, Whose wounds and passion you acknowledge with thankful devotion, deliver you from your sufferings.

IN GREAT LANGUOR OR EXHAUSTION.

In the Name, &c.
Our FATHER, &c.　I believe, &c.

℣. As many as I love, I rebuke and chasten. ℟. Be zealous, therefore, and repent. ℣. O GOD, &c. ℟. O LORD, &c. ℣. Glory, &c. ℟. As it was, &c.

Ant. The LORD GOD is my strength.

Ps. 6. O LORD, rebuke me not, &c.
18 (1—7.) I will love . . . . ears.
40 (v. 14.) Withdraw not, &c.
61. Hear my crying, &c.
77 (to v. 13.) I will cry . . . . our GOD.
109 (v. 20.) Deal Thou with me, &c.
130. Out of the deep, &c.

Ant. The LORD GOD is my strength, and He will make my feet like hinds' feet, and He will make me to walk upon mine high places.

The Chapter. Isa. xl.

Hast thou not known, hast thou not heard, that the everlasting GOD, the LORD, the Creator of the ends of the earth, fainteth not, neither is weary? there is no searching of His understanding. He giveth power to the faint; and to them that have no might He increaseth strength. Even the youths shall faint and be weary, and the young men shall utterly fall: but they that wait upon the LORD shall renew their strength; they shall mount up with wings as eagles; they shall run, and not be weary; and they shall walk, and not faint.

[Ep. 1st S. in L.; Tu. b. East.; 2nd S. a. East.; 16th S. a. T. Gosp. 3rd S. a. East.; S. Mark. App. 3, 4, 13, 53, 65.]

℣. But Thou, &c. ℟. Thanks, &c. ℣. The LORD is my light and my salvation, whom then shall I fear? ℟. The LORD is the strength of my life, of whom then shall I be afraid? ℣. Glory, &c. ℟. As it was, &c. ℣. I will bind up that which was broken. ℟. And will strengthen that which was sick. ℣. The LORD, &c. ℟. And with, &c. ℣. Let us pray.

LORD, have mercy, &c.
Our FATHER, &c.

℣. Strengthen the weak hands, O LORD. ℟. And confirm the feeble knees. ℣. Be Thou merciful unto me, O LORD. ℟. And raise Thou me up again. ℣. Let not the water-flood drown me. ℟. Neither let the deep swallow me up. ℣. LORD, hear, &c. ℟. And let, &c. ℣. Let us pray.

224. O LORD Almighty, King of Saints, Who correctest us, but givest us not over unto death, Who upholdest all such as fall, and liftest up all those that are down, and Who orderest the bodily afflictions of men; we pray Thee to send Thy mercy upon this Thy servant, for the healing of *his* body and soul, and to cleanse and deliver *him* from all suffering, disease, and weakness. Be Thou *his* Physician, raise *him* from the bed of sickness and couch of infirmity, and restore *him* whole and sound to Thy Church, that *he* may please Thee and do Thy will. Through.

[Coll. 3rd S. a. Epiph.; 2nd S. in L.; 1st S. a. T. **337, 338.**]

Benediction. The Lamb of GOD, Who was slain in weakness, and rose again with power, mightily deliver you from all afflictions of the flesh.

In the Name, &c.
Our FATHER, &c.   I believe, &c.

℣. In returning aud rest shall ye be saved. ℞. In quietness and confidence shall be your strength. ℣. O GOD, &c. ℞. O LORD, &c. ℣. Glory, &c. ℞. As it was, &c.

Ant. Thou art a place to hide me in.

Ps. 3. LORD, how are they increased, &c.
7. O LORD my GOD, in Thee, &c.
26. Be Thou my Judge, &c.
28. Unto Thee will I cry, &c.
42. Like as the hart, &c.
86. Bow down Thine ear, &c.

Ant. Thou art a place to hide me in, Thou shalt preserve me from trouble.

The Chapter. Isa. xxxii.

Behold, a king shall reign in righteousness, and princes shall rule in judgment. And a man shall be as an hiding-place from the wind, and a covert from the tempest; as rivers of water in a dry place; as the shadow of a great rock in a weary land. And the eyes of them that see shall not be dim; and the ears of them that hear shall hearken. Then judgment shall dwell in the wilderness, and righteousness remain in the fruitful field. And the work of righteousness shall be peace; and the effect of righteousness, quietness and assurance for ever. And My people shall dwell in a peaceable habitation, and in sure dwellings, and in quiet resting-places.

[Ep. 5th S. a. Epiph.; 4th S. a. T.; 16th S. a. T. Gosp. 4th S. a. Epiph., ending "obey Him;" 15th S. a. T.; SS. Phil. and Jas. App. 3, 13, 54, 65.]

℣. But Thou, &c. ℞. Thanks, &c. ℣. Peace I leave with you, My peace I give unto you. ℞. Not as the world giveth, give I unto you. ℣. Glory, &c. ℞. As it was, &c. ℣. Let not your heart be troubled. ℞. Neither let it be afraid. ℣. The LORD, &c. ℞. And with, &c. ℣. Let us pray.

LORD, have mercy, &c.
Our FATHER, &c.

℣. O LORD GOD and King, spare Thy people. ℞. Turn our sorrow into joy, that we may live. ℣. Make Thyself known in time of our affliction. ℞. And help them that are desolate. ℣. Hear the voice of the forlorn. ℞. And deliver us out of our fear. ℣. LORD, hear, &c. ℞. And let, &c.

225. O LORD, turn not Thine ear from our sighing, nor withdraw Thy Face from a contrite heart; but come to give us help, that we who are conformed to Thy sufferings, may be comforted by Thy gifts. Who.

[Coll. 2nd Matins; 2nd S. a. Epiph.; 4th S. a. Epiph.; 2nd S. in L.; 3rd S. a. T. **301, 303, 373, 378.**]

Benediction. The Only-begotten SON of GOD deliver you from evil, and so enlighten you with the rays of His brightness, that He may enrich you with the prize of glory and the gifts of eternity.

FOR ONE INSENSIBLE OR DERANGED.

In the Name, &c.
Our FATHER, &c.   I believe, &c.

℣. Deliver us, O LORD our GOD. ℟. That we may give thanks unto Thy holy Name.   ℣. O GOD, make speed, &c.   ℟. O LORD, make haste, &c.   ℣. Glory, &c.   ℟. As it was, &c.

Ant. I became dumb, and opened not my mouth.

Ps. 31 (10—20.)   Have mercy upon me, &c.
38. Put me not to rebuke, &c.
60 (1—5.)   O GOD, Thou hast cast, &c.
65 (1—8.)   Thou, O GOD, art praised, &c.
123. Unto Thee lift I up, &c.

Ant. I became dumb, and opened not my mouth, for it was Thy doing.

For one Insensible.

The Chapter.   Acts xx.

And upon the first day of the week, when the disciples came together to break bread, Paul preached unto them, ready to depart on the morrow; and continued his speech until midnight. And there were many lights in the upper chamber, where they were gathered together. And there sat in a window a certain young man named Eutychus, being fallen into a deep sleep; and as Paul was long preaching, he sunk down with sleep, and fell down from the third loft, and was taken up dead. And Paul went down, and fell on him, and embracing him said, Trouble not yourselves: for his life is in him. When he therefore was come up again, and had broken bread, and eaten, and talked a long while, even till break of day, so he departed. And they brought the young man alive, and were not a little comforted.

For one Deranged.

The Chapter.   S. Matt. xvii.

And when they were come to the multitude, there came to Him a certain man, kneeling down to Him, and saying, LORD, have mercy on my son: for he is a lunatick, and sore vexed: for ofttimes he falleth into the fire, and oft into the water. And I brought him to Thy disciples, and they could not cure him. Then JESUS answered and said, O faithless and perverse generation, how long shall I be with you? how long shall I suffer you? bring him hither to Me. And JESUS rebuked the devil; and he departed out of him: and the child was cured from that very hour. Then came the disciples to JESUS apart, and said, Why could not we cast him out? And JESUS said unto them, Because of your unbelief: for verily I say unto you, If ye have faith as a grain of mustard seed, ye shall say unto this mountain, Remove hence to yonder place; and it shall remove; and nothing shall be impossible unto you. Howbeit, this kind goeth not out but by prayer and fasting.

℣. But Thou, &c.   ℟. Thanks, &c.   ℣. He will not alway be chiding.   ℟. Neither keepeth He His anger for ever.   ℣. Glory, &c.   ℟. As it was, &c.   ℣. He sent His Word and healed them.   ℟. And they were saved from their destruction.   ℣. The LORD, &c.   ℟. And with, &c.   ℣. Let us pray.

LORD, have mercy, &c.
Our FATHER, &c.

℣. Have mercy upon us, and that soon.   ℟. For we are come to great misery.   ℣. Help us, O GOD of our salvation.   ℟. And for the glory of Thy Name deliver us, and be merciful unto our sins, for Thy Name's

sake. ℣. According to the greatness of Thy power. ℟. Preserve
Thou those that are appointed to
die. ℣. Lord, hear, &c. ℟. And
let, &c. ℣. Let us pray.

For one Insensible.

226. O Lord, we beseech Thee,
have mercy upon Thy servant, who
is like unto them that lie in the
grave. Open *his* eyes to behold
Thy wonders; open *his* ears to hear
Thy Word; loose *his* tongue, that
he may make *his* prayer unto Thee:
raise *him* up, that *he* may serve
Thee, and of Thy great goodness
restore *him* whole to Thy Church.
Through.

For one Deranged.

227. O Lord God, Who art the
Fountain of wisdom, mercifully restore the understanding of Thy servant, that *he* may glorify Thy holy
Name. Lay not to *his* charge whatever of evil *he* may do or say in the
time of *his* affliction, but of Thy
great goodness visit *him* and heal
him, that *he* may sit in *his* right
mind at Thy feet. Who livest.

[Coll. 2nd S. in L.; 8th S. a. T.
361—364.]

Benediction. God, Who for us
bore the sufferings of the Cross, renew you by the joy of His Resurrection.

IN SLEEPLESSNESS.

In the Name, &c.
Our Father, &c. I believe, &c.

℣. There remaineth a rest. ℟.
To the people of God. ℣. O God,
make speed, &c. ℟. O Lord,
make haste, &c. ℣. Glory, &c. ℟.
As it was, &c.

Ant. I have thought upon Thy
Name, O Lord, in the night season.

Ps. 4. Hear me, &c.
16. Preserve me, &c.
63. O God, Thou art my God, &c.
77. I will cry unto God, &c.

Ant. I have thought upon Thy
Name, O Lord, in the night season,
and have kept Thy law.

The Chapter. Job vii.

Is there not an appointed time to
man upon earth? are not his days
also like the days of an hireling?
As a servant earnestly desireth the
shadow, and as an hireling looketh
for the reward of his work: so am
I made to possess months of vanity,
and wearisome nights are appointed
to me. When I lie down, I say,
When shall I arise, and the night

be gone? and I am full of tossings
to and fro unto the dawning of the
day.

[Ep. 4th S. a. T. Gosp. S. Matthias; S. Barth. App. 50, 54.]

℣. But Thou, &c. ℟. Thanks,
&c. ℣. O my God, I cry in the
day-time, but Thou hearest not.
℟. And in the night season also I
take no rest. ℣. Glory, &c. ℟.
As it was, &c. ℣. When thou liest
down, thou shalt not be afraid. ℟.
Yea, thou shalt lie down, and thy
sleep shall be sweet. ℣. The Lord,
&c. ℟. And with, &c. ℣. Let us
pray.

Lord, have mercy, &c.
Our Father, &c.

℣. Come unto us, O Lord, and
give us rest. ℟. For we are weary
and heavy laden. ℣. Grant us
Thy peace, O Lord. ℟. And give
Thy beloved sleep. ℣. Let the
saints be joyful with glory. ℟.
Let them rejoice in their beds.
℣. Lord, hear, &c. ℟. And let,
&c. ℣. Let us pray.

228. O Lord Jesu Christ, Who didst suffer agony and wakefulness on the night before Thy Passion; we beseech Thee, of Thine infinite mercies, look upon Thy servant, grant *him* repose for *his* body and peace for *his* soul, and bring *him* finally into that place where the weary are at : Who livest.

[Coll. S. a. As

Benediction. fulfil for good y sires, and grant to your soul.

AFTER AN ATTEMPTED SUICI

In the Name, &c.
Our Father, &c.   I believe, &c.

℣. Thou hast destroyed thyself. ℟. But in Me is thine help. ℣. O God, make speed, &c. ℟. O Lord, make haste, &c. ℣. Glory, &c. ℟. As it was, &c.

Ant. Deliver me from blood-guiltiness, O God.

Ps. 14. The fool hath said, &c.
51. Have mercy upon me, &c.
88. O Lord God of my salvation, &c.
130. Out of the deep, &c.

Ant. Deliver me from blood-guiltiness, O God, Thou that art the God of my health, and my tongue shall sing of Thy righteousness.

The Chapter.   S. Matt. xxvii.

Then Judas, which had betrayed Him, when he saw that He was condemned, repented himself, and brought again the thirty pieces of silver to the chief priests and elders, saying, I have sinned, in that I have betrayed the innocent blood. And they said, What is that to us? see thou to that. And he cast down the pieces of silver in the temple, and departed, and went and hanged himself.

[*If the Patient be much depressed at the remembrance of his sin, instead of this reading, use* Ep. 1st S. in Adv.; Ash-Wed.; Purif. Gosp. 2nd S. in Adv.   App. 18, 22, 24.]

℣. But Thou &c.   ℣. I will out of your gr shall know that ℣. Glory, &c. ℣. I have no pl of him that die turn yourselves The Lord, &c. ℣. Let us pray.

Lord, have m Our Father,

℣. For Thy N ℟. Be merciful is great. ℣. O soul with the sir life with the bl Thy judgment ℟. And cast no in displeasure. adversity and forgive me all hear, &c. ℟. Let us pray.

229. O Alm givest us our lif we may prepare have pity, we b this Thy servant have thrown a as Thou hast *his* designs, so d *him* time and gr Through.

230. O Lord Captain of our s

ordained that we should serve under Thy banner, as faithful soldiers, unto our life's end; have mercy upon this Thy servant, who hath deserted the post which Thou didst assign unto *him*, and endeavoured to flee away from the face of the enemy. Restore *him* by Thy grace, strengthen *him* with Thy might, and give *him* victory through Thy merits, Who livest.

[Coll. Septuag.; 4th S. in L. **304, 316, 321—325, 360.**]

Benediction. CHRIST the LORD, Who by dying triumphed over death, make you victorious over your sins.

FOR ONE WHO HAS LIVED CARELESSLY OR SINNED GREATLY.

In the Name, &c.
Our FATHER, &c.   I believe, &c.

℣. We have sinned with our fathers. ℟. We have done amiss and dealt wickedly. ℣. O GOD, make speed, &c. ℟. O LORD, make haste, &c. ℣. Glory, &c. ℟. As it was, &c.

Ant. My flesh trembleth for fear of Thee.

Ps. 14. The fool hath said, &c.
. 15. LORD, who shall dwell, &c.
25. Unto Thee, O LORD, &c.
51. Have mercy upon me, &c.
52. Why boastest thou thyself, &c.
53. The foolish body, &c.
112. Blessed is the man, &c.
119 (1—8.) Blessed are those, &c.

Ant. My flesh trembleth for fear of Thee, and I am afraid of Thy judgments.

The Chapter. Ezek. xviii.

The soul that sinneth, it shall die, ... But if the wicked will turn from his sins that he hath committed, and keep all My statutes, and do that which is lawful and right, he shall surely live, he shall not die ... Because he considereth and turneth away from all his transgressions that he hath committed, he shall surely live, he shall not die.

Repent, and turn yourselves from all your transgressions; so iniquity shall not be your ruin. Cast away from you all your transgressions, whereby ye have transgressed: and make you a new heart and a new spirit: for why will ye die, O house of Israel? For I have no pleasure in the death of him that dieth, saith the LORD GOD: wherefore turn yourselves, and live ye.

[Ep. 1st S. in Adv.; 1st, 2nd, 3rd, 4th S. a. Epiph.; Ash-W.; 3rd S. in L. Gosp. 2nd S. in Adv.; Exhort. in Commination Serv. App. 20—25.]

℣. But Thou, &c. ℟. Thanks, &c. ℣. Return ye now every one from his evil way. ℟. And make your ways and your doings good. ℣. Glory, &c. ℟. As it was, &c. ℣. Though your sins be as scarlet, they shall be as white as snow. ℟. Though they be red like crimson, they shall be as wool. ℣. The LORD, &c. ℟. And with, &c. ℣. Let us pray.

LORD, have mercy, &c.
Our FATHER, &c.

℣. I said, LORD, be merciful unto me. ℟. Heal my soul, for I have sinned against Thee. ℣. Turn Thee again, O LORD, at the last. ℟. And be gracious unto Thy servant. ℣. In the midst of judgment remember mercy. ℟. And cast not Thy servant away in displeasure. ℣. O remember not the sins and offences of my youth. R̝. But according to Thy mercy think Thou upon me, O LORD, for Thy goodness. V̓. LORD, hear, &c. R̝. And let, &c. V̓. Let us pray.

231. O Almighty and most merciful GOD, Who broughtest forth a fountain of living waters from the rock of flint; bring forth from the hardness of our hearts tears of sorrow, that we may bewail our sins committed against Thee, and by Thy mercy obtain pardon for them. Through the merits.

[Coll. Septuag.; 4th S. in L.; 1st S. a. East. **315—325.**]

Benediction. The LORD Almighty open your heart to His Law, and humble your soul to receive His holy Commandments.

WITH A MARRIED WOMAN AFTER CHILDBIRTH.

In the Name, &c.
Our FATHER, &c.

V̓. I will receive you, and be a Father unto you. R̝. And ye shall be My sons and daughters, saith the LORD Almighty. V̓. O GOD, &c. R̝. O LORD, &c. V̓. Glory, &c. R̝. As it was, &c.

Ant. O Israel, trust in the LORD.

Ps. 113. Praise the LORD, ye servants, &c.

Ant. O Israel, trust in the LORD, from this time forth for evermore.

The Chapter. S. John xvi. 21.

A woman when she is in travail hath sorrow, because her hour is come: but as soon as she is delivered of the child, she remembereth no more the anguish, for joy that a man is born into the world.

V̓. But Thou, &c. R̝. Thanks, &c. V̓. Lo, children, and the fruit of the womb. R̝. Are an heritage and gift that cometh of the LORD. V̓. Glory, &c. R̝. As it was, &c. V̓. Like as the arrows in the hand of the giant. R̝. Even so are the young children. V̓. The LORD, &c. R̝. And with, &c. V̓. Let us pray.

232. Almighty GOD, our Heavenly FATHER, Who didst appoint unto our first mother, Eve, after her transgression, that in sorrow she should bring forth children, but didst promise redemption through her seed, even JESUS CHRIST, Thy SON, our LORD; favourably regard this Thine handmaid whom Thou hast preserved through the pains and perils of childbirth [and hast made the living mother of a living child, filling her heart with joy and gladness]. Stretch forth Thine hand to heal and restore her; endue her with renewed strength both in body and soul: sanctify her by Thy HOLY SPIRIT, and bring her again in peace into Thy holy Church, that she may praise Thy Name in the midst of Thy congregation. Hide her under the shadow of Thy wings from this day forward. Grant her the increase of faith, charity, and holiness with sobriety; and guarding her from all evil, bring her at length unto Thine everlasting salvation. Through the same.

BENEDICTION OF THE INFANT.

233. O GOD, Who for our salvation didst vouchsafe to send down from heaven Thine Only-begotten SON, to be born of Blessed Mary ever Virgin, and to be laid an Infant in the manger; and Who hast further said by the same Thy well-beloved SON, that in heaven the angels of little children do always behold Thy face; we humbly beseech Thee to embrace in the everlasting arms of Thy loving-kindness this infant on whom we now set the si+gn of our redemption, in token of Thy good will towards *him* through the Cross and Passion of our LORD JESUS CHRIST. Vouchsafe unto *him* the gift of Thy heavenly blessing. Defend *him* from the power and assaults of the devil.

Protect *him* by Thy good Providence from all harm of body and soul. Grant that *he* may be born again unto Thee in holy Baptism, be made partaker of Thy heavenly grace, abide Thy faithful soldier and servant unto *his* life's end, and finally may be admitted to Thine eternal glory. Through.

[*See Office* After a Miscarriage, p. 66.]

WITH AN UNMARRIED WOMAN AFTER CHILDBIRTH.

In the Name, &c.
Our FATHER, &c.

℣. There is no health in my flesh, because of Thy displeasure. ℟. Neither is there any rest in my bones by reason of my sin. ℣. O GOD, make speed, &c. ℟. O LORD, make haste, &c. ℣. Glory, &c. ℟. As it was, &c.

Ant. Thou shalt purge me with hyssop, and I shall be clean.

Ps. 51. Have mercy upon me, &c.

Ant. Thou shalt purge me with hyssop, and I shall be clean : Thou shalt wash me, and I shall be whiter than snow.

The Chapter. Rom. xiii.

The night is far spent, the day is at hand : let us therefore cast off the works of darkness, and let us put on the armour of light. Let us walk honestly, as in the day : not in rioting and drunkenness, not in chambering and wantonness, not in strife and envying. But put ye on the LORD JESUS CHRIST, and make not provision for the flesh, to fulfil the lusts thereof.

℣. But Thou, &c. ℟. Thanks, &c. ℣. Resist the devil, and he will flee from you. ℟. Draw nigh unto GOD, and He will draw nigh unto you. ℣. Glory, &c. ℟. As it was, &c. ℣. Humble yourself in the sight of the LORD. ℟. And He will lift you up. ℣. The LORD, &c. ℟. And with, &c. ℣. Let us pray.

LORD, have mercy, &c.
Our FATHER, &c.

℣. Turn Thee unto me, and have mercy upon me. ℟. For I am desolate and in misery. ℣. The sorrows of my heart are enlarged. ℟. O bring Thou me out of my troubles. ℣. For Thy Name's sake, O LORD. ℟. Be merciful unto my sin, for it is great. ℣. Look upon my adversity and misery. ℟. And forgive me all my sin. ℣. LORD, hear, &c. ℟. And let, &c. ℣. Let us pray.

234. O LORD, be gracious to the supplication of Thy servant, and heal the weakness of her body and soul, that she, obtaining pardon of her sin, may ever rejoice in Thy blessing. Through.

[315, 316, 335.]

Benediction. The LORD put away from you the perils of all temptations, and of His tender mercy protect you from all dangers and troubles.

FOR A PENITENT.

In the Name, &c.

Our FATHER, &c.   I believe, &c.

℣. I am not come to call the righteous.   ℟. But sinners to repentance.   ℣. O GOD, &c.   ℟. O LORD, &c.   ℣. Glory, &c.   ℟. As it was, &c.

Ant. O let Thy merciful kindness be my comfort.

The Penitential Psalms.

Ps. 6. O LORD, rebuke, &c.
32. Blessed is he, &c.
38. Put me not to rebuke, &c.
51. Have mercy upon me, &c.
102. Hear my prayer, &c.
130. Out of the deep, &c.
143. Hear my prayer, &c.

Or any of the following.

Ps. 25. Unto Thee, O LORD, &c.
55. Hear my prayer, &c.
86. Bow down Thine ear, &c.
88. O LORD GOD of my salvation, &c.

Ant. O let Thy merciful kindness be my comfort, according to Thy word unto Thy servant.

The Chapter.   Mic. vii.

I will look unto the LORD : I will wait for the GOD of my salvation : my GOD will hear me.   Rejoice not against me, O mine enemy : when I fall, I shall arise ; when I sit in darkness, the LORD shall be a light unto me.   I will bear the indignation of the LORD, because I have sinned against Him, until He plead my cause, and execute judgment for me : He will bring me forth to the light, and I shall behold His righteousness . . . . Who is a GOD like unto Thee, that pardoneth iniquity, and passeth by the transgression of the remnant of His heritage ?   He retaineth not His anger for ever, because He delighteth in mercy. He will turn again, He will have compassion upon us ; He will sub-

due our iniquities ; and Thou wilt cast all their sins into the depths of the sea.

[Ep. S. Jno. Ev. ; 6th S. a. Epiph. ; Septuag. ; 3rd S. in L. ; East. D. Gosp. Sex. ; ·3rd, 19th S. a. T. App. 28—41.]

℣. But Thou, &c.   ℟. Thanks, &c.   ℣. I am He that blotteth out thy transgressions.   ℟. And will not remember thy sins.   ℣. Glory, &c.   ℟. As it was, &c.   ℣. Reckon ye also yourselves to be dead indeed unto sin.   ℟. But alive unto GOD, through JESUS CHRIST our LORD. ℣. The LORD, &c.   ℟. And with, &c.   ℣. Let us pray.

LORD, have mercy, &c.

Our FATHER, &c.

℣. I said, LORD, be merciful unto me.   ℟. Heal my soul, for I have sinned against Thee.   ℣. Turn Thee again, O LORD, at the last.   ℟. And be gracious unto Thy servant.   ℣. O remember not the sins and offences of my youth.   ℟. But according to Thy mercy think Thou upon me, O LORD, for Thy goodness.   ℣. Let Thy merciful kindness, O LORD, be upon us.   ℟. Like as we do put our trust in Thee.   ℣. LORD, hear, &c.   ℟. And let, &c.   ℣. Let us pray.

235. O LORD JESU CHRIST, Who broughtest home the lost sheep to the fold on Thy shoulders ; Who wast appeased by the prayers and confessions of the Publican ; be favourable also, O LORD, unto Thy servant, and graciously hearken to *his* prayers.   Who livest.

[Coll. 5th S. a. Epiph. ; Ash-W. 24th S. a. T. **273—277, 284 292—297, 321—325.**]

Benediction. The Lamb of God Who came to take away the sins of the world, remove from you all stain of wickedness.

BEFORE RECEIVING HOLY COMMUNION.

In the Name, &c.
Our FATHER, &c.   I believe, &c.

℣. He gave them Bread from heaven. ℟. So man did eat angels' food. ℣. O GOD, &c. ℟. O LORD, &c. ℣. Glory,&c. ℟. As it was, &c.

Ant. I will wash my hands in innocency, O LORD.

Ps. 23. The LORD is my Shepherd, &c.
24. The earth is the LORD's, &c.
43. Give sentence with me, &c.
116 (ver. 10.) I believed, and therefore, &c.

Ant. I will wash my hands in innocency, O LORD ; and so will I go to Thine Altar.

The Chapter. 1 Cor. xi.

For I have received of the LORD that which also I delivered unto you, that the LORD JESUS the same night in which He was betrayed took bread: and when He had given thanks, He brake it, and said, Take, eat; this is My Body, which is broken for you: this do in remembrance of Me. After the same manner also He took the cup when He had supped, saying, This cup is the new Testament in My Blood: this do ye, as oft as ye drink it, in remembrance of Me. For as often as ye eat this Bread and drink this Cup, ye do show the LORD's death till He come.

[Ep. 1st S. a. T. Gosp. 4th S. in L.; S. Barn. App. 40, 41.]

℣. But Thou, &c. ℟. Thanks, &c. ℣. The eyes of all wait upon Thee, O LORD. ℟. And Thou givest them their meat in due season. ℣. Glory, &c. ℟. As it was, &c. ℣. Thou openest Thine hand. ℟. And fillest all things living with plenteousness. ℣. The LORD, &c. ℟. And with, &c. ℣. Let us pray.

LORD, have mercy, &c.
Our FATHER, &c. .

℣. Deal Thy Bread, O LORD, to the hungry. ℟. And hide not Thyself from Thine own flesh. ℣. Give strong drink to him that is ready to perish. ℟. And wine unto those that be of heavy hearts. ℣. Give meat unto Thy household, O LORD. ℟. And a portion unto Thy servants. ℣. LORD, hear, &c. ℟. And let, &c. ℣. Let us pray.

O GOD, Who in this wonderful Sacrament hast left unto us a Memorial of Thy Passion; grant to us, we beseech Thee, so to venerate the Sacred Mysteries of Thy Body and Blood, that we may always perceive in ourselves the fruit of Thy Redemption. Who livest.

[Coll. 6th S. a. T.; 21st S. a. T. **381—384.**]

Benediction. CHRIST fulfil your desires by showing you His Presence, and graciously accept your devotion.

THE COMMUNION OF THE SICK.

(WITH THE RESERVED SACRAMENT.)

Prayer on taking the Reserved Sacrament from the Tabernacle.

236. O Almighty GOD, Who didst send an Angel to feed Thy servant Elijah with wondrous food and drink to strengthen him for his journey through the wilderness ; grant unto me, Thine unworthy servant and messenger, that I may fitly and reverently bear the blessed Sacrament of Thine Only-begotten Son unto Thy sick servant *N.*, that it may be unto *him* Food by the way in *his* pilgrimage through the wilderness of this world and the valley of the shadow of death, that *he* may be so strengthened therewith as to attain unto the Mount of God, to the heavenly Jerusalem, to the innumerable company of the Angels, to the spirits of just men made perfect, and to Jesus the Mediator of the New Covenant. To Whom with Thee and the Holy Ghost.

———

In the Name, &c.
Our Father, &c.

[℣. O Lord, save Thy servant. ℟. Who putteth *his* trust in Thee. ℣. Send *him* help from Thy holy place. ℟. And strengthen *him* out of Sion. ℣. Let not the enemy prevail against *him*. ℟. Nor the son of wickedness approach to hurt *him*. ℣. Be Thou to *him*, O Lord, a strong tower. ℟. From the face of the enemy. ℣. O Lord, hear, &c. ℟. And let, &c. ℣. The Lord, &c. ℟. And with, &c. ℣. Let us pray.

237. O God, Who alone canst strengthen the weakness of man, show forth Thy mighty help unto this Thy sick servant, that by Thy merciful aid *he* may be restored whole to Thy Church. Through.]

The Priest then recites the Confession, in which the sick person joins, if able so to do.

Almighty God, Father of our Lord Jesus Christ, Maker of all things, Judge of all men; We acknowledge and bewail our manifold sins and wickedness, which we, from time to time, most grievously have committed, by thought, word, and deed, against Thy Divine Majesty, provoking most justly Thy wrath

and indignation against us. We do earnestly repent, and are heartily sorry for these our misdoings; the remembrance of them is grievous unto us; the burden of them is intolerable. Have mercy upon us, have mercy upon us, most merciful Father; for Thy Son our Lord Jesus Christ's sake forgive us all that is past; and grant that we may ever hereafter serve and please Thee in newness of life, to the honour and glory of Thy Name. Through Jesus Christ our Lord. Amen.

The Absolution.

Almighty God, our Heavenly Father, Who of His great mercy hath promised forgiveness of sins to all them that with hearty repentance and true faith turn unto Him; have mercy upon you; pardon and deliver you from all your sins; confirm and strengthen you in all goodness; and bring you to everlasting life. Through Jesus Christ our Lord. Amen.

Prayer of Humble Access.

We do not presume to come to this Thy Table, O merciful Lord, trusting in our own righteousness, but in Thy manifold and great mercies. We are not worthy so much as to gather up the crumbs under Thy Table. But Thou art the same Lord, Whose property is always to have mercy: Grant us therefore, gracious Lord, so to eat the Flesh of Thy dear Son Jesus Christ, and to drink His Blood, that our sinful bodies may be made clean by His Body, and our souls washed through His most precious Blood, and that we may evermore dwell in Him, and He in us. Amen.

The Priest then takes the Blessed Sacrament out of the Pyx, and holding it before the sick person, says:

Behold the Lamb of God, that taketh away the sins of the world.

He kneels down, and adds :

LORD, I am not worthy that Thou shouldest come under my roof, but speak the word only, and my soul shall be healed.

He rises, and communicates the sick person, saying :

The Body of our LORD JESUS CHRIST, which was given for thee, preserve thy body and soul unto everlasting life. R̸. Amen.

When the sick person is communicated with the reserved Chalice, the Priest elevates it, saying :

The Precious Blood of CHRIST, as of a Lamb without blemish and without spot.

He kneels and adds :

I will receive the Cup of Salvation, and will call upon the Name of the LORD.

He rises, and communicates the sick person, saying :

The Blood of our LORD JESUS CHRIST, which was shed for thee, preserve thy body and soul unto everlasting life. R̸. Amen.

When both kinds are reserved by dipping the Species of Bread in the Chalice, the Priest shall say,

The Body and Blood of our LORD JESUS CHRIST, which were given for thee, preserve, &c.

When the sick person has communicated, the Priest says,

Let us pray.

LORD, have mercy, &c.
Our FATHER, &c.

238. O LORD, Holy FATHER, Almighty, Everlasting GOD, we humbly beseech Thee that the Holy Communion of the Body and Blood of Thy SON JESUS CHRIST our LORD may be for the salvation of soul and body to this our *brother* who hath received it. Through the same.

The peace of GOD, which passeth all understanding, keep your hearts and minds in the knowledge and love of GOD, and of His SON JESUS CHRIST our LORD: and the blessing of GOD Almighty, the FATHER, the SON, and the HOLY GHOST, be amongst you and remain with you always. Amen.

If it be desirable to shorten the Service, the part in brackets may be omitted.

AFTER RECEIVING HOLY COMMUNION.

In the Name, &c.
Our FATHER, &c. I believe, &c.

℣. He hath fed us with the finest wheat flour. R̸. And with honey out of the stony rock hath He satisfied us. ℣. O GOD, &c. R̸. O LORD, &c. ℣. Glory, &c. R̸. As it was, &c.

Ant. He rained down Manna upon them for to eat.

Ps. 34. I will always give thanks, &c.

103. Praise the LORD, O my soul, &c.

146. Praise the LORD . . . . while I live, &c.

Ant. He rained down Manna upon them for to eat, and gave them Food from heaven.

The Chapter. S. John vi.

Then said JESUS unto them, Verily, verily, I say unto you, Except ye eat the flesh of the Son of Man, and drink His blood, ye have no life in you. Whoso eateth My flesh and drinketh My blood, hath eternal life; and I will raise him up at the last day. For My flesh is meat indeed, and My blood is drink indeed. He that eateth My flesh and drinketh My blood, dwelleth in Me, and I in him. As the living FATHER hath sent Me, and I live by the FATHER: so he that eateth Me, even he shall live by Me. This is that bread which came down from heaven; not as your fathers did eat manna, and are dead: he that eateth of this bread shall live for ever.

[Ep. 5th S. in L. Gosp. S. Mark.]

℣. But Thou, &c. ℟. Thanks, &c. ℣. The merciful and gracious LORD hath so done His marvellous works. ℟. That they ought to be had in remembrance. ℣. Glory, &c. ℟. As it was, &c. ℣. He hath given Meat unto them that fear Him. ℟. He will always be mindful of His covenant. ℣. The LORD, &c. ℟. And with, &c. ℣. Let us pray.

LORD, have mercy, &c.
Our FATHER, &c.

℣. LORD, what is man that Thou art mindful of him? ℟. And the son of man that Thou visitest him? ℣. My soul shall be satisfied even as it were with marrow and fatness. ℟. When my mouth praiseth Thee with joyful lips. ℣. Not unto us, O LORD, not unto us. ℟. But unto Thy Name give the praise. ℣. LORD, now lettest Thou Thy servant depart in peace, according to Thy word. ℟. For mine eyes have seen Thy salvation. ℣. LORD, hear, &c. ℟. And let, &c. ℣. Let us pray.

239. O LORD, we pray Thee, let the heavenly Table from which we have been fed hallow us, and so cleanse us from our sins that we may be made fit for Thy promised joys above. Through.

[Coll. 6th and 7th S. a. T.; All SS. **386—389.**]

Benediction. GOD, Who hath washed you with the water from His Side, and redeemed you by the shedding of His Blood, confirm in you the grace of that redemption wherein you have been made to share.

SPIRITUAL COMMUNION.

In the Name, &c.
Our FATHER, &c. I believe, &c.

℣. If any man hear My voice, and open the door. ℟. I will come in to him and will sup with him, and he with Me. ℣. O GOD, &c. ℟. O LORD, &c. ℣. Glory, &c. ℟. As it was, &c.

Ant. Blessed are they which do hunger and thirst after righteousness.

Ps. 23. The LORD is my Shepherd, &c.
42. Like as the hart, &c.

43. Give sentence with me, &c.
84. O how amiable, &c.

Ant. Blessed are they which do hunger and thirst after righteousness, for they shall be filled.

The Chapter. Deut. viii.

And He humbled thee, and suffered thee to hunger, and fed thee with manna, which thou knewest not, neither did thy fathers know; that He might make thee know that man doth not live by bread only, but by every word that proceedeth out of the mouth of the LORD doth man live.

[Ep. 2nd S. a. T. (*begin* "Beloved, if.") Gosp. 24th S. a. T.]

℣. But Thou, &c. ℟. Thanks, &c. ℣. Unto him that overcometh. ℟. Will I give to eat of the hidden manna. ℣. Glory, &c. ℟. As it was, &c. ℣. They shall hunger no more, neither thirst any more. ℟. For the Lamb which is in the midst of the throne shall feed them, and shall lead them unto living fountains of water. ℣. The LORD, &c. ℟. And with, &c. ℣. Let us pray.

LORD, have mercy, &c.
Our FATHER, &c.

℣. O LORD, prepare a table before me. ℟. Against them that trouble me. ℣. Feed me in a green pasture. ℟. And lead me forth beside the waters of comfort. ℣. Satisfy the empty soul. ℟. And fill the hungry soul with goodness. ℣. LORD, hear, &c. ℟. And let, &c. ℣. Let us pray.

240. Grant, O LORD JESU CHRIST, that as the hem of Thy garment touched in faith healed the woman who could not touch Thy Body, so the soul of Thy servant may be healed by like faith in Thee, Whom [by reason of weakness] *he* cannot now receive. Through Thy tender mercy, Who livest.

[Coll. 4th S. a. East.; 6th and 12th S. a. T. **390.**]

Benediction. The grace of Almighty GOD protect you, satisfy your hunger with spiritual food, bedew your thirst with the streams of righteousness, and pour the savour of His sweetness into your soul.

FOR ONE RECOVERING.

In the Name, &c.
Our FATHER, &c. I believe, &c.

℣. The LORD hath chastened and corrected me. ℟. But He hath not given me over unto death. ℣. O GOD, &c. ℟. O LORD, &c. ℣. Glory, &c. ℟. As it was, &c.

Ant. I will thank the LORD.

Ps. 34. I will alway give, &c.
40. I waited patiently, &c.
119 (65.) O LORD, Thou hast dealt graciously, &c.
121. I will lift up mine eyes, &c.
126. When the LORD turned, &c.

Ant. I will thank the LORD for giving me warning.

The Chapter. Isa. xlviii.

For My Name's sake will I defer Mine anger, and for My praise will I refrain for thee, that I cut thee not off. Behold, I have refined thee, but not with silver; I have chosen thee in the furnace of affliction . . . . Thus saith the LORD, thy Redeemer, the Holy One of Israel; I am the LORD thy GOD, which teacheth thee to profit, which leadeth thee by the way that thou shouldest go.

(*When recovery is unexpected, add,*)
Tobit viii.

O GOD, Thou art worthy to be praised with all pure and holy praise; therefore let Thy saints praise Thee with all Thy creatures; and let all Thine angels and Thine elect praise Thee for ever. Thou art to be praised, for Thou hast made me joyful; and that is not come to me which I suspected; but Thou hast dealt with us according to Thy great mercy.

[Ep. 1st S. in L.; 3rd and 6th S. a. T. Gosp. 3rd S. in Adv.; Sex. App. 42, 43.]

℣. But Thou, &c. ℟. Thanks, &c. ℣. The eyes of the LORD are upon them that love Him. ℟. He is their mighty protection and strong stay. ℣. Glory, &c. ℟. As it was, &c. ℣. He raiseth up the soul, and lighteneth the eyes. ℟. He giveth health, life, and blessing. ℣. The LORD, &c. ℟. And with, &c. ℣. Let us pray.

LORD, have mercy, &c.
Our FATHER, &c.

℣. Consider and hear me, O LORD my GOD. ℟. Lighten mine eyes that I sleep not in death. ℣. I said, LORD, be merciful unto me. ℟. Heal my soul, for I have sinned against Thee. ℣. O be Thou our help in trouble. ℟. For vain is the help of man. ℣. Thou art my helper and my Redeemer. ℟. O LORD, make no long tarrying. ℣. LORD, hear, &c. ℟. And let, &c. ℣. Let us pray.

241. O most mighty GOD, Who bringest down to the grave and liftest up; suffer not our enemies to triumph over us, but strengthen us by Thy might, that, our heaviness being turned into joy, we may ever give thanks unto Thee for the remembrance of Thy mercy. Through.

[Coll. 4th S. a. Epiph.; 3rd S. a. T.; 2nd Post-Comm. **391.**]

Benediction. The LORD our GOD, Who hath brought you out of the pit of corruption, bring you also to the Tree of Life.

THANKSGIVING FOR RECOVERY.

In the Name, &c.
Our FATHER, &c. I believe, &c.

℣. When I called upon Thee Thou heardest me. ℟. And enduedst my soul with much strength. ℣. O GOD, &c. ℟. O LORD, &c. ℣. Glory, &c. ℟. As it was, &c.

Ant. Blessed is he that hath the GOD of Jacob for his help.

Ps. 30. I will magnify Thee, &c.
33. Rejoice in the LORD, &c.
71. In Thee, O LORD, &c.
103. Praise the LORD, &c.
116. I am well pleased, &c.
118. O give thanks, &c.

Isa. xxxviii. 10—21. The Song of Hezekiah. [App. 45.]

Ant. Blessed is he that hath the GOD of Jacob for his help, and whose hope is in the LORD his GOD.

The Chapter. 2 Kings xx.

In those days was Hezekiah sick unto death. And the prophet Isaiah the son of Amoz came to him, and said unto him, Thus saith the LORD, Set thine house in order; for thou shalt die, and not live. Then he turned his face to the wall, and prayed unto the LORD, saying, I beseech Thee, O LORD, remember now how I have walked before Thee in truth and with a perfect heart, and have done that which is good in Thy sight. And Hezekiah wept sore. And it came to pass, afore Isaiah was gone out into the middle court, that the word of the LORD came to him, saying, Turn again, and tell Hezekiah the captain of My people, Thus saith the LORD, the GOD of David thy father, I have heard thy prayer, I have seen thy tears; behold, I will heal thee: on the third day thou shalt go up unto the house of the LORD. And I will add unto thy days fifteen years; and I will deliver thee and this city out of the hand of the king of Assyria; and I will defend this city for Mine own sake, and for My servant David's sake. And Isaiah said, Take a lump of figs. And they took and laid it on the boil, and he recovered.

[Ep. 1st S. iu L. Gosp. 14th S. a. T. App. 42, 43.]

℣. But Thou, &c. ℟. Thanks, &c. ℣. When my soul fainted within me, I remembered the LORD. ℟. And my prayer came in unto Thee into Thy holy Temple. ℣. Glory, &c. ℟. As it was, &c. ℣. I will sacrifice unto Thee with a voice of thanksgiving. ℟. I will pay that that I have vowed. ℣. The LORD, &c. ℟. And with, &c. ℣. Let us pray.

LORD, have mercy, &c.
Our FATHER, &c.

℣. I did call upon the LORD with my voice. ℟. And He heard me out of His holy hill. ℣. Praised be the LORD. ℟. For He hath heard the voice of my humble pe-titions. ℣. Thy mercy, O LORD, reacheth unto the heavens. ℟. And Thy faithfulness unto the clouds. ℣. O continue forth Thy lovingkindness unto them that know Thee. ℟. And Thy righteousness unto them that are true of heart. ℣. LORD, hear, &c. ℟. And let, &c. ℣. Let us pray.

242. O LORD JESU CHRIST, the Life and strength of all who put their trust in Thee; mercifully grant that as Thou hast been pleased to restore Thy servant to *his* bodily health, so Thou mayest endue *his* soul with all heavenly graces, and perseverance in good works, of Thy tender mercy. Who livest.

[Coll. 7th, 13th, and 25th S. a. T.; Last Thanksgiving Collects. **392, 393.**]

Benediction. The merciful LORD, in Whose hand is all prosperity, grant you ever the increase of blessing and peace.

FOR ONE UNLIKELY TO RECOVER.

In the Name, &c.
Our FATHER, &c. I believe, &c.

℣. GOD is our GOD for ever and ever. ℟. He shall be our Guide unto death. ℣. O GOD, &c. ℟. O LORD, &c. ℣. Glory, &c. ℟. As it was, &c.

Ant. Save me, O GOD.

Ps. 16. Preserve me, O LORD, &c.
23. The LORD is my Shepherd, &c.
27. The LORD is my light, &c.
39. I said, I will take, &c.
130. Out of the deep, &c.

Ant. Save me, O GOD, for the waters are come in, even unto my soul.

The Chapter. S. John v.

Verily, verily, I say unto you, He that heareth My word, and believeth on Him that sent Me, hath everlasting life, and shall not come into condemnation; but is passed from death unto life. Verily, verily, I say unto you, The hour is coming, and now is, when the dead shall hear the voice of the SON of GOD; and they that hear shall live.

[Ep. 1st and 4th S. in Adv.; S. Steph.; S. John Ev.; 6th S. a. Epiph.; Trin. S.; 1st and 6th S. a. T. Gosp. 2nd S. iu Adv.; Sept.; 5th S. a. East.; Whits. M. App. 46, 47, 53—55.]

℣. But Thou, &c. ℟. Thanks, &c. ℣. What is my strength that I should hope? ℟. And what is mine end that I should prolong my life? ℣. Glory, &c. ℟. As it was, &c. ℣. My days are gone like a shadow. ℟. And I am withered like grass. ℣. The LORD, &c. ℟. And with, &c. ℣. Let us pray.

LORD, have mercy, &c.
Our FATHER, &c.

℣. I said, LORD, be merciful unto me. ℟. Heal my soul, for I have sinned against Thee. ℣. Turn Thee again, O LORD, at the last. ℟. And be gracious unto Thy servants. ℣. Let Thy merciful kindness, O LORD, be upon us. ℟. As we do put our trust in Thee. ℣. LORD, hear, &c. ℟. And let, &c. ℣. Let us pray.

243. Assist us mercifully, O LORD, in these our supplications, and accept the prayers which we make before Thee in behalf of Thy servant, who asketh of Thee health and salvation of soul. Grant *him*, we beseech Thee, pardon of all *his* sins, that *his* soul may be rescued by Thy holy Angels, and may safely attain unto Thy kingdom and glory. Through.

[Coll. 1st S. in Adv.; 3rd S. a. Epiph.; S. a. Asc.; 12th S. a. T. **307, 309—314.**]

Benediction. The LORD, Whom you beseech, hear your prayers, and with His wonted mercy forgive you all your offences.

BEFORE MAKING A WILL.

In the Name, &c.
Our FATHER, &c. I believe, &c.

℣. The LORD Himself is the portion of mine inheritance and of my cup. ℟. Thou shalt maintain my lot. ℣. The lot is fallen unto me in a fair ground. ℟. Yea, I have a goodly heritage. ℣. Glory, &c. ℟. As it was, &c.

Ant. I love Thy commandments.

Ps. 15. LORD, who shall dwell, &c.
82. GOD standeth, &c.
112. Blessed is the man, &c.

Ant. I love Thy commandments above gold and precious stone.

The Chapter. Ecclus. xiv.

My son, according to thy ability do good to thyself, and give the LORD His due offering. Remember that death will not be long in coming, and that the covenant of the grave is not showed unto thee. Do good unto thy friend before thou die, and according to thy ability stretch out thy hand and give to him. Defraud not thyself of the good day, and let not the part of a good desire overpass thee. Shalt thou not leave thy travails unto another? and thy labours to be divided by lot? Give, and take, and sanctify thy soul; for there is no seeking of dainties in the grave . . . Every work rotteth and consumeth away, and the worker thereof shall go withal. Blessed is the man that doth meditate good things in wisdom, and that reasoneth of holy things by his understanding. He that considereth her ways in his heart shall also have understanding in her secrets.

℣. But Thou, &c. ℟. Thanks, &c. ℣. The ungodly borroweth and payeth not again. ℟. But the righteous is merciful and liberal. ℣. Glory, &c. ℟. As it was, &c. ℣. I will take heed unto the thing that is right. ℟. For that shall bring a man peace at the last. ℣. The LORD, &c. ℟. And with, &c. ℣. Let us pray.

Lord, have mercy, &c.
Our Father, &c.

℣. Teach me to do the thing that pleaseth Thee. ℟. For Thou art my God. ℣. Defend the poor and fatherless. ℟. See that such as are in need and necessity have right. ℣. Incline my heart unto Thy testimonies. ℟. And not to covetousness. ℣. Lord, hear, &c. ℟. And let, &c. ℣. Let us pray.

244. O Lord, Whose lovingkindness is everlasting, and Whose justice is infinite; mercifully grant Thy Holy Spirit unto Thy servant, that *he* may be a faithful steward of that which Thou hast committed unto *his* charge, so as not to wrong any to whom *he* is bound by kindred or duty, and that showing compassion unto Thy poor, *he* may obtain Thy mercy. Through.

[Coll. S. Matth.]

Benediction. The Lord make ready for Himself a place in your heart by good works in this life, that, justified for ever, you may reign with Christ.

THE ANOINTING OF THE SICK.

The Priest begins the Antiphon.

Ant. O Saviour of the world.

Ps. 31. In Thee, O Lord, &c.

Ant. O Saviour of the world, Who by Thy Cross and Precious Blood hast redeemed us, save us and help us, we humbly beseech Thee, O Lord.

℣. The Lord, &c. ℟. And with, &c. ℣. Let us pray.

245. Almighty, Everlasting God, Who spakest by Thy blessed Apostle James, saying, "Is any sick among you? Let him call for the Elders of the Church; and let them pray over him, anointing him with Oil in the Name of the Lord; and the prayer of faith shall save the sick, and the Lord shall raise him up, and if he have committed sins they shall be forgiven him;" vouchsafe to anoint this Thy sick servant *N.* at our hands with hallowed Oil, and to restore *him* to *his* former health by the might of Thy blessing, that what is outwardly done by our ministry, Thy Divine power and Thine invisible healing may spiritually make effective within. Through.

Then the Priest, approaching the sick person, begins the following Psalm, which the clerks or people continue, as they do also with the other Psalms.

Ps. 13. How long, &c.

While this Psalm is sung by the clerks or people, the Priest shall take the Oil of the Sick on his right thumb, and therewith touch the sick person, making the sign of the Cross, upon each eye, beginning with the right, and saying,

Through this anointing, and His most loving mercy, the Lord pardon thee whatever thou hast sinned by sight.
℟. Amen.

Ps. 30. I will magnify Thee, &c.

Then upon the ears, saying,

Through this anointing, and His most loving mercy, the Lord pardon thee whatever thou hast sinned by hearing.
℟. Amen.

Ps. 43. Give sentence with me, &c.

Then upon the lips, saying,

Through this anointing, and His most loving mercy, the LORD pardon thee whatever thou hast sinned by taste and unlawful words.

Ŗ. Amen.

Ps. 54. Save me, O GOD, &c.

Then upon the nostrils, saying,

Through this anointing, and His most loving mercy, the LORD pardon thee whatever thou hast sinned by smelling.

Ŗ. Amen.

Ps. 70. Haste Thee, O GOD, &c.

Then upon the hands, saying,

Through this anointing, and His most loving mercy, the LORD pardon thee whatever thou hast sinned by touch.

Ŗ. Amen.

Ps. 86. Bow down Thine ear, &c.

Then upon the feet, saying,

Through this anointing, and His most loving mercy, the LORD pardon thee whatever thou hast sinned by the gait of thy feet.

Ŗ. Amen.

Then the Priest, rising, washes his hands.
Afterwards he shall say the Blessing over the sick person in this wise.

In the Name of the FATHER, the SON, and the HOLY GHOST; let this Anointing of Oil be to thee for the purifying of soul and body, and for a bulwark and defence against the darts of unclean spirits.

Ŗ. Amen.

Ps. 141. LORD, I call upon Thee, &c.

℣. The LORD, &c. Ŗ. And with, &c. ℣. Let us pray.

246. O LORD GOD, our SAVIOUR, Who art the true Health and Medicine from Whom all soundness and healing come, and Who hast taught us by the precept of Thine Apostle James to anoint in prayer the sick; graciously look on this Thy servant *N.*, and let the medicine of Thy grace restore to health, after chastisement, *him* whom weakness leadeth unto death, and failure of strength draweth on to dissolution. Assuage in *him*, most merciful GOD, all feverish heat, all searching pains, all suffering from weakness. Heal with Thy medicine, *his* reins, *his* inward parts, and the joints of *his* marrow. Efface the old scars of *his* frame and members. Restrain *his* bitter sufferings. Let the perfect substance of that flesh and blood which Thou hast made be renewed in *him*, and let Thy lovingkindness ever so preserve *him*, that soundness may never lead *him* to sinfulness, nor sickness to destruction, but that this holy Anointing of Oil may quickly drive from *him his* present disease and weakness, and obtain for *him* that pardon of all *his* sins which *he* desires : through Thee, O SAVIOUR of the world, Who livest and reignest with the FATHER, and the HOLY GHOST, one GOD, world without end.

Ŗ. Amen.

The cottons shall be reverently burnt by the Priest.

————

Or the following short Form from the First Prayer Book of Edward the Sixth may be substituted, if more convenient.

If the sick person desire to be anointed, then shall the Priest anoint him upon the forehead and breast only, making the sign of the Cross, saying thus,

As with this visible oil thy body outwardly is anointed : so our heavenly FATHER, Almighty GOD, grant of His infinite goodness, that thy soul inwardly may be anointed with the HOLY GHOST, Who is the

Spirit of all strength, comfort, relief, and gladness; and vouchsafe for His great mercy (if it be His blessed will), to restore unto thee thy bodily health, and strength, to serve Him; and send thee release of all thy pains, troubles, and diseases, both in body and mind. And howsoever His goodness (by His divine and unsearchable providence) shall dispose of thee; we, His unworthy ministers and servants, humbly beseech the Eternal Majesty to do with thee according to the multitude of His innumerable mercies, and to pardon thee all thy sins and offences, committed by all thy bodily senses, passions, and carnal affections; Who also vouchsafe mercifully to grant unto thee ghostly strength, by His HOLY SPIRIT, to withstand and overcome all temptations and assaults of thine adversary, that in no wise he prevail against thee, but that thou mayest have perfect victory and triumph against the devil, sin, and death, through CHRIST our LORD; Who by His death hath overcome the prince of death, and with the FATHER and the HOLY GHOST evermore liveth and reigneth GOD, world without end. Amen.

Ps. 13. How long wilt Thou forget me, &c.

FOR A DYING COMMUNICANT.

In the Name, &c.
Our FATHER, &c. I believe, &c.

℣. The LORD is my refuge. ℟. And my GOD is the strength of my confidence. ℣. O GOD, &c. ℟. O LORD, &c. ℣. Glory, &c. ℟. As it was, &c.

Ant. Go not far from me, O GOD.

Ps. 23. The LORD is my shepherd, &c.
70. Haste Thee, O LORD, to deliver me, &c.
90. LORD, Thou hast been our refuge, &c.

Nunc dimittis. LORD, now lettest Thou, &c.

Ant. Go not far from me, O GOD; my GOD, haste Thee to help me.

The Chapter. Isa. lx.

The sun shall be no more thy light by day; neither for brightness shall the moon give light unto thee: but the LORD shall be unto thee an everlasting light, and thy GOD thy glory. Thy sun shall no more go down; neither shall thy moon withdraw itself: for the LORD shall be thine everlasting light, and the days of thy mourning shall be ended.

[Ep. S. Jno. Ev.; All SS. Gosp. Whits. T. App. 66—72, 49—52.]

℣. But Thou, &c. ℟. Thanks, &c. ℣. In Thy Presence is the fulness of joy. ℟. And at Thy right hand there is pleasure for evermore. ℣. Glory, &c. ℟. As it was, &c. ℣. O that I had wings like a dove. ℟. For then would I flee away and be at rest. ℣. The LORD, &c. ℟. And with, &c. ℣. Let us pray.

LORD, have mercy, &c.
Our FATHER, &c.

℣. Into Thy hands, O LORD, I commend my spirit. ℟. For Thou hast redeemed me, O LORD, Thou GOD of Truth. ℣. Keep me, O LORD, as the apple of an eye. ℟. Hide me under the shadow of Thy wings. ℣. O CHRIST, arise, help us. ℟. And deliver us, for Thy Name's sake. ℣. LORD, hear, &c. ℟. And let, &c. ℣. Let us pray.

247. O LORD JESU CHRIST, Who by the mouth of Thy Prophet hast said, I have loved thee with an everlasting love, therefore with lovingkindness have I drawn thee: we pray Thee that Thou wouldest offer that same love of Thine, which brought Thee from heaven to earth to suffer the bitterness of Thy Passion, and present it to the FATHER, GOD Almighty, for the soul of this Thy servant, and deliver *him* from all the pains and penalties which *he* fears that *he* has deserved for *his* sins. Who livest.

[Coll. 2nd at Matins; 6th S. a. Epiph.; Palm S.; Asc. Day. **394—429.**]

Benediction. GOD, Who reneweth us unto everlasting life through the Resurrection of His SON, clothe you at His coming again with the gladness of eternity.

FOR A DYING NON-COMMUNICANT.

In the Name, &c.
Our FATHER, &c. I believe, &c.

℣. The sorrows of my heart are enlarged. ℟. O bring Thou me out of my troubles. ℣. O GOD, &c. ℟. O LORD, &c. ℣. Glory, &c. ℟. As it was, &c.

Ant. Hide not Thy face from me.

Ps. 88. O LORD GOD of my salvation, &c.
 90. LORD, Thou hast been, &c.
 102. Hear my prayer, &c.
 130. Out of the deep, &c.
 142. I cried unto the LORD, &c.

Ant. Hide not Thy face from me, lest I be like unto them that go down into the pit.

The Chapter. 1 S. John ii.

If any man sin, we have an Advocate with the FATHER, JESUS CHRIST the righteous: and He is the propitiation for our sins: and not for ours only, but also for the sins of the whole world.

[Ep. 3rd S. a. T. Gosp. 3rd S. a. T. App. 61.]

℣. But Thou, &c. ℟. Thanks, &c. ℣. GOD sent not His SON into the world to condemn the world. ℟. But that the world through Him might be saved. ℣. Glory, &c. ℟. As it was, &c. ℣. We have One GOD, and One Mediator between GOD and man. ℟. The Man CHRIST JESUS. ℣. The LORD, &c. ℟. And with, &c. ℣. Let us pray.

LORD, have mercy upon us, &c.
Our FATHER, &c.

℣. LORD, I call upon Thee, haste Thee unto me. ℟. And consider my voice when I cry unto Thee. ℣. Let not the water-flood drown me, neither let the deep swallow me up. ℟. And let not the pit shut her mouth upon me. ℣. O remember not the sins and offences of my youth. ℟. But according to Thy mercy, think Thou upon me, O LORD, for Thy goodness. ℣. According to the greatness of Thy power. ℟. Preserve Thou those that are appointed to die. ℣. LORD, hear, &c. ℟. And let, &c. ℣. Let us pray.

248. O most merciful LORD JESU CHRIST, Who didst die for us upon the Cross; we pray Thee by all Thy sufferings and sorrows which Thou barest for us, miserable sinners, on the bitter tree, especially when Thy most holy soul departed from its pure and virgin dwelling of Thy Body: we pray Thee that Thou wouldest offer and present them to God the Father Almighty against all the pains and sufferings of Thy servant, and deliver *him* in this hour of *his* departure from all the pains and penalties which *he* fears *he* hath incurred for *his* sins, of Thy tender mercy.　Who livest.

[Coll. Septuag.; Ash-Wed.; 12th and 24th S. a. T. **270, 271, 275 —278, 291, 298, 316—325.**]

Benediction. Almighty God wash away the stains of your sins, and enlighten you with His blessing.

COMMENDATION OF A DEPARTING SOUL.

Lord, have mercy, &c.

Be merciful.　Spare *him*, O Lord.
Be merciful.　Deliver *him*, O Lord.

From Thy wrath,
From the peril of death,
From an evil death,
From the power of the devil,
By Thy Nativity,
By Thy Cross and Passion,
By Thy Death and Burial,
By Thy Glorious Resurrection,
By Thy Wonderful Ascension,
By the grace of the Holy Ghost, the Comforter,
In the Day of Judgment,

Good Lord, deliver him.

We sinners beseech Thee to hear us.

We beseech Thee to hear us, good Lord.

That Thou mayest spare *him;*
We beseech Thee to hear us, good Lord.

Lord, have mercy, &c.
Our Father, &c.

249. Go forth, Christian soul, from this world, in the Name of God the Father, Who created thee, of Jesus Christ, the Son of the Living God, Who suffered for thee, of the Holy Ghost, Who is poured upon thee; in the name of the Angels and Archangels; in the name of the Thrones and Dominations; in the name of the Principalities and Powers; in the name of the Cherubim and Seraphim; in the name of the Patriarchs and Prophets; in the name of the holy Apostles and Evangelists; in the name of the holy Martyrs and Confessors; in the name of the holy Monks and Hermits; in the name of the holy Virgins, and of all the Saints of God; may thy place to-day be in peace and thy dwelling in Sion.　Through the Same.

250. O God of mercy, God of pity, Who according to the multitude of Thy mercies blottest out the sins of the penitent, and by the gift of pardon doest away with the guilt of past offences; look graciously upon this Thy servant *N.,* and hearken to *him*, entreating with hearty confession the remission of all *his* sins, renew in *him*, most merciful Father, whatever in *him* hath been corrupted by earthly frailty, or hurt by the fraud of the devil, and join the member which Thou hast redeemed to the unity of the Church's body.　Have mercy, O Lord, upon *his* sighs; have mercy upon *his* tears, and as *he* trusteth only in Thy mercy, grant that *he* may be reconciled unto Thee.　Through.

251. I commend thee, dearest *brother,* to Almighty God, and I commit thee to Him Whose creature thou art, that when thou shalt pay the debt of nature at the arrival of death, thou mayest return to thy Maker, Who formed thee out of the dust of the earth.　Therefore as thy soul goeth forth from the body, let the bright host of angels meet thee; let the Apostles who shall judge the world come unto thee; let the conquering army of white-robed Martyrs welcome thee; let the lily-crowned band of shining Confessors compass thee; let the choir of rejoicing Virgins greet thee; let the Patriarchs receive thee to rest happily in their bosom; let CHRIST JESUS look upon thee in gentleness and joy, and set thee for ever amongst them who stand before Him. Mayest thou know nothing of the horrors of darkness, of the roaring of flames, of the torture of pangs. Let Satan the evil one yield before thee with his ministers: let him fear thee as thou comest with the angels as thy guard, and flee away into the dread abyss of everlasting night. Let GOD arise, and let His enemies be scattered, let them also that hate Him flee before Him. Like as the smoke vanisheth, so shalt Thou drive them away, and like as wax melteth at the fire, so let the ungodly perish at the presence of GOD. But let the righteous be glad and rejoice before GOD. Let all the legions of hell be confounded and put to shame, and the ministers of Satan not dare to stop thy way. CHRIST Who was crucified for thee, deliver thee from torment. CHRIST, Who vouchsafed to die for thee, deliver thee from eternal death. CHRIST, the SON of the living GOD, set thee in the ever pleasant pastures of His Paradise, and may He, the good Shepherd, number thee amongst His sheep. He loose thee from all thy sins, and set thee at His right hand in the heritage of His elect. Mayest thou see thy Redeemer face to face, and ever standing in His Presence behold the truth revealed to thy gladdened eyes. Set therefore amidst the company of the blessed, mayest thou enjoy the sweetness of the Light of GOD for ever and for evermore.

℟. Amen.

252. Receive, O LORD, Thy servant into the place of salvation, which *he* hopes to obtain from Thy mercy. Amen.

Deliver, O LORD, the soul of Thy servant, from all the perils of hell, and from the bonds of the penalty of sin, and from all tribulations. Amen.

Deliver, O LORD, the soul of Thy servant, as Thou deliveredst Enoch and Elias from the death common to all men. Amen.

Deliver, O LORD, the soul of Thy servant, as Thou deliveredst Noah from the flood. Amen.

Deliver, O LORD, the soul of Thy servant, as Thou deliveredst Abraham from Ur of the Chaldees. Amen.

Deliver, O LORD, the soul of Thy servant, as Thou deliveredst Job from his sufferings. Amen.

Deliver, O LORD, the soul of Thy servant, as Thou deliveredst Isaac from the sacrifice, and from the hand of his father.

Deliver, O LORD, the soul of Thy servant, as Thou deliveredst Lot from Sodom and from the flame of fire. Amen.

Deliver, O LORD, the soul of Thy servant, as Thou deliveredst Moses from the hand of Pharaoh king of Egypt. Amen.

Deliver, O LORD, the soul of Thy servant, as Thou deliveredst Daniel from the lions' den. Amen.

Deliver, O LORD, the soul of Thy servant, as Thou deliveredst the Three Children from the fiery furnace. Amen.

Deliver, O LORD, the soul of Thy servant, as Thou deliveredst Susannah from a false accusation. Amen.

Deliver, O LORD, the soul of Thy servant, as Thou deliveredst David from the hand of King Saul, and from the hand of Goliath. Amen.

Deliver, O LORD, the soul of Thy servant, as Thou deliveredst Peter and Paul from their prisons. Amen.

And as Thou didst deliver Thy

Martyrs from their most bitter pains, so vouchsafe to deliver the soul of this Thy servant, and to make it rejoice with Thee in heaven. Amen.

253. We commend unto Thee, O LORD, the soul of Thy servant N., and we beseech Thee, O LORD JESU CHRIST, SAVIOUR of the world, that as Thou didst come down to earth in mercy to seek it, so Thou wouldst not refuse to place it in the bosom of Thy Patriarchs : Acknowledge, O LORD, Thy creature, not made by strange gods, but by Thee the one Living and True GOD, for there is no GOD beside Thee, nor any works like Thy works. Make glad, O LORD, *his* soul in Thy sight, and remember not *his* old sins, and the passions which wrath or the heat of evil desire has stirred up. Remember not, O LORD, we beseech Thee, the sins and ignorances of *his* youth, but according to Thy great mercy be mindful of *him* in the brightness of Thy glory. Let the heavens be open to *him*, let the angels rejoice with *him*, receive, O LORD, Thy servant into Thy kingdom. Let S. Michael, the Archangel of GOD, the chief of the heavenly army, receive *him*. Let the Holy Angels of GOD come to meet *him*, and lead *him* to the heavenly city Jerusalem. Let blessed Peter the Apostle, to whom GOD gave the keys of the Kingdom of Heaven, receive *him*. Let Paul the Apostle, the worthy and elect vessel, aid *him*. Let S. John, the chosen Apostle of GOD, to whom the secrets of GOD were revealed, intercede for *him*. May all the holy Apostles of GOD, to whom the LORD hath given the power of binding and loosing, pray for *him*. Let all the Saints and elect of GOD, who for the Name of GOD suffered torments in this world, intercede for *him*, that loosed from the chains of the flesh *he* may reach the glory of the Heavenly Kingdom, through the mercy of our LORD JESUS CHRIST. Who.

CHRIST, Who hath called thee, receive thee, and bid His angels lead thee into Abraham's bosom.

℣. Eternal rest grant unto *him*, O LORD. ℟. And light perpetual shine upon *him*.

· LORD, have mercy, &c.
Our FATHER, &c.

℣. Eternal rest, &c. ℟. And light, &c. ℣. From the gates of hell, &c. ℟. Deliver *his* soul, O LORD. ℣. May *he* rest in peace. ℟. And, &c. ℣. The LORD hear, &c. ℟. And let, &c. ℣. The LORD, &c. ℟. And with, &c. ℣. Let us pray.

254. We commend to Thee, O LORD, the soul of Thy servant, that dead unto the world it may live unto Thee, and whatsoever sins it hath committed through the weakness of the flesh in this mortal life, wash away by the pardon of Thy merciful love. Through.

The Penitential Psalms (6, 32, 38, 51, 102, 130, 143,) may be read aloud if occasion requires.

WITH THE FRIENDS OF THE DEPARTED.

In the Name, &c.
Our FATHER, &c. I believe, &c.

℣. The LORD gave, and the LORD hath taken away. ℟. Blessed be the Name of the LORD. ℣. O GOD, make speed, &c. ℟. O LORD, make haste, &c. ℣. Glory, &c. ℟. As it was, &c.

Ant. O put thy trust in GOD.

Ps. 27. The LORD is my Light, &c.

90. LORD, Thou hast been, &c.
102. Hear my prayer, &c.
121. I will lift up, &c.
130. Out of the deep, &c.

Ant. O put thy trust in GOD, for I will yet give Him thanks, Which is the help of my countenance and my GOD.

The Chapter. 1 Thess. iv.

But I would not have you to be ignorant, brethren, concerning them which are asleep, that ye sorrow not, even as others which have no hope. For if we believe that JESUS died and rose again, even so them also which sleep in JESUS will GOD bring with Him. For this we say unto you by the word of the LORD, that we which are alive and remain unto the coming of the LORD shall not prevent them which are asleep. For the LORD Himself shall descend from heaven with a shout, with the voice of the archangel, and with the trump of·GOD : and the dead in CHRIST shall rise first : then we which are alive and remain shall be caught up together with them in the clouds, to meet the LORD in the air : and so shall we ever be with the LORD. Wherefore comfort one another with these words.

[Gosp. East. Eve. App. 48, 49, 50.]

℣. But Thou, &c. ℞. Thanks, &c. ℣. I heard a Voice from heaven saying unto me. · ℞. Blessed are the dead that die in the LORD. ℣. Glory, &c. ℞. As it was, &c. ℣. Whoso feareth the LORD, it shall go well with him at the last. ℞. And he shall find favour in the day of his death. ℣. The LORD, &c. ℞. And with, &c. ℣. Let us pray.

LORD, have mercy, &c.
Our FATHER, &c.

℣. Turn Thee, O LORD, and deliver *his* soul. ℞. O save *him*, for Thy mercy's sake. ℣. Enter not into judgment with Thy servant. ℞. For in Thy sight shall no man living be justified. ℣. Eternal rest grant unto *him*, O LORD. ℞. And Light perpetual shine upon *him*. ℣. From the gates of hell. ℞. Deliver *his* soul. ℣. LORD, hear, &c. ℞. And let, &c. ℣. Let us pray.

255. O LORD, the GOD of spirits and of all flesh, Who didst put death under Thy feet, didst destroy the power of the devil, and gavest Thy life for the world ; grant rest, O LORD, to the soul of Thy departed servant in the place of light and refreshment, whence pain and sorrow and sighing are done away ; and in Thy goodness and mercy pardon every sin committed by *him* in thought, word, and deed, Thou Who art the Resurrection and the Life, and Who livest.

When the death has been sudden.

256. Almighty GOD, the GOD of the spirits of all flesh, Who killest and makest alive, Who bringest down to the grave, and liftest up, have pity upon all those who are mourning for friends suddenly called away, and as Thy mercy rejoices over Thy justice, so do Thou pour into the hearts of the survivors the precious balm of Thy consolation, that they may abound in hope through the power of the HOLY GHOST. Through.

[Coll. East. Eve. **430—438.**]

Benediction. The LORD JESUS CHRIST cherish *him* in the pleasant land of Paradise, and strengthen you in holiness of life.

[*For the death of a child, see Office after a Miscarriage, p.* 66, *with* **432.**]

Appendix.

SCRIPTURE READINGS FOR THE SICK.

1. *In Sorrow or Trouble.*

Jer. xxxi., &c.

Therefore they shall come and sing in the height of Zion, and shall flow together to the goodness of the LORD, for wheat, and for wine, and for oil, and for the young of the flock and of the herd : and their soul shall be as a watered garden ; and they shall not sorrow any more at all. Then shall the virgin rejoice in the dance, both young men and old together ; for I will turn their mourning into joy, and will comfort them, and make them rejoice from their sorrow. And I will satiate the soul of the priests with fatness, and My people shall be satisfied with My goodness, saith the LORD. . . . Fear thou not ; for I am with thee : be not dismayed, for I am thy GOD : I will strengthen thee ; yea, I will uphold thee with the right hand of My righteousness. . . . When the poor and needy seek water, and there is none, and their tongue faileth for thirst, I the LORD will hear them, I the GOD of Israel will not forsake them. I will open rivers in high places, and fountains in the midst of the valleys : I will make the wilderness a pool of water, and the dry land springs of water.

2. *In Depression.*

2 Esd. vii.

I answered then, and said, I know, LORD, that the Most High is called merciful, in that He hath mercy upon them which are not yet come into the world, and upon those also that turn to His law ; and that He is patient, and long suffereth those that have sinned, as His creatures ; and that He is bountiful, for He is ready to give where it needeth ; and that He is of great mercy, for He multiplieth more and more mercies to them that are present, and that are past, and also to them which are to come. For if He shall not multiply His mercies, the world would not continue with them that inherit therein. And He pardoneth ; for if He did not so of His goodness, that they which have committed iniquities might be eased of them, the ten thousandth part of men should not remain living. And being Judge, if He should not forgive them that are cured with His word, and put out the multitude of contentions, there should be very few left peradventure in an innumerable multitude.

3. 2 Esd. xvi., &c.

Hear, O ye My beloved, saith the LORD : behold the days of trouble are at hand, but I will deliver you from the same. Be ye not afraid, neither doubt ; for GOD is your guide, and the guide of them who keep My commandments and precepts, saith the LORD GOD : let not your sins weigh you down, and let not your iniquities lift up themselves. . . . And therefore shake off thy great heaviness, and put away the multitude of sorrows, that the Mighty may be merciful unto thee again, and the Highest shall give thee rest and ease from thy labour.

4. *When recovery is delayed.*

Isaiah xxx.

Thus saith the LORD GOD, the Holy One of Israel ; In returning and rest shall ye be saved ; in quietness and confidence shall be your strength ; and ye would not. . . . And therefore will the LORD wait, that He may be gracious unto you, and therefore will He be exalted, that He may have mercy upon you : for the LORD is a GOD of judgment : blessed are all they that wait for Him. For the people shall dwell in Zion at Jerusalem : thou shalt weep no more : He will be very gracious unto thee at the voice of thy cry ; when He shall hear it, He will answer thee. And though the LORD give you the bread of adversity, and the water of affliction, yet shall not thy teachers be removed into a corner any more, but thine eyes shall see thy teachers : and thine ears shall hear a word behind thee, saying, This is the way, walk ye in it, when ye turn to the right hand, and when ye turn to the left.

5. *In long Sickness.*

Mal. iii., &c.

Then they that feared the LORD spake often one to another : and the LORD hearkened, and heard it, and a book of remembrance was written before Him for them that feared the LORD, and that thought upon His Name. And they shall be Mine, saith the LORD of hosts, in that day when I make up My jewels ; and I will spare them, as a man spareth his own son that serveth him. Then shall ye return, and discern between the righteous and the wicked, between him that serveth GOD and him that serveth Him not. . . . Because thou hast kept the word of My patience, I also will keep thee from the hour of temptation, which shall come upon all the world, to try them that dwell upon the earth. Behold, I come quickly : hold that fast which thou hast, that no man take thy crown. Him that overcometh will I make a pillar in the temple of My GOD, and he shall go no more out : and I will write upon him the Name of My GOD, and the name of the city of My

GOD, which is New Jerusalem, which cometh down out of heaven from My GOD : and I will write upon him My new Name.

6. *In long Suffering.*

2 Tim. ii.

Consider what I say ; and the LORD give thee understanding in all things. Remember that JESUS CHRIST of the seed of David was raised from the dead according to my Gospel. . . . It is a faithful saying : For if we be dead with Him, we shall also live with Him ; if we suffer, we shall also reign with Him ; if we deny Him, He also will deny us : if we believe not, yet He abideth faithful : He cannot deny Himself.

7. *For the Infirm or Blind.*

Isaiah xxxv.

Strengthen ye the weak hands, and confirm the feeble knees. Say to them that are of a fearful heart, Be strong, fear not : behold, your GOD will come with vengeance, even GOD with a recompense ; He will come and save you. Then the eyes of the blind shall be opened, and the ears of the deaf shall be unstopped. Then shall the lame man leap as an hart, and the tongue of the dumb sing : for in the wilderness shall waters break out, and streams in the desert. . . . And the ransomed of the LORD shall return, and come to Zion with songs and everlasting joy upon their heads : they shall obtain joy and gladness, and sorrow and sighing shall flee away.

8. *For the Aged.*

Wisd. v.

The hope of the ungodly is like dust that is blown away with the wind ; like a thin froth that is driven away with the storm ; like as the smoke which is dispersed here and there with a tempest, and passeth away as the remembrance of a guest that tarrieth but a day. But the righteous live for evermore ; their reward also is with the LORD, and the care of them is with the Most High. Therefore shall they receive a glorious kingdom, and a beautiful crown from the LORD's hand : for with His right hand shall He cover them, and with His arm shall He protect them.

9. Wisd. ix.

What man is he that can know the counsel of GOD? or who can think what the will of the LORD is ? For the thoughts of mortal men are miserable, and our devices are but uncertain. For the corruptible body presseth down the soul, and the earthly tabernacle weigheth down the mind that museth upon many things. And hardly do we guess aright at things that are upon earth, and with labour do we find the things that are before us : but the things that are in heaven, who hath searched out ? And Thy counsel who hath known, except Thou give wisdom, and send Thy HOLY SPIRIT from above ?

10. *For the Blind.*
Isaiah xlii.

I will bring the blind by a way that they knew not ; I will lead them in paths that they have not known : I will make darkness light before them, and crooked things straight. These things will I do unto them, and not forsake them.

11. *For a Sick Woman in Childbed.*
2 Esd. ii.

Mother, embrace thy children, and bring them up with gladness, make their feet as fast as a pillar ; for I have chosen thee, saith the LORD. And those that be dead will I raise up again from their places ; and bring them out of the graves ; for I have known My Name in Israel. Fear not, thou mother of the children : for I have chosen thee, saith the LORD.

12. *Before an Operation.*
Ecclus. xxxviii.

Honour a physician with the honour due unto him for the uses which ye may have of him ; for the LORD hath created him. For of the Most High cometh healing, and he shall receive honour of the king. The LORD hath created medicines out of the earth ; and he that is wise will not abhor them. Was not the water made sweet with wood, that the virtue thereof might be known ? And He hath given men skill, that He might be honoured in His marvellous works. With such doth He heal men, and taketh away their pains. My son, in thy sickness be not negligent : but pray unto the LORD, and He will make thee whole. Leave off from sin, and order thine hands aright, and cleanse thy heart from all wickedness. Give a sweet savour, and a memorial of fine flour ; and make a fat offering, as not being. Then give place to the physician, for the LORD hath created him : let him not go from thee, for thou hast need of him. There is a time when in their hands there is good success. For they shall also pray unto the LORD that He would prosper that, which they give for ease and remedy to prolong life.

13. *In Pain or Desolation.*
Isaiah lv., &c.

For a small moment have I forsaken thee ; but with great mercies will I gather thee. In a little wrath I hid My face from thee for a moment ; but with everlasting kindness will I have mercy on thee, saith the LORD thy Redeemer. . . . For I the LORD thy GOD will hold thy right hand, saying unto thee, Fear not ; I will help thee. . . And thou shalt rejoice in the LORD, and shalt glory in the Holy One of Israel. . . . And I will bring the third part through the fire, and will refine them as silver is refined, and will try them as gold is tried : they shall call on My Name, and I will hear them : I will say, It is My people : and they shall say, The LORD is my GOD.

14. S. James i., &c.

Blessed is the man that endureth temptation : for when he is tried, he shall receive the crown of life, which the LORD hath promised to them that love Him. . . . Be patient therefore, brethren, unto the coming of the LORD. Behold, the husbandman waiteth for the precious fruit of the earth, and hath long patience for it, until he receive the early and latter rain. Be ye also patient ; stablish your hearts : for the coming of the LORD draweth nigh. Grudge not one against another, brethren, lest ye be condemned ; behold, the Judge standeth before the door. Take, my brethren, the prophets, who have spoken in the Name of the LORD, for an example of suffering affliction, and of patience. Behold, we count them happy which endure. Ye have heard of the patience of Job, and have seen the end of the LORD : that the LORD is very pitiful, and of tender mercy.

15. Rev. vii.

And one of the elders answered, saying unto me, What are these which are arrayed in white robes ? and whence came they ? And I said unto him, Sir, thou knowest. And he said to me, These are they which came out of great tribulation, and have washed their robes and made them white in the Blood of the Lamb. Therefore are they before the throne of GOD, and serve Him day and night in His temple : and He that sitteth on the throne shall dwell among them. They shall hunger no more, neither thirst any more : neither shall the sun light on them, nor any heat. For the Lamb Which is in the midst of the throne shall feed them, and shall lead them unto living fountains of waters : and GOD shall wipe away all tears from their eyes.

16. *God's care for His people.*

S. Matt. vi. .

JESUS said, Take no thought for your life, what ye shall eat, or what ye shall drink ; nor yet for your body, what ye shall put on. Is not the life more than meat, and the body than raiment ? Behold the fowls of the air : for they sow not, neither do they reap, nor gather into barns ; yet your heavenly FATHER feedeth them. Are ye not much better than they ? Which of you by taking thought can add one cubit to his stature ? And why take ye thought for raiment ? Consider the lilies of the field, how they grow ; they toil not, neither do they spin : and yet I say unto you, That even Solomon in all his glory was not arrayed like one of these. Wherefore, if GOD so clothe the grass of the field, which to-day is, and to-morrow is cast into the oven, shall He not much more clothe you, O ye of little faith ? Therefore take no thought, saying, What shall we eat ? or, What shall we drink ? or, Wherewithal shall we be clothed ? (for after all these things do the Gentiles seek :) for your heavenly FATHER knoweth that ye have need of all these things. But seek ye first the kingdom of GOD, and His righteousness ; and all these things shall be added unto you. Take therefore no thought for the morrow : for the morrow shall take thought for the things of itself. Sufficient unto the day is the evil thereof.

17. *In Fever.*

Song of the Three Children, v. 26.

But the Angel of the LORD came down into the oven together with Azarias and his fellows, and smote the flame of the fire out of the oven ; and made the midst of the furnace as it had been a moist whistling wind, so that the fire touched them not at all, neither hurt nor troubled them. Then the three, as out of one mouth, praised, glorified, and blessed God in the furnace, saying, Blessed art Thou, O Lord God of our fathers : and to be praised and exalted above all for ever. And blessed is Thy glorious and holy Name : and to be praised and exalted above all for ever. Blessed art Thou in the temple of Thine holy glory : and to be praised and glorified above all for ever. Blessed art Thou that beholdest the depths, and sittest upon the cherubims : and to be praised and exalted above all for ever. Blessed art Thou on the glorious throne of Thy kingdom : and to be praised and glorified above all for ever. Blessed art Thou in the firmament of heaven : and above all to be praised and glorified for ever.

18. *After attempted Suicide.*

1 Sam. xii.

And Samuel said unto the people, Fear not : ye have done all this wickedness : yet turn not aside from following the Lord, but serve the Lord with all your heart : and turn ye not aside : for then should ye go after vain things, which cannot profit nor deliver ; for they are vain. For the Lord will not forsake His people for His great Name's sake : because it hath pleased the Lord to make you His people. Moreover as for me, God forbid that I should sin against the Lord in ceasing to pray for you : but I will teach you the good and the right way : only fear the Lord, and serve Him in truth with all your heart : for consider how great things He hath done for you. But if ye shall still do wickedly, ye shall be consumed, both ye and your king.

19. *For one who has sinned greatly.*

Deut. iv., &c.

If thou shalt seek the Lord thy God, thou shalt find Him, if thou seek Him with all thy heart and with all thy soul. When thou art in tribulation, and all these things are come upon thee, even in the latter days, if thou turn to the Lord thy God, and shalt be obedient unto His voice : (for the Lord thy God is a merciful God ;) He will not forsake thee, neither destroy thee, nor forget the covenant of thy fathers which He sware unto them. . . . O Israel, return unto the Lord thy God ; for thou hast fallen by thine iniquity. Take with you words, and turn to the Lord : say unto Him, Take away all iniquity, and receive us graciously ; so will we render the calves of our lips. . . . I will ransom them from the power of the grave : I will redeem them from death : O death, I will be thy plagues : O grave, I will be thy destruction : repentance shall be hid from Mine eyes . . . . I will heal their backsliding, I will love them freely : for Mine anger is turned away from him. . . . Who is wise, and he shall understand these things ? prudent, and he shall know them ; for the ways of the Lord are right, and the just shall walk in them : but the transgressors shall fall therein.

20. Isaiah lv., &c.

Seek ye the Lord while He may be found, call ye upon Him while He is near : let the wicked forsake his way, and the unrighteous man his thoughts : and let him return unto the Lord, and He will have mercy upon him, and to our God, for He will abundantly pardon . . . A new heart also will I give you, and a new spirit will I put within you : and I will take away the stony heart out of your flesh, and I will give you an heart of flesh. And I will put My Spirit within you, and cause you to walk in My statutes, and ye shall keep My judgments, and do them. . . . Then shall ye remember your own evil ways, and your doings that were not good, and shall loathe yourselves in your own sight for your iniquities and for your abominations. . . . What fruit had ye then in those things whereof ye are now ashamed? for the end of those things is death.

21. Ecclus. vi., &c.

Let thy mind be upon the ordinances of the LORD, and meditate continually in His commandments; He shall establish thine heart, and give thee wisdom at thine own desire. . . . . Say not, I have sinned, and what harm hath happened unto me? for the LORD is long-suffering, He will in no wise let thee go. Concerning propitiation, be not without fear to add sin unto sin: and say not, His mercy is great; He will be pacified for the multitude of my sins: for mercy and wrath come from Him, and His indignation resteth upon sinners. Make no tarrying to turn to the LORD, and put not off from day to day: for suddenly shall the wrath of the LORD come forth, and in thy security thou shalt be destroyed, and perish in the day of vengeance.

22. *When he excuses his sin.*

Ecclus. xv.

Say not thou, It is through the LORD that I fell away: for thou oughtest not to do the things that He hateth. Say not thou, He hath caused me to err: for He hath no need of the sinful man. The LORD hateth all abomination; and they that fear GOD love it not. He Himself made man from the beginning, and left him in the hand of his counsel; if thou wilt, to keep the commandments, and to perform acceptable faithfulness. He hath set fire and water before thee: stretch forth thy hand unto whether thou

wilt. Before man is life and death; and whether him liketh shall be given him. For the wisdom of the LORD is great, and He is mighty in power, and beholdeth all things; and His eyes are upon them that fear Him, and He knoweth every work of man. He hath commanded no man to do wickedly, neither hath He given any man licence to sin.

23. Ecclus. xvii., &c.

Return unto the LORD, and forsake thy sins, make thy prayer before His face, and offend less. Turn again to the Most High, and turn away from iniquity; for He will lead thee out of darkness into the light of health, and hate thou abomination vehemently. . . . . . The mercy of man is toward his neighbour; but the mercy of the LORD is upon all flesh: He reproveth, and nurtureth, and teacheth, and bringeth again, as a shepherd his flock. He hath mercy on them that receive discipline, and that diligently seek after His judgments. Be of good comfort, O my children, and cry unto GOD: for ye shall be remembered of Him that brought these things upon you. For as it was your mind to go astray from GOD: so, being returned, seek Him ten times more. For He that hath brought these plagues upon you shall bring you everlasting joy again with your salvation.

24. Ecclus. xxi., &c.

My son, hast thou sinned? do so no more, but ask pardon for thy former sins. Flee from sin as from the face of a serpent: for if thou comest too near it, it will bite thee: the teeth thereof are as the teeth of a lion, slaying the souls of men . . . . A prayer out of a poor man's mouth reacheth to the ears of GOD, and His judgment cometh speedily. He that hateth to be reproved is in the way of sinners: but he that feareth the LORD will repent from his heart. . . . . Know therefore this day, and consider it in thine heart, that the LORD He is GOD in heaven above, and upon the earth beneath ; there is none else. Thou shalt keep therefore His statutes, and His commandments, which I command thee this day, that it may go well with thee, and with thy children after thee, and that thou mayest prolong thy days upon the earth, which the LORD thy GOD giveth thee, for ever.

25. *For the Careless.*

Rev. iii.

He that hath an ear, let him hear what the Spirit saith unto the churches. . . . . These things saith the Amen, the faithful and true witness, the beginning of the creation of GOD ; I know thy works, that thou art neither cold nor hot, I would thou wert cold or hot. So then because thou art lukewarm, and neither cold nor hot, I will spue thee out of My mouth. Because thou sayest, I am rich, and increased with goods, and have need of nothing ; and knowest not that thou art wretched, and miserable, and poor, and blind, and naked : I counsel thee to buy of Me gold tried in the fire, that thou mayest be rich ; and white raiment, that thou mayest be clothed, and that the shame of thy nakedness do not appear ; and anoint thine eyes with eyesalve, that thou mayest see. As many as I love, I rebuke and chasten : be zealous therefore, and repent. Behold, I stand at the door, and knock ; if any man hear My voice, and open the door, I will come in to him, and will sup with him, and he with Me. To him that overcometh will I grant to sit with Me in My throne, even as I also overcame, and am set down with My FATHER in His throne.

26. *For arousing the Careless.*

Lev. xxvi., &c.

If ye shall despise My statutes, or if your soul abhor My judgments, so that ye will not do all My command-

ments, but that ye break My covenant : I will also do this unto you ; I will even appoint over you terror, consumption, and the burning ague, that shall consume the eyes, and cause sorrow of heart : . . . And ye shall sow your seed in vain, for your enemies shall eat it. And I will set My face against you, and ye shall be slain before your enemies : they that hate you shall reign over you ; and ye shall flee when none pursueth you. And if ye will not yet for all this hearken unto Me, then I will punish you seven times more for your sins. . . . . . The LORD searcheth all hearts, and understandeth all the imaginations of the thoughts : if thou seek Him, He will be found of thee ; but if thou forsake Him, He will cast thee off for ever.

27. Prov. i.

Because I have called, and ye refused ; I have stretched out My hand, and no man regarded ; but ye have set at nought all My counsel, and would none of My reproof : I also will laugh at your calamity ; I will mock when your fear cometh ; when your fear cometh as desolation, and your destruction cometh as a whirlwind ; when distress and anguish cometh upon you. Then shall they call upon Me, but I will not answer ; they shall seek Me early, but they shall not find Me : for that they hated knowledge, and did not choose the fear of the LORD : they would none of My counsel : they despised all My reproof. Therefore shall they eat of the fruit of their own way, and be filled with their own devices. For the turning away of the simple shall slay them, and the prosperity of fools shall destroy them. But whoso hearkeneth unto Me shall dwell safely, and shall be quiet from fear of evil.

28. *For a Penitent.*

Isa. i., &c.

Come now, and let us reason together, saith the LORD : though your sins be as scarlet, they shall be as white as snow ; though they be red like crimson, they shall be as wool. . . . For the mountains shall depart, and the hills be removed; but My kindness shall not depart from thee, neither shall the covenant of My peace be removed, saith the LORD that hath mercy on thee. . . . In righteousness shalt thou be established : thou shalt be far from oppression; for thou shalt not fear: and from terror; for it shall not come near thee. . . . . For I know the thoughts that I think toward you, saith the LORD, thoughts of peace, and not of evil, to give you an expected end. Then shall ye call upon Me, and ye shall go and pray unto Me, and I will hearken unto you. And ye shall seek Me, and find Me, when ye shall search for Me with all your heart.

29. Isa. xii.

In that day thou shalt say, O LORD, I will praise Thee : though Thou wast angry with me, Thine anger is turned away, and Thou comfortedst me. Behold, GOD is my salvation; I will trust and not be afraid : for the LORD JEHOVAH is my strength and my song; He also is become my salvation. Therefore with joy shall ye draw water out of the wells of salvation. And in that day shall ye say, Praise the LORD, call upon His Name, declare His doings among the people, make mention that His Name is exalted. Sing unto the LORD; for He hath done excellent things : this is known in all the earth. Cry out and shout, thou inhabitant of Zion : for great is the Holy One of Israel in the midst of thee.

30. Isa. xliii., &c.

But now thus saith the LORD that created thee, O Jacob, and He that formed thee, O Israel, Fear not : for I have redeemed thee, I have called thee by thy name ; thou art Mine. When thou passest through the waters, I will be with thee ; and through the rivers, they shall not overflow thee : when thou walkest through the fire, thou shalt not be burned ; neither shall the flame kindle upon thee . . . I, even I, am the LORD ; and beside Me there is no Saviour. . . . I, even I, am He that blotteth out thy transgressions for Mine own sake, and will not remember thy sins. . . . . For thus saith the high and lofty One that inhabiteth eternity, Whose Name is Holy ; I dwell in the high and holy place, with him also that is of a contrite and humble spirit, to revive the spirit of the humble, and to revive the heart of the contrite ones. For I will not contend for ever, neither will I be always wroth : for the spirit should fail before Me, and the souls which I have made.

31. Isa. lxi.

The Spirit of the LORD GOD is upon me ; because the LORD hath anointed me to preach good tidings unto the meek ; He hath sent me to bind up the brokenhearted, to proclaim liberty to the captives, and the opening of the prison to them that are bound; to proclaim the acceptable year of the LORD, and the day of vengeance of our GOD ; to comfort all that mourn ; to appoint unto them that mourn in Zion, to give unto them beauty for ashes, the oil of joy for mourning, the garment of praise for the spirit of heaviness; that they might be called trees of righteousness, the planting of the LORD, that He might be glorified. . . . For your shame ye shall have double; and for confusion they shall rejoice in their portion : therefore in their land they shall possess the double : everlasting joy shall be unto them.

32. Zeph. iii., &c.

In that day shalt thou not be ashamed for all thy doings wherein thou hast transgressed against Me : for then I will take away out of the midst of thee them that rejoice in thy pride, and they shall no more be haughty because of My holy mountain. I will also leave in the midst of thee an afflicted and poor people, and they shall trust in the Name of the LORD. The remnant of Israel shall not do iniquity, nor speak lies ; neither shall a deceitful tongue be found in their mouth : for they shall feed and lie down, and none shall make them afraid . . . . O LORD, the Hope of Israel, all that forsake Thee shall be ashamed, and they that depart from me shall be written in the earth, because they have forsaken the LORD, the fountain of living waters. Heal me, O LORD, and I shall be healed ; save me, and I shall be saved : for Thou art my praise. . . . Be not a terror unto me : Thou art my hope in the day of evil.

33. *Confession of Sin.*

2 Sam. xii.

The LORD sent Nathan unto David. And he came unto him, and said unto him, There were two men in one city; the one rich, and the other poor. The rich man had exceeding many flocks and herds : but the poor man had nothing, save one little ewe lamb, which he had bought and nourished up : and it grew up together with him, and with his children ; it did eat of his own meat, and drank of his own cup, and lay in his bosom, and was unto him as a daughter. And there came a traveller unto the rich man, and he spared to take of his own flock and of his own herd, to dress for the wayfaring man that was come unto him ; but took the poor man's lamb, and dressed it for the man that was come to him. And David's anger was greatly kindled against the man ; and he said to Nathan, As the LORD liveth, the man that hath done this thing shall surely die : and he shall restore the lamb fourfold, because he did this thing, and because he had no pity. And Nathan said to David, Thou art the man. Thus saith the LORD GOD of Israel, I anointed thee king over Israel, and I delivered thee out of the hand of Saul ; and I gave thee thy master's house, and thy master's wives into thy bosom, and gave thee the house of Israel and of Judah ; and if that had been too little, I would moreover have given unto thee such and such things. Wherefore hast thou despised the commandment of the LORD, to do evil in His sight ? thou hast killed Uriah the Hittite with the sword, and hast taken his wife to be thy wife, and hast slain him with the sword of the children of Ammon. Now therefore the sword shall never depart from thine house ; because thou hast despised Me, and hast taken the wife of Uriah the Hittite to be thy wife. Thus saith the LORD, Behold, I will raise up evil against thee out of thine own house, and I will take thy wives before thine eyes, and give them unto thy neighbour, and he shall lie with thy wives in the sight of this sun. For thou didst it secretly : but I will do this thing before all Israel, and before the sun. And David said unto Nathan, I have sinned against the LORD. And Nathan said unto David, The LORD also hath put away thy sin ; thou shalt not die. Howbeit, because by this deed thou hast given great occasion to the enemies of the LORD to blaspheme, the child also that is born unto thee shall surely die.

34. *The Prayer of Manasses.*

Thou, O LORD, according to Thy great goodness, hast promised repentance and forgiveness to them that have sinned against Thee ; and of Thine infinite mercies hast appointed repentance unto sinners, that they may be saved. . . . . My transgressions, O LORD, are multiplied : my transgressions are multiplied, and I am not worthy to behold and see the height of heaven for the multitude of mine iniquities. I am bowed down with many iron bands, that I cannot lift up mine head, neither have any release: for I have provoked Thy wrath, and done evil before Thee: I did not Thy will, neither kept I Thy commandments: I have set up abominations, and have multiplied offences. Now therefore I bow the knee of mine heart, beseeching Thee of grace. I have sinned, O LORD, I have sinned, and I acknowledge mine iniquities; wherefore I humbly beseech Thee, forgive me, O LORD, forgive me, and destroy me not with mine iniquities. Be not angry with me for ever, by reserving evil for me; neither condemn me into the lower parts of the earth. For Thou art the GOD, even the GOD of them that repent; and in me Thou wilt show all Thy goodness: for Thou wilt save me that am unworthy, according to Thy great mercy. Therefore I will praise Thee for ever all the days of my life: for all the powers of the heavens do praise Thee, and Thine is the glory for ever and ever. Amen.

35. *The Forgiveness of Sins.*

S. Luke v.

Behold, men brought in a bed a man which was taken with a palsy: and they sought means to bring him in, and to lay him before Him. And when they could not find by what way they might bring him in because of the multitude, they went upon the housetop, and let him down through the tiling with his couch into the midst before JESUS. And when He saw their faith, He said unto him, Man, thy sins are forgiven thee. And the scribes and the Pharisees began to reason, saying, Who is this which speaketh blasphemies? Who can forgive sins, but GOD alone? But when JESUS perceived their thoughts, He answering said unto them, What reason ye in your hearts? Whether

is easier, to say, Thy sins be forgiven thee; or to say, Rise up and walk? but that ye may know that the Son of Man hath power upon earth to forgive sins (He said unto the sick of the palsy), I say unto thee, Arise, and take up thy couch, and go into thine house. And immediately he rose up before them, and took up that whereon he lay, and departed to his own house, glorifying GOD. And they were all amazed, and they glorified GOD, and were filled with fear, saying, We have seen strange things to-day.

36. *The Prodigal pardoned.*

S. Luke xv.

JESUS said, A certain man had two sons: and the younger of them said to his father, Father, give me the portion of goods that falleth to me. And he divided unto them his living. And not many days after the younger son gathered all together, and took his journey into a far country, and there wasted his substance with riotous living. And when he had spent all, there arose a mighty famine in that land; and he began to be in want. And he went and joined himself to a citizen of that country; and he sent him into his fields to feed swine. And he would fain have filled his belly with the husks that the swine did eat: and no man gave unto him. And when he came to himself, he said, How many hired servants of my father's have bread enough and to spare, and I perish with hunger! I will arise and go to my father, and will say unto him, Father, I have sinned against heaven and before thee, and am no more worthy to be called thy son: make me as one of thy hired servants. And he arose and came to his father. But when he was yet a great way off, his father saw him, and had compassion, and ran, and fell on his neck, and kissed him. And the son said unto him, Father,

I have sinned against heaven, and in thy sight, and am no more worthy to be called thy son. But the father said to his servants, Bring forth the best robe, and put it on him; and put a ring on his hand, and shoes on his feet: and bring hither the fatted calf, and kill it; and let us eat, and be merry: for this my son was dead, and is alive again: he was lost, and is found. And they began to be merry.

37. *Delaying Repentance.*

S. Matt. xxv.

JESUS said, The kingdom of heaven is likened unto ten virgins, which took their lamps, and went forth to meet the bridegroom. And five of them were wise, and five were foolish. They that were foolish took their lamps, and took no oil with them: but the wise took oil in their vessels with their lamps. While the bridegroom tarried, they all slumbered and slept. And at midnight there was a cry made, Behold, the bridegroom cometh; go ye out to meet him. Then all those virgins arose, and trimmed their lamps. And the foolish said unto the wise, Give us of your oil; for our lamps are gone out. But the wise answered, saying, Not so; lest there be not enough for us and you: but go ye rather to them that sell, and buy for yourselves. And while they went to buy, the bridegroom came; and they that were ready went in with him to the marriage: and the door was shut. Afterward came also the other virgins, saying, Lord, Lord, open to us. But he answered and said, Verily I say unto you, I know you not. Watch therefore, for ye know neither the day nor the hour wherein the Son of Man cometh.

38. *The Last Judgment.*

S. Matt. xxv.

When the Son of Man shall come in His glory, and
with Him, then
the throne of Hi
Him shall be ga
and He shall s
from another, as
eth his sheep fr
He shall set the
hand, but the
Then shall the K
on His right han
of My FATHER, i
prepared for yo
tion of the world
gered, and ye ga
thirsty, and ye
was a stranger, a
naked, and ye c
sick, and ye visi
prison, and ye
Then shall the
Him, saying, L
Thee an hunger
or thirsty, and
When saw we T
took Thee in? or
Thee? Or wher
or in prison, and
And the King sl
unto them, Veri
Inasmuch as ye
one of the least
ren, ye have d
Then shall He
on the left hand
ye cursed, into e
pared for the de
for I was an hui
Me no meat: I
gave Me no drin
and ye took Me
ye clothed Me
prison, and ye
Then shall they
saying, LORD,
an hungered,
stranger, or na
prison, and did
Thee? Then she
saying, Verily I
asmuch as ye d
the least of the
Me. And these
everlasting pun
righteous into li

39. S. Luke xii.

JESUS said, Let your loins be girded about, and your lights burning; and ye yourselves like unto men that wait for their lord, when he shall return from the wedding; that when he cometh and knocketh, they may open unto him immediately. Blessed are those servants, whom the lord when he cometh shall find watching : verily I say unto you, that he shall gird himself, and make them sit down to meat, and will come forth and serve them. And if he shall come in the second watch, or come in the third watch, and find them so, blessed are those servants. And this know, that if the goodman of the house had known what hour the thief would come, he would have watched, and not have suffered his house to be broken through. Be ye therefore ready also : for the Son of Man cometh at an hour when ye think not.

40. *Sacramental Power.*

2 Kings v.

Naaman, captain of the host of the King of Syria, was a great man with his master, and honourable, because by him the LORD had given deliverance unto Syria : he was also a mighty man in valour, but he was a leper. And the Syrians had gone out by companies, and had brought away captive out of the land of Israel a little maid ; and she waited on Naaman's wife. And she said unto her mistress, Would GOD my lord were with the prophet that is in Samaria ! for he would recover him of his leprosy. . . . . So Naaman came with his horses and his chariot, and stood at the door of the house of Elisha. And Elisha sent a messenger unto him, saying, Go and wash in Jordan seven times, and thy flesh shall come again to thee, and thou shalt be clean. But Naaman was wroth, and went away, and said, Behold,

I thought, He will surely come out to me, and stand, and call on the Name of the LORD his GOD, and strike his hand over the place, and recover the leper. Are not Abana and Pharpar, rivers of Damascus, better than all the waters of Israel? may I not wash in them, and be clean ? So he turned and went away in a rage. And his servants came near, and spake unto him, and said, My father, if the prophet had bid thee do some great thing, wouldest thou not have done it? how much rather then, when he saith to thee, Wash, and be clean ? Then went he down, and dipped himself seven times in Jordan, according to the saying of the man of GOD : and his flesh came again like unto the flesh of a little child, and he was clean. And he returned to the man of GOD, he and all his company, and came, and stood before him : and he said, Behold, now I know that there is no GOD in all the earth, but in Israel.

41. *The Blessings of Holy Communion.*

S. John vi.

JESUS said, Verily, verily, I say unto you, He that believeth on Me hath everlasting life. I am that bread of life. Your fathers did eat manna in the wilderness, and are dead. This is the bread which cometh down from heaven, that a man may eat thereof, and not die. I am the living bread which came down from heaven : if any man eat of this bread, he shall live for ever : and the bread that I will give is My Flesh, which I will give for the life of the world. The Jews therefore strove among themselves, saying, How can this man give us His flesh to eat? Then JESUS saith unto them, Verily, verily I say unto you, Except ye eat the Flesh of the Son of Man, and drink His Blood, ye have no life in you. Whoso eateth My Flesh, and drinketh My Blood, hath eternal life;

and I will raise him up at the last day. For My Flesh is meat indeed, and My Blood is drink indeed. He that eateth My Flesh and drinketh My Blood, dwelleth in Me, and I in him. As the Living FATHER hath sent Me, and I live by the FATHER: so he that eateth Me, even he shall live by Me.

42. *For one recovering.*

Ecclus. li.

They compassed me on every side, and there was no man to help me: I looked for the succour of men, but there was none. Then thought I upon Thy mercy, O LORD, and upon Thy acts of old, how Thou deliveredst such as wait for Thee, and savest them out of the hands of the enemies. Then lifted I up my supplication from the earth, and prayed for deliverance from death. I called upon the LORD, the FATHER of my LORD, that He would not leave me in the days of my trouble, and in the time of the proud, when there was no help. I will praise Thy Name continually, and will sing praise with thanksgiving; and so my prayer was heard: for Thou savedst me from destruction, and deliveredst me from the evil time: therefore will I give thanks and praise Thee, and bless Thy Name, O LORD.

43. *From dangerous sickness.*

2 Cor. i.

Blessed be GOD, even the FATHER of our LORD JESUS CHRIST, the FATHER of mercies, and the GOD of all comfort; Who comforteth us in all our tribulation, that we may be able to comfort them which are in any trouble, by the comfort wherewith we ourselves are comforted of GOD. For as the sufferings of CHRIST abound in us, so our consolation also aboundeth by CHRIST. . . . We were pressed out of measure, above strength, insomuch that we despaired even of life: but we had the sentence of death in ourselves, that we should not trust in ourselves, but in GOD Which raiseth the dead: Who delivered us from so great a death, and doth deliver: in Whom we trust that He will yet deliver us.

44. *Thanksgiving.*

1 Sam. ii.

Hannah prayed, and said, My heart rejoiceth in the LORD, mine horn is exalted in the LORD: my mouth is enlarged over mine enemies; because I rejoice in Thy salvation. There is none holy as the LORD: for there is none beside Thee: neither is there any rock like our GOD. Talk no more so exceeding proudly; let not arrogancy come out of your mouth; for the LORD is a GOD of knowledge, and by Him actions are weighed. The bows of the mighty men are broken, and they that stumbled are girded with strength. They that were full have hired out themselves for bread; and they that were hungry ceased; so that the barren hath born seven; and she that hath many children is waxed feeble. The LORD killeth and maketh alive: He bringeth down to the grave, and bringeth up. The LORD maketh poor, and maketh rich: He bringeth low, and lifteth up. He raiseth up the poor out of the dust, and lifteth up the beggar from the dunghill, to set them among princes, and to make them inherit the throne of glory: for the pillars of the earth are the LORD's, and He hath set the world upon them. He will keep the feet of His saints, and the wicked shall be silent in darkness; for by strength shall no man prevail. The adversaries of the LORD shall be broken to pieces; out of heaven shall He thunder upon them: the LORD shall judge the ends of the earth; and He shall give strength unto His king, and exalt the horn of His anointed.

45. Isaiah xxxviii.

I said in the cutting off of my days, I shall go to the gates of the grave: I am deprived of the residue of my years. I said, I shall not see the LORD, even the LORD, in the land of the living: I shall behold man no more with the inhabitants of the world. Mine age is departed, and is removed from me as a shepherd's tent: I have cut off like a weaver my life: He will cut me off with pining sickness: from day even to night wilt Thou make an end of me. I reckoned till morning, that, as a lion, so will He break all my bones: from day even to night wilt Thou make an end of me. Like a crane or a swallow, so did I chatter: I did mourn as a dove: mine eyes fail with looking upward: O LORD, I am oppressed; undertake for me. What shall I say? He hath both spoken unto me, and Himself hath done it: I shall go softly all my years in the bitterness of my soul. O LORD, by these things men live, and in all these things is the life of my spirit; so wilt Thou recover me, and make me to live. Behold, for peace I had great bitterness: but Thou hast in love to my soul delivered it from the pit of corruption: for Thou hast cast all my sins behind Thy back. For the grave cannot praise Thee, death cannot celebrate Thee: they that go down into the pit cannot hope for Thy truth. The living, the living, he shall praise Thee, as I do this day: the father to the children shall make known Thy truth. The LORD was ready to save me: therefore we will sing my songs to the stringed instruments all the days of our life in the house of the LORD.

46. *For one unlikely to recover.*

2 Esd. iv.

We pass away out of the world as grasshoppers, and our life is astonishment and fear, and we are not worthy to obtain mercy. What will He then do unto His Name whereby we are called? of these things have I asked. Then answered he me and said, The more thou searchest, the more thou shalt marvel; for the world hasteth fast to pass away, and cannot comprehend the things that are promised to the righteous in time to come; for this world is full of unrighteousness and infirmities. . . . . As for the tokens whereof thou askest me, I may tell thee of them in part: but as touching thy life, I am not sent to show it thee; for I do not know it.

47. *For a Dying Communicant.*

Rev. xix.

I heard a great voice of much people in heaven, saying, Alleluia; Salvation, and glory, and honour, and power, unto the LORD our GOD. . . . . And the four and twenty elders and the four beasts fell down and worshipped GOD that sat on the throne, saying, Amen; Alleluia. And a voice came out of the throne, saying, Praise our GOD, all ye His servants, and ye that fear Him, both small and great. And I heard as it were the voice of a great multitude, and as the voice of many waters, and as the voice of mighty thunderings, saying, Alleluia: for the LORD GOD omnipotent reigneth. Let us be glad and rejoice, and give honour to Him: for the marriage of the Lamb is come, and His wife hath made herself ready. And to her was granted that she should be arrayed in fine linen, clean and white: for the fine linen is the righteousness of saints. And he saith unto me, Write, Blessed are they which are called unto the marriage supper of the Lamb. And he saith unto me, These are the true sayings of GOD.

48. *With the Friends of one departed.*

Wisd. iii.

The souls of the righteous are in

the hands of GOD, and there shall no torment touch them. In the sight of the unwise they seemed to die: and their departure is taken for misery, and their going from us to be utter destruction: but they are in peace. For though they be punished in the sight of men, yet is their hope full of immortality. And having been a little chastised, they shall be greatly rewarded: for GOD proved them, and found them worthy for Himself. As gold in the furnace hath He tried them, and received them as a burnt-offering. . . . They shall judge the nations, and have dominion over the people, and their LORD shall reign for ever.

49. *With Mourners.*

S. John xi.

Martha said unto JESUS, LORD, if Thou hadst been here, my brother had not died. But I know, that even now, whatsoever Thou wilt ask of GOD, GOD will give it Thee. JESUS saith unto her, Thy brother shall rise again. Martha saith unto Him, I know that he shall rise again in the resurrection at the last day. JESUS said unto her, I am the resurrection and the life: he that believeth in Me though he were dead, yet shall he live: and whosoever liveth and believeth in Me shall never die. Believest thou this? She saith unto Him, Yea, LORD: I believe that Thou art the CHRIST, the SON of GOD, which should come into the world.

50. *For Patience.*

Lam. iii.

It is of the LORD'S mercies that we are not consumed, because His compassions fail not. They are new every morning: great is Thy faithfulness. The LORD is my portion, saith my soul; therefore will I hope in Him. The LORD is good unto them that wait for Him, to the soul that seeketh Him. It is good that a man should both hope and quietly wait for the salvation of the LORD. It is good for a man that he bear the yoke in his youth. He sitteth alone and keepeth silence, because he hath borne it upon him. He putteth his mouth in the dust; if so be there may be hope. He giveth his cheek to him that smiteth him; he is filled full with reproach. For the LORD will not cast off for ever. But though He cause grief, yet will He have compassion according to the multitude of His mercies; for He doth not afflict willingly, nor grieve the children of men.

51. *When the Patient trusts over-much to Medical skill.*

2 Chron. xvi., &c.

And Asa in the thirty and ninth year of his reign was diseased in his feet, until his disease was exceeding great: yet in his disease he sought not to the LORD, but to the physicians. And Asa slept with his fathers, and died in the one and fortieth year of his reign. . . . . Thus saith the LORD; Cursed be the man that trusteth in man, and maketh flesh his arm, and whose heart departeth from the LORD.

52. *For Trust.*

Job v.

Although affliction cometh not forth of the dust, neither doth trouble spring out of the ground; yet man is born unto trouble, as the sparks fly upward. I would seek unto GOD, and unto GOD would I commit my cause: Which doeth great things and unsearchable: marvellous things without number: Who giveth rain upon the earth, and sendeth waters upon the fields: to set up on high those that be low; that those which mourn may be exalted to safety. . . . So the poor hath hope, and iniquity stoppeth her mouth. Behold, happy is the man whom GOD correcteth: therefore despise not thou the chastening of the Almighty: for He maketh sore, and bindeth up: He woundeth, and His hands make whole; He shall deliver thee in six troubles: yea in seven there shall no evil touch thee. . . . Thou shalt come to thy grave in a full age, like as a shock of corn cometh in in his season. Lo this, we have searched it, so it is, hear it, and know thou it for thy good.

53. Isa. xxvi., &c.

Thou wilt keep him in perfect peace whose mind is stayed on Thee: because he trusteth in Thee. Trust ye in the LORD for ever: for in the LORD JEHOVAH is everlasting strength. . . . Blessed is the man that trusteth in the LORD, and whose hope the LORD is. For he shall be as a tree planted by the waters, and that spreadeth out her roots by the river, and shall not see when heat cometh, but her leaf shall be green; and shall not be careful in the year of drought, neither shall cease from yielding fruit.

54. Ecclus. xxxiv.

The spirit of those that fear the LORD shall live; for their hope is in Him that saveth them. Whoso feareth the LORD shall not fear nor be afraid: for He is his hope. Blessed is the soul of him that feareth the LORD: to whom doth he look? and who is his strength? For the eyes of the LORD are upon them that love Him, He is their mighty protection and strong stay, a defence from heat, and a cover from the sun at noon, a preservation from stumbling, and an help from falling. He raiseth up the soul, and lighteneth the eyes: He giveth health, life, and blessing.

55. *Confidence in God.*

S. Matt. x.

JESUS said, Fear not them which kill the body, but are not able to kill the soul: but rather fear Him which is able to destroy both soul and body in hell. Are not two sparrows sold for a farthing? and one of them shall not fall on the ground without your FATHER. But the very hairs of your head are all numbered. Fear ye not therefore, ye are of more value than many sparrows. Whosoever therefore shall confess Me before men, him will I confess also before My FATHER which is in heaven. But whosoever shall deny Me before men, him will I also deny before My FATHER which is in heaven.

56. *For one in Poverty.*

Hab. iii., &c.

Although the fig tree shall not blossom, neither shall fruit be in the vines; the labour of the olive shall fail, and the fields shall yield no meat; the flock shall be cut off from the fold, and there shall be no herd in the stalls: yet I will rejoice in the LORD, I will joy in the GOD of my salvation. The LORD GOD is my strength, and He will make my feet like hinds' feet, and He will make me to walk upon mine high places. . . . . Marvel not at the works of sinners; but trust in the LORD, and abide in thy labour: for it is an easy thing in the sight of the LORD on the sudden' to make a poor man rich. The blessing of the LORD is in the reward of the godly, and suddenly He maketh His blessing to flourish. Say not, What profit is there of my service? and what good things shall I have hereafter? . . . . For it is an easy thing unto the LORD in the day of death to reward a man according to his ways.

57. S. John vi.

JESUS said, Labour not for the meat which perisheth, but for that meat which endureth unto everlasting life, which the Son of Man shall give unto you: for Him hath GOD the FATHER sealed. Then said they unto Him, What shall we do, that we might work the works of God? Jesus answered and said unto them, This is the work of God, that ye believe on Him whom He hath sent. They said therefore unto Him, What sign showest Thou then, that we may see, and believe Thee? what dost Thou work? Our fathers did eat manna in the desert; as it is written, He gave them bread from heaven to eat. Then Jesus said unto them, Verily, verily, I say unto you, Moses gave you not that bread from heaven; but My Father giveth you the true bread from heaven. For the Bread of God is He which cometh down from heaven and giveth life unto the world. Then said they unto Him, Lord, evermore give us this bread. And Jesus said unto them, I am the Bread of Life: he that cometh to Me shall never hunger; and he that believeth on Me shall never thirst.

58. *For one in Hatred.*

Ecclus. xxviii., &c.

He that revengeth shall find vengeance from the Lord, and He will surely keep his sins in remembrance. Forgive thy neighbour the hurt that he hath done unto thee, so shall thy sins also be forgiven when thou prayest. One man beareth hatred against another, and doth he seek pardon from the Lord? He showeth no mercy to a man, which is like himself: and doth he ask forgiveness of his own sins? If he that is but flesh nourish hatred, who will entreat for pardon of his sins? Remember thy end, and let enmity cease; remember corruption and death, and abide in the commandments. .... Put on therefore, as the elect of God, holy and beloved, bowels of mercies, kindness, humbleness of mind, meekness, longsuffering; forbearing one another, and forgiving one another, if any man have a quarrel against any: even as Christ forgave you, so also do ye.

And above all these things put on charity, which is the bond of perfectness.

59. *Brotherly Forgiveness.*

S. Matt. xviii.

Jesus said, If thy brother shall trespass against thee, go and tell him his fault between thee and him alone: if he shall hear thee, thou hast gained thy brother. But if he will not hear thee, then take with thee one or two more, that in the mouth of two or three witnesses every word may be established. And if he shall neglect to hear them, tell it unto the church: but if he neglect to hear the church, let him be unto thee as an heathen man and a publican. Verily I say unto you, Whatsoever ye shall bind on earth shall be bound in heaven: and whatsoever ye shall loose on earth shall be loosed in heaven. Again I say unto you, that if two of you shall agree on earth as touching any thing that they shall ask, it shall be done for them of My Father which is in heaven. For where two or three are gathered together in My name, there am I in the midst of them. Then came Peter to Him, and said, Lord, how oft shall my brother sin against me, and I forgive him? till seven times? Jesus saith unto him, I say not unto thee, Until seven times; but, Until seventy times seven.

General Readings.

60. 1 Sam. ii.

There is none holy as the Lord: for there is none beside Thee: neither is there any rock like our God. .... The Lord killeth and maketh alive: He bringeth down to the grave, and bringeth up. The Lord maketh poor, and maketh rich: He bringeth low, and lifteth up. He raiseth up the poor out of the dust, and lifteth up the beggar from the dunghill, to set them among princes, and to make them inherit the throne of glory : for the pillars of the earth are the LORD's, and He hath set the world upon them. He will keep the feet of His saints, and the wicked shall be silent in darkness : for by strength shall no man prevail.

61. Job xxxiii.

GOD speaketh once, yea twice, yet man perceiveth it not. In a dream, in a vision of the night, when deep sleep falleth upon men, in slumberings upon the bed ; then He openeth the ears of men, and sealeth their instruction. . . . He looketh upon men, and if any say, I have sinned, and perverted that which was right, and it profited me not ; He will deliver his soul from going into the pit, and his life shall see the light. Lo, all these things worketh GOD oftentimes with man, to bring back his soul from the pit, to be enlightened with the light of the living.

62. Isa. liii.

Who hath believed our report ? and to whom is the arm of the LORD revealed ? For He shall grow up before Him as a tender plant, and as a root out of a dry ground : He hath no form nor comeliness ; and when we shall see Him, there is no beauty that we should desire Him. He is despised and rejected of men ; a Man of Sorrows and acquainted with grief : and we hid as it were our faces from Him ; He was despised, and we esteemed Him not. Surely He hath borne our griefs, and carried our sorrows : yet we did esteem Him stricken, smitten of GOD, and afflicted. But He was wounded for our transgressions, He was bruised for our iniquities : the chastisement of our peace was upon Him ; and with His stripes we are healed. All we like sheep have gone astray ; we have turned every one to his own way ; and the LORD hath laid on Him the iniquity of us all. He was oppressed, and He was afflicted, yet He opened not His mouth : He is brought as a lamb to the slaughter, and as a sheep before her shearers is dumb, so He openeth not His mouth. He was taken from prison and from judgment : and who shall declare His generation ? for He was cut off out of the land of the living : for the transgression of My people was He stricken. And He made His grave with the wicked, and with the rich in His death ; because He had done no violence, neither was any deceit in His mouth. Yet it pleased the LORD to bruise Him ; He hath put Him to grief : when Thou shalt make His soul an offering for sin, He shall see His seed, He shall prolong His days, and the pleasure of the LORD shall prosper in His hand. He shall see of the travail of His soul, and shall be satisfied : by His knowledge shall My righteous servant justify many ; for He shall bear their iniquities. Therefore will I divide Him a portion with the great, and He shall divide the spoil with the strong ; because He hath poured out His soul unto death : and He was numbered with the transgressors ; and He bare the sin of many, and made intercession for the transgressors.

63. Isa. lxi., &c.

The Spirit of the LORD GOD is upon me : because the LORD hath anointed me to preach good tidings unto the meek ; He hath sent me to bind up the brokenhearted, to proclaim liberty to the captives, and the opening of the prison to them that are bound ; to proclaim the acceptable year of the LORD, and the day of vengeance of our GOD ; to comfort all that mourn ; to appoint unto them that mourn in Zion, to give unto them beauty for ashes, the oil of joy for mourning, the garment of praise for the spirit of heaviness ; that they might be called trees of righteousness, the planting of the LORD, that He might be glorified. . . . For the LORD GOD will help me; therefore shall I not be confounded: therefore have I set my face like a flint, and I know that I shall not be ashamed. He is near that justifieth me; who will contend with me? let us stand together: who is mine adversary? let him come near to me. Behold, the LORD GOD will help me; who is he that shall condemn me? Who is among you that feareth the LORD, that obeyeth the voice of His servant, that walketh in darkness, and hath no light? let him trust in the Name of the LORD, and stay upon his GOD.

64. Ezek. xxxiv.

For thus saith the LORD GOD; Behold I, even I, will both search My sheep, and seek them out. As a shepherd seeketh out his flock in the day that he is among his sheep that are scattered, so will I seek out My sheep, and will deliver them out of all places where they have been scattered in the cloudy and dark day. And I will bring them out from the people, and gather them from the countries, and will bring them to their own land, and feed them upon the mountains of Israel by the rivers, and in all the inhabited places of the country. I will feed them in a good pasture, and upon the high mountains of Israel shall their fold be: there they shall lie in a good fold, and in a fat pasture shall they feed upon the mountains of Israel. I will feed My flock, and I will cause them to lie down, saith the LORD GOD. I will seek that which was lost, and bring again that which was driven away, and I will bind up that which was broken, and will strengthen that which was sick, but I will destroy the fat and the strong: I will feed them with judgment.

65. Zeph. iii., &c.

The LORD thy GOD in the midst of thee is mighty; He will save, He will rejoice over thee with joy: He will rest in His love, He will joy over thee with singing. I will gather them that are sorrowful for the solemn assembly, who are of thee, to whom the reproach of it was a burden. Behold, at that time I will undo all that afflict thee: and I will save her that halteth, and gather her that was driven out; and I will get them praise and fame in every land where they have been put to shame. At that time will I bring you again, even in the time that I gather you: for I will make you a name and a praise among all people of the earth, when I turn back your captivity before your eyes, saith the LORD. . . . And it shall come to pass in the day that the LORD shall give thee rest from thy sorrow, and from thy fear, and from the hard bondage wherein thou wast made to serve.

66. 2 Esd. ii.

Look for your Shepherd, He shall give you everlasting rest; for He is at hand that shall come in the end of the world. Be ready to the reward of the kingdom, for the everlasting light shall shine upon you for evermore. . . . . Arise up and stand, behold the number of those that be sealed in the feast of the LORD; which are departed from the shadow of the world, and have received glorious garments of the LORD. . . . I Esdras saw upon the mount Sion a great people, whom I could not number, and they all praised the LORD with songs. And in the midst of them there was a young man of high stature, taller than all the rest, and upon every one of their heads he set crowns, and was more exalted; which I marvelled at greatly. So I asked the angel, and said, Sir, what are these? He answered and said unto me, These be they that have put off the mortal clothing, and put on the immortal, and have confessed the Name of GOD: now are they crowned, and receive palms.

Then said I unto the angel, What young person is it that crowneth them, and giveth them palms in their hands? So he answered and said unto me, It is the Son of God, Whom they have confessed in the world. Then began I greatly to commend them that stood so stiffly for the Name of the Lord. Then the angel said unto me, Go thy way, and tell my people what manner of things, and how great wonders of the Lord thy God thou hast seen.

67. Tobit xiii.

O Jerusalem, the holy city, He will scourge thee for thy children's works, and will have mercy again on the sons of the righteous. Give praise to the Lord, for He is good: and praise the everlasting King, that His tabernacle may be builded in thee again with joy, and let Him make joyful there in thee those that are captives, and love in thee for ever those that are miserable. Many nations shall come from far to the Name of the Lord God with gifts in their hands, even gifts to the King of heaven; all generations shall praise thee with great joy. Cursed are all they which hate thee, and blessed shall all be which love thee for ever. Rejoice and be glad for the children of the just: for they shall be gathered together, and shall bless the Lord of the just. O blessed are they which love thee, for they shall rejoice in thy peace: blessed are they which have been sorrowful for all thy scourges; for they shall rejoice for thee, when they have seen all thy glory, and shall be glad for ever. Let my soul bless God the great King. For Jerusalem shall be built up with sapphires, and emeralds, and precious stone: thy walls and towers and battlements with pure gold. And the streets of Jerusalem shall be paved with beryl and carbuncle and stones of Ophir. And all her streets shall say, Alleluia: and they shall praise Him, saying, Blessed be

God, which hath extolled it for ever.

68. S. Luke vii.

One of the Pharisees desired Him that He would eat with him. And He went into the Pharisee's house, and sat down to meat. And, behold, a woman in the city, which was a sinner, when she knew that Jesus sat at meat in the Pharisee's house, brought an alabaster box of ointment, and stood at His feet behind Him weeping, and began to wash His feet with tears, and did wipe them with the hairs of her head, and kissed His feet, and anointed them with the ointment. Now when the Pharisee which had bidden Him saw it, he spake within himself, saying, This man, if He were a prophet, would have known who and what manner of woman this is that toucheth Him: for she is a sinner. And Jesus answering said unto him, Simon, I have somewhat to say unto thee. And he said, Master, say on. There was a certain creditor which had two debtors: the one owed five hundred pence, and the other fifty. And when they had nothing to pay, he frankly forgave them both. Tell Me therefore, which of them will love him most? Simon answered and said, I suppose that he, to whom he forgave most. And He said unto him, Thou hast rightly judged. And He turned to the woman, and said unto Simon, Seest thou this woman? I entered into thine house, thou gavest Me no water for My feet: but she hath washed My feet with tears, and wiped them with the hairs of her head. Thou gavest Me no kiss: but this woman since the time I came in hath not ceased to kiss My feet. My head with oil thou didst not anoint: but this woman hath anointed My feet with ointment. Wherefore I say unto thee, Her sins, which are many, are forgiven; for she loved much: but to whom little is forgiven, the same loveth little. And He said unto her, Thy sins are forgiven. And they that sat at meat with Him began to say within themselves, Who is this that forgiveth sins also? And He said to the woman, Thy faith hath saved thee; go in peace.

69. S. John iv.

Then cometh JESUS to a city of Samaria, which is called Sychar, near to the parcel of ground that Jacob gave to his son Joseph. Now Jacob's well was there. JESUS therefore, being wearied with His journey, sat thus on the well: and it was about the sixth hour. There cometh a woman of Samaria to draw water: JESUS saith unto her, Give Me to drink. (For His disciples were gone away unto the city to buy meat.) Then saith the woman of Samaria unto Him, How is it that Thou, being a Jew, askest drink of me, which am a woman of Samaria? for the Jews have no dealings with the Samaritans. JESUS answered and said unto her, If thou knewest the gift of GOD, and who it is that saith to thee, Give Me to drink; thou wouldest have asked of Him, and He would have given thee living water. The woman saith unto Him, Sir, Thou hast nothing to draw with, and the well is deep: from whence then hast Thou that living water? Art Thou greater than our father Jacob, which gave us the well, and drank thereof himself, and his children, and his cattle? JESUS answered and said unto her, Whosoever drinketh of this water shall thirst again: but whosoever drinketh of the water that I shall give him shall never thirst; but the water that I shall give him shall be in him a well of water springing up into everlasting life.

70. Rev. xxi., &c.

And there came unto me one of the seven angels which had the seven vials full of the seven last plagues, and talked with me, saying, Come hither, I will show thee the bride, the Lamb's wife. And he carried me away in the spirit to a great and high mountain and showed me that great city, the holy Jerusalem, descending out of heaven from GOD, having the glory of GOD: and her light was like unto a stone most precious, even like a jasper stone, clear as crystal. . . . And the twelve gates were twelve pearls: every several gate was of one pearl: and the street of the city was pure gold, as it were transparent glass. And I saw no temple therein: for the LORD GOD Almighty and the Lamb are the temple of it. And the city had no need of the sun, neither of the moon to shine in it: for the glory of GOD did lighten it, and the Lamb is the light thereof. And the nations of them which are saved shall walk in the light of it: and the kings of the earth do bring their glory and honour into it. And the gates of it shall not be shut at all by day: for there shall be no night there. And they shall bring the glory and honour of the nations into it. And there shall in no wise enter into it any thing that defileth, neither whatsoever worketh abomination, or maketh a lie: but they which are written in the Lamb's book of life. And he showed me a pure river of water of life, clear as crystal, proceeding out of the throne of GOD and of the Lamb. In the midst of the street of it, and on either side of the river, was there the tree of life, which bare twelve manner of fruits, and yielded her fruit every month: and the leaves of the tree were for the healing of the nations. And there shall be no more curse: but the throne of GOD and of the Lamb shall be in it; and His servants shall serve Him: and they shall see His face: and His Name shall be in their foreheads. And there shall be no night there; and they need no candle, neither light of the sun; for the LORD GOD giveth them light: and they shall reign for ever and ever.

71. *The Power of the Cross.*

Numb. xxi.

They journeyed from mount Hor by the way of the Red Sea, to compass the land of Edom: and the soul of the people was much discouraged because of the way. And the people spake against GOD, and against Moses, Wherefore have ye brought us up out of Egypt to die in the wilderness? for there is no bread, neither is there any water; and our soul loatheth this light bread. And the LORD sent fiery serpents among the people, and they bit the people; and much people of Israel died. Therefore the people came to Moses, and said, We have sinned, for we have spoken against the LORD, and against thee; pray unto the LORD, that He take away the serpents from us. And Moses prayed for the people. And the LORD said unto Moses, Make thee a fiery serpent, and set it upon a pole: and it shall come to pass, that every one that is bitten, when he looketh upon it, shall live. And Moses made a serpent of brass, and put it upon a pole, and it came to pass, that if a serpent had bitten any man, when he beheld the serpent of brass, he lived.

72. *The Passion (Harmonized).*

(A.) *The Agony.*

JESUS saith unto them, All ye shall be offended because of Me this night: for it is written, I will smite the shepherd, and the sheep of the flock shall be scattered abroad. But after I am risen again, I will go before you into Galilee. Peter answered and said unto Him, Though all men shall be offended because of Thee, yet will I never be offended. And JESUS saith unto him, Verily I say unto thee, that this day, even in this night, before the cock crow twice, thou shalt deny Me thrice. But he spake the more vehemently, If I should die with Thee, I will not deny Thee in any wise. Likewise also said all the disciples. Then cometh JESUS with them unto a place called Gethsemane, where was a garden, into the which He entered, and His disciples. And when He was at the place, He said unto them, Pray that ye enter not into temptation. Sit ye here, while I go and pray yonder. And He was withdrawn from them about a stone's cast. And He took with Him Peter and the two sons of Zebedee, James and John, and began to be sorrowful and very heavy. Then saith He unto them, My soul is exceeding sorrowful, even unto death: tarry ye here, and watch with Me. And He went a little further, and kneeled down, and fell on His face on the ground, and prayed, that, if it were possible, the hour might pass from Him. And He said, Abba, FATHER, all things are possible unto Thee; O My FATHER, if it be possible, if Thou be willing, remove this cup from Me: nevertheless, not My will, but Thine, be done. And there appeared an angel unto Him from heaven, strengthening Him. And being in an agony He prayed more earnestly: and His sweat was as it were great drops of blood falling down to the ground. And He cometh unto the disciples, and findeth them asleep, and saith unto Peter, Simon, sleepest thou? What! could ye not watch with Me one hour? Watch and pray, that ye enter not into temptation: the spirit indeed is willing, but the flesh is weak. He went away again the second time, and prayed, and spake the same words: saying, O My FATHER, if this cup may not pass away from Me, except I drink it, Thy will be done. And when He returned, He found them asleep again (for their eyes were heavy), neither wist they what to answer Him. And He left them, and went away again, and prayed the third time, saying the same words. And He cometh the third time to His disciples, and saith unto them, Sleep on now, and take your rest; it is enough, behold, the hour is at hand, and the Son of Man is betrayed into the hands of sinners. Rise, let us be going: behold, he is at hand that doth betray Me. And when He rose up from prayer, and was come to His disciples, He found them sleeping for sorrow, and said unto them, Why sleep ye? rise and pray, lest ye enter into temptation. And Judas also, which betrayed Him, knew the place: for JESUS ofttimes resorted thither with His disciples.

℣. But Thou, &c. ℟. Thanks, &c. ℣. Be not Thou far from Me, O LORD. ℟. Thou art My succour, haste Thee to help Me. ℣. Glory, &c. ℟. As it was, &c. ℣. Now is My soul troubled, what shall I say? ℟. FATHER, save Me from this hour.

(B.) *The Betrayal.*

And immediately, while He yet spake, cometh Judas, one of the twelve, and with him a great multitude with swords and staves, from the chief priests, and the scribes, and the elders of the people. JESUS therefore, knowing all things that should come upon Him, went forth, and said unto them, Whom seek ye? They answered Him, JESUS of Nazareth. JESUS saith unto them, I am He. And Judas also, which betrayed Him, stood with them. As soon then as He had said unto them, I am He, they went backward, and fell to the ground. Then asked He them again, Whom seek ye? And they said, JESUS of Nazareth. JESUS answered, I have told you that I am He: if therefore ye seek Me, let these go their way: that the saying might be fulfilled, which He spake, Of them which Thou gavest Me have I

lost none. Now he that betrayed Him gave them a sign, saying, Whomsoever I shall kiss, that same is He: hold Him fast, and lead Him away safely. And as soon as he was come, he goeth straightway and drew near unto JESUS to kiss Him, and saith, Hail, Master, and kissed Him. And JESUS said unto him, Friend, wherefore art thou come? Betrayest thou the Son of Man with a kiss? Then came they, and laid their hands on JESUS, and took Him. When they which were about Him saw what would follow, they said unto Him, LORD, shall we smite with the sword? And one of them which stood by with JESUS stretched out his hand, and drew his sword, and struck a servant of the high priest, and cut off his right ear. And the servant's name was Malchus. And JESUS answered and said, Suffer ye thus far. And He touched his ear, and healed him. Then said JESUS unto Peter, Put up thy sword into the sheath: for all they that take the sword shall perish with the sword: the cup which My FATHER hath given Me, shall I not drink it? Thinkest thou that I cannot now pray to My FATHER, and He shall presently give Me more than twelve legions of angels? But how then shall the Scriptures be fulfilled, that thus it must be? In that same hour JESUS said unto the chief priests, and captains of the temple, and the elders, which were come to Him, Be ye come out as against a thief, with swords and staves for to take Me? When I was daily with you in the temple, ye stretched forth no hands against Me: but this is your hour, and the power of darkness. But all this was done that the Scriptures of the prophets might be fulfilled. Then all the disciples forsook Him and fled. And there followed Him a certain young man, having a linen cloth cast about his naked body; and the young men laid hold on him: and he left the linen cloth, and fled from them naked. Then

the band and the captain and officers of the Jews took JESUS, and
bound Him, and led Him away to
Annas first: for he was father in
law to Caiaphas, which was the
high priest that same year. Now
Caiaphas was he which gave counsel
to the Jews, that it was expedient
that one man should die for the
people. And they that had laid hold
on JESUS led Him away to Caiaphas
the high priest, and brought Him
into the high priest's house. And
Simon Peter followed JESUS, and so
did another disciple: that disciple
was known unto the high priest,
and went in with JESUS into the
palace of the high priest. But
Peter stood at the door without.
Then went out that other disciple,
which was known unto the high
priest, and spake unto her that kept
the door, and brought in Peter.

℣. But Thou, &c.   ℟. Thanks,
&c.   ℣. It is not an open enemy
that hath done Me this dishonour.
℟. But it was even thou, My companion, My guide, and Mine own
familiar friend.   ℣. Glory, &c.   ℟.
As it was, &c.   ℣. Have I not chosen
you twelve, and one of you is a
devil?   ℟. He spake of Judas Iscariot, which should betray Him.

(C.) *Before the High Priest.*

The high priest then asked JESUS
of His disciples, and of His doctrine.   JESUS answered him, I spake
openly to the world; I ever taught
in the synagogue, and in the temple,
whither the Jews alway resort; and
in secret have I said nothing. Why
askest thou Me? ask them which
heard Me, what I have said unto
them: behold, they know what I
said.   And when He had thus spoken, one of the officers which stood
by struck JESUS with the palm of
his hand, saying, Answerest Thou
the high priest so? JESUS answered
him, If I have spoken evil, bear
witness of the evil: but if well, why
smitest thou Me?   Now Annas had

sent Him bound unto Caiaphas the
high priest, and with him were
assembled all the chief priests and
the elders and the scribes.   And
Peter followed Him afar off, even
into the palace of the high priest.
And when they had kindled a fire
in the midst of the hall, and were
set down together, Peter sat down
among the servants, and warmed
himself at the fire, to see the end.
Now the chief priests and elders,
and all the council, sought false
witness against JESUS, to put Him
to death; but found none: yea,
though many false witnesses came,
yet found they none; their witness
agreed not together.   At the last
came two false witnesses, saying,
We heard Him say, "I am able to
destroy this temple of GOD, that is
made with hands, and within three
days I will build another made
without hands."   But neither so did
their witness agree together.   And
the high priest stood up in the
midst, and asked JESUS, saying,
Answerest Thou nothing? what is
it which these witness against Thee?
But He held His peace, and answered nothing.   Again the high
priest asked Him, and said unto
Him, I adjure Thee by the living
GOD, that Thou tell us whether
Thou be the CHRIST, the SON of
GOD? JESUS saith unto him, Thou
hast said: nevertheless I say unto
you, Hereafter shall ye see the Son
of Man sitting on the right hand of
power, and coming in the clouds of
heaven.   Then the high priest rent
his clothes, saying, He hath spoken
blasphemy: what further need have
we of witnesses? behold, now ye
have heard His blasphemy.   What
think ye? And they all condemned
Him to be guilty of death.   And
the men that held JESUS mocked
Him, and smote Him.   And some
began to spit on Him, and to cover
His Face, and to buffet Him; and
when they had blindfolded Him,
they struck Him on the Face, and
others smote Him with the palms
of their hands, saying, Prophesy

unto us, Thou Christ, who is he that smote Thee? And many other things blasphemously spake they against Him. And as Peter was beneath in the palace, there cometh one of the maids of the high priest (the damsel that kept the door), and when she saw Peter she looked upon him, and said, And thou also wast with Jesus of Nazareth. Art not thou also one of this Man's disciples? But he denied before them all, saying, Woman, I know Him not, neither understand I what thou sayest. And he went out into the porch; and the cock crew. And the servants and officers stood there, who had made a fire of coals: for it was cold; and they warmed themselves: and Peter stood with them, and warmed himself. And after a little while, when he was gone out into the porch, another maid saw him, and said unto them that were there, This fellow was also with Jesus of Nazareth. They said therefore unto him, Art not thou also one of His disciples? And again he denied with an oath, I do not know the Man. And about the space of one hour after, another confidently affirmed, saying, Of a truth this fellow also was with Him; for he is a Galilæan. And they that stood by said again to Peter, Surely thou art one of them: for thou art a Galilæan, and thy speech agreeth thereto. One of the servants of the high priest, being his kinsman, whose ear Peter cut off, said, Did not I see thee in the garden with Him? Peter then began to curse and to swear, saying, I know not this Man of Whom ye speak. And immediately, the second time while he yet spake, the cock crew. And the Lord turned, and looked upon Peter. And Peter remembered the word of the Lord, how He had said unto him, Before the cock crow twice, thou shalt deny Me thrice. And when he thought thereon, he went out, and wept bitterly.

℣. But Thou, &c. ℟. Thanks, &c. ℣. False witnesses did rise up. ℟. They laid to My charge things that I knew not. ℣. Glory, &c. ℟. As it was, &c. ℣. Consider Him that endured such contradiction of sinners against Himself. ℟. Lest ye be weary and faint in your minds.

(D.) *Before the Sanhedrim and Pilate.*

And as soon as it was day, the elders of the people and the chief priests and the scribes came together, and led Him into their council, saying, Art Thou the Christ? tell us. And He said unto them, If I tell you, ye will not believe: and if I also ask you, ye will not answer Me, nor let Me go. Hereafter shall the Son of Man sit on the right hand of the power of God. Then said they all, Art Thou then the Son of God? And He said unto them, Ye say that I am. And they said, What need we any further witness? for we ourselves have heard of His own mouth. And straightway when the morning was come, all the chief priests held a consultation with the elders of the people, and scribes, and the whole council against Jesus to put Him to death. And when they had bound Him, the whole multitude of them arose, and led Him away from Caiaphas unto the hall of judgment, and delivered Him to Pontius Pilate the governor: and it was early. Then Judas which had betrayed Him, when he saw that He was condemned, repented himself, and brought again the thirty pieces of silver to the chief priests and elders, saying, I have sinned, in that I have betrayed the innocent blood. And they said, What is that to us? see thou to that. And he cast down the pieces of silver in the temple, and departed, and went and hanged himself. And the chief priests took the silver pieces, and said, It is not lawful for to put them into the treasury, because it is the price of blood. And they took counsel, and bought with them the potter's field to bury strangers in. Wherefore that field was called, The field of blood, unto this day. Then was fulfilled that which was spoken by Jeremy the prophet, saying, And they took the thirty pieces of silver, the price of Him that was valued, Whom they of the children of Israel did value : and gave them for the potter's field, as the LORD appointed me. And they themselves went not into the judgment hall, lest they should be defiled ; but that they might eat the passover. Pilate then went out unto them, and said, What accusation bring ye against this Man ? They answered and said unto him, If He were not a malefactor, we would not have delivered Him np unto thee. Then said Pilate unto them, Take ye Him, and judge Him according to your law. The Jews therefore said unto him, It is not lawful for us to put any man to death : that the saying of JESUS might be fulfilled, which He spake, signifying what death He should die. Then Pilate entered into the judgment hall again, and called JESUS, and said unto Him, Art Thou the King of the Jews? JESUS answered him, Sayest thou this thing of thyself, or did others tell it thee of Me? Pilate answered, Am I a Jew? Thine own nation and the chief priests have delivered Thee unto me : what hast Thou done? JESUS answered, My kingdom is not of this world : if My kingdom were of this world, then would My servants fight, that I should not be delivered to the Jews ; but now is My kingdom not from hence. Pilate therefore said unto Him, Art Thou a king then? JESUS answered, Thou sayest that I am a king. To this end was I born, and for this cause came I into the world, that I should bear witness unto the truth. Every one that is of the truth heareth My voice. Pilate saith unto Him, What is truth? And when he had said this he went out again unto the Jews, and saith

unto them, I find in Him no fault at all. But ye have a custom, that I should release unto you one at the Passover : will ye therefore that I release unto you the King of the Jews ? Then cried they all again, saying, Not this Man, but Barabbas. Now Barabbas was a robber.

℣. But Thou, &c. ℟. Thanks, &c. ℣. The kings of the earth stood up, and the rulers took counsel together. ℟. Against the LORD, and against His Anointed. ℣. Glory, &c. ℟. As it was, &c. ℣. CHRIST JESUS, Who before Pilate witnessed a good confession. ℟. He is the faithful Witness, and the Prince of the kings of the earth.

(E.) *The Trial.*

Then Pilate therefore took JESUS, and scourged Him. And the soldiers platted a crown of thorns, and put it on His head : and they put on Him a purple robe, and said, Hail, King of the Jews ! and they smote Him with their hands. Pilate therefore went forth again, and saith unto them, Behold I bring Him forth to you, that ye may know that I find no fault in Him. Then came JESUS forth, wearing the crown of thorns, and the purple robe. And Pilate saith unto them, Behold the Man ! When the chief priests therefore and officers saw Him, they cried out, saying, Crucify Him, crucify Him. Pilate saith unto them, Take ye Him, and crucify Him : for I find no fault in Him. The Jews answered him, We have a law, and by our law He ought to die, because He made Himself the SON of GOD. When Pilate therefore heard that saying, he was the more afraid, and went again into the judgment hall, and saith unto JESUS, Whence art Thou ? But JESUS gave him no answer. Then saith Pilate unto Him, Speakest Thou not unto me ? knowest Thou not that I have power to crucify Thee, and have power to release Thee? JESUS answered, Thou couldest have no power at all against Me except it were given thee from above: therefore he that delivered Me unto thee hath the greater sin. And from thenceforth Pilate sought to release Him: but the Jews cried out, saying, If thou let this Man go, thou art not Cæsar's friend: whosoever maketh himself a king, speaketh against Cæsar. When Pilate therefore heard that saying, he brought JESUS forth, and sat down in the judgment seat, in a place that is called the Pavement, but in the Hebrew Gabbatha. And it was the preparation of the Passover, and about the sixth hour. And JESUS stood before the governor: and they began to accuse Him, saying, We found this fellow perverting the nation, and forbidding to give tribute to Cæsar, saying, that He Himself is CHRIST a king. And Pilate the governor asked Him saying, Art Thou the King of the Jews? And JESUS said unto him, Thou sayest it. And the chief priests accused Him of many things: and when He was accused of the chief priests and elders, He answered nothing. And Pilate asked Him again, saying, Answerest Thou nothing? Behold, hearest Thou not how many things they witness against Thee? And He answered him to never a word; insomuch that the governor marvelled greatly. Then said Pilate to the chief priests and to the people, I find no fault in this Man. And they were the more fierce, saying, He stirreth up the people, teaching throughout all Jewry, beginning from Galilee to this place. When Pilate heard of Galilee, he asked whether the Man were a Galilean. And as soon as he knew that He belonged unto Herod's jurisdiction, he sent Him to Herod, who himself also was at Jerusalem at that time.

℣. But Thou, &c. ℟. Thanks, &c. ℣. Consider Mine enemies, how many they are, and they bear a tyrannous hate against Me. ℟. O keep my soul, and deliver me. ℣. Glory, &c. ℟. As it was, &c. ℣. They have seen and hated both Me and My FATHER. ℟. That the word might be fulfilled which is written in their law, They hated Me without a cause.

(F.) *The Condemnation.*

And when Herod saw JESUS, he was exceeding glad: for he was desirous to see Him of a long season, because he had heard many things of Him; and he hoped to have seen some miracle done by Him. Then he questioned with Him in many words; but He answered him nothing. And the chief priests and scribes stood and vehemently accused Him. And Herod with his men of war set Him at nought, and mocked Him, and arrayed Him in a gorgeous robe, and sent Him again to Pilate. And the same day Pilate and Herod were made friends together: for before they were at enmity between themselves. And Pilate saith unto the Jews, Behold your King! But they cried out, Away with Him, away with Him; crucify Him. Pilate said unto them, Shall I crucify your King? The chief priests answered, We have no king but Cæsar. And Pilate, when he had called together the chief priests and the rulers and the people, said unto them, Ye have brought this Man unto me, as one that perverteth the people: and, behold I having examined Him before you, have found no fault in this Man touching those things whereof ye accuse Him: no, nor yet Herod: for I sent you to him: and lo, nothing worthy of death is done by Him. I will therefore chastise Him, and release Him. Now at that feast the governor was wont to release unto the people one prisoner, whomsoever they desired. (For of necessity he must release one unto them at the feast.) And they had then a notable prisoner called Barabbas, which lay bound with them that had made insurrection with him, who had committed murder in the insurrection. And the multitude crying aloud, began to desire him to do as he had ever done unto them. Therefore when they were gathered together, Pilate said unto them, Whom will ye that I release unto you? Barabbas, or JESUS which is called CHRIST? For he knew that the chief priests had delivered Him for envy. When he was set down on the judgment seat, his wife sent unto him, saying, Have thou nothing to do with that just Man: for I have suffered many things this day in a dream because of Him. But the chief priests and elders persuaded the multitude that they should ask that he should rather release Barabbas unto them, and destroy JESUS. And they cried out all at once, saying, Away with this Man, and release unto us Barabbas. Pilate therefore, willing to release JESUS, spake again unto them, Whether of the twain will ye that I release unto you? They said, Barabbas. Pilate saith unto them, What shall I do then with JESUS which is called CHRIST? unto Him whom ye call the King of the Jews? And they cried out again, saying, Crucify Him. And the governor said unto them the third time, Why, what evil hath He done? I have found no cause of death in Him: I will therefore chastise Him, and let Him go. And they were instant with loud voices, requiring that He might be crucified. And they cried out the more exceedingly, Crucify Him. When Pilate saw that he could prevail nothing, but that rather a tumult was made, he took water, and washed his hands before the multitude, saying, I am innocent of the blood of this just Person: see ye to it. Then answered all the people, and said, His blood be on us, and on our children. And the voices of them and of the chief priests prevailed. And so Pilate,

willing to content the people, gave sentence that it should be as they required. And he released unto them him that for sedition and murder was cast into prison, whom they had desired; but he delivered JESUS, when he had scourged Him, to their will, to be crucified.

℣. But Thou, &c. ℟. Thanks, &c. ℣. And a man of Belial said, We have no part in David. ℟. Neither have we inheritance in the son of Jesse. ℣. Glory, &c. ℟. As it was, &c. ℣. Ye denied the Holy One and the Just. ℟. And desired a murderer to be granted unto you.

(G.) *The Crucifixion.*

Then the soldiers of the governor took JESUS into the common hall, called Prætorium; and gathered unto Him the whole band of soldiers. And they stripped Him, and put on Him a scarlet robe. And when they had platted a crown of thorns, they put it upon His head, and a reed in His right hand: and they bowed the knee before Him, and began to salute Him, and mocked Him, saying, Hail, King of the Jews! And they smote Him on the head with a reed, and did spit upon Him, and bowing their knees worshipped Him. And when they had mocked Him, they took off the purple robe from Him, and put His own clothes on Him, and led Him out to crucify Him. And as they led Him away, they laid hold upon one Simon, a Cyrenian, who passed by, coming out of the country, and on him they laid the cross, that he might bear it after JESUS. And there followed Him a great company of people, and of women, which also bewailed and lamented Him. But JESUS, turning unto them, said, Daughters of Jerusalem, weep not for Me, but weep for yourselves, and for your children. For, behold, the days are coming, in the which they shall say, Blessed are the barren, and the wombs that never bare, and the paps which never gave suck. Then shall they begin to say to the mountains, Fall on us; and to the hills, Cover us. For if they do these things in a green tree, what shall be done in the dry? And there were also two other, malefactors, led with Him to be put to death. And He bearing His cross went forth, and when they were come unto a place called Golgotha, which is, being interpreted, The place of a skull, they gave Him vinegar to drink mingled with gall: and when He had tasted thereof, He would not drink. There they crucified Him, and the two malefactors with Him, one on the right hand, and the other on the left, and JESUS in the midst. Then said JESUS, FATHER, forgive them; for they know not what they do. And Pilate wrote a title, and put it on the cross. And the writing was, JESUS OF NAZARETH, THE KING OF THE JEWS. This title then read many of the Jews: for the place where JESUS was crucified was nigh to the city: and it was written in Hebrew, and Greek, and Latin. Then said the chief priests of the Jews to Pilate, Write not, The King of the Jews; but that He said, I am King of the Jews. Pilate answered, What I have written, I have written. Then the soldiers, when they had crucified JESUS, took His garments, and made four parts, to every soldier a part; and also His coat: now the coat was without seam, woven from the top throughout. They said therefore among themselves, Let us not rend it, but cast lots for it, whose it shall be: that the scripture might be fulfilled, which was spoken by the prophet, They parted My garments among them, and for My vesture did they cast lots. These things therefore the soldiers did. And it was the third hour, and they crucified Him. And sitting down they watched Him there.

℣. But Thou, &c. ℟. Thanks, &c. ℣. Abraham took the wood of the burnt offering. ℟. And laid it upon Isaac his son. ℣. Glory, &c. ℟. As it was, &c. ℣. We look unto JESUS, the Author and Finisher of our faith. ℟. Who for the joy that was set before Him endured the Cross, despising the shame.

(H.) *On the Cross.*

And with Him they crucify two thieves; the one on His right hand, and the other on His left. And the scripture was fulfilled, which saith, And He was numbered with the transgressors. And the people stood beholding. And they that passed by railed on Him, wagging their heads, and saying, Ah, Thou that destroyest the temple, and buildest it in three days, save Thyself. If Thou be the SON of GOD, come down from the cross. Likewise also the chief priests mocking Him, with the scribes and elders, derided Him, saying, He saved others; Himself He cannot save. Let Him save Himself, if He be CHRIST, the chosen of GOD. If He be the King of Israel, let Him now come down from the cross, that we may see, and we will believe Him. He trusted in GOD; let Him deliver Him now, if He will have Him: for He said, I am the SON of GOD. And the soldiers also mocked Him, coming to Him, and offering Him vinegar, and saying, If Thou be the King of the Jews, save Thyself. The thieves also, which were crucified with Him, cast the same in His teeth. And one of the malefactors which were hanged railed on Him, saying, If Thou be CHRIST, save Thyself and us. But the other answering rebuked him, saying, Dost not thou fear GOD, seeing thou art in the same condemnation? And we indeed justly; for we receive the due reward of our deeds: but this Man hath done nothing amiss. And he said unto JESUS, LORD, remember me when Thou comest into Thy kingdom. And JESUS said unto him, Verily I say unto thee, To-day shalt thou be with Me in paradise. Now there stood by the cross of JESUS His Mother, and His Mother's sister, Mary the wife of Cleophas, and Mary Magdalene. When JESUS therefore saw His Mother, and the disciple standing by whom He loved, He saith unto His Mother, Woman, behold thy son! Then saith He to the disciple, Behold thy Mother! And from that hour that disciple took her unto his own home.

℣. But Thou, &c. ℟. Thanks, &c. ℣. He was wounded for our transgressions, He was bruised for our iniquities. ℟. The chastisement of our peace was upon Him, and with His stripes we are healed. ℣. Glory, &c. ℟. As it was, &c. ℣. Who His Own Self bare our sins in His Own Body on the tree. ℟. That we being dead to sin should live unto righteousness.

(I.) *The Death and Piercing.*

And when the sixth hour was come, there was darkness over the whole land until the ninth hour. And the sun was darkened, and about the ninth hour JESUS cried with a loud voice, saying, ELI, ELI, LAMA SABACHTHANI? which is, being interpreted, My GOD, My GOD, why hast Thou forsaken Me? And some of them that stood by, when they heard it, said, Behold, He calleth for Elias. After this, JESUS, knowing that all things were now accomplished, that the scripture might be fulfilled, saith, I thirst. Now there was set a vessel full of vinegar; and straightway one of them ran, and took a sponge, and filled it with vinegar, and put it on a reed, and gave Him to drink. The rest said, Let be, let us see whether Elias will come to save Him. When JESUS therefore had received the vinegar, He said, It is finished : and the veil of the temple was rent in the midst. And when JESUS had cried with a loud voice, He said, FATHER, into Thy hands I commend My Spirit : and having said thus, He bowed His Head, and gave up the ghost. And, behold, the veil of the temple was rent in twain from the top to the bottom; and the earth did quake, and the rocks rent ; and the graves were opened ; and many bodies of the saints which slept arose, and came out of the graves after His Resurrection, and went into the holy city, and appeared unto many. And when the centurion, which stood over against Him, and they that were with him watching JESUS, saw the earthquake, and those things that were done, and saw that He so cried out, and gave up the ghost, they feared greatly, saying, Truly this was the SON of GOD. And all the people that came together to that sight, beholding the things which were done, smote their breasts, and returned. And all His acquaintance, and the women that followed JESUS from Galilee, ministering unto Him, stood afar off, beholding these things ; among whom was Mary Magdalene, and Mary the mother of James the less, and of Joses and Salome (who also, when He was in Galilee, followed Him, and ministered unto Him), and many other women which came up with Him unto Jerusalem. The Jews therefore, because it was the preparation, that the bodies should not remain upon the cross on the Sabbath-day (for that Sabbath-day was an high-day), besought Pilate that their legs might be broken, and that they might be taken away. Then came the soldiers, and brake the legs of the first, and of the other which was crucified with Him. But when they came to JESUS, and saw that He was dead already, they brake not His legs : but one of the soldiers with a spear pierced His Side, and forthwith came thereout blood and water. And he that saw it bare record, and his record is true : and he knoweth that he saith true, that ye might believe. For these things were done, that the Scripture should be fulfilled, A bone of Him shall not be broken. And again another Scripture saith, They shall look on Him Whom they pierced.

℣. But Thou, &c. ℟. Thanks,

&c. ℣. Your lamb shall be without blemish. ℟. And all the congregation of Israel shall kill it in the evening. ℣. Glory, &c. ℟. As it was, &c. ℣. In the midst of the Throne stood a Lamb as it had been slain. ℟. Blessing, and honour, and glory, and power be unto the Lamb for ever and ever.

PRAYERS FOR THE SICK.

General Prayers.

257. O CHRIST our GOD, Who didst endure mocking and scourging in Thy Body; cleanse from all manner of stain our souls which are beset with temptations, that with perfect health dwelling in our flesh we may attain unto the Crown which Thou hast prepared. Who.

258. O GOD, from Whose Face no man's desires or groanings are hid; haste Thee to help us, and turn away from us the fierceness of Thine anger, that we who put our trust in Thee may not fall into the snares of the enemy. Through Thy mercy, O our GOD, Who art blessed, and livest.

259. O GOD, Whose eyes behold the poor; give Thy help to our soul which trusteth in Thee, that we who pray for healing through the wounds of Thy Passion, may by Thine assistance be delivered from our sufferings. Through Thy mercy.

260. Have mercy upon us, O LORD, have mercy upon us, lest the disease of our sins should bring death upon us. Heal us, O LORD, that our souls which are troubled through our offences may obtain peace through grace, and pour Thy medicine upon the sick by granting them pardon for their transgressions. Through.

261. O LORD, help us in our tribulation, hearken and save us, that Thy beloved may be renewed by the Hand which created them, and that by the aid of that Arm which hath laid them low they may attain to the healing which they desire. Through.

262. O LORD, let our souls give thanks to Thee, and all that is within us praise Thy holy Name, that hearkening unto our prayers Thou mayest come to heal our weakness, and to deliver our souls from death, to satisfy our desire with good things, and to crown us with mercy and lovingkindness. Through.

263. Be near, O LORD, to them that call upon Thee, and fulfil the desire of them that fear Thee, uphold all such as fall, and lift up all those that are down, that we who are falling headlong into death, may arise in safety through Thy help. Who livest.

264. O LORD, let our soul ever praise Thee, forasmuch as Thy mercy is ever present in our afflictions, since Thou dost chasten us with correction, and cherish us with lovingkindness, dost heal us by smiting, and strengthen us by healing: grant therefore unto us that as we have tasted Thy sweetness in faith, we may obtain the fulness of Thy delights in reward. Through.

265. O God, make haste to help us, that we who ardently long to share in Thy Passion may find Thee our Helper in our own sufferings. Through Thy mercy.

266. O Lord, Who didst suffer the shame of the Cross; deliver us from the lion's mouth, that giving thanks unto Thee in the midst of the congregation we may declare Thy Name unto our brethren, Who alone didst overcome death, and Who livest.

267. O Lord and Ruler of the universe, Physician and Helper of them that are in trouble, Redeemer and Saviour of those that are diseased; grant healing, we beseech Thee, unto Thy sick servant, have mercy and pity upon *him* who hath sinned much, and deliver *him* from *his* offences, that *he* may glorify Thy divine power. Who.

268. O Lord, we beseech Thee, give unto Thy servant patience in *his* sorrows, comfort in *his* sickness, and restore *him* to health, if it seem good to Thee. But howsoever Thou shalt determine concerning *him*, yet make *his* repentance perfect and *his* passage safe, *his* faith strong, and *his* hope sure, that when Thou shalt call *his* soul from the dwelling of the body, it may enter into the rest of the sons of God. Through.

269. O God, the Life of the faithful, the glory of the lowly, and the Blessedness of the righteous; graciously hear the prayers of Thy servants, that the souls which thirst after Thy promises may be filled with the abundance of Thy love. Through.

For Faith.

270. Lighten our eyes, O Lord, that our faith may fix her sight upon Thee, and our soul may take counsel in the sweetness of Thy love, and Thy fear implant true penitence in our heart. Through Thy mercy, O our God, Who art blessed, and livest.

271. O God, the Truth, and the Everlasting Light, Who hast made faith the beginning of man's salvation, and the foundation of all righteousness; enlighten and strengthen our hearts by Thy Spirit, that believing Thy Word, and confessing that which we believe, we may attain unto the end of our faith, even the salvation of our souls. Through.

For Trust in God's Care.

272. O God, our Light and Defence, remove from us the night of sorrow and ignorance: give us the light of truth and knowledge, that all our trust may remain fixed on Thee. Grant that we may be set upon the Rock which is Christ, that being made strong in Him we may be built up in faith and love. Through Thy mercy, O our God, Who art blessed and livest.

273. Teach us, O Lord, to submit ourselves both now and ever to Thy will and providence, and to cast all our care upon Thee, Who never leavest those that love Thee; and grant that we may so seek the kingdom of God and His righteousness, that all good things may be added unto us. Through.

For Trust.

274. O Blessed Saviour, Who in that great heaviness of Thy soul which Thou sustainedst before Thy Passion, didst fall down upon Thy face in prayer unto Thy heavenly Father; give us grace and the aid of Thy Holy Spirit, that we likewise, in all heaviness of mind and troubles of this world, may seek evermore, by most humble and earnest prayer, the aid and comfort of our heavenly Father. Hear us, our Saviour Christ, for Thy Name's sake. Who.

For Hope.

275. O God, Who never forsakest those that hope in Thee; grant that we may ever keep that hope which Thou hast given us by Thy Word, as an anchor of our souls, sure and steadfast, to preserve us unshaken and secure in all the storms of this life. Through.

276. O GOD, of wonderful goodness and power, Who by Thy words and works dost command us, though unworthy servants, to hope for true and everlasting blessings in Thee and from Thee; grant unto us Thy servants such fervent hope in Thee as may rouse us to diligent labour to make our calling and election sure. In Thee, O LORD, have we trusted, let us never be confounded.

277. O GOD, our Salvation and Protection, arm us with the helmet of hope, and the shield of Thy glorious defence, that we, being helped by Thee in all time of our necessity, may enter into the joy of them that love Thee. Through.

Against Despair.

278. Many a one there be that say of my soul, There is no help for him in his GOD: but Thou, O LORD, art my Defender, Thou art my worship, and the lifter up of my head. Depart not from me in the time of my need, but defend Thou me until this tyranny be overpast. Through.

For Love.

279. O GOD, Who makest all things work together for good to them that love Thee; pour into our hearts the unchanging tenderness of Thy love, that those desires which spring from Thine inspiration may not be disturbed by any temptation. Through.

For Gentleness.

280. O CHRIST, SON of GOD, Who didst patiently endure the reproaches of Thine adversaries when, like roaring lions, they gnashed upon Thee with their teeth; grant, we beseech Thee, that we, following Thine example, and the pattern of Thy longsuffering, may become

gentle to all. Through Thy mercy, O our GOD, Who art blessed, and livest.

For Patience.

281. O GOD, Who by the Passion and Death of Thine Only-begotten SON didst crush the pride of our enemy the devil; grant to Thy faithful servants, when they are in trouble, to bear in mind His sufferings, and cheerfully to endure all adversities. Through the same.

Against Murmuring and Impatience.

282. O LORD, Who knowest all the necessities and all the infirmities of Thy servant; give unto *him*, we beseech Thee, such graces as *he* needs to bear the burden which Thou hast been pleased to lay upon *him*. Take from *him* all undue affection for the things of this world, and fill *his* heart with Thy love, and a desire for eternal life. Through.

For Patient Submission.

283. Almighty GOD, our heavenly FATHER, we humbly beseech Thee to grant, that, as Thine Only-begotten SON, our SAVIOUR JESUS CHRIST, according to His blessed will, suffered willingly Death and bitter Passion for our salvation; so we, in like manner, whensoever it may be Thy pleasure to lay like cross and affliction upon us, may also willingly and patiently bear it, in the trial of our faith for the latter day, unto Thine everlasting glory. Through.

For Grace.

284. O LORD, we beseech Thee, look mercifully upon Thy people, and bestow upon us the abundance of Thy heavenly grace, that assisted by Thy comfort here, we may ever strive more earnestly after everlasting happiness. Through.

Against Self-Sufficiency.

285. O GOD, in Whose sight the very heavens are unclean, and Who chargest even Thine Angels with folly; mercifully enlighten our souls that we may see our weakness and sin, and with all lowliness of heart turn unto Thee, the only Giver of all goodness. Through.

286. O GOD, Who gavest such grace of humility unto Thy holy Apostle S. Paul, that he acknowledged himself the chief of sinners; grant that we, who are still lagging behind in the race of salvation, may so bewail our sins and offences, as to find mercy with Thee. Through.

287. O LORD JESU CHRIST, Who hast declared that when we have done all that is commanded us we are still unprofitable servants; give us grace so to fix our eyes on Thy most pure and holy life, that we may know our own impurity and sin, and seek in all humility to be conformed unto Thy will. Who livest.

288. Pour into our hearts, O LORD, we beseech Thee, the grace of penitence, prayer, and lowliness, that mortifying the flesh and living by the Spirit, and always meditating on heavenly things, we may think meanly of ourselves, and ever find our rest and glory in Thee alone. Who livest.

Against Presumption.

289. Almighty GOD, our heavenly FATHER, Who didst suffer Thine Apostle, S. Peter, presuming on his own power, miserably to fall, even so as to deny his Master; grant to us, we beseech Thee, that we may never presume on our own might and power, but being in our hearts humble and lowly, acknowledging our own infirmity, frailty, and weakness, may ever, in all our doings, receive at Thy mighty hand the strength and comfort which we need, to the due performance of Thy holy will. Through.

For Enlightenment.

290. Shed, we beseech Thee, O merciful Word of GOD, Thy Divine radiance on the souls that seek Thee early with desire, that they may know Thee, the very GOD, Who callest them out of the darkness of their sins, and Who livest.

291. Most gracious GOD, to know and love Whose will is righteousness; enlighten our souls with the brightness of Thy Presence, that we may both know Thy will, and be enabled to perform it. Through.

292. O GOD, Who enlightenest every man that cometh into the world; enlighten, we beseech Thee, the heart of Thy servant with the brightness of Thy grace, that *he* may ponder and love those things that are acceptable unto Thy Divine Majesty. Through.

For Purity of Heart.

293. O merciful LORD JESU CHRIST, Who being made in the likeness of sinful flesh, hast borne our sins in Thy Body, to cleanse us by Thy death, and to make us new creatures acceptable unto GOD; purify us, we beseech Thee, from those stains of sin whereby our souls daily are defiled, and grant us grace to maintain the cleanness which Thou shalt mercifully impart, that both in name and in profession we may be worthy to be called Thine. Who livest.

For Newness of Life.

294. O GOD, the Fountain and Source of everlasting life; pour down upon us, we beseech Thee, the abundance of Thy mercy, that we, being filled with the plenteousness of Thy house, may evermore eschew all guile and superfluity of naughtiness. Through.

For Fruitfulness in Good Works.

295. Increase in us, O LORD, the fruit of good works, that *he* who has been [*or* is being] restored to health by Thy power, may by Thy grace be enabled to attain that place of blessedness, where Thou, with the FATHER.

296. O Lord, suffer not Thy servant to be any more conformed to this world, and grant that by Thy merciful chastisement *he* may be so renewed in the spirit of *his* mind, that *he* may henceforth approve those things which are excellent, and be preserved sincere and without offence unto the day of Jesus Christ Thy Son, our Lord. Who with Thee.

For Holiness.

297. O Father of mercies, Who hast foreordained Thine elect to be conformed to the image of Thy Son; so conform us, we beseech Thee, unto Him in holiness, that when He shall appear, we may be made like unto Him in glory. Through the same.

For the gift of Prayer.

298. O Almighty God, help Thou our weakness, and because we can neither perform nor even pray for what is right of ourselves as of ourselves, arouse by Thy Holy Spirit in our hearts groanings of prayer which cannot be uttered, that by Thy lovingkindness there may be given unto us both the will to ask and the power to accomplish what is well pleasing unto Thee, through Jesus Christ our Lord. Who liveth.

Against Evil Thoughts.

299. O most merciful and gracious Lord God, we beseech Thee to hear our prayers and to deliver our hearts from the temptation of evil thoughts, that by Thy goodness we may become a fitting habitation for Thy Holy Spirit. Through.

Against Evil Desires.

300. O Lord, the great Physician of our mortal hurts and wounds; send, we beseech Thee, Thy salvation upon our weakness, that with Thee on our side, and fighting for us, we may overcome the assaults of the enemy, and pouring forth all our tears and sorrows before Thee, may prevail against the motions of our sins. Through.

Against Sloth.

301. O Lord Jesu Christ, Who hast said, My Father worketh hitherto, and I work; grant us, we beseech Thee, such zeal in Thy service, that we may never be weary in well doing, but may labour steadfastly unto the end. Through Thy mercy.

Against Sins of the Tongue.

302. We beseech Thee, O Lord Jesu, by those sacred words which in Thy last Agony Thou didst utter upon the Cross, that Thou wouldest keep our tongues from evil, and our lips that they speak no guile, that as Thy holy Angels ever sing Thy praises in heaven, so with our tongues may we at all times glorify Thee on earth. Who livest.

For Peace of Mind.

303. O Lord Jesu Christ, Who in Thine Agony wast sore troubled; look, we beseech Thee, mercifully upon Thy servant, grant unto *his* body relief from pain, and to *his* mind that peace which passeth all understanding, that *he* may rest on Thee for evermore. Who livest.

Against direct Temptations of the Flesh.

304. O God, Who art the Healer both of soul and body; send forth Thy salvation, and make us whole; that while we deplore all our sickness and all our infirmity, we may by Thy strength overcome the temptations of the enemy. Through.

For Perseverance.

305. O God of hope, fill us, we beseech Thee, with all joy and peace in believing, that abounding in hope through the power of the Holy Ghost, we may steadily press on to those good things which Thou hast promised to those that shall endure unto the end.   Through.

306. O GOD, the Blessedness of all who put their trust in Thee, Who art both the Helper and the Judge of them that contend in the way of righteousness; we pray Thee that Thou wouldest so keep them from falling in this life that Thou mayest crown them in the life to come.   Through.

For Resignation.

307. O LORD JESU CHRIST, Who didst willingly yield Thyself up to shame and torture and death for us miserable sinners; grant unto Thy servant so readily to drink the bitter cup of sorrow which Thou puttest to *his* lips, that *he* may at length attain unto the full sweetness of Thy heavenly blessings. Who livest.

For Obedience.

308. Work Thy work in us, O LORD, of Thyself, that we may ever obey Thee, our SAVIOUR, not in servile fear, but with true affection and love of righteousness, and thus through obedience reign with Thee for ever, Who, obedient to Thy FATHER even unto death, livest and rulest all creation, world without end.

For Preparation for the Judgment.

309. O GOD, Who givest and takest away according to Thine own good pleasure; grant unto us, we beseech Thee, such a measure of Thy grace, that mindful of Thy warnings, we may so live unto Thee in this life, that when Thou shalt call us to depart from the body we may be received by thy holy Angel, cleansed from all our offences. Through.

310. Grant, O LORD, that we may never sleep in sin, nor in death eternal, but that we may have our part in the second resurrection, and that the second death may have no power over us.   Through.

311. O LORD, in the day when Thou makest up Thy jewels, remember Thy servants for good and not for evil, that our souls may be numbered among the righteous. Who.

312. O LORD GOD, FATHER Almighty, purify the secrets of our hearts, and mercifully wash out the stains of our sins; and grant, O LORD, that being cleansed from our offences by Thy mercy, we may without terror await the fearful coming of JESUS CHRIST our LORD. Who liveth.

313. O LORD JESU CHRIST, Who hast promised to come at a time when we look not for Thee, and at an hour when we are not aware; mercifully grant that we, following Thy precepts and example in this life, may at Thy coming be found among the number of Thy faithful ones, evermore to dwell with Thee. Who livest.

314. O LORD JESU CHRIST, Who art coming again at the end of the world to judge the quick and the dead; have mercy upon us, miserable sinners, and so temper Thy justice with mercy, that we may not be cast out in that day, but, together with those who have served Thee faithfully in their generation, may be admitted into the inner courts of Thy house, there with Saints and Angels and just men made perfect to praise Thee for evermore. Who livest.

For a sense of Sin.

315. O GOD, Who art of purer eyes than to behold iniquity; mercifully grant unto us such a sense of sin, that we may receive cleansing, and such cleansing, that we may be made pure in heart, and may see Thee for evermore.   Through.

For true Contrition.

316. O LORD JESU CHRIST, Who forgavest the sinful woman; grant unto Thy servant so to bewail *his* sins at Thy feet, that *he* may not fail to obtain Thy merciful pardon. Who livest.

For Penitence.

317. O GOD, Restorer and Lover of innocency, Who hast said by the mouth of Thy Prophet, As I live, I desire not the death of a sinner, but rather that he may be converted and live; we humbly and devoutly pray Thee to stretch forth Thy merciful hand unto Thy fallen servants, to lift them out of the dust, and to cleanse and save them from all their sins. Through.

318. Hearken, O LORD, to the prayers of Thy servants, and graciously hear the supplication of them that cry unto Thee; and through the light of Thy tender mercy pour upon us sorrow for our sins, that by Thy loving guidance we may salve the wounds of our earthly pleasures with the bitter medicine of penitence, and by the corrective discipline of the HOLY GHOST may obtain pardon from Thee. Through.

319. Hear our prayers, O LORD, and let not the compassion of Thy mercy be far from Thy servants; heal their wounds, pardon their sins, that no iniquities may part them from Thee, but that they may ever cleave unto Thee their GOD. Through. .

320. O Holy Trinity, One GOD, Who cleansest man's heart from sin, and makest it whiter than snow; pour down Thy mercy upon us; renew in us, we beseech Thee, Thy HOLY SPIRIT, that we may show forth Thy praise, and strengthened by Thy free Spirit, may attain a place in the heavenly Jerusalem. Through.

For Pardon.

321. O most merciful GOD, remember not, we beseech Thee, the sins of our youth, nor the transgressions of our after years; and those things by which we, in our wilfulness, have offended Thee, do Thou of Thy great mercy pardon. Through.

322. O GOD of compassion, GOD of pity, GOD Who according to the multitude of Thy great mercies, washest away the sins of the penitent, and by the grace of remission doest away the guilt of past offences; look graciously upon this Thy servant, and hearken unto *him* entreating for the forgiveness of all *his* sins. Through.

323. We beseech Thee, O LORD, in Thy goodness, to show us Thine unspeakable mercy; that Thou mayest both set Thy servant free from *his* sins, and rescue *him* from the punishment which for those sins *he* deserves. Through.

324. Almighty, Everlasting GOD, Who declaredst unto Adam, when he transgressed Thy commandment and acknowledged not his sin, that dust he was, and unto dust he should return; we humbly beseech Thee to spare us who truly confess our sins, and grant that we may obtain pardon, so as to pass from sin unto righteousness, from corruption to incorruption, and from death unto eternal life. Through.

325. O LORD JESU CHRIST, SON of the living GOD, Who reignest with the FATHER and the HOLY GHOST; vouchsafe to give us faith, hope, and charity, humility and purity of body and soul, patience, true obedience, and amendment of life. Grant us, O merciful and gracious GOD, full pardon and remission for all our sins and offences committed by day or night, that through Thy grace we may attain the glory of Thy kingdom, O SAVIOUR of the world. Where Thou livest.

For Profit by Sickness.

326. O LORD, look upon Thy servant, restore the soul which Thou hast created, that, chastened by Thy punishments it may be healed by Thy medicine. Through.

327. O Lord Jesu Christ, the only Physician of our souls; create in us a pure heart, O God, and renew a right spirit within us. Bind up the wounds of our souls, wash them with the wine of Thy Precious Blood, and anoint them with the oil of Thy holiness. Repair that Heavenly Image which is defaced in us through sin, and adorn it again with Thine Own righteousness, that we being restored by Thee may sing praises acceptably to Thee in Thy Holy Church. Who.

328. O Lord Jesu Christ, Who smotest Saul with blindness that Thou mightest make the persecutor an Apostle; mercifully grant unto Thy servant so to feel Thy chastisement in this world, that Thy loving correction may make *him* great in the kingdom of heaven. Where with the Father.

329. O God, Who dost correct us with Thy judgments, yet in Thy mercy willest our salvation, Who scourgest sinners that they may turn again, and Who dost constantly warn us lest we should fall away; grant, we beseech Thee, that grace may be given to Thy servant from heaven unto newness of life, equal to the faith and fervour with which we have cried to Thee from earth. Through.

For Acceptance of Sickness.

330. O most merciful Lord, Who healest the inward man by outward afflictions, and by troubles in this world dost prepare us for eternal joys in the world to come; by that Cup of sorrow which Thou drankest for us, and by that weary path which Thou troddest, grant that we may willingly drink of Thy Cup, and cheerfully follow Thee along the road where Thou hast gone before. Who with the Father.

When Sickness increases.

331. O Lord Jesu Christ, for our sakes wast Thou born, for our sakes didst Thou hunger and thirst, for our sakes didst Thou teach and pray, for our sakes didst Thou suffer, and give Thy life over unto death. As Thou dost make Thy servant to share in Thy sufferings, make *him* to share also in Thy merits. May Thy Blood wash away the stains of *his* sins. May Thy righteousness cleanse away *his* unrighteousness. May Thy merits plead for *him* when *he* stands before Thee as Judge. As sickness increases on *him*, so do Thou increase unto *him* Thy grace. Let not *his* faith waver, nor *his* hope fail, nor *his* love wax cold. Let not the dread of death cause *him* to cast away *his* confidence in Thee, or to place it anywhere but in Thee, but looking steadfastly unto Thee to the last let *him* say, "Into Thy hands, O Lord, I commend my spirit." To Whom be honour and praise, world without end. Amen.

332. By Thy overflowing mercy, heal, O merciful Lord, the pains, the weakness, and the increasing sickness of this Thy servant, whose strength faileth *him* through the sharpness of *his* sufferings, that being delivered *he* may gratefully give thanks unto Thee. Through.

In great Pain.

333. O Lord Jesu Christ, Who for the salvation of the world wast willing to bear patiently sorrows and agony, passion and death; grant, we beseech Thee, that we, mindful of all that Thou hast borne for us, may bear our light afflictions for Thy sake, so that, sharing in Thy pain and sorrow, Thou mayest make us also partakers of Thy rest and glory. Who livest.

For Acceptance of Pain or Sorrow.

334. O Lord Jesu Christ, give us grace to receive from Thy hand all the pains and sorrows which we endure in the flesh, as so many portions of Thy holy Cross given unto us by Thee. May we receive and embrace them, and bear them with patience in the tabernacles of our body and soul, for Thy sake, Who didst suffer and die for us, and now livest.

That Pain may be profitable.

335. O LORD JESU CHRIST, Rest of the Saints and most joyful Salvation of all that hope in Thee; Who in the night of Thy fearful Passion didst pray to Thy FATHER, saying, "Let this cup pass from Me; nevertheless, not My will, but Thine, be done," and Who in that hour wast in such agony that Blood poured forth from Thy Blessed Body; we pray Thee, O loving JESU, so to aid the soul of this Thy servant with Thine accustomed mercy, that *he* may be moved with such hearty repentance for *his* sins, as without dread to meet Thee at Thy second Coming, through Thy help, O JESU CHRIST, by Whose Passion *he* hath been redeemed. And Who.

For Relief from Pain.

336. O JESU, the Good Samaritan, Who pourest into our wounds the sharp wine of affliction to purge away our sins, whilst Thou allayest the smart with the oil of Thy comfort; mercifully regard the sufferings of Thy servant, and temper the bitterness of Thy punishment with the gift of Thy consolation, mindful both of what is needful for *his* correction, and of what *his* weakness can bear. Who livest.

In Exhaustion from Pain.

337. O Almighty and merciful GOD, Who didst send Thine Angel from heaven to strengthen Thy SON, our LORD JESUS CHRIST, when fainting in His Agony; send, we beseech Thee, Thy strengthening grace upon this Thy servant, that *he* may be refreshed both in body and soul. Through the same.

In great Languor.

338. O LORD, Who art the rest of the weary and heavy laden; mer-cifully grant Thy loving help and refreshment to the suffering body [and burdened soul] of Thy servant, that *he*, renewed by Thy power, may glory in Thy salvation. Who livest.

For a Blessing on Remedies.

339. O Almighty GOD, Who by a plaster of figs didst cure the disease of Thy servant Hezekiah, and Who didst Thyself anoint with clay the eyes of the blind man, that his sight might be restored; send Thy blessing, we beseech Thee, upon the means now used for the recovery of Thy servant, and grant unto them such success, that *he* may be restored whole to Thy Church, and may praise and glorify Thy holy Name. Who livest.

340. O LORD JESU CHRIST, the great Physician, Who gavest unto Thine Apostles power to heal all manner of sickness, and all manner of disease; assist with the Spirit of wisdom the endeavours of him who is striving to work the cure of Thy servant, and grant that the means employed by his skill may be blessed by Thy power. Who livest.

For a Restoration to Health.

341. O GOD, Who addedst fifteen years of life to Thy servant Hezekiah; so by Thy power raise this Thy servant from the bed of sickness unto health. Through.

342. O GOD, Who 'didst send Thy blessed Apostle S. Peter to Dorcas Thy servant, that she might be raised to life by his prayers; hear us, we beseech Thee, and of Thy great mercy speedily restore to health this Thy servant, whom we, who have no power without Thee, visit in Thy Name. Through.

343. Almighty and everlasting GOD, Who helpest them that are in trouble and necessity, and graciously minglest mercy with Thy chastisements; we humbly beseech Thee, O LORD, that Thou wouldest mercifully raise this Thy servant from the sickness by which *he* is held, and present *him* sound to Thy holy Church, to the praise and glory of Thy great Name. Who livest.

344. O Thou Who in mercy and compassion healest the diseases of our souls and the wounds of our bodies, O Thou Great Physician, heal *him* who lieth here in sickness, and grant *him* Thy salvation. Who livest.

345. O Thou Who art good, and the fountain of mercy to all who with fervent faith come unto Thee; deliver Thy servant from all *his* infirmities, heal *his* sickness, and grant unto *him* Thy divine grace from on high. Where Thou.

346. O Lord Jesu Christ, Who art the true Physician and the heavenly Medicine; be gracious unto us and help us. Heal, O Lord, all weakness and sickness in Thy people. Take from us the diseases of body and mind. Remove all plagues and disorders, and graciously prevent the causes of our wounds, that whilst Thou dost turn away our iniquities, Thou mayest cure our sufferings. Who livest.

347. O Lord, Holy Father, Physician of our souls and bodies, Who didst send Thine Only Begotten Son, our Lord Jesus Christ, to heal all sickness, and to ransom us from death; heal this Thy servant from the infirmity of *his* soul and body, through the grace of Thine Anointed, and quicken *him* so to perform Thy good pleasure, that *he* may in all holiness give Thee due thanks and adoration. Through the same.

348. O Lord, forgive our sins, and grant us Thy mercy, that, hearkening unto the prayer of our lips, Thou mayest look upon the lowliness and suffering of Thy servant. Loose *his* bonds, blot out *his* offences, regard *his* suffering, drive away *his* trouble, and in Thy boun-teous mercy fulfil our petitions. Through.

In a Hospital.

349. Almighty and merciful God, we beseech Thee of Thy great goodness to visit these Thy servants who lie weary in this house, that as Thou didst visit Tobit and Sara, Peter's wife's mother, and the Centurion's servant, so these also, restored to their former health of mind and body, may give thanks unto Thee in Thy Church. Through.

For the Aged.

350. O Lord Jesu Christ, Who saidst unto Thy disciples, "A little while and ye shall not see Me, and again a little while and ye shall see Me;" grant unto Thine aged servant that when the little while of exile and darkness which remains for *him* here is passed, *he* may see Thee in *his* home for evermore. Where Thou.

351. O Lord Jesu Christ, the Strength of them that put their trust in Thee; vouchsafe unto Thy servant increase of spiritual might as *his* bodily vigour faileth, and grant that as *his* eyes become dim, and *his* ears dull to earthly things, *his* affections may be the more set on things above. Through Thy mercy, Who.

352. O Lord Jesu Christ, Who didst hearken unto the prayer of Thy two disciples, and didst abide with them when it was towards evening, and the day was far spent; abide, we pray Thee, with Thine aged servant in the evening of *his* life. Make Thyself fully known unto *him*, and whensoever *he* shall pass through the valley of the shadow of death, be with *him* until the end. Who livest.

For the Deaf.

353. O Lord Jesu Christ, Who at the intercession of Thy disciples didst heal one that was deaf, and had an impediment in his speech;

graciously hearken unto our prayers in behalf of this Thy servant, and so open *his* ears unto discipline that *he* may in all things be ready to fulfil Thy holy commandments. Who livest.

In Blindness.

354. O GOD, Who hast been pleased that Thy servant should be sightless [from birth] that *he* may from within look on Thee alone with the enlightened eyes of the heart; be Thou the light of our eyes, that we may be rid of the darkness of this world, and reach the land of everlasting brightness, where all imperfections shall be done away. Through.

For the Infirm.

355. O LORD, Whose strength is made perfect in weakness; mercifully look upon Thy servant, remove *his* feebleness, renew *his* vigour, and grant that *he* may with recovered might praise and serve Thee. Through.

For an unbaptized Sick Person.

356. O LORD our heavenly FATHER, Almighty, everlasting GOD, Who givest help in peril, and restrainest the scourge when Thou chastenest; we entreat Thy healing power, humbly beseeching Thee to raise up this Thy servant from *his* sickness, that the enemy may not prevail to tempt *his* soul; appoint *him* a limit, as Thou didst for Job, lest the enemy should begin to triumph over this soul without the redemption of Baptism. [Delay, O LORD, the time of *his* death.] Extend the span of *his* life, and relieve *him* whom Thou wilt bring to the grace of Thy holy Baptism. Through.

In Fever.

357. O LORD JESU CHRIST, Who at the prayer of Thine Apostle S. Peter didst rebuke the fever of his wife's mother; hear, we beseech Thee, our supplications for this Thy servant, and mercifully grant *him* ease and refreshment, Thou Who art a River of Water in a dry place, and the Shadow of a great Rock in a weary land. And Who livest.

When Sleepless.

358. O LORD JESU CHRIST, Who hast commanded us to watch and pray; grant unto Thy servant so to rest in the sleep of the body, that *his* soul may wake in prayer to Thee. Who livest.

359. O LORD GOD Almighty, Whom Angels praise without ceasing day or night, and Who hast framed the stars, that faint not in their watches; grant unto Thy servant that, in the watches of the night *his* soul may be so stayed on Thee, that *he* may continually praise and bless Thy holy Name. Through.

When Injured in Body.

360. O LORD, Who rulest over all, Thou Who art the Physician and Helper in sickness, the Deliverer and SAVIOUR from pain; heal this Thy servant who hath suffered grievous injury of body; show compassion and mercy upon *him* who hath in many things offended Thee, and deliver *him*, O JESU CHRIST, both from sin and from its punishment, that *he* may glorify Thy Divine power, and bless Thy holy Name. Who.

For one Insensible.

361. O most merciful LORD JESU CHRIST our SAVIOUR, Who, to do away our offences, didst not only bear cruel stripes, and shameful insults, and mocking, and a painful crown of thorns, but wast willing also to be fastened naked to the Cross like a thief; we pray Thee, by these Thy sufferings, that Thou wouldest hear us in behalf of this Thy servant, who, through weakness of mind and body, cannot now plead for *himself*. We pray Thee, by the merits of Thy bitter Passion and Death, that Thou wouldest mercifully regard *his* infirmity, pardon all *his* sins, and bring *him* to everlasting joy. Who livest.

For one subject to Fits.

362. O merciful LORD, look, we pray Thee, with pity upon this Thy servant, whose power oftentimes leaveth *him*, and whose understanding departeth from *him*; give Thy holy Angels charge over *him* to preserve *him* from harm, and if it shall please Thee to withdraw this grievous affliction from *him*, grant that, relieved by Thy mercy, *he* may be ever mindful of Thy love. Who livest.

For the Hysterical.

363. O LORD JESU CHRIST, the Prince of Peace; grant rest unto the soul and body of this Thy servant, that *he* may be no more vexed and torn with the violence of *his* sickness, but in quietness and confidence may find strength in Thee. Who livest.

For Idiots.

364. O LORD, Whose ways are past finding out; we pray Thee of Thy great goodness to look upon this Thy servant whom Thou hast afflicted with weakness and darkness of mind: grant unto *him* to be strengthened and enlightened with Thy SPIRIT in the inner man, that *he* to whom Thou hast denied earthly wisdom may be filled within with that knowledge of Thee which passeth all understanding. Through.

Before an Operation.

365. We beseech Thee, O LORD JESU CHRIST, by those wounds and bruises which Thou barest for us in Thy Sacred Body, to look graciously upon the suffering body of this Thy servant; bless the means employed for working out *his* cure, and grant that *he* may so patiently endure *his* sufferings in the flesh, that the wounding of *his* body may

be for the salvation of *his* soul. Through Thy mercy. Who livest.

In Childbed.

366. O LORD, Who for the sin of our first mother didst ordain that women should bring forth children in sorrow; regard, we pray Thee, the supplications of this Thy servant, who turneth unto Thee in trust and lowliness, and grant that she being protected by Thy power and blessed with Thy grace, may speedily have her sorrow turned into joy. Through.

367. O LORD, Who lookest always lovingly upon Thy creatures; bow down Thine ears to our prayers, and mercifully look upon Thy servant suffering under great weakness of body; visit her with Thy salvation, grant unto her the medicine of Thy heavenly grace, and by Thine Almighty power preserve her offspring both in body and soul. Through.

368. O GOD, Who madest man in the beginning, and gavest him an help meet for him, that Thy people might increase and multiply upon the earth; grant Thy mercy unto this Thy servant, that she may bring forth safely. Through.

For a new born Infant.

369. O GOD, Who didst send Thine Only-begotten SON into the word as a little Child; mercifully look upon this infant, and protect *him* with Thy heavenly grace; vouchsafe unto *him* soundness of body and mind, and grant that *he*, increasing in wisdom and stature, may evermore find favour with Thee. Through the same.

For a Sick Child.

370. O LORD JESU CHRIST, Who although Very GOD, wast subject unto Thine earthly parents; grant unto this Thy child grace to be gentle and docile, that *he* may bear cheerfully what Thou art pleased to lay upon *him*, and readily obey those set over *him* by Thee. Who livest.

For a Sick Child who has been Wicked.

371. O GOD, the Creator and Redeemer of mankind, Who according to Thy great goodness restorest Thine image and likeness in that which Thou hast made; graciously look upon this Thy servant, and of Thy lovingkindness pardon *him* for whatever *he* hath done amiss through the malice of the enemy, that as *he* hath not yet a perfect knowledge of Thy will, nothing may be laid to *his* charge, but that by Thy merciful pardon *he* may be made a faithful member of Thy Church. Through.

For a Dying Child.

372. O LORD JESU CHRIST, Who didst take little children in Thine arms and bless them; bless, we beseech Thee, this child; take *him* into the arms of Thine everlasting mercy, keep *him* from all evil, and bring *him* into the company of those who ever behold the face of Thy FATHER Which is in heaven. With Whom.

In Trouble.

373. O LORD, we pray Thee that the thought of the country towards which we are travelling may make us forgetful of the weariness of the journey; and if Thou addest a weight of troubles, give us also strength that we may not faint under the burden. Thou, O LORD, hast gone before us, bearing Thy Cross, make us to bear ours after Thee, ever looking unto Thee, and putting our trust in Thee, O LORD, alone. Who livest.

374. O GOD, Refuge of the poor, Hope of the lowly, and Salvation of the miserable; graciously hearken unto the prayers of Thy servants, that they whom the justice of Thy punishment has afflicted may in the abundance of Thy mercy be comforted. Through.

375. O LORD GOD, Who showest unto us Thine anger that Thou mayest also give us Thy help, Who threatenest that Thou mayest spare; stretch forth Thy hand to the fallen, and help the weary with Thy manifold compassion, that they who are redeemed by Thee may by Thy governance be preserved unto the hope of eternal life. Through.

376. O GOD, Who resistest the proud, and givest grace unto the humble; in all our troubles and adversities hear our prayers, and have mercy upon us, for Thou only art mighty, and there is none that can gainsay Thee. Help us, O GOD Almighty, and we shall be saved. Through.

In Heaviness of Mind.

377. O LORD JESU CHRIST, Who in the sorrow of Thy soul didst fall down upon Thy face in prayer; give us grace that we likewise in all our sorrows may betake ourselves with humble and earnest prayer to our heavenly FATHER for aid and comfort and relief. Hear us, O SAVIOUR JESU CHRIST, for Thy Name's sake. Who livest.

When Unhappy.

378. O most merciful LORD JESU, Consolation of the unhappy, Who, in Thy Body, didst bear all our sins and sorrows; we beseech Thee, by that Thy wondrous love, that Thou wouldest heal the wounds of this Thy servant, and pour the oil of comfort into *his* soul, that, strengthened with spiritual consolation, *he* may joyfully serve Thee, and at the last be brought to taste of Thy joys in Thine eternal kingdom. Where.

In Poverty.

379. O merciful FATHER, grant us Thy grace, and the quickening and powerful might of Thy HOLY

SPIRIT, that in our manifold crosses, poverty, sickness, adversity, and affliction, we may ever acknowledge Thy Fatherly will in our hearts, and peaceably accept it with holy patience, to Thy glory. Through.

In Desolation.

380. O most merciful LORD JESU, Who in the awful night of Thy Passion, abandoned by Thy disciples, stoodest alone among Thine enemies; we pray Thy mercy that Thou wilt not leave the soul of Thy servant [in *his* departure] alone in the hands of evil spirits, or destitute of Thy help, but that Thou wilt ever guard it by Thy might, and the companionship of Thy holy Angels, and through the power of Thy Blood restore it to peace and gladness, and in the end bring it to the place where all is happiness and joy. And where.

Before Holy Communion.

381. O LORD JESU CHRIST, SON of the Living GOD, Who by the will of the FATHER and the power of the HOLY GHOST hast given life unto the world by Thy Death; deliver us by Thy sacred Body and Blood from all our sins, and keep us from all evil. Make us to abide always in Thy commandments, and suffer us not to be ever separated from Thee. Who livest.

382. O King of heaven and earth, rich in mercy, behold, we are poor and needy. Thou knowest how greatly we are in need, and Thou alone art able to help and enrich us. O LORD, look graciously upon us, and from the treasures of Thy goodness succour the poverty of our souls. Through.

383. O LORD, let our souls perceive the sweetness of Thy presence, let them taste and see how gracious Thou art, that filled with Thy love, they may seek nothing out of Thee wherein to rejoice; for

Thou, O LORD, art the joy of our heart, and our portion for ever.

For a Penitent before Holy Communion.

384. We pray Thy Majesty, Holy LORD, Almighty FATHER, Eternal GOD, Who always desirest the life, not the death of a sinner, to look graciously upon Thy servant mourning for the sins of *his* past life, and to turn *his* heaviness into joy. Rend the sackcloth of *his* sins, and clothe *him* with the gladness of Thy salvation, that after the long hunger of *his* pilgrimage, *he* may be filled from Thy holy Altar, and entering into the King's chamber, may in Thy courts ever bless Thy glorious Name. Through.

For a Blind Man before Holy Communion.

385. O LORD GOD, with Whom is the fountain of life, and in Whose light we shall see light; increase in us the brightness of Thy knowledge, that when we are thirsty we may receive from Thee the fountain of living waters, and when we are dark we may be enlightened with the brightness of Thy understanding. Through.

After Holy Communion.

386. O Almighty GOD, vouchsafe that the holy Gifts which we have received may cleanse away our sin, and work in us the effects of a pure and holy life. Through.

387. Grant, we beseech Thee, O LORD, that we, whom Thou dost feed with heavenly dainties, may evermore desire that Food through which alone we truly live, even JESUS CHRIST, Thy SON, our LORD. Who.

388. O LORD, we pray Thee by Thine aid to sustain those whom Thou dost renew through Thy holy Sacraments; and as Thou dost refresh us with temporal blessings, so Thou mayest feed us also with those that endure unto eternal life. Through.

389. O Lord, we beseech Thee, graciously with mercy hear our supplications, that we who in sorrow and trouble have received Thy Gifts, may thereby be comforted, and increase in love for Thee. Through.

For Spiritual Communion.

390. Soul of Christ, sanctify me.

Body of Christ, save me.

Blood of Christ, inebriate me.

Water out of the side of Christ, wash me.

Passion of Christ, strengthen me.

O good Jesu, hear me;

Within Thy wounds hide me.

Suffer me not to be separated from Thee;

From the malicious enemy defend me;

At the hour of my death call me,

And bid me come unto Thee,

That with Thy saints I may praise Thee

For all eternity. Amen.

When beginning to recover.

391. O most mighty and merciful God, fulfil, we beseech Thee, the work of healing which Thou hast so graciously begun, and grant that Thy servant may be restored whole to Thy Church to show forth Thy praise, and taking Thy easy yoke and light burden upon *him*, may henceforth serve Thee in reverence and godly fear all the days of *his* life. Through.

Thanksgiving for Relief, or Recovery.

392. O God, Whose mercies are without number, and the treasure of Whose goodness is infinite; we give Thee hearty thanks for the blessings which Thou hast bestowed upon Thy servant; and we humbly beseech Thee that, as Thou hast granted that for which we prayed, so Thou wouldst continue Thy goodness towards us, and prepare us by Thy blessings in this life for the enjoyment of eternal happiness in the life to come. Through.

For the performance of Vows.

393. O Lord, Who hast shown compassion upon Thy servant [and lifted *him* up from the gates of death]; mercifully grant *him* Thy grace, that *he* may offer unto Thee the sacrifice of thanksgiving, and pay Thee the vows which *he* promised with *his* lips and spake with *his* mouth when *he* was in trouble. Through.

For one whose mind is feeble [before Death.]

394. O Lord Jesu Christ, Crown and glory of the Saints, Who hanging on the Cross didst pray for Thy crucifiers, saying, " Father, forgive them, for they know not what they do;" we pray Thy mercy, O Lord Jesu, that Thou wouldest deign to revive the force of Thy prayer in behalf of this Thy servant, that *he* may obtain pardon for all *his* offences from the Eternal Father; and as Thou wast then heard, so now with the Father hear our prayers for Thy afflicted servant, who knoweth not what *he* does through feebleness of mind and body. O merciful Jesu, we pray Thee that [in *his* departure] Thou wilt forgive *him* all *his* offences, and that by Thy bitter Passion *he* may be brought to the fellowship of the Angels. Through Thy mercy.

For one too weak to pray.

395. O God, Who art graciously pleased to accept a ready mind, and to reward us according to that we have, not according to that we have not; be merciful unto this Thy servant, who by reason of weakness cannot now pray unto Thee, nor fix *his* mind upon Thee, and as Thou knowest *his* desires, so do Thou in Thy bounty fulfil them. For the sake.

For true Faith to the last.

396. O most glorious LORD JESU CHRIST, Who on the Cross didst pour the true light of faith into the heart of the thief; preserve, we beseech Thee, true faith in the heart of Thy servant [whose hour of departure now seems near], that, armed by the merits of Thy most holy Passion, *he* may resist all the attacks of the evil spirits, and joyfully enter into Thine eternal glory. Where Thou.

For Resignation in the Hour of Death.

397. O most merciful LORD JESU CHRIST, the Crown of those that fight, Who, dying upon the Cross, didst teach us to pray briefly in the hour of our death, saying, "FATHER, into Thy hands I commend My Spirit;" we entreat Thy Majesty that by the power of Thy HOLY SPIRIT, Thou wouldest imprint that same prayer upon the mind of this Thy servant, that by constantly repeating it *he* may at the hour of *his* departure cheerfully commit *himself* into Thy most holy Hands. Who.

For God's Care of Widow and Orphan.

398. O GOD, Who art the FATHER of the fatherless, and defendest the cause of the widow; comfort, we beseech Thee, the soul of Thy servant with a full trust in Thy care and love, and grant that those whom *he* shall leave behind *him* here on earth, may be ever protected by Thine Almighty power. Through.

On the Approach of Death.

399. O holy and most gracious SAVIOUR JESU CHRIST, we humbly commend the soul of Thy servant into Thy most merciful hands. Let

Thy blessed Angels keep guard over *him* to defend *him* from the malice of *his* ghostly enemies, and to drive far from *him* the spirits of darkness.

400. LORD, receive the soul of this Thy servant. Enter not into judgment with Thy servant. Spare *him* whom Thou hast redeemed with Thy most precious Blood. Deliver *him* from all evil, for whose sake Thou didst suffer all evil. From the crafts and assaults of the devil, from the fear of death, and from death eternal, good LORD, deliver *him*.

401. Count not against *him*, O LORD, the errors of *his* youth, nor the sins and shortcomings of *his* after years, but strengthen *him* in *his* agony. Let not *his* faith waver, nor *his* hope fail, nor *his* love grow cold. Let the enemy have no advantage over *him*, O LORD; but let *him* die in peace, and rest in hope, and rise in glory.

402. Let *his* portion be with Abraham, Isaac, and Jacob, with David, the man after GOD'S own heart, and with holy Job, with the Prophets, and Apostles, with the Martyrs and all the holy Saints, in the arms of CHRIST, in the bosom of happiness, in the kingdom of GOD for ever and ever. Amen.

In the Name of a Dying Person.

403. O LORD JESU, SON of GOD made Flesh, Who hast vouchsafed for our salvation to be born in a manger, to live in poverty, to suffer toil and want, and to die by the pangs of the Cross; say, I beseech Thee, to Thy Divine FATHER at the moment of my death, "FATHER, forgive *him*;" say to Thy beloved Mother, "Behold thy son;" say unto my soul, "To-day shalt thou be with Me in Paradise." My GOD, my GOD, forsake me not in that hour. "I thirst," yea, my GOD, my soul thirsteth for Thee Who art the Fountain of living waters.

My life passeth away like a shadow, yet a little while and all things shall come to an end; wherefore, O my adorable SAVIOUR, from this moment unto all eternity, "Into Thy hands I commend my spirit," LORD JESU, receive my soul. Amen.

Sarum Blessing.

404. GOD the FATHER bless thee, Who created all things in the beginning; the SON of GOD heal thee; the HOLY GHOST enlighten thee, guard thy body, save thy soul, direct thy thoughts, and bring thee safe to the heavenly country; Who liveth and reigneth GOD, in a perfect Trinity throughout all ages.

Prayers on the Passion.
(*For use with Harmony*, pp. 120—129.)

405. [A.] We believe, O LORD JESU CHRIST, that Thou didst toil for us sinners in the groans of Thine Agony, and we therefore pray Thee that the wondrous example of Thy patience may avail for the profit of our souls, and that we may so wash our bed and water our couch with our tears, that, sharing in Thy Passion, we may share also in Thy glory. Who.

406. O merciful JESU, have pity upon us sinners. O JESU, deliver us. O JESU, be gracious unto us. O JESU, help us, and grant that we may be joined to the ranks of Thine elect. O JESU, SAVIOUR of all who hope in Thee, believe in Thee, and love Thee, Thou Who art the Refuge of all who trust in Thee with their whole heart, have mercy upon us, O JESU, Who art the Propitiation for our sins. And Who.

407. [B.] O CHRIST, SON of GOD, Who without sin wast delivered unto death, and caught in the snare of the hunters; grant that through Thine unmerited death the death which we merit may be overcome, that Thou, Who, though innocent, wast given up for us, may-

est through the gift of innocency make us come at length in blessedness to Thee. Who.

408. O most loving JESU, Who didst create us and redeem us by Thy Blood, Who madest us out of nothing, and didst restore us when lost, suffer us not to fall into the pains of eternal death. Let not our sins destroy us whom Thy mercy hath made partakers of Thy heavenly grace. Look, O LORD, on that in us which is Thine, take from us all that is our own. Who.

409. [C.] O JESU, our GOD, Who gavest Thy cheek to the smiters, and wast overwhelmed with reproach for us; grant unto us Thy miserable servants that, taught by the example of Thy Passion, we may be enabled to bear Thy light yoke, and learning from Thee how meek and lowly Thou art, may so share in Thy sufferings that in Thee we may obtain the gift of everlasting blessedness. Where Thou.

410. O CHRIST JESU, pour Thy grace upon us; bestow on us a true and lively hope; give us of the fount of Thy grace, and grant us love, purity, and lowliness, and patience in all trouble and distress. Make us to love Thee with all our hearts, and so truly and without deceit or guile to glory in Thee, that we may draw all our pleasure and all our joy from Thee alone. Who.

411. [D.] O GOD, SON of GOD, Who lovedst them who hated Thee, and sparedst them who demanded Thy death, Who wast gracious and merciful to Thy persecutors; grant that our offences may be atoned for by the wounds of Thy Passion, that Thou, Who in Thy humility didst suffer death, mayest in Thy glory bestow on us everlasting light. Where.

412. O CHRIST, O SON of GOD, Whom Thy FATHER delivered up for us all when He accepted Thee as the true Oblation for us; hearken to the prayers of Thy people, save those whom Thou hast purchased, quicken those whom Thou hast freed, suffer not to go into everlasting mourning those whom Thou didst come to redeem lest they should perish eternally. Thou Who didst endure the Cross for us, pierce our hearts with the nails of Thy fear, that here we may obtain remission of our sins, and in the world to come eternal joy, through Thee Whom we believe to have been crucified for all, and Who livest.

413. [E.] O most merciful LORD JESU CHRIST, Very GOD, full of lovingkindness and truth, have pity on us according to the multitude of Thy mercies. We pray Thee, by Thy most Precious Blood which Thou didst shed upon the altar of the Cross for us miserable sinners, take away our sins, and turn not Thyself from us, who, though unworthy, humbly entreat Thee, and call for mercy upon Thy most holy Name.

414. O CHRIST, GOD of our salvation, Who by Thy Passion quenchest our passions; grant to us Thy servants, O LORD JESU CHRIST, confessing our transgressions and iniquities, pardon for our offences, and remission of our sins, that we may obtain eternal life from Thy hands. Who.

415. [F.] O JESU, most loving Fountain of life and mercy, by that sentence of death pronounced against Thee by Pilate, to which Thou didst willingly submit for us, condemn us not, we pray Thee, in the day of judgment to eternal death. Through Thy mercy.

416. O CHRIST, Only-begotten SON of the Unbegotten FATHER, the innocent One, Who wast slain by wicked men, remember the price of Thy Blood, and blot out the sins of all Thy people. Thou Who didst vouchsafe for us to bear spitting, reproaches, bonds, smitings, blows, and scourgings, the Cross, the nails, the bitter draught, death, the spear, and burial at the last; grant to us miserable sinners, for whom Thou didst suffer all these, the infinite bliss of the kingdom of heaven, that we, who humbly adore Thy Passion, may be raised to heavenly blessings through the gladness of Thy Resurrection. Who.

417. [G.] O LORD JESU CHRIST, write Thy wounds upon our hearts in Thy most precious Blood, that in them we may read Thy sorrow and Thy love, so as to bear cheerfully for Thee all earthly troubles and adversities. Make us, we pray Thee, to share in Thy holy Passion and most bitter pain, which Thou barest in Thy sore and long hanging upon the Cross, when Thy blessed hands were nailed by wicked men, and Thy sacred feet fastened to the cruel tree. There too Thy whole Body was so strained that all Thy bones might be numbered, and when Thou didst yield up Thy most holy Spirit, Thy side was so pierced with the soldier's spear that blood and water flowed thereout for the redemption of the world. By those Thy sufferings, deliver us, Thy guilty servants, from everlasting death, and remember us, Thou Who hast come into Thy kingdom, and Who livest.

418. [H.] O LORD JESU CHRIST, Who wast given up for us unto death, wast hung upon the Cross, and didst drink the cup of vinegar and gall; hear the sighs of Thy servants; grant Thy help in their distress, and let Thy holy Name ever be marked upon us. Who.

419. O LORD JESU CHRIST, we adore Thee hanging upon the Cross, wearing the crown of thorns upon Thy Head. We pray Thee that Thy Cross may save us from the destroying Angel.

420. O LORD JESU CHRIST, we adore Thee wounded upon the Cross, and given vinegar and gall to drink ; we pray Thee that Thy wounds may be the healing of our souls.

421. [I.] O LORD JESU CHRIST, we beseech Thee by the bitterness of Thy Passion which Thou didst endure in the hour of death, especially when Thy most holy Soul departed from Thy blessed Body, have mercy upon our souls in their departure from our bodies, and lead them unto eternal life.

422. O LORD JESU CHRIST, we adore Thee laid in the tomb and embalmed with myrrh and spices. We pray Thee that Thy death may be our life.

423. O LORD JESU CHRIST, we adore Thee descending into hell, and preaching the glad tidings of redemption to the prisoners of hope. Grant that when we depart this life we may enter with Thy faithful into the paradise of rest.

424. O LORD JESU CHRIST, we adore Thee rising again from death, ascending into heaven, and sitting on the right hand of the FATHER. We pray Thee that we may follow Thee thither, and stand before Thy Face.

425. O LORD JESU CHRIST, Good Shepherd, preserve the righteous, justify sinners, have mercy upon all the faithful, and be gracious unto us miserable and unworthy sinners. Amen.

For Future Happiness.

426. O merciful LORD JESU CHRIST, Who didst redeem us with Thy precious Blood ; have mercy upon the soul of this Thy servant in this hour of *his* departure, and graciously bring *him* to the joyful dwellings of Paradise, that *he* may there love Thee with that unspeakable love which can never be separated from Thee and Thine elect. Who livest.

For a Happy Death.

427. O LORD JESU CHRIST, Who by Thy death didst take away the sting of death ; grant unto us Thy servants so to follow in faith where Thou hast led the way, that we may at length fall asleep peacefully in Thee, and awaking up after Thy likeness, may be satisfied with it. Through Thy mercy. Who livest.

Prayer of Commendation.

428. O GOD, FATHER of mercies, and GOD of all consolation, Who willest not that any that trusteth and hopeth in Thee should perish ; graciously look upon Thy servant, whom true faith and Christian hope commend unto Thee. Visit *him* with Thy salvation, and, through the Passion and Death of Thine Only-begotten SON, mercifully grant unto *him* pardon and remission of all *his* sins, that *his* soul in the hour of *his* departure may find Thee a pitying Judge, and washed from all spot in the Blood of JESUS CHRIST, may pass into eternal life. Through.

429. Into Thy merciful hands, O LORD, we commend the soul of this Thy servant now departing from the body ; acknowledge, we meekly beseech Thee, a work of Thine hands, a sheep of Thine own fold, a lamb of Thine own flock, a sinner of Thine own redeeming. Receive *him* into the blessed arms of Thine unspeakable mercy, into the sacred rest of Thine everlasting peace, and into the glorious estate of Thy chosen saints in heaven.

GOD the FATHER, Who hath created thee ; GOD the SON, Who hath redeemed thee ; GOD the HOLY GHOST, Who hath poured down His grace upon thee ; be now and evermore thy defence, assist thee in this thy last trial, and bring thee into the way of everlasting life. Amen.

CHRIST, Who redeemed thee with His Agony and bloody Death, have mercy upon thee, and strengthen thee in this agony of death. Amen.

CHRIST JESUS, Who rose the third day from death, raise up thy body again in the resurrection of the just. Amen.

CHRIST, Who ascended into heaven, and now sitteth on the right hand of GOD, bring thee unto the place of eternal happiness and joy. Amen.

GOD the FATHER preserve and keep thee. GOD the SON assist and strengthen thee. GOD the HOLY GHOST defend and aid thee. GOD the Holy Trinity be ever with thee, that thy death may be precious in the sight of the LORD, with Whom thou shalt live for ever. Amen.

To be repeated until the Soul be departed.

Turn unto Thy rest, O my soul, for the LORD hath upholden thee.

O Blessed LORD, Who scourgest every son whom Thou receivest, let me not be weary of Thy correction.

From death to life; from sorrow to joy: from a vale of misery to a Paradise of mercy.

O CHRIST, Who didst suffer so grievously, and then enteredst into Thy glory, make me to suffer with Thee, that I may also be glorified with Thee.

I know that my Redeemer liveth, and that I shall be raised again at the last day.

I shall walk before the LORD in the land of the living.

O JESU, Who didst die upon the Cross for me, may that bitter death of Thine sweeten the bitterness of mine.

Into Thy hands I commend my spirit, for Thou hast redeemed me, O LORD, Thou GOD of truth.

Make me to be numbered with Thy saints in glory everlasting.

O receive me into that place of rest where all tears shall be wiped from my eyes, where there shall be no more death, nor sorrow, nor crying, nor pain.

O take me where I may ever behold Thy face, and follow the Lamb whithersoever He goeth.

O LORD, in Thee is my trust: O cast not out my soul.

O LORD, let it be Thy pleasure to deliver me: make haste, O LORD, to help me.

Thou art my Helper and my Redeemer; O LORD, make no long tarrying.

Come, LORD JESU, come quickly.

LORD JESU, receive my spirit.

When the Soul has departed.

O Thou Lamb of GOD, that takest away the sins of the world: Grant *him* Thy peace.

430. O LORD, with Whom do live the spirits of them that die, and by Whom the souls of Thy servants, after they are delivered from the burden of the flesh are in joy and felicity; we most humbly beseech Thee for this Thy servant, that having received forgiveness of all *his* sins which *he* hath committed in this world, *he* may escape the gates of hell, and the pains of eternal darkness; that *he* may for ever dwell with Abraham, Isaac, and Jacob in the region of light and Thy blessed Presence, where there is neither weeping nor heaviness; and that when the dreadful day of the general judgment shall come, *he* may rise again with the just, and receive this dead body, which must now be buried in the earth, to be joined with *his* soul, and be made pure and incorruptible for ever after in Thy glorious kingdom. For the merits.

431. O LORD, receive the soul of Thy servant, which Thou hast been pleased to call out of the prison of this world; deliver it from the place of punishment, and grant that it may enjoy the blessedness of everlasting rest and light with Thine elect saints in the glory of the Resurrection. Through.

On the Death of a Child.

432. O LORD JESU CHRIST, Who takest the righteous away from the evil to come, and hast been pleased to call a child from this family unto Thyself; comfort, we beseech Thee, the hearts of *his* parents; and as Thou gavest Thy beloved disciple to console Thy Blessed Mother when she stood by Thy Cross, so now grant that these mourners may be consoled by the ministry of Thy holy Word. Who livest.

For the Repose and Blessedness of the Departed.

433. Absolve, O LORD, we beseech Thee, the soul of Thy servant, that dead unto the world it may live unto Thee, and whatsoever sins it hath committed through the weakness of the flesh in this mortal life, wash away by the pardon of Thy merciful love. Through.

434. O GOD, the Bestower of pardon, Who desirest the salvation of mankind; we beseech Thy mercy that Thou wouldst cause the soul of Thy servant departed from this world to attain with all Thy saints to fellowship in everlasting blessedness. Through.

435. Bow down Thine ear, O LORD, to our prayers with which we suppliantly entreat Thy mercy, that Thou wouldst place in the abode of peace and light the soul of Thy servant, which Thou hast caused to depart from this world, and unite it to the fellowship of Thy saints. Through.

436. O LORD JESU CHRIST, Who by Thy death broughtest help unto the dead; mercifully hear our prayers for the faithful departed, and grant that we may obtain salvation for ourselves and rest for them, so that the faith by which we and they alike believe in Thee may justify us from our sins and deliver them from all tribulation. Through Thy mercy, O our GOD, Who art blessed and livest.

437. O GOD, perfect Love and loving Truth, unwearied in goodness and mercy, Who willest to save us from death, and madest our LORD JESUS CHRIST to undergo death that His descent into hell might be our ascension into heaven; we humbly entreat Thee that, granting pardon of all *his* sins to Thy servant whom Thou hast called from the toils and pilgrimage of this world, Thou wouldst place *his* soul in Abraham's bosom. Through the same.

For the Coming of Christ's Kingdom.

438. O LORD JESU CHRIST, Who hast promised to come again in like manner as Thou didst go into heaven; we pray Thee to hasten the time of Thine Advent, that sin and death may be overcome, and that we, with all Thy faithful departed, may be perfected in blessedness in that day when Thou makest up Thy jewels. Through Thy mercy, O our GOD, Who art blessed and livest.

HYMNS FOR THE SICK.

I.

Jesu! The very thought is sweet!
In that dear Name all heart-joys meet!
But O than honey sweeter far
The glimpses of His Presence are.

No word is sung more sweet than this:
No name is heard more full of bliss:
No thought brings sweeter comfort nigh,
Than Jesus, Son of God most high.

Jesu! the Hope of souls forlorn!
How good to them for sin that mourn!
To them that seek Thee, O how kind!
But what art Thou to them that find?

Jesu, Thou sweetness, pure and blest,
Truth's Fountain, Light of souls dis-
    tressed,
Surpassing all that heart requires,
Exceeding all that soul desires!

No tongue of mortal can express,
No letters write its blessedness:
Alone who hath thee in his heart
Knows, Love of Jesus! what thou art.

I seek for Jesus in repose,
When round my heart its chambers close:
Abroad, and when I shut the door,
I long for Jesus evermore.

With Mary in the morning gloom,
I seek for Jesus at the tomb;
For Him, with Love's most earnest cry,
I seek with heart, and not with eye.

Jesus, to God the Father gone,
Is seated on the Heavenly Throne:
My heart hath also passed from me,
That where He is, there *it* may be.

We follow Jesus now, and raise
The voice of prayer, the hymn of praise,
That He at last may make us meet
With Him to gain the Heavenly Seat.
                    Amen.

II.

Art thou weary, art thou languid,
    Art thou sore distressed?
"Come to Me," saith One, "and coming,
        Be at rest!"

Hath He marks to lead me to Him,
    If He be my Guide?
"In His Feet and Hands are Wound-
    prints
        And His Side."

Is there Diadem as Monarch,
    That His Brow adorns?
"Yea, a Crown in very surety,
        But of Thorns!"

If I find Him, if I follow,
    What His guerdon here?
"Many a sorrow, many a labour,
        Many a tear."

If I still hold closely to Him,
    What hath He at last?
"Sorrow vanquished, labour ended,
        Jordan passed!"

If I ask Him to receive me,
    Will He say me nay?
"Not till earth, and not till heaven
        Pass away!"

Finding, following, keeping, struggling,
    Is He sure to bless?
"Angels, Martyrs, Prophets, Virgins,
        Answer, Yes!"

III.

O happy band of pilgrims,
    If onward ye will tread
With Jesus as your Fellow,
    To Jesus as your Head!

O happy if ye labour
    As Jesus did for men:
O happy, if ye hunger
    As Jesus hungered then!

The Cross that Jesus carried
    He carried as your due:
The Crown that Jesus weareth
    He weareth it for you.

The faith by which ye see Him,
    The hope in which ye yearn,
The love that through all trouble
    To Him alone will turn,—

What are they but forerunners
    To lead you to His sight;
What are they save the effluence
    Of uncreated Light?

The trials that beset you,
    The sorrows ye endure,
The manifold temptations
    That death alone can cure,—

What are they but His jewels,
    Of right celestial worth?
What are they but the ladder
    Set up to heaven on earth?

O happy band of pilgrims,
    Look upward to the skies,
Where such a light affliction
    Shall win you such a prize.

IV.

JESU, Name all names above,
  JESU, best and dearest,
JESU, Fount of perfect love ;
  Holiest, tenderest, nearest;
JESU, Source of grace completest,
JESU, purest, JESU sweetest,
  JESU, well of power Divine,
  Make me, keep me, seal me Thine !

JESU, open me the gate
  That of old he entered,
Who, in that most lost estate,
  Wholly on Thee ventured ;
Thou Whose wounds are ever pleading,
And Thy Passion interceding,
  From my misery let me rise
  To a Home in Paradise !

Thou didst call the Prodigal,
  Thou didst pardon Mary :
Thou Whose words can never fail,
  Love can never vary ;
LORD, to heal my lost condition,
Give—for Thou canst give—contrition;
  Thou canst pardon all mine ill,
  If Thou wilt : O say, "I will !"

Woe, that I have turned aside,
  After fleshly pleasure !
Woe, that I have never tried
  For the Heavenly Treasure !
Treasure, safe in Homes supernal ;
Incorruptible, eternal !
  Treasure no less price hath won
  Than the Passion of the SON !

JESU, crowned with thorns for me,
  Scourged for my transgression,
Witnessing through agony,
  That Thy good confession !
JESU, clad in purple raiment,
For my evils making payment :
  Let not all Thy woe and pain,
  Let not Calvary, be in vain !

When I reach death's bitter sea,
  And its waves roll higher,
Help the more forsaking me
  As the storm grows nigher :
JESU, leave me not to languish,
Helpless, hopeless, full of anguish !
  Tell me—"Verily I say,
  Thou shalt be with Me to-day !"

V.

Rock of Ages, cleft for me,
Let me hide myself in Thee :
Let the Water and the Blood,
From Thy riven side which flowed,
Be of sin the double cure,
Cleanse me from its guilt and power.

Not the labours of my hands,
Can fulfil Thy law's demands ;
Could my zeal no respite know,
Could my tears for ever flow,
All for sin could not atone ;
Thou must save, and Thou alone.

Nothing in my hand I bring,
Only to Thy Cross I cling ;
Naked, come to Thee for dress ;
Helpless, look to Thee for grace ;
Vile, to David's fountain fly :
Cleanse me, SAVIOUR, or I die.

While I draw this fleeting breath,
When mine eye-strings break in death,
When I soar through tracts unknown,—
See Thee on Thy Judgment-throne,
Rock of Ages, cleft for me,
Let me hide myself in Thee. Amen.

VI.

JESU, Lover of my soul,
  Let me to Thy bosom fly,
While the nearer waters roll,
  While the tempest still is high :
Hide me, O my SAVIOUR, hide,
  Till the storm of life is past ;
Safe into the haven guide ;
  O receive my soul at last !

Other refuge have I none ;
  Hangs my helpless soul on Thee :
Leave, ah ! leave me not alone,
  Still support and comfort me :
All my trust on Thee is stayed ;
  All my help from Thee I bring;
Cover my defenceless head
  With the shadow of Thy wing.

Plenteous grace with Thee is found,
  Grace to cover all my sin :
Let the healing streams abound,
  Make and keep me pure within.
Thou of Life the Fountain art,
  Freely let me take of Thee ;
Spring Thou up within my heart,
  Rise to all eternity. Amen.

VII.

Let every faithful heart rejoice,
And render thanks to GOD on high :
And with each power of soul and voice
Extol His praises worthily.

Into this dark world JESUS came,
And all men might His Form behold;
While to the limits of the same
He passed, that we might be consoled.

To all He showed that gentle Face ;
On good and bad alike it shone :
Its perfect loveliness and grace
The LORD of all concealed from none.

O love of CHRIST beyond all love !
O clemency beyond all thought !
O grace all praise of men above,
Whereby such gifts to men are brought !

O Blessed Face, Whose praise we sing !
Here in the Way we worship Thee :
That in the Country of our King
Filled with Thy glory we may be !

To GOD on High be glory meet !
Equal to Thee, Eternal SON !
Equal to Thee, Blest PARACLETE,
While never-ending ages run ! Amen.

VIII.

Sweet the moments, rich in blessing,
  Which before the Cross I spend,
Life, and death, and peace possessing,
  From the sinner's dying Friend.

Here I rest, for ever viewing
  Mercy poured in streams of Blood;
Precious drops, my soul bedewing,
  Plead and claim my peace with God.

Truly blessed is the station,
  Low before His Cross to lie,
While I see Divine compassion
  Floating in His languid eye.

Love and grief my heart dividing,
  With my tears His feet I'll bathe,
Constant still in faith abiding,
  Life deriving from His death.

IX.

Sun of my soul, Thou Saviour dear,
It is not night if Thou be near;
O may no earth-born cloud arise
To hide Thee from Thy servant's eyes.

When the soft dews of kindly sleep
My weary eyelids gently steep,
Be my last thought, how sweet to rest
For ever on my Saviour's breast.

Abide with me from morn till eve,
For without Thee I cannot live;
Abide with me when night is nigh,
For without Thee I dare not die.

If some poor wandering child of Thine
Have spurned to-day the voice divine,
Now, Lord, the gracious work begin;
Let him no more lie down in sin.

Watch by the sick; enrich the poor
With blessings from Thy boundless store;
Be every mourner's sleep to-night,
Like infant's slumbers, pure and light.

Come near and bless us when we wake,
Ere through the world our way we take;
Till in the ocean of Thy love
We lose ourselves in heaven above.
           Amen.

X.

O come and mourn with me awhile,
See, Mary calls us to her side;
O come and let us mourn with her:
Jesus, our Love, is Crucified!

Have we no tears to shed for Him,
While soldiers scoff and Jews deride?
Ah! look how patiently He hangs:
Jesus, our Love, is Crucified!

How fast His hands and feet are nailed,
His blessèd tongue with thirst is tied!
His failing eyes are blind with blood:
Jesus, our Love, is Crucified!

His Mother cannot reach His Face;
She stands in helplessness beside;
Her heart is martyred with her Son's:
Jesus, our Love, is Crucified!

Seven times He spoke, Seven Words of
  Love;
And all three hours His silence cried
For mercy on the souls of men:
Jesus, our Love, is Crucified!

Death came, and Jesus meekly bowed:
His failing eyes He strove to guide
With mindful love to Mary's face:
Jesus, our Love, is Crucified!

O break! O break, hard heart of mine!
Thy weak self-love and guilty pride
His Pilate and His Judas were:
Jesus, our Love, is Crucified!

Come, take thy stand beneath the Cross,
And let the blood from out that side
Fall gently on thee, drop by drop:
Jesus, our Love, is Crucified!

A broken heart, a fount of tears,
Ask, and they will not be denied;
A broken heart love's cradle is:
Jesus, our Love, is Crucified!

O love of God! O sin of man!
In this dread act your strength is tried;
And victory remains with love:
Jesus, our Love, is Crucified!

XI.

Saviour, when in dust to Thee
Low we bow the adoring knee;
When, repentant, to the skies
Scarce we lift our weeping eyes;
O by all Thy pains and woe
Suffered once for man below,
Bending from Thy throne on high,
Hear our solemn Litany!

By Thy helpless infant years,
By Thy life of want and tears,
By Thy days of sore distress
In the savage wilderness;
By the dread mysterious hour
Of the insulting tempter's power,
Turn, O turn a favouring eye,
Hear our solemn Litany!

By the sacred grief that wept
O'er the grave where Lazarus slept;
By the boding tears that flowed
Over Salem's loved abode;
By the anguished sigh that told
Treachery lurked within Thy fold;
From Thy seat above the sky,
Hear our solemn Litany!

By Thine hour of dire despair;
By Thine agony of prayer;
By the Cross, the nail, the thorn,
Piercing spear, and torturing scorn;
By the gloom that veiled the skies
O'er the dreadful Sacrifice;
Listen to our humble cry,
Hear our solemn Litany!

By Thy deep expiring groan;
By the sad sepulchral stone;
By the vault, whose dark abode
Held in vain the rising God:
O from earth to heaven restored,
Mighty re-ascended Lord,
Listen, listen to the cry
Of our solemn Litany!   Amen.

XII.

Christ, of the Holy Angels Light and
   gladness,
Maker and Saviour of the human race,
O may we reach the world unknown to
   sadness,
       And see Thy Face.

Angel of peace, may Michael to our
   dwelling
Down from high heaven in mighty
   calmness come,
Breathing all peace, and hideous war
   dispelling
       To hell's dark gloom.

Angel of might, may Gabriel swift descending
Far from our gates our ancient foe
   repel,
And, as of old, o'er Zacharias bending,
       In temples dwell.

Angel of health, may Raphael lighten
   o'er us,
To every sick bed speed his healing
   flight,
In deeds of doubt direct the way before
   us,
       Guide us aright.

Mary, the harbinger of peace supernal,
   Mother of God, with all the Angel
   train,
All Saints be with us, till the bliss eternal
       In Christ we gain.

Be this by Thy thrice Holy Godhead
   granted,
   Father, and Son, and Spirit ever
   blest:
Whose glory by the Angel host is chanted,
       By all confess'd.   Amen.

XIII.

Loving Shepherd, kind and true,   ·
   Wilt Thou not in pity come
To Thy lamb? As shepherds do,
   Bear me in Thy bosom home;
Take me hence from earth's annoy
To Thy home of endless joy.

See how I have gone astray
   In this earthly wilderness;   ·
Come and take me soon away
   To Thy flock who dwell in bliss,
And Thy glory, Lord, behold,
Safe within Thy heavenly fold.

For I fain would gaze on Thee,
   With the lambs to whom 'tis given
That they feed, from danger free,
   In the happy fields of heaven;
Praising Thee, all terrors o'er,
Never can they wander more.

Here I live in sore distress,
   Fearing, watching, hour by hour;
For my foes around me press,
   And I know their craft and power:
Lord, Thy lamb can never be
Safe one moment, but with Thee.

O Lord Jesu, let me not
   'Mid the ravening wolves e'er fall,
Help me as a shepherd ought,
   That I may escape them all:
Bear me homeward in Thy breast,
To Thy fold of endless rest.

XIV.

Sweet Saviour, bless us ere we go;
   Thy Word into our minds instil;
And make our lukewarm hearts to glow
   With lowly love and fervent will.
Through life's long day and death's dark
   night,
O gentle Jesu, be our Light.

The day is gone, its hours have run,
   And Thou hast taken count of all,
The scanty triumphs grace hath won,
   The broken vow, the frequent fall.
Through life's long day and death's dark
   night,
O gentle Jesu, be our Light.

Grant us, dear Lord, from evil ways
   True absolution and release;
And bless us more than in past days,
   With purity and inward peace.
Through life's long day and death's dark
   night,
O gentle Jesu, be our Light.

Do more than pardon; give us joy,
   Sweet fear, and sober liberty,
And simple hearts without alloy
   That only long to be like Thee.
Through life's long day and death's dark
   night,
O gentle Jesu, be our Light.

Labour is sweet, for Thou hast toiled;
   And care is light, for Thou hast cared;
Ah! never let our work be soiled
   With strife, or by deceit ensnared.
Through life's long day and death's dark
   night,
O gentle Jesu, be our Light.

For all we love, the poor, the sad,
   The sinful, unto Thee we call;
O let Thy mercy make us glad;
   Thou art our Jesus, and our All.
Through life's long day and death's dark
   night,
O gentle Jesu, be our Light.   Amen.

XV.

There is a fountain filled with blood,
  Drawn from Immanuel's veins ;
And sinners, plunged beneath that flood,
  Lose all their guilty stains.

The dying thief rejoiced to see
  That fountain in his day :
And there would I, as vile as he,
  Wash all my sins away.

Blest dying Lamb ! Thy precious Blood
  Shall never lose its power,
Till all the ransomed Church of God
  Be saved, to sin no more.

E'er since by faith I saw the stream
  Thy flowing wounds supply,
Redeeming love has been my theme,
  And shall be till I die.

Then in a nobler, sweeter song
  I'll sing Thy power to save ;
When this poor lisping, mortal tongue
  Lies silent in the grave.

XVI.

When I survey the wondrous Cross,
  On which the Prince of glory died,
My richest gain I count but loss,
  And pour contempt on all my pride.

Forbid it, Lord, that I should boast,
  Save in the Cross of Christ my God ;
All the vain things that charm me most,
  I sacrifice them to His Blood.

See from His Head, His Hands, His Feet,
  Sorrow and love flow mingling down ;
Did e'er such love and sorrow meet,
  Or thorns compose so rich a crown ?

Were the whole realm of nature mine,
  That were an offering far too small ;
Love so amazing, so divine,
  Demands my life, my soul, my all.

To Christ, Who won for sinners grace
  By bitter grief and anguish sore,
Be praise from all the ransomed race,
  For ever and for evermore. Amen.

XVII.

When our heads are bowed with woe,
When the bitter tears o'erflow,
When we mourn in sorrow drear,
Jesu, Son of Mary, hear.

Thou our throbbing flesh hast worn,
Thou our mortal griefs hast borne,
Thou hast shed the human tear,
Jesu, Son of Mary, hear.

When the sullen death-bell tolls
For our own departed souls ;
When our final doom is near,
Jesu, Son of Mary, hear.

Thou hast bowed the dying Head,
Thou the Blood of Life hast shed,
Thou hast filled a mortal bier,
Jesu, Son of Mary, hear.

When the heart is sad within
With the sense of all its sin,
When the spirit sinks in fear,
Jesu, Son of Mary, hear.

Thou the shame and grief hast known,
Though the sins were not Thine own,
Thou hast deigned their load to bear,
Jesu, Son of Mary, hear.

XVIII.

There is a stream, whose waters rise
Amidst the hills of Paradise,
Where foot of man hath never trod,
Proceeding from the throne of God :
Oh, give me sickness here, or strife,
So I may reach that spring of life !

There is a Rock that, nigh at hand,
Gives shadow in a weary land ;
Who in that Stricken Rock hath rest,
Finds waters gushing from its breast ;
Oh, grant me, when this scene is o'er,
Their lot who thirst not any more.

There is a people, who have cast
The strife and toil away at last ;
On whom—so calm their rest and sweet-
The sun lights not, nor any heat ;
Give me with them at length to be,
And send me here what pleaseth Thee !

O Thou, Who camest Death to spoil,
And barest weariness and toil ;
And just before his chains were burst,
Fulfilling Scripture, saidst, " I thirst !"
Who call'st Thy weary servants o'er
The same rough road Thou trodd'st be
  fore ;

Thou only Good ! Thou only Wise !
Who dost so lovingly chastise,
To give more strength, and add mor
  grace,—
Grant me Thy Spirit to embrace,
The more,—the more that nature faints,-
The glorious portion of all Saints !

Thou wouldst not, Lord, ascend to reig
But first on earth Thou suffered'st pain
And now, O Father, at Thy side
For us He pleads, for us Who died ;
Shading from storm, and blast, and hea
With that Eternal Paraclete !

XIX.

Why marvelling though the clouds t
  black,
  The path be rough to tread ?
Why thus impatient for a track
  Of pleasure in its stead ?

His Path, on Whom we fix our eye,
  Was never strewn with flowers :

How can we think on Calvary,
  And give one thought to ours?

And was the Cross so soft a bed,
  The Reed so fair a gem,
The Crown of Thorns that wreathed His
      Head,
  So bright a diadem?

Oh, who could bear to dwell at ease,
  Rememb'ring what He bore !
Oh, who would sigh for what might please,
  When He was tried so sore ?

The Cross was borne by all the rest
  Of His Elected Seed:
They clasped it bravely to their breast,—
  And why should we be freed ?

Yea, in Thy Mercy, not Thy wrath,
  Our trials Thou dost send ;
Lest if we should not tread their path,
  We might not share its end.

Praise in the Church's highest strain,
  To God the FATHER be :
And to the LAMB that once was slain,
  And HOLY GHOST, to Thee !

XX.

Thou only Refuge from the heat,
Thou only Rock wherein to hide,
Thou only Shade when tempests beat,
The Suffering, the Crucified !
Captain of our Salvation, that couldst be
Made perfect only through Thine Agony.

  My sin is great,—my pain is sore,—
  My strength is gone,—my spirit fails ;—
  For me the Cross Thy great Love bore,
  For me the Scourge, for me the Nails ;
For me the Crown around Thy Temples
      set,
For me the Agony and Bloody Sweat ;

  Oh, while I tread these hard rough ways,
  Ways smooth to *Thy* way,—lead mine
      eye
  With holy yet with steadfast gaze
  Into Thy Passion's Sanctuary ;
Thy Wounds my cure,—my more than
      trust art Thou ;
Hadst Thou not borne them, where had I
      been now ?

  Hear me, and save me when I call,
  By all those woes now passed away,
  Thy precious Death and Burial,
  Thy Resurrection the third day ;
Thy triumph over death and all his host ;
And by the coming of the HOLY GHOST.

  LORD, if Thou wilt, Thou canst for-
      give,
  Speak the word only ; set me free
  From sin, that so my soul may live,
  From suffering,—if it pleaseth Thee !
Or make Thou here whate'er Thou wilt
      my part,
If there I may but see Thee as Thou art.

XXI.

JESUS lives ! no longer now
  Can thy terrors, Death, appal us ;
JESUS lives ! by this we know
  Thou, O Grave, canst not enthral us.
              Alleluia !

JESUS lives ! henceforth is death
  But the gate of Life immortal ;
This shall calm our trembling breath,
  When we pass its gloomy portal.
              Alleluia !

JESUS lives ! for us He died ;
  Then, alone to JESUS living,
Pure in heart may we abide,
  Glory to our SAVIOUR giving.
              Alleluia !

JESUS lives ! for us He died ;
  Nought from us His love shall sever ;
Life, nor death, nor powers of hell
  Tear us from His keeping ever.
              Alleluia !

JESUS lives ! to Him the Throne
  Over all the world is given :
May we go where He is gone,
  Rest and reign with Him in Heaven.
              Alleluia !   Amen.

XXII.

JESU, my LORD, my GOD, my all,
Hear me, blest SAVIOUR, when I call !
Hear me, and from Thy dwelling place
Pour down the riches of Thy grace ;
  JESU, my LORD, I Thee adore,
  O make me love Thee more and more.

JESU, too late I Thee have sought,
How can I love Thee as I ought ?
And how extol Thy matchless fame,
The glorious beauty of Thy Name ?
  JESU, my LORD, &c.

JESU, what didst Thou find in me,
That Thou didst deal so lovingly ?
How great the joy that Thou hast brought,
So far exceeding hope or thought !
  JESU, my LORD, &c.

JESU, of Thee shall be my song,
To Thee my heart and soul belong ;
All that I am or have is Thine,
And Thou, blest SAVIOUR, Thou art mine.
  JESU, my LORD, I Thee adore,
  O make me love Thee more and more.
              Amen.

XXIII.

Abide with me ; fast falls the even-tide :
The darkness deepens ; LORD, with me
    abide ;
When other helpers fail, and comforts flee,
Help of the helpless, O abide with me.

Swift to its close ebbs out life's little day;
Earth's joys grow dim, its glories pass
  away;
Change and decay in all around I see:
O Thou Who changest not, abide with me.

I need Thy presence every passing hour;
What but Thy grace can foil the Tempter's
  power?
Who like Thyself my guide and stay can
  be?
Through cloud and sunshine, Lord, abide
  with me.

I fear no foe with Thee at hand to bless;
Ills have no weight, and tears no bitter-
  ness;
Where is death's sting? where, grave, thy
  victory?
I triumph still, if Thou abide with me.

Hold Thou Thy Cross before my closing
  eyes;
Shine through the gloom, and point me
  to the skies;
Heaven's morning breaks, and earth's
  vain shadows flee;
In life, in death, O Lord, abide with me.
                    Amen.

XXIV.

O how soft that bed must be,
Made in sickness, Lord, by Thee;
And that rest,—how calm, how sweet—
Where Jesus and the sufferer meet!

It was the Good Physician now,
Soothed my cheek and chafed my brow;
Whispering, as He raised my head,
"It is I, be not afraid."

God of glory, God of grace,
Hear from Heav'n, Thy dwelling-place;
Hear in mercy, and forgive,
Bid Thy child believe and live.

Bless me, and I shall be blest;
Soothe me, and I shall have rest;
Fix my heart, my hopes above,
Love me, Lord, for Thou art Love!

XXV.

O Jesu, in Thy torture,
  Nailed to the bitter tree,
My soul's true Guide and Nurture,
  I yearn to be with Thee.

How can I taste of pleasure,
  Whilst Thou dost hang in pain,
Jesu, mine only treasure,
  Mine everlasting gain?

O Jesu, may Thy sadness,
  Thine agony and tears,
Win for my spirit gladness
  Throughout the endless years.

With Thine Own Body feed me,
  Life to my soul accord,
Then to Thy pierced Heart lead me,
  And hide me there, O Lord.

And in my dying hour,
  By those sharp wounds, I pray,
Lord, may Thy Passion's power
  Wash all my sins away.

XXVI.

Brief life is here our portion;
  Brief sorrow, short-lived care;
The life that knows no ending,
  The tearless life, is *there.*

O happy retribution!
  Short toil, eternal rest:
For mortals and for sinners
  A mansion with the blest.

That we should look, poor wand'rers,
  To have our Home on high!
That worms should seek for dwellings
  Beyond the starry sky!

To all one happy guerdon
  Of one celestial grace;
For all, for all who mourn their fall,
  Is one eternal place:

And martyrdom hath roses
  Upon that heavenly ground;
And white and virgin lilies
  For virgin-souls abound.

There grief is turned to pleasure;
  Such pleasure, as below
No human voice can utter,
  No human heart can know.

And after fleshly scandal,
  And after this world's night,
And after storm and whirlwind,
  Is calm, and joy, and light.

And now we fight the battle,
  But then shall wear the crown
Of full and everlasting
  And passionless renown:

And now we watch and struggle,
  And now we live in hope,
And Sion, in her anguish,
  With Babylon must cope:

But He Whom now we trust in
  Shall then be seen and known,
And they that know and see Him
  Shall have Him for their own.

XXVII.

For thee, O dear dear Country,
  Mine eyes their vigils keep;
For very love, beholding
  Thy happy name, they weep:

The mention of thy glory
  Is unction to the breast,
And medicine in sickness,
  And love, and life, and rest.

O one, O onely Mansion !
  O Paradise of Joy !
Where tears are ever banished,
  And smiles have no alloy ;

Beside thy living waters
  All plants are, great and small,
The cedar of the forest,
  The hyssop of the wall :

With jaspers glow thy bulwarks :
  Thy streets with emeralds blaze ;
The sardius and the topaz
  Unite in thee their rays :

Thine ageless walls are bonded
  With amethyst unpriced :
Thy Saints build up its fabric,
  And the corner-stone is CHRIST.

The Cross is all thy splendour,
  The Crucified thy praise :
His laud and benediction
  Thy ransomed people raise.

XXVIII.

Jerusalem the Golden,
  With milk and honey blest,
Beneath thy contemplation
  Sink heart and voice oppressed :
I know not, O, I know not,
  What social joys are there !,
What radiancy of glory,
  What light beyond compare !

They stand, those halls of Syon,
  Conjubilant with song,
And bright with many an angel,
  And all the martyr-throng :
The Prince is ever in them ;
  The daylight is serene :
The pastures of the blessed
  Are decked in glorious sheen.

There is the throne of David,—
  And there, from care released,
The song of them that triumph,
  The shout of them that feast ;
And they who, with their Leader,
  Have conquered in the fight,
For ever and for ever
  Are clad in robes of white !

XXIX.

Jerusalem the glorious !
  The glory of the Elect !
O dear and future vision
  That eager hearts expect :
Even now by faith I see thee :
  Even here thy walls discern :
To thee my thoughts are kindled,
  And strive and pant and yearn.

O mine, my golden Syon !
  O lovelier far than gold !
With laurel-girt battalions,
  And safe victorious fold !
O sweet and blessed Country,
  Shall I ever see thy face ?
O sweet and blessed Country,
  Shall I ever win thy grace ?
I *have* the hope within me
  To comfort and to bless !
Shall I ever win the prize itself ?
  O tell me, tell me, yes !

Exult, O dust and ashes,
  The LORD shall be thy part :
His only, His for ever,
  Thou shalt be, and thou art !
Exult, O dust and ashes !
  The LORD shall be thy part :
His only, His for ever,
  Thou shalt be, and thou art !

XXX.

JESU, grant me this, I pray,
Ever in Thy Heart to stay :
Let me evermore abide
Hidden in Thy wounded Side.

If the evil one prepare,
Or the world, a tempting snare,
I am safe when I abide
In Thy Heart and wounded Side.

If the flesh, more dangerous still,
Tempt my soul to deeds of ill,
Nought I fear when I abide
In Thy Heart and wounded Side.

Death will come one day to me ;
JESU, cast me not from Thee :
Dying let me still abide
In Thy Heart and wounded Side.
  Amen.

XXXI.

Thee we adore, O hidden SAVIOUR, Thee,
Who in Thy Sacrament dost deign to be ;
Both flesh and spirit at Thy presence fail,
Yet here Thy Presence we devoutly hail.

O blest memorial of our dying LORD,
Who living Bread to men doth here afford,
O may our souls for ever feed on Thee,
And Thou, O CHRIST, for ever precious be.

Fountain of Goodness, JESU, LORD and
  GOD,
Cleanse us, unclean, with Thy most
  cleansing Blood ;
Increase our faith and love, that we may
  know
The hope and peace which from Thy pre-
  sence flow.

O CHRIST, Whom now beneath a veil we
  see,
May what we thirst for soon our portion be,

To gaze on Thee, and see with unveiled
	face
The vision of Thy glory and Thy grace.
					Amen.

XXXII.

Christ, the Light that knows no waning,
	Gives to us His Flesh as food,
Drink He gives us also, deigning
	To refresh us with His Blood.

Christ, Thou radiance ever glowing,
	Who upon the Cross didst bleed,
Light on all Thy Saints bestowing,
	With Thyself Thy flock dost feed.

Flesh, which we are now receiving,
	Of a Virgin took the Word,
And the Blood we drink believing
	He for sinful man outpoured.

In this rite, our souls to nourish,
	To the Word made Flesh we come,
Hence our faith in strength doth flourish,
	Hence we reach our heavenly home.

Bread of sweetness, ever holy,
	Full art Thou of pure delight;
Saviour, born of Maiden lowly,
	King art Thou of perfect might!

May we ever eat in gladness
	Of this rich, angelic Bread,
May we, in death's hour of sadness,
	With this sweetest Gift be fed.

He was, at the third day-hour,
	Led a Victim forth to die,
When He bore His Cross of power,
	His elect to raise on high.

Lead us, Giver of Salvation,
	To our home Thyself beside,
Where eternal jubilation
	Dwelleth through the Lamb that died.

Evermore we there the story
	Of Thy wondrous deeds will raise,
Reigning with Thy saints in glory,
	We will offer gifts of praise.

Sacrifice and hymns in union,
	God we bring this festal day,
May He with Divine communion
	Feed us in His love for aye. Amen.

XXXIII.

O Thou, Who rising long before the day,
				Went'st forth to pray
On the cold mount by weariness opprest,
				That we might rest
With Thee hereafter; though my lot de-
	nies
				Sleep to mine eyes,—
Blessed Redeemer, how can I repine,
				Remembering Thine?

O Thou, Who at the fourth watch of the
	night
				Didst come in sight

Of Thine Apostles, toiling on the wave;
				And swift to save
From peril and from fear, saidst, drawing
	nigh,
				" Peace! it is I!"
O still my thoughts, tempestuous as that
	sea!
				Speak peace to me!

O Thou, Who didst not roughly chide Thy
	Saint
				With faith too faint
To walk the waters, but with outstretched
	Hand
				Didst bid him stand;
My faith is weak: according to Thy Word
				Help me, O Lord!
Afraid of every danger; not afraid
				To seek Thine aid!

O give Thy servant patience, to be still,
				And bear Thy Will;
Courage to venture wholly on the Arm
				That will not harm;
The wisdom that will never let me stray
				Out of my way;
The love that, now afflicting, knoweth
	best
				When I should rest!

Thy time is not yet come. Enough for me!
				Thy time will be
The safest and the best; and how can I
				Wish it more nigh?
If e'er Thou settest me among Thy blest,
				Enough of rest!
Meanwhile, although Thou bidd'st my
	pains not cease,
				Grant me Thy Peace!

The peace, O God the Father, that
	alone
				Surrounds Thy throne;
The peace, O God the Son, Thy last be-
	quest
				To hearts distressed;
O God the Holy Ghost, from age to age
				Thine heritage!

XXXIV.

Holy Father, from Thy throne
Hear a lowly suppliant moan;
Yea, though wrath be all my meed,
Break not Thou the bruised reed:
	Let the bitter Agony
	Of my Jesu plead for me.

Hear by Him, Who bowing low
'Neath our sins' o'erwhelming woe,
His Soul's Blood in anguish poured:
Lo! those drops on high are stored:
	Let the bitter Agony
	Of my Jesu groan for me.

In that Flood my soul embathe,
In that love my spirit swathe;
Bid that shower of bitter Tears
Thrill my heart through livelong years:
	Let the bitter Agony
	Of my Jesu weep for me.

Give me from that Fount of might,
Grace to brave the powers of night;
With a child's reposing faith,
Thine to be in life or death:
    Let the bitter Agony
    Of my Jesu strive for me.

Holy Father, Strong and Just,
Hear Thy suppliant from the dust;
May that overflowing love
Thee to gentle pity move:
    Let the bitter Agony
    Of my Jesu sue for me.

XXXV.

Behold, the Bridegroom cometh in the middle of the night,
And blest is he whose loins are girt, whose lamp is burning bright;
But woe to that dull servant whom his Master shall surprise
With lamp untrimmed, unburning, and with slumber in his eyes.

Do thou, my soul, beware, beware lest thou in sleep sink down,
Lest thou be given o'er to death, and lose the golden crown:
But see that thou be sober, with watchful eye, and thus,
Cry, Holy, Holy, Holy God, have mercy upon us.

That day, the day of fear, shall come; my soul, slack not thy toil,
But light thy lamp, and feed it well, and make it bright with oil;
Who knowest not how soon may sound the cry at eventide,
Behold the Bridegroom comes. Arise! Go forth to meet the Bride.

Beware, my soul: take thou good heed, lest thou in slumber lie,
And, like the five, remain without, and knock, and vainly cry;
But watch, and bear thy lamp undimmed, and Christ shall gird thee on
His own bright Wedding Robe of Light— the Glory of the Son.

XXXVI.

God comes: and who shall stand before His fear?
Who bide His Presence when He draweth near?
    My soul, my soul, prepare
    To kneel before Him there.

Haste,—weep,—be reconciled to Him, before
The fearful judgment knocketh at the door:
    Where in the Judge's eyes,
    All bare and naked lies.

Have mercy, Lord, have mercy, Lord, I cry,
When with Thine Angels Thou appear'st on high:
    And each a doom shall herit,
    Aceording to his merit.

How can I bear Thy fearful anger, Lord,
I, that so often have transgressed Thy Word?
    But put my sins away,
    And spare me in that day.

O miserable soul, return, lament,
Ere earthly converse end, and life be spent:
    Ere, time for sorrow o'er,
    The Bridegroom close the door.

Yea, I have sinned, as no man sinned beside:
With more than human guilt my soul is dyed;
    But spare and save me here
    Before that day appear.

Three Persons in One Essence uncreate,
On Whom, both Three and One, our praises wait,
    Give everlasting light
    To them that sing Thy might.

XXXVII.

Lead, Kindly Light, amid the encircling gloom,
    Lead Thou me on!
The night is dark, and I am far from home—
    Lead Thou me on!
Keep Thou my feet; I do not ask to see
The distant scene,—one step, enough for me.

I was not ever thus, nor prayed that Thou
    Shouldst lead me on:
I loved to choose and see my path; but now
    Lead Thou me on!
I loved the garish day, and, spite of fears,
Pride ruled my will: remember not past years.

So long Thy power hath blest me, sure it still
    Will lead me on,
O'er moor and fen, o'er crag and torrent, till
    The night is gone,
And with the morn those Angel faces smile
Which I have loved long since, and lost awhile.

XXXVIII.

Woe is me! what is existence below?
Trouble on trouble, and blow upon blow!
What is in this world save sorrowful years,
Much tribulation, and plentiful tears?

"Dust of the earth, dost thou wail and repine?
For that, in sundry ways, trial is thine?

Leisure and softness—to these hast thou
  right ?
Draw the sword—grasp the shield—gird
  thee for fight!

"As in the furnace the gold must be
  proved,
So, by affliction, the son that is loved:
For My true followers trouble is stored;
Nor is the servant above his own LORD.

"Hast thou forgotten the tale thou hast
  read ?
I, when on earth, had no place for My
  head:
This was the Cross all My life long I bare,
When, the world's Maker, I exiled Me
  there.

"Wouldst thou but ponder the promise
  I make,
Willingly, joyfully, pain wouldst thou
  take:
That in My kingdom the joys thou may'st
  see
Of the Confessors who suffered for Me."

Grant Thou this patience, O JESU, to me!
Grant Thou Thy graces, my safeguard to
  be !
So that in all things Thy will may be
  mine,
Bearing all troubles, because they are
  Thine.

Still let me study like Thee to appear,—
Still let me seek to be crucified here :
That, if my anguish, like Thine, is in-
  creased,
I may sit also with Thee at Thy Feast.

XXXIX.

GOD the FATHER, from on high,
Look on me with loving eye,
Hearken to my feeble cry.
    LORD, be merciful to me.

GOD the SON, Who from Thy throne,
Camest down to seek Thine own,
Hearken to my piteous moan.
    LORD, be merciful to me.

GOD the SPIRIT, ever blest,
Comforter and Healer best,
Hearken to my prayer for rest.
    LORD, be merciful to me.

Holy Trinity Divine,
Unity in Persons trine,
Grant to me Thine aid benign.
    LORD, be merciful to me.

CHRIST, Who from the Red Sea wave
Didst Thy chosen people save,
Lift Thy servant from the grave.
    LORD, be merciful to me.

Thou, Whose ever mighty Hand
Breaks the battle and the brand,
Loose disease's iron band.
    LORD, be merciful to me.

Thou, with Whom the Children Three
In the flames walked safe and free,
Help me too in agony.
    LORD, be merciful to me.

Thou, Who didst Thine Angel send
Blinded Tobit to befriend,
Bring my troubles to an end.
    LORD, be merciful to me.

Thou, Who in Thy tender care
Didst Thyself our sorrows bear,
JESU, now in pity spare.
    LORD, be merciful to me.

By Thine hour of pain and dread,
By the Life-blood Thou hast shed,
By Thy burial with the dead,
    LORD, be merciful to me.

By Thine own victorious might,
By Thy Resurrection bright,
By Thy rising to the height,
    LORD, be merciful to me.

Thou, Who wilt again appear
On the last great Day of fear,
Save me then, Redeemer dear.
    LORD, be merciful to me.

By this chastisement of pain
Wean me from affections vain,
Cleanse my heart from guilty stain.
    LORD, be merciful to me.

Grant me spotless purity,
Patience in adversity,
And a peaceful end in Thee.
    LORD, be merciful to me.

Then, O Shepherd Good and Wise,
Let me see Thee with mine eyes
In Thy fold of Paradise.
    LORD, be merciful to me.

XL.

CHRIST, Who didst for sinners suffer
  In Thy perfect innocence;
By Thine Agony and Passion,
  Give us refuge and defence.

By the cords that bound Thee closely,
  Closer bind our hearts to Thee;
By the stripes that scourged Thee sharply
  Scourge us into purity.

By the stripping of Thy garments,
  Strip us of all false delight;
By Thy royal robe of purple,
  Clothe us with Thy kingly might.

By the crown of thorns Thou worest,
  Pierce our brows with penitence ;
By the sceptre-reed Thou borest,
  Govern every thought and sense.

By Thine unjust condemnation,
  Spare us in the Judgment Day ;
By Thy road to Crucifixion,
  Lead us in the narrow way.

By Thy carrying the Rood-tree,
　Help us sorrow to endure;
By Thy bitter cup of mocking,
　Give Thy medicine to cure.

By Thine awful crucifying,
　Nail upon Thy Cross our pride;
By Thy painful exaltation,
　Draw us sinners to Thy Side.

By Thy pardoning the robber,
　Grant that we may pardon win;
By the seven words Thou spakest,
　Keep our tongues from words of sin.

By Thy yielding up Thy Spirit,
　Grant that we to guilt may die;
By the stream of Blood and water,
　All uncleanness purify.

So that we, in tribulation
　Following Thy steps of woe,
May at length Thy full salvation
　And Thy joys eternal know.

XLI.

LORD JESU, Who for us didst bear
　Such anguish and distress,
And all our many trials share,
　And all our sicknesses:

For this dear end Thou barest woe,
　That by such pain and shame
Thy people's sufferings Thou might'st
　　know,
　As having felt the same.

Thou well canst make our easier bed,
　To such a hard one bound;
Thou pitiest every aching head,
　For Thine with thorns was crowned.

Thou feltest anguish long and keen,
　And weakness at its worst;
Thou know'st what burning fevers mean,
　For Thou hast said, " I thirst."

Thine hands made whole the child from
　　harm,
　Whom demons sore oppressed;
And children taken in Thine Arms,
　By Thy dear words were blest.

No pulse that moved, no breath that
　　stirred,
　Her life had reached its close;
Talitha cumi was Thy word,
　And straight the maid arose.

Thou chosest innocents to be
　First martyrs here below;
They gave their little lives for Thee,
　Whose name they could not know.

Thousands since then have learned. to
　　bear
　The worst that pain could do;
In Thine affliction having share,
　But in Thy glory too.

Thou knowest all my future lot,
　Sweet Mary's sweetest Son;
O raise me up again—yet not
　My will, but Thine be done.

O raise me up to be Thine own,
　Or, if Thou take me hence,
Give me a place beneath Thy throne,
　Among the Innocents.

XLII.

LORD, Who in pain and weariness
Thy path of sorrow here didst tread;
Who, scorned of man, and shelterless
Couldst find no place to lay Thy Head;
　Grant Thy shelter, JESU meek,
　To Thy poor, who refuge seek.

LORD, Who through long and saddened
　　years,
Didst toil for suffering mankind;
Didst bind their wounds, didst calm their
　　fears,
Didst cure the sick, the halt, the blind!
　Grant Thy healing, JESU blest,
　To the faint, who long for rest.

LORD, Who wast merciful to spare,
And madest leprous sinners clean,
Who freely, at her tearful prayer,
Forgavest Mary Magdalene;
　Grant Thy pardon, JESU sweet,
　To the mourners at Thy Feet.

LORD, Who didst die upon the Rood,
That we might ever die to sin,
Who givest us Thyself as Food,
To make us strong the goal to win;
　Grant Thy patience, JESU dear,
　Unto all who suffer here.

LORD, Who from burial didst arise,
That we might rise to life in Thee,
And hence ascended to the skies,
Dost rule all things in majesty;
　Grant Thy glory, JESU pure,
　To the faithful who endure.

XLIII.

CHRIST, on Whose Face the soldiers
　Spat in their mockery;
Who hungest, faint and bleeding,
　On the atoning Tree!
Who heardest the revilings
　Of them that cursed Thy Name,
And watched, in bitter hatred,
　Beneath the Cross of shame:

·Look down, we pray, in mercy
　On weary souls below,
Who turn to Thee, their SAVIOUR,
　For comfort in their woe,
O let their piteous crying
　Pierce through the angels' song,
That cry of desolation,
　" How long, O LORD, how long ?"

Christ, Who art throned in heaven,
 Supremest over all,
Before Whose Face archangels
 In adoration fall;
Who hearest the sweet singing
 Of them that tell Thy fame,
And tread, amidst their harping,
 The sea of glass and flame;

O lift us, by Thy Passion,
 Up from the bed of sin;
O bring us, by Thy Rising,
 The heavenly gates within;
That with the angel choirs,
 We there may raise the strain
Of glory, laud, and honour,
 To Thee, for sinners slain.

XLIV.

Lord Jesu, by Thy Passion,
 To Thee I make my prayer,
Thou Who in mercy smitest,
 Have mercy, Lord, and spare.

O wash me in the fountain,
 That floweth from Thy Side,
O clothe me in the raiment
 Thy Blood hath purified.

O hold Thou up my goings,
 And lead from strength to strength,
That unto Thee in Sion
 I may appear at length.

O hearken to my knocking,
 And open wide the door,
That I may enter freely,
 And never leave Thee more.

O bring me, loving Jesu,
 To that most blessed place,
Where angels and archangels
 Look ever on Thy Face;

Where gladsome Alleluias
 Unceasingly resound,
Where martyrs, now triumphant,
 Walk robed in white, and crowned.

O make my spirit worthy
 To join that ransomed throng,
O teach my lips to utter
 That everlasting song.

O give that last, best blessing,
 That even Saints can know,
To follow in Thy footsteps
 Wherever Thou dost go.

Not wisdom, might, or glory
 I ask to win above;
I ask for Thee, Thee only,
 O Thou Eternal Love.

XLV.

Christ, from the Father sent to bring
us healing,
Truest Physician, stronger than the
grave,
Look on Thy people suppliantly kneeling,
 Hearken, and save.

Lo, unto Thee we humbly make petition,
For all whom sickness grieveth with its
pain.
In mercy from their suffering condition
 Lift them again.

Thou Who didst quickly cure of burning
fever
Peter's wife's mother and the noble's
son,
Of the centurion's servant the reliever,
 Mightiest One;

Heal soul and body, give Thy perfect
curing
Unto those causes whence diseases
spring,
Let not the gnawing pangs we are en-
during
 Uselessly sting.

Vigour upon Thy drooping people send-
ing,
Thy full salvation ever on them pour,
Grant, as of old, to feeble ones amending,
 Help and restore.

Hearken, O God, in pity to our crying,
Aid all for whom to Thee we make com-
plaint,
Be Thy refreshment felt by each one lying
 Weary and faint.

Banish each pang which makes the body
perish,
Bid every throe of agony be still,
Let welcome health the tortured mem-
bers cherish,
 Strengthen from ill.

So that on earth, by suffering's sharp
training,
Counted with them whom Thou in love
dost try,
They may attain where Thou, O Lord,
art reigning,
 Crowned upon high.

XLVI.

My heart to Thee I give for aye,
 O Jesu, sweetest, best;
Thy Heart to me give Thou, I pray,
 O Jesu loveliest.
Our hearts alone Thou dost require,
Our hearts alone Thou dost desire,
Make me love Thee as Thou dost me,
O Jesu, Fount of Charity.

What for Thy grace can I repay,
 God, Who for me wast born?
What for Thy love before Thee lay,
 Man, Who didst suffer scorn?
"Thy heart," Thou sayest, "give Me
here;"
Take Thou my heart, O Jesu dear,
Make me love Thee as Thou dost me,
O Jesu, Fount of Charity.

For me Thy heart is opened wide,
 That I may entrance find,

And there my own within it hide,
  And close in union bind.
Thou, Jesu blest, by love possessed,
Thyself didst give, that I might live ;
Make me love Thee as Thou dost me,
O Jesu, Fount of Charity.

  Here is the heart's true bulwark found,
    And here is rest secure,
  And here is love's most certain ground,
    And here salvation sure.
In this cleft Rock, once rent for all,
And in this Heart's protecting wall,
May I confide, may I abide,
O Jesu, Saviour glorified.

XLVII.

The clouds of sorrow rest upon mine eyes,
  Grieving and faint, I yearn to see the
    day;
O Sun of Righteousness, in glory rise,
  And drive the night of trouble far
    away.

The tempest gathers round me in its rage,
  And wildly surge the foaming waves of
    ill ;
Come quickly, Lord, Who canst their
    wrath assuage,
  And speak Thy word of power, "Peace,
    be still."

The wolves are howling close beside the
    fold,
  Striving to slay and rend Thy feeble
    sheep;
O loving Shepherd, hearken and behold,
  And Thine own flock in perfect surety
    keep.

Weary of groaning, now my throat is
    dry,
  I thirst and languish in the burning
    heat;
Fountain of Life, Thy cooling streams
    supply,
  And pour upon my soul refreshment
    sweet.

My days are like a shadow, quickly past,
  The might of youth abides no more in
    me ;
O Strength Eternal, come Thou at the
    last,
  And take me home to dwell in peace
    with Thee.

XLVIII.

God the Lord has heard our prayer,
God has lightened all our care;
To His glorious throne on high
Rose His children's mournful cry,—
Alleluia ! praises sing !
To our Father and our King !

Helpless, Lord, Thy Face we sought,
Thou hast our deliverance wrought ;

God, Who gave us faith to pray,
Gives us thankful hearts to-day.
Alleluia ! Lord, to Thee
Sing we, though unworthily.

Now the night of grief is gone,
Now with joy breaks forth the morn ;
Trust in God if ye would prove
All the riches of His love.
Alleluia! praise the Lord !
Trust His love and plead His Word.

Praise to God, Who heard our cry :
Praise to Christ, Who pleads on high ;
Praise the Spirit blest, Who gave
Strength our Father's help to crave !
Alleluia ! glory be
To the Eternal Trinity ! Amen.

XLIX.

My sins, my sins, my Saviour !
  They take such hold on me,
I am not able to look up,
  Save only, Christ, to Thee ;
In Thee is all forgiveness,
  In Thee abundant grace,
My shadow and my sunshine
  The brightness of Thy Face.

My sins, my sins, my Saviour !
  How sad on Thee they fall,
Seen through Thy gentle patience,
  I tenfold feel them all ;
I know they are forgiven,
  But still, their pain to me
Is all the grief and anguish
  They laid, my Lord, on Thee.

My sins, my sins, my Saviour !
  Their guilt I never knew
Till with Thee, in the desert
  I near Thy passion drew ;
Till, with Thee, in the garden
  I heard Thy pleading prayer,
And saw the sweat-drops bloody,
  That told Thy sorrow there.

Therefore my songs, my Saviour,
  E'en in this time of woe,
Shall tell of all Thy goodness
  To suffering man below ;
Thy goodness and Thy favour,
  Whose presence from above,
Rejoice those hearts, my Saviour,
  That live in Thee and love.

L.

O Jesu, Lord most merciful,
  Low at Thy Cross I lie.
O sinner's Friend, most pitiful,
  Hear my bewailing cry.
I come to Thee with mourning,
  I come to Thee in woe ;
With contrite heart returning,
  And tears that overflow.

O gracious Intercessor !
  O Priest within the Veil !

Plead, for a lost transgressor,
 The Blood that cannot fail.
I spread my sins before Thee,
 I tell them one by one;
O for Thy Name's great glory,
 Forgive all I have done.

O by Thy Cross and Passion,
 Thy tears and agony,
And crown of cruel fashion,
 And death on Calvary :—
By all that untold suffering
 Endured by Thee alone ;—
O Priest ! O Spotless Offering !
 Plead for me, and atone !

And in this heart now broken
 Re-enter Thou and reign :
And say, by that dear token,
 I am absolved again.
And build me up, and guide me,
 And guard me day by day ;
And in Thy presence hide me,
 And keep my soul alway. Amen.

LI.

To Calvary ascending
 With Jesus let us go,
Beneath the shadow bending
 Of all His mighty woe :
The Chief of our salvation,
 Should we not follow nigh,
With all His tribulation,
 In all His death to die ?

The rereward's faint wayfarer
 Must stagger with his load,
Where still the standard-bearer
 Leads up the mountain road :
Wrung out from life's affliction,
 Death has no bitter cup,
So sharp, but crucifixion
 Has brimmed its sorrows up.

Does life's last fever burning
 Thy couch with anguish toss ?
His racked limbs had no turning,
 His death-bed was the Cross :
Each vein of life-drops streaming
 From soul to crown Divine,
Has, Death, for thy redeeming
 A deeper pang than thine.

Art poor ? in all thy toiling
 See how the Master sped,
His robe, His vesture-spoiling,
 His naked, homeless Head :
The fox his hole, the sparrow
 Has where to lay her nest,
Those rude beams, hard and narrow,
 Are all the Saviour's rest.

Have evil-tongued oppressors
 Thy reputation torn ?
Hark ! numbered with transgressors
 He bears the robbers' scorn :
The sharpened nails assailing
 Less need the opiate bowl,
Than those fell tongues, impaling
 Their iron in His soul.

Dost fear the pains of dying,
 When Death has poised his dart ?
See ! all those arrows flying
 Are gathered in His heart :
A moist wind gently sighing
 Is now that furnace blast :
Death, in His bitter crying,
 Thy bitterness is past.

LII.

I heard the voice of Jesus say,
 "Come unto Me and rest ;
Lay down, thou weary one, lay down
 Thy head upon My breast."
I came to Jesus as I was—
 Weary and worn and sad ;
I found in Him a resting place,
 And He has made me glad.

I heard the voice of Jesus say,
 "Behold I freely give
The living water—thirsty one,
 Stoop down, and drink, and live."
I came to Jesus, and I drank
 Of that life-giving stream ;
My thirst was quenched, my soul re-
  vived,
 And now I live in Him.

I heard the voice of Jesus say,
 "I am this dark world's Light,
Look unto Me, thy morn shall rise,
 And all thy day be bright."
I looked to Jesus, and I found
 In Him my Star, my Sun :
And in that light of life I'll walk,
 Till pilgrimage is done.

LIII.

Jerusalem, my happy home !
 When shall I come to thee ?
When shall my labours have an end ?
 Thy joys when shall I see ?

O happy harbour of the Saints,
 O sweet and pleasant soil,
In thee no sorrow may be found,
 No grief, no care, no toil !

In thee no sickness may be seen,
 No hurt, no ache, no sore ;
There is no death, nor ugly dole,
 But Life for evermore.

No dampish mist is seen in thee,
 No cold nor darksome night ;
There every soul shines as the sun ;
 There God Himself gives light.

There lust and lucre cannot dwell,
 There envy bears no sway ;
There is no danger, heat, nor cold,
 But pleasure every way.

Jerusalem ! Jerusalem !
 God grant I once may see
Thy endless joys, and of the same
 Partaker aye to be.

Thy walls are made of precious stones,
  Thy bulwarks diamonds square,
Thy gates are of right orient pearl,
  Exceeding rich and rare.

Thy turrets and thy pinnacles,
  With carbuncles do shine,
Thy very streets are paved with gold,
  Surpassing clear and fine.

Thy houses are of ivory,
  Thy windows crystal clear,
Thy tiles are made of beaten gold,
  —O GOD, that I were there!

LIV.

Ah, my sweet home, Jerusalem,
  Would GOD I were in thee!
Would GOD my woes were at an end,
  Thy joys that I might see!

Thy Saints are crowned with glory great,
  They see GOD face to face;
They triumph still, they still rejoice,
  Most happy is their case.

We that are here in banishment
  Continually do moan,
We sigh and sob, we weep and wail,
  Perpetually we groan.

Our sweet is mixed with bitter gall,
  Our pleasure is but pain;
Our joys scarce last the looking on,
  Our sorrows still remain.

But there they love in such delight,
  Such pleasure and such play,
As that to them a thousand years
  Doth seem as yesterday.

Thy vineyards and thy orchards are
  Most beautiful and fair,
Full furnished with trees and fruit,
  Exceeding rich and rare.

Thy gardens and thy gallant walks
  Continually are green;
There grow such sweet and pleasant
    flowers
  As nowhere else are seen.

Quite through the streets with silver
    sound
  The Flood of Life doth flow,
Upon whose banks on every side
  The Wood of Life doth grow.

There trees for evermore bear fruit,
  And evermore do spring;
There evermore the Angels sit,
  And evermore do sing.

Our Lady sings *Magnificat*,
  With tones surpassing sweet,
And all the Virgins bear their part,
  Sitting about her feet.

Jerusalem, my happy home!
  Would GOD I were in thee,
Would GOD my woes were at an end,
  Thy joys that I might see!

LV.

Rest of the weary,
  Joy of the sad,
Hope of the dreary,
  Light of the glad;
Home of the stranger,
  Strength to the end,
Refuge from danger,
  SAVIOUR and Friend.

Pillow where, lying,
  Love rests its head,
Peace of the dying,
  Life of the dead;
Path of the lowly,
  Prize at the end,
Breath of the holy,
  SAVIOUR and Friend.

When my feet stumble,
  I'll to Thee cry;
Crown of the humble,
  Cross of the high.
When my steps wander,
  Over me bend,
Truer and fonder,
  SAVIOUR and Friend.

Ever confessing
  Thee, I will raise
Unto Thee blessing,
  Glory and praise;
All my endeavour,
  World without end,
Thine to be ever,
  SAVIOUR and Friend.

LVI.

When day's shadows lengthen,
  JESU, be Thou near;
Pardon, comfort, strengthen,
  Chase away my fear;
Love and hope be deepened,
  Faith more strong and clear.

When the night grows darkest,
  And the stars are pale,
When the foe assembles
  In death's misty vale,
Be Thou Sword and Buckler,
  Be Thou Shield and Mail.

Come, Thou Food of Angels,
  Source of every Grace,
In Thy FATHER'S Mansions
  Give me soon a place,
That unveiled in splendour
  I may see Thy Face.

By the Jordan's ripples,
  Passing through the shade,

' Let me hear that promise
Once for ever made—
It is I, thy Jesus,
Be not thou afraid.

Then be near me, Jesu,
Enemies shall flee;
Hidden God and Saviour,
Thou my Comfort be,
Food, and Priest, and Victim,
Let me feed on Thee.

So shall no fears chill me
On that unknown shore,
For in death He conquered
And can die no more.
His Hand guards and guides me
To the City's door.

Blesséd warfare over,
Endless Rest alone,
Tears no more, nor sorrow,
Neither sigh nor moan,
But a song of triumph
Round about the Throne.

LVII.

Captain of Salvation,
Victor o'er the grave,
In our tribulation
Come with speed to save.

Enemies malignant
Close around us throng,
We are few and weary,
They are fierce and strong.

Some with torments dire
Pierce the shrinking frame,
Some with hot desire
Set the heart aflame.

Some with wiles ensnaring
Lure us from the goal,
Some with fears despairing
Vex the fainting soul.

Thou alone canst help us
In our sore distress,
Who Thyself wast tempted
In the wilderness.

Thou alone canst give us
Medicine to cure,
Who the thorns and scourging
Didst Thyself endure.

Thou alone canst rout them,
Drive them back with loss,
Who didst triumph o'er them
On the saving Cross.

Let angelic armies
Guard us on each side,
But Thyself as Leader
First in battle ride,

Thou Whose Name is Faithful,
Thou Whose vesture glows
White with perfect pureness,
Red with blood of foes;

Be our strong Defender
In the time of fear;
Be Thou Shield and Helmet,
Breastplate, Sword, and Spear.

Give us strength victorious
Till the strife be o'er;
Then, Christ Jesu glorious,
Peace for evermore.   Amen.

LVIII.

Into Thy Hands, O Lord,
This precious soul we give,
A jewel, 'mid Thy glistening hoard
Of quickening stones to live;
Now let Thy mild Fraternal eyes
Our darling deign to recognize,
A work of Thy creative mould,
A sheep of Thine Apostles' fold,
A sinner from the fiery flood
Redeemed by Thine own Flesh and Blood.

Receive, with arms outspread,
A Prize that cost Thee dear!
'Tis Easter round this dying bed
When our true life draws near!
The thought of Thy forsaken tomb
With brightness cheers this awful gloom;
The stifling, sickening hours of death
Are freshened by Thine odorous breath;
And Hades' gates are glorified
At sight of Him that lives, and died.

Out of this world of tears,
O Christian soul, depart!
Farewell to pain, and grief, and fears,
And wants that rend the heart!
Go thou where those can come no more,
Within the Cherub-guarded door,
Nor dread to change a world like this
For quiet deepening into bliss,
For Eden's dwellings calm and fair—
Pass forth and take thy portion there!

Out of this world of sin,
O Christian soul, depart!
The stainless call thee; pass thou in,
Full-pardoned as thou art!
O crown of joys! no more to stray,
No more to take thy own wild way,
No more thy dearest Friend to leave,
No more His loving Spirit grieve,
What promise sweet or boon secure
Can match those words—" I make thee
pure?"

Now let the Lord arise
And put thy foes to flight,
Let all the immortal Panoplies
Array thee in their might!
Fenced round about by holiest things,
From Satan screened by angel-wings,
To God Who made thee, God Who
bought,
And God Whose grace thy cleansing
wrought,
That hell no part in thee should claim—
Go forth, sweet soul, in Jesu's Name!

LIX.

Gentle Shepherd, Thou hast stilled
Now Thy little lamb's long weeping;
  Ah, how peaceful, pale, and mild,
In its narrow bed 'tis sleeping,
  And no sigh of anguish sore
  Heaves that little bosom more.

In this world of care and pain,
Lord, Thou wouldst no longer leave it,
  To the sunny heavenly plain
Dost Thou now with joy receive it;
  Clothed in robes of spotless white,
  Now it dwells with Thee in light.

Ah, Lord Jesu, grant that we
Where it lives may soon be living,
  And the lovely pastures see
That its heavenly food are giving,
  Then the gain of death we prove
  Though Thou take what most we love.

Hymns for the Dead.

LX.

With pain earth's joys are mingled,
  Earth's glories will not stay,
And, feebler than a shadow,
  Like dreams they fade away.
In one brief, sudden moment
  Death comes to take their place;
But Thee we pray, Lord Jesu,
  With Thine unclouded Face,
And with Thine own sweet beauty,
  Thou Who hast loved us best,
Look on *him* Thou hast chosen,
  And grant Thy servant rest.

Woe for the bitter struggle
  That racks the parting soul!
Woe for the tears she poureth
  When none can make her whole!
She looketh to the Angels,
  But supplicates in vain;
Her hands to men she stretcheth,
  But thence no help may gain.
Then mindful, dearest brethren,
  How soon this life must cease,
Pray we to Christ for mercy,
  And for our *brother's* peace.

Vain, vain are all possessions
  That man can gather here,
They last for us no longer
  When death is coming near;
Our wealth hath no abiding,
  Fame may not with us go,
When death is hasting onward,
  They vanish with their show;
And so to Christ Eternal
  Cry we, of His dear grace,
To grant our *brother* quiet
  In His glad dwelling-place.

Where are the world's affections,
  Where dreams of earthly gain,
Where are the gold and silver,
  And where the serving train?
All, all are dust and ashes,
  All are but as a shade,
So to the King Eternal
  Be our petition made,
Grant, Lord, Thy ceaseless blessings
  To *him* now called away;
And give *him* joys unfading,
  And rest that lasts for aye.

LXI.

O Lord, to Whom the spirits live
Of all the faithful passed away,
Unto their path that brightness give
  Which shineth to the perfect day.
    Light Eternal, Jesu blest,
    Shine on them, and grant them rest.

Bless Thou the dead which die in Thee,
  And make their painful labours cease,
O purge them from impurity,
  And give them everlasting peace.
    Light Eternal, Jesu blest,
    Shine on them, and grant them rest.

In Thy green, pleasant pastures feed
  The sheep which Thou hast summoned
    hence,
And by the still, cool waters lead
  Thy flock in loving providence.
    Light Eternal, Jesu blest,
    Shine on them, and grant them rest.

Heal Thou the wounds of earthly strife,
  Pouring upon the faint Thy balm,
The wearied with the toils of life
  Place in the breast of Abraham.
    Light Eternal, Jesu blest,
    Shine on them, and grant them rest.

How long, O Holy Lord, how long
  Must we and they expectant wait
To hear the gladsome bridal song,
  To see Thee in Thy royal state?
    Light Eternal, Jesu blest,
    Shine on them, and grant them rest.

O hearken, Saviour, to their cry,
  O rend the heavens and come down,
Make up Thy jewels speedily,
  And set them in Thy golden crown.
    Light Eternal, Jesu blest,
    Shine on them, and grant them rest.

Direct us with Thine Arm of might,
  And bring us, perfected with them,
To dwell within Thy city bright,
  The Heavenly Jerusalem.
    Light Eternal, Jesu blest,
    Shine on them, and grant them rest.

LITANY FOR THE SICK.

[May be shortened by omitting the clauses marked *.]

LORD, have mercy, &c.
CHRIST, &c.   LORD, &c.

O GOD the FATHER, of heaven,
O GOD the SON, &c.,
O GOD the HOLY GHOST, &c.,
Holy Trinity, One GOD,
O Thou, Who healest those that are broken in heart, Who woundest and makest whole, Who killest and makest alive, Who bringest down to the grave and bringest up,

O Thou Who art wont to heal those who pray in their sickness, and Who of Thy great mercy savest all that put their trust in Thee,

* O . . . didst heal Job when smitten with grievous sores, and savedst Hezekiah in his sickness when he called upon Thee,

* O . . . madest Tobit to see the light of heaven, and heardest the Canaanitish woman entreating for her daughter,

* O . . . didst deliver Peter's wife's mother from the fever, and didst raise up to perfect health the woman bowed with an infirmity eighteen years,

* O . . . didst save the nobleman's son when dying of a fever, and Who didst heal the Centurion's servant by a word,

O . . . didst heal and cleanse the palsied and the lepers, and didst set free those who were possessed with the devil,

O . . . madest the deaf to hear, and the dumb to speak, the lame to walk, and the blind to see,

* O . . . by the touch of Thy garments didst cure the woman with the issue of blood, and by Thine own touch didst heal the sick and weakly of their infirmities and plagues,

O . . . carriest all our sorrows, and refreshest the weary and heavy laden,

* O . . . didst deliver the dead son to his mother, and didst restore the daughter of Jairus to life, and didst raise Lazarus from the grave after four days,

O . . . didst visit the sick, and didst promise eternal rewards to those that visit them,

* O . . . by the shadow of Peter didst deliver many from their diseases, and didst cure many sick by the napkins and girdles of Paul, and Who didst recall a dead man to life through the bones of Elisha,

O GOD, our helper and our protection, our aid and our deliverer, our strength and patience, our SAVIOUR and Redeemer, the horn also of our salvation, and our refuge,

Have mercy upon us.

Be merciful and spare us, O LORD.
Be merciful and hear us, O LORD.
Be merciful and deliver us, O LORD.

From all evil and sin, from all weakness and sickness, from all murmuring and impatience.
Good LORD, *deliver us.*
* From all contagion and pestilence, from the snares of the devil, from sudden death, and from everlasting damnation,
Good LORD, *deliver us.*
By Thy fasting and temptation, by Thy tears and sorrows, by Thy

labours and weariness, by Thy fear and grief,

By Thine Agony and Bloody Sweat, by Thy most holy Wounds, by the desolation which Thou didst feel, and by the thirst which Thou didst endure,

By Thy Cross and Passion, by Thy death and burial, by Thy glorious Resurrection, and by Thy wonderful Ascension, *Good LORD, deliver us.*

In the day of judgment, we sinners beseech Thee to hear us.

That Thou mayest spare and pardon us;

That Thou mayest grant us time for true repentance with sorrow of heart;

That Thou mayest visit and comfort us, granting unto us health of mind and body, and pardon and remission of all our sins;

That Thou wouldst pour into us the grace and comfort of Thy HOLY SPIRIT, and give us true and Christian patience in all our troubles and adversities;

*That . . . protect us in the hour of our death from all the *We beseech Thee to hear us, good LORD.*

snares of the devil, that we may die in Thy grace and persevere unto the end;

That . . . bless and hallow our last end, and receive our spirit into Thy hands, and after death bid us enter into the gates of Paradise with joy;

That . . . hearken unto us, O SON of GOD; *We beseech Thee, &c.*

O Lamb of GOD, &c.,
Spare us, JESU.
O Lamb of GOD, &c.,
Hear us, JESU.
O Lamb of GOD, &c.,
Have mercy upon us.

O CHRIST, hear us. LORD, have mercy, &c. CHRIST, &c. LORD, &c. Our FATHER, &c.

℣. O LORD, save Thy servants. ℟. Which put, &c. ℣. Be Thou our helper, leave us not. ℟. Neither forsake us, O GOD of our salvation. ℣. Help us, O GOD our SAVIOUR. ℟. And for the glory of Thy Name deliver us, and be merciful unto us sinners for Thy Name's sake. ℣. LORD, hear, &c. ℟. And let, &c. ℣. Let us pray.

[*Select the Collect according to circumstances.*]

SHORT LITANY.

SUITABLE FOR ANY SICK ADULT.

O GOD the FATHER, of heaven,
Have mercy upon *him.*
Keep and defend *him.*
O GOD the SON, Redeemer, &c.,
Have mercy upon *him.*
Save *him* and deliver *him.*
O GOD the HOLY GHOST, &c.,
Have mercy upon *him.*
Strengthen and comfort *him.*
O holy, blessed, and glorious TRINITY,
Have mercy upon *him.*

Remember not, LORD, *his* offences, nor the offences of *his* forefathers; but spare *him,* good LORD, spare this Thy servant, whom Thou hast redeemed with Thy most Precious Blood, and be not angry with *him* for ever.
Spare him, *good* LORD.

From Thy wrath and heavy indignation; from the fear of death; from the guilt and burden of *his* sins; and from the dreadful sentence of the last judgment,

From the sting and terrors of conscience; from distrust or despair; from anguish or agony, that may in any way withdraw *his* mind from Thee,

From the bitter pangs of eternal death; from the powers of darkness; and from the assaults of our ghostly enemy,

By Thy manifold and great mercies; by the manifold and great merits of JESUS CHRIST Thy SON; by His Agony and Bloody Sweat; by His strong crying and tears; by His bitter Cross and Passion; by His glorious Resurrection and Ascension; by His effectual and most acceptable Intercession; and by the graces and comforts of Thy HOLY SPIRIT,

In the time of extremity; in *his* last and greatest need; in the hour of death, and in the day of judgment,

Good LORD, deliver him.

We sinners beseech Thee to

hear us, O LORD GOD: that it may please Thee to assuage *his* pains, and give *him* patience to bear *his* sickness; and when Thou shalt call *him* home, give *him* a quiet and joyful departure;

That it may please Thee to make *him* a partaker of all Thy mercies and promises in CHRIST JESUS;

That it may please Thee, after this life, to bestow upon *him* the state of joy, bliss, and happiness, with all Thy blessed saints in Thy heavenly kingdom;

We beseech Thee to hear us, good LORD.

SON of GOD, we beseech Thee to hear us.

     O Lamb of GOD, that takest, &c.,
        Grant him *Thy peace.*
     O Lamb of GOD, &c.,
        Have mercy upon him.

O CHRIST, hear us. LORD, have mercy, &c. CHRIST, &c. LORD, &c. Our FATHER, &c.

[For Versicles, Responses, and Collect, see the previous Litany.]

LITANY FOR THE DYING.

LORD, have mercy, &c.
O GOD the FATHER, &c.,
     Have mercy upon the soul of Thy servant.
O GOD the SON, &c.,
     Have mercy, &c.
O GOD the HOLY GHOST, &c.,
     Have mercy, &c.
Holy TRINITY, One GOD,
     Have mercy, &c.
One and the same merciful GOD,
     Have mercy, &c.
O GOD, Holy SAVIOUR of the world,
     Have mercy, &c.
Be merciful, O LORD;
     Consider and hear him.
Be merciful, O LORD;
     Spare and pardon him.

Be merciful, O LORD;
     Save and defend him.

From all evil, and from the power of sin,
     Good LORD, deliver him.

From the snares of the devil, and the deceits of the world,

From the terror of death, and from Thy wrathful indignation,

By Thy most holy and suffering life,

By Thy most holy and loving death,

By Thy mysterious descent into hell,

By Thy glorious Resurrection and by Thy wonderful Ascension,

Deliver his soul, O LORD.

By the gift of the HOLY GHOST, the Comforter of souls,
Deliver his *soul, O* LORD.
By Thy coming to Judgment in power and glory,
Deliver his *soul, O* LORD.

We sinners do beseech Thee to hear us.

That it may please Thee to deliver *his* soul from the princes of darkness and from the place of punishment ;
That . . . not to remember the sins and offences of *his* youth ;
That . . . graciously to forgive *him* for whatsoever *he* hath done amiss ;
That . . . to loose the bands of *his* sins ;
That . . . to deal mercifully with *him* at the last great day ;
That . . . to deliver *him* from the pains of hell ;
That . . . to grant *him* admission into the place of rest and peace ;
That . . . that *he* may have a foretaste of eternal bliss ;
That . . . to grant *him* peace and fellowship with Thy Saints and elect in Thy kingdom ;

We sinners do beseech Thee to hear us.

That . . . to vouchsafe to *him* the blessedness of Thy light, and the brightness of Thy glory ;
We sinners, &c.
That . . . to show *him* in mercy Thy holy, glorious, and beloved Face ;
We sinners, &c.

Lamb of GOD, &c. *Have mercy on* his *soul.* Lamb of GOD, &c. *Have mercy, &c.* Lamb of GOD, &c. *Grant* him *Thy peace, eternal happiness and everlasting glory.* O CHRIST, hear us. LORD, have mercy, &c. Our FATHER, &c.

℣. Eternal rest grant unto *him,* O LORD. ℟. And light perpetual shine upon *him.* ℣. From the gates of hell. ℟. Deliver *his* soul. ℣. Let *him* depart in peace. ℟. In the Name of the LORD. ℣. LORD, hear our prayer. ℟. And let, &c. ℣. Let us pray.

439. O most loving JESU, Who camest into the world to save sinners ; deal mercifully with this Thy servant. Let not the princes of darkness prevail against *him,* but with Thy Hand bring *him* unto the place of rest and peace, where with Saints and Angels, and the spirits of just men made perfect, Thou livest.

LITANY FOR THE DEAD.

LORD, have mercy.
CHRIST, &c. LORD, &c.
O CHRIST, hear us.
O CHRIST, graciously hear us.

O GOD the FATHER, of heaven,
Have mercy on the souls of the faithful departed.
O GOD the SON, Redeemer of the world,
Have mercy, &c.
O GOD the HOLY GHOST,
Have mercy, &c.
Holy TRINITY, One GOD,
Have mercy, &c.

Be merciful : spare them, O LORD.
Be merciful : hear them, O LORD.

From all evil,
From Thy wrath,
From the strictness of Thy justice,
From the power of evil spirits,
From the gnawing worm of conscience,
From eternal anguish,
From cruel flames,
From intolerable cold,
From fearful darkness,

Good LORD, *deliver them.*

From dreadful weeping and gnashing of teeth,

By Thy wonderful Conception,

By Thy holy Birth,

By Thy sweetest Name,

By Thy Baptism and Holy Fast,

By Thy deep Humility,

By Thy ready Obedience,

By Thy Purity,

By Thine utter Poverty,

By Thy loving Meekness,

By Thy boundless Love,

By Thy Pains and Anguish,

By Thy bloody Sweat,

By Thy leading away Captive,

By Thy Flagellation,

By Thy Coronation,

By Thy bearing of the Cross,

By Thy bitter Death,

By Thy most holy Wounds,

By Thy Cross and bitter Passion,

By Thy glorious Resurrection,

By Thy wonderful Ascension,

By the Coming of the HOLY GHOST,

In the Day of Judgment,

Good LORD, deliver them.

We sinners beseech Thee to hear us.

Who didst pardon Mary,
We beseech Thee to hear us.
Who heardest the prayer of the publican,
We beseech Thee to hear us.
Who givest grace for grace,
We beseech Thee to hear us.
Who hast the keys of death and of hell,
We beseech Thee to hear us.
That Thou wouldst save the souls of our parents, relations,

friends, and benefactors from the pains of hell,

That Thou wouldst deliver all the faithful departed from eternal damnation,

That Thou wouldst have mercy on the souls whose memory is lost on earth,

That Thou wouldst spare them, and be gracious to them all,

That Thou wouldst fulfil their desire,

That Thou wouldst bring them into the company of Thine Elect,

King of tremendous Majesty,

SON of GOD,

We beseech Thee to hear us.

O Lamb of GOD, &c.,
Grant them rest.
O Lamb of GOD, &c.,
Grant them eternal rest.

O CHRIST, hear us.
O CHRIST, graciously hear us.
LORD, have mercy.
CHRIST, &c. LORD, &c.
Our FATHER, &c.

℣. From the gates of hell. ℟. Deliver their souls, O LORD. ℣. LORD, hear, &c. ℟. And let, &c.

440. O GOD, to Whom all things do live, mercifully look upon the souls of the faithful departed [especially . . .,] and grant that they may be purified from all stain of sin, and, entering into Thy rest, may pass from glory to glory till they come to the full light of the Beatific Vision; to which we beseech Thee to bring us also. Through.

℣. Eternal rest grant unto them, O LORD. ℟. And light perpetual shine upon them. ℣. May they rest in peace. ℟. Amen.

LITANY OF THE NAME OF JESUS.

LORD, have mercy upon us.
CHRIST, &c.   LORD, &c.

O GOD the FATHER, of Heaven,
O GOD the SON, Redeemer of the world,
O GOD the HOLY GHOST,
O Holy TRINITY, One GOD,
JESU, SON of the Living GOD,
JESU, most mighty,
JESU, most powerful,
JESU, most perfect,
JESU, most glorious,
JESU, most wonderful,
JESU, most dear,
JESU, brighter than the sun,
JESU, fairer than the moon,
JESU, more shining than the stars,
JESU, most admirable,
JESU, most delectable,
JESU, most honourable,
JESU, most humble,
JESU, most poor,
JESU, most gentle,
JESU, most patient,
JESU, most obedient,
JESU, most chaste,
JESU, Lover of chastity,
JESU, Lover of peace,
JESU, Mirror of life,
JESU, Pattern of Virtues,
JESU, Lover of souls,
JESU, our Refuge,
JESU, Father of the poor,
JESU, Consolation of the afflicted,
JESU, Treasure of the faithful,
JESU, precious Gem,
JESU, Shrine of perfection,
JESU, Good Shepherd of the sheep,
JESU, Star of the sea,
JESU, true Light,
JESU, eternal Wisdom,
JESU, infinite Goodness,
JESU, Joy of the Angels,
JESU, King of the Patriarchs,
JESU, Theme of the Prophets,
Have mercy upon us.

JESU, Master of the Apostles,
JESU, Teacher of the Evangelists,
JESU, Strength of the Martyrs,
JESU, Light of the Confessors,
JESU, Bridegroom of the Virgins,
JESU, Crown of all Saints,
Have mercy, &c.

Be merciful : spare us, JESU.
Be merciful : hear us, JESU.

From all evil,
From all peril,
From Thy wrath,
From the snares of the devil,
From plague, famine, and war,
From the transgression of Thy commandments,
From the attacks of all evils,
By Thine Incarnation,
By Thine Advent,
By Thy Nativity,
By Thy Circumcision,
By Thy Woes,
By Thy Scourges,
By Thy Death,
By Thy Resurrection,
By Thine Ascension,
By Thy Joys,
By Thy Glory,
Deliver us, JESU.

O Lamb of GOD, that takest, &c.,
Spare us, JESU.
O Lamb of GOD, &c.,
Hear us, JESU,
O Lamb of GOD, &c.,
Have mercy on us, JESU.

LORD, have mercy, &c.
CHRIST, &c.   LORD, &c.
Our FATHER, &c.

℣. Blessed be the Name of the LORD. ℟. From this time forth for evermore. ℣. O LORD, hear, &c. ℟. And let, &c. ℣. The LORD, &c. ℟. And with, &c. ℣. Let us pray.

441. GOD, Which hast made the glorious Name of JESUS CHRIST

Thy Son our Lord most dear to Thy faithful people, and most terrible to evil spirits; grant, we beseech Thee, that all we who worship this Name on earth, may receive in this life the sweetness of Thy holy consolations, and in the world to come, the joy of exultation, and of eternal blessedness in heaven; through the same Jesus Christ our Lord. Who liveth, &c.

LITANY OF THE HOLY CHILDHOOD.

FOR A SICK CHILD.

Lord, have mercy upon us.
Christ, &c. Lord, &c.

O Holy Child Jesu, One with the Father and the Holy Ghost,
Have mercy upon us.

O Holy Child Jesu, Power of God,
O . . . our Brother,
O . . . Giver of Life, yet fed from Thy Mother's breast,
O . . . Eternal Word, yet too young to speak,
O . . . Lord of heaven and earth, yet lying in a manger,
O . . . clothed with glory, yet wrapped in swaddling clothes,
O . . . King of kings, and Lord of Lords, yet housed in a stable,
O . . . Strong in Thy Weakness,
O . . . Author of the blessings of heaven,
O . . . Healer of the sufferings of earth,
Have mercy upon us.

From the chains of sin,
From the snares of the devil,
From all temptations,
From pride and disobedience,
From obstinacy and perverseness,
From hardness of heart,
By Thy Holy Incarnation,
By Thy lowly Birth,
By Thy hunger and cold,
Deliver us, O Holy Child Jesu.

By Thy sobs and tears,
By the first shedding of Thy Precious Blood,
By Thy holy Name Jesus,
By the offerings of the Wise Men,
By Thy Presentation in the Temple,
By Thy Flight into Egypt,
By Thine obedience to Thy Holy Mother,
Deliver us, &c.

O Lamb of God, &c.,
Spare us, O Holy Child Jesu.
O Lamb of God, &c.,
Hear us, &c.
O Lamb of God, &c.,
Have mercy, &c.

Lord, have mercy upon us.
Christ, &c. Lord, &c.
Our Father, &c.

℣. Give the King Thy judgments, O God. ℟. And Thy righteousness unto the King's Son. ℣. Send Thy Word and heal us. ℟. And save us from our destruction. ℣. Lord, &c. ℟. And let, &c. ℣. The Lord, &c. ℟. And with, &c. ℣. Let us pray.

442. O Lord Jesu Christ, Who wast born for us, didst take upon Thee human Childhood, wast wrapped in swaddling clothes, and laid in a manger; vouchsafe to quicken us by Thy Nativity, to clothe us with the garment of heavenly virtues, and to be the inmost food of our souls. Who livest.

LORD, have mercy upon us.
CHRIST, &c.   LORD, &c.
O CHRIST, hear us.

O GOD the FATHER, &c.,
O GOD the SON, &c.,
O GOD the HOLY GHOST, &c.,
Holy TRINITY, One GOD,
Living Bread, which camest down from heaven,
Hidden GOD and SAVIOUR,
Perpetual Sacrifice,
Pure Oblation,
Lamb without spot,
Food of Angels,
Hidden Manna,
Daily Bread,
WORD made Flesh, and dwelling in us,
Sacred Victim,
Bread of Life,
Cup of blessing,
Mystery of the Faith,
True Propitiation for the living and the dead,
Heavenly Antidote, to keep us from sin,
Fulness of Divine love,
Medicine of immortality,
Bread made Flesh by the Power of the Word,
Bond of charity,
Priest and Victim,
Hope of penitents,
Refreshment of holy souls,
Food by the way for those that die in the LORD,
Pledge of glory in the life to come,

Have mercy upon us.

Be merciful unto us.
Spare us, good LORD.
Be merciful unto us.
Hear us, good LORD.

From unworthy reception of Thy Body and Blood,
Good LORD, *deliver us.*
From the lust of the flesh,
Good LORD, *deliver us.*

From the lust of the eye,
From the pride of life,
From all occasions of sin,
By the desire which Thou hadst to eat the Passover with Thy disciples,
By the deep humility with which Thou didst wash the disciples' feet,
By that great love with which Thou didst institute this Holy Sacrament,
By Thy most sacred Body and precious Blood, Which Thou hast left us in the Sacrament of the Altar,
By the wounds which Thou receivedst for us, and by Thy death upon the Cross,

Good LORD, *deliver us.*

We sinners do beseech Thee to hear us.

That it may please Thee to preserve and increase in us faith, reverence, and devotion, with regard to this wonderful Sacrament;
That . . . to forgive us for having received It at any time without due preparation of heart;
That . . . to bring us by a true confession of our sins to a frequent and worthy use of this Holy Eucharist;
That . . . to deliver us from all heresy, unbelief, and hardness of heart;
That . . . to grant unto us the precious and heavenly fruits of this most Holy Sacrament;
That . . . to comfort and defend us in the hour of our death, with this Heavenly Food for our journey;

We beseech Thee to hear us, good LORD.

SON of GOD, we beseech Thee to hear us.
O Lamb of GOD, &c.,
Grant us Thy peace.

O Lamb of God, &c.,
Have mercy upon us.

O Christ, hear us.
Lord, have mercy, &c.
Our Father, &c.

℣. The eyes of all wait upon Thee, O Lord. ℟. And Thou givest them their meat in due season. ℣. Thou openest Thine hand. ℟. And fillest all things living with plenteousness. ℣. The Lord, &c. ℟. And with, &c. ℣. Let us pray.

443. O God, Who in this wonderful Sacrament hast left unto us a Memorial of Thy Passion; grant to us, we beseech Thee, so to venerate the sacred Mysteries of Thy Body and Blood, that we may always perceive in ourselves the fruit of Thy Redemption: Who livest.

LITANY OF THE PASSION.

Ant. Our Lord Jesus Christ humbled Himself, and became obedient unto death, even the death of the Cross. Wherefore God hath highly exalted Him, and given Him a Name which is above every name, that at the Name of Jesus every knee should bow, of things in heaven, and things in earth, and things under the earth, and that every tongue should confess that Jesus Christ is Lord, to the glory of God the Father.

Lord, have mercy upon us.
Christ, &c. Lord, &c.

O God the Father, &c.,
O God the Son, &c.,
O God the Holy Ghost, &c.,
Holy Trinity, One God,
Jesu, Son of the Living God,
Have mercy upon us, miserable sinners.

From all evil,
　O Jesu, deliver us.

From sudden, unprepared, or evil death,
From the snares of the devil,
From anger, hatred, or ill will,
From everlasting death,
By the mystery of Thy Holy Incarnation,
By Thy most Holy Life and Conversation,
By Thy most bitter Passion and Death,
By Thine Agony and Bloody Sweat,
By Thy thrice repeated Prayer,
By the resignation of Thy human Will,
By Thy bonds and stripes,
By Thy Sacred Body buffeted and smitten,
By Thy cruel mockings and scourgings,
By the spitting upon Thine adorable Face,
By the false judgment pronounced on Thee by Caiaphas,
By Thy being set at nought by Herod,
By the shameful stripping off of Thy garments,
By Thy painful crown of thorns,
By Thy purple robe of mockery,
By Thy most unjust condemnation,
By Thy bearing Thine Own Cross,
By Thy footprints traced in Blood,
By the tearing off of Thy garments,
By the cruel straining of Thy sacred Limbs,
By Thy dread Crucifixion,
By the upraising of Thy Cross,
By the anguish which Thou didst suffer,
By the insults which Thou didst endure,
By Thy prayers and tears,
O Jesu, deliver us.

By the shedding of Thy most precious Blood,

By Thy patience and humility,

By the love wherewith Thou didst love us unto the end,

O Jesu, &c.

We sinners beseech Thee, O Jesu, to hear us.

That being dead unto sin, we may live unto righteousness,

That we may not glory save in the Cross of our Lord Jesus Christ,

That we may take up our cross daily, and follow Thee,

That Thy Blood may cleanse us from dead works, to serve the living God,

That looking unto Thine example, we may follow Thy steps,

That being partakers of Thy sufferings, we may be also of Thy glory,

Jesu, we beseech Thee to hear us.

Lamb of God, that takest, &c.,
O Jesu, *spare us.*
Lamb of God, that takest, &c.,
O Jesu, *hear us.*
Lamb of God, that takest, &c.,
O Jesu, *have mercy upon us.*

Ant. O Saviour of the world, Who by Thy Cross and precious Blood hast redeemed us, save us and help us, we humbly beseech Thee, O Lord.

℣. We adore Thee, O Jesu, we bless Thee. ℟. Because by Thy Cross and Passion Thou hast redeemed the world. ℣. Remember, O Lord, Thy tender mercies. ℟. And Thy lovingkindnesses which have been ever of old. ℣. Look upon mine adversity and misery. ℟. And forgive me all my sin. ℣. Lord, hear, &c. ℟. And let, &c. ℣. Let us pray.

Lord, have mercy, &c.
Our Father, &c.

Let us pray.

444. O Lord Jesu Christ, Son of the Living God, Who at the sixth hour wast lifted up upon the Cross for the Redemption of the world, and didst shed Thy Blood for the remission of our sins; we humbly beseech Thee that by the virtue and merits of Thy most holy Life, Passion, and Death, Thou wouldst grant us to enter into the gates of Paradise with joy. Who livest.

LITANY OF THE RESURRECTION.

Lord, have mercy, &c.
Christ, &c. Lord, &c.

O God the Father, &c.,
O God the Son, &c.,
O God the Holy Ghost, &c.,
O Holy Trinity, One God,
O Lord Jesu Christ, the True Paschal Lamb,
Jesu, Who didst build up in three days the temple of Thy Body,
Jesu, Who, according to Thy Word, didst rise the third day from the grave,

Have mercy upon us, miserable sinners.

Jesu, Whose Resurrection an Angel announced to the women at the Sepulchre,
Jesu, Who didst show Thyself to Thy disciples after Thy Resurrection,
Jesu, Who didst manifest the truth of Thy Resurrection with unnumbered miracles,
Jesu, Whose Resurrection the Apostles preached, and confirmed with their blood,
Jesu, Who through Thy Resurrection hast given us a sure hope of eternal life,
Jesu, Who after Thy Resur-

Have mercy, &c.

rection didst continue forty days with Thy disciples,

JESU, Who didst ascend from the Mount of Olives to Thy FATHER and ours,

JESU, Who hast prepared mansions in Thy FATHER's House for Thy servants,

JESU, Who wilt come again at the end of time to judge the quick and the dead,

Have mercy, &c.

We sinners beseech Thee to hear us, JESU.

That we may truly rise from the grave of our sins,

That we may conquer our evil desires, and die to our sins,

That we may grow in knowledge and love of Thy holy teaching,

That we may serve Thee in holiness and righteousness all the days of our life,

We beseech Thee to hear us, JESU.

That our sorrows may, like Thine, one day be turned into eternal joy,

That we may not seek after things on earth, but things in heaven,

That we may awake at length from the grave to the Resurrection of eternal life,

That at the general Resurrection we may have a share in Thy kingdom,

We beseech, &c.

SON of GOD, we beseech, &c.
Lamb of GOD, that takest, &c.
LORD, have mercy, &c.
Our FATHER, &c.

℣. Lighten mine eyes, O LORD. ℟. That I sleep not in death. ℣. Help me now, O LORD. ℟. O LORD, send us now prosperity. ℣. O LORD, hear, &c. ℟. And let, &c. ℣. Let us pray.

Easter Coll. Almighty GOD, Who through.

LITANY OF THE HOLY GHOST.

LORD, have mercy, &c.

O GOD the FATHER, &c.,
O GOD the SON, &c.,
O GOD the HOLY GHOST, &c.,
Holy TRINITY, One GOD,
O HOLY SPIRIT, by Whose wondrous power the Incarnation of our LORD was wrought in the Virgin's womb,
O HOLY SPIRIT, Who teachest us all things, and guidest us into all truth,
O HOLY SPIRIT of Wisdom and understanding, of counsel and strength, of knowledge and godliness, and of holy fear,
O HOLY SPIRIT of power, of love, and of a sound mind,
O HOLY SPIRIT of all virtues,
O HOLY SPIRIT, Who makest intercession for us with groanings which cannot be uttered,

Have mercy upon us.

O HOLY SPIRIT, by Whom we are born again, and made heirs of eternal life,
O HOLY SPIRIT, Who helpest our infirmities,
O HOLY SPIRIT, Who quickenest us, and purifiest our hearts by faith,
O HOLY SPIRIT, Who art a discerner of the thoughts and intents of the heart,

Have mercy upon us.

From all evil,
Deliver us, O HOLY SPIRIT.
Be merciful unto us,
Spare us, O HOLY SPIRIT.
Be merciful unto us,
Hear us, O HOLY SPIRIT.

From all sins of thought, word, and deed,
Deliver us, O HOLY SPIRIT.

From the crafts and assaults of the devil,
From presumption and despair,
From unbelief and hardness of heart,
From uncleanness of heart and life,
From anger, hatred, and ill-will,
From obstinacy and impenitence,
By Thine invisible anointing,
By the abundance of Thy grace,
Deliver us, O HOLY SPIRIT.

We sinners do beseech Thee to hear us, O HOLY SPIRIT.

That Thou mayest spare us,
That we, through the Spirit, may mortify the deeds of the body,
That we may keep the unity of the SPIRIT in the bond of peace,
That sowing to the SPIRIT, we may of the SPIRIT reap life everlasting,
That Thou wouldst vouchsafe to create in us a clean heart, and renew a right spirit within us,
That we may patiently bear all things for the love of GOD,
That we grieve not the HOLY SPIRIT of GOD, whereby we are sealed unto the day of redemption,
That Thou wouldst grant us to persevere unto the end in faith, hope, and charity,
We beseech Thee to hear us, O HOLY SPIRIT.

Lamb of GOD, &c.,
Pour into our hearts the Spirit of love.
Lamb of GOD, &c.,
Enlighten our minds with the Spirit of truth.
Lamb of GOD, &c.,
Give unto us the Spirit of peace.

LORD, have mercy, &c.
Our FATHER, &c.

℣. Make me a clean heart, O GOD. ℟. And renew a right spirit within me. ℣. Cast me not away from Thy Presence. ℟. And take not Thy HOLY SPIRIT from me. ℣. O give me the comfort of Thy help again. ℟. And stablish me with Thy free Spirit. ℣. LORD, hear, &c. ℟. And let, &c. ℣. Let us pray.

445. O GOD the HOLY GHOST, Who proceedest from the FATHER and the SON, enrich us with the gift of Thy blessing, that, stablished with Thy free Spirit, we may be daily delivered by Thy heavenly influence. Let Thy blessing rest upon us, and ever strengthen us therewith, through the unspeakable might of the TRINITY; that the Spirit of holiness may dwell in us, the Spirit of counsel renew us, the Spirit of might confirm us, so that we, strengthened by the FATHER, and renewed by the SON, may rejoice in the protection of the HOLY SPIRIT. Through Thy mercy, O our GOD, Who art blessed and livest.

LITANY OF PENITENCE.

LORD, have mercy, &c.
O CHRIST, hear us.

O GOD the FATHER, &c.,
Have mercy upon us.
O GOD the SON, &c.,
Have mercy upon us.

O GOD the HOLY GHOST, &c.,
Holy TRINITY, One GOD,
O GOD, Who wouldst not the death of a sinner, but rather that he should be converted and live,
Have mercy upon us.

Who sparedst not the Angels
that sinned, but didst cast them
down to hell,

Who calledst Adam, after his
fall, to penitence and acknowledgment of his sin,

Who didst fearfully punish
Pharaoh, feigning repentance,
yet hardened in heart,

Who forgavest Thy disobe-
dient people at the prayer of
Moses,

Who forgavest the Nine-
vites, repenting in sackcloth
and ashes,

Who by Thy Prophet Na-
than broughtest David to a
sense of sin,

Who didst put away his sin
when he humbly confessed it,

Who sparedst Ahab when he
humbled himself before Thee,

Who camest into the world
to save sinners,

Who broughtest salvation to
the house of Zaccheus when he
restored fourfold,

Who mercifully heardest the
Canaanitish woman when she
persevered in prayer,

Who receivedst publicans and
sinners, and didst eat with them,

Who freely forgavest the sins
of Mary Magdalene who loved
much,

Who in mercy lookedst upon
Peter who denied Thee, thus
moving him to confess his sin,
and to shed tears of penitence,

Who on the Cross didst promise Paradise to the penitent
thief,

Who Thyself didst no sin,
yet barest our sins in Thine
Own Body on the tree,

Who wast bruised for our
transgressions, and wounded for
our iniquities,

Who wouldst not that any
should perish, but that all should
come to repentance,

Who camest to seek and to
save that which was lost,

Who after our repentance rememberest our sins no more,

Have mercy upon us.

Be merciful and spare us, good
LORD.

From all evil and wicked-
ness,

From sudden, unprepared, or
evil death,

By Thy Blood, which Thou
didst shed for the remission of
sins,

In time of trouble, in the hour
of death, and in the day of
Judgment,

Good LORD, deliver us.

We sinners do beseech Thee to
hear us.

That it may please Thee to
bring us to true repentance,

That condemning ourselves
we may escape Thy condemnation,

That we may bring forth
worthy fruits of penitence,

That we may not give place
to the devil, nor let the sun go
down upon our wrath,

That denying ungodliness and
worldly lusts, we may live soberly, righteously, and godly in
this present world,

That being dead unto sin, we
may live unto righteousness,

That we may work out our
salvation with fear and trembling,

That coming boldly to the
throne of grace, we may obtain
mercy and find grace to help in
time of need,

We beseech Thee to hear us, Good LORD.

O Lamb of GOD, &c.
    Spare us, O LORD.
O Lamb, &c. *Hear us, &c.* O
Lamb, &c. *Have mercy, &c.* O
CHRIST, hear us. LORD, have mer-
cy, &c. Our FATHER, &c.

℣. O LORD, deal not with us
after our sins. ℟. Neither reward
us after our iniquities. ℣. O LORD,
remember not our old sins. ℟.
But have mercy upon us, and that
soon, for we are brought very low.
℣. Help us, O GOD our SAVIOUR.
℟. And for the glory of Thy Name
deliver us, and be merciful unto

our sins for Thy Name's sake. ℣. Cleanse us, O Lord, from our secret faults. ℟. And keep Thy servants from presumptuous sins. ℣. Lord, hear, &c. ℟. And let, &c. ℣. Let us pray.

446. O Lord Jesu Christ, Saviour of the world, Who gavest Thyself to death upon the Cross to save sinners, have mercy upon us, and be not angry with us for ever. Accept our contrition, pardon our offences, hear our prayers, that freed from the bondage of our sins, we may evermore cleave unto Thee in this life, and finally be received by Thee unto life eternal. Where Thou.

LITANY OF THANKSGIVING.

Lord, have mercy, &c. Christ, &c. Lord, &c.

O God the Father, &c.,
O God the Son, &c.,
O God the Holy Ghost, &c.,
O Holy Trinity, One God, &c.,
O God, Who hast decreed from eternity to do good unto us,
Who hast employed Thy Power, Wisdom, and Love for our benefit,
Who in a moment dost bestow new blessings upon us,
Who hast not withdrawn Thy bounteous Hand from us, though we have sinned against Thee, — *Have mercy upon us.*

Because Thou hast made us in Thine own Image,
Because Thou hast raised us up to an aim and end beyond this life,
Because Thou hast given us an immortal soul,
Because Thou hast made it able to know Thee, love Thee, and enjoy Thee for ever,
Because Thou hast given so many creatures for our service,
Because Thou hast kept and nourished us hitherto in Thy Fatherly goodness,
Because Thou hast given us the holy Apostles as our guardians and helpers,
Because Thou hast redeemed us from the captivity of hell by the Passion of Thy dear Son,
Because Thou hast made us members of Thy holy Catholic Church,
Because Thou hast given us the holy Sacraments for our salvation,
Because Thou hast given us so many other means of grace,
Because Thou hast not rejected and condemned us for so many past sins,
Because Thou hast saved us from innumerable sins of soul and body, — *We thank Thee, O Lord.*

For all Thy gifts and blessings, natural and supernatural,
For all our inward and outward sufferings,
For all Thy fatherly correction and chastisement,
For all Thy gifts and blessings which we have never yet fully known,
For all Thy gifts and blessings which we have never yet duly treasured up,
For all Thy gifts and blessings which we have so often sinfully misused, — *We thank Thee, O Lord.*

For all Thy gifts and blessings which Thou hast bestowed on our relations, benefactors, friends and enemies,

For all Thy gifts and blessings which Thou hast bestowed on all the family of mankind,

In union with the thanksgivings which the Church militant here on earth pays Thee, and will pay Thee till the end of the world,

In union with the thanksgivings which the Church triumphant in heaven pays Thee, and will pay Thee for evermore,

We thank Thee, O Lord.

Son of God, we beseech, &c.
Lamb of God, that takest, &c.
Lord, have mercy, &c.
Our Father, &c.

℣. Thou art my God, and I will thank Thee. ℟. Thou art my God, and I will praise Thee. ℣. All Thy works praise Thee, O Lord. ℟. And Thy saints give thanks unto Thee. ℣. The Lord, &c. ℟. And with, &c. ℣. Let us pray.

447. O God, Who hast been pleased to show us, Thine unworthy creatures, the riches of Thy love and bounty in all their greatness, so add Thy priceless grace and blessing unto them, that we may henceforth at all times truly know them, duly treasure them, and so employ them for Thine honour and our salvation, that through holy use of them, and thankful love in return for them, we may at length reach that place where, with all Thy Saints and elect, we shall praise and bless Thy boundless goodness and mercy for evermore. Through.

Miscellaneous.

NOTES ON THE VISITATION OF THE SICK.

1. The Clergyman should remember that he visits the sick as a Priest, not as a mere sympathising friend. He has to do for the soul of the sick man what the physician has to do for his body,—to ascertain the disease, and apply the remedies.

2. All bodily as well as spiritual sickness is the consequence of sin, personal or original, therefore the time of sickness especially calls for the ministration of the physician of the soul.

3. The soul and body react upon one another, so that in sickness of the body the soul also suffers from torpor or undue sensitiveness, for either of which the Priest must make allowance in drawing his conclusions as to the spiritual condition of the sick man.

4. Therefore the Priest should visit at a time when the patient is least under these disturbing influences, i.e., generally speaking, from 11 a.m. to 3 p.m., of course avoiding the patient's meal time. Evening visits often destroy his night's rest, and should never be made except in case of great urgency.

5. In the evening the mind of the sick man is most of all out of tune. Expressions of religious feelings are then especially untrustworthy, being usually the result of mere physical excitement or exhaustion.

6. A quarter of an hour is generally long enough for a visit. When the patient is very languid, a much shorter one is desirable.

7. Never, except in extreme cases, visit a sick man more than *once a*

day. (1) Because too frequent calls lower his estimate of the religious character of the act. (2) Because they are mostly a source of both mental and physical distress and irritation to him.

8. If you have made an appointment for a sick call, be very punctual, for the strain of watching for a delayed visit is exciting and hurtful.

9. Never allow a patient to be awakened.

10. On entering, give the salutation, "Peace be to this house."

11. Enter and leave the sick chamber without lingering, but also without abruptness or hurry.

12. Avoid all noise, as the sudden closing of doors, loud talking, &c., do not speak too low to the patient himself, nor whisper to his friends in the room such things as he is not intended to hear. This is especially important if the person be *seemingly* unconscious, for the sense of hearing is often retained in such cases.

13. Clear the room if crowded.

14. Do not sit on nor touch the bed.

15. Never let a patient stand.

16. Vary your visits, in long cases, as much as possible, by bringing pictures, books, &c.

17. Avoid gossip, but if you can give pleasant intelligence do so.

18. Speak calmly and gently, but decidedly and concisely. Read slowly and distinctly.

19. Never preach or pray *at* the sick. In the case of hardened sinners trust to private intercession, and when with them pray in the first person—"we," "us,"—not in the third.

20. Do not begin arguing with sick dissenters: find some point of agreement with them, and so lead them on.

21. Avoid giving false encouragement as to recovery, and also over-commiseration.

22. Find or suggest some occupation for the sick person, if feasible.

23. Encourage the sick man, if at variance with any one, to send a verbal message of kindliness by the Priest.

24. The Priest should not write a will for a sick person, save under most exceptional circumstances, and when no one else competent can be procured. He should not recommend special legacies, but urge the sick person in general terms to justice and charity.

25. A summons to a private Baptism should be attended to without the least delay. The Priest is advised to take a surplice, stole, vessel, and fair linen cloth.

26. On first visiting a new case he should ascertain whether the patient has been baptized. If not, he should at once begin to instruct him for Baptism, as the Office for the Visitation of the Sick is intended only for the baptized.

27. If the sick person be near death, he is to be briefly instructed in the following truths: the Holy Trinity, the Incarnation, the Atonement, and its application through the Sacraments.

28. On the sick man's expression of belief in these truths, and of sorrow for his past sins, the Priest may proceed to baptize him.

29. The Office to be used will be the Office for the Baptism of those of Riper Years, with such abridgment as may be necessary.

30. Very ignorant persons, unfamiliar with prayers, should be taught short Acts of Devotion. The following may serve:

I. *Act of Faith.*

I believe in Thee, O GOD the FATHER, my Maker. I believe in Thee, O GOD the SON, my SAVIOUR, I believe in Thee, O GOD the HOLY GHOST, my Helper. Glory be to Thee, O Holy TRINITY, Three Persons and One GOD. Amen.

II. *Act of Hope.*

O merciful GOD, in Thee is my

hope; O cast not out my soul, but save it for JESUS CHRIST'S sake. Amen.

III. *Act of Love.*

I love Thee, O FATHER, Who didst give Thy SON for me. I love Thee, O CHRIST, Who didst die for me. I love Thee, O HOLY GHOST, Who dost bless me. Amen.

IV. *Act of Sorrow.*

O GOD, I repent of all my sins against Thee, forgive me, and make me holy, for JESUS CHRIST'S sake. Amen.

Some of the Ejaculations, pp. 9 and 148, may also be taught to the sick.

31. The Priest should instruct those lay persons who are much about the persons of the sick (and especially nurses and midwives), how to act when there is great danger of a child or adult dying unbaptized.

32. If there appear no hope of an infant surviving until the Priest can be fetched, the nurse, midwife, or other person present should take a little pure water, and pour it three times on the child's head, saying, " I baptize thee in the Name," &c. It is not *necessary* to name the child, though this too may be done if the parents' wish be known.

33. If it be uncertain whether the child be alive, or if it appear as a monster, and not of human shape, the baptism should take place as above, only changing the form thus: " *If thou art capable*, I baptize thee," &c.

34. The case of adults is of very much rarer occurrence. Still it may, in most exceptional instances, happen that a person whose baptism has been neglected or deferred may desire that Sacrament when dying in the absence of a Priest. This may possibly occur in seasons of epidemic. The attendant in that case should ask the sick person these three questions :—1. Do you believe in GOD the FATHER, GOD the SON, and GOD the HOLY GHOST? 2. Do you repent of all your sins? 3. Is it your wish to be baptized? On receiving affirmative answers, the Sacrament may be administered as in 32, but this is not to be done if the Priest can be brought before the patient is likely to expire.

35. On a first visit the Priest should impress upon the patient that sickness is of GOD'S permission, and is the consequence of sin, original or personal. The Exhortation in the Visitation Office, read with comments, is suitable for this purpose.

36. The sick poor are generally more struck with what is read out of *their own* Bible and Prayer Book. This should be remembered if what is to be read is likely to be strange to them.

37. When a general idea of sin has been impressed on the patient, the fact of his own personal sinfulness should be urged on him.

38. With those who assert that they have never done any harm, the Priest should explain that sins of omission are as bad as sins of commission ; e.g., to starve a child is as bad as to poison it.

39. In examination of conscience the Priest may employ the Notes on the Commandments (p. 195). The explanation of our duties in the Catechism, if used, would recall early teaching.

40. Many who are prejudiced against the *word* "Confession" will gladly avail themselves of the *thing*, if suggested to them with tact, and without abruptness.

41. To do this, the Priest may suggest to the patient such considerations as the comfort of making a clean breast ; the danger to himself of underrating or ignoring real evils ; and the greater likelihood that the Priest can give him useful advice and real consolation, if he knows what kind of life he has hitherto led. Quotations from the

Exhortation to Communion may be cited with advantage.

42. In case the sick man has wronged another either by word or deed, the fullest restitution possible should be urged upon him.

43. Where enmity has existed, the sick man shall be asked whether he can fully and freely assent to the following declaration of forgiveness:

" I humbly beg forgiveness of all whom I have injured ; I heartily forgive all who have injured me, that I myself may be forgiven my sins, for JESUS CHRIST'S sake. Amen."

44. The Communion of the Sick should be celebrated, as regards altar furniture and ritual, with as much resemblance as possible to the service in Church. This will impress the identity of the rite on the sick.

45. The Priest should carry with him the vessels, &c., and would do well to take not only the Wine, but also the Bread and the Water. He should have a spoon with which to communicate the sick, in case of difficulty of swallowing. Small pocket Communion plate is undesirable.

46. The same amount of intelligent faith in the Holy Eucharist is not to be exacted from all classes of persons. It suffices that a communicant should believe that our LORD JESUS CHRIST feeds our souls with His Body and Blood, and that he come to the Sacrament with sorrow for past sins, and resolve of amendment.

47. It is well to have a district visitor or other fit person to make the responses, who might also be instructed to prepare the sick room for the Celebration.

48. The Priest should inquire as to the sick person's capability of swallowing or retaining food. If the answers are so unsatisfactory as to involve the risk of any irrever-

once, he should confine himself, for the time being, to the use of the Office for Spiritual Communion (p. 86.)

49. If the patient be unable to swallow solids, a very small particle of the species of Bread should be put into a spoon with the species of Wine, and the two be administered simultaneously with the single formula, "The Body and Blood," &c.

50. If he be unable to take Wine, the species of Bread may be tinged with a single drop from the Chalice, and administered as in the last case. When this is impossible, Communion under one kind becomes necessary.

51. When nausea or fear of infection prevents the Priest from swallowing the ablutions, they should be carefully poured into the fire. When a spoon has been employed, it should be placed in a cup of water, which may be used subsequently for the ablutions.

52. Before beginning to celebrate, he should inquire who among those present design to communicate, and should arrange them conveniently.

53. In chronic cases the sick should communicate at least as frequently as during previous health. The Collect, Epistle, and Gospel *for the day* may be fitly used.

54. Unconfirmed children, if intelligent, and otherwise fitly disposed, should be communicated, however young, when in danger of death.

55. Adults of feeble mind, and deaf and dumb persons, may also be communicated, if they show faith and penitence according to the measure of their capacity.

56. Insane persons may be communicated during lucid intervals, provided their previous life has not made them unfit.

57. Idiots, and insane persons, during aberration, are never to be communicated.

58. During the death-agony spiritual consolation is especially needed. The Priest should therefore endea-

vour to be present at each death-bed in his parish. To insure this, he should instruct the friends of persons in dangerous sickness to summon him when death seems to be approaching.

59. As a visit of this nature may be indefinitely protracted, the devotions used must be such as can be made to extend over a considerable time.

60. The Harmonized Passion Lections should always be used, and three or four Passion Collects inserted after each portion. Hymns and Litanies may also be fitly introduced.

61. The Priest would often do well to confer with the medical attendant as to the exact condition of the sick person. He may thus, by reminding those about the sick of the medical instructions as to diet, ventilation, visits of friends, &c., assist the cure, and also aid in checking infection and panic in epidemic cases. He may often prevent the spread of sickness by recommending attention to personal cleanliness, drainage, ventilation (especially in bed-rooms), warm clothing, &c.

62. Wine or brandy should not be provided without the permission of the medical man.

63. As a personal precaution, the Priest should take food before visiting infectious cases, except, of course, when about to celebrate the Holy Communion, and should stand to "windward" of such patients.

64. In case of sudden insensibility from faintness or loss of blood, *with pallor of face*, let the patient be laid horizontally, and the head low. Loose the dress about the throat and chest, and give warm brandy and water. If accompanied with struggling and *redness of face*, the head should be raised, after loosening the dress, and no stimulants be given. The room must be cleared, and cold water sprinkled on the face.

65. In case of poisoning, the stomach should be relieved by copious draughts of warm salt and water or mustard and water. If by opium, keep the patient awake by any means till the arrival of the medical man ; e.g., by making him walk barefoot on a stone floor. No antidotes should be given without medical advice.

NOTES ON SINS, AND THEIR REMEDIES.

Sins.

Selfishness, in one form or another, will be found to be at the root of all personal sin. The following are the forms in which sin most commonly violates the commandments :

First Commandment.

Determining to disbelieve in GOD through a desire to follow sin, or through pride of intellect—Making a mock of religion or of sin—Putting some friend in the place of GOD—Doing wrong things, or omitting right things, in order to please man — Adopting a conventional standard in religious practice, for fear of giving offence—Pursuing steadily, as the main object in life, something from which religion is banished—Showing disbelief in GOD's mercy by despairing, or in His justice by presuming—Putting off repentance from sloth or self-will.

Second Commandment.

Neglect of Public Worship—of Baptism—Confirmation—Holy Eucharist—Private Prayer—Going to church from a wrong motive, e.g., respectability, vanity, curiosity, or gossip, merely for the music or sermon—Improper thoughts or behaviour at church—Attending Dissenting worship or religious meetings—Unnecessary perusal of unsound books, or conversation on religious topics with unsound persons.

Third Commandment.

Profane swearing—Careless or irreverent use of holy names, writings, or things—Superstitious use of the same—Using as oaths phrases resembling or suggesting holy names—Hypocrisy—Mechanical recitation of prayers—Talking too freely on religious subjects, even if not in a bad spirit.

Fourth Commandment.

Laziness or misspending time—Procrastination—Unnecessary work on Sundays or Festivals—Missing church, or causing others to miss it, on Sundays.

Fifth Commandment.

Disobedience or disrespect to parents—Inattention to their wishes or wants—Eye-service towards employers—Neglect of family duties and claims—Of direction or advice of teachers—Harshness to inferiors, or neglect of their temporal or spiritual wants—Setting a bad example.

Sixth Commandment.

Hatred — Sullenness — Pride — Spitefulness—Vindictiveness—Injuring others in body or mind—Quickness of Retort — Reviling — Cruelty to men or animals—Causing anger in others.

Seventh Commandment.

Impure thoughts, words, or deeds —Perusal of coarse, lax, or sensual books—Looking at immodest pictures, or similar objects—Unsuitable or immodest dress—Personal vanity—Attempting to attract the notice of the opposite sex—Overeating—Daintiness—Drunkenness, or frequent use of stimulants — Using opium—Physical self-indulgence — Flirting — Ostentation — Corrupting others—Marriage with divorced persons, or within the prohibited degrees, or from merely worldly motives.

Eighth Commandment.

Stealing—Receiving stolen goods — Pilfering — In *buying*, beating down an article below its fair value; in *selling*, taking advantage of the ignorance of a customer—Borrowing without returning—Extravagance—Contracting debts without having a reasonable prospect of paying—Giving insufficient wages or payment to servants or workpeople—Giving short time or imperfect work for full payment—Adulteration—Using false weights and measures—Omitting tithes and almsgiving—Failing to make restitution—Wasting food, or anything useful—Taking credit due to another.

Ninth Commandment.

Lying, deception, or equivocation—Breaking vows or promises—Acting a lie—Betraying trust or secrets—Making unreal excuses—Defending oneself when in the wrong—Prying—Slander—Gossip—Putting an evil construction on the words or acts of others—Taking pleasure in the evil of others—Hinting evil or concealing good of others—Speaking of the evil of others apart from imperative duty—Habitual exaggeration.

Tenth Commandment.

Discontent—Envy—Grumbling—Worldliness—Stinginess—Eager speculation—Gambling.

REMEDIES FOR SIN.

To uproot sin, uproot selfishness (Rom. xiii. 10); for he who lives for others will have less time and inclination for following his own sins.

As a help to self-mortification, some voluntary act may be performed, in addition to the prescribed practice of the virtue directly contrary to the sin which is to be overcome.

It is, as a general rule, inexpedient to impose additional devotions by way of penance, as this tends to degrade prayer into a formal and irksome task: some act involving self-denial will be found more useful.

When a sinful use has been made of things lawful, abstain from the innocent use of such things.

The Seven Deadly Sins will be found to include almost all ordinary offences.

I. PRIDE, i.e., thinking too highly of oneself, is the commonest form of selfishness. It includes unbelief, ostentation, vanity, disobedience, and disrespect, harshness to inferiors, spiritual self-conceit. Its contrary virtue is Humility.

Remedies.—Discover the exact subject of the pride, in order to localize the treatment.

If *power* or *influence*, compare your influence with that of kings and emperors, and theirs in turn with GOD's. Test the *degree* of your influence by trying to overcome some settled abuse; its *extent* by change of scene to some place where you are unknown; its *duration* by considering how long your labours are likely to survive you.

If *knowledge* or *intellect*, compare yours with that of illustrious scholars, and theirs with GOD's omniscience. Sir I. Newton spoke of himself as a child picking up shells on the shore of the ocean of knowledge. Begin the study of a new and difficult subject. Seek the conversation of those superior to you in learning; avoid the company of those who are likely to place you first.

If *wealth*, consider how many things, and those the most valuable, it cannot buy, as health or peace of mind. It is not a possession, but a trust. Consider the poverty of our LORD and His Apostles.

If *rank*, consider that its origin was due to merit in the first possessors, and that rank without merit is a disgrace. Our LORD, though of royal descent, chose the life of an artisan, and refused to be made a king.

If *physical gifts*, consider their short duration, and their liability to be lost by sickness or age.

If *character* or *reputation*, consider whether people would praise you if they knew all your faults. Is your name known beyond a small circle? How soon will your place be filled up when you die?

Where pride has shown itself by disrespect or discourtesy, frank and ample apology should form part of the amends.

II. ANGER. Neglecting Public Worship out of pique—Violent language—Sullenness—Spite—Cruelty—Provoking others to anger—Quarrelling—Bitter or irritating language—Vindictiveness. Its contrary virtue is Patience.

In case of a temptation to anger, be silent for a few moments before speaking. Say the LORD's Prayer secretly. If there be no time to do this, make the sign of the Cross on your lips. Do some kind act for the person with whom you are angry. Mention him in your private prayers.

III. COVETOUSNESS, the contrary virtue to which is Liberality, was the sin of Judas Iscariot, the only man of whose damnation we are quite certain. Practise regular and systematic almsgiving.

IV. LUST, the contrary virtue to

which is Chastity, is a part of man's physical nature, and therefore the more difficult to overcome. Hence flight from the objects of temptation is safer than battle. The chief encouragements to lust are idleness, high living, and languor, whether constitutional or brought on by sloth. The more vigorous is the health of the body, the less is it usually subject to lust. The preventives are—(1.) To bring some other thought before the mind, when tempted, or to engage the body in some immediate and active occupation. The bitter taste of a chip of quassia will often serve to drive away the first motions of evil thoughts. (2.) Early rising. (3.) Cold bathing. (4.) For *men*, bracing exercise and out-of-door occupation. For *women*, change of employment without much exercise, and when the temptation comes on in solitude, mixing in society. (5.) Moderate fasting. The remedies are—(1.) In *sudden* cases, ejaculatory prayer, and the use of the Sign of the Cross. (2.) In *prolonged* ones, severe fasting and hard lying, even on the floor. (3.) In *extreme* cases, self-inflicted and sharp physical suffering.

V. GLUTTONY and DRUNKENNESS. Its contrary virtue is Temperance. —Observe the fasts of the Church with regularity and devotion. Compute the money saved by so doing, and give it to the poor. Take somewhat less food than you are inclined to take, and of a coarser or less favourite kind. Meals should be few in number, and eating at other times should be avoided. If drink is sought for necessary excitement, seek a change of excitement in variety of scene or society, in music, active exercise, &c. If taken to drown thought, the Priest should endea-vour to discover the cause, and apply remedies to that. The desire for drink may often be checked by an appetizing diet: in winter by warm food; in summer by the abundant use of fruit. Where excessive use of spirit or opium has become habitual, their sudden cessation is fraught with great physical and moral dangers: very gradual but steady diminution should be recommended. Where the penitent sees no safety save in total abstinence, the Priest should not check him. A loathing for alcoholic liquor has been created by mixing it with every article of food or drink for a short time.

VI. ENVY. Its contrary virtue is Love. Its remedies are persistence in Intercessory Prayer; doing kind actions, or speaking kind words in behalf of the object of our envy: seeking out those who are less favoured than ourselves, and trying to help them.

VII. SLOTH, the contrary virtue to which is Diligence, gives rise to both lust and theft. Begin by fixing the times of morning and evening prayer, the former at an early hour, and take care not to swerve from them without positive necessity. Select some one piece of work to be done each day at a fixed time, and involving some labour. When this has become a habit, add another task, until the day is mapped out. Where fixed duties already exist, do first that which is nearest in point of order, not that which is liked best. Employ amusement as relaxation after work, not as the business of life. The formation of habits is the only way to secure spiritual advancement, and this must be acquired by the faithful discharge of petty every-day duties.

NOTES ON THE PRACTICE OF HOLINESS.

The Three Theological Virtues are Faith, Hope, and Charity. The Four Cardinal Virtues are Justice, Prudence, Temperance, and Fortitude. The Three kinds of Good Works are, Fasting, Prayer, and Almsdeeds. The Seven Gifts of the HOLY GHOST are, the Spirit of Wisdom, Understanding, Counsel, Ghostly Strength, Knowledge, True Godliness, and Holy Fear. The Twelve Fruits of the HOLY GHOST are, Love, Joy, Peace, Patience, Mercy, Goodness, Longsuffering, Meekness, Faith, Modesty, Chastity, Sobriety. The Spiritual Works of Mercy are to instruct the ignorant (Dan. xii. 3), to correct offenders (S. James v. 19, 20), to counsel the doubtful (Gal. vi. 1), to comfort the afflicted (Rom. xii. 15), to suffer injuries with patience (S. Matt. v. 39), to forgive offences and wrongs (S. Luke vi. 37), to pray for the living and the dead (S. James v. 16; 2 Tim. i. 18). The Corporal Works of Mercy are, to feed the hungry (S. Matt. xxv. 35), to give drink to the thirsty (Ib.), to clothe the naked (Ib. 36), to harbour the stranger and poor (Isa. lviii. 7), to visit the sick (S. Matt. xxv. 36), to minister to prisoners (Ib.), to bury the dead (Tobit xii. 12, 13).

As all Christian excellence consists in likeness to CHRIST's obedience, the practice of Humility is at the root of all holiness. Its exercise, as in the case of all other virtues, consists in (1) meditation on the life of CHRIST, and the comparison of our own with it. (2.) Prayer for grace. (3.) Outward and inward acts of self-abnegation.

When praise or self-esteem has excited vanity, think of your greatest sin, and make at once the following

Act of Humility.

Woe is me that pride hath blinded mine eyes. Show me my sins in Thy light, O LORD: humble me and save me for JESUS CHRIST's sake. Amen.

Avoid making excuses when found fault with, even to yourself.

If vain of freedom from some particular fault, examine narrowly (1.) Whether the fact really is so. (2.) Whether the freedom is due to successful resistance, or merely to the absence of temptation. (3.) Whether the contrary sin is not the dominant one of your character. A blind man is not pure merely because he does not sin through the lust of the eyes.

When slighted or insulted, think of your LORD's rejection by the Jews.

Practise courtesy to all as a Christian duty.

Avoid giving unnecessary trouble in all cases.

Do not insist obstinately on your just rights, unless those of others, or some principles, are involved.

When tempted to spiritual pride, change your usual form of self-examination for a more searching one; note down all deviations from the strict line of Christian duty, and compare the result with the obedience of the Saints and Angels, ending with an act of humility.

The three stages of humility are to endure (1) Patiently, (2) Willingly, (3) Joyfully.

Humility teaches to serve others, and is therefore the parent of good works and kindness. It prompts to the subjugation of the body, and thus encourages chastity and temperance. It teaches a reliance upon GOD rather than on ourselves, and thus confers patience and fortitude.

Each of these virtues must however be promoted by special acts of meditation and prayer, of which those made at the celebration of the Holy Eucharist are most efficacious. Humility will inspire self-distrust, and hence constant watchfulness in guarding against little relapses, and will banish all publicity and ostentation from good works.

Frequent ejaculatory prayers offered throughout the day as well as in all moments of temptation, will serve to keep the soul on the alert.

The greater portion of the prayers offered up should be intercessory, lest prayer itself should take the form of selfishness.

When troubled with wandering in prayer, recommence the interrupted devotion. If it continues change the posture of the body, and assume an inconvenient one. If the distractions are chronic, change the devotions for very short and fervent forms, especially such as refer to the Passion.

Take care that your prayers be not that your own will may be done.

When prayer seems to be unanswered, it is from one of two reasons: either the thing prayed for would be hurtful to you, or the gift sought is withheld to try your faith.

In either case change the form of devotion to one simply asking GOD to do His good pleasure.

Dryness and coldness of devotion are not necessarily signs of unspirituality. They may result from (1) Disordered physical condition; (2) Reaction after exceptional religious excitement or devotion; (3) Secret sin; (4) A desire on GOD's part to try us as He tried His SON.

Those affected in this manner should by no means remit or shorten their customary devotions, but add to them at stated periods Ps. xxii. Devotional poetry will often relieve the soul of its burdens. To omit our devotions at such times as we cease to feel pleasure in performing them, is to treat them as personal luxuries rather than as acts of positive duty towards GOD.

As the practice of holiness has for its object the future enjoyment of GOD's visible Presence, so we should make acts of His Presence in prayer and meditation a part of our regular spiritual training. These acts should at first be made weekly, and gradually increased in number and continuity, until they become habitual, and at length bring the whole daily life into close relation to Divine things.

INSTRUCTIONS ON CHRISTIAN DOCTRINE.

The Holy Trinity, one GOD, was not plainly revealed to the Jews, lest they should fall into the error of the heathen, and imagine that there were more Gods than One. Still the doctrine was shadowed forth in the Old Testament (Gen. i.; ii. 22; xi. 7; Ps. xxxiii. 6; cx. 1; Isa. vi. 3).

The knowledge of the mystery was not *necessary* until the Second Person of the Holy Trinity had become Man, and the Third Person was about to become the Teacher of the Church (S. John xiv. 26). Therefore the revelation was made to us at the Baptism of CHRIST, when His public ministry began.

In the New Testament GOD is revealed to us as Three *Persons*, FATHER, SON, and HOLY GHOST (S. Matt. xxviii. 19; 2 Cor. xiii. 14), all equal (S. John v. 17, 18; x. 30; xiv. 9, 11; Acts v. 3, 4), but still as only one GOD (1 Cor. viii. 4; Eph. iv. 6). GOD the FATHER is revealed to us as the First Cause of all things (1 Cor. viii. 6) ; GOD the SON as the Creator (S. John i. 1, 3 ; Col. i. 16) and Redeemer (Rom. iv. 24, 25 ; 1 Cor. xv. 3 ; 1 S. Pet. ii. 24) ; GOD the HOLY GHOST as the Life Giver (S. John vi. 63 ; Rom. viii. 2, 11 ; 2 Cor. iii. 6), Teacher (S. John xvi. 13 ; 2 S. Pet. i. 21), and Sanctifier (Gal. vi. 8).

THE CREED.

I. *I believe in God . . . earth ;* i.e. I am thoroughly persuaded as being GOD'S truth that He is to be looked upon as a FATHER (2 Chron. xx. 20 ; Heb. xi. 6) ; 1, as the Creator of all things (1 Cor. viii. 6 ; Eph. iv. 6) ; 2, as the FATHER of JESUS CHRIST (S. John i. 18 ; iii. 16 ; 2 Cor. i. 3) ; 3, as the FATHER of the Baptized (Rom. viii. 15 ; 1 S. John iii. 1) ; of infinite Power (Jer. xxxii. 17, 18, 27 ; Dan. iv. 35 ; S. Matt. xix. 26) ; Knowledge (Ps. cxxxix. 4 ; Prov. xv. 3 ; Rom. xi. 33 ; Heb. iv. 13) ; Truth (Ps. xxxi. 5 ; S. John iii. 33 ; vii. 28 ; Rom. iii. 4) ; Holiness (1 Sam. ii. 2 ; 1 S. Pet. i. 15) ; Justice (Gen. xviii. 25 ; Job xxxvii. 23 ; Rom. ii. 2) ; Goodness (Ps. xxxiv. 8 ; Jer. ix. 24 ; Mic. vii. 18) ; Love (Exod. xxxiv. 6 ; Deut. iv. 30, 31 ; Ps. c. 4 ; ciii. 8 ; 1 S. John iv. 8—10). Hence the duty of hoping and trusting in Him at all times and under all circumstances (1 S. Pet. iv. 19).

II. *In Jesus Christ . . . our Lord ;* i.e., we believe this not only as a fact, but accept Him as He is set before us in Scripture. First as GOD, equal to the FATHER (S. John v. 18 ; x. 30) ; and then as *our* SAVIOUR (Acts iv. 12 ; 1 Cor. iii. 11) ; and therefore that we should renounce our own merits, and trust entirely to His ; *our* Prophet (Acts iii. 22), and therefore accept His teaching in all things ; *our* Priest (Ps. cx. 4 ; Heb. iv. 14 ; vii. 25), and therefore look to His Sacrifice alone for salvation ; *our* LORD and

King (Isa. ix. 6 ; xiv. 9), and ther all things (2 Co died for each one 2 S. Pet. ii. 1). LORD, LORD," ¿ 46.)

III. *Conceived . . . Mary.* Her tery of the Incarn Perfect Godhead 1 Tim. iii. 16) Manhood (S. Lu Heb. ii. 14, 17). that He might without sheddin (Heb. ix. 22), an nature which ha 14) ; that He with man's infirm and leave us an 5—7 ; 1 S. Pet. is our *duty* to ho sion (Heb. iv. 14 that we may ap fullest confidence

IV. *Suffered u . . . . . hell :* i.e not only in fulfiln cies (Isa. liii. 4 ; Acts iii. 18), and xxii. 6 ; S. John xxi. 9 ; S. John (Gal. iii. 13 ; 1 18), and thereby v. 9).

A belief in C death, and burial flect that ours a parison (cf. 2 Co xxvi. 38), nothin serve (1 S. Pet. we partake of C (2 Cor. iv. 10 ; I are called to bea crucified with Cr v. 24 ; vi. 14) ; t (S. Luke ix. 23). sin, we crucify vi. 6). Being b Baptism, we sho ness of life (Ro are partakers of shall be also of His consolation (2 Cor. i. 5; 2 Tim. ii. 11, 12). Present sufferings are not comparable with future glory (Rom. viii. 18). By them we are prepared for future glory (Rom. vi. 3, 5, 8, 9).

V. *The third day . . . . dead*, as He had foretold (S. Mark viii. 31; x. 34), His Resurrection being a token of His Divinity (Rom. i. 4), of full satisfaction having been made for sin (S. Luke xxiv. 46, 47; Rom. iv. 25; 1 S. Pet. i. 3, 21), and of our resurrection (Rom. vi. 5; viii. 11; 1 Thess. iv. 14).

VI. *He ascended . . . the Father Almighty.* This expresses our belief that our LORD's Human Body is in heaven, as well as His soul and Divinity (S. Luke xxiv. 39, 51; Acts iv. 9, 10). He ascended in order to send the Comforter (S. John xvi. 7) to abide in, and guide the Church (S. John xiv. 16, 17); to present His Sacrifice to the FATHER (Heb. vii. 17, 24, 25; viii. 1; ix. 24), thus making intercession for us (Rom. viii. 34), and being our Mediator (1 Tim. ii. 5) and Advocate with the FATHER (1 S. John ii. 1). He thus also is shown to be our Prince and SAVIOUR (Acts v. 31), the Head of His Church (Eph. i. 22); and will remain at GOD's right hand until all His enemies are put under His feet (Heb. x. 13).

A belief in these two articles of the Creed requires of us that we should arise from the death of sin (Eph. v. 14; Col. iii. 1, 2), and henceforth have our conversation in heaven (Phil. iii. 20), looking forward hopefully to CHRIST's reappearance (Tit. ii. 13; Heb. vi. 19, 20), and trusting now to His intercession (Heb. vii. 25), and in the Comforter Whom He has sent to help us to live a risen and heavenly life (S. John xiv. 26; Rom. v. 5; viii. 26; Eph. ii. 18).

VII. *From thence He . . . dead.* Hence we believe that all men, living (1 Thess. iv. 15, 17) and dead (Ib. iv. 16) must appear before the judgment-seat of CHRIST (2 Cor. v. 10; Acts x. 42), to give account for all things, however secret (Eccl. xii. 14); thoughts (1 Cor. iv. 5; Acts viii. 22), words (S. Matt. xii. 36, 37; S. Jude 15), works (S. Matt. xvi. 27; Rom. ii. 6; Rev. xx. 12, 13), and omissions (S. Matt. xxv. 42; S. Luke xii. 47; S. James iv. 17). The Judgment will be sudden (S. Mark xiii. 35—37; 2 S. Pet. iii. 10), and the final lot of all then pronounced (S. Matt. xxv. 34, 41, 46); a motive to repentance (Acts xvii. 30, 31; 2 Cor. v. 9, 10; 2 S. Pet. iii. 9).

VIII. *I believe in the Holy Ghost.* That He is not only a real Person, distinct from the FATHER and the SON (S. John xv. 26), Very and Eternal GOD (Acts v. 3, 4), but that He is also the Giver of spiritual life (Rom. viii. 2; 2 Cor. iii. 6), by regenerating us in Holy Baptism (S. John iii. 5; Titus iii. 5), strengthening us in Confirmation (Acts viii. 17; Eph. iii. 14, 16), giving His mysterious energy to the Holy Eucharist (S. John vi. 63), enlightening our understanding (S. Luke xii. 12; Eph. i. 17, 18), sanctifying our will (1 Cor. vi. 11; 1 S. Pet. i. 2), working in us a lively faith (1 Cor. xii. 9); making our faith fruitful (Gal. v. 22; Rom. v. 5); guiding us (Rom. xiii. 14); comforting us (S. John xiv. 16); quickening us (Rom. viii. 10, 11); interceding for us, and teaching us to pray (Rom. viii. 26).

Hence we must pray for His influence and assistance, with the intention of using them (1 Cor. xii. 7), for He is often grieved (Eph. iv. 30), and His influence may be quenched (1 Thess. v. 19); since GOD will not always strive with man (Gen. vi. 3).

IX. *In the Holy Catholic Church, the Communion of Saints.* The Church, which is the Body of CHRIST (Eph. i. 22, 23), and the

pillar and ground of the truth
(1 Tim. iii. 15), embraces the baptized (Acts ii. 41, 47), who hold the
true faith (Rom. vi. 17; 2 Tim. i.
13). It is essential that we should
belong to the Church (Acts ii. 47),
because it is the Body of CHRIST,
and severed ($\chi\omega\rho\ell s$) from Him we
can do nothing (S. John xv. 5, 6),
He is the Door (S. John x. 9), and
the only way of access to the FA-
THER (Ib. xiv. 6; Eph. ii. 18—20).
Wilful separation is a sin (2 Thess.
iii. 6). We are warned against it
(Rom. xvi. 17; 1 Cor. i. 10), because it is contrary to CHRIST's
prayer (S. John xvii. 20—23), and
because the Body is One (1 Cor. xii.
12; Eph. iv. 3—6).

The Church is holy, though containing many unholy members (1
Cor. xi. 17—19); compare the
Jewish nation (Exod. xix. 6; Deut.
vii. 6). Members of the Church
called "saints," at the same time
that they are accused of grievous
sins (Phil. i. 1; iii. 18).

Hence follows a belief in the
first privilege of the Church, i.c. the
Communion of Saints; a mysterious bond of union wrought in the
Church by the Sacraments, Holy
Baptism (1 Cor. xii. 13), the Holy
Eucharist (1 Cor. x. 17). This communion is with the FATHER (S.
John xiv. 23; xvii. 21; 1 S. John
i. 3); the SON (Gal. iii. 27, 28);
the HOLY GHOST (1 Cor. iii. 16; xii.
13; Phil. ii. 1); the Holy Angels
(S. Matt. xviii. 10; S. Luke xv. 7,
10; Heb. i. 14); the Saints living
(Rom. xii. 5; 1 Cor. xii. 26), and departed (Col. i. 12; Rev. vi. 9—11).
But without holiness true communion cannot be perfectly maintained
(1 S. John i. 6, 7).

X. *The Forgiveness of Sins*, original (Rom. v. 8—10, 12, 19), and
actual (Acts v. 31), is the second
privilege of the Church; for CHRIST
is the SAVIOUR of the Body (Eph.
v. 23). This forgiveness is ordinarily dispensed through the ordinances of the Church;—Holy Bap-

tism (S. Mark xv
xxii. 16); Holy
Matt. xxvi. 28)
Matt. xvi. 19;
xx. 21, 23; 2 Co
This belief sh
faith (Acts x. 4
Luke xxiv. 47; A
sion (1 S. John i.
vii. 47); forgiven
23—35; S. Luke
The unpardon
rejection of CHRI
(S. John iii. 36
obstinate and fin
Luke xiii. 3; Re

XI. *The Resur*
[*Flesh.*] Foresho
ing the dead (S.
S. Luke vii. 12,
11, &c.), and by F
tion (S. Luke xxi
declared (S. Joh
2; xxiv. 15; xx
20, &c.; 2 Cor. iv
14, &c.; Rev. xx
rise to happiness
(Dan. xii. 2; S.
46; S. John v. 28
of the just will
iii. 21; 1 S. John
shadowed by th
(S. Matt. xvii. 2)
cere Christians, de
no terrors for us
not, the greatest
14).

XII. *The Life*
perfect happiness
Matt. xiii. 43; 1
vii. 16, 17; xiv. 1
to the wicked (S
Rev. xiv. 10, 11;
8); in either case
(S. Matt. xxv. 46
—48; 2 Thess. i.
though there will
grees of happine
27; xx. 23; S. Jc
xv. 41, 42) and of
xii. 40; S. Luke x

THE COMMANDMENTS.

Sin is the transgression of the law (1 S. John iii. 4) : it is necessary therefore to know what the law is, and CHRIST has said that the baptized are to be taught it (S. Matt. xxviii. 20), and that eternal life depends on our keeping it (S. Matt. xix. 17—19) : further summing it up under two great heads (S. Matt. xxii. 36—39 ; S. Luke x. 25—28). The keeping of the Commandments is a test of our love of GOD (1 S. John ii. 3—6).

Rules for Interpreting the Ten Commandments.

1. When a duty is commanded, the contrary sin is forbidden, and *vice versâ*.
2. When a general rule is given, it includes all duties and sins which come under that head, as well as everything which leads to them (Ps. cxix. 96).
3. They are to be understood in the spirit as well as in the letter, as CHRIST has shown (S. Matt. v. 17, &c.)
4. They enjoin duties as well as forbid sins, and therefore condemn acts of omission as well as those of commission (S. Luke xii. 47 ; S. James iv. 17).
5. They are couched in the *second person singular*, to show that each of us individually is bound to keep them.

The First Commandment.

Forbids unbelief of all kinds (S. John viii. 24) ; hypocrisy (S. Matt. xiii. 5, 14 ; 2 Tim. iii. 5) ; carelessness about religion (Exod. v. 2 ; Ps. l. 4) ; pride (S. James iv. 6) ; presumption (Job xv. 25) ; despair (Ps. lii. 6, 7). It enjoins on us to believe in GOD (2 Chron. xx. 20 ; Heb. xi. 6) ; fear Him (Deut. x. 12 ; S. Luke xii. 5 ; Heb. xii. 28) ; love Him (S. Luke x. 27 ; 1 Cor. xvi. 22 ; 1 S. John v. 3) ; and to give our *heart* to GOD (Prov. xxiii. 26).

The Second Commandment.

Forbids us to put anything in the place of GOD (Exod. xxxiv. 14 ; Isa. xlii. 8 ; Jer. xvii. 5) ; to try to serve GOD and Mammon (S. Matt. vi. 24) ; to neglect His worship (Heb. x. 25) ; to worship Him in a wrong way (Lev. x. 1 ; 2 Thess. iii. 6). It enjoins us to worship Him (2 Kings xvii. 36 ; S. Matt. iv. 10 ; S. John ix. 31) ; give Him thanks (Ps. l. 14 ; 1 Thess. v. 18 ; Eph. v. 20) ; put our whole trust in Him (Prov. iii. 5 ; Isa. l. 10 ; Jer. xvii. 7 ; 1 S. Pet. v. 7) ; and call upon Him (Ps. l. 15 ; Isa. lv. 6 ; Rom. x. 13).

That children suffer *temporal* punishment for their parents' sins, we see in the case of extravagant or profligate parents, but not *eternal* punishment (Ezek. xviii. 19, 20).

The Third Commandment.

[The *Name* of GOD, often used for GOD Himself (S. Matt. vi. 9 ; S. Luke i. 49 ; S. John i. 12 ; Acts iv. 7).] Forbids false oaths (Lev. xix. 12 ; Zech. viii. 17 ; S. Matt. v. 33) ; profane swearing (S. Matt. v. 34—37 ; S. James v. 12) ; and cursing (S. Matt. v. 44 ; Rom. iii. 14) ; blasphemy and irreverence (Lev. xix. 12 ; xxi. 6 ; xxii. 2 ; Col. iii. 8). It enjoins reverence for GOD, especially in speaking of Him, (Ps. xxix. 2 ; cxix. 6 ; Phil. ii. 10, 11) ; His house (Lev. xix. 30 ; S. Matt. xxi. 12 ; 1 Cor. xi. 22) ; ministers (1 Thess. v. 12, 13 ; 1 Tim. v. 17) ; Scriptures (Acts xvii. 11 ; Rom. xv. 4 ; 2 Tim. iii. 15—17 ; S. James i. 21, 22) ; ordinances (S. John vi. 53—58 ; 1 Cor. xi. 23 —29) ; keeping vows (Deut. xxiii. 23 ; Eccl. v. 4).

The Fourth Commandment.

Forbids the waste or improper use of time (Prov. vi. 6, 9 ; Rom. xii. 11 ; Eph. iv. 28 ; 1 Thess. iv. 11). Enjoins especially the due observance of the LORD's day.

The Jewish holy seasons were part of that ceremonial law fulfilled in CHRIST (Col. ii. 16, 17), Who is LORD of the Sabbath (S. Matt. xii. 8). The *spirit* of the Commandment is that one day in seven should be devoted to the worship of GOD. The precise day altered by the Church, probably by CHRIST'S command (S. John xxi. 25; Acts i. 3), certainly by His sanction: for He appeared to the Apostles when assembled for worship on this day (S. John xx. 19, 26). The HOLY GHOST descended (Acts ii. 1—4). The first day afterwards the special day for worship (Acts xx. 7; 1 Cor. xvi. 1, 2). The LORD'S day to be observed by attendance on public worship (Deut. xxxi. 12, 13; S. Matt. xviii. 20; Heb. x. 25); by abstaining from the ordinary business of life (Neh. xiii. 15, 16), except in cases of necessity (S. Matt. xii. 1, 11, 12; S. Mark ii. 27). The Jews' Sabbath was not to be a day of gloom (Isa. lviii. 13, 14), much less the Christian Sunday. Acts of worship should be performed with joyfulness (S. James v. 13; Eph. v. 19; Col. iii. 16), being the employment of the Angels (S. Luke ii. 13), and the heavenly host (Rev. iv. 8—11; v. 11, 12).

The Fifth Commandment.

The last six Commandments summed up (S. Matt. vii. 12; xxii. 39; Rom. xiii. 9), mean that we should love our neighbours in the same way, consistently with the Gospel, not in the same degree, that we love ourselves. Enjoins children to love and honour (Deut. xxi. 18—21; Prov. i. 8, 9; S. Matt. xv. 4; S. Luke ii. 51), and succour (Gen. xlvii. 12; S. Mark vii. 10—13; 1 Tim. v. 4) their parents. To obey rulers and magistrates (Titus iii. 1; 1 S. Pet. ii. 13; 2 S. Pet. ii. 10,) and teachers (Prov. v. 10—13). It includes also the duties of the clergy to their flocks (Acts xx. 28), and *vice versâ* (Mal. ii. 7; S. Luke x. 16; 1 Cor. iv. 1; Heb. xiii. 7, 17); superiors to inferiors (Rom. xii. 16; 1 Tim. vi. 17, 18), and *vice versâ* (Rom. xiii. 7); the old to the young (Titus ii. 4—8), and *vice versâ* (Lev. xix. 32; Job xxxii. 4; 1 S. Pet. v. 5). The respective duties of parents and children, husbands and wives, masters and servants, treated of (Eph. v. and vi.; Col. iii. and iv.; Titus ii.) The wickedness of persons in authority no excuse for disobeying them (S. Matt. xxiii. 2, 3), unless they command us to do what is sinful (Acts iv. 19; v. 28, 29, 41, 42). Punishment threatened to bad children (Prov. xx. 20).

The Sixth Commandment.

Forbids not only personal violence (S. Luke iii. 14), but revenge, hatred, malice, &c., in the heart (S. Matt. xv. 19; S. Mark vii. 21—23), and their expression by the mouth (Eph. iv. 26, 31, 32).

The bodily injury of another being thus forbidden, much more is injury to his soul by evil deeds, words, or example.

The taking away of life is justifiable in *Magistrates* passing sentence (Rom. xiii. 4); *War*, which is not spoken of with disapproval in Scripture (S. Luke iii. 14; 2 Tim. ii. 4); *Self-defence* (Exod. xxii. 2).

The Seventh Commandment.

Sins against purity, whatever form they may take, are in Scripture condemned in the strongest language (Gal. v. 19, 21; Eph. v. 5; Rev. xxii. 15). The Commandment embraces not only acts of impurity (1 Cor. vi. 9, 18), but also impure thoughts (S. Matt. v. 28) and words (Eph. iv. 29; Col. iii. 8), immodest behaviour (Isa. iii. 16, &c.), intemperance, which provokes lust (Prov. xxiii. 31, 33; Rom. xiii. 13), and in a word all things which tend to inflame the passions either of ourselves or of others (1 S. Pet. iv. 3).

The Eighth Commandment.

Forbids robbery of all kinds,

whether secret or open (S. Mark x. 19; Lev. xix. 13, 35, 36; Titus ii. 9, 10); overreaching in trade (Prov. xx. 10, 14, 17); non-payment of debts (Lev. xxv. 14), or loans (Ps. xxxvii. 21); neglect of almsgiving (Deut. xv. 11).

The Ninth Commandment.

Forbids lying, false witness, and mischief-making (Prov. vi. 16, 19; Rev. xxi. 8, 27), slander (Ps. ci. 5), talebearing (Lev. xix. 16), and, to speak generally, all sins of the tongue (S. Matt. xii. 36; S. James i. 19, 26; iii.)

The Tenth Commandment.

Forbids covetousness and discontent (1 Tim. vi. 6—10; Heb. xiii. 5.)

Man was made at first in the "Image of God" (Gen. i. 27), i.e., in perfect purity (Eph. iv. 24); the expression used of JESUS CHRIST (2 Cor. iv. 4; Col. i. 15); Adam was thus the friend of GOD, and would have been immortal (Rom. v. 12) had he been obedient. He chose to listen to the devil rather than to GOD, and fell (Gen. iii.)

I. Adam sold himself to Satan for one sin. By this he not merely lost Paradise, but involved all his posterity in his fall (Rom. v. 12; vii. 14).

We fell in Adam (comp. Gen. xiv. 20; Heb. vii. 9, 10). *Ill.* If a man buy an acorn and plant it in his own ground, the tree which springs from that acorn, and all the acorns produced by that tree, and the trees produced by those acorns, belong to the original purchaser.

II. But by the Fall Adam not only became *subject to Satan*, but *corrupted human nature* (Gen. v. 3; also Job xiv. 4; Ps. li. 5; Eph. ii. 3). *Ill.* A child may be born a pauper through the extravagance, or diseased through the profligacy, of his parents.

Man, having thus sold himself by his sin, could not redeem himself by a perfectly pure life; because (1) his corrupted nature made it impossible that his life should be quite pure. (2) Even if he committed no more sin, he was merely abstaining from contracting fresh debt, and doing nothing towards cancelling the old one. This old debt could only be paid by the offering up of a perfectly spotless human being.

To provide such a being, GOD the SON became Man (S. John i. 14); was a real child of Adam (Heb. ii. 14); perfectly Man (Gal. iv. 4; Heb. ii. 17); perfectly spotless (1 S. Pet. i. 19; ii. 22); and "gave Himself a ransom for all" (1 Tim. ii. 6).

But, in order to work out the true end of the Incarnation, which is the union of the Divine and human natures, so as to knit GOD and man together, some means for extending the effect of it became necessary. Otherwise CHRIST would have been, as Man, only a great Example and Teacher, instead of being what is much more, the Second Adam (1 Cor. xv. 45), head of a new creation (Rev. iii. 14) and the Everlasting Father of His children (Isa. ix. 6). As the natural man requires union with a woman to propagate his race, so the Divine Man must have a Bride also, to be "the mother of all living" (Gen. iii. 20). As Eve was born from the side of Adam while he slept (Gen. ii. 21,) so the Church, which is the Bride of CHRIST (Rev. xix. 7; xxi. 9, 10), was born from the side of CHRIST as He slept in death upon the Cross. This Bride is the collective body of the faithful, who "continue in the Apostles' doctrine and fellowship, and in the breaking of bread, and in prayer" (Acts ii. 42), and who are symbolically spoken of as a "chaste Virgin betrothed to CHRIST" (2 Cor. xi. 2), and as His "Body" (Eph. i. 23; Col. i. 24). As the Gospel recognizes only one wife in true marriage, and as a man can have but one body, so the Church can be only One (Rom. xii. 5; 1 Cor. x. 17; xii. 12; Gal. iii. 28; Eph. iv. 4). As it consists of all servants of GOD, whether Angels or men, quick or dead, it is, however, classified under two heads, as Triumphant in heaven, or Militant on earth. Some add a third division, that of Expectant, denoting the Saints in Paradise, who await their perfection. The Church Militant, as it consists of living men, endued with bodies as well as souls, must needs be visible, and it is visible also for another reason, that it may be a beacon to the world, and an example, such as no secret society could be. Accordingly it is always spoken of in prophecy and in the Gospels as a thing plainly to be seen (Isa. ii. 2; Ezek. xvii. 22; Mic. iv. 1; S. Matt. v. 1). As the kingdom of CHRIST on earth (S. Luke xvii. 21) the Church has its own laws (S. Matt. xviii. 18), courts (1 Cor. vi. 2), officers (Eph. iv. 11; 1 Tim. iii. 1), and regular public assemblies (1 Cor. xi. 20).

The Church is not only to be known by its being One, but has other notes or marks whereby it is to be distinguished from counterfeits. It is Holy (1 Cor. vi. 11; Eph. v. 26) as setting forth pure and wholesome doctrine and training its children in saintliness, though not as containing none but the holy, since sinners form part of it (S. Matt. xiii.) It is Catholic, as extending over all lands and nations (Col. i. 5, 6; iii. 11), lasting through all time (S. Matt. xxviii. 20; Eph. iii. 21), and adapting itself to all needs and temperaments. It is Apostolic, as continuing to teach the same doctrine as that given by the Apostles (2 Tim. ii. 2) and as transmitting in unbroken succession the commission of ministry intrusted by CHRIST to them.

The functions of the Church are threefold, (a) to be the preserver

and witness of tl
livered to the Sair
Tim. i. 13; S. Jud
be the " pillar an
truth;" (b) to be
faithful (Gal. iv. 2
the children of C
converting unbeli
the channel throu
pernatural gifts o
for everlasting life
the faithful.

For the better c
functions, too im
cult to be perfor
body of the faith
Head of the Chu
appointed officers
Thess. v. 12; 1
xiii. 17), in His
Apostles, and then
degree (Eph. iv. 1
mitting to them tl
ing, baptizing (S.
20), celebrating
rist (S. Luke xxi
24), and remitting
(S. John xx. 22).
take upon himse
minister of the Ch
senger of GOD; s
called specially to
Heb. v. 4), eithe
tokens like S. Pe
by the ordinary
powers through
the hands of thos
to convey the o
Apostles, or thei
Bishops (1 Tim.
6; Tit. i. 5). Mi
appointed by the
be their officers, n

The various me
the Church emplo
to CHRIST and to
to them are tl
preaching, and sa

Sacraments are
dained or renewe
bestow invisible g
ble signs. There
rites, of which
Holy Eucharist a
Confirmation, Pen

Holy Orders, and Unction of the Sick, the secondary ones, recognized by the Church Universal. Matrimony and Holy Orders are voluntary sacraments, to which no one is necessarily obliged to have recourse. Confirmation, Penance, and Unction, though salutary and profitable to the soul, are not of such peremptory and general obligation as the two greater Sacraments, which were enjoined by CHRIST in a more specific manner than any of the others.

The redemption which CHRIST thus wrought for the whole world (1 S. John ii. 2) is applied to individual souls through the Sacraments of the Christian Church, which are intended to bring us into union with His Incarnation (1 S. John v. 5, 6). In Holy Baptism we are made members of His Mystical Body (1 Cor. xii. 13) ; in Holy Communion we are fed with His Flesh and Blood (S. John vi. 56), and are thus joined to Him (1 Cor. x. 16) and to one another (1 Cor. x. 17).

GOD had prepared man for the Christian Sacraments by certain ordinances of the Jewish Church. i. *Circumcision;* the seal of admission into the Jewish Church and its privileges (Gen. xvii. 14). This prefigured Holy Baptism, of which CHRIST said (S. John iii. 5). ii. *The Passover;* without which there could be no continuance of the Jewish Church. This prefigured the Holy Eucharist, of which CHRIST said (S. John vi. 53).

The Jewish ordinances were merely outward signs. At length CHRIST came, "full of grace and truth" (S. John i. 14), by His Circumcision showed that the ordinances pointed to Him, and the descent of the HOLY SPIRIT at His Baptism showed that Christian rites would receive energy from that HOLY SPIRIT, and be means of grace (S. John iii. 5; vi. 63).

To impress this idea on men's minds CHRIST used outward means in working His miracles. Some of these seem especially to point to the virtue of the Sacraments. Baptism, S. John ii. 6, 7; Holy Eucharist, S. Matt. xiv. 19; xv. 36.

The Element of Water is an important feature in the Old Testament. The SPIRIT "moved on the waters" at the Creation. When wickedness increased, the earth was washed by the Flood (Gen. vi., vii., 1 S. Pet. iii. 20, 21). The Israelites saved by passing through the sea (Exod. xiv. 21, &c.; 1 Cor. x. 2). Baptism foreshadowed in Levitical rites (Lev. xiv. 5 ; xxii. 6) ; in the cleansing of Naaman (2 Kings v. 10) ; and foretold (Zech. xiii. 1). CHRIST's first miracle was wrought on Water (S. John ii. 7) ; notice also His discourse with the woman of Samaria (Ib. iv. 5, &c.), His healing the blind man by bidding him wash in Siloam (Ib. ix. 7). The sick healed at the pool of Bethesda (Ib. v. 4). The washing of the disciples' feet (Ib. xiii. 4, &c.), and the Blood and Water from CHRIST's Side (Ib. xix. 34).

We find CHRIST giving commission to His Apostles to baptize (S. Matt. xxviii. 19 ; S. Mark xvi. 16), and the Apostles acting upon it (Acts ii. 37, &c. ; viii. 36; ix. 18; x. 47; xxii. 16).

Christian Baptism is administered by the application of water to a person in the Name of the HOLY TRINITY (S. Matt. xxviii. 19). Immersion, though desirable, is not essential; the tongues of fire merely rested on the heads of those who were baptized with the HOLY GHOST (S. Matt. iii. 11 ; Acts ii. 3). The Christian Sacrament must be distinguished from S. John's Baptism, which was a Jewish ordinance, and merely typical.

The effects of Baptism are—i. The remission of all sin original and personal, provided that no bar to a right reception be interposed (Acts ii. 38; xxii. 16). ii. Regeneration or new birth from a state of nature in the family of Adam (Ps. li. 5;

Rom. v. 12 ; Eph. ii.) to a state of grace in the Body of CHRIST (1 Cor. xii. 13, 27), making us members of CHRIST (Ib.), and consequently children of GOD (Gal. iii. 26, 27), and inheritors of the kingdom of heaven (Rom. viii. 17). This is the work of GOD'S HOLY SPIRIT (S. John iii. 5 ; Eph. ii. 18, 19), for we can neither make ourselves GOD'S adopted children, nor cleanse ourselves from sin. We are then placed in a state of salvation, from which, however, we may fall by wilful sin.

It may thus be compared to what in the civil order is known as "letters of naturalization," which are a grant from the sovereign of a country giving to a foreigner the same rights and privileges of citizenship in that country as if he had been born to them ; an act which necessitates on his part a renunciation of his former nationality.

That the salvation of the baptized is not final, but conditional, is thus shown. The same converts who are *all* addressed as buried and risen with CHRIST in Baptism (Col. ii. 11), made members of CHRIST by the SPIRIT (1 Cor. vi. 15, 19 ; xii. 13, 27 ; Eph. v. 29—33 ; Col. i. 24, 27, 28), partakers of the SPIRIT (1 Cor. vi. 19 ; 1 Thess. iv. 7, 8), and clothed with CHRIST in Baptism (Gal. iii. 27), are addressed as those who might be falling from grace (Gal. iii. 1 ; v. 4), quenching the SPIRIT (1 Thess. v. 19), receiving the grace of GOD in vain (2 Cor. vi. 1), and committing deadly sin (Eph. v. 1—5 ; Col. iii. 5, 6).

Baptism or Regeneration (Tit. iii. 5) is that by which we are brought into a new relationship to GOD, and differs from Conversion, which is the act of a penitent soul, either before or after Baptism, turning from sin unto GOD. In the case of an unbaptized adult, Conversion must precede Baptism, or the Sacrament is profaned. In that of one baptized in infancy, if he afterwards fall into wilful sin, Conversion must follow, otherwise he will be lost.

Conversion is, in short, the exercise of faith and penitence on the part of one who has been living in a state of sin.

That CHRIST connected Regeneration with Baptism is evident from the *order* which He adopted in His discourse with Nicodemus. When His first declaration (S. John iii. 3) was misunderstood, He added in His second one the word " Water," to make His meaning quite clear (Ib. iii. 5). Had He reversed this order, using the word " Water" in His first and omitting it in His second declaration, the Calvinistic interpretation might hold good, but not as it stands now.

Baptism cannot be repeated (Eph. iv. 5). As we are born but once naturally, so we can only be born once of water and the Spirit.

Baptism is *generally* necessary (i.e., *for all* : thus " *General Fast*," " *General Thanksgiving*") to salvation (S. Mark xvi. 16). The insertion of the word " Baptized" in the second clause of this verse would be superfluous, as one who did not believe would not be baptized.

As Baptism was to take the place of Circumcision (Col. ii. 11, 12), there was no occasion to order the Baptism of Infants. If they were not to be baptized, a distinct prohibition would have been necessary. In this latter case children would have been worse off under the Christian than under the Jewish dispensation, as being no longer permitted to enter into covenant with GOD. This would have been quite inconsistent with the favour which CHRIST ever showed towards children (S. Matt. xviii. 3 ; xix. 13 ; S. Mark x. 14 ; S. Luke xviii. 15).

Again ; if children can be guilty of original sin while unconscious, they can be partakers of grace while unconscious. And further, there is greater difficulty in believing in the due reception of the grace of Baptism by an adult than by an infant, who can place no bar in the way of such reception.

Baptism is made perfect and complete by the rite of Confirmation, which is administered by the laying on of the hands of the Bishop, the successor of the Apostles. In Baptism the HOLY GHOST comes to us as the Giver of spiritual life, making us Christians (1 Cor. xii. 13); in Confirmation, as the Comforter, to strengthen us, that we may live as good Christians (Acts viii. 16; Rom. viii. 11—13). As one of the "first principles of the doctrine of CHRIST" (Heb. vi. 1, 2), it was probably ordained by Him (Acts i. 3). The first recorded Confirmation, Acts viii. 17. The result of the laying on of the Apostles' hands was to convey—1. The ordinary gifts of the SPIRIT, which enabled men to resist temptation, and to live a Christian life (Gal. v. 16—22; Eph. iii. 16); 2. His extraordinary gifts, which enabled them to work miracles, &c. (Acts xix. 6; 1 Cor. xii. 4). The ordinary gifts only are to be looked for in Confirmation now, but these are of the most importance (1 Cor. xii. 31; xiii. 1, 2); e.g., Judas Iscariot had better have been a good man than merely a worker of miracles (S. Luke ix. 1, 2). These ordinary gifts of the SPIRIT are— 1, the spirit of *wisdom*, which makes us seek after GOD (Rom. viii. 14); 2, of *understanding*, which teaches us the truths of our religion (1 S. John ii. 27); 3, of *counsel*, which teaches us which of two ways to choose when they are set before us (Ps. lxxiii. 23, 24; Phil. i. 9—11); 4, of *ghostly strength*, to enable us to do our Christian duties (Eph. vi. 10); 5, of *knowledge*, which teaches us the will of GOD (Col. i. 9); 6, of *true godliness*, which teaches us how to live pious lives (1 S. Pet. i. 22); 7, of *holy fear*, which teaches us reverence for GOD (Isa. xi. 2, 3; Heb. xii. 28).
We approach this rite in order to have something done to us, i.e., *to be confirmed*, to be made firm or strong. The public acknowledgment which we make of our baptismal vow is merely to satisfy the congregation that we are fit to be admitted to the higher blessings of the Church. In itself it is simply a repetition of an acknowledgment which we have made every time that we have said the Catechism. See the answer to the question, "Dost thou not think," &c. Our baptismal vows are binding upon us so soon as we know right from wrong (Prov. xx. 11). The use of Confirmation is to give us special strengthening grace to enable us to keep our vows. Penitence and faith are necessary to the right reception of this grace.

If persons fall into sin after Baptism, they cannot be re-baptized (Heb. iv. 4—6), but a remedy for such sin is provided in Absolution, coming from GOD, but through the channel of the Priesthood (1 Cor. iv. 1; Col. i. 25). As under the old dispensation GOD appointed Moses as His delegate, and to be to the Israelites "instead of a mouth, ... instead of GOD" (Exod. iv. 16), so under the Christian covenant even higher privileges are entrusted to the Priesthood for the benefit of GOD's children (2 Cor. iii. 9), for, in the Person of CHRIST He gave power unto men to forgive sins (S. Matt. ix. 6—8), and CHRIST gave to His Apostles and their successors in the Church that same power (S. John xx. 21—23; 2 Cor. v. 18—20). Here we have shown (1) that GOD is the sole source of pardon; (2) that this pardon comes to us through CHRIST, Who purchased it for us by His Blood; (3) that He has made His ministers the stewards of this gift.
This gift of pardon was first conveyed to us in Baptism (Acts ii. 38). Pardon for post-baptismal sin is conveyed to us in Absolution.
The practice of the Apostles is shown in the case of the incestuous

Corinthian. S. Paul first "retains" his sin by excommunication (1 Cor. v. 4), and afterwards, when satisfied with his repentance, he "remits" it (2 Cor. ii. 10) as the representative of CHRIST.

The delegated power of the Priesthood to absolve is very positively stated in the Prayer Book. (See Exhort. in Communion Serv., Office for Vis. of Sick, and Ordinal.) Sick persons, and those who, in preparing themselves for Holy Communion, are unable to quiet their consciences, are urged to confess their sins to a Priest, in order to receive the benefit of absolution.

The Holy Eucharist is the Body and Blood of CHRIST under the forms of bread and wine (S. John vi. 51). CHRIST instituted It just before His Crucifixion (S. Matt. xxvi. 26—28), and empowered and bade His Apostles and their successors, the Priests of His Church, to "DO this" (S. Luke xxii. 19), i.e. offer this Sacrifice, as He had done, until the end of time. CHRIST did so, that even after the withdrawal of His visible Presence He might still really be with His Church (S. Matt. xxviii. 20). Therefore when the Priest breaks the Bread and blesses the Cup, as CHRIST did, and says in the Consecration prayer the words which CHRIST said, the Bread and Wine become "verily and indeed" the Body and Blood of CHRIST.

The outward elements of Bread and Wine do not sensibly cease to be what they were before, but they *become* what they were not before; even as in the beginning "GOD breathed the breath of life" into that body of clay, which He had created, and "man *became* a living soul" (Gen. ii. 7); and as in the Incarnation, the WORD became flesh, and two Natures were united in one Person, without "confusion of substance." (Athan. Creed.)

We cannot tell how the Bread and Wine become the Body and Blood of CHRIST, except that it is by the power of the HOLY GHOST, exerted in the act of Consecration through the agency of the Priests of the Church, to whom CHRIST gave authority (1 Cor. xi. 24; Heb. v. 4).

This is the doctrine of the Real Presence. That which we see on the Altar after Consecration is not a picture of CHRIST's Body now in Heaven, but the visible sign of His invisible Presence with us on earth. A picture, however perfectly drawn, could not possibly be said to be "verily and indeed" the object which it represents. At most it is merely the image of something absent. As CHRIST after His Resurrection showed Himself to His disciples under various "forms" (S. Mark xvi. 12; S. John xx. 14, 15; xxi. 4), so He shows Himself as really to us under the forms of Bread and Wine. The consecrated Sacrament is the same Body which was crucified, only presented to our sight under another "form."

CHRIST instituted the Holy Eucharist to be (1) the Sacrifice of the Church continually offered up before GOD as a memorial of His Passion; (2) the Food of baptized members of His Body, to strengthen and refresh their souls.

The word "sacrifice," like the words "church," "school," &c., has two significations. It signifies (1) the act of slaying a victim; (2) the victim itself which has been slain. In the first sense we speak of the Sacrifice on the Cross; in the second of the Sacrifice in the Eucharist. The Body of CHRIST was sacrificed once for all on the Cross (Heb. vii. 27; ix. 26, 28), but is continually offered to GOD, as *the* Sacrifice, by CHRIST Himself in heaven, naturally (Rom. viii. 3, 4; Heb. x. 21; 1 S. John ii. 1, 2), by the Church on earth in the Holy Eucharist, supernaturally.

The ceremonies on the great day of Atonement (Lev. xvi. 11, 14, 15) typified the twofold nature of

CHRIST'S Sacrifice. He, the Great High Priest, offered Himself to die on the Cross (Heb. vii. 27) near Jerusalem, GOD'S Holy Place (Ps. ii. 6; xlviii. 2; S. Matt. v. 35), and then went up to Heaven, the Most Holy Place (Heb. ix. 24; x. 20), to offer His Blood in the Presence of His FATHER (Ib. ix. 12, 23, 24).

So far as pain and death are concerned, our LORD'S sacrifice of Himself is over, for He suffered once for all (Rom. vi. 10; Heb. vii. 27; ix. 12, 26, 28; x. 12); but He is now continually re-presenting Himself as the Lamb once slain, *the* Sacrifice, before GOD'S Throne, as a propitiation for our sins (Rom. viii. 3, 4; Heb. x. 2; 1 S. John ii. 1, 2). He will continue to do so until He comes again in glory (1 Cor. xi. 26), because we are always sinning (Ps. xiv. 1, 3; liii. 3; Prov. xxiv. 16; Rom. iii. 10), and are therefore always needing propitiation for our sins (Heb. ix. 22; 1 S. John i. 7).

That which CHRIST is doing in heaven, the Church, which is His Body (Eph. i. 22, 23), does on earth, by celebrating the Holy Eucharist, and thus " showing forth," not before men, but before GOD, His Death (1 Cor. xi. 26). Hence this is the Church's great Act of Worship, and is dependent upon the *reality* of our LORD'S Presence. It is the doing in *act* what we say in *words* at the end of our prayers, " through JESUS CHRIST."

In addition to being a re-presentation of CHRIST'S Sacrifice, the Eucharist is a Sacrament of Communion (1 Cor. x. 16), in which CHRIST unites Himself to us (Rev. iii. 20), by feeding us with His Body and Blood (S. John vi. 55, 56); and thus, in Him, we are united to all His members (1 Cor. x. 17).

The chief type of the Eucharist under this aspect was the Passover, in which the Jews ate of a Lamb which had been slain (Exod. xii. 3); and therefore CHRIST is called " our Passover" (1 Cor. v. 7), for we feed (S. John vi. 54) upon Him Who is the Lamb of GOD (S. John i. 29, 36; 1 S. Pet. i. 19; Rev. v. 6).

Other types of the Eucharist were the bread and wine which Abram received at the hand of Melchizedek (Gen. xiv. 18, 19); the blessing of corn and wine given to Jacob, but withheld from Esau (Gen. xxvii. 37); the manna, " What is this?" mysterious food (Exod. xvi. 15); the flour and the wine, which, together with the lamb, formed the continual burnt-offering (Exod. xxix. 40; Lev. xxiii. 13); the cake of barley bread which fell into the camp of Midian, and caused Gideon to overthrow his enemies (Judg. vii. 13); the cake which strengthened Elijah until he reached the mount of GOD (1 Kings xix. 6).

Preparation for communicating worthily consists of self-examination (1 Cor. xi. 28) as to our—I. Faith in the reality of CHRIST'S Presence (Ib. xi. 29; Heb. x. 21); II. Penitence (Ps. cxxxix. 23, 24; Lam. iii. 40; Tit. ii. 11, 12); III. Gratitude (1 Cor. xi. 26; Col. i. 12—14); IV. Charity (S. Matt. v. 23, 24; 1 Cor. v. 7, 8; 1 S. John iv. 11).

By communicating unworthily (1 Cor. xi. 29) we eat and drink our own damnation, i.e. judgment, ordinarily temporal; if we do not repent, eternal (Ib. xi. 30). The reason is because we receive the Body of CHRIST into a soul unfit for Its reception. *Ill.* A dish of strong meat partaken of by two men, one in vigorous health, the other sickly and weak, will refresh the one, but will seriously disagree with and injure the other. The state of the eater's health makes no difference as to' the character of the meat, but makes all the difference as to the benefit which he receives by eating. The Sacrament is delivered to worthy and unworthy communicants alike with the words " The Body," &c., " The Blood," &c. All alike receive the same

Thing, but with different results. Hence the danger of receiving unworthily. It is not our worthiness which makes the Bread and Wine become the Body and Blood of CHRIST, but the power of the HOLY GHOST through the act of consecration by the Priest.

CLASSIFIED TABLE OF PSALMS, COLLECTS, EPISTLES, AND GOSPELS IN THE BOOK OF COMMON PRAYER.

THE PSALMS.

I. PSALMS OF PRAYER.

a. Against the enemies of CHRIST and His faithful. 3, 7, 10, 28, 35, 44, 56, 59, 64, 70, 71, 79, 83, 94, 109, 137.

b. Against errors of life and doctrine. 5, 12, 17, 26, 36, 55, 58, 82, 120, 140, 141.

c. In time of urgent need. 39, 42, 43, 54, 69, 77, 88, 142.

d. Against the backsliding and danger of the Church. 12, 74, 79, 80, 94.

e. Penitential Psalms. 6, 32, 38, 51, 102, 130, 143.

f. For the preservation and advancement of the Church. 36, 74, 80, 84.

g. For GOD'S blessing, consolation, and grace. 13, 25, 31, 57, 60, 67, 71, 85, 86, 90, 121, 123, 141, 144.

h. For divers orders in the Church.
(1.) For teachers, 132, 134.
(2.) For magistrates and rulers. 20, 61, 101.
(3.) For households. 127, 128.

II. PSALMS OF CONSOLATION.

a. In oppression and persecution. 4, 11, 52, 56, 91.

b. In great need and temptation. 39, 42, 43.

c. Comfort in union with GOD. 16, 27, 46, 84, 115.

d. Comfort in GOD'S help and guidance. 23, 40, 62, 63, 75, 76, 77, 90, 91, 106, 108, 121, 124, 125, 129, 139.

e. When the ungodly prosper. 37, 49, 73.

f. GOD'S might and holiness. 21, 47, 48, 52, 61, 76, 82, 93, 99, 146.

g. The victory, glory, and sure foundation of the Church. 46, 84, 87, 122, 129.

III. PSALMS OF PRAISE AND THANKSGIVING.

a. For the spread and defence of the Church. 9, 75, 76, 117, 118, 124, 125, 149.

b. For the gifts and preservation of the Word and the Sacraments. 23, 33, 46, 48, 84, 117.

c. For deliverance from perils of soul and body. 18, 30, 66, 103, 105, 107, 116, 135, 138.

d. For spiritual and temporal graces. 34, 65, 111, 113, 136, 144, 147.

e. Praise of the Divine power and grace. 19, 29, 47, 95, 96, 97, 98, 99, 100, 104, 111, 113, 114, 134, 138, 145—150.

f. Joy of the Saints in GOD. 8, 33, 68, 84, 87, 92, 97, 122.

IV. PSALMS OF COUNSEL.

a. In GOD'S law. 78, 119.

b. Knowledge of sin. 14, 49, 53, 90.

c. Knowledge of CHRIST and His kingdom.
(1.) In suffering. 22, 40, 69.
(2.) In triumph. 2, 16, 19, 21, 24, 45, 47, 72, 89, 109, 110.

d. For the practice of holiness. 1, 15, 41, 101, 112, 131, 133, 139.

e. For the due performance of Divine Service. 50, 81, 84, 101, 132.

THE COLLECTS.

CHRIST, Benefits of the Death of. Annun.

CHRIST, Imitation of. 2nd S. a. East.

The Church and Clergy. Coll. for Clergy and people; Ember Colls.; 3rd S. in Adv.; 5th S. a. Epiph.; 1st and 2nd G. Frid.; 5th, 16th, and 22nd S. a. Trin.; S. Matthias; S. Pet.; S. Barth.; SS. Sim. and Jude; Colls. in Ordinal.

Contrition. Ash-Wed.

Conversion of Heathen. 3rd Good Frid.

Courage, Christian. S. John Bapt.

Faith. Trin. Sund.; 14th S. a. Trin.; S. Thos.; S. Mark.

Final blessedness. S. John Ev.; Epiph.; S. a. Asc. Day; All Saints.

Guidance and grace. 4th S. in Adv.; Christmas D.; 1st S. a. Epiph.; 5th S. in Lt.; East. D.; 5th S. a. East.; Whitsun D.; 1st, 4th, 9th, 11th, 13th, 17th, 19th, 25th S. a. Trin.; SS. Ph. and Jas.; S. Barn.; 1st, 2nd, and 4th Post-Comm. Colls.

Heavenly-mindedness. 4th S. a. East.; Asc. D.

Help in trouble or danger. 2nd and 3rd Matins; 3rd Evensong; Colls. in Lit.; 3rd and 4th S. a. Epiph.; Septuag.; 2nd and 3rd S. in Lt.; 2nd, 3rd, 8th, 15th, and 20th S. a. Trin.; S. Mich.

Love. S. Steph.; Quinquag.

Love of GOD. 6th and 7th S. a. Trin.

Love of GOD's Word. 2nd S. in Adv.; S. Paul; S. Luke; 3rd Post-Comm.

Pardon. "Almighty GOD, Whose Nature;" Septuag.; 4th S. in L.; 12th, 21st, and 24th S. a. Trin.; Collects in Commin. Serv.

Patience. 6th S. in L.

Peace. 2nd Matins; 2nd Evensong; 2nd S. a. Epiph.

Perseverance. 3rd S. a. East.

Prayer, Acceptance of. 10th and 23rd S. a. Trin.; 5th and 6th Post-Comm.

Preparation for Judgment. 1st and 3rd S. in Adv.

Purity of heart and life. H. Inn.; Circum.; 6th S. a. Epiph.; 1st S. in L.; East. Eve; 1st S. a. East.; 18th S. a. Trin.; Purif.; S. James; 1st in Commun. Serv.

Readiness of will. S. And.

Unworldliness. S. Matt.

THE EPISTLES.

The Incarnation. Christmas Day; 25th S. a. Trin.; Annun.

Humility of CHRIST. Palm S.; 2nd S. a. East.

Redemption. M. b. East.; East. Eve; Purif.; S. John Bapt.

Holy Eucharist. Thurs. b. East.

Sacrifice of CHRIST. 5th S. in L.; Tues. and Wed. b. East.; Good Frid.

Resurrection. East. Mon. and Tues.; 11th S. a. T.

Ascension. Asc. Day.

HOLY SPIRIT. Whitsun Mond. and Tues.; 10th and 14th S. a. T.

Sonship in CHRIST. S. a. Christmas; 8th S. a. T.

Fellowship with GOD in CHRIST. S. John Evang.; Epiph.; 6th S. a. Epiph.; 1st and 6th S. a. T.

CHRIST the Ruler of the Gentiles. 2nd S. in Adv.; 25th S. a. T.

Glory of the Gospel Ministration. 12th S. a. T.

Freedom in CHRIST. 4th S. in L.; 13th and 15th S. a. T.

Preparation for Judgment. 1st and 3rd S. in Adv.; 23rd S. a. T.; S. Luke.

Fasting and Penitence. Ash-Wed.; 8th S. a. T.

Endurance, Suffering, and Martyrdom. S. Steph.; Sexag.; 1st S. in L.; 4th S. a. T.; SS. Ph. and Jas.

Prayer for Grace. 16th, 22nd, 24th S. a. T.

Patience and Joy in Prayer. 4th S. in Adv.; 5th S. a. Epiph.; 20th and 21st S. a. T.

Steadfast Faith the Root of Holiness. Circum.; 1st S. a. East.; 18th S. a. T.; S. And.; S. Mark; SS. Sim. and Jude.

Perseverance in Good Works. Sept.; 5th S. a. East.; 3rd and 21st S. a. T.

Purity of Life and Will. 1st S. a. Epiph.; 2nd and 3rd S. in L.; East. D.; 4th S. a. East.; 7th and 19th S. a. T.; S. Matt.

Christian Brotherhood and Love. 2nd, 3rd, and 5th S. a. Epiph.; Quinq.; S. a. Asc.; 1st, 2nd, 5th, 17th, and 22nd S. a. T.; S. Thos.

Obedience to Superiors. 4th S. a. Epiph.; 3rd S. a. East.

Revelation of Heaven and Bliss of the Saints. H. Inn.; Trin. S.; S. Mich.; All SS.

Historical. S. Paul; S. Matthias; S. Barn.; S. Pet.; S. Jas.; S. Barth.

Example from Jewish History. 9th S. a. T.

THE GOSPELS.

NARRATIVE.

The Incarnation. Annun.; Christmas Day.

Birth of S. John Bapt. S. John B.

Nativity. S. a. Christmas; Circum.

Presentation in the Temple. Purif.

Adoration of the Magi. Epiph.

Flight into Egypt. H. Inn. D.

CHRIST with the Doctors. 1st S. a. Epiph.

Temptation of CHRIST. 1st S. in L.

Testimony of S. John B. 4th S. in Adv.

SS. Andrew and Peter called. S. And.

S. Matthew called. S. Matt.

S. Peter's Confession. S. Pet.

The Seventy sent. S. Luke.

CHRIST Anointed before Death. M. b. East.

Entry into Jerusalem. 1st S. in Adv.

Weeping over Jerusalem. 10th S. a. T.

Last Supper. M. and W. b. East.

Agony in the Garden. W. b. East.

Betrayal. M. and W. b. East.

Crucifixion. Palm S.; Tu. and Th. b. East.; Good Frid.

Burial. East. Eve.

Resurrection. East. D.

Emmaus. East. M.

First Appearance to the Apostles. East. T.

Second Appearance to the Apostles. 1st S. a. East.

S. Thomas. S. Thos.

Summons to S. Peter. S. John Ev.

Ascension. Asc. D.

PARABLES.

Tares in the Field. 5th S. a. Epiph.

Labourers in the Vineyard. Septuag.

Sower. Sexag.

Dives and Lazarus. 1st S. a. T.

Great Supper. 2nd S. a. T.

Lost Sheep. 3rd S. a. T.

Unjust Steward. 9th S. a. T.

Pharisee and Publican. 11th S. a. T.

Good Samaritan. 13th S. a. T.

Lowest Place. 17th S. a. T.

Wedding Garment. 20th S. a. T.

Two Debtors. 22nd S. a. T.

Tribute Money. 23rd S. a. T.

MIRACLES.

Water made Wine. 2nd S. a. Epiph.

Healing Leper. 3rd S. a. Epiph.

Centurion's Servant. 3rd S. a. Epiph.

Two Demoniacs. 4th S. a. Epiph.

Blind. Quinquag.

Syrophenician's Daughter. 2nd S. in L.

Dumb. 3rd S. in L.

Deaf and Dumb. 12th S. a. T.

Ten Lepers. 14th S. a. T.

Dropsy. 17th S. a. T.

Palsy. 19th S. a. T.

Nobleman's Son. 21st S. a. T.
Issue of Blood. 24th S. a. T.
Raising Widow's Son. 16th S. a. T.
Jairus's Daughter. 24th S. a. T.
Stilling Tempest. 4th S. a. Epiph.
Feeding Thousands. 4th S. in L. ; 7th S. a. T. ; 25th S. a. T.
Miraculous Draught. 5th S. a. T.

HORTATORY.

Character of S. John B. 3rd S. in Adv.
Light of the World. Whitsun M.
Sinlessness of CHRIST. 5th S. in Lent.
Good Shepherd. 2nd S. a. East. ; Whitsun T.
Approach of Passion. Quinquag.

Unbelief of Jews. S. Stephen.
Second Advent. 2nd S. in Adv. ; 6th S. a. Epiph.
Last Discourse. SS. Phil. and Jas.; Whitsun D.; S. Mark ; S. Barn.; SS. Sim. and Jude ; S. a. Asc. ; 4th, 3rd, and 5th S. a. East.
New Birth. Trin. S.
Fasting. Ash-Wed.
Mercy and Brotherly Love. 4th, 6th, and 22nd S. a. T.
False Prophets. 8th S. a. T.
Trust in GOD. 15th S. a. T.
Two Commandments. 18th S. a. T.
Reward of Saints. S. Paul.
Teaching of the Lowly. S. Matthias.
Humility of Saints. S. Jas.; S. Barth.
Duty of being Childlike. S. Mich.
Beatitudes. All Saints.

OCCASIONAL OFFICES, ETC.

OFFICE FOR A RURIDECANAL SYNOD OR CLERICAL MEETING.

In the Name of the FATHER, &c.
Our FATHER, &c.
I believe, &c.

℣. O GOD, make speed, &c. ℟. O LORD, make haste, &c. ℣. Glory, &c. ℟. As it was, &c.

Here may be said or sung the Hymn
COME, HOLY GHOST, our souls inspire.

Ant. Blessed be the Name of the LORD.

Ps. 113. Praise the LORD, ye servants, &c.
133. Behold how good and joyful, &c.

Ant. Blessed be the Name of the LORD from this time forth for evermore.

The Chapter. 1 S. Pet. v.

The elders which are among you I exhort, who am also an elder, and a witness of the sufferings of CHRIST, and also a partaker of the glory that shall be revealed: feed the flock of GOD which is among you, taking the oversight thereof, not by constraint, but willingly; not for filthy lucre, but of a ready mind: neither as being lords over GOD's heritage, but being ensamples to the flock. And when the Chief Shepherd shall appear, ye shall receive a crown of glory that fadeth not away.

℣. But Thou, O LORD, have mercy upon us. ℟. Thanks be to GOD. ℣. Take heed unto yourselves, and to all the flock. ℟. Over the which the HOLY GHOST hath made you overseers. ℣. Glory, &c. ℟. As it was, &c. ℣. Feed the Church of GOD. ℟. Which He hath purchased with His Own Blood. ℣. The LORD be with you. ℟. And with thy spirit.

LORD, have mercy, &c.
Our FATHER, &c.

℣. I said, LORD, be merciful unto me. ℟. Heal my soul, for I have sinned against Thee. ℣. Turn Thee again, O LORD, at the last. ℟. And be gracious unto Thy servants. ℣. O LORD, let Thy mercy be showed upon us. ℟. As we do put our trust in Thee. ℣. Let Thy Priests be clothed with righteousness. ℟. And let Thy saints sing with joyfulness. ℣. LORD, hear our prayer. ℟. And let our cry come unto Thee. ℣. Let us pray.

448. Pour, we beseech Thee, O LORD GOD, the spirit of truth and peace upon Thy servants, that we may fully know what is pleasing unto Thee, and may follow that which we know in perfect harmony of will. Through.

GOD, Who . . . . didst teach the hearts, &c. (Collect for Whitsun Day.)

[*Here add special prayer, according to the object of the Meeting.*]
Prevent us, O LORD, &c.

At the conclusion of the Meeting.
℣. Stablish the thing, O LORD, that Thou hast wrought in us. ℟. For Thy Temple's sake at Jerusalem. ℣. Let us depart in peace. ℟. In the Name of the LORD. Amen.

OFFICE FOR THE ADMISSION OF A CHORISTER.

In the Name, &c.
Our FATHER, &c.

℣. I will give great thanks unto the LORD with my mouth. ℟. And praise Him among the multitude. ℣. O GOD, make speed, &c. ℟. O LORD, make haste, &c. ℣. Glory, &c. ℟. As it was, &c. Alleluia.

Ant. It is a good thing to give thanks unto the LORD.

Ps. 101. My song shall be, &c. 108 (1—7.) O GOD, my heart is ready . . . hear Thou me.

Ant. It is a good thing to give thanks unto the LORD; and to sing praises unto Thy Name, O most Highest.

The Chapter. 2 Chron. xx.

And when he had consulted with the people, he appointed singers unto the LORD, and that should praise the beauty of holiness, as they went out before the army, and to say, Praise the LORD, for His mercy endureth for ever. And when they began to sing and to praise, the LORD set ambushments against the children of Ammon, Moab, and Mount Seir, which were come against Judah; and they were smitten.

℣. But Thou, &c. ℟. Thanks, &c. ℣. Praise the LORD with harp. ℟. Sing praises unto Him with the lute, and instrument of ten strings. ℣. Glory, &c. ℟. As it was, &c. ℣. Sing unto the LORD a new song. ℟. Sing praises lustily unto Him with a good courage.

The Candidate, vested in a cassock, is brought forward between two choristers, in cassocks and surplices, and presented to the Priest, who says as follows :

P. Dost thou desire to enter into the ranks of this choir?
A. I do.
P. Dost thou promise obedience in all things lawful to its rules and officers?
A. I do.
P. I admit thee into this choir, in the Name, &c.

Then putting the surplice on the new chorister, he shall say :

I clothe thee in the white garment of the surplice, and see that thou serve GOD, and sing His praise, that thou mayest hereafter be admitted into the ranks of those who, having washed their robes, and made them white in the Blood of the Lamb, stand before the Throne of GOD serving Him day and night continually.

He gives the chorister the Psalter, saying,

See that what thou singest with thy mouth, thou believe in thy heart, and show forth by thy works.

Ant. Lift up your hands in the sanctuary.

Ps. 84. O how amiable, &c. 122. I was glad, &c.

Ant. Lift up your hands in the sanctuary, and praise the LORD.

℣. The LORD, &c. ℟. And with, &c. ℣. Let us pray.

LORD, have mercy, &c.
Our FATHER, &c.

℣. Hear me, O LORD, and have mercy upon me. ℟. LORD, be Thou my helper. ℣. O send out Thy light and truth, that they may lead me. ℟. And bring me unto

Thy holy hill and to Thy dwelling. ℣. Let Thy priests be clothed with righteousness. ℞. And let Thy saints sing with joyfulness. ℣. LORD, hear, &c. ℞. And let, &c. ℣. Let us pray.

449. O LORD GOD Almighty, behold and sanctify this Thy servant, grant that he may in all wisdom and understanding sing Thy praises, and keep him in the holy fellowship of the saints, through the mercy and lovingkindness of Thine Only-begotten SON, Who liveth and reigneth with Thee in the unity of the HOLY GHOST, One GOD, world without end. Amen.

Benediction. CHRIST, the Lamb of GOD, Whose Name you celebrate on earth, grant you to sing His new song amongst the choirs of angels in heaven.

OFFICE FOR ADMITTING A SERVER.

In the Name, &c.
Our FATHER, &c.

℣. I had rather be a doorkeeper in the house of my GOD. ℞. Than to dwell in the tents of ungodliness. ℣. Glory, &c. ℞. As it was, &c.

Ant. My voice shalt Thou hear betimes, O LORD.

Ps. 5. Ponder my words, &c.

Ant. My voice shalt Thou hear betimes, O LORD, early in the morning will I direct my prayer unto Thee, and will look up.

The Priest addresses the candidate.

P. My son, what dost thou desire?
A. I desire to minister to the Priests of the LORD at His holy Altar.
P. Dost thou promise to be reverent in thought and act in the discharge of such ministry?
A. I do, GOD being my helper.
P. Dost thou promise cheerful obedience to all directions given thee by due authority for the execution of thine office?
A. I do promise.
P. Dost thou promise regularity and punctuality of attendance during thy term of service?

A. I do so promise.
P. GOD, Who has given thee a good will, graciously fulfil the same in thee. And I admit thee to serve at the Altar in this church, in the Name, &c.

Ant. LORD, I have loved the habitation of Thy house.

Ps. 26. Give sentence, &c.

Ant. LORD, I have loved the habitation of Thy house, and the place where Thine honour dwelleth.

LORD, have mercy, &c.
Our FATHER, &c.

℣. O send out Thy light and Thy truth, that they may lead me. ℞. And bring me unto Thy holy hill, and to Thy dwelling. ℣. And that I may go unto the Altar of GOD. ℞. Even unto the GOD of my joy and gladness. ℣. LORD, hear, &c. ℞. And let, &c. ℣. Let us pray.

450. Bless, O LORD, this Thy servant, as Thou didst bless Samuel who ministered to Thine High Priest Eli, and Elisha who ministered to Thy Prophet Elijah, and grant him so devoutly to serve at Thine Altar on earth, that he may be counted worthy at length to worship at the golden Altar before Thy throne in heaven.   Through.

Blessing. The LORD grant unto thee clean hands and a pure heart, and give thee blessing and rightcousness, and make thee at the last a pillar in the temple of thy GOD, that thou go no more out.

OFFICE FOR THE ADOPTION OF A CHILD.

The Priest, vested in surplice and stole, stands before the altar, with the child who is to be adopted, kneeling within the altar-rails, holding a lighted taper in his hand.   The adopter, also holding a lighted taper, kneels outside the rails.

In the Name, &c.
Our FATHER, &c.

℣. He is a FATHER to the fatherless.   ℟. And defendeth the cause of the widows.   ℣. O GOD, &c. ℟. O LORD, &c.   ℣. Glory, &c. ℟. As it was, &c.

Ant. When my father and my mother forsake me.

Ps. 27. The LORD is my light, &c.
113. Praise the LORD, &c.
127. Except the LORD, &c.

Ant. When my father and my mother forsake me, the LORD taketh me up.

The Chapter.   Exodus ii.

And the daughter of Pharaoh came down to wash herself at the river ; and her maidens walked along by the river's side : and when she saw the ark among the flags, she sent her maid to fetch it.   And when she had opened it, she saw the child : and, behold, the babe wept.   And she had compassion on him, and said, This is one of the Hebrews' children.   Then said his sister to Pharaoh's daughter, Shall I go and call to thee a nurse of the Hebrew women, that she may nurse the child for thee? And Pharaoh's daughter said to her, Go.   And the maid went and called the child's mother.   And Pharaoh's daughter said unto her, Take this child away, and nurse it for me, and I will give thee thy wages.   And the woman took the child, and nursed it.   And the child grew, and she brought him unto Pharaoh's daughter, and he became her son.   And she called his name Moses : and she said, Because I drew him out of the water.

℣. But Thou, &c.   ℟. Thanks be to GOD.   ℣. I will be a FATHER unto you.   ℟. And ye shall be My sons and daughters, saith the LORD Almighty.   ℣. Glory, &c.   ℟. As it was, &c.   ℣. Leave thy fatherless children, I will preserve them alive. ℟. And let thy widows trust in Me.

Then the Priest, addressing the adopter, asks :

Dost thou desire to adopt this child for thine own?
A. I do.
P. Wilt thou be to *him* a father (*or* mother) in spirit and in deed?
A. I will.
P. Wilt thou deal with *him* as with thine own offspring, and never forsake *him* nor cast *him* off?
A. I will.
P. Wilt thou bring *him* up in the knowledge, fear, and love of the LORD?

A. I will, GOD being my helper.

P. GOD, Who hath put into thy heart to do these things, give thee grace to fulfil it unto the end.

[*Then, addressing the child, if old enough, the Priest adds :*

P. N., wilt thou go with this man (*or* woman) to be *his* child?

A. I will.

P. Wilt thou be obedient and loving unto *him?*

A. I will, GOD being my helper.

P. GOD, the SON of GOD, Who was obedient to His foster-father, Joseph, give thee grace so to do.]

℣. The LORD, &c. ℟. And with, &c. ℣. Let us pray.

LORD, have mercy, &c.
Our FATHER, &c.

℣. Defend the poor and father-less. ℟. See that such as are in need and necessity have right. ℣. Show Thy servants Thy work. ℟. And their children Thy glory. ℣. Not unto us, O LORD, not unto us. ℟. But unto Thy Name give the praise. ℣. LORD, hear, &c. ℟. And let, &c.

451. O LORD our GOD, Who through Thy beloved SON, our LORD JESUS CHRIST, hast called us to be the children of GOD by adoption and the grace of Thine Almighty and HOLY SPIRIT, Who hast said, I will be to him a Father, and he shall be to Me a son; look down, O merciful King, from Thy holy dwelling-place on these Thy servants, and unite them [though by natural birth strangers to each other] as *father* and *son* by Thy HOLY SPIRIT. Stablish them in Thy love, bind them together with Thy good favour, bless them in Thy glory, confirm them in Thy faith, that they may ever keep, and not make void, the promises of their lips, and Thyself receive their pledge, which they have vowed before Thee, that they may preserve it unbroken and truly unto their lives' end, living unto Thee, our living and Very GOD, and may be heirs of Thy heavenly king-dom. Through.

The Priest takes the child by the right hand (or, if it be an infant, in his arms), and gives it to the adopter, saying,

Our LORD JESUS CHRIST hath said : Whoso shall receive one such little child in My Name, receiveth Me.

The child, if old enough, kneels before the adopter, who raises it up, saying,

The Angel which redeemed me from all evil, bless the child, and let my name be named upon *him.*

℣. The LORD, &c. ℟. And with, &c. ℣. Let us pray.

452. O LORD GOD, Creator of all the world, Who in the first Adam didst institute fleshly kinship, and hast made us Thy kindred through grace, in Thy beloved SON JESUS CHRIST our LORD; look on these Thy servants, who humbly beseech Thy blessing, and as they have bound themselves one to another as *father* and *son*, united in Thee, so grant that by perseverance in holiness they may obtain those good things which they desire, and be fitted for adoption in Thee, to the honour and praise of Thy holy Name. Through.

Blessing. The Almighty GOD, Who hath predestinated us unto the adoption of children by JESUS CHRIST unto Himself, make you heirs of GOD, and joint-heirs with CHRIST, that ye may be glorified together. Amen.

FORM OF RECONCILIATION OF A PENITENT.

In the Name, &c.
Our FATHER, &c.

℣. Our old man is crucified with Him. ℟. That the body of sin might be destroyed. ℣. O GOD, make speed, &c. ℟. O LORD, make haste, &c. ℣. Glory, &c. ℟. As it was, &c.

Ant. I said, I will confess my sins unto the LORD.

Ps. 32. Blessed is he, &c.
51. Have mercy upon me, &c.
130. Out of the deep, &c.

Ant. I said, I will confess my sins unto the LORD, and so Thou forgavest the wickedness of my sin.

The Chapter. Ezek. xviii.

The soul that sinneth, it shall die. The son shall not bear the iniquity of the father, neither shall the father bear the iniquity of the son: the righteousness of the righteous shall be upon him, and the wickedness of the wicked shall be upon him. But if the wicked will turn from all his sins that he hath committed, and keep all My statutes, and do that which is lawful and right, he shall surely live, he shall not die. All his transgressions that he hath committed, they shall not be mentioned unto him: in his righteousness that he hath done he shall live. Have I any pleasure at all that the wicked should die? saith the LORD GOD; and not that he should return from his ways and live?

℣. But Thou, &c. ℟. Thanks, &c. ℣. Let the wicked return unto the LORD, and He will have mercy upon him. ℟. And to our GOD, for He will abundantly pardon. ℣.

Glory, &c. ℟. As it was, &c. ℣. To the LORD our GOD belong mercies and forgiveness. ℟. Though we have rebelled against Him. ℣. The LORD, &c. ℟. And with, &c. ℣. Let us pray.

LORD, have mercy, &c.
Our FATHER, &c.

℣. I said, LORD, be merciful unto me. ℟. Heal my soul, for I have sinned against Thee. ℣. Turn Thee again, O LORD, at the last. ℟. And be gracious unto Thy servants. ℣. Let Thy merciful kindness be upon us. ℟. As we do put our trust in Thee. ℣. O remember not our old sins. ℟. But have mercy upon us, and that soon. ℣. Help us, O GOD of our salvation, for the glory of Thy Name. ℟. O deliver us, and be merciful unto our sins, for Thy Name's sake. ℣. LORD, hear, &c. ℟. And let, &c. ℣. Let us pray.

O LORD, we beseech Thee, mercifully hear our prayers, and spare all those who confess their sins unto Thee; that they whose consciences by sin are accused, by Thy merciful pardon may be absolved. Through.

453. O LORD our GOD, Who art not wearied out by our sins, but art gracious when we repent; look upon this Thy servant who confesseth that *he* hath grievously sinned against Thee. Thou Who willest not the death of a sinner, but rather that he should turn from his wickedness, canst alone wash away our offences and pardon our iniquities. Grant, therefore, that *he* may serve Thee in true repentance, and amending *his* ways may give Thee thanks for everlasting blessings. Through.

454. Hear us, O LORD, and as

Thou wast pleased with the confession and prayer of the publican, so likewise be gracious to this Thy servant, and mercifully hear *his* prayers, that *he*, abiding in contrite acknowledgment of *his* sins, and in fervent supplication, may speedily obtain Thy mercy, and restored to the communion of Thine Altar, may once more be partaker of heavenly glory. Through.

Benediction. The LORD grant thee remission of all thy sins, and eternal life.

R̵. Amen.

FORM OF RECONCILIATION OF A LAPSED CHURCHMAN.

In the Name, &c.
Our FATHER, &c.

℣. In returning and rest shall ye be saved. R̵. In quietness and confidence shall be your strength. ℣. They also that erred in spirit shall come to understanding. R̵. And they that murmured shall learn doctrine. ℣. O GOD, &c. R̵. O LORD, &c. ℣. Glory, &c. R̵. As it was, &c. Alleluia.

HYMN. *Veni Creator.*

Ant. What man is he that feareth the LORD.

Ps. 25. Unto Thee, O LORD, &c.
51. Have mercy, &c.
116. I am well pleased, &c.
122. I was glad, &c.

Ant. What man is he that feareth the LORD : him shall He teach in the way that He shall choose.

The Chapter. Jer. xlii.

Thus saith the LORD, the GOD of Israel, unto Whom ye sent me to present your supplication before Him ; If ye will still abide in this land, then will I build you, and not pull you down ; and I will plant you, and not pluck you up : for I repent Me of the evil that I have done unto you. Be not afraid of the king of Babylon, of whom ye are afraid ; be not afraid of him, saith the LORD : for I am with you to save you, and to deliver you from his hand. And I will show mercies unto you, that he may have mercy upon you, and cause you to return to your own land. But if ye say, We will not dwell in this land, neither obey the voice of the LORD our GOD, saying, No ; but we will go into the land of Egypt, where we shall see no war, nor hear the sound of the trumpet, nor have hunger of bread ; and there will we dwell : and now therefore hear the word of the LORD, ye remnant of Judah ; thus saith the LORD of hosts, the GOD of Israel, If ye wholly set your faces to enter into Egypt, and go to sojourn there ; then it shall come to pass, that the sword, which ye feared, shall overtake you there in the land of Egypt; and the famine whereof ye were afraid, shall follow close after you there in Egypt; and there ye shall die.

℣. But Thou, &c. R̵. Thanks, &c. ℣. I will give you pastors according to My heart. R̵. Which shall feed you with knowledge and understanding. ℣. Glory, &c. R̵. As it was, &c. ℣. Ask for the old paths, where is the good way. R̵. Walk therein, and ye shall find rest for your souls.

The Priest addresses the penitent.

N., dost thou desire to return unto the fold of the Church ?
R̵. That is my desire.

P. Dost thou repent and abjure the schisms and errors in which thou didst sometime live?

℟. I renounce them all.

P. Repeat the confession of thy faith.

℟. I believe in one GOD, &c.

P. The LORD grant thee to believe with the heart unto righteousness, what thou hast confessed with the mouth unto salvation.

℟. Amen.

℣. The LORD, &c. ℟. And with, &c. ℣. Let us pray.

LORD, have mercy, &c.
Our FATHER, &c.

℣. Bring my soul out of prison. ℟. That I may give thanks unto Thy Name. ℣. Teach me, O LORD, the way of Thy statutes. ℟. And I shall keep it unto the end. ℣. Bring me unto Thy holy hill, and to Thy dwelling. ℟. That I may go unto the Altar of GOD. ℣. LORD, hear, &c. ℟. And let, &c.

455. Almighty and most merciful GOD, unwearied in loving-kindness, Who didst bear with Thy rebellious people, and heal their backslidings, graciously accept the prayers and contrition of this Thy servant, and granting *him* remission of all *his* offences, restore *him* whole to Thy Church. Through.

456. Grant, O LORD, we beseech Thee, the gift of Thy HOLY SPIRIT to this Thy servant, that forsaking all errors and false belief, *he* may abide steadfast in the faith, and come to the full knowledge of Thee. Through.

The Priest lays his hand on the penitent's head, saying,

Our LORD JESUS CHRIST, gracious and longsuffering, grant thee pardon and remission of thy sins, and by His authority committed unto me, I absolve and release thee from all spiritual censures and condemnations which thou hast incurred, and restore thee to the communion of the Church. In the Name.

Benediction. CHRIST, the SON of GOD, the Good Shepherd of the sheep, bear thee on His shoulders out of the wilderness unto His everlasting fold, that thou mayest there find pasture, and go out no more.

FORM OF RECONCILIATION OF A BAPTIZED DISSENTER.

In the Name, &c.
Our FATHER, &c.

℣. Return and obey the voice of the LORD. ℟. And do all His commandments which I command thee this day. ℣. O GOD, make speed, &c. ℟. O LORD, make haste, &c. ℣. Glory, &c. ℟. As it was, &c.

HYMN.

Come, HOLY GHOST, our souls inspire.

The Priest, standing before the penitent, addresses him.

Wilt thou be received into communion with the Catholic Church?

℟. That is my desire.

Priest. Dost thou renounce the errors and schisms of [*Here name the sect*] in which thou didst heretofore live?

℟. I renounce them all.

Priest. Repeat the Confession of thy faith.

℟. [*He recites the Nicene Creed. If he cannot read, the Priest repeats the Creed to him, and he makes answer,* Amen. All this I steadfastly believe.]

The Priest kneels and recites,

Ant. O pray for the peace of Jerusalem.

Ps. 51. Have mercy, &c.
120. When I was in trouble, &c.
122. I was glad, &c.
133. Behold, how good, &c.

Ant. O pray for the peace of Jerusalem : they shall prosper that love thee.

The Chapter. 1 Cor. i.

Now I beseech you, brethren, by the name of our LORD JESUS CHRIST, that ye all speak the same thing, and that there be no divisions among you; but that ye be perfectly joined together in the same mind and in the same judgment. For it hath been declared unto me of you, my brethren, by them which are of the house of Chloe, that there are contentions among you. Now this I say, that every one of you saith, I am of Paul; and I of Apollos; and I of Cephas; and I of CHRIST. Is CHRIST divided? was Paul crucified for you? or were ye baptized in the name of Paul?

℣. But Thou, &c. ℟. Thanks, &c. ℣. Thy teachers shall not be removed into a corner any more. ℟. But thine eyes shall see thy teachers. ℣. Glory, &c. ℟. As it was, &c. ℣. And thine ears shall hear a word behind thee, saying. ℟. This is the way, walk ye in it. ℣. The LORD, &c. ℟. And with, &c.

℣. LORD, &c. Our FATHER, &c.
℣. O LORD, save Thy servant, &c.

Let us pray.

457. O GOD, Who by Thine Only-

Begotten SON didst restore man, made in Thine Image, when deceived by the craft of the serpent, mercifully look upon Thy servant N. . . ., who desires to come out of the darkness of error into the light of Thy truth, that whatever in *him* hath been decayed through the malice and fraud of the devil, may be restored by Thy loving-kindness. Through the same.

458. Almighty and merciful GOD, graciously receive this Thy sheep, saved from the jaws of the wolf, and of Thy great mercy number *him* in Thy flock, that the enemy may not rejoice against *him*, but that Thy Church may be glad in *his* conversion and deliverance, and receive as a mother her child which was dead and is alive again, which was lost and is found. Through.

The Priest rises and lays his hand on the penitent's head saying,

Our LORD JESUS CHRIST, Who hath commanded that repentance and remission of sins should be published in His Name among all nations, of His great mercy give unto thee true repentance, and forgive thee all thy sins. And I, His Priest, by His authority committed unto me, do absolve thee from all ecclesiastical censures, which thou hast or mayest have incurred by reason of thy former errors, heresy and schism. And I restore thee to the full communion of the Catholic Church, in the Name, &c.

He then gives the Benediction, Unto GOD's gracious mercy, &c.

The person reconciled shall be presented to the Bishop for Confirmation so soon as may be.

OFFICE ON BEHALF OF THOSE AT SEA IN A STORM.

In the Name, &c. Our FATHER, &c. I believe, &c. ℣. Thy way is in the sea. ℟. And Thy paths in the great waters. ℣. O GOD, &c. ℟. O LORD, &c. ℣. Glory, &c. ℟. As it was, &c.

HYMN. 222 Ancient and Modern, or 329 People's Hymnal.

Ant. Thou rulest the raging of the sea.

Ps. 65. Thou, O GOD, &c.
93. The LORD is King, &c.
107 (23—33). They that go down
. . . . elders.

Ant. Thou rulest the raging of the sea: Thou stillest the waves thereof when they arise.

The Chapter. S. Matt. viii.

And when He was entered into a ship, His disciples followed Him. And, behold, there arose a great tempest in the sea, insomuch that the ship was covered with the waves: but He was asleep. And His disciples came to Him, and awoke Him, saying, LORD, save us: we perish. And He saith unto them, Why are ye fearful, O ye of little faith? Then He arose, and rebuked the winds and the sea; and there was a great calm. But the men marvelled, saying, What manner of man is this, that even the winds and the sea obey Him?

℣. But Thou, &c. ℟. Thanks, &c. ℣. It is the LORD that commandeth the waters. ℟. It is the glorious GOD that maketh the thunder. ℣. Glory, &c. ℟. As it was, &c. ℣. The LORD sitteth above the water-flood. ℟. And the LORD remaineth a King for ever. ℣. The LORD, &c. ℟. And with, &c. ℣. Let us pray.

LORD, have mercy, &c. Our FATHER, &c. ℣. O LORD, save Thy servants. ℟. Which put their trust in Thee. ℣. Send them help from Thy holy place. ℟. And evermore mightily defend them. ℣. Let not the waterflood drown them. ℟. Neither let the deep swallow them up. ℣. Stretch Thine hand over the sea. ℟. And say unto the storm, Peace, be still. ℣. Be as an hiding-place from the wind. ℟. And a covert from the tempest. ℣. LORD, hear, &c. ℟. And let, &c. ℣. Let us pray.

459. O LORD GOD Almighty, Who walkest upon the wings of the wind, and bindest the floods from overflowing, mercifully protect Thy servants from perils in the sea, as Thou didst save Noah in the ark, Peter when he was sinking, and Paul in time of shipwreck, that they may always praise Thy holy Name, and when they leave their ships may follow Thy SON for evermore. Through the same.

Benediction. The LORD, the LORD GOD, Who divided the seas with His power, and brought His people over on dry ground; bless, protect, and deliver His servants on the deep, and lead them finally into that place which is called the Fair Havens, nigh whereunto is the City of the LORD. Amen.

Benedictions.

THE FORM OF BLESSING OF WATER.

The Priest shall bless the salt on this wise.

We humbly implore Thee, Almighty and Everlasting GOD, that of Thy bountiful goodness Thou wouldst be pleased to bl✝ess and sanc✝tify this creature of salt, which Thou hast created for the service of men, that it may profit for the health both of soul and body of them that take it, and that whatsoever is touched or sprinkled therewith may be freed from all uncleanness, and from all attacks of spiritual wickedness; through JESUS CHRIST our LORD. *Amen.*

He shall then bless the water on this wise.

O GOD, Who in ordaining divers mysteries for the salvation of mankind, hast been pleased to employ the element of water in the chiefest of Thy Sacraments; give ear to our prayers, and pour upon this water the might of Thy bles✝sing, that as it serves Thee in those holy mysteries, so by Thy divine grace it may here avail for the casting out of devils, and the driving away of diseases; that whatsoever in the houses or places of the faithful is sprinkled therewith may be freed from all uncleanness, and delivered from hurt. Let not the breath of pestilence therein abide, nor the destroying blast; let all snares of the enemy be dispersed, and all that does despite to the safety and quietness of Thy people be removed; let them seek health by the invocation of Thy Name, and be defended from all ill; through JESUS CHRIST our LORD. *Amen.*

Here let him cast the salt into the water in the form of a cross, saying,

Let this mixture of salt and water be made, in the Name of the FATHER, and of the SON, and of the HOLY GHOST. *Amen.*

℣. The LORD be with you.
℟. And with thy spirit.

Let us pray.

O GOD, the Author of victorious might, King of everlasting Empire, eternal and glorious Conqueror, Who pullest down the strength of the adversary, overcomest the rage of Satan, and by Thy power destroyest his wicked imaginations; we humbly entreat Thee to accept this creature of salt and water, and with the dew of Thy bles✝sing illuminate and sanctify it, that wheresoever Thy people shall sprinkle it and call upon the Name of the LORD, they may be preserved from every malice of the unclean spirit, and from the snare of the poisonous serpent, and that the presence of the HOLY SPIRIT may be vouchsafed us in every place, when we ask Him of Thy tender mercy; through JESUS CHRIST our LORD. *Amen.*

AN ORDER FOR LAYING THE FOUNDATION-STONE OF A CHURCH OR CHAPEL.

All things being ready, the Priest (or the Bishop, being present,) shall say,

℣. Our help is in the Name of the LORD. ℟. Who hath made heaven and earth. ℣. O LORD, hear our prayer. ℟. And let our cry come unto Thee. ℣. Blessed be the Name of the LORD. ℟. From this time forth for evermore. Alleluia.

Ps. 84. O how amiable, &c.

And after that, these Prayers following, all devoutly kneeling, the Minister first pronouncing with a loud voice,

℣. The LORD, &c. ℟. And with, &c. ℣. Let us pray.

LORD, have mercy, &c.
Our FATHER, &c.

Then the Priest standing up shall say,

460. O Almighty LORD GOD, Whom the heavens and earth cannot contain, yet Who disdainest not to dwell with Thy Church here on earth ; mercifully grant that all evil may depart from this place whereon we are about to lay the foundation of a house to the honour and praise of Thy most holy Name ; through JESUS CHRIST our LORD, Who ever liveth and reigneth.

Then the Priest, laying his hand upon the Foundation-stone, shall say,

Let us pray.

461. O LORD JESU CHRIST, SON of the Living GOD, Who art the brightness of the FATHER'S glory, and the express image of His Person ; the chief corner-stone hewn from the mountain without hands ; the immutable foundation ; strengthen this stone about to be laid in Thy Name ; and Thou, Who art the beginning and the end, by Whom in the beginning GOD created all things, be, we beseech Thee, the beginning, the increase, and the consummation of this our work, which is undertaken to the glory of Thy Name. Who, with the FATHER.

462. Almighty and everlasting GOD, mercifully be pleased to bless this stone which we are about to place for a foundation in the Name and strength of Him Who is the tried and precious stone ; and grant that all they who to the furtherance of this work shall have faithfully offered to Thee of their substance, may ever be preserved, both in both and soul.   Through.

Here all standing up the Priest shall begin :

℣. Behold, I lay in Zion a chief corner-stone, elect, precious. ℟. And he that believeth in Him shall not be confounded. ℣. The stone which the builders refused. ℟. Is become the head-stone of the corner. ℣. This is the LORD'S doing. ℟. And it is marvellous in our eyes. ℣. Other foundation can no man lay than that is laid. ℟. Which is JESUS CHRIST. ℣. Praise ye the LORD. ℟. The LORD'S Name be praised.

Then shall be sung or said this Psalm following :

Ps. 127. Except the LORD, &c.

Then, the lime being prepared, and all things ready, the Priest shall assist the architect and builder in placing the stone, saying,

In the faith of JESUS CHRIST, we place this foundation-stone in the Name of GOD the FATHER, GOD the SON, and GOD the HOLY GHOST.

R︦. Amen.

Priest. Here let true faith, the fear of GOD, and brotherly love ever remain : this place is consecrated to prayer and to the praise of the most holy Name of the same our LORD JESUS CHRIST. Who ever liveth.

R︦. Amen.

After which shall be said or sung this Anthem.

O how dreadful is this place !
This is none other than the House of GOD : this is the gate of heaven.

And these Psalms following :
Ps. 87. Her foundations, &c.
122. I was glad, &c.

℣. The LORD, &c. R︦. And with, &c. ℣. Let us pray.

463. O GOD, Who art the shield and defence of Thy people, be ever at hand, we beseech Thee, to protect and succour the builders of this house ; that the work which, through Thy mercy, hath now been begun, may by their labour be brought to a happy end. Through.

Prevent us, O LORD, in all our doings, with Thy most gracious favour, and further us with Thy continual help ; that in all our works begun, continued, and ended in Thee, we may glorify Thy holy Name, and finally by Thy mercy obtain everlasting life. Through.

464. O GOD, Who hast built the living temple of Thy Church upon the foundation of the Apostles and Prophets, JESUS CHRIST Himself being the chief corner-stone ; grant unto the work of Thine own hands continual increase of glory and spiritual strength, and daily make Thy people more meet for the eternal tabernacle of Thy rest in the heavens ; through JESUS CHRIST our LORD, to Whom.

The grace of our LORD, &c.

FORM OF SERVICE FOR THE BENEDICTION OF A CHAPEL.

While the Choir and Clergy walk from the place where they vest to the chapel, a Processional Hymn may be sung.
On arriving at the chapel-door, shall be said,

In the Name, &c.
Our FATHER, &c.

℣. O GOD, make speed, &c. R︦. O LORD, make haste, &c. ℣. Glory, &c. R︦. As it was, &c.

Then while the Choir and Clergy walk round the chapel, shall be said or sung,

Ant. Thou shalt purge me with hyssop, and I shall be clean.

Ps. 51. Have mercy upon me, O GOD.

Ant. Thou shalt purge me with hyssop, and I shall be clean : Thou shalt wash me, and I shall be whiter than snow.

Let us pray.

465. O LORD GOD, Who, although Heaven and earth cannot contain Thee, yet condescendest to have habitations upon earth, where we may continually call upon Thy Name ; visit, we beseech Thee, this place with Thy wonderful loving-kindness, cleanse it by Thy grace from all pollution, and ever keep it pure : and as Thou didst accept the devotion of Thy servant Solomon, so vouchsafe to send Thy blessing upon this our work, to accomplish our desires, and to drive hence all spiritual wickednesses. Through.

R̲. Amen.

The Choir and the Clergy will then pass into the chapel, at the entrance of the nave of which shall be said,

℣. Our help is in the Name of the LORD. R̲. Who hath made Heaven and earth. ℣. Blessed be the Name of the LORD. R̲. Henceforth world without end. ℣. The LORD be with you. R̲. And with thy spirit. ℣. Let us pray.

466. Almighty and merciful GOD, Who hast granted such grace unto Thy Priests, that whatsoever they do fitly in Thy Name is held as done by Thee; we entreat Thy great goodness that Thou wouldst visit what we visit, and bless what we bless, and grant that as we enter this place in lowliness of heart, the evil spirits may be put to flight, and the Angel of Peace enter in. Through.

R̲. Amen.

Ant. Have respect unto the prayer of Thy servant.

Ps. 48. Great is the LORD.

Ant. Have respect unto the prayer of Thy servant and to his supplication, and hallow this house which we have built to Thy honour and glory, that Thine eyes may be upon it day and night.

℣. The LORD be with you. R̲. And with thy spirit.

Let us pray.

467. O GOD, Who hallowest places dedicated to Thy Name, pour Thy grace, we beseech Thee, upon this House of Prayer; sanc✝tify and bl✝ess it, that all who shall call upon Thee here, may feel the help

of Thy gracious mercy and protection. Through.

R̲. Amen.

The Choir and Clergy passing on to the Altar, shall sing,

Ant. Thou, O GOD, art praised in Sion.

Ps. 23. The LORD is my Shepherd, &c.

121. I will lift up mine eyes, &c.

Ant. Thou, O GOD, art praised in Sion, and unto Thee shall the vow be performed in Jerusalem.

℣. The LORD, &c. R̲. And with, &c. ℣. Let us pray.

All kneeling.

LORD, have mercy, &c.
CHRIST, have mercy, &c.
LORD, have mercy, &c.

Our FATHER, &c.

℣. My soul hath longed for Thy salvation. R̲. And I have a good hope because of Thy word. ℣. Let the freewill offering of my mouth please Thee, O LORD. R̲. And teach me Thy judgments. ℣. Hide me from the gathering together of the froward. R̲. And from the insurrection of wicked doers. ℣. Hold Thou me up, and I shall be safe. R̲. Yea, my delight shall be ever in Thy statutes. ℣. LORD, hear our prayer. R̲. And let our cry come unto Thee. ℣. Let us pray.

468. Blessed be Thy Name, O LORD, that it hath pleased Thee to put into the hearts of Thy servants to build this House to Thy praise and honour. Let Thy blessing be upon them, their families, and their substance, and accept their pious and charitable work. Remember them concerning this : wipe not out this kindness which they have done, and grant that all they who shall hereafter enjoy the benefit of this pious work, may show forth their thankfulness, by rightly using it, to the glory of Thy Blessed Name. Through.

R7. Amen.

Turning to the people, the Priest shall pronounce the Dedication.

Forasmuch as Almighty GOD accepted the purpose of His servants David and Solomon to build His temple at Jerusalem, and nothing doubting but that He favourably alloweth this charitable work of ours in having built this House of prayer which we now set apart to His glory : We, therefore, on behalf of His Church and people dedicate this Chapel to bear henceforth the name of [. . . .] To the honour and glory of the Holy and Eternal Trinity, the FATHER, 'the SON, and the HOLY GHOST.

R7. Amen.

Standing as before, the Priest shall say,

Let us pray.

(*Collect for All Saints' Day.*)

O Almighty GOD, Who hast knit together Thine elect, &c.

469. O GOD, Who hast built the living temple of Thy Church upon the foundation of the Apostles and Prophets, JESUS CHRIST Himself being the chief corner stone ; grant unto the work of Thine own hands continual increase of glory and spiritual strength, and daily make Thy people more meet for the eternal tabernacle of Thy rest in the heavens. Through.

470. Grant, we beseech Thee, Almighty GOD, that those for whom this House of prayer is provided may be so filled with the Spirit of Thy grace that they may ever do Thy will with a pure heart and a ready mind, to the glory of Thy Name and the good of their own souls. Through.

Let us pray.

471. Give ear, LORD, unto the prayers which shall be offered unto Thee in this place, and with Thy mighty arm protect those who offer them. Be ever present with Thy children, and pour upon them bountifully all blessings both to their souls and bodies, and grant that they may so serve Thee in this life that in the world to come they may have life everlasting, and be made glad with the joy of Thy countenance. Where Thou livest.

472. Enlarge, O LORD, the hearts of Thy faithful people, that like as the Israelites Thy people of old offered willingly to Thee of their substance, so we, remembering that our days on earth are but as a shadow, that here we have no abiding place, and that all things come of Thee, may with perfect hearts offer willingly each according to his ability to the continual support of Thy holy service this day begun in this House of prayer. Through.

Then the Priest turning to the people shall pronounce this Benediction.

GOD the FATHER, GOD the SON, GOD the HOLY GHOST, bless, preserve, and keep you now and for evermore.

R7. Amen.

Then shall follow the Celebration of the Holy Communion.

BENEDICTION OF A COLLEGE, OR RELIGIOUS HOUSE.

To be used at the first opening, and afterwards annually on the Feast of the Epiphany.

Ant. O LORD, protect this house. and let Thy holy Angels guard it, and drive away all evil from it.

Ps. 67. GOD be merciful, &c.

Ant. O LORD, protect this house, V. LORD, I have loved the habitation of Thy house. R℣. And the place where Thine honour dwelleth. ℣. LORD, hear, &c. R℣. And let, &c. ℣. The LORD, &c. R℣. And with, &c. ℣. Let us pray.

Almighty and merciful GOD, Who hast granted such grace unto Thy Priests, that whatsoever they do fitly in Thy Name is held as done by Thee; we entreat Thy great goodness that Thou wouldst visit whatsoever we shall visit, and bless whatsoever we shall bless, and grant that as we enter this place in lowliness of heart, the evil spirits may be put to flight, and the Angels of peace enter in. Through.

While the Procession is moving from room to room through the building, Psalms or Hymns proper of the season shall be sung.

IN THE DORMITORIES.

Ant. Save us, O LORD, watching, guard us sleeping, that we may watch with CHRIST, and rest in peace.

℣. I will lay me down in peace. R℣. And take my rest. ℣. LORD, hear, &c. R℣. And let, &c. ℣. The LORD, &c. R℣. And with, &c. ℣. Let us pray.

473. O LORD GOD, the Keeper of Israel, Who neither slumberest nor sleepest; bless, we beseech Thee, this dormitory of Thy servants, and as they rest in this place after their labours, keep them from the illusions and deceits of the devil, that when they wake they may meditate upon Thy commandments, and when they sleep they may be guarded by Thy protecting help. Through.

IN THE INFIRMARY.

Ant. O LORD, look down upon Thy holy house, and consider us: bow down Thine ear, O LORD, to hear us: open Thine eyes, and behold our affliction.

℣. O GOD, save Thy servants. R℣. Which put their trust in Thee. ℣. LORD, hear, &c., (*as before.*)

Let us pray.

474. Almighty and merciful GOD, we beseech Thy boundless loving-kindness, that as Thou didst visit Tobit, Peter's wife's mother, and the centurion's servant, so Thou wouldst vouchsafe mercifully to visit this infirmary, and to bless it with Thy right hand, that Thy sick servants abiding in it, may attain health of body and soul, and when they die may be protected by the guardianship of Thine Angels. Through.

IN THE REFECTORY.

Ant. The eyes of all wait upon Thee, O LORD, and Thou givest them their meat in due season. Thou openest Thine hand, and fillest all things living with plenteousness.

℣. The poor shall eat and be satisfied. R℣. They that seek after the LORD shall praise Him. ℣. LORD, hear, &c. &c.

Let us pray.

475. Almighty and everlasting GOD, Who in Thy loving bounty nourishest Thy servants, and sustainest them in this place of bodily refreshment; we beseech Thy great goodness that Thou wouldst vouchsafe to bless this dining hall, and grant to Thy servants, that, through Thy blessing, they may receive meat and drink with thanksgiving, and at length attain unto eternal joys. Through.

IN THE SUPERIOR'S ROOM.

Ant. Obey them that have the rule over you, and submit yourselves, for they watch for your souls as they that must give account, that they may do it with joy, and not with grief.

℣. Know them which labour among you, and are over you in the LORD. R℣. And esteem them very highly in love for their work's sake. ℣. LORD, hear, &c. &c.

Let us pray.

476. O LORD, we beseech Thee, grant the spirit of counsel and might to the Superior of this House, and vouchsafe Thy blessing upon this chamber, that the orders issued hence may be for Thy glory, and the spiritual and temporal benefit of the community. Through.

In the Common Room.

Ant. Be kindly affectioned one to another with brotherly love, in honour preferring one another, not slothful in business, fervent in spirit, serving the LORD.

℣. Above all things have fervent charity among yourselves. ℟. For charity shall cover the multitude of sins. ℣. LORD, hear, &c. &c.

Let us pray.

477. O LORD GOD Almighty, we beseech Thee to make the dwellers in this place of one heart and of one soul, that knit together in true fellowship here on earth, they may finally be joined with the communion of Thy Saints in heaven. Through.

In the Library.

Ant. Every scribe which is instructed unto the kingdom of heaven is like unto a man that is an householder, which bringeth forth out of his treasures things new and old.

℣. Give instruction to a wise man, and he will be yet wiser. ℟. Teach a just man, and he will increase in learning. ℣. LORD, hear, &c. &c.

Let us pray.

478. O GOD the HOLY GHOST, Teacher Who leadest into all truth, grant us so to give attendance to reading, to exhortation, to doctrine, and so to meditate in Thy law, that we may be filled with the knowledge of Thy will in all wisdom and spiritual understanding. Through.

In the Workroom.

Ant. Study to be quiet, and to do your own business, and to work with your own hands, that ye may walk honestly towards them that are without, and that ye may have lack of nothing.

℣. Work your work betimes. ℟. And in His time He will give you your reward. ℣. LORD, hear, &c. &c.

Let us pray.

479. O LORD JESU CHRIST, Who hast said, My FATHER worketh hitherto, and I work; grant us so to labour diligently while it is called to-day, that when the night cometh wherein no man can work, we may enter into the rest which remaineth for the people of GOD. Through Thy mercy.

In the Visitors' Room.

Ant. Be not forgetful to entertain strangers, for thereby some have entertained angels unawares.

℣. The LORD your GOD loveth the stranger, in giving him food and raiment. ℟. Love ye therefore the stranger, for ye were strangers in the land of Egypt. ℣. LORD, hear, &c. &c.

Let us pray.

480. O LORD JESU CHRIST, Who by Thine Apostle hast commanded us to use hospitality one to another without grudging; enter into this guest-chamber with us Thy disciples, and bless it, that all who sojourn herein may be fulfilled with Thy grace, and at the end of their pilgrimage be led into the inner chambers of Thy palace, to go out thence no more. Who livest.

In the Store-rooms.

Ant. Behold, I will send you corn and wine and oil, and ye shall be satisfied therewith: be glad then, and rejoice in the LORD your GOD.

℣. O LORD, send Thy blessing upon these storehouses. ℟. And on the works of Thine hands. ℣. LORD, hear, &c. &c.

Let us pray.

481. Almighty and merciful GOD, Who by Thy servant Moses didst say, If thou shalt hearken unto the voice of the LORD thy GOD, the LORD shall command the blessing upon thee and thy storehouses; we humbly beseech Thy Majesty that Thou wouldst in Thy loving-kindness visit this store, to drive away all evil from it, and to pour down the abundance of Thy blessing upon all that is contained in it. Through.

IN THE KITCHEN.

Ant. He shall feed me in a green pasture.

℣. Thou, O GOD, hast of Thy goodness prepared for the poor. ℟. Thou Who makest men to be of one mind in a house. ℣. LORD, hear, &c. &c.

Let us pray.

482. O eternal GOD, before Whose Face the Angels serve, by Whose will all things are governed, and Who, in Thy goodness, dost not cease to provide for the wants of human weakness; we humbly beseech Thee that Thou wouldst pour down upon this kitchen Thy blessing, wherewith, by the hand of the Prophet Elisha, Thou madest sweet the bitter taste of the pot, and that Thy servants, ever here abounding in the fulness of Thy blessing, may praise Thee Who givest food to all flesh, and fillest all things living with plenteousness, O SAVIOUR of the world. Who livest.

IN THE CLOISTER.

Ant. The love of CHRIST hath gathered us into one, let us fear and love CHRIST our GOD: where charity and love are, there is GOD.

℣. Behold, how good and joyful a thing it is. ℟. Brethren, to dwell together in unity. ℣. LORD, hear, &c. &c.

Let us pray.

483. Almighty, everlasting GOD, Who by Thy special grace hast mer-cifully gathered us together in this house; grant to us Thy servants through the power of this solemn benediction, so worthily to praise Thee herein, that living in brotherly love, and continuing in peace, we may at length, through Thy mercy, attain unto that pleasant land where all things are calm and unshaken. Through.

AT THE GATE.

Ant. The LORD hath made fast the bars of thy gates, and hath blessed thy children within thee.

℣. This is the gate of the LORD. ℟. The righteous shall enter into it. ℣. LORD, hear, &c. &c.

Let us pray.

484. O LORD JESU CHRIST, Who at the entering in of Jerusalem, didst hallow its twelve gates with the glory of jewels, and with the names of Thy twelve Apostles in their foundations, and Who by the mouth of Thy Prophet hast said, Praise the LORD, O Jerusalem, for He hath made fast the bars of thy gates, and hath blessed thy children within thee; we beseech Thy mercy that Thou wouldest make peace in all the borders of this house, and that Thy Word, running very swiftly, may fill us with the flour of wheat, and that the HOLY SPIRIT may defend us, and that the enemy may not prevail to hurt us, but that all who dwell in this house may praise Thee in voice, heart, and work, knowing that Thou art the great GOD and our LORD JESUS CHRIST, and great is Thy power, and Thy wisdom is infinite. Who livest.

Proceeding to the Chapel they kneel before the Altar and say,

Ant. Whoso dwelleth under the defence of the Most High shall abide under the shadow of the Almighty.

LORD, have mercy, &c. &c.
Our FATHER, &c.

℣. O Lord, think upon Thy congregation. ℟. Whom Thou hast purchased and redeemed of old. ℣. Lord, hear, &c. &c.

Let us pray.

485. O God, Who in all places of Thy dominion art ever present, and alone workest in us; hear, we beseech Thee, our prayers, and grant that the benediction of this house may abide inviolate, and that the whole body which beseeches Thee may obtain Thy bountiful gifts.

486. Almighty, everlasting God, direct our actions in accordance with Thy will, that in the Name of Thy beloved Son we may abound in good works. Through the same.

And the blessing of God Almighty, the Father, the Son, and the Holy Ghost, descend upon us and upon this house, and abide for evermore. Amen.

BENEDICTION OF A PARISH OR MISSION ROOM.

Hymn 335, H. A. M., (*as they enter the building.*)

Priest. Be kindly affectioned one to another; with brotherly love, in honour preferring one another; not slothful in business; fervent in spirit; serving the Lord.

℣. Above all things, have fervent charity among yourselves. ℟. For charity shall cover the multitude of sins. ℣. Lord, hear our prayer. ℟. And let our cry come unto Thee. ℣. Let us pray.

487. O Lord God Almighty, we beseech Thee to make those who meet in this place of one heart and of one soul, that knit together in true fellowship here on earth, they may finally be joined with the communion of Thy saints in heaven. Through.

488. Almighty, everlasting God, who by Thy special grace hast mercifully gathered us together in this [. . . .], grant to us Thy servants, through the power of this solemn benediction, so worthily to glorify Thee herein, that continuing in brotherly love and grace, we may at length, through Thy mercy, attain unto that pleasant land where all things are calm and unshaken. Through.

489. Blessed be Thy Name, O Lord, that it hath pleased Thee to put into the hearts of Thy servants to build (*or* set apart) this [. . .] to Thy praise and honour. Let Thy blessing be upon them, their families, and their substance, and accept their pious and charitable work. Remember them concerning this: wipe not out this kindness which they have done, and grant that all they who shall hereafter enjoy the benefit of this pious work, may show forth their thankfulness by rightly using it, to the glory of Thy blessed Name. Through.

490. O Lord God, Who art the Giver of all wisdom, and willest that children should be brought up in the fear and love of Thy holy Name; pour down, we beseech Thee, the gift of Thy loving-kindness upon this place, that all who shall be gathered together in it for [Sunday School and other meetings,] may grow in Thy grace, and be delivered from all evils of body and soul. Through.

Lord, have mercy, &c.
Our Father, &c.

℣. O satisfy us with Thy mercy, and that soon. ℟. So shall we rejoice and be glad all the days of our life. ℣. Show Thy servants Thy work. ℟. And their children

Thy glory. ℣. Let them say alway, Blessed be the LORD. ℟. Who hath pleasure in the prosperity of His servant. ℣. Let us pray.

491. Almighty and merciful GOD, we beseech Thy great goodness that Thou wouldst visit what we visit and bless what we bless, that all evil spirits may be driven from this place, and that it may be the abode of peace. Through.

492. O LORD JESUS CHRIST, Who hast said that none shall enter into the kingdom of heaven, except they become as little children; grant unto us, and to all who shall be gathered here, so to serve Thee with a childlike heart, that we may at length attain to that blessed place where Thou livest.

The grace of our LORD, &c.

OFFICE FOR LAYING THE FIRST STONE OF A CLERGY-HOUSE.

In the Name, &c.
Our FATHER, &c.

℣. Be Thou my strong Rock and house of defence. ℟. That Thou mayest save me. ℣. O GOD, make speed, &c. ℟. O LORD, make haste, &c. ℣. Glory, &c. ℟. As it was, &c.

Alleluia.

Ant. Mark well her bulwarks.

Ps. 48. Great is the LORD, &c.

Ant. Mark well her bulwarks, set up her houses, that ye may tell them that come after.

℣. The LORD, &c. ℟. And with, &c. ℣. Let us pray.

493. O LORD, Who by Thy servant Elisha didst bless the sons of the prophets in building their habitations; bless, we beseech Thee, this place with Thy mercy, that it may be pure from all stain, and that those who shall dwell within it may be fulfilled with Thy heavenly grace and benediction. Through.

℣. Our help is in the Name of the LORD. ℟. Who hath made heaven and earth. ℣. Blessed be the Name of the LORD. ℟. From this time forth for evermore. ℣. The stone which the builders rejected. ℟. Is become the head of the corner. ℣. Glory, &c. ℟. As it was, &c. ℣. Let us pray.

Almighty and everlasting GOD, mercifully be pleased to bless this stone, which we are about to place for a foundation in the Name of Him Who is the tried and precious Stone; and grant that all they who, to the furtherance of this work, shall have faithfully offered to Thee of their substance, may ever be preserved both in body and soul. Through.

Then the Priest makes the sign of the Cross on the stone, saying,

In the Name, &c.

Let us pray.

Bless, O LORD, this stone, and grant, by the invocation of Thy holy Name, that whosoever piously aideth in the erection of this house, may obtain health of body and soul. Through.

When the mortar is ready, the Priest begins the Antiphon:

Ant. Through wisdom is our house builded.

Ps. 127. Except the LORD, &c.

Ant. Through wisdom is our house builded, and by understanding is it established.

Then the Priest fixes the stone in its place, saying,

In the faith of JESUS CHRIST we place this headstone in the foundation, in the Name of the FATHER, the SON, and the HOLY GHOST, that here true faith, the fear of GOD, and brotherly love may dwell, and that this place may be set apart as the dwelling of those who shall minister at His altars, and for the honour of the Name of the same our LORD JESUS CHRIST. Who liveth.

Ant. Thou shalt purge me with hyssop, and I shall be clean.

Ps. 51. Have mercy upon me, &c.

Ant. Thou shalt purge me with hyssop, and I shall be clean : Thou shalt wash me, and I shall be whiter than snow.

Ant. The righteous shall flourish like a palm tree, and shall spread abroad like a cedar in Libanus.

℣. The LORD, &c. ℟. And with, &c. ℣. Let us pray.

Almighty and merciful GOD, we beseech Thy great goodness that Thou wouldst visit what we visit, and bless what we bless, and that all evil spirits may be driven from this place, and that it may be the abode of the Angel of peace. Through.

494. Grant, O LORD, we beseech Thee, that those for whom we build this house may be so filled with Thy Spirit, that they may ever accomplish their ministry with a pure heart and a ready will, to the glory of Thy Name and the benefit of Thy holy Church. Who livest.

The peace of GOD, &c.

BENEDICTION OF A CLERGY-HOUSE.

For the Benediction of particular chambers in the Clergy-House, see the Office for the Benediction of a College.

In the Name, &c.
Our FATHER, &c.

℣. Whoso dwelleth under the defence of the Most High. ℟. Shall abide under the shadow of the Almighty. ℣. O GOD, make speed, &c. ℟. O LORD, make haste, &c. ℣. Glory, &c. ℟. As it was, &c.
Alleluia.

Ant. My people shall dwell in a peaceable habitation.

Ps. 15. LORD, who shall dwell, &c.
65. Thou, O GOD, art praised, &c.
133. Behold, how good, &c.

Ant. My people shall dwell in a peaceable habitation, and in sure dwellings, and in quiet resting-places.

Priest. Let us pray, beloved brethren, unto the LORD our GOD, that He may enlighten this dwelling with His loving-kindness, fill it with holy inmates, and grant unto His servants the protection of His Divine Majesty.

℣. The LORD, &c. ℟. And with, &c. ℣. Let us pray.

LORD, have mercy upon us, &c.
Our FATHER, &c.

℣. O pray for the peace of Jerusalem. ℟. They shall prosper that love thee. ℣. Peace be within thy walls. ℟. And plenteousness within thy palaces. ℣. Let Thy Priests be clothed with righteousness. R/. And let Thy saints sing with joyfulness. V/. LORD, hear, &c. R/. And let, &c. V/. Let us pray.

495. We beseech Thee, O LORD, to bless the goings out and the comings in of the dwellers in this house; to keep them in purity and health; to send Thy holy Angel to be their defence; to drive away darkness; to grant light; to give the enemy no advantage against them; to bestow on them sufficiency of food and raiment; to enrich them with all works of faith; and to encompass them with the unity of the Blessed Trinity. Through.

496. Let this house be hallowed, and the unclean spirit be driven from it through the might of our LORD JESUS CHRIST; and to those who abide within it let health, cheerfulness, and gladness be vouchsafed, and let them be kept and preserved therein by Thy Majesty, O Almighty GOD. Through.

497. O LORD our heavenly FATHER, Almighty, everlasting GOD, hear us, and vouchsafe to send Thy holy Angel, to guard, cherish, protect, visit, and defend all who dwell in this habitation. Through.

498. Almighty GOD, bless this dwelling and household, and as Thou didst bless the house of Abraham, Isaac, and Jacob, so vouchsafe to bless and hallow this house, and all who abide in it. Through.

The blessing of GOD Almighty, the FATHER, the SON, and the HOLY GHOST, be upon this house, and all who dwell within it. Amen.

This Office may be used for the Benediction of any Dwelling-House.

OFFICE FOR LAYING THE FOUNDATION-STONE OF A SCHOOL.

In the Name, &c.
Our FATHER, &c.

V/. My seed shall serve Him. R/. They shall be counted unto the LORD for a generation. V/. O GOD, make speed, &c. R/. O LORD, make haste, &c. V/. Glory, &c. R/. As it was, &c.

Alleluia.

Ant. O let me have understanding.

Ps. 101. My song shall be of mercy, &c.

Ant. O let me have understanding in the way of godliness.

V/. The LORD, &c. R/. And with, &c. V/. Let us pray.

499. O LORD GOD, Who art the Giver of all wisdom, and willest that children should be brought up in the fear and love of Thy holy Name; pour down, we beseech Thee, the gift of Thy loving-kindness upon this place, that all who shall be gathered together in it may grow in Thy grace, and be delivered from all evils of body and soul. Through.

V/. Our help is in the Name of the LORD. R/. Who hath made heaven and earth. V/. Blessed be the Name of the LORD. R/. From this time forth for evermore. V/. The stone which the builders rejected. R/. Is become the head of the corner. V/. Glory, &c. R/. As it was, &c. V/. Let us pray.

Almighty and everlasting GOD, mercifully be pleased to bless this stone which we are about to place for a foundation in the Name and strength of Him Who is the tried and precious Stone; and grant that all they who to the furtherance of this work shall have faithfully offered to Thee of their substance may ever be preserved both in body and soul. Through.

Then the Priest makes the sign of the Cross on the stone, saying,

In the Name of the FATHER, &c.

Let us pray.

Bless, O LORD, this stone, and grant by the invocation of Thy holy Name, that whosoever piously aideth in the erection of this school may obtain health of body and soul. Through.

When the mortar is ready, the Priest begins the Antiphon.

Ant. He shall bring forth the headstone thereof.

Ps. 127. Except the LORD, &c.

Ant. He shall bring forth the headstone thereof with shoutings, crying, Grace, grace unto it.

Then the Priest fixes the stone in its place, saying,

In the faith of JESUS CHRIST we place this headstone in the foundation, in the Name of the FATHER, the SON, and the HOLY GHOST, that here true faith, the fear of GOD, and brotherly love may dwell, and that this place may be set apart for the instruction of the young, and for the honour of the Name of the same our LORD JESUS CHRIST. Who liveth.

Ant. Thou shalt purge me with hyssop, and I shall be clean.

Ps. 51. Have mercy upon me, &c.

Ant. Thou shalt purge me with hyssop, and I shall be clean : Thou shalt wash me, and I shall be whiter than snow.

Ant. Do well, O LORD.

Ps. 125. They that put their trust, &c.

Ant. Do well, O LORD, unto those that are good and true of heart.

℣. The LORD, &c. ℟. And with, &c. ℣. Let us pray.

LORD, have mercy, &c.
Our FATHER, &c.

℣. O satisfy us with Thy mercy, and that soon. ℟. So shall we rejoice and be glad all the days of our life. ℣. Show Thy servants Thy work. ℟. And their children Thy glory. ℣. Let them say alway, Blessed be the LORD. ℟. Who hath pleasure in the prosperity of His servant. ℣. Let us pray.

Almighty and merciful GOD, we beseech Thy great goodness that Thou wouldst visit what we visit and bless what we bless, that all evil spirits may be driven from this place, and that it may be the abode of the Angel of peace. Through.

O LORD JESU CHRIST, Who hast said that none shall enter into the kingdom of heaven except they become as little children; grant unto us, and to all who shall be gathered here, so to serve Thee with a child-like heart, that we may at length attain to that blessed place, where Thou livest.

BENEDICTION OF A NEW SCHOOL-HOUSE.

In the Name, &c.
Our FATHER, &c.

℣. Our help is in the Name of the LORD. ℟. Who hath made heaven and earth. ℣. O GOD, make speed, &c. ℟. O LORD, make haste, &c. ℣. Glory, &c. ℟. As it was, &c.

Alleluia.

HYMN.

Ant. Come, ye children, and hearken unto me.

Ps. 8. O LORD, our Governor, &c. 119 (9—16). Wherewithal, &c.

Ant. Come, ye children, and hearken unto me: I will teach you the fear of the LORD.

℣. The LORD, &c. ℟. And with, &c. ℣. Let us pray.

LORD, have mercy, &c.
Our FATHER, &c.

℣. Teach me, O LORD, the way of Thy statutes. ℟. And I shall keep it unto the end. ℣. Give me understanding, and I shall keep Thy law. ℟. Yea, I shall keep it with my whole heart. ℣. LORD, hear, &c. ℟. And let, &c. ℣. Let us pray.

500. Almighty and merciful GOD, graciously bow down Thine ear to the petitions of Thy humble servants, hallow with the might of Thy blessing this school-house, erected for the instruction of Thy children, and vouchsafe the gift of Thy grace to all who come to learn within it, that they may grow up in Thy faith and fear, and obtain remission of all their sins. Through.

501. O GOD the HOLY GHOST, pour down, we pray Thee, Thy mercy upon this place, that it may be blessed and hallowed by Thy Presence, and that the fulness of Thy sevenfold gifts may rest upon all Thy children. Through.

The blessing of GOD Almighty, the FATHER, the SON, and the HOLY GHOST, descend and rest upon this place, and all who learn and teach in it, now and for evermore.

INDUCTION OF A SCHOOL TEACHER.

In the Name, &c.
Our FATHER, &c.

℣. Take fast hold of instruction, let her not go. ℟. Keep her, for she is thy life. ℣. O GOD, &c. ℟. O LORD, &c. ℣. Glory, &c. ℟. As it was, &c.

Ant. Come, ye children, and hearken unto Me.

Ps. 119 (25—40). My soul cleaveth, &c.

Ant. Come, ye children, and hearken unto Me: I will teach you the fear of the LORD.

The Priest, turning to the candidate, says,

N., you have been appointed to the office of Master (*or* Mistress) of this school of ——. Do you promise to deal with the children as one who must give account for them at the last day?

℟. I promise.

Do you promise to bring them up in the admonition and fear of the LORD?

℟. I promise, GOD being my helper.

Will you be steadfast in upholding the necessary discipline of the school?

R⁷. I will.

Will you deal justly and fairly with the children, not ruling by caprice or favouritism, but sincerely?

R⁷. I will, God being my helper.

Will you always pause and reflect before punishing, lest you should do so rather in anger than for correction?

R⁷. I promise so to do.

Will you strive in all things to set a good and cheerful example to the children, remembering that your conduct is their chief lesson?

R⁷. I will so endeavour myself, with the help of God.

God, Who has given you a good desire, enable you to fulfil it unto the end.

R⁷. Amen.

Then the Priest delivering the school register into the teacher's hands, shall say,

Receive this Register of the School in token of your admission as *Master*, and see that you rule the children with firmness, gentleness, and discretion.

V̄. The Lord, &c. R⁷. And with, &c. V̄. Let us pray.

Lord, have mercy, &c.

Our Father, &c.

V̄. O Lord, save Thy servant. R⁷. Who putteth *his* trust in Thee. V̄. Send *him* help from the sanctuary. R⁷. And strengthen *him* out of Sion. V̄. Grant *him his* heart's desire. R⁷. And fulfil all *his* mind. V̄. Lord, hear, &c. R⁷. And let, &c. V̄. Let us pray.

502. O Lord God, Father Almighty, grant Thy grace to this Thy servant, that *he* may wisely and devoutly fulfil the charge committed unto *him*, and so train the children intrusted to *his* care that they may fully learn their duty towards God and man, and with *him* attain a final reward. Through.

503. We beseech Thee, O Lord, to pour Thy heavenly grace on the children of this school, that, after the lowly example of Thy Son, our Lord Jesus Christ, they may be docile, obedient, and diligent, and may profit by the instructions of the teacher set over them. Through the same.

Benediction. The Lord increase you more and more, you and your children, and be ye blessed of the Lord, Who made heaven and earth. Amen.

OFFICE FOR THE CIRCUIT OF A PARISH IN ROGATION-TIDE.

When the Priest, Clerks, and people are assembled, before they proceed to the Church the Priest shall say,

Dearly beloved, let us beseech God the Father Almighty to purify the world from all errors, to repel diseases, avert famine, loose captives, break the chains, grant safe return to travellers, health to the sick, a sure haven to those at sea, to give peace in our days, to drive back our enemies who rise against us, and to deliver us from the hand of the evil one, for His Name's sake. Alleluia.

As they proceed to the Church, Psalms 44 and 65 shall be sung, the Priest saying the Antiphon.

Ant. O Lord, arise, help us.

Ps. 44. We have heard with our ears, &c.

65. Thou, O God, art praised, &c.

Ant. O Lord, arise, help us, and deliver us for Thy Name's sake.

On reaching the Church The Litany shall be said or sung, after which the Procession shall leave the Church singing a Hymn for Rogation-tide. At the close of the Hymn they shall proceed to make the Circuit of the Parish, singing Ps. 104, the Priest beginning with the following

Ant. He watereth the hills from above: the earth is filled with the fruit of Thy works.

Ps. 104. Praise the Lord, O my soul, &c.

Ant. He watereth the hills from above: the earth is filled with the fruit of Thy works. He bringeth forth grass for the cattle, and green herb for the service of men; that He may bring food out of the earth, and wine that maketh glad the heart of man, and oil to make him a cheerful countenance, and bread to strengthen man's heart.

After the Priest has repeated the Antiphon at the close of the Psalm, the Procession shall stop, and the Priest and Clerks shall say as follows :

In the Name, &c.
Our Father, &c.

℣. The Lord shall show loving-kindness. ℟. And our land shall give her increase. ℣. When Thou lettest Thy breath go forth they shall be made. ℟. And Thou shalt renew the face of the earth. ℣. Lord, hear, &c. ℟. And let, &c. ℣. The Lord, &c. ℟. And with, &c. ℣. Let us pray.

504. May God, even our own God, give us His blessing, and the earth bring forth her increase abundantly, that the sower may sow in joy, and the reapers gather their sheaves in gladness, and ever bless His Name.   Through.

The Psalms shall be sung while the Procession is moving ; after each Psalm it shall halt at some convenient place while the Priest says the succeeding prayer : after which it shall again move on as before.

Ant. Thou, O God, sentest a gracious rain upon Thine inheritance.

Ps. 68. Let God arise, &c.

Ant. Thou, O God, sentest a gracious rain upon Thine inheritance, and refreshedst it when it was weary.

℣. The Lord, &c. ℟. And with, &c. ℣. Let us pray.

505. Almighty God, we beseech Thy mercy that Thou wouldst vouchsafe to bless the lands and multiply the harvests of Thy servants, as Thou didst bless those of the Patriarchs, Abraham, Isaac, and Jacob, that Thy servants may have plenty, and that the poor and needy may bless Thy glorious Name. Through.

Ant. I am the Lord thy God, Who brought thee out of the land of Egypt.

Ps. 81. Sing we merrily, &c.

Ant. I am the Lord thy God, Who brought thee out of the land of Egypt : open thy mouth wide, and I shall fill it.

℣. The Lord, &c. ℟. And with, &c. ℣. Let us pray.

506. Almighty God, we humbly beseech Thy mercy that Thou wouldest vouchsafe to bless, sanctify, and water the fields and crops of Thy servants, and to defend them from all assaults of the enemy, that Thou mayest satisfy their need with the abundance of Thy blessing, and that they may ever offer praises unto Thee, Who givest food to all flesh. Through.

Ant. The merciful goodness of the Lord endureth for ever and ever upon them that fear Him.

Ps. 103. Praise the Lord, &c.

Ant. The merciful goodness of the Lord endureth for ever and ever upon them that fear Him, and His righteousness upon children's children.

℣. The Lord, &c.   ℟. And with, &c.   ℣. Let us pray.

507. O God, the Lord of heaven and earth, we humbly entreat Thee that Thou wouldst send Thine angel to guard and defend the fields and crops of Thy servants from all the attacks of the enemy, and that Thou wouldst so satisfy their hunger with good things, that they may ever praise Thy Name, and obtain salvation here and for evermore. Through.

Ant. O all ye green things upon the earth, bless ye the Lord.

Benedicite. O all ye works, &c.

Ant. O all ye green things upon the earth, bless ye the Lord, praise Him, and magnify Him for ever.

When they have completed the half circuit of the Parish, the Procession shall enter a field, and the Priest shall pronounce the following Benedictions on the crops.

508. Almighty God, we beseech Thy mercy that Thou wouldst water with the rain of Thy blessing these firstlings of Thy creatures, which Thou hast been pleased to nourish with the mingling of wind and rain, and grant Thy people over to give Thee thanks for Thy gifts, that those who hunger by reason of the barrenness of the earth may be so filled with good things, that the poor and needy may praise Thy glorious Name. Through.

509. Almighty and everlasting God, Ruler of the universe, Who governest the world which hangeth upon nothing, and Who hast commanded us to till the land with our labour for the support of mankind and the sustenance of the body; we humbly beseech Thy mercy that Thou wouldst graciously look upon whatsoever good seed is sown or planted in these fields; give temperate weather, keep them from all weeds and thorns, make the crops plentiful, and grant that they may arrive at full perfection, that we, Thy servants, thankfully receiving the abundant fruit of Thy gifts, may pay due and acceptable praise to Thy Name. Through.

510. We pray and beseech Thee, O Lord, that Thou wouldst vouchsafe to look graciously and propitiously upon these crops of [wheat, &c., . . .] and grant us the help of Thy grace to bless them, that no hail may beat them down, no storm may lay them, no tempest break them off, no drought parch them up, no floods destroy them, no blight or mildew waste them, but bring them in safety and abundance to full maturity for the use of mankind. Through.

Benediction. The blessing of God Almighty, the Father, the Son, and the Holy Ghost, descend and abide on these crops.
℟. Amen.

The Procession now moves on to complete the circuit of the Parish, the Priest saying,

Ant. We have sinned, O Lord, and Thou wast angry with us.

Ps. 89. My song shall be alway, &c.

Ant. We have sinned, O Lord, and Thou wast angry with us, and there is none that can deliver out of Thine hand, but we pray that Thy mercy may come upon us; Thou Who didst spare the Ninevites, have mercy upon us, O Lord our God.

Lord, have mercy, &c.
Our Father, &c.

℣. O Lord, save Thy servants and Thine handmaids. ℟. Which put their trust in Thee. ℣. The sorrows of our heart are enlarged. ℟. O bring Thou us out of our troubles. ℣. We have sinned with our fathers. ℟. We have done amiss and dealt wickedly. ℣. Have mercy upon us, O Lord, have mercy upon us. ℟. For we are utterly despised. ℣. O Lord, let Thy mercy be showed upon us. ℟. As we do put our trust in Thee. ℣. Be not Thou far from us, O Lord. ℟. Thou art our succour, haste Thee to help us. ℣. Remember, O Lord, Thy congregation. ℟. Whom Thou hast purchased and redeemed of old. ℣. Lord, hear, &c. ℟. And let, &c. ℣. The Lord, &c. ℟. And with, &c. ℣. Let us pray.

511. O Lord, mercifully hear the prayers of those who cry unto Thee, and as Thou sparedst the Ninevites when they afflicted themselves, so vouchsafe to help us in our penitent sorrow. Through.

Ant. O how plentiful is Thy goodness, which Thou hast laid up for them that fear Thee.

Ps. 31. In Thee, O Lord, &c.

Ant. O how plentiful is Thy goodness, which Thou hast laid up for them that fear Thee, and that Thou hast prepared for them that put their trust in Thee, even before the sons of men.

℣. The Lord, &c. ℟. And with, &c. ℣. Let us pray.

512. Grant us, O Lord, joy after our sorrow, that while we are punished for our sins, we may be refreshed by Thy mercy; and being mindful of Thy goodness may walk before Thee in holiness and righteousness all the days of our life. Through.

Ant. Such as are blessed of God shall possess the land.

Ps. 37. Fret not thyself, &c.

Ant. Such as are blessed of God shall possess the land, and they that are cursed of Him shall be rooted out.

℣. The Lord, &c. ℟. And with, &c. ℣. Let us pray.

513. O Lord, we beseech Thee, help Thy people which prayeth unto Thee, and mercifully grant Thine aid unto the weak, that serving Thee with a pure heart they may rejoice in this world and in the world to come. Through.

Ant. There shall be a heap of corn in the earth, high upon the hills.

Ps. 72. Give the king, &c.

Ant. There shall be a heap of corn in the earth, high upon the hills; his fruit shall shake like Libanus, and shall be green in the city, like grass upon the earth.

℣. The Lord, &c. ℟. And with, &c. ℣. Let us pray.

514. O God, Who desirest not the death of a sinner, but that of his sins; restrain Thine anger which we have deserved, and pour down upon us that loving-kindness for which we pray, that after our grief we may attain the gladness of Thy mercy. Through.

Ant. He giveth food to all flesh.

Ps. 136. O give thanks, &c.

Ant. He giveth food to all flesh, for His mercy endureth for ever.

On returning to the Church the Priest shall celebrate the Holy Eucharist.

If the above Office be not long enough to occupy the time required for the circuit of the parish, additional Psalms and Hymns [of thanksgiving when going out, and of supplication when returning] shall be added at the discretion of the Priest.

OFFICE FOR THE BLESSING OF CANDLES.

TO BE USED ON THE FEAST OF THE PURIFICATION.

Before the Procession, let the Priest and his ministers vest as for the Eucharist. Which done, let him bless the candles in this wise.

℣. The LORD be with you. ℟. And with thy spirit. ℣. Let us pray.

515. O LORD, Holy FATHER, Almighty, Everlasting GOD, Who didst create all things out of nothing, and hast willed that by the labour of bees this fluid should be brought to the perfection of wax; and who on this day didst fulfil the desire of righteous Simeon; vouchsafe, we beseech Thee, to bl+ess and sanc+tify these candles, fashioned for the service of men; and mercifully hear from heaven Thy dwelling-place the voice of this Thy congregation who desire reverently to bear them in their hands to the praise and exaltation of Thy Name; and show mercy to all that call upon Thee, whom Thou hast redeemed with the precious Blood of Thy dear SON. Who with Thee.

℣. Lift up your hearts. ℟. We lift them up unto the LORD. ℣. Let us give thanks unto our LORD GOD. ℟. It is meet and right so to do.

516. It is very meet, right, and our bounden duty, that we should at all times and in all places, give thanks unto Thee, O LORD, Holy FATHER, Almighty, Everlasting GOD, Fountain and Source of light, Who hast enlightened the world with the beams of Thy brightness, by sending to us from the womb of a pure Virgin Thy Only-begotten SON our LORD. Him Whom of old Thou didst promise by the mouth of Thy holy prophets Thou hast sent in these last days, a Light to the people that sat in darkness. We pray Thee, therefore, O LORD, to hal+low with Thy blessing these candles prepared for the honour of Thy Name, Who hast translated us from darkness into light; and Who hast fulfilled the desire of holy Simeon, that he should not see death before his eyes had seen incarnate the same CHRIST Thy SON, the light and salvation of the whole world; and so fill us with the brightness of Thy light that all clouds of error and unbelief may be driven away. And as on this day Thou didst let Thy servant depart in peace, even so vouchsafe to guide us in the peace of Thy holy Church, that we may come to the haven of everlasting rest; so shall the true Light pour its beams upon us, and in the last day with angels and archangels we shall joyfully behold the face of the Sun that never goeth down, even JESUS CHRIST. Who with Thee.

Here let the candles be sprinkled and censed, and let fire be blessed as follows:

℣. The LORD be with you. ℟. And with thy spirit. ℣. Let us pray.

517. O Holy LORD, Almighty FATHER, unfailing Light, and Maker of all light, bl+ess this light to be borne by Thy people to the honour of Thy Name, that, being sanctified by Thee and blessed by the brightness of Thy light, we may be kindled and illuminated: and as Thou didst cause the face of Thy servant Moses to shine therewith, so illumine also our hearts and senses that we may be found meet to attain to the vision of eternal brightness. Through.

518. Almighty and everlasting GOD, Who didst send into the world Thy Only-begotten SON, begotten before all worlds, but in time made flesh in the womb of the Virgin Mary, to be the true and unfailing light to dispel the darkness of mankind, and to kindle the light of faith and truth; mercifully grant that like as our eyes are enlightened by this natural light, so Thy spiritual beams may shine upon our souls. Through.

The candles shall then be distributed to the choir, and to others as may be appointed. During the dis-tribution the following shall be sung.

Ant. A light to lighten the Gentiles: and to be the glory of Thy people Israel.

LORD, now lettest Thou Thy servant depart in peace : according to Thy word.

Ant. A light, &c.

For mine eyes have seen : Thy salvation.

Ant. A light, &c.

Which Thou hast prepared : before the face of all people.

Ant. A light, &c.

Glory be, &c. A light, &c. As it was, &c. A light, &c.

OFFICE FOR THE BLESSING OF ASHES.

TO BE USED ON THE FIRST DAY OF LENT.

Let the ashes be placed in suitable vessels, and let the Priest say,

℣. Our help is in the Name of the LORD. ℟. Who hath made heaven and earth. ℣. The LORD be with you. ℟. And with thy spirit. ℣. Let us pray.

519. Almighty and everlasting GOD, Who hast compassion upon all men, and hatest nothing that Thou hast made, and dost forgive the sins of them that are penitent; Who also succourest them that are in need; vouchsafe to bl+ess and sanc+tify these ashes, which after the manner of the Ninevites, Thy people bear upon their heads in token of repentance : and grant that all they that shall so bear them for the entreating of Thy mercy, may be accounted worthy to receive from Thee pardon of all their sins, and may so begin this day their holy fast that with pure minds they may be admitted to the Paschal feast, and at length may receive everlasting life. Through.

Here let the ashes be sprinkled with Holy Water.

℣. The LORD be with you. ℟. And with thy spirit. ℣. Let us pray.

520. O GOD, Who desirest not the death of a sinner, but rather that he should be converted and live; graciously look upon the frailty of our condition, and of Thy loving-kindness vouchsafe to bl+ess and sanc+tify these ashes which, in token of humility and contrition, we place on our heads; that we whom Thou hast taught that we are but dust and ashes, and who know that by reason of our depravity we shall return unto dust, may mercifully be thought worthy to obtain the pardon of all our sins, and the rewards promised to them that unfeignedly repent. Through.

Then the Officiant, having been signed with the Ashes on his forehead by the Priest next in dignity, shall proceed to sign the rest of the clergy, and then the laity in order, as they shall present themselves.

When he signs any one he shall say,

Remember, O man, that thou art dust, and unto dust shalt thou return. In the Name, &c.

During the signing the Choir shall sing the following Antiphons.

Let us change our garments for sackcloth and ashes; let us fast and weep before the LORD, for our GOD is ever merciful to put away our sins.

Let the Priests, the ministers of the LORD, weep between the porch and the altar, and let them say, Spare, O LORD, spare Thy people, and turn not away the faces of those who cry unto Thee.

Let us amend the sins which we have committed through ignorance, lest, being suddenly overtaken by the day of our death, we seek a place of repentance, and be not able to find it.

Hear us, O LORD, for Thy loving-kindness is comfortable; turn Thee unto us according to the multitude of Thy mercies.

Save me, O GOD, for the waters are come in, even unto my soul. Glory, &c. As it was, &c. ℣. The LORD be with you. ℟. And with, &c. ℣. Let us pray.

521. O GOD, Who, when we humble ourselves before Thee, dost turn towards us, and Who art appeased when we make satisfaction for our sins; incline the ear of Thy mercy to our prayers, and pour upon the heads of Thy servants, covered with these ashes, the grace of Thy blessing, that Thou mayest fill them with the spirit of compunction, grant them the things which they shall ask aright, and make them to abide steadfastly in those things which Thou dost grant. Through.

522. Almighty, everlasting GOD, Who forgavest the Ninevites when they repented in sackcloth and ashes; mercifully grant unto us so to imitate them in their penitence that with them we may obtain the pardon of our sins. Through.

If the Holy Communion do not follow here, the Priest shall proceed as follows:

Ant. Remember not, LORD, our offences.

Ps. 6. O LORD, rebuke me not, &c.
32. Blessed is he, &c.
38. Put me not to rebuke, &c.
51. Have mercy upon me, &c.
102. Hear my prayer, &c.
130. Out of the deep, &c.
143. Hear my prayer, &c.

Ant. Remember not, LORD, our offences, neither take Thou vengeance on our sins.

LORD, have mercy, &c.
Our FATHER, &c.

℣. LORD, save Thy servants and Thine handmaids. ℟. Who put their trust in Thee. ℣. Send them help from the sanctuary. ℟. And strengthen them out of Sion. ℣. Let the enemy have no advantage over them. ℟. Nor the son of wickedness approach to hurt them. ℣. Be unto them, O LORD, a tower of strength. ℟. From the face of the enemy. ℣. Turn us again, O LORD GOD of hosts. ℟. Show the light of Thy countenance, and we shall be whole. ℣. LORD, hear, &c. ℟. And let, &c. ℣. The LORD, &c. ℟. And with, &c. ℣. Let us pray.

523. Be present, O LORD, to our prayers, and let not Thy mercy be far from Thy servants, heal their wounds, and take away their sins, that freed from all iniquity they may evermore cleave unto Thee. Through.

Other penitential prayers may follow.

Benediction. JESUS CHRIST, Who endured temptation, so clothe you with the armour of spiritual power, that you may overcome all the assaults of the enemy.

OFFICE FOR THE BLESSING OF PALMS AND FLOWERS.

TO BE USED BEFORE THE PROCESSION ON THE SIXTH SUNDAY IN LENT.

Let the Palms for the Clergy be placed by themselves, and those for the people by themselves, and let the Priest stand where he may conveniently minister.

Let us pray.

524. Almighty and everlasting GOD, Who in the flood didst announce to Thy servant Noah the restoration of peace to the earth by the means of a dove bearing an olive branch in her mouth; we humbly beseech Thee to sanc+tify these flowers and palm branches (*or* boughs of trees) which we offer to Thy divine Majesty; that Thy faithful people bearing them in their hands may obtain the grace of Thy heavenly benediction. Through.

525. O GOD, Whose SON for the salvation of mankind came down from heaven, and when the hour of His Passion was at hand willed to enter into Jerusalem riding upon an ass, and to be hailed as King by the multitude; increase the faith of them that trust in Thee, and mercifully hear the prayers of Thy suppliants. Let Thy blessing come upon us; and vouchsafe to bl+ess these branches of palms and other trees, that all who carry them may be fulfilled with Thy benediction. And grant that as the Hebrew children met the same Thy SON our LORD JESUS CHRIST with branches of palms in their hands, crying, Ho-

sanna in the highest; so we also, carrying these boughs of trees, may with good works go forth to meet CHRIST, and attain to everlasting felicity. Through the same.

Here let the flowers and leaves be sprinkled and censed. After which, let the Priest say,

The LORD be with you. R̸. And with thy spirit.

Let us pray.

526. O LORD JESU CHRIST, SON of the living GOD, Maker and Redeemer of the world, Who for us men and for our salvation wast pleased to come down from heaven, to take our flesh, and to undergo Thy Passion; and Who of Thine own will when approaching the place of that Thy Passion didst deign to be blessed and praised, and to be hailed a King blessed coming in the Name of the LORD; receive now the service of our praises, and vouchsafe to bl+ess and sanc+tify these branches of palms and other trees and flowers, that whosoever shall carry anything hence in honour of Thy power, may be sanctified by Thy heavenly benediction, and be counted worthy to attain the remission of sins and the rewards of everlasting life; through Thee, O SAVIOUR JESU CHRIST, Who with the FATHER and the HOLY GHOST livest and reignest, ever one GOD, world without end. Amen.

OFFICE FOR THE WASHING OF THE ALTAR,

TO BE PERFORMED AFTER EVENSONG ON THE THURSDAY BEFORE EASTER.

After Evensong, let the Altar be stripped, and water having been blessed in the usual manner privately outside the choir, let two Priests of highest rank, with deacon and subdeacon (one ministering wine, the other water) and taper-bearer, all in albs and amices, approach the Altar and wash it, pouring on it wine and water: the choir meanwhile standing before the Altar and singing this responsory with its verse, and without Gloria Patri.

Resp. On the Mount of Olives I prayed to the FATHER: FATHER, if it be possible, let this Cup pass from Me; the spirit indeed is willing, but the flesh is weak. Thy will be done.

℣. Nevertheless, not as I will, but as Thou wilt. Thy will be done.

Let the Priest of highest rank then say in a low voice the Collect of that Saint in whose honour the Church is dedicated, without The LORD be with you, *but with* Let us pray.

Resp. II. My soul is exceeding sorrowful even unto death: tarry ye here and watch with Me: now shall ye see the multitude that shall compass Me about. Ye shall flee, but I go to be sacrificed for you.

℣. Behold, the hour is at hand, and the Son of Man shall be delivered into the hands of sinners: ye shall flee, but I go to be sacrificed for you.

Resp. III. Lo, we have seen He hath no form nor comeliness; there is no beauty in Him; He hath borne our sins, and carried our sorrows. He was wounded for our iniquities, and by His stripes we are healed.

℣. Surely He hath borne our griefs, and carried our sorrows. And by His stripes we are healed.

When the Altar or Altars have been washed, let the choir sing this Responsory.

Resp. Lying men compassed me about; they scourged me without a cause; but Thou, O LORD my defender, avenge my cause.

℣. For trouble is hard at hand, and there is none to help. But Thou, O LORD my defender, avenge my cause.

Let the Deacon read the Gospel (S. John xii. 1—15), and a sermon may follow.

OFFICE FOR THE BENEDICTION OF A LIFE-BOAT.

In the Name, &c.
Our FATHER, &c.

℣. The waves of the sea are mighty and rage horribly. ℟. But yet the LORD Who dwelleth on high is mightier. ℣. O GOD, make speed, &c. ℟. O LORD, make haste, &c. ℣. Glory, &c. ℟. As it was, &c.

Ant. Thou rulest the raging of the sea.

Ps. 46. GOD is our hope, &c.

107 (23—32). They that go down . . . elders.

124. If the LORD Himself, &c.

Ant. Thou rulest the raging of the sea, Thou stillest the waves thereof when they arise.

The Chapter. S. Mark vi.

And when even was come, the ship was in the midst of the sea, and He alone on the land. And He saw them toiling in rowing: for the wind was contrary unto them: and about the fourth watch of the night He cometh unto them, walking upon the sea, and would have passed by them. But when they saw Him walking upon the sea, they supposed it had been a spirit, and cried out: for they all saw Him, and were troubled. And immediately He talked with them, and saith unto them, Be of good cheer: it is I, be not afraid. And He went up unto them into the ship; and the wind ceased: and they were sore amazed in themselves beyond measure, and wondered. For they considered not the miracle of the loaves: for their heart was hardened.

Ry. Thanks be to GOD.

Ꝟ. Our help, &c. Ry. Who hath made, &c. Ꝟ. LORD, hear our prayer. Ry. And let our cry, &c. Ꝟ. The LORD, &c. Ry. And with, &c. Ꝟ. Let us pray.

527. O LORD GOD Almighty, Who savedst Noah and his family in the ark from perishing by water, Who didst deliver Jonah from the sea-monster, and Thine Apostle Paul from perils of the deep; bl+ess, we beseech Thee, this boat, that it may, by Thy help, assist in the preservation of human life, and that those whom it rescues may ever thankfully praise Thy holy Name. Through. Ry. Amen.

528. O LORD JESU CHRIST, Man Whom the winds and sea obey, Who savest Thy disciples even when Thou seemest to sleep; aid with Thy strong right hand the crew of this boat, that their toils may be blessed, and they themselves guarded by Thee in all time of need; through Thy mercy, O blessed LORD, Who with the FATHER and the HOLY GHOST livest and reignest one GOD, world without end. Ry. Amen.

Benediction. GOD, the SON of GOD, Who measureth the waters in the hollow of His hand, bl+ess and keep you for evermore. Ry. Amen.

HYMNS. 222, Ancient and Modern; 329, 482, People's Hymnal.

OFFICE FOR MAKING A CATECHUMEN,

PRIOR TO INSTRUCTION FOR BAPTISM.

Ant. Wash you, make you clean.

Ps. 23. The LORD is my Shepherd, &c.

70. Haste Thee, O LORD, &c.

Ant. Wash you, make you clean: put away the evil of your doings from before Mine eyes, cease to do evil, learn to do well.

The Priest turning to the Catechumen, says,

My *son*, what dost thou ask of me?

Ans. I ask of thee Christian teaching and Holy Baptism.

Priest. It is needful for all men who are admitted into the fellowship of CHRIST's religion to worship One

GOD in Three Persons, FATHER, SON, and HOLY GHOST, and renounce all idols and false gods: to live a sober, honest, pure, and godly life, to be in peace and charity with all men, to help those who are in need and distress, to deny themselves, to be constant as well in private prayer as in the public worship of GOD in His Church.

I ask therefore,

Dost thou promise to worship and serve One GOD only, putting away all idols and false gods?

Ans. I promise.

Dost thou renounce the evil spirit and all his works?

Ans. I do.

Dost thou promise to abstain from all uncleanness, gluttony, and drunkenness?

Ans. I do.

Dost thou promise to abstain from all anger, strife, lying, fraud, and covetousness?

Ans. I do.

Benediction. GOD, the FATHER of our LORD JESUS CHRIST, Who is the Way, the Truth, and the Life, and Who hath put these holy desires into thine heart, so to seek for His grace in Baptism, of His great mercy grant thee to persevere therein unto the end, and fulfil in thee the good pleasure of His will. Amen.

Let us pray.

LORD, have mercy, &c.
Our FATHER, &c.

℣. Wash me throughly from my wickedness, O GOD. ℟. And cleanse me from my sin. ℣. Purge me with hyssop, and I shall be clean. ℟. Wash me, and I shall be whiter than snow. ℣. Turn Thy face from my sins. ℟. And put out all my misdeeds. ℣. LORD, hear, &c. ℟. And let, &c.

Let us pray.

529. O LORD GOD Almighty, we beseech Thee, look upon this Thy servant who desires to come out of darkness into light, and out of the bondage of *his* sins into the glorious liberty of the children of GOD, that being no more a servant but a son, *he* may in Thy Presence find fulness of joy. Through.

530. O LORD JESU CHRIST, Good Shepherd, Who didst lay down Thy life for the sheep; mercifully receive this wanderer into Thy fold. Join *him* with Thine own flock, and lead *him* to the pleasant pastures of everlasting life. Through Thy mercy.

531. O GOD the HOLY GHOST, LORD of love and Giver of life, lead this Thy servant from the dry and barren land of ignorance unto Thy waters of comfort, that *he* may be washed clean from all offence and begin a new life in Thee. Who livest.

THE EXORCISM.

The Priest standing before the kneeling candidate, and lifting his right hand, shall say:

GOD, the SON of GOD, Who having spoiled principalities and powers triumphed over them on His Cross, Who by death destroyed death, and overcame him that had the power of death; beat down Satan quickly under thy feet, deliver thee from all his works, drive from thee every evil and unclean spirit, the spirit of error, the spirit of wickedness, the spirit of idolatry and all covetousness, the spirit of lying and all uncleanness, and cause them to depart from thee henceforth and for ever, that thou mayest be made a child of GOD, a member of CHRIST, a temple of the HOLY GHOST, and an heir, with all His saints, of the kingdom of heaven.

The Priest then puts a Crucifix round the catechumen's neck.

Receive this Cross in token that CHRIST JESUS, Who died for thee upon the Cross, is stretching out His arms to receive and bless thee for evermore.

Benediction. GOD, the SON of GOD, Who hath called thee to follow Him, pour water upon thee that art thirsty, and floods upon the dry ground of thy soul, [pour His Spirit upon thy seed and His blessing upon thine offspring.]

OFFICE FOR THE RENEWAL OF BAPTISMAL VOWS.

This Office, when employed in Retreats or Missions, should be preceded by an explanatory Address, and should conclude with an Exhortation to perseverance. The people should be desired to kneel down, and repeat the following Act of Contrition after the Priest :

O most mighty GOD, &c. (See Commination Service.)

Then shall be sung Hymn 346 (People's Hymnal), or other suitable Hymn, all still kneeling.
All standing up, the Priest shall say,

Christian men, Christian women, Christian children, Do you here in the presence of GOD, &c. (See Confirmation Service.)

Every one shall audibly answer,
I do.
Dost thou renounce the devil, &c. (See Baptismal Service.)
Ans. I renounce them all.
Dost thou believe in GOD, &c. (See Baptismal Service.)
Ans. All this I steadfastly believe.
Wilt thou then obediently, &c. (See Baptismal Service.)
Ans. I will endeavour so to do, GOD being my helper.

Then shall the Priest say,

O merciful GOD, grant, &c.
Grant that all carnal affections, &c.
Grant that they may have power, &c.
Grant that *those who have been* dedicated, &c. (See Baptismal Service.)

Hymn (No. 543, People's Hymnal).

℣. The LORD, &c. ℟. And with, &c. ℣. Let us pray.

LORD, have mercy, &c.
Our FATHER, &c.

We yield Thee humble thanks, O heavenly FATHER, that Thou hast vouchsafed to call us to the knowledge of Thy grace and faith in Thee. Increase this knowledge, and confirm this faith in us evermore. Give Thy HOLY SPIRIT to these persons, that having been born again and made heirs of everlasting salvation through our LORD JESUS CHRIST, they may continue Thy servants and attain Thy promises : through the same Thy SON JESUS CHRIST, Who liveth and reigneth with Thee in the unity of the same HOLY SPIRIT everlastingly. Amen.

OFFICE FOR CHURCH DECORATORS.

In the Name, &c.
Our FATHER, &c.

℣. The palace is not for man. ℟. But for the LORD GOD. ℣. O GOD, make speed, &c. ℟. O LORD, make haste, &c. ℣. Glory, &c. ℟. As it was, &c.

Alleluia.

Ant. How goodly are thy tents, O Jacob.

Ps. 122. I was glad, &c.

Ant. How goodly are thy tents, O Jacob, and thy tabernacles, O Israel.

· *The Chapter.* Isa. lx.

The glory of Lebanon shall come unto thee, the fir tree, the pine tree, and the box together, to beautify the place of My sanctuary; and I will make the place of My feet glorious. The sons also of them that afflicted thee shall come bending unto thee; and all they that despised thee shall bow themselves down at the soles of thy feet; and they shall call thee, The city of the LORD, The Zion of the Holy One of Israel.

℣. But Thou, &c. ℟. Thanks, &c. ℣. Jerusalem shall be built up with sapphires and emeralds, and precious stones. ℟. Thy walls, and towers, and battlements with pure gold. ℣. Glory, &c. ℟. As it was, &c. · ℣. And the streets of Jerusalem shall be paved with beryl, and carbuncle, and stones of Ophir. ℟. And all her streets shall say,

Alleluia. ℣. The LORD, &c. ℟. And with, &c. ℣. Let us pray.

LORD, have mercy, &c.
Our FATHER, &c.

℣. O LORD my GOD, hearken unto the cry and to the prayers of Thy servant and of Thy people. ℟. That Thine eyes may be open towards this House night and day. ℣. Bring us to Thy holy mountain. ℟. And make us joyful in Thy House of Prayer. ℣. Ascribe unto the LORD the honour due unto His Name. ℟. Bring presents, and come into His courts.

Let us pray.

532. O LORD GOD Almighty, Who didst put wisdom and understanding into the hearts of Bezaleel and Aholiab, to know how to work all manner of work for the sanctuary, and Who, by the mouth of David the King, taughtest Solomon to adorn Thy temple; mercifully bless the labours of Thy servants; and grant that, as they offer willingly for the service of Thy house on earth, they may attain at length unto that house not made with hands, eternal in the heavens. Through.

Benediction. The Name of the GOD of Jacob defend you, strengthen you out of Sion, remember all your offerings, grant you your heart's desire, and fulfil all your mind. Amen.

OFFICE FOR THE BURIAL OF CHILDREN.

The Priest and Clerks meeting the Corpse at the entrance of the church-yard, and going before it, either into the church, or towards the grave, shall say, or sing,

Suffer the little children to come unto Me, and forbid them not : for of such is the kingdom of GOD.

Verily, I say unto you, Whosoever shall not receive the kingdom of GOD as a little child, he shall not enter therein. And He took them up in His arms, put His hands upon them, and blessed them.

Come, ye blessed of My FATHER, inherit the kingdom prepared for you from the foundation of the world.

Rejoice and be glad for the children of the just, for they shall be gathered together, and shall bless the LORD of the just.

The LORD gave, and the LORD hath taken away, blessed be the Name of the LORD.

After they are come into the church, shall be read one or more of these Psalms following :

Ps. 8. O LORD our Governor, &c.
23. The LORD is my Shepherd, &c.
24. The earth is the LORD's, &c.

The Lesson. Epistle for Holy Innocents.

R̷. Thanks be to GOD.

When they come to the grave, while the corpse is made ready to be laid into the earth, the Priest shall say,

A voice was heard in Ramah, lamentation, and bitter weeping ; Rahel weeping for her children refused to be comforted for her children, because they were not. Thus saith the LORD ; Refrain thy voice from weeping, and thine eyes from tears : for thy work shall be rewarded, saith the LORD ; and they shall come again from the land of the enemy. And there is hope in thine end, saith the LORD, that thy children shall come again to their own border.—Jer. xxxi. 15.

Not by works of righteousness which we have done, but according to His mercy He saved us, by the washing of regeneration, and renewing of the HOLY GHOST ; Which He shed on us abundantly through JESUS CHRIST our SAVIOUR ; that, being justified by His grace, we should be made heirs according to the hope of eternal life.—Titus iii. 5.

Therefore are they before the throne of GOD, and serve Him day and night in His temple : and He that sitteth on the throne shall dwell among them. They shall hunger no more, neither thirst any more ; neither shall the sun light on them, nor any heat. For the Lamb, which is in the midst of the throne, shall feed them, and shall lead them unto living fountains of waters ; and GOD shall wipe away all tears from their eyes.—Rev. vii. 15.

Then shall the Priest say,

Let this grave be hallowed, in the Name, &c.

He casts dust or earth on the coffin.

Remember, man, that thou art dust, and unto dust thou shalt return.

When the coffin is covered, he makes the sign of the Cross, saying,

The sign of our LORD and SAVIOUR JESUS✠CHRIST, be signed✠

upon thee, Who in this sign redeemed + thee, and suffer not the destroying angel to enter in for evermore. Peace be unto thee. Amen.

Dearly beloved in CHRIST the LORD, forasmuch as a token of human frailty and mortality is given unto us through this innocent child, let us faithfully call on GOD the LORD, and beseech Him of His Divine grace that we in this world may lead a holy and spotless life, may have a happy death, and finally with this child, and all GOD's Saints and elect, attain the crown of everlasting joy and felicity.

Let us pray.

LORD, have mercy, &c.
CHRIST, have mercy, &c.
LORD, have mercy, &c.

Our FATHER, &c.

℣. Our soul is escaped even as a bird out of the snare of the fowler. ℟. The net is broken, and we are delivered. ℣. With the holy thou shalt be holy. ℟. And with a perfect man thou shalt be perfect. ℣. They shall see His Face. ℟. And His Name shall be in their foreheads. ℣. The LORD, &c. ℟. And with, &c. ℣. Let us pray.

533. Almighty and most merci-
ful GOD, Who straightway bestowest everlasting life on all children born again in the laver of Baptism, without any merits of their own, when they depart from this world, as we believe Thou hast done this day for the soul of this little child ; grant, we beseech Thee, that we may serve Thee here with pure minds, and be joined for evermore in Paradise with Thy blessed children. Through.

534. O GOD, Who hast hastened to take to Thyself the soul of this happy child, dear unto Thee; grant to us who are still in our pilgrimage and who walk as yet by faith, that enlightened by the heavenly food which nourisheth us, we be not corrupted with the evil, nor deceived by the craft, of this world. Through.

535. Almighty, everlasting GOD, lover of holy purity, Who hast been mercifully pleased to call the soul of this child to-day into the kingdom of heaven; deal, we pray Thee, LORD, with us in like mercy, that through the merits of Thy most holy Passion, Thou mayest cause us evermore to rejoice in that same kingdom with all Thy saints and elect. Who livest.

Benedicite. Blessing.

ABRIDGED OFFICE FOR HOLY COMMUNION.

When necessary, the Office for Holy Communion may be materially shortened, without interfering with the reverence or validity of the rite. The following order may fitly be employed.

Collect, Epistle, and Gospel.

[Church Militant Prayer.]
Confession and Absolution.
Sursum Corda, Preface, and *Sanctus.*
Consecration.
Communion.
Our FATHER.
Blessing.

COLLECTS, EPISTLES, GOSPELS, AND POST-COMMUNIONS FOR SPECIAL PURPOSES.

I. For Confirmation Candidates.

Coll. **66**.
Ep. Whitsun Tuesd.
Gosp. 4th S. a. East.
Post-Comm. **536**. Grant, we beseech Thee, O Lord, that Thy servants may faithfully renew that vow which they pledged to Thee in their baptism, renouncing the devil and all his works, and firmly resolving to fulfil the law of Christ: and vouchsafe that they may receive at Thine Altar the pledge of that life immortal which Thou hast promised us, and derive therefrom continual increase in the life of holiness which they have vowed. Through.

II. For Ember-tide.

Coll. ⎫
Ep. ⎬ See "Ordering of Priests."
Gosp. ⎭
Post-Comm. 2nd Emb. Coll. "Almighty God, the Giver," &c.

III. For Missionaries.

Coll. **74**.
Ep. 2 Cor. ii. 14 to end.
Gosp. S. Matt. xxviii. 18 to end.
Post-Comm. **203**.

IV. During the Vacancy of a See.

Coll. **46**.
Ep. Acts xiii. 1—4.
Gosp. S. John xv. 16—22.
Post-Comm. **40**.

V. For a Church Synod.

Coll. **35**.
Ep. Acts xx. 17—37.
Gosp. S. Matt. xviii. 15—21.
Post-Comm. **571**.

VI. For Parliament.

Coll. in Pr. Bk., " Most gracious God," &c., [with any verbal change to fit for Colonial Legislatures.]
Ep. 1 Thess. v. 12—15.
Gosp. S. Luke xix. 12—27.
Post-Comm. **537**. Almighty God, by Whom alone kings reign and princes decree justice ; and from Whom alone cometh all counsel, wisdom, and understanding ; we Thine unworthy servants, here gathered together in Thy Name, do most humbly beseech Thee to send down Thy Heavenly Wisdom from above to direct and guide the Legislature of this country in all its consultations : and grant that, having Thy fear always before its eyes, and laying aside all private interests, prejudices, and partial affections, the result of all its counsels may be to the glory of Thy blessed Name, the maintenance of true religion and justice, the safety, honour, and happiness of the Queen, the public wealth, peace, and tranquillity of the Realm, and the uniting and knitting together of the hearts of all persons and estates within the same in true Christian love and charity one towards another, through Jesus Christ our Lord and Saviour. Amen.

VII. For Schools and Colleges.

Coll. **538**. O God the Son, Eternal Wisdom of the Father, Who wast Thyself the Teacher of Thine Apostles and of the multitude of the Jews, and Who didst send Thy Holy Spirit to lead Thy Church into all truth ; visit, we beseech Thee, with Thy gracious favour, all places set apart for the pursuit of knowledge : and grant unto all those who teach and those who learn therein, a right understanding in all things, that they may so use the talents committed to their charge as to bring unto Thee Thine own with usury, and, proving all things, may hold fast that which is good, laying up in store for themselves a good foundation against the time to come, that they may lay hold on eternal life. Through Thy mercy.

Ep. 1 Tim. iv. 12 to end.
Gosp. S. Matt. v. 13—17.
Post-Comm. **539**. O GOD, the Father of lights, and Source of all knowledge, from Whom cometh down every good and perfect gift; feed, we beseech Thee, Thy servants with the bread of understanding, and give them the water of wisdom to drink, that their eyes may be enlightened unto counsel and knowledge, and that they may show forth that which they have learned, and glory in the law of Thy covenant. Through.

VIII. AGAINST OPPRESSORS OF THE CHURCH.

Coll. **79**.
Ep. Acts xxvi. 9—21.
Gosp. S. John xviii. 1—10.
Post-Comm. **28**.

IX. THE INSTITUTION OF THE HOLY EUCHARIST.

Coll. **15**.
Ep. 1 Cor. xi. 23—30.
Gosp. S. John vi. 55—58.
Post-Comm. **239**.

X. FOR A MARRIAGE.

Coll. **155**.
Ep. Eph. v. 22 to end.
Gosp. S. Matt. xix. 3—10.
Post-Comm. **540**. O LORD, we beseech Thee, mercifully hear our prayers, and graciously bless this Thine ordinance, that the union which is formed by Thine institution may be preserved unbroken by Thine aid. Through.

XI. AFTER CHILDBIRTH.

Coll. **221**.
Ep. 1 Sam. i. 20—28.
Gosp. S. Luke ii. 22—33.
Post.-Comm. **541**. O GOD, Who vouchsafest that the sorrow of a woman in travail should be turned into joy when a man is born into the world; receive the thanksgivings and prayers of Thy Church, and grant Thy grace unto both mother and child, that they may be stablished in holiness, and attain Thine everlasting kingdom. Through.

XII. FOR THE SICK.

Coll. **268**.
Ep. S. James v. 14—17.
Gosp. S. Luke vii. 1—11.
Post-Comm. **262**.

XIII. FOR THE DYING.

Coll. See Service for Vis. of Sick in Pr. Bk. "O FATHER of mercies," &c.
Ep. 2 Cor. v. 1—11.
Gosp. S. Luke xxii. 39—45.
Post-Comm. **399**.

XIV. AT A FUNERAL.

Coll. See Burial Serv. in Pr. Bk. "O merciful GOD," &c.
Ep. 1 Thess. iv. 13 to end.
Gosp. S. John vi. 37—40.
Post-Comm. **435**.

XV. FUNERAL OF CHILDREN.

Coll. **533**.
Ep. Titus iii. 4—8.
Gosp. S. Mark x. 13—17. As in Bapt. Off.
Post-Comm. **534**.

XVI. For Travellers.

Coll. Post-Comm. in Pr. Bk. "Assist us mercifully," &c.
Ep. Isa. xxxv. 8 to end.
Gosp. S. Luke xiii. 24—31.
Post-Comm. **24**.

XVII. For those at Sea.

Coll. **542**. Almighty and everlasting God, Who didst bid Blessed Peter Thine Apostle to come unto Thee upon the waters; be present with Thy servants who voyage by sea, and who put their trust in Thy mercy, that aided thereby they may in all safety and without hindrance reach the place whither they would go, and finally attain unto the haven of everlasting salvation. Through.
Ep. Jonah ii. 1—10.
Gosp. S. Mark iv. 35 to end.
Post-Comm. **92**.

XVIII. For Fair Weather.

Coll. in Pr. Bk. "O Almighty Lord God," &c.
Ep. Gen. ix. 11—17.
Gosp. S. Luke viii. 22—26.
Post-Comm. **543**. Grant us, we beseech Thee, O Lord, such favourable weather as may be beneficial to the fruits of the earth, and profitable to the bodily health of Thy people. Through.

XIX. For Rain.

Coll. in Pr. Bk. "O God, heavenly Father," &c.
Ep. S. James v. 16—19.
Gosp. S. Matt. v. 43—46.
Post-Comm. **544**. O God, Who waterest the hills from above, and sendest Thy springs into the valleys; mercifully satisfy our soul in drought, and make of the thirsty land pools of water, that we may receive the fruits of the earth in their season, and may give thanks unto Thee. Through.

XX. For the Crops.

Coll. **506**.
Ep. Deut. xi. 13—18.
Gosp. S. Matt. vii. 7—12.
Post-Comm. **545**. Pour, we beseech Thee, O Lord our God, Thy blessing upon Thy people, that of Thy bountiful goodness the earth may yield her fruits, and we, gathering them in, may use them to the praise and honour of Thy holy Name. Through.

XXI. Rogation-tide.

Coll. **506**.
Ep. S. James v. 7—12.
Gosp. S. Luke xi. 5—11.
Post-Comm. **507**.

XXII. Harvest Thanksgiving.

Coll. **546**. Grant us, O Lord, so to bless Thee with grateful hearts for the bounty of Thine earthly harvest, that fulfilled with Thy love we may bring forth fruit to Thee a hundredfold in this life, and in that harvest where the angels are the reapers we may be gathered as wheat into Thy garner. Through.
Ep. Deut. xvi. 13—16.
Gosp. S. Luke xii. 16—22.
Post-Comm. **547**. O God, Who pourest upon us the gifts of Thy mercy, grant us, we beseech Thee, so to use Thy temporal bounties that they may be comforts for the way as we hasten back to our country, and not temptations to linger here. Through.

XXIII. In Time of Famine.

Coll. 1st of Occ. Prayers in Pr. Bk. "O God, heavenly Father," &c.
Ep. 1 Kings viii. 37—41.
Gosp. S. Matt. xv. 32—39.
Post-Comm. 2nd of Occ. Prayers in Pr. Bk. "O God, merciful Father," &c.

XXIV. In War Time.

Coll. in Pr. Bk. "O Almighty God, King," &c.

Ep. S. James iv. 1—7.
Gosp. S. Matt. xxiv. 1—9.
Post-Comm. **548**. O Lord God Almighty, Who dost refrain the spirit of princes, and art wonderful among the kings of the earth; mercifully decide the issues of this war according unto righteousness, and then break the arrows of the bow, the shield, the sword, and the battle, that Thy people may rest in peace under Thy shelter. Through.

XXV. Thanksgiving for Victory.

Coll. **549**. O God of Hosts and God of Peace, Who givest victory not according to strength of arms, but as is pleasing in Thy sight; accept the humble petitions of Thy thankful people, and forgiving alike the sins of the victors and the vanquished, turn their hearts unto peace. Through.

Ep. 2 Chron. xx. 14—28.
Gosp. S. Luke vi. 31—38.
Post-Comm. **550**. O God, Who hast vouchsafed to bestow on us victory over our visible enemies; grant, we beseech Thee, that by this Holy Sacrament we may be fortified against the attacks of our invisible enemies. Through.

XXVI. For Peace.

Coll. 2nd Coll. at Matins. "O God, Who art the Author," &c.

Ep. S. James iii. 13 to end.
Gosp. S. John xiv. 27—31.
Post-Comm. 2nd Coll. at Evensong. "O God, from Whom," &c.

XXVII. In Time of Pestilence.

Coll. in Pr. Bk. "O Almighty God, Who in Thy wrath," &c.

Ep. 2 Chron. vi. 28—32.

Gosp. S. Luke iv. 38—44.
Post-Comm. **551**. O Lord, Who smitest that Thou mayest heal, mercifully spare Thy people, and grant us so to profit by Thy Fatherly chastisement, that we may return to Thee from all our sins, and not incur fresh guilt by neglect of Thy warnings. Through.

XXVIII. For Penitents.

Coll. in Pr. Bk. "O God, Whose nature and property," &c.

Ep. Gal. vi. 1—5.
Gosp. S. Matt. ix. 10—14.
Post-Comm. **317**.

XXIX. In any Trouble.

Coll. in Lit. "O God, merciful Father," &c.

Ep. 2 Cor. i. 3—6.
Gosp. S. John xxi. 20—23.
Post-Comm. **374**.

XXX. At a Retreat or Mission.

Coll. **552**. O Lord Jesu Christ, Who didst withdraw Thyself unto a mountain for prayer, and didst bring Thine Apostles apart from the multitude, that they might rest a while with Thee; be graciously present, we beseech Thee, with those who are gathered together in Thy Name, and grant that they, profitably meditating in Thy Word, and inspired thereby with a good will to serve Thee, may diligently fulfil the same. Through.

Ep. Phil. iv. 4—10.
Gosp. S. Mark vi. 30—33.
Post-Comm. **271**.

XXXI. For a Guild.

Coll. **205**.
Ep. for 5th S. aft. Epiph.
Gosp. S. John xvii. 24 to end.

Post-Comm. **553**. O God, Who art perfect love, grant unto Thy servants to bear one another's burdens with sincere affection, that Thy peace, which passeth all understanding, may keep our hearts and minds. Through Thy Son. Who with Thee.

XXXII. For the Reunion of Christendom.

Coll. **34**.
Ep. for 17th S. aft. Trin.
Gosp. S. John xvii. 11 to end. " Holy Father," &c.
Post-Comm. Coll. in Accession Service. " O God, the Father," &c.

XXXIII. For Prisoners.

Coll. **554**. O Lord Jesu Christ, Who didst preach to the spirits in prison, and breaking the gates of brass, and smiting the bars of iron in sunder, didst lead captivity captive ; look, we beseech Thee, in compassion on those that are holden in bonds or imprisonment, comfort them in all their afflictions, and as Thou didst bring Joseph out of his dungeon in Egypt, Daniel from the den of lions, and Peter out of the hands of Herod, so proclaim deliverance unto the captives, and bring them unto the glorious liberty of the children of God. Who livest.
Ep. 1 Kings viii. 46—51.
Gosp. S. Luke iv. 16—22.
Post-Comm. **171**.
Post-Comm. for Prisoners of War, **281**.

XXXIV. For one Condemned to Death.

Coll. ⎫
Ep. ⎬See Office, p. 41.
Gosp. ⎭
Post-Comm. **555**. Almighty God, come, we beseech Thee, to the help of Thy servant now near to the hour of *his* death, that the power of the devil may not prevail against *him*, but that repenting *him* of all *his* sins *he* may at length find mercy with Thee. Through.

XXXV. A General Thanksgiving.

Coll. **556**. O God, of Whose mercy there is no end, and the treasure of Whose bounty is infinite ; we give thanks to Thy Divine Majesty for the gifts of Thy loving-kindness, humbly beseeching Thee that the praise and thanksgiving which we begin here on earth we may, with all Thy ransomed saints, continue in heaven. Through.
Ep. Isa. xii. 1 to end.
Gosp. S. Luke xvii. 11—22.
Post-Comm. **557**. O God, Whose mercy not only bestows bounties on the undeserving, but also puts into our hearts the desire of thanksgiving ; grant us who partake of this holy mystery, that filled with the gifts of Thy loving-kindness, we may never cease to offer those praises which we cannot sufficiently render. Through.

NOTES ON CONFESSION.

1. The Confessional is the tribunal of mercy, not that of justice.

2. The practice of CHRIST in dealing with sinners is the pattern which a Confessor should set before him.

3. Therefore the qualities of a good Confessor are (1) gentleness in receiving sinners ; (2) penetration in dealing with them; (3) vigour in rebuking and applying remedies.

4. The church, or at least its vestry, is the proper place for hearing Confessions. Avoid hearing them, especially those of women, in private houses, save in the case of sick persons.

5. Let all be done with as little mystery as possible, and as openly as is consistent with the nature of the ordinance.

6. The Priest, when hearing Confessions, should be vested in cassock, surplice, and violet or black stole.

7. A quarter of an hour is usually a sufficient time for an ordinary Confession.

8. Cases may occur when a longer time is required, such as a first Confession or a general Confession made at a subsequent period. The Priest should not hurry the penitent, nor betray weariness or impatience at the time which is occupied.

9. Therefore it is well not to fix such a time for hearing Confession as must insure great briefness, e.g., just before Divine Service.

10. Before hearing the Confession of a stranger, it is expedient to inquire his occupation and position in life ; whether he have ever confessed before, and if so, how long ago, and why he has changed his Confessor ; whether he have complied with the directions last given him ; whether, if he be an ignorant person, he knows the Creed and the Ten Commandments ; but the Priest *has no right to ask his name*.

11. In ordinary cases, it is well that the heads (but only the heads) of the confession be written down by the Penitent, that the Priest may refer to them in making his comments. The order of the Decalogue is the most convenient.

12. Penitents who come without previous preparation should be sent back, unless the want of preparation arises from ignorance, or from some sudden cause needing prompt attention.

13. The Priest should pay special attention to *class* sins ; e.g., dishonesty amongst traders, drunkenness amongst the poor, sloth and luxury amongst the rich, formalism amongst the clergy, &c.

14. He is not to interrupt the penitent, as a rule, so long as he goes on with his confession, but he may interpose to help when fear or ignorance has checked him.

15. He is to interrupt in any of the following cases : (1) if the penitent import the name of any person into his confession—he is there to confess his own sins, not another's ; (2) if he begin making excuses for himself ; (3) if he be prolix, or wandering from the point ; (4) if he be coarse.

16. The Priest is to be especially careful not to allow any token of astonishment or disgust to escape him, lest he should repel or dishearten the penitent.

17. As a general rule, he is to avoid questioning the penitent (except in case of absolute necessity), and especially as to kinds of sin to which he has made no reference in his confession. Questions are worse than useless when he can gather as

much as is needful for him to know without them.

18. He should always inquire whether the penitent has performed the penance last enjoined him, and whether he has tried to make amends in case of wrong-doing. Other cases in which he should question are— (1) when a penitent is too ignorant, too nervous, or too timid to make a continuous statement; (2) when the Priest has reason to suspect that some important particular, which either aggravates the offence or is necessary to account for it, is kept back; (3) when it is needful for him to know whether the sin confessed is an isolated act or part of a chain of habit; (4) when he has from other sources knowledge of sin which the penitent has not confessed; (5) when he has reason to believe that the penitent is unconscious of, or underrates some sin. In a word, the duty of the confessor is to ascertain what is the real burden on the penitent's soul.

19. The Priest should take most especial care not to suggest any new sinful idea to the mind of the penitent, nor to teach him any evil formerly unknown to him. This is unspeakably important in the case of very young persons, since for them ignorance of evil is often better even than knowledge of good.

20. When a penitent is afraid to confess any particular sin, the Priest may often encourage him by assuming that the sin is much graver than any which he is likely to have committed.

21. A frequent change of Confessors is to be discouraged : for such change is often due to mere caprice, or to an unwillingness to break off habits which the former confessor has condemned, and which it is hoped that the new one may overlook.

22. Cases in which Absolution should be refused or deferred are as follows : (1) when the Confession appears to be merely formal, without any real penitence ; (2) when the penance enjoined at a previous Confession has been wilfully neglected ; (3) when no efforts have been made to overcome the besetting sin ; (4) when the penitent declines to avoid company and places, out of the path of his duty, which tempt him to sin ; (5) when he continues, without absolute necessity, in a calling which tends to lead him into sin ; (6) when no attempt at forgiveness, amends, or restitution has been made in the case of enmity, scandal, or wrongdoing ; (7) when the Priest knows that the penitent is keeping back some sin which he ought to confess, unless such knowledge is derived from the confession of another person, in which case he has no right to use it against the penitent.

23. The Priest should carefully impress upon penitents that penances are in no respect payment or atonement for sin. They are merely (1) tests of contrition, by showing readiness on the part of the penitent to undergo punishment ; (2) remedies to prevent the repetition of sin.

24. Penances must be adapted to the age, sex, condition, and spiritual needs of each penitent ; e.g., fasting is unsuitable for invalids and children, and long forms of devotion for the ignorant.

25. The spiritual questions to be considered in imposing penances are (1) the degree of sinfulness; (2) the condition of the penitent ; (3) the amount of correction needful. The severity as well as the kind of penance will vary according to these conditions.

26. A good penance is one which is at once punitive, remedial, and simple.

27. A penance is a bad one which is unduly severe or lax, or which consists of minute or complicated details difficult to be carried out.

28. Remedial penances commonly consist of acts of a nature directly opposite to that of the sins

committed. For examples, see pp. 188, 189.

29. In estimating the gravity of a fault, the Confessor should remember that its heinousness depends rather on the premeditation with which it has been committed, than upon the consequences which it involves.

30. The Confessor should endeavour to ascertain what is the besetting sin of the penitent, and should direct his efforts and arrange his penances rather for its eradication than for the suppression of any casual manifestation of sin.

31. It is sacrilege of the very gravest kind for the Priest to disclose what has been revealed to him in Sacramental Confession. His silence must extend (1) to all things actually confessed, of which he may not speak, out of the confessional, even to the penitent himself, except by the desire or permission of the latter; (2) to the offences of other persons casually referred to in confession, and not otherwise known to the Priest; (3) to all hints, innuendoes, or indirect references as to the matter of confession, and, as a rule, to the names of the penitents. If the Priest meet with a case with which he does not know how to deal, and for whose treatment he must seek advice, he should state it in such broad and general terms as to avoid any probability of identifying the person on whose behalf he makes the inquiries. The obligation to silence on the part of the Priest does not terminate with the death of the penitent, but is perpetually binding.

NOTES ON DIRECTION.

1. The object of Direction is to form JESUS CHRIST in the soul (Gal. iv. 19), and especially to give a religious tone to secular life.

2. Direction, therefore, is guidance in questions of practical action, afforded to Christians in doubt or difficulty, by one who is wiser in spiritual matters than they.

3. Therefore, unlike the Sacramental rites of the Church, the efficacy of Direction depends on the personal character and abilities of the Director.

4. It follows that although a Priest may not decline the office of Confessor, which is part of his ordinary ministerial duty, he is at liberty to decline that of a Director if he feel himself incompetent to fulfil its requirements.

5. There is thus no necessary connexion between the office of Director and Confessor, although for convenience' sake they are frequently combined. Thus the Exhortation in the Communion Office implies that "ghostly counsel and advice" are to be sought for from the Priest who pronounces "Absolution."

6. As no sacerdotal character is necessary for giving advice in spiritual things, the office of Director may be, and often has been, exercised by Laymen.

7. The natural Director of a wife is her husband, of a child its parents, and nothing but grave faults of omission or commission can excuse the interposition of any other person, even of a Priest.

8. Direction has chiefly to do with adjusting the conflicting claims of Society and of the Church, of conventional laws and of Evangelical precepts, and, in general, where temporal and spiritual well-being seem to be opposed.

9. The advice given should be of an eminently practical nature, and

take as a rule the common-sense view of a subject.

10. Therefore, while the best Director is one who combines deep spirituality with profound intellect, yet, when these qualifications are not to be found united, mental power and experience should have the preference.

11. A Director should confine himself to general guidance, and enter as little as possible into minute details. He should endeavour rather to instil maxims and principles, than to construct a code of minute observances.

12. The amount of detail will vary according to the intelligence of the inquirer; the less instructed he is, the more definite must be the rules laid down for his guidance.

13. The Director should aim at strengthening the sense of personal responsibility in those who consult him, and at increasing the sensitiveness and vigour of their consciences.

14. Over-direction commonly weakens the conscience by leading persons to lean rather upon external aid than upon those natural instincts of right and wrong which have been implanted in them by GOD. A wise physician will discourage the habitual use of drugs, and will rather urge attention to regimen and exercise.

15. The Director should therefore reserve his aid for matters of real difficulty. If applied to in simple and obvious cases he should rather, by appealing to the conscience of the inquirer, endeavour to draw the answer from his lips.

16. To avoid the grave perils of over-direction, the Director will take care that the interviews which he grants shall be short and infrequent.

17. In matters of doubt or of conflicting duties, the less pleasant way is usually the safer.

18. Persons often imagine that they are compelled to commit one of two sins, and will seek counsel as to which is the less heinous. The Director must always point out that such an alternative of moral evil is impossible. There must always be a right path, since otherwise GOD would be the compeller to sin.

19. As the Director has to deal chiefly with external modes of action, his counsels must be indefinitely modified according to the condition of those who consult him.

20. He should remember that whilst it is impossible to fix the moral standard too high, yet the practical standard in such matters as devotions, almsgivings, acts of self-denial, &c., must fluctuate according to individual needs and circumstances.

21. In dealing with persons who are troubled with unnecessary scruples, the Director will do well to suggest some course of active employment for both mind and body which shall aim at the benefit or pleasure of another, in order to draw them out of themselves.

22. In the case of persons of a demonstrative temperament, if the Director has reason to suppose them unreal and sentimental, he may ascertain the truth, and often effect a cure, by counselling them to undertake some benevolent work of a routine and uninteresting description.

23. With persons of highly-wrought and enthusiastic temperament, he should point out that the most obvious and commonplace duties, as they are the nearest, are also the most imperative, but if there be no signs of extravagance or neglect of local duties, the Director should be careful not to check devotion which passes the ordinary standard.

24. A constant change of Directors is unadvisable, but there are two cases in which it is desirable to sever the connexion between guide and pupil. (1) When constraint has grown up between them, and

they are no longer on a footing of mutual confidence. (2.) When the pupil exhibits too blind and slavish a compliance with the suggestions of the Director, and appears to be substituting his dictates for the operations of conscience.

NOTES ON MISSIONS.

The object of a Mission is to rouse in the careless a sense of sin, and a desire for pardon, and to excite all who attend it to greater earnestness in the work of salvation.

If possible, the Mission should be conducted by two Priests who may assist one another, each taking that part of the work for which he has a special capacity.

When an exceptional effort, such as a Mission, is undertaken, no pains should be spared to secure the work being done thoroughly.

It is desirable that the Mission should be conducted by strangers, (1) because their arguments and appeals from the pulpit will, by reason of their freshness, be more likely to affect and influence the congregation than those of the Parish Priest, whose ordinary manner and train of thought are more or less familiar to the people. (2) Because those who may become convinced of grievous secret sins will have less scruple in confessing them to a stranger than to one whom they will be frequently seeing afterwards.

The time occupied should not be less than a week. It is well for a short Mission to begin on the evening of one Sunday and end with a general Communion on the morning of the Sunday following. Every effort should be made to ensure a good beginning and a good ending to the Mission.

During the fortnight previous to the Mission the Parishioners should be carefully visited,—leaflets and tracts distributed, and the people urged personally and individually to avail themselves of the advantages which it offers.

The Mission Priests will naturally consult with the Parochial Clergy as to the general plan of the spiritual campaign, which will necessarily vary according to the circumstances of the parish. They should not, however, be hampered by restrictions, but be allowed to do their own work in their own way.

There should be at least one Celebration of the Blessed Sacrament at an early hour every morning—two are preferable, the former being not later (say) than six o'clock.

Matins and Evensong will of course be said, but it will be better for these to be independent of the Mission services.

The more freedom that characterizes the Mission Services, within reason, the better. Metrical Litanies, and other Hymns of a rousing and emotional character, should be very freely employed. Mere routine and conventionality should be scrupulously eschewed. Sensationalism, within such limits as good sense will dictate, will be effective, when commonplace would be utterly powerless.

The chief agencies employed in a Mission are Preaching—Meditations—Bible Classes—Prayer Meetings—Public and Private Conferences—and the Confessional.

Sermons should, of course, be extempore, delivered with as much life and vigour as may be, and containing a good supply of illustration and anecdote. Directness and plain speaking should be their character-istics, and they should not exceed half-an-hour in duration. It is often advisable to call upon the congregation to kneel, if a fit op-portunity offers, in the course of the sermon, the preacher inviting his hearers to join with him in say-ing the *Veni Creator*, or similar appropriate devotion. Aspirations and Colloquies may be fitly intro-duced.

The other agencies above men-tioned have been treated of so well in a small publication by the Evan-gelist Fathers, entitled, "Sugges-tions as to the Conduct of a Mis-sion," (Knott, Greville Street, E.C.) that it is thought superfluous to speak of them here in detail.

The Mission should close with a General Communion. At the evening service immediately pre-ceding this there should be a so-lemn renewal of Baptismal Vows, and so far as possible each person who has attended should make some special resolution, suggested by the Mission.

It is found a good plan to give to each person who has made a first Confession during the Mission, or who has otherwise distinguished himself by earnestness and devo-tion, a medal or cross as a me-mento.

The greatest possible facility should be afforded to persons wish-ing to consult the priest, who ought to be easily accessible at all times, and to all persons.

NOTES ON RETREATS.

The object of a Retreat is to deepen the Spiritual sense of those who are already living religious lives. The means employed are Retirement from the world; Si-lence; Meditations conducted by a Priest; and Mental Prayer.

A Retreat commonly lasts three whole days, in addition to an open-ing address on the first evening, and a general Communion on the last morning. Thus if the opening address be given on Tuesday even-ing, the Communion will be on Saturday morning. Sometimes cir-cumstances may not admit of more than one day being given up to a Retreat. Other modifications as to time, &c., are adopted as occasion requires.

A College or Religious House is the best place in which to hold a Retreat.

Retreats may be either for men or women, but should not be for both on the same occasion.

It is usual for the Priest Con-ductor to give three Meditations a day, but sometimes an "Instruc-tion," explanatory of some question which has come up in the course of the previous Meditations, takes the place of the midday Meditation.

Some one special object is usu-ally taken on which all the Medi-tations have a bearing, more or less direct.

The Conductor, kneeling, begins each Meditation by reciting the *Veni Creator*, in which all join. After this he says the Collect for Whitsun Day, and any other ap-propriate prayer. He then, after stating the subject, gives the "Pre-lude," which is frequently a word-picture of some event, Scriptural or otherwise, illustrative of the grace which he desires to enforce.

This is intended to place the minds of those present in a proper attitude for profiting by what is to follow. After this all take their seats—the Conductor, sitting down, begins his Meditation, which generally lasts about three quarters of an hour. At its conclusion, all again kneel, the Conductor recites the *Anima Christi*, with any appropriate Collect. He then retires to the Sacristy or other fit place where any of those present may resort to him for advice or Confession.

Persons in Retreat generally provide themselves with a note-book and pencil to take down anything that especially strikes them in the Meditation.

After a Meditation those in Retreat remain in the Chapel, and occupy themselves in Mental Prayer or Spiritual Reading.

Every Retreat should finish with a distinct Resolution made by each person present according to his needs. Printed papers arranged with blanks for filling up are usually provided for this purpose. These are signed kneeling, before the Blessed Sacrament, and are to be kept by each person for future reference.

Sometimes a general renewal of Baptismal vows is made on the evening before the closing Communion, but this appears more suitable for a Mission than for a Retreat. In the latter, excitement is not advisable.

An admirable Paper on Retreats, from the pen of the Rev. T. T. Carter, will be found in the volume of Essays entitled "The Church and the World," 1866. This should be carefully studied by any one who desires to make himself acquainted with the spirit and routine of such exercises. In the arrangement of materials for Meditations, the "Manresa" by S. Ignatius Loyola will be found most useful.

JUSTIFICATION.

Justification is the process by which fallen man is admitted to and retained in a state of grace, and of acceptance with GOD.

To justify is a legal or forensic term, signifying, strictly taken, to declare a person righteous when he is not righteous.

But when GOD is the Justifier, a further idea is involved. His eyes cannot away with iniquity. He cannot declare that a man is righteous when he is not so, nor look with favour upon an unholy creature. Further, as man did not become guilty except by becoming sinful, so he cannot become innocent except by becoming holy.

GOD's Word, which is with power, is the instrument of His deed. The Voice of the LORD is mighty in operation, and therefore when He says, "Let the soul be just," it becomes just.

So that Justification is an announcement or fiat of Almighty GOD, declaring the soul righteous, and by that declaration conveying pardon for the past and making it actually righteous. Hence those who are counted righteous by GOD are actually made righteous in being counted so (comp. 2 Thess. i. 5 ; Rev. iii. 4).

Thus GOD does not belie Himself by accounting us righteous when we are not so, but He makes us righteous by an inward renovation of the soul (S. John i. 29 ; Acts iii. 19 ; Rom. viii. 1 ; Eph. v. 8).

Justification, being needed, could be had either by GOD's dispensing with obedience, or by His enabling us to fulfil it. He does not annihilate the Law; but He creates in us new wills and powers for the observance of it (Rom. viii. 1—4).

This capacity of serving GOD acceptably is not a name, but a power, wrought by "the ministration of the Spirit" which writes the Law on our inward hearts. Thus with Justification comes the power of well-doing, as S. Paul says, "The GOD of grace make you perfect in every good work to do His will, working in you (not *imputing to you*) that which is well-pleasing in His sight, through JESUS CHRIST." Justification, therefore, does not come to us direct from GOD, but through ourselves, being wrought in us by the power of GOD, and consequently we see how that " by works a man is justified, and not by faith only."

Justification is the application of the Atonement to us severally and individually. Its source is the Resurrection of CHRIST (Rom. iv. 25), in whom human nature rose. Its accomplishment is wrought by the HOLY SPIRIT, which is a " Spirit of holiness" (Rom. i. 4), by whose presence we can obey unto Justification.

Thus Justification and Sanctification are substantially the same thing, saving that the former term is usually restricted to the earliest stage of the process.

Hence we may gather the true meaning of "Justification by Faith."

Justification being the work of the HOLY GHOST, i.e., a spiritual gift or presence in the heart—faith, which is a grace resident in the heart, alone can discern it, and prepare the recipient for it, for " with the heart man believeth unto righteousness."

Faith, therefore, which is a lively faith, trusting, loving, working, is the sole *internal* mean or instrument of Justification, being now the qualification for the reception of spiritual blessings, as it was for the reception of temporal blessings when CHRIST was on earth.

Baptism, by which we are admitted into close relationship with GOD through the Atonement, is the *external* mean or instrument of Justification.

In a word, Faith continues what Baptism begins, as the Apostle says, " after having been begotten again we are kept by the power of GOD through Faith unto salvation" (1 S. Pet. i. 3—5), and it keeps us in that justified condition, for " by Faith we stand."

ANGLICAN ORDERS.

At the Restoration of Charles II. in 1660, after Episcopal government had been suspended for seventeen years under the Commonwealth, there were eight prelates of the Anglican Church still surviving.

From these the existing line is derived, and it is convenient, therefore, to narrow the inquiry to the validity of their succession.

They were Juxon of London (at once translated to Canterbury), Frewen of York, Duppa of Winchester, Wren of Ely, King of Chichester, Skinner of Oxford, Warner of Rochester, and Roberts of Bangor.

All of these, except King and Frewen, were consecrated by Archbishop Laud with sometimes four, and sometimes five co-consecrators. The two others, raised to the mitre while Laud was in prison, were severally consecrated by Juxon with three other bishops, and by Williams, Archbishop of York, with four others, including Duppa.

Laud and Williams were consecrated within a week of each other, one by six bishops, the other by five of those six. Amongst them were George Monteigne of London and Nicolas Felton of Ely, who had been consecrated in 1617 by Marc Antonio de Dominis, Archbishop of Spalato, assisting Abbot of Canterbury, and four others. Another of their consecrators was Field of Llandaff, one of whose consecrators was George, Bishop of Derry; and a fourth was Howson of Oxford, who derived, through Morton of Durham, from Hampton, Archbishop of Armagh. Morton and Bancroft of Oxford (who had been consecrated by William Murray of Kilfenora) were amongst Duppa's consecrators.

Thus, in the present line of Anglican prelates, three successions meet, the Italian, the Irish, and the English. No allegation of loss of continuity is urged against the two former, and thus, even if the third be imperfect, the cord is unbroken.

That the English strand is as perfect as the two others is easy of proof. At the death of Cardinal Pole, Archbishop of Canterbury, in 1558, leaving the English primacy canonically vacant, the Crown nominated Matthew Parker to the Chapter for election, and he was elected on August 1st, 1559. The temporal act of confirmation took place on September 7th, and he was consecrated in Lambeth Chapel on Sunday, December 17th, 1559, by William Barlow, Bishop of Chichester, John Hodgkins, Suffragan Bishop of Bedford, Miles Coverdale, illegally deprived Bishop of Exeter, and John Scory, Bishop of Hereford. Of these four, Barlow and Hodgkins had been made Bishops in Henry VIII.'s reign, under the old Pontifical, and Coverdale and Scory in Edward VI.'s time (1551) by Cranmer and

two suffragans. ...
all save Barlow a...
evidence for the ...
Parker's consecrati...

A. The register ...
archives of Lambet...
same hand as the r...
mer and Pole, and ...
same Notaries Pub...
record.

B. A contempor...
of this register in ...
Office.

C. Another conte...
the register in the ...
Christi College, Ca...

D. Parker's auto...
in the same library ...
consecration on De...

E. The casual ...
fact, as an item ...
contemporary MS. ...
Machyn, preserved ...
Museum.

F. The contemp...
rich Letters," testi...
fact, and but lately ...

G. The conduct ...
ner, in his suit ag...
shop of Winchest...
based his objectio...
thority on the grou...
consecration was n...
law, because the ...
nal, abolished by ...
had not been exp...
by Elizabeth when ...
secrated according ...
of the consecration ...
allowed by Bonne...

H. The precise ...
the event into the ...
cate series of civil (...
documents require ...
evidence of Park...
barony, revenues, ...
of Lords, and coe...
in his province.

I. The manner ...
porary writers, s...
Holinshed, &c., ta...
notorious and und...

Against this cu...
evidence, only or...
adduced, that kno...

Head Fable." According to this account, first published by Christopher Holywood, a Jesuit, in 1604 (forty-five years after the event), Parker and others with him met at the Nag's Head Tavern in Cheapside, where Scory laid his hands upon them, and then they in turn laid their hands upon Scory, to make him a Bishop. As the record of Scory's own consecration, by Cranmer, Ridley, and Hodgkins, at Croydon, on August 30, 1551, is still extant, there is at least one manifest falsehood in this version, which professes to be given as hearsay from Thomas Neale, Hebrew lecturer at Oxford, who died in 1590, fourteen years before the story came out, without ever publishing it himself. There are five other forms of the tale, varying from one another on fundamental points, all of them avowedly based on hearsay alone, and not only contradicting the diverse and independent testimonies cited above, but also ascribing to Elizabeth, Cecil, and Parker, the suicidal folly of countenancing an act which would have had no validity whatsoever in law, any more than in theology, when they had every church in England open to them, an Ordinal at hand, and plenty of Bishops, English and Irish, able and ready to officiate.

There is, however, a second objection raised. Granting the *fact* of Parker's consecration, its *validity* is contested on two separate grounds. (*a*) That Barlow, who acted as chief consecrator, was himself never consecrated, and that this deficiency could not be made up by his co-consecrators, because as they merely coincided in what he was doing, they effected nothing if his act was an empty form. (*b*) That the Edwardine Ordinal is an invalid rite.

As regards the office of co-consecrators, the fact is that the primeval and Nicene Canons requiring three Bishops to take part in every consecration, were intended expressly to guard against any chance of heresy or invalidity, so that B and C might supply any defect of A. And so Liguori lays down, Theol. Mor. vi. 2, 755, that Priests who have been ordained by a Bishop, himself consecrated by one Bishop only, are doubtfully ordained, which of course would not hold if, in fact, only one Bishop consecrates in each particular case, his colleagues being merely witnesses. Martene, on the other hand, is express in defining the assisting Bishops to be co-consecrators, and not mere witnesses. The theory that the junior Bishops at a consecration are only witnesses is based on a false analogy between the form for the Consecration of Bishops and that for the ordination of Priests. In the latter, Presbyters join with the Bishop in the laying on of hands, but this only by way of attestation and consent, since, were the Bishop absent, their imposition of hands would not be accepted as valid; but where Bishops are the assistants, each of them has power singly to consecrate or ordain, and accordingly, the notion that they are mere witnesses in the rite lands us in the absurdity of supposing that the mere presence of a superior in rank, though equal in office, takes away, for the time being, from all the others their inherent powers as Bishops. Further, in the special case of Parker, each of the four Bishops, as the Register expressly mentions, recited aloud the formula of consecration when laying hands on him, and thereby acted independently, though in concert, and thus any possible defect in Barlow was fully supplied.

The evidence as respects Barlow himself is as follows. The actual record of his consecration is missing, as are those of eight other prelates out of forty-five in Cranmer's carelessly-kept Register. But Barlow's *confirmation* is entered, as are those of four of the other Bishops whose consecrations are omitted.

Two of these consecrations are found recorded in diocesan registers, but Barlow's registers at S. Asaph's and S. David's are both lost. There exist, however, the documents which prove his nomination, election, and confirmation, all of which, by English law, must precede consecration, and his installation, his recovery of the temporalities, his summons to the House of Lords, his sitting and voting there and in Convocation, and his share in consecrating other Bishops, in 1539 and 1542; most, if not all of which, by law, could not take place unless he had been consecrated. One link is absent, but the rest of the chain is complete, and the loss of one small parchment is of little weight. For supposing Cranmer and Barlow, from their Erastian views, ever so willing to have neglected the ceremony of consecration, they were faced by a then brand-new statute, 25 Hen. VIII. cap. 20, which directs the Archbishop and other Bishops to whom the election of any person to a See in virtue of the Crown's letters missive has been signified, to invest and consecrate the said person within twenty days under pain of Præmunire. And Præmunire was far too formidable a weapon under Henry VIII. for Cranmer to neglect Barlow's consecration, or for Barlow himself to act as Bishop without it, especially as the King was a great stickler for legal punctilio in all matters, particularly ecclesiastical ones, even when the spirit of justice was most absent from his proceedings. It has also been urged that Henry VIII.'s view of his powers as Supreme Head of the Church of England led him to consider a Royal Patent as sufficient to make a man a valid Bishop without episcopal consecration. Yet not only is there no scrap of evidence that he did hold this opinion, but, had he done so, he would certainly have taken pains to give effect to the opinion in the most public fashion by appointing Bishops in this very way, whereas no example of the sort took place in the whole of his reign, in all the latter years of which the practice was ruled by the statute cited above. The inference is that Barlow was consecrated between April 21 and April 25, 1536, for he was confirmed in person at Bow Church on the former day, had the temporalities restored on the latter, and two days later received the writ of summons to the House of Lords. This was when Bishop of S. David's. He had been six months previously elected and confirmed to S. Asaph, but never obtained its temporalities, nor was called to the Lords and to Convocation in virtue of those events, whence it follows that some act in addition must have been added to give him full episcopal rank when he was promoted to S. David's. Besides this plain inference, there is some direct evidence. Bishop Gardiner, writing to Protector Somerset, speaks of Barlow as " Bishop," and as his " brother of S. David's," and Mary's *congé d'élire* naming Gilbert Bourne to the see of Bath and Wells, specifies the resignation of William Barlow, last Bishop thereof, as the cause of the vacancy. If Barlow had never been really Bishop, that reason would not appear in the deed. Several autograph letters of Barlow himself have been lately (1869) discovered in the State Paper Office, which refer to his episcopal character, besides a State paper which expressly mentions his installation at S. David's, a ceremony fixed by 26 Henry VIII. c. 14, to follow necessarily on consecration, which consecration is recited in all contemporary mandates to the Chapters. And against the conceivable plea that Cranmer and Barlow, both Erastians, might have agreed to omit the ceremony of consecration, (though to do so would have made every episcopal act of Barlow's null and void in civil matters,) stands the fact that under Edward VI., when an act of the kind would have been far less perilous 'than under Henry VIII., Hooper was forced by Cranmer to submit to consecration, though openly protesting against the ritual and the form of the office.

The theory that Barlow was not consecrated was never broached till 1616, forty-seven years after his death, and eighty after his accession to the see of S. David's. It was utterly unknown to all his contemporaries under Henry VIII., Edward VI., Mary I., and Elizabeth, and even to the generation which succeeded him. And no argument has ever been adduced for it except the loss of a paper which may be found some day even now.

Further, even were it proved that neither Parker nor Barlow was ever consecrated, yet the succession would be unbroken. For Parker held a consecration of four new Bishops on Dec. 21, 1559, in which Scory and Hodgkins joined as well as Barlow; and the prelates then made transmitted their orders to the next series.

The question of the validity of the Edwardine Ordinal meets its answer in the admitted fact that only two Sacraments are tied to express forms of words and particular matter by Divine appointment. Baptism must be in the Name of the Holy Trinity, and with water. The Eucharist must be attended with recitation of the words of Institution and be celebrated with wheaten bread and grape-wine. But no such rule exists for Holy Orders. Provided there be the imposition of hands by a competent officer, and a formula employed which in one place or another specifies the intention of the rite, all is done which is necessary or enjoined by the most ancient rites. In the Edwardine Ordinal there are three such specifications: (*a*) the words used by the Bishop who presents the elect to the Archbishop; (*b*) the oath taken by the Bishop-elect; (*c*) a prayer said in the Litany. The office of Bishop is not specified in the actual words of consecration, but neither was it in the Sarum Pontifical, nor is it in the Roman Pontifical either. And all the essential acts of consecration prescribed by the African Canons of the Fourth Council of Carthage, were precisely complied with by the Book of 1552. The various accretions on the rite, chiefly Western, were intended to add dignity and pomp, but not validity. They are merely analogous to the incense and music at a High Mass, which do not lift it in any sense above a low one. And if the Edwardine rite be rejected for its simplicity, the consecrations of the first thousand years of Christianity fall with it.

These considerations settle the validity of Anglican Orders, which indeed has been recognized by the authorities of the Roman Church in two ways. (*a*) Pope Julius III. addressed a Brief to Cardinal Pole in 1554 desiring him to absolve and reconcile Bishops and Priests made in Edward VI.'s time, but not directing him to re-ordain them. (*b*) The Council of Trent was asked by Pius IV. to declare the Elizabethan Bishops unlawful, and it expressly refused to do so.

But a fresh question now arises, as to their *regularity*, whether full mission and jurisdiction belong to them. Here too proof is not deficient. Mission, starting from the sending of the Apostles, means the office of preaching the Gospel and setting up the Church in a heathen land. Only two possible events can occur which make a fresh act of mission needful, the total disappearance of Christianity (as when the early teachers of Greenland and their disciples all died of plague), or the abandonment by Christians themselves of the Apostolic ministry, so as to lose the Sacraments of Order, Penance, and the Eucharist, as in Denmark and other Presbyterian countries. But so long as a Christian remnant, episcopally ruled, continues, fresh mission is impossible. Such is obviously the case in England. It has not ceased to be Christian, its Church has never ceased to be episcopally transmitted, and no other body can have true mission so long as this state of things continues.

Jurisdiction means the legal, as distinguished from the spiritual, right of publicly discharging the functions acquired by consecration, and of exercising rule in a definite place. Thus it is not a divine grace, making part of the gift of Holy Orders, but a human limitation of the exercise of that gift. By ordination or consecration a man is made a Priest or a Bishop of the whole Catholic Church, his acts being equally valid everywhere. By the ecclesiastical law of jurisdiction he is barred from exercising those powers outside of a given area; and thus jurisdiction is in no sense a spiritual grace, but a human arrangement for administrative convenience. By the most ancient code of the Church, the African Canons already mentioned, jurisdiction is lodged in a Metropolitan by the assent of his comprovincials, and is communicated from the Metropolitan to all newly-made Bishops in his province. This Metropolitan might be, as in some Churches, the senior Bishop, in years or in date of consecration, or as in other Churches, including England, the holder of a particular See. The See of Canterbury had enjoyed this pre-eminence ever since the mission of S. Augustine, and a Papal Brief of Boniface V. is recorded by William of Malmesbury, anathematizing any person who should ever interfere with or resist its primatial rights, *no matter what changes time might bring about in human affairs.* This Brief, on Roman principles, disposes of the claims of the titular See of Westminster, to

which, in fact, no jurisdiction is annexed, as its occupant is compelled to refer all matters of the *forum externum* to Rome. There is thus, even since the setting up of the Anglo-Roman hierarchy in 1850, no rival jurisdiction to contest the claims of Lambeth. When Parker was canonically elected to the vacancy left by Pole's death, he entered, on consecration, into all the Metropolitical and Primatial rights of his predecessor, including that of giving jurisdiction to his suffragans. If Pole had lived, and been uncanonically deposed, this would not have been so, since Parker, if intruded in his place, would have been in an irregular position, but as matters actually were, his rights are unimpeachable. Only one thing could have impugned them, and that was not forthcoming, to wit, a protest against his authority by the suffragans of his province, with the putting forward another claimant of the Primacy. His consecrators were precisely the surviving representatives of the Episcopate of 1553, which had been illegally, (even if deservedly) deprived by the State—not by Canon law—under Mary. And death was singularly busy amongst the Marian Bishops. When Queen Mary died, seven sees were vacant, six in the south, and one in the north. Nine more Bishops were dead before the middle of January, 1560, that is to say, within little more than a twelvemonth after Parker's consecration. Only eight Marian prelates then survived. Three of these quitted England, and never returned, the five who stayed made no sign, and did not interfere in any way. Thus, even the six sees into which men had been intruded were canonically filled one by one, and when Scambler, the intrusive Bishop of Peterborough, who had supplanted Poole, died in 1585, and was canonically succeeded by Howland, the last trace of irregularity vanished. No schism, such as that of the Nonjurors, no protest, like that of 36 of the 135 French Bishops deprived unlawfully by Pius VII., acting as the tool of Napoleon I. in 1801, is to be found in this period of English Church history. The Roman Church allowed the case to go by default, and the breach to heal itself in twenty-seven years, making no effort to start a rival claim till 1850, three centuries too late for any show of canonical validity, and even then, by not venturing to set up an Archbishop of Canterbury, professing to be the true successor of Pole, it left the new titular Primate under the operation of Boniface V.'s anathema. And ever since Parker's time the episcopal registers of England show a regular adhesion to the Nicene rule of at least three consecrators, which contrasts forcibly with the frequent relaxations of it in the Roman obedience (as, for example, in the consecration of the first Roman Catholic Bishop for the United States, who had but one consecrator, an English Vicar-Apostolic with a merely titular see of Ragal), and testifies completely to the care with which the succession has been fenced and preserved.

PONTIFICAL.

CONFIRMATION OF A BISHOP ELECT.

Before the Confirmation of any Bishop Elect full and sufficient public notice shall be given, and the ceremony shall be fixed at such a place and hour as will admit of the greatest possible publicity.

The Metropolitan (or some Bishop acting under his commission) and at least two Suffragan Bishops, shall be seated in chairs in the nave of the Church, vested in their episcopal habits.

The Dean, or the Archdeacon, of the vacant Cathedral, accompanied by two Canons, all vested in alb and cope, shall then present themselves, and kneeling before the Metropolitan, say,

Sir, pray for a blessing.

Metr. The Almighty and merciful LORD preserve and govern us, and bring us to the bliss of heaven.

My son, what desirest thou?

Dean. That the LORD GOD may grant us a Pastor.

Metr. Is he of your own Diocese, or of another?

Dean. Our own [*or otherwise, as the case may be*].

Metr. What has caused you to elect him?

Dean. His godly conversation in CHRIST and good repute amongst the brethren.

Metr. Have you the deed of election?

Dean. We have.

Metr. Let it be read.

The Dean, or some official appointed by him, reads as follows:

To the Most Reverend Father in CHRIST, the Lord *N.* Metropolitan of the See *N.*, the Chapter [*or* Synod] of the Church *N.* humbly greeting.

As is known unto your Grace, the Church of *N.* is deprived of its pastor. Therefore, lest in the absence of a ruler of its own, the flock of the LORD should be exposed to the ravening of treacherous wolves, and be a prey to the wicked spoiler, we have by joint vote and assent elected as Bishop, *N.* Priest of our Church [*or*, of the Church *N.*], a prudent man, given to hospitality, virtuous, chaste, sober, and courteous, pleasing in all things to GOD and man, whom we have caused to be brought hither to your Grace, with one accord asking and beseeching you, Most Reverend Father, to consecrate him Bishop, that by the LORD's goodness, he may rule over us, and be profitable to us, and that we, under his wise governance, may always fight as we should the battles of the LORD. And that you may know that the votes of us all are agreed in this election, we have signed our names with our own hands in confirmation of this deed.

Then the Metropolitan shall say,

If any man know of any just cause or impediment, either by reason of simony, defective election, heretical pravity, immoral conduct, or the like, why *N.* should not be consecrated to the office of Bishop of the Church *N.*, let him now declare it.

The Metropolitan shall have no power of refusal to receive any objection, though he may require it to be put in writing, and attested by the signature of the objector.

If any one or more of the Consecrating Bishops consider the objection to be a valid one, proceedings must be stayed until the question be decided by the Provincial Synod. But if the objection be overruled, or no objection be alleged, the Metropolitan shall proceed.

Then the Dean and Canons withdraw to the sacristy, and return thence conducting the Bishop elect, who kneels before the Metropolitan, saying,

Sir, pray for a blessing.

Metr. CHRIST, the Light of the FATHER'S Light, shine on you with His brightness.

My son, what desirest thou ?

Elect. Most Reverend Father, my brethren have elected me (albeit unworthy) to be their Pastor.

Metr. Of what order art thou ?

Elect. Of the Priesthood [*as the case may be*].

Metr. Dost thou accept and undertake the office of Bishop of the See *N.*, to which thou hast been canonically elected ?

Elect. Since the Chapter [*or Synod*] of the diocese has judged me worthy to undertake this charge, I give thanks therefore, and do undertake it, and in no wise gainsay it.

Metr. I require and charge thee,

as thou shalt answer at the day of judgment, that if thou knowest any just impediment by reason of thy faith, morals, or share in bringing about thine election, why thou shouldest not be consecrated to this office, thou do now declare it.

Elect. I declare, and that without reservation, that I know not of any such impediment. So help me GOD. Amen.

Metr. And I, by the authority committed unto me, hereby confirm thine election as Bishop of *N.*, in the Name, &c.

Then shall be sung Ps. lxviii., *with the Antiphon :*

Stablish the thing, O GOD, that Thou hast wrought in us, for Thy temple's sake, which is in Jerusalem. Let GOD arise, &c.

Then the Metropolitan, rising from his seat, and standing before the kneeling Bishop elect, shall say,

℣. O GOD, save Thy servant.
℟. Who putteth his trust in Thee.
℣. Be unto him a strong tower.
℟. From the face of the enemy.
℣. Let not the enemy prevail against him. ℟. Nor the son of wickedness approach to hurt him.
℣. LORD, hear, &c. ℟. And let, &c.
℣. The LORD, &c. ℟. And with, &c.

Let us pray.

558. Almighty, everlasting GOD, have mercy on this Thy servant *N.*, and lead him according to Thy goodness, in the way of eternal salvation, that of Thy grace, he may desire that which is well-pleasing unto Thee, and fulfil the same with all his power. Through.

Prevent us, &c.

The blessing, &c.

℣. Let us depart in peace.

℟. In the Name + of the LORD. Amen.

OFFICE FOR THE ENTHRONIZATION OF A BISHOP.

When the Bishop arrives at the place appointed, he is met by the Dean, Canons, and other functionaries of the Cathedral, and exhibits the documents testifying to his due Consecration. The Procession is then formed, the Bishop being conducted by the Dean and Archdeacon, and preceded by his Chaplains, one of whom shall bear the Pastoral Staff. When they arrive at the west door, and during their passage to the Altar, the Choir shall sing the following Antiphon and Psalm.

Ant. To the most high and adorable Trinity be all glory, honour, and power, world without end.

Ps. 122. I was glad, &c.

Ant. To the most high and adorable Trinity be all glory, honour, and power, world without end. Amen.

When they reach the sanctuary the Bishop shall kneel at a faldstool with a Chaplain on either side, while the Dean, or chief officiant, shall stand in the midst of the Altar with his face to the people and shall say,

LORD, have mercy, &c.
Our FATHER, &c.

℣. O LORD, save Thy servant *N.*, our Bishop. ℞. Who putteth his trust in Thee. ℣. Send him help from Thy holy place. ℞. And strengthen him out of Zion. ℣. Let not the enemy prevail against him. ℞. Nor the son of wickedness approach to hurt him. ℣. Be unto him, O LORD, a strong tower. ℞. Against the face of the enemy. ℣. LORD, hear, &c. ℞. And let, &c. ℣. Let us pray.

559. Grant, we beseech Thee, O LORD, to this Thy servant *N.*, our Bishop, that in preaching and doing those things which be right, he, by the example of his godly life, may teach the souls of those committed to his care, and finally receive the reward of eternal life from the Great Shepherd of the flock, JESUS CHRIST our LORD. Who.

560. O LORD GOD, FATHER Almighty, Who by the unspeakable bounty of Thy grace alone, hast appointed this Thy servant *N.* to rule over Thy people; grant him, we beseech Thee, by the grace of Thy Holy Spirit, fitly to discharge the ministry of the priestly office before Thee, duly to dispense the Sacraments of the Church, and worthily to govern the flock entrusted to him, to the glory of Thy holy Name. Through.

The Bishop is then led up to the Altar in procession, the Choir singing,

Ps. 89, vv. 20—30. Thou spakest . . . . . . days of heaven.

℣. Glory, &c. ℞. As it was, &c.

The Bishop shall then make aloud the following promise:

I, *N.*, Bishop of ——, do hereby promise to respect, maintain, and defend the rights, privileges, and liberties of this Church and diocese, and to rule therein with truth, justice, and charity, not lording it over GOD's heritage, but showing myself in all things an example to the flock. So help me GOD. Amen.

The Dean then says,

℣. The LORD be with you. ℞. And with, &c. ℣. Let us pray.

And turning to the Altar:

561. O LORD, we beseech Thee, mercifully hear our prayers, and bestow the grace of Thy blessing on Thy servant *N.*, our Bishop, whom Thou hast vouchsafed to advance to the High Priesthood, and as he surpasses others in the Church in honour of rank, so may he excel likewise in holiness and good works. Through.

Then turning to the Bishop, he says,

In the Name of GOD. Amen.

I, *N.*, Dean of this Church of —— [or I, *N.*, by the authority of the Dean and Chapter of this Church committed to me for that purpose], enthrone thee, Lord Bishop, in this Church of ——, and therewith give thee all possession, authority, and jurisdiction which pertain to the Bishop of this See, wherein may the LORD JESUS CHRIST preserve thy coming in from this time forth for evermore, and mayest thou abide in justice and sanctity, and adorn the place delegated to thee by GOD. GOD is mighty, and may He increase thy grace.

The Dean then conducts the Bishop to his throne, and returns to the Altar. The Choir shall then sing the Benedictus, *after which the Dean shall say,*

℣. The LORD, &c. ℟. And with, &c.

Let us pray.

562. O GOD, Who makest Thy Church glad with the manifold bounty of Thy gifts; vouchsafe to Thy servant *N.*, whom Thou hast this day given unto us, to bear the glory, to sit and rule upon his throne, and to be a priest upon his throne; stablish him with the counsel of peace, that he may be mighty in good works, shining with the grace of holiness and zeal, may worthily and faithfully guide, strengthen, and comfort the flock entrusted to him, and overcoming the world, may with happiness reach the pastures of everlasting life. Through.

Benediction. GOD, Whose grace hath called thee to this office, be thine aid, and grant thee thine heart's desire, endue thee with judgment, knowledge, bounty, purity, lowliness, and patience, stablish thee in righteousness and holiness, and evermore grant thee His peace. Through.

℟. Amen.

The blessing of GOD Almighty, the FATHER, the SON and the HOLY GHOST, descend and abide upon thee now and for evermore.

℟. Amen.

Then shall follow the Holy Eucharist.

THE VISITATION OF A BISHOP.

When the Bishop comes to the entrance of a village, if in the country, or to the door of the Church in towns, the Priests and lay-clerks shall meet him in procession, preceded by the Cross, and singing the Antiphon, with one or more of the Psalms following.

Ant. Blessed be He that cometh.

Ps. 48. Great is the LORD, &c.
84. O how amiable, &c.

99. The LORD is King, the earth, &c.

101. My song shall be of mercy, &c.

122. I was glad, &c.
132. LORD, remember David, &c.
147. O praise the LORD, &c.

Ant. Blessed be He that cometh in the Name of the LORD.

On entering the Church the Bishop proceeds to a faldstool in front of

*the High Altar, where he kneels.
The parish Priest, or the ecclesi-
astic of highest rank in the diocese, stands at the Epistle corner,
facing west, and begins the Office:*

In the Name, &c.   R⁊. Amen.

LORD, have mercy, &c.
Our FATHER, &c.

℣. Behold, O GOD our defender.
R⁊. And look upon the face of Thine
Anointed.   ℣. O GOD, save Thy
servant. R⁊. Who putteth his trust
in Thee.   ℣. Send him help from
Thy holy place. R⁊. And strength-
en him out of Sion.   ℣. Let not the
enemy prevail against him. R⁊. Nor
the son of wickedness approach to
hurt him.   ℣. O LORD, hear, &c.
R⁊. And let, &c.   ℣. The LORD,
&c. R⁊. And with, &c.   ℣. Let
us pray.

Almighty and everlasting GOD,
Who alone workest great mar-
vels ; send down upon Thy servant
N., our Bishop, and all congregations committed to his charge, the
healthful spirit of Thy grace, and
that they may truly please Thee,
pour upon them the continual dew
of Thy blessing.   Grant this, O
LORD, for the honour of our Advocate and Mediator, JESUS CHRIST.
Amen.

563. O GOD, Who visitest the
lowly, and comfortest them with
Thy fatherly love ; vouchsafe Thy
grace to our congregation, that we
may perceive Thy coming in the
persons of those in whom Thou
dwellest.   Through.

564. We beseech Thee, Almighty
GOD, so to endue Thy servant *N.,*
our Bishop, with Thy power and
benediction, that what he visits
Thou mayest visit, that he may
with all wisdom, justice, and charity, inquire, counsel, and amend,
as need shall be, and that we may
gladly obey his godly admonitions,

through the mercies and merits of
the great Shepherd and Bishop of
our souls, Thy SON JESUS CHRIST
our LORD, Who liveth.

*Then shall be sung the Psalms fol-
lowing, with the Antiphon.*

Ant. The LORD prosper you.

Ps. 20. The LORD hear thee, &c.
26. Be Thou my judge, &c.
43. Give sentence, &c.

Ant. The LORD prosper you : we
wish you good luck in the Name of
the LORD.

*Then the Bishop, rising up, shall go
to the midst of the Altar, and say,*

℣. The LORD, &c. R⁊. And with,
&c.   ℣. Let us pray.

Collect for Whitsun Day.

Prevent us, &c.

*Then he shall proceed to hold his
Visitation.   And if it be a local
one, he shall himself examine in
the sacristy the sacred vessels,
vestments, linen, books, and other
ornaments of the Church and the
ministers, which shall be there laid
ready for inspection, and shall
make all further inquiries, as need
may be.   If it be a general Visitation of the diocese, he shall
seat himself in front of the High
Altar, and shall cause the clergy
and churchwardens of the diocese
to be cited before him, to make answer to his Articles of Visitation,
and to present such other matters
as fall within their province.
This ended, he shall deliver his
Charge, if there be one.   Then he
shall say,*

℣. Stablish the thing, O LORD,
which Thou hast wrought in us.
R⁊. For Thy Temple's sake in Jerusalem.

The peace, &c.   R⁊. Amen.

INSTALLATION OF A DEAN OR PROVOST.

The Chapter being assembled in the Chapter House or Sacristy, the Senior Canon present shall administer this oath following to the Dean elect:

I, *N.*, chosen Dean [*or Provost*] of the Church of *N.*, promise faithfulness in the discharge of my office; and that I will observe my appointed term of residence; maintain its statutes, customs, and usages; uphold and defend all its rights and liberties; be a just steward of its goods, a watchful guardian of its fabric, a zealous minister of its services, and a willing counsellor in its Chapter. And I further promise to observe lowliness and patience in my own person, and to exhibit justice and courtesy to all those who are set under me; so help me GOD.

Then shall they go in procession to the Dean's stall; and the Senior Canon, taking the Dean elect by the right hand, shall induct him therein, saying,

By the authority committed to me for that end, I assign to thee, *N.*, the stall pertaining to the office of Dean in this Church, and induct thee into possession thereof with all its rights and belongings. The LORD preserve thy going out and coming in from this time forth for evermore. Stand in righteousness and holiness, and keep the place committed to thee by GOD; and may the Holy GOD grant thee increase of grace to discharge the duties thereto belonging. Through.

Ant. The LORD send thee help from the sanctuary.

Ps. 20. The LORD hear thee, &c.
99. The LORD is King, &c.
133. Behold, how good, &c.

Ant. The LORD send . . . . and strengthen thee out of Sion.

℣. The LORD, &c.
℞. And with, &c.

Let us pray.

Our FATHER, &c.

℣. O LORD, save Thy servant.
℞. Who putteth his trust in Thee.
℣. Be Thou to him a strong tower.
℞. From the face of the enemy.
℣. Let not the enemy prevail against him. ℞. Nor the son of wickedness approach to hurt him.
℣. Remember Thy congregation.
℞. Which Thou hast purchased and redeemed of old. ℣. LORD, hear, &c. ℞. And let, &c. ℣. Let us pray.

565. Grant, we beseech Thee, Almighty GOD, the gift of Thy grace to Thy servant *N.*, chosen to bear rule in this Church. Grant that he may well and fitly discharge his office, and that of Thy great goodness both he and we may be well-pleasing unto Thee. Through.

Then shall follow the To Deum.

INSTALLATION OF A CANON OR PREBENDARY.

The Dean or Senior Canon, and the Chapter Clerk, shall receive the Canon elect in the Chapter House or Sacristy; then shall the Dean say to him,

My brother, what dost thou desire?

Canon Elect. I desire admission to the Canonry [*or* Prebend] of —— in this Church.

Dean. On what ground dost thou claim admission thereto ?

Canon Elect. By virtue of this Mandate, which I now tender.

Then shall the mandate be read aloud by the Chapter Clerk ; which ended, the Dean shall say,

Dost thou promise faithful compliance with the laudable customs of this Church, and maintenance of its just rights and privileges ?

Can. Elect. I do.

Dean. Wilt thou duly observe such term of residence as is enjoined on thee by the Statutes of this Church ?

Can. Elect. I will.

Dean. Wilt thou diligently perform any specific duties which are now or may be hereafter by lawful authority annexed to thy stall ?

Can. Elect. I will, GOD helping me.

Dean. Wilt thou be a just steward of the goods [and patronage] of this Church ; administering them for the common benefit of all, and not for private advantage or profit ?

Can. Elect. I will so be, the LORD being my helper.

Dean. Wilt thou be at all times ready and willing to aid thy brethren of this Chapter with true and helpful brotherly counsel in all matters spiritual and temporal on which ye may be called to deliberate ?

Can. Elect. I will.

Dean. Dost thou promise as well due respect to those set over thee in this place, as fitting courtesy and good will to those below thee ?

Can. Elect. I do so promise.

Then shall the Dean say,

The LORD, Who hath given thee a good will, of His great mercy grant thee grace and power to fulfil the same ; and I, by the authority committed unto me, admit thee as a Canon [*or* Prebendary] of this Church, in the Name, &c.

Then shall they go into the Church in procession, and the Canon Elect shall kneel at the faldstool, where the Litany is wont to be said. The Dean and Canons shall go to their respective stalls. Then shall be sung the following Antiphon and Psalm.

Ant. Behold how good and joyful.

Ps. 101. My song shall be of mercy, &c.

Ps. 133. Behold how good, &c.

Ant. Behold . . . . a thing it is, brethren, to dwell together in unity.

LORD, have mercy, &c.

Our FATHER, &c.

℣. O LORD, save Thy servant. ℟. Who putteth his trust in Thee. ℣. Send him help from Thy Sanctuary. ℟. And strengthen him out of Sion. ℣. Let Thy Priests be clothed with righteousness. ℟. And let Thy saints sing with joyfulness. ℣. LORD, hear, &c. ℟. And let, &c.

Then shall the Dean, or in his absence the Senior Canon, say,

Let us pray.

566. Almighty and everlasting GOD, look graciously upon this Thy servant, and according to Thy mercy lead him in the way of everlasting salvation, that he, desiring those things that are acceptable in Thy sight, may daily proceed in all virtue and godliness of life. Through.

Prevent us, &c.

Then shall the Dean or Senior Canon come from his stall to the faldstool, and taking the Canon Elect by the right hand, shall lead him to his place in the Choir, and shall say,

By virtue of sufficient authority committed to me in this behalf, I assign thee this stall in this Church of ——.

*Then setting him down in the stall,
he shall add,*

N., I induct thee into the real and corporal possession of the same ; with all rights, goods, and privileges thereunto belonging, inclusive of a place and voice in the Chapter; and may the LORD preserve thy going out and coming in from this time forth for evermore.

R̷. Amen.

Then shall follow the Te Deum.

ORDER FOR A PROVINCIAL OR DIOCESAN SYNOD.

After the Celebration of Holy Communion, those members of the congregation who are not to take part in the Synod shall leave the Church.

At a Provincial Synod, the Metropolitan shall be seated in front of the Altar with his comprovincials ranged on either hand.

At a Diocesan Synod, the Bishop shall be seated in front of the Altar, with his suffragans (if any), Dean, Archdeacon, Vicars-General, and other chief diocesan officials seated on either hand. The clergy, vested in cassock and biretta, shall be placed according to their seniority by ordination. After these shall be ranged the lay delegates (if any).

Then the President standing and facing the Altar shall say,

In the Name, &c.

℣. The LORD, &c. R̷. And with, &c. ℣. Let us pray.

O GOD, Who didst teach the hearts of Thy faithful people, &c. (*Collect for Whitsun Day*).

Then, all kneeling shall say,

Come, HOLY GHOST, our souls inspire, &c.

All rising, the following Psalm with its Antiphon shall be sung.

Ant. Lead me, O LORD, in Thy righteousness, because of mine enemies.

Ps. 19. The heavens declare, &c.

Ant. Lead me, O LORD, in Thy righteousness, because of mine enemies : make Thy way plain before my face.

Then one of the Archdeacons shall read the following Gospel.

S. Luke ix. 1—6.

Then JESUS called His twelve disciples together, and gave them power and authority over all devils, and to cure diseases. And He sent them to preach the kingdom of GOD, and to heal the sick. And He said unto them, Take nothing for your journey, neither staves, nor scrip, neither bread, nor money ; neither have two coats apiece. And whatsoever house ye enter into, there abide, and thence depart. And whosoever will not receive you, when ye go out of that city, shake off the very dust from your feet for a testimony against them. And they departed, and went through the towns, preaching the Gospel, and healing everywhere.

R̷. Praise be to Thee, O CHRIST.

The Bishop, turning to the Altar, shall say,

567. We are here, O LORD the HOLY GHOST, we are here, though tied by the heinousness of our sins, yet specially assembled in Thy Name. Come unto us, help us, vouchsafe to glide into our hearts, teach us what to do, show us whither to go, work in us that which we are to accomplish. Mayest Thou alone prompt and execute our judgments, Who alone possessest the Name of glory with GOD the FATHER and His SON. Thou Who chiefly lovest equity, suffer us not to pervert righteousness; let not ignorance lead us astray; let not favour warp us; let no gifts or personal influence corrupt us: but unite us throughly to Thyself, by the gift of Thy grace alone, that we may be one in Thee, and in nought depart from the truth, and that guided by Thy lovingkindness, we may so in all things hold to righteousness, that our judgment here may vary in nought from Thy will, and that in the world to come we may obtain everlasting rewards for that which we have well done. Through Thy grace, Who alone with GOD the FATHER and His SON livest and reignest GOD for ever and ever.

LORD, have mercy, &c.
Our FATHER, &c.

℣. Give peace in our time, O LORD. ℟. Because there is, &c. ℣. Peace be within thy walls. ℟. And plenteousness, &c. ℣. We have sinned with our fathers. ℟. We have done amiss, &c. ℣. O LORD, deal not with us after our sins. ℟. Neither reward us, &c. ℣. O LORD, save the Queen. ℟. And mercifully hear, &c. ℣. O LORD, save Thy servants and handmaidens. ℟. Which put their trust, &c. ℣. O LORD, save Thy people. ℟. And bless, &c. ℣. Let Thy merciful kindness, O LORD, be upon us. ℟. As we do put, &c. ℣. Let Thy Priests be clothed with righteousness. ℟. And let Thy Saints, &c. ℣. Let us pray for the faithful departed. ℟. Eternal rest grant unto them, O LORD, and Light perpetual shine upon them. ℣. O LORD, hear our prayer. ℟. And let, &c. ℣. Let us pray.

Prevent us, O LORD, &c.

568. O most loving GOD, Who didst promise that Thou wouldst be in the midst of Thy faithful gathered together in Thy Name; mercifully vouchsafe to inspire us with that which is for the true well-being of Thy Church, and the assembly of Thy Priests; and as Thou hast conferred upon us, though unworthy, the task of piloting Thy ship, make haste to walk on the waters, and to come to the aid of its rowers beset with grievous perils, that inasmuch as we have at Thy calling taken upon us duties to discharge at the risk of our souls, we may, through Thy mercy going before, accompanying, and following us, accomplish our toils, and make an acceptable offering unto Thee with all holy devotion.   Through.

The Bishop shall then address the members of the Synod as follows:

Dearly beloved, seeing that we are gathered here in the Name of GOD to hold counsel on behalf of His Church, for His glory, and for the furtherance of His Gospel unto the salvation of souls, I pray and beseech you, in His most blessed Name, that you give due heed and attention to the matters that shall come before you, and that you hearken with courtesy and good will to that which shall be spoken by any amongst you. Set a watch before your own lips, that you say nothing contrary to the will of GOD or brotherly kindness. Order yourselves reverently both within and without the Synod during the whole time of its Session, that you may be void of offence, as fits the solemn work in which you are engaged. Keep steadfastly the faith once delivered to the Saints. Give diligent care to the reformation of abuses, and for the devising such measures as may be needed for the wants of our time. If aught that is said or done displease any of you, let him, nothing doubting, bring the matter before us all for common consideration, that by the help of GOD he may either teach us or be taught himself. Let each one of you make his prayer to Almighty GOD that he may not be swayed by personal feeling, by error of mind, or by fear of man in forming his judgment, that our united decisions may be according to the will of GOD and the teaching of Holy Church, and be profitable to all the faithful members of CHRIST'S Body.

Then silence shall be kept for a short space, during which the members of the Synod shall betake themselves to private prayer, all kneeling. After this the business of the Synod shall begin.
After the business of the day is concluded, the Bishop shall say,

℣. The LORD, &c. ℟. And with, &c. ℣. Let us pray.

569. O GOD, Who didst vouchsafe to enlighten the minds of the disciples by the outpouring of the Spirit of the Comforter; fulfil us with Thy blessing, and make us to abound in the gifts of the same Spirit. Through.

Benediction. GOD, Who vouchsafed to bring the various nations and languages into one by the confession of the one Faith, make you to persevere in the same Faith, and thereby to attain from hope to happiness.

SECOND DAY.

Prayers as on the First Day, except the Psalm, Lesson, and Collect, as below, the Bishop's address being omitted.

Ant. We make our boast of GOD all the day long.

Ps. 46. GOD is our hope and strength, &c.

Ant. We make our boast of GOD all the day long: and will praise Thy Name for ever.

S. Luke x. 1—9.

After these things the LORD appointed other seventy also, and sent them two and two before His face into every city and place, whither He Himself would come. Therefore said He unto them, The harvest truly is great, but the labourers are few: pray ye therefore the LORD of the harvest, that He would send forth labourers into His harvest. Go your ways: behold, I send you forth as lambs among wolves. Carry neither purse, nor scrip, nor shoes: and salute no man by the way. And into whatsoever house ye enter, first say, Peace be to this house. And if the son of peace be there, your peace shall rest upon it: if not, it shall turn to you again. And in the same house remain, eating and drinking such things as they give: for the labourer is worthy of his hire. Go not from house to house. And into whatsoever city ye enter, and they receive you, eat such things as are set before you: and heal the sick that are therein, and say unto them, The kingdom of GOD is come nigh unto you.

570. O GOD, Who hast commanded us to speak righteousness and to do that which is good; grant us that there be neither iniquity found in our mouths nor evil in our minds, that our speech may be pure, and agree with the pureness of our hearts, that righteousness may be manifested in our works, that there be no guile in our tongue, and that we may bring forth the truth in our hearts. Through.

After business is concluded, the Bishop shall say,

℣. The LORD, &c. ℟. And with, &c. ℣. Let us pray.

571. Grant, we beseech Thee, O merciful GOD, that Thy Church which is assembled in the HOLY GHOST may be disturbed by no assaults of the enemy. Through.

Benediction. The LORD, Who taught the faith unto His Apostles, nourish you with faith in this life present, and bring you hereafter unto everlasting rest.

LAST DAY.

Ant. Set up Thyself, O GOD, above the heavens.

Ps. 111. I will give thanks, &c.

Ant. Set up Thyself, O GOD, above the heavens: and Thy glory above all the earth.

S. Matt. xviii. 15—22.

JESUS said unto His disciples, If thy brother shall trespass against thee, go and tell him his fault between thee and him alone: if he shall hear thee, thou hast gained thy brother. But if he will not hear thee, then take with thee one or two more, that in the mouth of two or three witnesses every word may be established. And if he shall neglect to hear them, tell it unto the Church: but if he neglect to hear the Church, let him be unto thee as an heathen man and a publican. Verily I say unto you, whatsoever ye shall bind on earth shall be bound in heaven: and whatsoever ye shall loose on earth shall be loosed in heaven. Again I say unto you, that if two of you shall agree on earth as touching anything that they shall ask, it shall be done for them of My FATHER which is in heaven. For where two or three are gathered together in My Name, there am I in the midst of them. Then came Peter to Him, and said, LORD, how oft shall my brother sin against me, and I forgive him? till seven times? JESUS saith unto him, I say not unto thee, Until seven times: but, Until seventy times seven.

572. Almighty and everlasting GOD, Who hast promised in the sacred teaching of Thy word that where two or three are gathered together in Thy Name, there Thou wouldst be in the midst of them; graciously be present with our assembly, and mercifully enlighten our hearts, that we may not go astray from the blessing of Thy lovingkindness, but alway keep to the straight path of Thy righteousness. Through.

573. There is no power, O LORD, in the knowledge of man which can without offending accomplish the judgments of Thy will, and therefore because Thine eyes beheld our imperfections, count, we beseech Thee, as perfect that which we desire to bring to a just and perfect end. We pray Thee to meet us at our setting out, we hope for Thee as our witness at this close of our decision, that Thou mayest spare our ignorance, pardon our errors, and bestow perfect and effectual working in answer to our perfected prayers; and because we are sore afraid by the warnings of our consciences lest ignorance should have drawn us into error, or hasty wilfulness have led us to swerve from that which is just; therefore we pray and beseech Thee, that if we have committed any offence against Thee in the assembly of this Synod, it may be remitted by Thy grace, that in this assemblage which we are about to dissolve we may be loosed from all the chains of our sins, that we who have transgressed may obtain pardon, and giving thanks to Thee, may hereafter receive an everlasting reward. Through.

LORD, have mercy, &c.

Our FATHER, &c.

Benediction. CHRIST, the SON of GOD, Who is the beginning and the end, grant you the fulness of love. Amen.

And He Who hath caused you to reach the end of this Synod deliver you from all contagion of guilt. Amen.

That, freed and loosed from every guiltiness by the gift of the HOLY GHOST, you may safely and unharmed return to your own homes. Amen.

Then shall follow the Itinerary, *see p.* 19.

ORDINATION OF READERS.

The Archdeacon, or the Priest of the parish where the Reader is to officiate, shall present the candidate, vested in cassock and surplice, to the Bishop, seated in his chair in front of the High Altar, and shall say,

Right Reverend Father in GOD, we present unto you this person, *N.,* here present, who seeks the imposition of your hands, to be ordained Reader for the Church *N.*

Bishop. Do ye testify that he is worthy of this office ?

Archd. We do so testify.

Bishop. If any man know of any impediment or crime, by reason of which *N.* ought not to be ordained Reader, for the avoiding of scandal and offence, let him now declare it.

If no objection be alleged, the Bishop shall proceed, saying,

My son, if thou wouldst be a Reader in the House of our GOD, learn what that office is, that thou mayest fulfil it, and that Almighty GOD may bestow upon thee the grace of everlasting perfection. It behoves a Reader to recite the Lessons, and otherwise, if so ordered, to aid the Priest in Divine Service. Give heed, therefore, to repeat the words of GOD distinctly and plainly, for the instruction and edification of the faithful, lest the true meaning of the Holy Scriptures should, through thy carelessness, be perverted, and fail to teach the hearers.

I ask therefore :

Bishop. Dost thou unfeignedly believe all the Canonical Scriptures of the Old and New Testament?

Ans. I do believe them.

Bishop. Wilt thou diligently read the same unto the people assembled in the Church where thou shalt be appointed to serve ?

Ans. I will.

Bishop. What then thou readest with thy mouth, believe with thy heart, and fulfil in thy works, that thou mayest instruct them that hear thee both by thy words and thine example, which may GOD accomplish of His grace.

℣. The LORD, &c. ℟. And with, &c. ℣. Let us pray.

LORD, have mercy, &c.

Our FATHER, &c.

℣. O GOD, save Thy servant. ℟. Who putteth his trust in Thee. ℣. Let his mouth be exercised in wisdom. ℟. And his tongue be talking of judgment. ℣. Then shall he teach Thy ways unto the wicked. ℟. And sinners shall be converted unto Thee. ℣. Open Thou his eyes. ℟. That he may see the wondrous things of Thy law. ℣. Guide him with Thy counsel. ℟. And after that receive him with glory. ℣. LORD, hear, &c. ℟. And let, &c.

Let us pray.

574. Almighty GOD, bountiful in Thy gifts, Who hast appointed divers grades and orders in Thy Church for the ministry thereof, and hast poured Thy grace on Thy servants ; vouchsafe now to hallow this Thy servant *N.,* and choose him to be a Reader, granting him with all wisdom and understanding to meditate upon and read the Divine Scriptures, filling him with Thy gifts, and keeping him pure and blameless, that he may worthily pronounce to Thy people Thy holy Word, which Thou hast given for our help and comfort and the salvation of our souls. Through.

Then the Bishop shall lay his hands on the candidate, and give him a Bible, saying,

Receive authority to read the Bible in the Church, and be thou a wise setter-forth of the Word of

GOD. And if thou fulfil this thy charge with a right heart and mind, thou shalt have a share in the fellowship of the Saints and elect of GOD.

Then shall the Archdeacon read the Gospel.

S. Luke iv. 16—21.

And JESUS came to Nazareth, where He had been brought up: and, as His custom was, He went into the synagogue on the sabbath-day, and stood up for to read. And there was delivered unto Him the book of the prophet Esaias: and when He had opened the book, He found the place where it was written, The Spirit of the LORD is upon me, because He hath anointed me to preach the Gospel to the poor; He hath sent me to heal the broken-hearted, to preach deliverance to the captives, and recovering of sight to the blind, to set at liberty them that are bruised; to preach the acceptable year of the LORD. And He closed the book, and He gave it again to the minister, and sat down. And the eyes of all them that were in the synagogue were fastened on Him. And He began to say unto them, This day is this Scripture fulfilled in your ears.

Ry. Thanks be to GOD.

The Gospel ended, the Bishop shall say,

Vy. The LORD, &c. Ry. And with, &c. Vy. Let us pray.

575. O Almighty GOD, Who didst choose Thy servant Ezra, and gavest him wisdom to read Thy Law unto the people; look graciously on this Thy servant, whom Thou hast chosen as a Reader of Thy Word. Make him wise in Thy commandments, and understanding in Thy statutes. Enlighten the eyes of his mind, that he may clearly know Thy precepts, and grant him with purity of heart and with faith unfeigned to meditate and read therein, unto the edifying of them that hear, so that they may declare the honour and glory of Thy kingdom, where with Thy SON and HOLY SPIRIT, Thou livest and reignest, GOD, for ever and ever.

Prevent us, &c. The peace, &c.

ORDINATION OF SUBDEACONS.

The Archdeacon shall present the candidates, vested in cassock, girdle, and surplice, to the Bishop, seated in his chair before the High Altar, and shall say,

Right Reverend Father in GOD, we present unto you these persons *NN.* here present, who seek the imposition of hands for the office of Subdeacon.

Bishop. Take heed that the persons whom ye present unto us, be apt and meet, for their learning and godly conversation, to exercise their Ministry duly, to the honour of GOD, and the edifying of His Church.

The Archdeacon shall answer,

I have inquired of them, and also examined them, and think them so to be.

Then the Bishop shall say unto the people,

Brethren, if there be any of you who knoweth any impediment, or notable crime, in any of these persons presented to be ordered Subdeacons, for the which he ought not to be admitted to that Office, let him come forth in the Name of God, and show what the crime or impediment is.

And if any great crime or impediment be objected, the Bishop shall surcease from Ordering that person, until such time as the party accused shall be found clear of that crime.

Then the Bishop (commending such as shall be found meet to be ordered to the prayers of the Congregation) shall, with the clergy and people present, sing or say the Litany, with the prayers following.

The Litany and special Suffrages.

(See Form of making Deacons in Book of Common Prayer.)

Then shall follow the Holy Eucharist, with the Collect, Epistle, and Gospel as under.

Collect.

576. O LORD our heavenly FATHER, Almighty, everlasting GOD, vouchsafe to bless *this* Thy servant, whom Thou hast chosen for the office of Subdeacon; make *him* diligent in Thy sanctuary, a vigilant watchman in the heavenly warfare, a faithful minister at Thy holy Altar, and cause to rest upon *him* the spirit of wisdom and understanding, the spirit of counsel and might, the spirit of knowledge and holiness, and fill *him* with the spirit of Thy fear; stablish *him* in the sacred ministry, that obedient in word and deed, *he* may obtain Thy grace. Through.

Epistle. 1 S. Pet. v. 5—11.

Likewise, ye younger, submit yourselves unto the elder; yea, all of you be subject one to another, and be clothed with humility: for GOD resisteth the proud, and giveth grace to the humble. Humble yourselves therefore under the mighty hand of GOD, that He may exalt you in due time; casting all your care upon Him; for He careth for

you. Be sober; be vigilant; because your adversary the devil, as a roaring lion, walketh about, seeking whom he may devour: whom resist steadfast in the faith, knowing that the same afflictions are accomplished in your brethren that are in the world. But the GOD of all grace, Who hath called us unto His eternal glory by CHRIST JESUS, after that ye have suffered awhile, make you perfect, stablish, strengthen, settle you: to Him be glory and dominion for ever and ever. Amen.

Gospel. S. Mark xiii. 33—37.

JESUS said unto His disciples, Take ye heed, watch and pray: for ye know not when the time is. For the Son of Man is as a man taking a far journey, who left his house, and gave authority to his servants, and to every man his work, and commanded the porter to watch. Watch ye therefore: for ye know not when the master of the house cometh, at even, or at midnight, or at the cock-crowing, or in the morning: lest, coming suddenly, he find you sleeping. And what I say unto you, I say unto all, Watch.

The Nicene Creed ended, the Bishop shall say,

Beloved, ye that seek the holy office of Subdeacon, must needs ponder carefully again and again what a duty it is that ye desire to take upon yourselves.

I demand therefore, Do you seek this office freely, not being constrained thereto, nor for the sake of gain, but for the honour and service of GOD?

Ans. I do so seek it.

Bishop. Do you believe that GOD Himself has called you to His service?

Ans. I do so believe.

Bishop. Will you be diligent in framing your life and conduct after the rule of CHRIST's doctrine?

Ans. I will, the LORD being my helper.

Bishop. Will you be zealous in discharging your office according to the laws of this Church of God?

Ans. I will do so, by the help of God.

Bishop. It belongeth to the office of a Subdeacon to aid the Deacon in his ministry; to serve at the Altar of God; to care for the holy vessels, linen and books thereof, keeping them in readiness, purity, and order; to read the Epistles in the Church; to minister the oblations at the offertory; to see that all things are prepared for Divine Service, and to perform such other duties in the Church and parish as shall be enjoined him by lawful authority. See therefore that ye be henceforth zealous, watchful, sober, pure, and devout, which may He grant you, Who liveth.

Then the Bishop laying his hands severally upon the head of every candidate, kneeling before him, shall say,

Receive the office of a Subdeacon in the Church of God. In the Name, &c.

Then shall the Archdeacon put into the hands of each of them the flagon or cruet, and the Book of Epistles, while the Bishop says,

Take heed to the ministry which is committed unto thee, and see that thou so fulfil it as shall be well-pleasing unto God.

Then shall follow the Offertory, and in the Post-Communion the Collect subjoined shall be said.

577. Almighty, everlasting God, Who hast given unction to kings, Who didst raise up and sanctify Thy prophets, Who calledst the just; so call and choose Thy servants for the office of a Subdeacon, that they may be good stewards in Thy Church, bestowing on them the gift of Thy HOLY SPIRIT, granting that they may love the beauty of Thy House, and the communion of Thy sacraments, and plant them as fruitful olive trees to bring forth the fruits of righteousness unto CHRIST JESUS our LORD. Who liveth.

INSTITUTION OF AN INCUMBENT OF A PARISH OR CHURCH.

The Bishop, (or in his absence, the Archdeacon or Rural Dean) shall be seated in a chair before the Altar. The new Incumbent shall kneel at the Litany-stool in front of him.

The Bishop.

Dearly beloved brethren, *N.,* elected Pastor of this Church, is present here to enter upon his office; wherefore we think fit that he shall be examined, according to the rule of the godly Fathers, in those things which belong to our holy religion and to the clerical state. Wherefore, before instituting him thereto, I require that if any of you do know of any just cause or impediment why he should not be instituted to this office, ye do now declare it.

If any objection be alleged, the Institutor, according to his discretion, shall suspend or continue the Service.

Brother, seeing that the grace of God, and the choice of the patron of this benefice [*or of the congregation, as may be the case,*] and thy former life and conversation have called thee to this office, we desire to know from thine own lips, whether thou art willing to dwell with thy flock in this place, to refrain thyself from all evil ways, and to devote thyself to all good works, as GOD shall grant?

Ans. I am willing.

Bishop. Wilt thou diligently observe and keep thy priestly vows and pledges, and instruct those set under thee?

Ans. I will, with the help of GOD.

Bishop. Wilt thou be a good steward of the goods of this Church, and guard them for the benefit of the brethren, the poor, and strangers?

Ans. I will.

Bishop. Wilt thou observe holiness and patience, and teach others the like?

Ans. I will, GOD being my helper.

Bishop. Wilt thou busy thyself in holy things, and shun earthly concerns and filthy lucre, so far as human frailty suffereth thee?

Ans. I will, with the help of GOD.

Bishop. Wilt thou be courteous and merciful to the poor and the stranger, and to all that are in need, for the honour of GOD's Name?

Ans. I will, with the help of GOD.

Bishop. Wilt thou yield canonical obedience in all things to the mother Church, *N.*?

Ans. I will.

He then makes his profession in the usual form, and signs his name to the document.

The Senior Churchwarden, or some other lay parishioner, shall deliver the keys of the Church to the new Incumbent, saying,

In the name of this Parish [*or* Church] I, A. B., acknowledge you, C. D., as Priest and Rector [Vicar *or* Perpetual Curate] of the same, and in token thereof give into your hands the keys of this Church.

Then the new Incumbent shall answer,

I, C. D., receive these keys of the House of GOD at your hands, as the pledge of my institution, and of your recognition, and I promise to be a faithful shepherd over you, in the Name of the FATHER, &c.

Bishop. Almighty GOD be thy Helper, in these and all other good things.

℣. The LORD, &c. ℟. And with, &c. ℣. Let us pray.

LORD, have mercy, &c.

Our FATHER, &c.

℣. O LORD, save Thy servant. ℟. Who putteth his trust in Thee. ℣. The LORD preserve thy coming in. ℟. From this time forth for evermore. ℣. The LORD preserve thee from all evil. ℟. The LORD Himself be the keeper of thy soul. ℣. Send thee help from His holy place. ℟. And strengthen thee out of Sion. ℣. O LORD, arise, help us. ℟. And deliver us for Thy Name's sake. ℣. The LORD, &c. ℟. And with, &c.

Let us pray.

578. Grant, we beseech Thee, Almighty GOD, the increase of Thy grace to this Thy servant, whom we have elected to the cure of souls, that by Thy bounty we, and the choice we have made, may be pleasing unto Thee. Through.

Let us pray.

579. O GOD, Who rulest all the kingdoms of the earth according to Thy divine pleasure; we humbly pray and beseech Thee to bless with the grace of heavenly sanctification this Thy servant *N.*, whom we have chosen as Pastor of this Church; that in his days holy discipline may revive, and that by Thy help, he may set a good example to his flock, and carrying on his warfare in Thy fear and with gentleness to his people, may be ever peacefully sheltered under the shield of Thy majesty. Vouchsafe to enrich him with Thy divine right hand, that he may be a wise steward, and able to help lovingly all them that need. Be Thou his worship, his joy in his home, his companion in his journeys, his comfort in sorrow, his counsel in doubt, his medicine in sickness, his helper in toil, his defence in adversity, his patience in tribulation. Let him learn in Thee forethought and wisdom, to rule prudently the flock entrusted to him, that ever prospered and rejoicing in the riches of Thy bountiful goodness, he may thankfully enjoy the temporal gifts of this present life, and finally be united in everlasting fellowship with the heavenly citizens and the choirs of angels. Through.

Let us pray.

580. Look down graciously, O LORD, we beseech Thee, on this Thy servant, and give him true knowledge, unshaken hope, right counsel, and holy doctrine, that he may be meet to receive the grace of Thy blessing, and, without offence, may follow the footsteps of Thy Saints, and cause his flock to follow him by his godly teachings, and that he may bear in mind that whoso taketh on himself the guidance of souls, must give an account for them all in the Judgment Day to our LORD JESUS CHRIST. Who.

Then the Bishop, turning to the Altar, shall kneel, and recite, with the clerks and people, the Veni Creator.

This ended, the Bishop shall seat himself again, addressing the new Incumbent, who kneels before him, and shall say,

In the Name, &c.

I, *N.*, Bishop of the See of ——, [*or* Archdeacon, &c., acting under commission from the Bishop of *N.*,] by the authority committed to me, do hereby give thee, *N.*, Institution and Mission [and cure of souls] as Pastor of this Church [*or* Parish,] and authority to preach the Word,

and to administer the Sacraments herein.

Then putting a Bible into the hand of the new Incumbent, he shall say,

I charge thee before GOD and the LORD JESUS CHRIST, Who shall judge the quick and the dead, at His appearing and His kingdom; preach the word; be instant in season, out of season; reprove, rebuke, exhort, with all longsuffering and doctrine.

He shall then lead him to his stall, and inducting him therein, say,

O praise the LORD for His goodness, and declare the wonders that He doeth for the children of men. Exalt Him also in the congregation of the people, and praise Him in the seat of the elders.

The Bishop, returning to the Altar, shall stand before it, facing the people, and say,

581. O GOD, the author of all good things, Who by Thine Apostle Paul didst ordain elders to bear rule in every Church; we humbly beseech Thee to guard with Thy gracious protection this Thy servant *N.*, instituted this day as pastor over Thy sheep in this place, and grant him, we pray Thee, so to rule those set under him, that he and they all may attain the kingdom of heaven, and that ever aided by Thy help, and stayed up by the doctrine of Thine Apostles, he may joyfully enter the gates of Paradise, bearing fruit an hundredfold, and there hear Thy commendation, Well done, good and faithful servant, thou hast been faithful over a few things, I will set thee over many things; enter thou into the joy of thy LORD. Which may He grant, Who with the FATHER, &c.

Te Deum.   Blessing.

OFFICE FOR SENDING FORTH A MISSIONARY.

The Bishop, or some other principal dignitary, shall be seated in front of the High Altar. Then shall some official appointed for that purpose present the candidate to him, saying,

Right Reverend [*or* Rev.] Father, I present unto thee this person, *N.*, who desires mission and benediction for the work of an Evangelist.

Bishop. Let the mandate of his appointment be read.

THE MANDATE.

I, *N.*, by Divine permission Bishop of ——, having duly examined *N. N.*, who is desirous of devoting himself to missionary labour, and having satisfied myself of his soundness in doctrine, godliness of life, sufficiency of knowledge, and zeal in the work of the ministry, hereby appoint him and authorize him to labour for the furtherance of the Gospel in ——, and give him mission to minister the Word therein. In the Name, &c.

(Signed) A. B., Bishop of ——.

Then shall the Bishop address the candidate as follows:

N., dost thou, in the sight of GOD and of this congregation, accept this appointment to labour in —— ?

Candidate. I do.

Bishop. Dost thou promise steadfastness, faithfulness, charity, and zeal for souls therein ?

Candidate. I do so promise, the LORD being my helper.

Bishop. GOD, Who hath given thee a good will, grant thee all grace and power to fulfil the same, and to persevere unto the end.

R̰. Amen.

Then shall be said or sung the following Antiphon and Psalm :

Ant. The LORD gave the Word.

Ps. 115. Not unto us, O LORD, &c.

Ant. The LORD . . . . great was the company of the preachers.

The Chapter. S. Luke x.

After these things the LORD appointed other seventy also, and sent them two and two before His face into every city and place, whither He Himself would come. Therefore said He unto them, The harvest truly is great, but the labourers are few : pray ye therefore the LORD of the harvest, that He would send forth labourers into His harvest. Go your ways : behold, I send you forth as lambs among wolves. Carry neither purse, nor scrip, nor shoes : and salute no man by the way. And into whatsoever house ye enter, first say, Peace be to this house. And if the son of peace be there, your peace shall rest upon it : if not, it shall turn to you again. And in the same house remain, eating and drinking such things as they give : for the labourer is worthy of his hire. Go not from house to house. And into whatsoever city ye enter, and they receive you, eat such things as are set before you : and heal the sick that are therein, and say unto them, The kingdom of GOD is come nigh unto you.

℣. But Thou, &c. R̰. Thanks, &c. ℣. The harvest truly is plenteous. R̰. But the labourers are few. ℣. Glory, &c. R̰. As it was, &c. ℣. Pray ye therefore the LORD of the harvest. R̰. That He will send forth labourers into His harvest.

LORD, have mercy, &c.
Our FATHER, &c.

℣. I will patiently abide alway. R℣. And will praise Thee more and more. ℣. My mouth shall daily speak of Thy righteousness and salvation. R℣. For I know no end thereof. ℣. I will go forth in the strength of the LORD GOD. R℣. And will make mention of Thy righteousness only. ℣. Thou, LORD, hast taught me from my youth up until now. R℣. Therefore will I tell of Thy wondrous works. ℣. Forsake me not, O LORD, in my old age, when I am greyheaded. R℣. Until I have showed Thy strength unto this generation, and Thy power unto all them that are yet for to come. ℣. LORD, hear, &c. R℣. And let, &c. ℣. Let us pray.

582. Almighty GOD, Who didst send Thine only-begotten SON into the world for the redemption of mankind, and that the Gospel of His kingdom might be made known unto men through the preaching of His Apostles; send, we pray Thee, Thy HOLY SPIRIT upon this Thy servant whom Thou hast called to labour in Thy vineyard. Anoint him to preach the Gospel to the poor, send him to heal the broken-hearted, to preach deliverance to the captives, and recovery of sight to the blind, to set at liberty them that are bruised, and to preach the acceptable year of the LORD. And grant that he may follow after righteousness, godliness, faith, love, patience, and meekness. Through.

583. O LORD JESU CHRIST, Who shalt judge the quick and the dead at Thine appearing and Thy kingdom; grant that this Thy servant N. may preach the Word, be instant in season and out of season, reprove, rebuke, exhort with all longsuffering and doctrine; watch in all things, endure afflictions, do the work of an evangelist, and make full proof of his ministry, that he may obtain the crown of righteousness which Thou the righteous Judge shalt give him in that day. Who livest.

584. O GOD the HOLY GHOST, Who art the Giver of all good gifts, mercifully bestow upon this Thy servant the spirit of wisdom and understanding, the spirit of counsel and might, the spirit of knowledge and true godliness, and the spirit of Thy holy fear, that in faith and love he may hold fast the form of sound words which has been committed unto him, and giving attendance to reading, to exhortation, and to doctrine, may be an example to believers in word, in conversation, in charity, in spirit, in faith, in purity, so that coming again with abundant fruit from the harvest of souls, he may be counted with them who having turned many to righteousness, shine as the stars for ever and ever. Who, with the FATHER, and the SON, livest.

Then shall the Bishop say to the candidate,

Receive thou mission and authority in the Name of the LORD to go forth into the place ———, now committed to thy charge, there to do the work of an Evangelist. The LORD Himself be a lantern unto thy feet, and a light unto thy paths, Himself go before thee and be thy rereward, stablish and comfort thine heart in all trouble and perplexity, and guarding thee from all peril of body and soul, preserve thy going out and coming in.

And the peace of GOD, &c.

FORM OF DEGRADATION FROM HOLY ORDERS.

No deprivation of any person in Holy Orders shall take place save for grave errors in doctrine or practice, which (if not confessed by the delinquent) must be duly proved by open trial in the Church Courts, and even after conviction in such Courts, the assent of the Diocesan Synod shall be necessary in the case of any Priest or Deacon, and that of the Provincial Synod in the case of any Bishop, before degradation from Holy Orders can be proceeded with.

The Bishop, attended by the diocesan officials, shall stand in front of the High Altar, facing the people, and shall say,

In the Name, &c.

Forasmuch as *N.* [Bishop, Priest, *or* Deacon], hath grievously offended against the law of GOD and the ordinances of the Holy Catholic Church, by open and notorious sin, whereof he hath been fully convicted [by his own confession, *or* by open trial], we therefore, by the counsel and with the assent of the [Diocesan *or* Provincial] Synod, have met here in the presence of GOD and this congregation, to depose him from the office he has misused, to take from him the trust which he hath violated, to deprive him of the privileges he hath forfeited; and that publicly, that others may be warned in time neither to receive his ministrations nor to follow his example. And that ye may know that this our act is justly and rightly done, the sentence shall now be read in your hearing.

Here the Bishop's Secretary, the Synod Clerk, or the Chancellor of the diocese, shall read aloud the sentence of the Court.

Then shall be said the Antiphon and Psalms following :

Ant. Thou shalt be no priest to Me.

Ps. 50, vv. 14—23. Offer unto GOD, &c.

73. Truly GOD is loving, &c.

101. My song shall be, &c.

Ant. Thou shalt . . . . seeing thou hast forgotten the law of thy GOD.

The Chapter. Malachi ii. 1—9.

And now, O ye priests, this commandment is for you. If ye will not hear, and if ye will not lay it to heart, to give glory unto My Name, saith the LORD of hosts, I will even send a curse upon you, and I will curse your blessings; yea, I have cursed them already, because ye do not lay it to heart. Behold, I will corrupt your seed, and spread dung upon your faces, even the dung of your solemn feasts; and one shall take you away with it. And ye shall know that I have sent this commandment unto you, that My covenant might be with Levi, saith the LORD of hosts. My covenant was with him of life and peace; and I gave them to him for the fear wherewith he feared Me, and was afraid before My Name. The law of truth was in his mouth, and iniquity was not found in his lips : he walked with Me in peace and equity, and did turn many away from iniquity. For the priest's lips should keep knowledge, and they should seek the law at his mouth : for he is the messenger of the LORD of hosts. But ye are departed out of the way; ye have caused many to stumble at the law; ye have corrupted the covenant of Levi, saith the LORD of hosts. Therefore have I also made you contemptible and base before all the people, according as ye have not kept My ways, but have been partial in the law.

℣. But Thou, O LORD, have mercy upon us. ℟. Thanks be to GOD. ℣. The LORD be with you. ℟. And with thy spirit. ℣. Let us pray.

LORD, have mercy, &c.

Our FATHER, &c.

℣. O LORD, to us belongeth confusion of face. ℟. For we have sinned against Thee. ℣. We have sinned, we have done amiss. ℟. And have dealt wickedly. ℣. Arise, O GOD, maintain Thine own cause. ℟. Remember how the foolish man blasphemeth Thee daily. ℣. Deliver us, O LORD, from the evil man. ℟. And preserve us from the wicked man. ℣. Break Thou the power of the ungodly and malicious. ℟. Take away his ungodliness and Thou shalt find none. ℣. Turn us again, O LORD GOD of hosts. ℟. Show the light of Thy countenance, and we shall be whole. ℣. O LORD, hear our prayer. ℟. And let our cry come unto Thee.

585. O LORD GOD, Who by Thy Prophet hast said, Be ye clean, that bear the vessels of the LORD; Who slewest Nadab and Abihu when they offered strange fire unto Thee; and sentest the sword upon the house of Eli, taking the priesthood from it for the guilt of Hophni and Phinehas; mercifully look upon Thy Church, and impute not unto her the sins of her rebellious children, but raise up in her faithful priests, who shall do according to that which is in Thine heart and in Thy mind; build them a sure house, and cause them to walk before Thine Anointed for ever. Through the same our LORD JESUS CHRIST. Who.

O Almighty GOD, Who into the place of the traitor Judas didst choose Thy faithful servant Matthias to be of the number of the twelve Apostles; grant that Thy Church, being alway preserved from false Apostles, may be ordered and guided by faithful and true pastors; through JESUS CHRIST our LORD. Amen.

[Then shall the deponend (if present), dressed in his ecclesiastical garb, be caused to kneel before the Bishop seated in front of the Altar, who shall say,

N., because thou hast violated GOD's law, and profaned His holy things, hast put no difference between the holy and profane, neither showed it between the unclean and the clean, so that GOD is profaned among us; know that thou shalt bear thine iniquity and not come near unto Him, to do the office of a priest unto Him, nor come near to any of His holy things in His holy place, but shalt bear thy shame, and the abominations thou hast committed.

If the deponend be a Bishop, then shall the pastoral staff be put into his hands and taken from him again, the Officiant saying,

Because thou hast been a hireling, and not a shepherd; because the diseased hast thou not strengthened, neither hast thou healed that which was sick, neither hast thou bound up that which was broken, neither hast thou brought again that which was driven away, neither hast thou sought that which was lost, but hast ruled with force and with cruelty; therefore the LORD refuses His flock at thine hand, and causes thee to cease from feeding the flock, and we, in token thereof, take from thee the pastoral staff, and the office of a Bishop in His Church. In the Name, &c.

If a Priest, a stole shall be put on his neck, and a chalice in his hands, which being taken from him, the Bishop shall say,

Because thou hast despised the easy yoke and light burden of CHRIST, hast refused to drink of His Cup, and hast counted the Blood of the covenant, wherewith thou wast sanctified, an unholy thing, we take from thee the office of the priesthood, and the right to minister at the altar of GOD. In the Name, &c.

If a Deacon, the Book of the Gospels is put into his hands, and withdrawn, with the words:

Because thou hast not obeyed the Gospel of CHRIST, whereof the dispensation was committed unto thee, we take from thee the office of Deacon, and the authority to read that Gospel in the Church. In the Name, &c.

Then shall the surplice be taken away, with these words:

Because, after escaping the pollutions of the world through the knowledge of the LORD and SAVIOUR JESUS CHRIST, thou hast been again entangled therein and overcome, defiling thy garments, we take from thee the white robe, the token of the righteousness of Saints, and therewith all right of ministration in the Church, that others may be warned, and thyself moved to repentance, that thou mayest be washed again from thy sins in the Blood of the Lamb. In the Name, &c.

Here note that the deponend shall be degraded successively from each Office in the ministry to which he has attained, beginning with the highest.]

[*But if the deponend be absent, the Bishop shall proceed as under:*

Because N. hath violated GOD'S law, and profaned His holy things, hath put no difference between the holy and profane, neither showed it between the unclean and the clean, so that GOD is profaned among us; he shall bear his iniquity, and not come near unto GOD, to do the office of a priest unto Him, nor come near to any of His holy things in His holy place, but shall bear his shame, and the abominations he hath committed.

Whereas our LORD JESUS CHRIST hath left to the ministers of His Church the power of binding and loosing, and hath declared of His own mouth that whoso will not hear the Church shall be unto us as a heathen man and a publican, and by His Apostle hath taught us to withdraw from every brother that walketh disorderly, and to put away from us wicked persons; we, by His authority committed to us, hereby deprive N. of all privileges and powers in the ministry of the Church, and depose him from his office of ——. In the Name, &c.]

Then, addressing the people, he shall add:

Forasmuch as N. is now deposed and thrust out from being a minister unto the LORD, we call on you, brethren, to bear witness unto the fact, and to keep yourselves and others from receiving any ministrations of the Church at his hands, lest ye be partakers of his evil deeds, but to have no company with him, that he may be ashamed.

And we do now erase and blot out his name from the register of the clergy of this Church (*Here shall the Bishop draw a pen through the name of the deposed clerk on the roll presented to him by an official,*) in token that if he repent not and amend, GOD will blot out his name out of the Book of Life. Amen.

But as GOD, Who hath taken this unfruitful branch away from His Vine, is able to purge it, that it may bring forth much fruit, and to graff it in again; let us pray to Him that He will, of His great mercy, vouchsafe conversion and amendment to our sinful brother, and restore him whole to the Church.

Then, all kneeling, shall be said the prayers following:

LORD, have mercy, &c.
Our FATHER, &c.

℣. I said, LORD, be merciful unto me. ℟. Heal my soul, for I have sinned against Thee. ℣. Turn

Thec again, O LORD, at the last. R̂. And be gracious unto Thy servants. V̂. Let Thy merciful kindness, O LORD, be upon us. R̂. As we do put our trust in Thee. V̂. We have sinned with our fathers. R̂. We have done amiss, and dealt wickedly. V̂. O LORD, deal not with us after our sins. R̂. Neither reward us according to our iniquities. V̂. Remember not our old sins. R̂. But have mercy upon us, and that soon.

Ps. 51. Have mercy, &c.
130. Out of the deep, &c.

Then shall the Bishop rise, and continue the Office standing at the Altar.

V̂. O LORD, hear our prayer. R̂. And let our cry come unto Thee. V̂. Let us pray.

586. O most merciful GOD, Who hast sent Thine Only-begotten SON into the world, to save sinners, to seek the lost sheep, and to purify for Himself an acceptable people, zealous in good works; Who desirest not the death of a sinner, but rather that he should be converted and live; grant Thy grace unto

Thy servant *N.* that his mind may be enlightened, and that he may come to a knowledge of his sin. Take from him all obstinacy and hardness of heart, give him a new heart and a new spirit, take from him his heart of stone, and give him an heart of flesh, and renew Thy Spirit within him, that denying all ungodliness and worldly lusts, he may live soberly, righteously, and godly in this present world, waiting for the blessed hope and glorious appearing of the great GOD our SAVIOUR JESUS CHRIST. Who with Thee. **[94—98.]**

[At the close of the prayers, if the deposed clerk be present, he shall be conducted out of the Church by two officials, the Bishop saying:

Go out of the sanctuary, for thou hast trespassed.]

Then shall be said,

Ps. 125. They that put their trust, &c.

V̂. Stablish the thing, O LORD, that Thou hast wrought in us. R̂. For Thy temple's sake at Jerusalem. V̂. Let us depart in peace. R̂. In the Name of CHRIST. Amen.

OFFICE FOR THE RECONCILIATION OF A LAPSED CLERIC.

In the Name, &c.
Our FATHER, &c.
V̂. Ye shall be named the Priests of the LORD. R̂. Men shall call you the ministers of our GOD. V̂. O GOD, &c. R̂. O LORD, &c. V̂. Glory, &c. R̂. As it was, &c. Alleluia.

Veni Creator.

Ant. Stablish me with Thy free Spirit.

Ps. 30. I will magnify, &c.
51. Have mercy, &c.
61. Hear my crying, &c.

Ant. Stablish me with Thy free Spirit: then shall I teach Thy ways unto the wicked.

The Chapter. S. Luke xxii. 54—63.

Then took they JESUS, and led Him, and brought Him into the High Priest's house. And Peter followed afar off. And when they had kindled a fire in the midst of the hall, and were set down together, Peter sat down among them. But a certain maid beheld him as he sat by the fire, and earnestly looked upon him, and said, This man was also with Him. And he denied Him, saying, Woman, I know Him not. And after a little while another saw him, and said, Thou art also of them. And Peter said, Man, I am not. And about the space of one hour after another confidently affirmed, saying, Of a truth this fellow also was with Him; for he is a Galilæan. And Peter said, Man, I know not what thou sayest. And immediately, while he yet spake, the cock crew. And the LORD turned, and looked upon Peter. And Peter remembered the word of the LORD, how He had said unto him, Before the cock crow, thou shalt deny Me thrice. And Peter went out, and wept bitterly.

℣. But Thou, &c. ℟. Thanks, &c. ℣. Then I said, I will not make mention of Him, nor speak any more in His Name. ℟. But His Word was in my heart as a burning fire. ℣. Glory, &c. ℟. As it was, &c. ℣. If thou return, then will I bring thee again, and thou shalt stand before Me. ℟. And if thou take forth the precious from the vile, thou shalt be as My mouth.

The Bishop addressing the penitent, says,

N., is it thy purpose to take upon thee again the yoke of the LORD, which thou didst cast off?
℟. That is my desire.
℣. Dost thou repent and abjure the schism and error into which thou hast fallen?
℟. I do.
℣. Wilt thou give thyself henceforth to the ministry of the Word and to prayer?
℟. I will, GOD being my helper.
℣. The LORD give thee the comfort of His help again, and stablish thee with His free Spirit.

℣. The LORD, &c. ℟. And with, &c. ℣. Let us pray.

LORD, have mercy, &c.
Our FATHER, &c.
℣. I said, LORD, be merciful unto me. ℟. Heal my soul, for I have sinned against Thee. ℣. Let Thy priests be clothed with righteousness. ℟. And Thy saints sing with joyfulness. ℣. O LORD, save Thy servant. ℟. Which putteth his trust in Thee. ℣. Remember all his offerings. ℟. And accept his burnt sacrifice. ℣. LORD, hear, &c. ℟. And let, &c.

587. O LORD, we beseech Thee to accept the contrition of this Thy servant, as Thou didst accept the repentance of Aaron Thine High Priest, and of Peter Thy chief Apostle, and to restore him to his former place, that he may serve in Thy courts all the days of his life. Through.

588. Almighty GOD, Who by Thy Prophet hast said, The priest's lips should keep knowledge, and they should seek the law at his mouth, for he is the messenger of the LORD of hosts; have mercy on this Thy servant, and put again into his mouth that Word which he cast away, that he may declare Thy wonders unto this generation, and that sinners may be converted unto Thee. Through.

He lays his hand on the penitent's head, saying,

The LORD JESUS CHRIST absolve and pardon thee, and by His authority committed to me I release thee from all spiritual censures which thou hast incurred, and restore thee to the office of a [. . . .] in the Church of GOD, in the Name, &c.

Benediction. CHRIST JESUS, King of kings, and LORD of lords, a Priest for ever after the order of Melchizedek, cause thine iniquity to pass from thee, clothe thee with change of raiment, send His Angel to stand by thee, and make thee a King and Priest unto Him for evermore.

THE ADMISSION OF A NOVICE INTO A BROTHERHOOD.

The Bishop or the Superior standing in front of the Altar, facing east, with the candidate kneeling on the lowest step, begins thus :

In the Name, &c.
Our FATHER, &c.

℣. The LORD, &c. ℟. And with, &c. ℣. Let us pray.

589. O GOD, Who turnest us from the vanity of the world, and kindlest us with desire for the prize of our high calling, and Who preparest mansions in heaven for them who renounce the world; enlarge the heart of this Thy servant with heavenly gifts, that he may be united with us in the bond of brotherly charity, that he may be of the same mind, steadfast, sober, guileless, and peaceable, may keep the rule of his Order, and by Thy help arrive at that perfection which he hath desired through Thine inspiration. Through.
℟. Amen.

Let us pray.

590. O LORD JESU CHRIST, our Captain, our Salvation, and our Strength, we humbly beseech Thee that as Thou hast separated Thy servant from the vanity of this world through the fervour of holy abhorrence of sin, so Thou wouldst also set him apart from worldly conversation, and bestow on him grace to persevere in Thee, that strengthened by the safeguard of Thy protection, he may fulfil through Thine assistance that which he desires through Thy gift, and that carrying out his devout resolution, he may happily attain to those things which Thou hast vouchsafed to promise unto them that persevere in Thee. Who livest.
℟. Amen.

Then shall the Officiant go to the Epistle corner, and standing there bless the Habit (if a special one be worn,) which shall lie on a side-table for that purpose.

℣. Our help, &c. ℟. Who hath made, &c. ℣. Blessed be the Name, &c. ℟. From this time forth, &c. ℣. O LORD, hear, &c. ℟. And let, &c. ℣. The LORD, &c. ℟. And with, &c. ℣. Let us pray.

591. O LORD JESU CHRIST, Who didst deign to put on the clothing of our mortality, we humbly beseech Thy boundless lovingkindness that Thou wouldst so vouchsafe to bl+ess and hal+low this Habit, the token of purity and of lowliness, that this Thy servant, who through pious devotion desires to put on the garb of holy religion, may be clothed with Thee within. Who livest.

The Girdle shall be blessed on this wise.

℣. Our help, &c. (*as before.*)

592. O GOD, Who to redeem the bondservant didst will that Thy SON should be bound by the hands of ungodly men, bl+ess, we beseech Thee, this girdle, and grant that Thy servant who is to be girt therewith may ever be mindful of the bonds of the same our LORD JESUS CHRIST, may alway persevere in the condition which he taketh upon him, and may unceasingly remember that he is ever bound to carry out Thy commandments. Through the same.

Then shall the Novice be led out to be clothed, the Officiant saying,

The LORD put off from thee the old man and his deeds.
℟. Amen.

On his return the Officiant shall say,

The LORD put on thee the new man, which after GOD is created in righteousness and true holiness.

Then he gives to the Novice a lighted Candle, saying,

Receive, dearly beloved Brother, the light of CHRIST, the token of thine immortality, that dead unto the world thou mayest live unto GOD. Arise from the dead, and CHRIST shall give thee light.

R/. Amen.

The Officiant, turning to the Altar, says,

V/. O LORD, save Thy servant. R/. Who putteth, &c. V/. Send him help, &c. R/. And strengthen him, &c. V/. Let not the enemy, &c. R/. Nor the son of wickedness, &c. V/. LORD, hear, &c. R/. And let, &c. V/. The LORD, &c. R/. And with, &c. V/. Let us pray.

593. We humbly beseech Thy Majesty, O LORD, that as we, trusting in Thy grace, have admitted Thy servant *N.* into this Brotherhood, so Thou wouldst vouchsafe to number him amongst Thy disciples, to clothe him with power from on high, to arm him with the breastplate of righteousness, and to cover him with the garment of salvation, that he may serve Thee perseveringly in lowliness, and attain the robe of immortality and glory.   Through.

Then all kneeling, the Veni Creator *shall be sung. This ended, the Officiant shall rise and say,*

V/. Stablish the thing, O GOD, which Thou hast wrought in us. R/. For Thy Temple's sake at Jerusalem. V/. The LORD, &c. R/. And with, &c. V/. Let us pray.

GOD, Who didst teach (*Collect for Whitsun Day.*)

V/. The LORD, &c. R/. And with &c. V/. Bless we the LORD. R/. Thanks be to GOD.

Benediction. The peace of GOD, &c.

THE PROFESSION OF A BROTHER.

The Bishop or Superior shall be seated before the Altar, and the Novice shall be caused to kneel before him : and the person who conducts the Novice shall say,

Reverend Father [in GOD], we present unto you this Novice, entreating you to admit him to Profession in the Brotherhood of *N.*

Officiant. Has he been duly elected?

Answer. He has been so elected.

Offic. Do you know him to be fit for his Profession?

Ans. I believe him to be fit.

Offic. If any one here present know of any cause or impediment why he should not be professed, let him now declare it.

If no impediment be alleged, he shall proceed, addressing the Novice :

Officiant. My son, what dost thou ask?

Novice. I ask the mercy of GOD, and leave to make my Profession in this Community.

Offic. Dost thou do so willingly and without constraint?

Nov. I do.

Offic. Hast thou studied the Rule and weighed the obligations which thou art about to take upon thee?

Nov. I have so done.

Offic. Dost thou promise faithful obedience in all things lawful to the Rule and to those set over thee by it?

Nov. I do so promise, GOD being my helper.

Offic. GOD, Who hath given thee a good will, give thee grace and strength to perform the same.

Then shall be sung the Veni Creator, *all kneeling.*

℣. When Thou lettest Thy Breath go forth they shall be made. ℟. And Thou shalt renew the face of the earth. ℣. Let us pray.

Prevent us, O LORD, &c.

Ant. O stablish me according to Thy Word, that I may live.

Ps. 15. LORD, Who shall dwell, &c. 133. Behold, how good, &c.

Ant. O stablish me according to Thy Word, that I may live: and let me not be disappointed of my hope.

LORD, have mercy, &c.
Our FATHER, &c.

℣. O LORD, save Thy servant. ℟. Who putteth, &c. ℣. Send him help, &c. ℟. And strengthen, &c. ℣. Let the enemy, &c. ℟. Nor the wicked, &c. ℣. Be Thou to him, &c. ℟. From the face, &c. ℣. Turn us again, &c. ℟. Show the light, &c. ℣. LORD, hear, &c. ℟. And let, &c. ℣. The LORD, &c. ℟. And with, &c. ℣. Let us pray.

594. O GOD, Who by Thy Co-eternal SON hast created all things, and hast vouchsafed through the mystery of His incarnation to renew the world grown old in sin; we pray Thee that Thou wouldst so vouchsafe to look upon this Thy servant our Brother *N.*, who hath resolved by a solemn vow at our hands to renounce to-day in this Thy holy temple the vanity of the world and the pomps of the devil, that renewed in the spirit of his mind he may put off the old man with his deeds, and put on the new man who is created after GOD. Through the same.

Let us pray.

595. O LORD JESU CHRIST, Who art the Way without which no man goeth to the FATHER; we humbly be-seech Thy mercy that Thou wouldst withdraw this Thy servant from fleshly desires, and lead him in the narrow and safe way of rule and discipline. And as Thou didst vouchsafe to call sinners, saying, Come unto Me all ye that labour and are heavy laden, and I will refresh you, grant that this voice of Thy calling may sound so loud within him, that laying down the burden of his sins, and tasting how sweet Thou art, he may be sustained by Thy consolation. Who livest.

Let us pray.

596. O HOLY SPIRIT, Who hast vouchsafed to reveal Thyself to mankind as GOD and LORD, we humbly beseech Thy lovingkindness that as Thou breathest where Thou willest, so Thou wouldst inspire the love of holy devotion in this Thy servant, our Brother *N.*, that as he is created by Thy wisdom, he may be ruled also by Thy providence, and that Thine anointing may teach him all things. Grant him to be so truly turned from the vanity of the world, that stablished in brotherly love he may of Thy help so righteously, devoutly, and godly fulfil with true humility and obedience what he begins to-day of Thine inspiration, that constantly persevering in his holy resolve he may obtain everlasting life. Through Thy mercy.

If there be a special Habit, it shall be blessed, as in the preceding Office.

597. Hearken, O LORD, to our supplications, and vouchsafe to bless this Thy servant, whom in Thy Holy Name we have clad in the Religious Habit, that of Thy grace he may persevere, devout and obedient, in his Community, and obtain everlasting life. Through.

598. We invoke Thee, O LORD, holy FATHER, Almighty, Everlasting GOD, upon this Thy servant, who hath vowed to serve Thee with a pure mind and clean heart, that Thou mayest vouchsafe to join him to those hundred and forty and four thousand who remain virgins, and in whose mouth is found no guile, and mayest cause him to remain without spot through Thine unspotted SON.   With Whom.

Then shall be said or sung the Te Deum.

℣. Stablish the thing, O GOD, which Thou hast wrought in us. ℟. For Thy Temple's sake at Jerusalem. ℣. The LORD, &c. ℟. And with, &c. ℣. Bless we the LORD. ℟. Thanks be to GOD.

Benediction. The peace of GOD, &c.

INSTALLATION OF THE SUPERIOR OF A BROTHERHOOD.

The Bishop, or other Officiant, shall sit in front of the Altar. The Senior Brother shall present the Superior-Elect to him, saying,

Reverend Father [in GOD], we present to you this our Brother *N.*, to be installed by you as Superior of the community of *M.*

Officiant. Hath he been duly elected according to the Rule ?

Answer. He hath been so elected.

Offic. Have you the schedule of election in writing ?

Ans. We have.

Offic. Read it.

This having been done, the Officiant shall proceed :

Officiant. We think it fit that he should first be examined as to his willingness to undertake and his fitness to discharge the duties of the office.

N., thou hast been elected to the Office of Superior of the Community of *M.*, art thou willing to undertake its duties ?

Superior-Elect. I am willing.

Offic. Dost thou promise to observe the Rule of thy Community, and to instruct thy brethren to do the like ?

Sup.-El. I do so promise, GOD helping me.

Offic. Wilt thou be a faithful steward of the goods of thy Society, and employ them for the use of the brethren, the poor, and strangers ?

Sup.-El. I will do so, by the help of GOD.

Offic. Dost thou promise not to take any steps affecting the welfare of thy Community without the consent of the Chapter ?

Sup.-El. I do promise.

Offic. Wilt thou endeavour to restore whatever has become relaxed or impaired through neglect or mishap ?

Sup.-El. I will do so.

Offic. Dost thou promise to rule with equity and kindness, not by favour and harshness, but to set a good example to thy brethren ?

Sup.-El. I do so promise.

Offic. GOD give thee faith and constancy, that thou mayest fulfil and keep these things.

℣. The LORD, &c. ℟. And with, &c.

LORD, have mercy, &c.
Our FATHER, &c.

℣. O LORD, save, &c. ℟. Who putteth, &c. ℣. The LORD preserve thy going out and coming in. ℟. From this time, &c. ℣. The LORD keep thee from all evil. ℟. Yea, may the LORD keep thy soul. ℣. O LORD, arise, &c. ℟. And deliver, &c. ℣. The LORD, &c. ℟. And with, &c. ℣. Let us pray.

599. Grant, we beseech Thee, Almighty GOD, the gift of Thy grace unto Thy servant, whom we have chosen to the rule of souls, that of Thy bounty this our choice may be pleasing unto Thee.   Through.

Let us pray.

600. We beseech Thee, O Lord, mercifully look upon this Thy servant, and give him true knowledge, steadfast hope, right judgment, and holy doctrine, that being found meet to receive the grace of Thy benediction, he may without offence follow the footsteps of the Saints, and by his godly admonitions cause those under him to do the like, knowing that he who taketh upon him the rule of souls must in the Day of Judgment give an account of them all to our Lord Jesus Christ. Who.

Then shall be sung the Veni Creator, all kneeling.
Then the Bishop rising shall give him the Rule.

Receive the Rule given to thee to govern the flock entrusted to thee by God, according as He shall give thee strength, and so far as human frailty shall permit.

Then the Staff shall be blessed, if this have not been previously done.

℣. Our help, &c. ℟. Who hath, &c. ℣. Let us pray.

601. O God, the stay of man's weakness, bl✠ess this Staff, and let Thy merciful lovingkindness inwardly work in the life of this Thy servant what is outwardly figured thereby.   Through.

Giving the Staff into the hands of the Superior, the Officiant shall say,

In the Name of our Lord Jesus Christ receive the Pastoral Staff to keep the flock, and to give it back to the Shepherd of shepherds.

Then the Bishop shall put him in his seat, saying,

Blessed be the Lord thy God, Whose pleasure it is to give thee the seat of honour, and to bless thee for evermore.   The Lord add unto thee length of days and years of life, and let not His mercy and truth fail thee.

Let us pray.

602. O God, the Fountain of all good things, Who rewardest the progress of the just; grant, we beseech Thee, that Thy servant may perform all the office which he hath obtained, and show by good works that it hath been given him by Thee.   Through.

Then shall follow the Te Deum.

℣. Stablish the thing, &c.   ℟. For Thy Temple's sake, &c.

Then shall the Bishop pronounce this Benediction :

God of heaven bless thee. Christ, the Son of the living God, help thee, and preserve thy body in His service.
℟. Amen.
He enlighten thy mind, keep thine understanding, grant thee His grace for the profit of thy soul.
℟. Amen.
Deliver thee from all evil, defend thee with His right hand, help thee as He hath ever helped His saints, and bring thee to the kingdom of heaven.
℟. Amen.
And the blessing of God Almighty, the Father, the Son,✠and the Holy Ghost, defend thee now and for evermore.
℟. Amen.

CLOTHING OF A NOVICE IN A SISTERHOOD.

The Bishop, or some one in his stead, vested in alb, stole, and cope, shall stand in front of the Altar. The Postulant shall kneel at a fald-stool at the entrance of the Sanctuary, in a secular dress. The Mother and Sisters shall be ranged in their places according to seniority.

The Officiant, turning to the people, shall say,

℣. The LORD, &c. ℟. And with, &c. ℣. Let us pray.

Then, all kneeling, the following Litany shall be sung.

LORD, have mercy, &c.
CHRIST, &c. LORD, &c.

O GOD the FATHER, of Heaven,
> *Have mercy upon us.*

O GOD the SON, Redeemer of the world,
> *Have mercy upon us.*

O GOD the HOLY GHOST,
> *Have mercy upon us.*

O Holy TRINITY, One GOD,
> *Have mercy upon us.*

From pride and vain glory,
From disobedience and self-will,
From murmuring and impatience,
From all forms of selfishness,
From wavering in faith,
From hesitating in duty,
From turning back from after Thee,
From the invention of our own hearts,
From the snares of the devil,
From all bitterness and wrath,
From jealousy and envy,
From all sins of the tongue,
From impure thoughts, } *Deliver us, O JESU.*

From eye-service as men-pleasers,
From distrust and despondency,
From weariness in devotion,
From slothful habits of body and soul, } *Deliver us, &c.*

By the mystery of Thy Holy Incarnation,
By Thy Holy Nativity,
By Thy Cross and Passion,
By Thy Death and Burial,
By Thy glorious Resurrection,
By Thy wonderful Ascension,
By the coming of the HOLY GHOST, } *Save us, O JESU.*

That this Community may be blessed with the fulness of Thy Love,
That Thou wouldst prosper the work whereunto Thou hast called us,
For our Mother, and for all that are in authority under her,
That Thou wouldst direct their counsels for the good of us all,
For the Sisters and Novices here gathered into one,
That unity and love may be promoted amongst us,
That in quietness and confidence our strength may be shown,
That we may incite one another by a holy example,
That Thou wouldst cause our hearts to long after perfection,
For N., Thine handmaiden, who desires to join us,
That Thou wouldst accept her devotion and increase her love,
That she may grow in grace and in the knowledge of Thee, } *We beseech Thee to hear us, O JESU.*

That in all things she may take pattern by Thy most holy Life,

That Thou alone mayest be the end of her desires,

That Thou wouldst grant her grace to persevere unto the end,

That Thou wouldst bring us all unto life eternal,

That Thou wouldst cause us to see Thy glorious Countenance,

We beseech Thee, &c.

O Lamb of GOD, &c.,
Pour into our hearts the Spirit of love.

O Lamb of GOD, &c.,
Enlighten our minds with the Spirit of truth.

O Lamb of GOD, &c.,
Grant unto us the Spirit of peace.

LORD, have mercy, &c.
CHRIST, &c. LORD, &c.
Our FATHER, &c.

℣. Let Thy loving mercy come also unto us, O LORD. ℟. Even Thy salvation, according to Thy Word. ℣. Be unto us, O LORD, a tower of strength. ℟. From the face of the enemy. ℣. Let us pray for this Sisterhood. ℟. Peace be within its walls, and plenteousness within its habitations. ℣. O stablish us according to Thy Word, that we may live. ℟. And let us not be disappointed of our hope. ℣. Let us pray for *N.*, who desires to join us [*or* to make her profession amongst us]. ℟. O LORD, save Thine handmaid, who putteth her trust in Thee. ℣. Send her help from the Sanctuary. ℟. And strengthen her out of Sion. ℣. Let the enemy have no advantage over her. ℟. Nor the wicked approach to hurt her. ℣. Give Thine Angel charge over her. ℟. To keep her in all Thy ways. ℣. Let us pray for the faithful departed. ℟. Eternal rest grant unto them, O LORD, and Light perpetual shine upon them. ℣. LORD, hear our prayer. ℟. And let our cry come unto Thee.

Let us pray.

O GOD, Who turnest us from earthly vanity and kindlest us with desire for the prize of our high calling, and Who preparest mansions in the heavens for them that renounce the world; gladden the heart of this Thine handmaid with heavenly gifts, that she may be united with us in the bonds of sisterly love, that so being of one mind, steadfast, sober, single-hearted, and peaceable, she may constantly observe her Rule, and attain by Thy help to that perfection of spirit whose first beginning she has received of Thine inspiration. Through.

Then shall follow the Benediction of the Candle, in this wise :

℣. Our help is in the Name of the LORD. ℟. Who hath made heaven and earth. ℣. Blessed be the Name of the LORD. ℟. From this time forth for evermore. ℣. The LORD, &c. ℟. And with, &c. ℣. Let us pray.

603. O LORD JESU CHRIST, true Light which lighteth every man which cometh into the world, we beseech Thee to bl✠ess this Candle, and grant that she who beareth it may never walk in darkness, but may have the light of life. Through Thy mercy, Who, with the FATHER and the HOLY GHOST, livest.
℟. Amen.

Then the Officiant shall light the Candle, and place it in the hand of the Postulant, saying,

Receive, my daughter, this light, a type of the light that should be within thee, to drive away all the darkness of ignorance and sin, that illumined with the rays of divine wisdom and the fervour of the HOLY GHOST, thou mayest ever be united to JESUS CHRIST, the Bridegroom of the Church. Who.

If there be a Sermon, it shall follow here, the Postulant seating herself on a chair placed behind her faldstool.

The Sermon being ended, the Veni Creator *shall then be sung kneeling, after which the Superior and Assistant Superior shall lead the Postulant to the Officiant, before whom she kneels whilst he addresses her.*

My daughter, what dost thou desire?

Postulant. I desire the mercy of God, and admission to the Religious life and habit.

Officiant. Dost thou believe that thou art called by God to this estate, and not moved by self-will or fancy?

Post. I do so believe.

Offic. Dost thou promise to remain in the holy estate of chastity [*or widowhood*] during the time of probation?

Post. I promise so to do, God being my helper.

Offic. Wilt thou during the same time submit thyself faithfully to the Rule of this Community?

Post. By God's help I will do so.

Offic. Is it thy desire that thou mayest be found worthy to persevere unto the end in this thy calling?

Post. I do so desire.

Offic. God, Who hath given thee a good will, give thee grace and strength to perform the same.

The LORD put off from thee the old man with his works.

℟. Amen.

And clothe thee with the new man, which after God is created in righteousness and true holiness.

℟. Amen.

Then shall the Novice's Habit be blessed as follows.

Our help, &c.

604. O God, Who dost most faithfully promise and most surely bestow everlasting blessings, Who hast promised unto Thy faithful the garments of salvation and the robe of eternal joy; we humbly beseech Thy mercy, that Thou wouldst vouchsafe to bl+ess this Habit, betokening lowliness of heart and contempt of the world, wherewith Thine handmaiden is to be visibly put in mind of her holy resolve, that through Thy protection, she may keep that purity which she has received of Thy grace, and as Thou dost clothe her here with the garments of promise, so grant her to be clad with everlasting blessedness. Through.

605. O Almighty God, hearken to our prayers, and pour down the abundant rain of Thy bless+ing upon these garments, wherewith Thine handmaiden desires to be clad, and as Thou didst pour upon the skirts of Aaron's clothing the blessing of the precious ointment which flowed down from his head to his beard, so mayest Thou vouchsafe to bl+ess and sanc+tify these garments, and grant that they may be unto Thine handmaiden a sure protection, a token of her profession, a beginning of holiness, and a strong defence against all the darts of the enemy, that persevering in chastity, she may be enriched with a hundredfold reward.   Through.

The Bishop shall then deliver the Habit to the Postulant, saying,

Receive this Habit, that thou mayest wear it unspotted before the Judgment seat of our LORD JESUS CHRIST, to Whom boweth every knee of things in heaven and things in earth, and things under the earth, and Who liveth.

The Novice is then led out to be clothed in the Habit: the Sacristan meantime taking charge of her Candle: during her absence some of the Gradual Psalms shall be sung, as time may require, with this Antiphon:

For my brethren and companions' sake: I will wish thee prosperity.

The Novice returning, clad in her Habit, and having received the Candle, shall be again led to the Altar-step to be invested with the Girdle, Veil, and Cross, which shall be blessed as follows :

THE GIRDLE.

Our help, &c.

Let us pray.

O GOD, Who to set the bondservant free, didst will that Thy SON should be bound by the hands of ungodly men, bl+ess, we beseech Thee, this Girdle, and grant that Thy handmaid who is to be girded therewith may ever be mindful of the bonds of our LORD JESUS CHRIST, and feel herself to be evermore bound unto Thy service. Through.

The Officiant shall then deliver the Girdle to the Novice, who shall be assisted in putting it on by the Mother, or her deputy, the Officiant saying,

The LORD turn thy heaviness into joy and gird thee with gladness, that thou mayest give thanks unto Him for ever.

THE VEIL.

Our help, &c.

Let us pray.

606. We humbly beseech Thee, O LORD, that Thy merciful bless+ing may descend upon this vestment to be placed upon the head of Thy servant, and that it may be bles+sed, hal+lowed, spotless and holy. Through.

Receive the white veil, the token of inward purity, that thou mayest follow the Lamb without spot, and walk with Him in white. In the Name.

THE CROSS.

Our help, &c.

Let us pray.

607. Bl+ess, O LORD, we beseech Thee, and sanc+tify this Cross, that she who weareth it, persevering in Thy service, may by the Cross attain unto the Crown. Through.

The Officiant shall put the Cross round her neck, saying,

Receive the Cross of our LORD JESUS CHRIST, as a Novice of this Community. In the Name.

℣. The LORD, &c. ℞. And with, &c. ℣. Let us pray.

608. We humbly beseech Thy majesty, O LORD, that Thou wouldst vouchsafe to clothe amongst Thy disciples with power from on high this Thy handmaid, upon whom we, trusting in Thy grace, have bestowed the Religious Habit; fortify her with the breastplate of righteousness, and cover her with the garment of salvation, that serving Thee steadfastly in this lowly Habit she may attain the robe of everlasting glory. Through.

609. O Almighty GOD, Who hast hallowed woman by the birth of Thine Only-begotten SON, our GOD, from a Virgin after the flesh, and Who hast given the grace and visitation of Thy HOLY SPIRIT not to men alone, but to women also; look now, O LORD, upon this Thy handmaid whom Thou hast called to devote herself unto Thy service. Send down upon her the rich gift of Thy HOLY SPIRIT, that continuing steadfast in the faith, she may fulfil her course in blameless conversation, according to Thy will. Of Thy mercy, O our GOD, Who art blessed, and livest, and reignest.

Then all shall rise, and the Mother and Sisters shall severally give to the Novice the Kiss of Peace, saying, " Peace to thee, Sister," the Choir in the mean time singing Ps. 133.

Behold, how good and joyful a thing it is : brethren, to dwell together in unity ! It is like the precious ointment upon the head, that ran down unto the beard : even unto Aaron's beard, and went down to the skirts of his clothing.

Behold, how good . . . . unity.

Like as the dew of Hermon : which fell upon the hill of Sion.

Behold, how good, &c.

For there the LORD promised His blessing : and life for evermore.

Behold, how good, &c.

℣. Glory, &c. ℞. As it was, &c. Behold, how good, &c.

℣. Stablish the thing, O LORD, which Thou hast wrought in us. ℞. For Thy Temple's sake at Jerusalem.

Benediction. GOD, the SON of GOD, make thee to be glad and to rejoice with all thine heart, O daughter of Jerusalem, and cast out thine enemy, so that thou shalt not see evil any more.

The peace of GOD, &c.

FORM FOR THE PROFESSION OF A SISTER.

The Bishop is to be seated in a chair in front of the Altar. The Sisters and Novices, either in their places in the Choir, or coming towards the Altar in procession, shall sing the following Antiphon and Psalm :

Ant. Behold the Bridegroom cometh.

Ps. 84. O how amiable.

Ant. Behold the Bridegroom cometh : go ye out to meet Him.

Then the Novice who is to be professed shall kneel at the entrance of the Sanctuary, and the Chaplain shall address the Bishop :

Right Reverend Father in GOD, the Community of S. —— and especially the Mother Superior, beseech you to bless and consecrate this devout woman, and admit her to full profession.

Bishop. Are you satisfied of her fitness and vocation ?

Priest. So far as human frailty and man's knowledge allow, I believe her to be fit.

Then the Bishop shall address the Superior.

Have you and the Chapter of your Community, consented that this Novice should make her profession amongst you ?

Superior. We have so consented.

Then the Bishop, addressing the Novice, shall say,

My daughter, what dost thou ask ?

Novice. The mercy of GOD, and liberty to make my profession in the Community of *N.*

Bishop. Dost thou ask this of thine own free will, and not of constraint ?

Nov. I do.

Bishop. Hast thou carefully studied the Rule of this Community, and duly weighed the obligations it would impose upon thee ?

Nov. I have so done.

Bishop. Dost thou truly and firmly believe that thou art called by GOD to this life, and art not influenced by passing fancy or caprice ?

Nov. I do so believe.

Bishop. Dost thou promise to remain henceforth in the holy estate of chastity [*or* widowhood] ?

Nov. I do so promise, by the help of GOD.

Bishop. Dost thou promise to [remain in a state of poverty, and to] practise obedience to thy Rule, and to those set over thee by it?

Nov. I do promise, GOD being my helper.

Bishop. Dost thou promise to devote every faculty of soul and body to GOD's service for ever?

Nov. I do promise, GOD being my helper.

Bishop. GOD grant thee perseverance in thy holy resolve, and vouchsafe of His mercy to bring it to good effect. In the Name.

Then shall follow the Litany as in the Office for Clothing a Novice, to the end of the Preces (see pp. 298, 299). After which shall be sung the Veni Creator, *all kneeling.*
If the Habit for a Professed Sister be different from that of the Noviciate, the Bishop shall proceed to bless it according to the form on p. 300, and shall deliver it with the words there used. During her absence the Gradual Psalms shall be sung as before. But if the Habits be the same, the Bishop shall bless the Veil and Ring immediately after the Veni Creator *as follows:*

℣. Our help is in the Name of the LORD. ℞. Who hath made heaven and earth. ℣. The LORD, &c. ℞. And with, &c. ℣. Let us pray.

610. O GOD, Who for our sakes didst vouchsafe to assume the Veil of our flesh, bl+ess, we beseech Thee, and sanc+tify this Veil, that she who is to wear it may be clothed with Thy love here, and be made worthy of Thy vision hereafter. Who.

Receive this Veil, the token of purity and modesty, whereby may the HOLY GHOST come upon thee and the power of the Most Highest overshadow thee, that thou mayest at last with the wise Virgins be ready to enter in to the joyful marriage of the Lamb. Through the same.

The Novice, taking the Veil, is assisted by the Superior in arranging it, saying at the same time,

The LORD hath clad me with a vesture of gold, and adorned me with priceless jewels.

℣. Our help, &c. ℞. Who hath made, &c. ℣. The LORD, &c. ℞. And with, &c. ℣. Let us pray.

611. Creator and Preserver of the human race, Giver of every spiritual benediction, Author of eternal Salvation, bl+ess, O LORD, we beseech Thee, and sanc+tify this Ring, that she who is to wear it may be fortified with heavenly virtue, may retain the faith undefiled, may persevere in every good resolution, and may inherit Thine everlasting kingdom. Through.

The Bishop shall then place the Ring on the fourth finger of the Novice, saying,

Receive the Ring of Faith, the Pledge of the HOLY GHOST, that thou mayest be called the Bride of GOD, and ever remain so from henceforth, and wear it in the Presence of the Lamb, thy Bridegroom, JESUS CHRIST, on the day of His heavenly marriage, if thou faithfully serve Him. In the Name.

Having received the Ring, the Sister shall say,

My LORD JESUS CHRIST hath betrothed me with His Ring, and adorned me as His Spouse with a Crown.

[The Garland of Flowers (which shall not be used for a widow) shall then be blessed as follows:

℣. Our help, &c. ℞. Who hath, &c. ℣. The LORD, &c. ℞. And with, &c. ℣. Let us pray.

612. Bl+ess, O LORD, this Garland, and grant, as we call upon Thy Name, that she who wears it may serve Thee faithfully, and receive in heaven that Crown which it typifies. Through.

Receive the crown of virginal dignity, that as thou art crowned by my hands on earth, so thou mayest also be a crown of glory in the hand of the LORD, and a royal diadem in the hand of thy GOD. Through.

Having received the Garland, the Sister shall say,

Henceforth there is laid up for me a crown of righteousness, which the LORD, the righteous Judge, shall give me in that day.]

℣. The LORD, &c. ℟. And with, &c. ℣. Let us pray.

613. Grant, we beseech Thee, Almighty GOD, that this Thy servant, who for the hope of an eternal reward hath desired to be consecrated to Thee, may remain firm unto the end of her life in this her holy resolution. Give her, O LORD, humility, chastity, obedience, charity, and plenteousness in good works, that she may attain everlasting life. Through.

The Sister shall then read aloud the Form of Profession according to the use of the Community, and shall sign her name thereto. This done, if it be so provided, she shall communicate.
Then the Sacristan shall put a lighted taper into her hand, and she shall kneel as before.

℣. The LORD, &c. ℟. And with, &c. ℣. Let us pray.

614. O LORD, mercifully look upon this Thine handmaid, that she may keep by Thy governance that holy resolution which she has made at Thine inspiration. Through.

℣. The LORD, &c. ℟. And with, &c. ℣. Lift up your hearts. ℟. We lift them up unto the LORD. ℣. Let us give thanks unto our LORD GOD. ℟. It is meet and right so to do.

615. It is very meet, right, and our bounden duty that we should at all times and in all places, give thanks unto Thee, O LORD, Holy FATHER, Almighty, Everlasting GOD. O LORD, Who graciously dwellest in the temple of pure bodies and lovest undefiled souls, mercifully look upon this Thy handmaid who has vowed her devotion and service unto Thee, and who beseeches Thine aid that she may be hallowed and stablished with Thy blessing, guarded and ruled by Thy protection, that the ancient enemy may in no wise prevail against her. Grant her by the gift of Thy HOLY SPIRIT modesty, wisdom, lovingkindness, gentleness, gravity, and prudence. Let her be fervent in charity, and love Thee above all things, live a praiseworthy life and not desire to be praised, glorify Thee in the sanctification of body and purity of soul. Be Thou her crown, her joy, her gladness, her comfort in sorrow, her counsel in doubt. Be her defence in suffering, her patience in trouble, her abundance in poverty, her food in fasting, her Physician and medicine in sickness. Grant her to keep that which she has vowed, and that she may please the Searcher of hearts, not in body only, but in soul. Admit her into the number of the wise virgins, that with oil ready and lamp burning she may await the heavenly Bridegroom, and untroubled at the sudden coming of the King may joyfully go forth to meet Him with the choirs of Virgins, and not be shut out with the foolish, but may be suffered to enter the King's gate with the wise Virgins, and abide in the perpetual fellowship of the Lamb, Thy SON our LORD. Through the same.

Then, turning to the newly professed, he shall pronounce this Benediction.

GOD, the FATHER, SON, ✠ and HOLY GHOST, bless thee with all spiritual benediction, that thou mayest abide incorrupt, inviolate, and spotless, after the example of

Blessed Mary, the Mother of our LORD JESUS CHRIST.

R̷. Amen.

The sevenfold Spirit of GOD rest upon thee, the Spirit of wisdom and understanding, the Spirit of counsel and might, the Spirit of knowledge and godliness, and the Spirit of the fear of the LORD fill thee.

R̷. Amen.

The LORD strengthen thy weakness, stablish thee in constancy of faith, confirm thee when· strong, uplift thee in His loving-kindness, keep thee in His mercy.

R̷. Amen.

He rule thy soul, direct thy ways, inspire holy thoughts within thee.

R̷. Amen.

He approve thy doings, perfect good works in thee, build thee up in charity, enlighten thee with wisdom, guard thee with chastity, teach thee with knowledge.

R̷. Amen.

He multiply thee with virtue, exalt thee in holiness, prepare thee for wisdom, subdue thee unto obedience, bring thee down in lowliness.

R̷. Amen.

He give thee strength to remain pure, guard thee in modesty, visit thee in weakness, lift thee up in pain, raise thee in temptation, keep thee in thy daily walk, restrain thee in prosperity, calm thee in anger, cleanse thee from all unrighteousness.

R̷. Amen.

He pour into thee His grace, pardon thine offences, grant thee His training, that stablished by these and the like virtues, and zealous in good works, thou mayest ever strive to do those good things which GOD counts worthy of an everlasting reward.

R̷. Amen.

Mayest thou have Him as witness Whom thou shalt have as Judge, and so study to prepare thyself that thou mayest carry a shining lamp in thine hand, and thus ready to enter the Bridegroom's chamber mayest go forth with joy to meet Him, that He may find in thee nothing foul, nothing stained, nothing corrupt, but a pure and snow-white soul in a shining and glorious body.

R̷. Amen.

Therefore when that awful day of the reward of the righteous and the punishment of the wicked cometh, let not the avenging flame find aught to burn in thee, but the loving-kindness of GOD somewhat to crown, in that thy devout conversation shall have purified thee altogether in this world.

R̷. Amen.

So that ascending to the Judgment-seat and the glorious palace of the King, thou mayest have thy portion with them that follow the Lamb, and who cease not to sing the new song, that there thou mayest have thy reward after toil, and ever abide in the land of the living, and He Himself bl✠ess thee from heaven, Who, by the Passion of His Cross on earth, vouchsafed to redeem mankind, JESUS CHRIST our LORD. Who.

Then the Sister shall rise, and the following Responsory shall be said or sung :

Choir. As the Bridegroom rejoiceth over the Bride : so shall thy GOD rejoice over thee.

Sister. He is my Beloved and He is my Friend : O daughters of Jerusalem.

Choir. Thy Maker is thine Husband : the LORD of Hosts is His Name.

Sister. My Beloved is mine and I am His : He feedeth among the lilies.

Choir. Hearken, O daughter, and consider, incline thine ear : forget also thine own people, and thy father's house.

Sister. My heart is inditing of a good matter : I speak of the things which I have made unto the King.

Choir. So shall the King have pleasure in thy beauty : for He is thy LORD GOD, and worship thou Him.

Sister. My soul doth magnify the LORD : for He hath regarded the lowliness of His handmaiden.

Choir. The King's daughter is all glorious within : her clothing is of wrought gold.

Sister. He shall give to mine head an ornament of grace : and a crown of glory shall He deliver unto me.

Choir. She shall be brought unto the King in raiment of needlework ; the virgins that be her fellows shall bear her company, and shall be brought unto Thee.

Sister. These are they that follow the Lamb whithersoever He goeth : and in their mouths was found no guile.

Choir. With joy and gladness shall they be brought : and shall enter into the King's palace.

Sister. The Lamb which is in the midst of the throne shall feed them : and shall lead them beside living fountains of water.

℣. Glory be, &c. ℟. As it was, &c. ℣. The LORD, &c. ℟. And with, &c. ℣. Let us pray.

LORD, have mercy, &c.
CHRIST, &c.   LORD, &c.
Our FATHER, &c.

℣. O LORD, save Thine handmaiden. ℟. Which putteth her trust in Thee. ℣. Be unto her a tower of strength. ℟. From the face of the enemy. ℣. Let not the enemy prevail against her. ℟. Nor the son of wickedness approach to hurt her. ℣. LORD, hear, &c. ℟. And let, &c. ℣. Let us pray.

616. O LORD GOD everlasting, Who hast mercifully redeemed both man and woman from the destruction of eternal death, through JESUS CHRIST Thy SON born of the Virgin Mary ; vouchsafe to bless with all spiritual benediction this Thine handmaid, who serveth Thee with devout mind, that she may keep her faith unbroken, ever persevere in the precepts of Thy law, despise earthly and temporal things, and with steadfast meditation love things which are unseen and eternal, that abiding in the number of Thy Saints she may faithfully go forth to meet her heavenly Bridegroom with the shining lamp of good works ; through His great mercy. Who liveth.

617. O GOD, Maker of body and soul, Who refusest no age, rejectest neither sex ; Who hast, moreover, promised a special crown to them who for Thy love embrace a special cross ; look upon this Thine handmaid. Arm her with the shield of Thy protection ; prepare her for every work of virtue and glory, to the end that refusing all earthly love she may be united to Thy well-beloved SON, our LORD JESUS CHRIST. Give her the invincible arms of Thy grace ; inspire her with the irresistible force of Thy love ; grant that the enemy may have no advantage over her, neither the son of wickedness approach to hurt her. Let the dew of Thy grace extinguish all worldly desires, the light of Thy love disperse all earthly darkness, the watchfulness of Thy mercy prevent every occasion of surprise. Grant her so to embrace poverty here that she may attain the City of Gold hereafter ; so to remain firm in chastity here that she may be one of the Lilies in Thy Paradise above : so to vow obedience here that she may be for ever an inhabitant of that Jerusalem which is free. Through.

Here shall follow the Te Deum, *unless this Office be used in the course of the Celebration of the Holy Eucharist, in which case it is sung just before the final blessing.*

Benediction. GOD the FATHER, GOD the SON, GOD the HOLY GHOST, bl✠ess and defend thee for evermore. He give thee the sevenfold Spirit of Grace ; He guard thee in temptation; He keep thee steadfast in adversity; He make thee watchful in prosperity; He cause thee to appear before Him not having spot, nor wrinkle, nor any such thing; He keep thy robe undefiled; He grant thee to enter the Eternal Palace, and to be the bride of the Eternal King. R̶. Amen.

The peace of GOD, &c.

The newly received Sister shall wear her veil [and coronal] during the remainder of the day.

INSTALLATION OF A MOTHER SUPERIOR.

The Bishop shall be seated in front of the Altar. The Chaplain of the Community, or other person appointed, shall present the Superior-Elect, attended by so many of the Sisters of the Community as can be present, to the Bishop, saying,

Right Reverend Father in GOD, the Community of *N.* entreats you by my mouth to affirm the appointment of Sister *M.* as Superior thereof, and to instal her with benediction.

Then shall the Bishop ask,

Has she been duly elected with the free consent of the Community?

Chaplain. She has been so elected.

Bishop. Produce the Schedule of Election.[1]

Then shall the Schedule of Election, signed by the requisite majority of the Electors in the Community, be delivered to the Bishop, who after examining it shall say,

If any of you know any just cause, either by defect in the election, or by unfitness for the office, for the which Sister *M.* should not be appointed as Superior of this Community of *N.*, I charge you that you do now declare it.

Then a pause shall be made, and if no objection be alleged, the Bishop shall proceed as follows :

My daughter, seeing that the grace of GOD, and the election of thy Sisters, have called thee to this office, we desire to know from thine own lips whether thou art willing to undertake it?

Superior-Elect. I am willing.

Bishop. Dost thou promise to observe thine own vows, and the Rules of thine House, and diligently to instruct those set under thee to do the like?

Sup.-El. I do so promise, by the help of GOD.

Bishop. Wilt thou be a careful and wise steward of the goods of thine House, and employ them for the use of the Church, of thy Sisters, of the poor, and of strangers?

Sup.-El. I will, GOD being my helper.

Bishop. Wilt thou observe lowliness and patience in thine own person, and teach others the like?

Sup.-El. I will, GOD being my helper.

---

[1] [FORM OF SCHEDULE.

We, the Sisters of the Community of *N.* assembled in free Chapter on —— [*such a day*] in —— [*such a place*] did then and there elect Sister *M.* to the Office of Superior of our Society [*or House*] for the term of —— years [*or for life*] without constraint, and of our own voluntary choice, believing her to be fitted for that office by reason of her piety, zeal, and discretion. And we do further testify that she received the necessary majority of votes required by the constitutions of our Society. In witness whereunto we have set our hands this —— day of —— in the year of our LORD ——

      (Signed)   A. B.
                 C. D.
                 E. F., &c.]

Bishop. Wilt thou always busy thyself in holy things, and avoid worldly occupation, so far as human frailty allows?

Sup.-El. I will, by the help of GOD.

Bishop. Wilt thou be courteous and gentle to the poor, and to strangers, and to all the needy, for GOD's sake?

Sup.-El. I will, GOD being my helper.

Bishop. Dost thou promise to decide no affairs which may affect the whole Community without the knowledge and assent of the Chapter?

Sup.-El. I do so promise.

Bishop. Wilt thou be strict in maintaining the discipline of the House, and in reforming whatever may have become relaxed or impaired through neglect or mishap?

Sup.-El. I will endeavour so to do, by GOD's help.

Bishop. Dost thou promise to rule by the law of kindness and equity, and not by favour and harshness?

Sup.-El. I do so promise, by the help of GOD.

Bishop. Dost thou promise to distribute all offices in the Community for the glory of GOD and the benefit of the House, and not by favour and partiality?

Sup.-El. I do so promise.

Bishop. Almighty GOD be thy helper in these and all other good things.

R̰. Amen.

Then shall the following be said, all kneeling :

℣. The LORD, &c. R̰. And with, &c. ℣. Let us pray.

LORD, have mercy, &c.
CHRIST, &c. LORD, &c.
Our FATHER, &c.

℣. O LORD, save Thine handmaiden. R̰. Who putteth her trust in Thee. ℣. The LORD preserve thy going out and coming in. R̰. From this time forth for evermore. ℣. The LORD preserve thee from all evil. R̰. And evermore keep thy soul. ℣. Send thee help from His holy place. R̰. And strengthen thee out of Sion. ℣. O LORD, arise, help us. R̰. And deliver us for Thy Name's sake. ℣. LORD, &c. R̰. And let, &c. ℣. The LORD, &c. R̰. And with, &c.

Let us pray.

618. Grant, we beseech Thee, Almighty GOD, Thy merciful help unto our prayers, and assist with the gift of Thy grace Thine handmaid whom we have elected to the rule of souls, that of Thy bounty we may, together with her, please Thee in whatsoever we do. Through.

Veni Creator.

Then shall the Bishop arise, and standing before the Superior-Elect, shall bless her as follows :

619. O LORD, hear our prayers, and pour the Spirit of Thy blessing upon this Thine handmaid, *M.*, that hallowed by Thy heavenly bounty, she may both attain Thy divine gifts, and be an example unto others in good works. Through.

Let us pray.

620. We humbly beseech Thine Almighty power, O LORD, that Thou wouldst graciously pour the gift of Thy benediction upon this Thy handmaid, whom Thou hast been pleased to call to an holy office, and bestow upon her such grace that she may under Thy guidance keep entire that which she receives. Through.

℣. The LORD, &c. R̰. And with, &c. ℣. Lift up your hearts. R̰. We lift them up unto the LORD. ℣. Let us give thanks unto our LORD GOD. R̰. It is meet and right so to do.

621. It is very meet, right, and our bounden duty, that we should at all times and in all places give thanks unto Thee, O LORD, Holy FATHER, Almighty, Everlasting

GOD. Hearken to our prayers and supplications, Thou Who wondrously orderest all things by the word of Thy might, Who always adornest Thy Church with divers flowers, in that Thou makest it bright with holy works and the lives of devout women, and Who hast been pleased, moreover, to unite to the number of Thy servants Thine handmaid *M.* Pour down upon her, whom we set apart, trusting faithfully in Thy divine confirmation, the grace of the HOLY SPIRIT, that her service may at all times be well-pleasing unto Thee, and vouchsafe to bless and hallow her for the noble work of Thy ministry with Thy right hand of power, that she may faithfully discharge the duty of her office, and may be strengthened by the might of the same sevenfold HOLY SPIRIT of grace. We pray Thee, O LORD, that there may rest upon her the Spirit of wisdom and understanding, the Spirit of counsel and strength, the Spirit of knowledge and godliness, and fill her with the Spirit of Thy fear. Grant her, moreover, gravity of conduct and strictness of life, that she may meditate on Thy law day and night, keep Thy commandments, obey Thy precepts, busy herself in devout reading, contemn worldly and temporal things, and at all times occupy herself in good works, overcome evil desires, be firm in her love of chaste purity, that she may meet with unquenchable lamp Thee her Bridegroom when Thou comest, and not be shut out with the foolish virgins, but be suffered to enter into the King's gate with the wise ones. Cause all virtue to abound in her. Let her be lowly in ruling, steadfast in modesty, innocent in purity, and observant in spiritual discipline. Let Thy precepts shine in her conduct, that by her example she may be a pattern for all those set under her, showing the testimony of a good conscience in sincerity, may abide firm and unshaken in CHRIST JESUS, and so

with Thy help discharge the office committed to her, that she may of Thy bounty attain an everlasting reward. Through the same.

Then shall the Bishop give the Rule and Keys of the House into her hands, saying,

Receive the Keys, the tokens of authority in this House, and the Rule of holy conversation, which brings with it blessing, that thou mayest through it appear unstained, with the flock entrusted to thee, before the LORD in the day of His awful judgment, and He vouchsafe to help thee, Who with the FATHER and the HOLY GHOST, liveth.

Then shall the Bishop proceed to bless the Pastoral Staff.

℣. Our help is in the Name of the LORD. ℟. Who hath made heaven and earth. ℣. The LORD, &c. ℟. And with, &c. ℣. Let us pray.

622. Almighty and merciful GOD, Who of Thine unspeakable goodness hearkenest to our supplications, and of Thine abundant loving kindness givest to us the desire to pray, plenteously pour the might of Thy bless✠ing upon this Staff which we dedicate in Thy Name, as a token of the pastoral office, that she who is furnished therewith may so diligently keep Thy people as to suffer none to stray from the unity of the Church, but may make whole that which is broken, stablish that which is shaken, and may keep herself together with her flock whole and undefiled for Thee. Through.

The Bishop shall deliver the Staff to the Superior-Elect, saying,

In the Name of our LORD JESUS CHRIST, receive the Pastoral Staff, to keep His sheep and to give them back to the Shepherd of shepherds. Amen.

Then shall he bless the Ring of Office.

Our help, &c.

623. O God, Creator of heaven and earth, and merciful restorer of mankind, Who givest all spiritual grace and blessing, and Who writest Thy holy Law in the hearts of believers with Thy finger, which is Thine Only-begotten Son; Bl✠ess, O Lord, and hal✠low this Ring, and send upon it Thy sevenfold Holy Spirit, that Thine handmaid, filled with Him, and pledged by the Ring of faith, may be kept without sin through the power of the most High, and that all the blessings of Holy Writ may plenteously descend upon her.   Through.

Then the Bishop adds,

Receive this Ring, the token of Faith, that thou mayest be called the Bride of the Holy Ghost, and so faithfully serve Him.   Through.

Let us pray.

624. Almighty, everlasting God, Who dost clothe them that are dedicated to Thee with the vestment of Thy service in this world, to the end that they may attain the robe of glory in the next; we pray Thee that Thou wouldst bestow on this Thine handmaid, whom in Thy Name we have received and blessed, and on whom we have invoked Thy mercy, all the graces that Thou requirest in a steward of Thine household. Make her, O Lord, patient as Sarah, faithful as Rebekah, courageous as Deborah; give her faith towards Thee, hope as concerneth Thy work, love towards her Sisters; grant that, in respect of this world, she may be a true Martha, labouring for Thee; as regards the next world, she may be a beloved Mary, kneeling at Thy Feet. Grant that in her that may be fulfilled which Thou didst foretell by Thy Prophet, the plenteousness of children which such as she is should offer to Thee; grant that she may be a blessing to this house, and that this house may be her title to reward at the Last Day.   Through.

625. O Lord God Almighty,

Who madest Miriam, the sister of Moses, leading the other virgins amidst the waters with timbrels and dances, to come in joy to the shore of the sea; we humbly entreat Thee for Thy faithful handmaid *M.*, who is to-day set on the Mother's seat over all those entrusted to her, that she may govern all Thine handmaidens with such godly rule as with Thy help to enter joyfully with all Thy saints into everlasting glory, and then, exulting with the angels and singing the new song, may follow whithersoever He goeth, the Lamb of God, Jesus Christ our Lord.   Who.

Then the Bishop shall put her into her seat, saying,

Receive full and free power of ruling this house and its Community, and all things spiritual and temporal which belong to its outer and inner government.

[*But if it be not in her own House, the Bishop shall say,*

Stand in righteousness and holiness, and keep the place committed to thee by God, for God is able to increase His grace in thee.]

Then shall be sung the Te Deum.

Benediction.

The merciful Lord grant thee such purity and gentleness, that never overcome by the evil one, thou mayest triumph in holiness over all evil things. R̷. Amen.

He grant thee, through prudence of spirit, to look down upon all the craftiness of carnal wisdom, and to show fitting honour and respect for the office which thou holdest under Christ our High Priest. R̷. Amen.

So that, with the centurion, by true confession of the Lord's power and of thine own lowliness, thou mayest through the steadfastness of thy faith obtain from Him the healing of all weakness in the household which is set under thee. R̷. Amen.

And the blessing of God, &c.

ADMISSION OF A DEACONESS.

The Candidate shall be presented to the Bishop 'by some Priest appointed for that purpose, with these words:

Right Reverend Father in GOD, I present to you this person to be admitted to the office and work of a Deaconess.

Bishop. Have you reason to believe her to be fit in body and mind, in zeal, piety, and perseverance, for the discharge of this office?

Priest. I believe her so to be.

Bishop. Dearly beloved, it belongeth generally to the office of a Deaconess to assist the Clergy in all such good works as shall be committed unto them; especially visiting and tending the sick and needy, teaching the ignorant, and taking order for the seemly maintenance of GOD's House, and of the things pertaining thereto. Art thou ready, of thine own free will, to undertake this work, and to give thyself faithfully thereto?

Candidate. I am ready, GOD being my helper.

Bishop. Wilt thou be obedient to them who are over thee in the LORD, cheerfully and faithfully performing the service that shall be appointed to thee?

Can. I will, by the help of GOD.

[If the Deaconess is to join a Community, the following questions may be added.

The Bishop shall ask the Superior of the Community, or her deputy:

Have you consented to admit *N.* into your Community?

Ans. We have so consented.

Then the Bishop shall ask the Candidate:

Wilt thou faithfully observe the rules of the Community, so long as thou remainest a member of it?

Can. I promise so to do.

Bishop. Wilt thou help thy Sisters in their work and labour of love? Wilt thou cultivate and preserve sisterly love towards thy fellow-helpers, and all others, and above all, endeavour to order thy life and conversation according to the doctrine of CHRIST, and to live in His faith and fear?

Ans. I will do so, the LORD being my helper.]

The Candidate shall then kneel in front of the Bishop, who shall pray as follows:

626. Almighty and everlasting GOD, Who hast hallowed women by the birth of Thine Only-begotten SON, our LORD, from a pure Virgin; look now, O LORD, on this Thine handmaid, call her to the work of Thy ministry, send down on her the rich gifts of Thy HOLY SPIRIT; keep her steadfast in the faith, and grant that she may always fulfil her office according to Thy good pleasure. Through.

The Bishop shall lay his hands on the head of each person to be made Deaconess, and say,

I admit thee, *N.*, to the office of Deaconess [and as Sister of —— Home], in the Name of the FATHER, and of the SON, and of the HOLY GHOST.

R⁊. Amen.

Then giving the Cross or Badge, the Bishop shall say,

Receive and wear this Cross [or Badge], a symbol of thy profession as a Deaconess. Be not ashamed to confess the faith of CHRIST crucified, and ever bear in thy heart the remembrance of His love Who died on the Cross for thee.

The Bishop shall then bless the Deaconess as follows :

GOD the FATHER, GOD the SON, GOD the HOLY GHOST bless, preserve, and sanctify thee, and so fill thee with all spiritual benediction and grace, with all faith, wisdom, and humility, that thou mayest serve before Him to the glory of His great Name, and to the benefit of His Church and people: make thee faithful unto death, and give thee the crown of everlasting life.

R⁊. Amen.

℣. Our help is in the Name of the LORD. R⁊. Who hath made heaven and earth. ℣. O LORD, bless Thine handmaid. R⁊. Who putteth her trust in Thee. ℣. Make her a clean heart, O LORD. R⁊. And renew a right spirit within her. ℣. Give Thine Angels charge over her. R⁊. To keep her in all Thy ways. ℣. O LORD, hear, &c. R⁊. And let, &c. ℣. The LORD, &c. R⁊. And with, &c. ℣. Let us pray.

Our FATHER, &c.

Let us pray.

627. Grant, O LORD, we beseech Thee, to Thine handmaid whom we have called to the office of Deaconess, the grace of perseverance in her ministry; bestow on her the gifts of wisdom and sound judgment, of simplicity and singleness of heart, of sympathy with those amongst whom she dwells and works, of ready obedience to all lawful rule and authority; of firmness when she herself is called to rule, and of courtesy and mildness towards all with whom she has to do. Be Thou, O LORD, her guide in all doubt, her support in weariness, and her comfort in sorrow, that Thou mayest be also unto her an exceeding great reward in the day of the revelation of Thine Only-begotten SON. To Whom with Thee and the HOLY GHOST, &c.

If the Holy Communion does not follow here, the Bishop may say,

Let us depart in peace.
Ans. In the Name of CHRIST.

ORDER FOR THE CONSECRATION OF A CHURCH.

The Bishop, attended by his Chaplains, and other officials and Clergy, shall vest in some building or tent near the Church. The petition for Consecration and other necessary legal documents, shall then be delivered to him. The Procession shall be formed and the following Antiphons, Psalms, and Prayers shall be sung, as they go to the Church.

Ant. But will GOD in very deed dwell with men on the earth?

Ps. 86. Bow down Thine ear, &c.

132. LORD, remember David, &c.

Ant. But will GOD in very deed dwell with men on the earth? Behold, heaven and the heaven of heavens cannot contain Thee; how much less this house which I have built!

LORD, have mercy, &c.
Our FATHER, &c.

℣. O LORD, show Thy mercy upon us. R⁊. And grant us Thy salvation. ℣. Be Thou unto us, O LORD, a strong tower. R⁊. From the face of the enemy. ℣. Not

unto us, O LORD, not unto us. R̷.
But unto Thy Name give the praise.
V̷. O LORD, save Thy servants. R̷.
Who put their trust in Thee. V̷.
LORD, hear, &c. R̷. And let, &c.
V̷. Let us pray.

Prevent us, &c.

628. O GOD, Who by Thy FA-
THER'S might didst burst the fiery
barriers of hell, and by Thy Blood
didst purchase unto Thyself a people for evermore; clothe us with
the spiritual arms of godliness and
the invincible power of the holy
Cross, to be our aid when in battle
against the devil, until we recover
Thine heritage for Thee from his
unrighteous grasp, and Thou Who
didst once come down in mercy to
the house of Zacchæus, vouchsafe
to come into this house also which
we are about to hallow, and enrich
with spiritual joy the people who
are assembled at its dedication, O
SAVIOUR of the world, LORD JESUS
CHRIST. Who livest.

Ant. It shall come to pass that
the mountain of the LORD'S house
shall be established in the top of
the mountains, and shall be exalted
above the hills; and all nations
shall flow unto it.

Ps. 48. Great is the LORD, &c.

Ant. It shall come to pass that
the mountain of the LORD'S house
shall be established in the top of
the mountains, and shall be exalted
above the hills; and all nations
shall flow unto it. And many people shall go and say, Come ye, and
let us go up to the mountain of the
LORD, to the house of the GOD of
Jacob; and He will teach us of
His ways, and we will walk in His
paths: for out of Zion shall go
forth the law, and the word of the
LORD from Jerusalem.

*The Bishop standing before the
Church door, and holding the Pastoral Staff in his hand, shall say,*

Let us pray.

629. Almighty, everlasting GOD,

Who art everywhere present, and
workest in all places throughout
Thy kingdom; hearken to our petitions, and as Thou hast founded this
House, so be now its Protector and
Defence. Let no rebel powers resist Thee here, but grant that by
the powerful working of the HOLY
GHOST there may be offered unto
Thee a pure service in godly freedom. Through.

Almighty and merciful GOD, Who
hast granted such grace unto Thy
Priests, that whatsoever they do
fitly in Thy Name is held as done
by Thee; we entreat Thy great
goodness that Thou wouldst visit
whatsoever we shall visit, and bless
whatsoever we shall bless, and grant
that as we enter this place in lowliness of heart, the evil spirits may
be put to flight, and the Angel of
peace enter in. Through.

*Then shall the Bishop strike three
times the threshold of the Church
door, saying,*

Lift up your heads, O ye gates,
and be ye lift up, ye everlasting
doors, and the King of Glory shall
come in.

The Deacon from within shall say,

Who is the King of Glory?

The Bishop replies,

It is the LORD, strong and mighty,
even the LORD mighty in battle. The
LORD of Hosts, He is the King of
Glory.

The Bishop shall then say,

Open.

*The Church doors shall then be
opened, and the Bishop, giving the
Pastoral Staff into the hands of
the Chaplain, shall receive a Cross,
and enter the Church, saying,*

Peace be to this house.

Ant. Blessed is He that cometh
in the Name of the LORD.

Ps. 122. I was glad, &c.

Ant. Blessed is He that cometh in the Name of the LORD: Hosanna in the highest.

Then the Bishop shall kneel at a faldstool in front of the chancel steps, the attendants kneeling on either side.

The Veni Creator *shall be said or sung.*

Then shall follow the Litany, said by one of the assistant Priests. After the Suffrage for the Holy Church Universal, the Bishop shall rise from his knees and say,

That it may please Thee to bless this place, and to give Thine Angels charge over it;

Ans. We beseech Thee to hear us, Good LORD.

Then stretching forth his hands to all parts of the Church, and making the sign of the Cross, he shall add,

That it may please Thee to bless and hallow this Church and Altar to be consecrated in Thine honour, and in the name of S. *N.*

Then shall the Bishop again kneel down, and the Litany proceed as before. At its close the Procession shall be again formed, and the Bishop, Clergy, and Choir, going round the Church, shall sing,

Ant. Thou shalt purge me with hyssop, and I shall be clean.

Ps. 51. Have mercy, &c.

Ant. Thou shalt purge me with hyssop, and I shall be clean : Thou shalt wash me, and I shall be whiter than snow.

Then the Bishop, returning to the faldstool, shall kneel, and say,

℣. The LORD, &c. ℟. And with, &c. ℣. Let us pray.

630. O GOD, Who hallowest places dedicated to Thy Name, pour forth Thy grace upon this House of Prayer, that Thy merciful help may be felt by all who call upon Thee here. Through.

631. O GOD, Almighty LORD of holiness, Whose lovingkindness hath no end ; O GOD, Who rulest heaven and earth alike, Who keepest Thy mercy for Thy people that walketh before the face of Thy glory ; hear the prayer of Thy servants, that Thine eyes may watch over this House day and night ; and of Thy great mercy hallow this Church, erected for holy mysteries in honour of the Blessed TRINITY, [and of S. *N.*,] enlighten it with Thy pity, glorify it with Thine own brightness, graciously accept and look upon every one who cometh to worship Thee in this place, and for Thy great Name's sake protect Thy suppliants in this house with Thy strong hand and Thy mighty arm ; hearken unto them, preserve them with Thine everlasting defence, that ever rejoicing and gladly trusting in Thee they may constantly persevere in the Catholic faith and in the confession of the Holy TRINITY. Through.

Then the Bishop shall ascend the Altar steps, and there shall follow,

Ant. I will go unto the Altar of GOD.

Ps. 43. Give sentence with me, &c.

Ant. I will go unto the Altar of GOD : even unto the GOD of my joy and gladness.

The legal instruments shall then be read aloud by the Chancellor, or Registrar, and shall be signed by the Bishop standing at the midst of the Altar. After signing, the Bishop shall direct them to be enrolled among the archives of the Diocese.

Then the Bishop shall say,

Dearly beloved brethren, let us

beseech the mercy of GOD the FATHER Almighty, that He, hearkening to our cry, may sanctify with His blessing this Altar now to be consecrated for spiritual sacrifices, that He may ever vouchsafe to bless and hallow the offerings of His servants placed thereon, in devout reverence for Him, and, well pleased with that spiritual incense, may be ready to hearken to His people, as they make their prayer through our LORD JESUS CHRIST. Who liveth.

℣. The LORD, &c. ℟. And with, &c. ℣. Let us pray.

632. O LORD, Holy FATHER, Almighty, gracious, and merciful GOD, we humbly beseech Thee that this Altar may be unto Thee as that on which Abel offered unto Thee the firstlings of his flock; let this Altar be unto Thee as that on which Thy High Priest Melchizedek foreshowed the form of our sacrifice, as that whereupon our father Abraham offered up his son, and as the stone which Jacob placed beneath his head, whereon he beheld the Angels ascending and descending. Through the same.

633. O GOD, Who, to hallow to Thyself Israel Thy firstborn people, didst show to Thy servant Moses a pattern of the tabernacle in Mount Sinai; mercifully bedew with the grace of Thy heavenly unction and consecration this Altar, set apart for celebrating the saving mysteries of redemption, that the offering thereupon, sanctified by Thy grace, may become the well-pleasing and sufficient sacrifice of the Body and Blood of our LORD JESUS CHRIST, and that the WORD made flesh may give us Himself in that Holy Offering, and become our everlasting Life. Through the same.

634. Almighty GOD, in Whose honour we Thine unworthy servants, invoking Thy Name, do consecrate this Altar; mercifully and graciously hearken to our humble petitions, bl+ess, hal+low, and sanc+tify it at our hands, and grant that the offerings on this Table may be acceptable and pleasing unto Thee, and be ever bedewed with the grace of Thy HOLY SPIRIT, that as Thy servants make their prayers to Thee in this place Thou mayest always relieve their distress, heal their sicknesses, hearken to their entreaties, accept their vows, confirm their desires, and grant their petitions. Through.

℣. Stablish the thing, O LORD, that Thou hast wrought in us. ℟. For Thy temple's sake at Jerusalem. Glory, &c. As it was, &c.

Then shall follow the Benediction of the Altar furniture, which has been previously placed on a side-table.

The Altar Cloths.

635. O LORD GOD Almighty, Who from the beginning hast created things useful and necessary to mankind, and hast willed that temples made with the hands of man should be dedicated to Thy Holy Name, and be called the places of Thy habitation; and Who by Thy servant Moses didst command vestments to be made for the High Priest, Priests, and Levites, and also other ornaments of divers kinds to deck and beautify Thy tabernacle and Altar; mercifully hear our prayers, and vouchsafe through our humble services to purify, bl+ess, hal+low, and con+secrate all these ornaments prepared for Thine honour and glory and for the use of Thy Church and Altar, that they may be meet for Divine Service and holy Mysteries, and for the ministration of the Sacrament of the Body and Blood of our LORD JESUS CHRIST. Who liveth.

[For the Cross, &c., p. 44.]

While the Altar is being vested, the Choir shall sing,

Ant. Awake, awake, put on thy strength, O Sion.

Ps. 45. My heart is inditing, &c.

Ant. Awake, awake, put on thy strength, O Sion : put on thy beautiful garments, O Jerusalem, the holy city.

The Corporal.

636. O most merciful GOD, Whose power is unspeakable, and Whose Sacraments are endued with wondrous might; grant, we beseech Thee, that this linen cloth may be hal+lowed by Thy gracious blessing, and be fitted for the consecration thereon of the Body of our GOD and LORD JESUS CHRIST Thy SON. Through the same.

The Paten.

637. Almighty and everlasting GOD, Who didst institute sacrifices under the Law, and didst among them command that fine flour should be offered on Thine Altar in gold and silver patens; vouchsafe to bl+ess, hal+low, and con+secrate this paten for the administration of the Eucharist of Thy SON JESUS CHRIST, Who for our salvation, and for that of all mankind, was pleased to offer Himself unto Thee, His FATHER, upon the Cross, and Who liveth.

The Chalice.

638. Vouchsafe, O LORD, our GOD, to bl+ess this Chalice, framed for the service of Thy ministry by the holy zeal of Thy servants, and pour down upon it that hallowing which Thou didst pour upon the holy cup of Thy servant Melchizedek, and grant that it, which neither art nor costliness can make meet for the service of Thine Altar, may be hal+lowed by Thy blessing. Through.

639. Almighty and everlasting GOD, pour, we beseech Thee, the aid of Thy blessing upon our hands, that this chalice and 'paten may be hal+lowed by our benediction, and through the grace of the HOLY SPIRIT may be made a new tomb for the Body and Blood of our LORD JESUS CHRIST. Who liveth.

Benediction of a Pyx, or Ciborium.

640. O LORD JESU CHRIST, Whom the heaven of heavens cannot contain, yet Who didst vouchsafe to make Thy tabernacle in the womb of a Virgin ; pour Thy benediction, we beseech Thee, upon this vessel, as a shrine for Thy Presence veiled under the form of Bread, which we now bl+ess, hal+low, and con+secrate, in the Name.

*If the Vestments be not all blessed together (as in **635**), the following Benedictions may be used singly.*

The Amice.

641. O LORD GOD Almighty, bl+ess, we beseech Thee, this Amice, and mercifully grant that whosoever places it upon his head may receive Thy blessing, be steadfast in faith, and stablished in holiness. Through.

The Alb.

642. O GOD, unconquered Author of might, Creator and hallower of all things, mercifully hear us and vouchsafe Thyself to bl+ess, hal+low, and con+secrate this Alb, and grant that all who use it and serve Thee in it devoutly and lovingly, may be worthy ministers of Thy Sacraments, and acceptable unto Thee. Through.

The Girdle.

643. Almighty, everlasting GOD, Who didst command Aaron and his sons to be girt about the loins with a girdle and belt in the priestly office ; hearken to our prayers, that all the ministers of Thy holy service, compassed with this girdle of righteousness, may strive and prevail to gird their loins with holy purity, that they may not fall into laxity or coldness, but rather by Thine aid may attain more and

more to be stablished and strengthened in that which is well pleasing
unto Thee. Through.

The Stole and Maniple.

644. O Lord Jesu, Son of the
Living God, gentle and merciful,
Who saidst with Thy holy and
blessed lips, Come unto Me, all ye
that travail and are heavy laden,
and I will refresh you, and ye shall
find rest for your souls, for My yoke
is easy, and My burden is light;
vouchsafe to bl+ess this Stole
and Maniple, which Thy servants
the Priests or Deacons are to wear
in token that they are bound to
Thy service, that they may feel as
they use them Thy yoke easy and
Thy burden light, and find rest
unto their souls, through Thee, O
Saviour of the world. Who livest.

The Chasuble.

645. O God, the Fountain of
lovingkindness and righteousness,
vouchsafe us, we beseech Thee, the
power and bless+ing of Thy grace,
that all those that are clad in this
Chasuble may be adorned within
with all virtues, and possess and
keep above all things the bond of
perfect charity, that they may offer
sacrifice well-pleasing unto Thee
for the living and the dead, and
may be able to attain that which
they desire with a devout mind,
through the bounty of our Lord
Jesus Christ. Who liveth.

*Then the Bishop and his Assistants
shall proceed to the Font, singing,*

Ant. The rivers of the flood thereof
shall make glad the city of God.

Ps. 46. God is our hope and
strength, &c.

Ant. The rivers . . . . . the holy
place of the tabernacle of the most
Highest.

Benediction of the Font.

646. Almighty God, hallow by
Thy heavenly visitation, and the
radiancy of Thy Holy Spirit, this
Baptistery [*or* Font], which we dedicate unto Thee, that whosoever
shall be laved in this Font [*or* here-
in], being cleansed by the three-
fold washing, may of Thy bounty
obtain the pardon of all their sins.
Through.

647. Multiply, O Lord, Thy
blessings, and by the gift of Thy
Holy Spirit, strengthen our faith,
that whoso goeth down into these
waters may be written in the Book
of Life. Through.

648. Almighty, everlasting God,
the Fount of all Virtues, and the
Fulness of Grace; vouchsafe by Thy
Divine Presence to hal+low this
Font prepared for Holy Baptism,
that we may feel Thee, Who art
everywhere present, to be especially
present here amidst our prayers,
and that whoso shall here receive
the benefit of the threefold Confession and of Holy Regeneration may
alway rejoice in the hope of everlasting gladness. Through.

*Then they shall proceed to the Pul-
pit, saying,*

Ant. I will talk of Thy commandments.

Ps. 119 (9—16.) Wherewithal,
&c.

Ant. I will . . . . . and have respect unto Thy ways.

Benediction of the Pulpit.

649. O Almighty God, Who dost
enlighten the minds of Thy servants
with the knowledge of Thy truth;
bl+ess, we beseech Thee, this pulpit, and give unto those who shall
stand therein the spirit of wisdom
and understanding, of counsel and
might, that they may speak those
things which belong unto eternal
life; and grant that Thy people,
taught in Thy ways, may so take
heed what they hear, as to fulfil all
wholesome precepts delivered to
them, so that by the word of truth
they may at length attain unto Him

Who is the Way, the Truth, and the Life, and Who liveth.

Then shall the Bishop return to the Altar, and standing at the entrance to the Sanctuary shall add the following prayers.

For Penitents.

650. Grant, O LORD, to Thy people, when they have sinned and turn again unto Thee, and confess, and pray, and make supplication unto Thee in this house, that they may be washed clean in the Blood of the Lamb and be justified by faith in our LORD JESUS CHRIST. Who liveth.

For those to be Confirmed.

651. O GOD, Who gavest the HOLY SPIRIT unto Thine Apostles, and didst will that, by them and their successors, He should be communicated to the rest of the faithful; mercifully accept our humble petitions, and grant that the same HOLY SPIRIT may come unto all who shall be here admitted to the Rite of Confirmation, and vouchsafe to dwell in them, making them a temple of His glory. Through.

For those to be Married.

652. Almighty and everlasting GOD, Who in the beginning of the creation, when Thou didst make man, in Thine own image, didst frame woman also out of his side to be his inseparable helpmeet, thereby teaching us that, as they were one at the first, so they should never be parted; and Who by this wonderful mystery didst in the marriage tie foreshadow the union between CHRIST and the Church; Thou in Whose hand alone is the power of the heart, Who so joinest that no man can put asunder, and so blessest that no man can curse; grant, we beseech Thee, that those united here in the Sacrament of Matrimony may be so truly joined together by Thy grace in heart and affection, that as Thou only art truly One and Almighty, so they may be one in Thee, loving, faithful, and chaste; see their children's children unto the third and fourth generation, and after a happy old age attain to the rest of the blessed and the kingdom of heaven. Through.

Almighty GOD, Who hast promised to hear the petitions of them that ask in Thy SON'S Name; we beseech Thee mercifully to incline Thine ears to us that have made now our prayers and supplications unto Thee; and grant, that those things, which we have faithfully asked according to Thy will, may effectually be obtained, to the relief of our necessity, and to the setting forth of Thy glory; through JESUS CHRIST our LORD.

The Bishop (holding the Pastoral Staff in his left hand) advancing to the entrance of the Church, and standing in the midst, facing the people, shall say,

By the authority committed unto us in the Church of GOD, we dedicate and set apart for ever, from all common and profane uses, this House, and whatsoever therein is consecrated by our prayer and benediction, for the ministration of the holy service and mysteries of the Church of GOD. And we hereby declare this House to be hallowed and consecrated, in the Name, &c.

℣. The LORD, &c. ℟. And with, &c. ℣. Stablish the thing, O LORD, that Thou hast wrought in us. ℟. For Thy temple's sake at Jerusalem.

Benediction. GOD, the Fountain and Source of blessing, fill you, gathered together in this House at the Festival of Dedication, with all wisdom and spiritual understanding, preserve in you soundness of faith, steadfastness of hope and charity, persevering unto the end with holy patience; hearken unto your prayers here and in all places, blot out your sins, drive afar your enemies, and bring you after this

Feast to the unending Festival of the Church above.

R̶̷. Amen.

Then shall follow the Holy Eucharist with the proper Collect, Epistle, Gospel, and Preface, as below. On the day of Consecration Mattins shall in no case be said, but the Proper Psalms, Lessons, and Hymns may be used during the other days of the Octave.

Introit. How dreadful is this place : this is none other than the house of GOD, and this is the gate of heaven.

Ps. xciii. 1. The LORD is King, and hath put on glorious apparel : the LORD hath put on His apparel, and girded Himself with strength. Glory, &c. As it was, &c.

How dreadful.

Collect.

653. O GOD, Who invisibly containest all things, and yet for the salvation of mankind showest forth visibly the tokens of Thy power; enlighten this Church with Thy mighty indwelling, and grant that whosoever shall come hither to make their prayer, in whatever trouble they cry unto Thee, may obtain the blessing of Thy consolation. Through.

Epistle. Rev. xxi. 2—5.

And I John saw the holy city, new Jerusalem, coming down from GOD out of heaven, prepared as a bride adorned for her husband. And I heard a great voice out of heaven saying, Behold, the tabernacle of GOD is with men, and He will dwell with them, and they shall be His people, and GOD Himself shall be with them, and be their GOD. And GOD shall wipe away all tears from their eyes ; and there shall be no more death, neither sorrow, nor crying, neither shall there be any more pain : for the former things are passed away. And He

that sat upon the throne said, Behold, I make all things new.

Gradual. Them will I bring to My holy mountain, and make them joyful in My house of prayer.

℣. Their burnt-offerings and their sacrifices shall be accepted upon Mine Altar ; for Mine house shall be called an house of prayer for all people. Alleluia, Alleluia.

℣. Blessed art Thou, O LORD, in the temple of Thine holy glory ; and to be praised and glorified above all for ever. Alleluia, Alleluia.

Sequence. (*People's Hymnal,* 310.)

" Fair Sion's feast is ready."

Gospel. S. Matt. xxi. 10—17.

And when He was come into Jerusalem, all the city was moved, saying, Who is this? And the multitude said, This is JESUS the prophet of Nazareth of Galilee. And JESUS went into the temple of GOD, and cast out all them that sold and bought in the temple, and overthrew the tables of the money-changers, and the seats of them that sold doves, and said unto them, It is written, My house shall be called the house of prayer ; but ye have made it a den of thieves. And the blind and the lame came to Him in the temple ; and He healed them. And when the chief priests and scribes saw the wonderful things that He did, and the children crying in the temple, and saying, Hosanna to the Son of David ; they were sore displeased, and said unto Him, Hearest Thou what these say? And JESUS saith unto them, Yea ; have ye never read, Out of the mouth of babes and sucklings Thou hast perfected praise? And He left them, and went out of the city into Bethany ; and He lodged there.

Or, S. Luke xix. 1—10.

And JESUS entered and passed through Jericho. And behold,

there was a man named Zacchæus, which was the chief among the publicans, and he was rich. And he sought to see JESUS who He was; and could not for the press, because he was little of stature. And he ran before, and climbed up into a sycomore tree to see Him: for He was to pass that way. And when JESUS came to the place, He looked up, and saw him, and said unto him, Zacchæus, make haste, and come down; for to-day I must abide at thy house. And he made haste, and came down, and received Him joyfully. And when they saw it, they all murmured, saying, That He was gone to be guest with a man that is a sinner. And Zacchæus stood, and said unto the LORD, Behold, LORD, the half of my goods I give to the poor; and if I have taken any thing from any man by false accusation, I restore him fourfold. And JESUS said unto him, This day is salvation come to this house, forsomuch as he also is a son of Abraham. For the Son of Man is come to seek and to save that which was lost.

Offertory. As for me, in the uprightness of mine heart I have willingly offered all these things; and now I have seen with joy Thy people, which are present here, to offer willingly unto Thee.

Hymn. (*People's Hymnal,* 307.)
" O GOD, Who lovest to abide."

Secret.

654. Almighty, everlasting GOD, hallow with Thy heavenly might and benediction this Church and Altar dedicated to Thy Name, and show forth Thy bountiful help to all who put their trust in Thee, that here they may obtain the grace of Thy Sacraments and answers to their prayers. Through.

Proper Preface.

Who enlightenest this Church, dedicated to Thy Name, and sendest it from heaven to earth, adorned with mystical virtues. For this, O LORD, is the mother of the living, the life and salvation of those that believe in Thee. This is the Bride of Thy Lamb, decked with His own wondrous glory, for whose sake, O most merciful FATHER, Thine Only-begotten endured the Cross and conquered the adversary. Wherefore she, now set on Thy right hand in the heavenly places, and adorned with the righteousness of her citizens, ceases not to invoke Thy Majesty in the three-fold hymn. Therefore, &c.

Post-Communion Collect.

655. We beseech Thee, Almighty GOD, open Thy merciful ears unto all who seek Thee in this place which we, Thine unworthy servants, have dedicated to Thy Name. Through.

656. O GOD, Who preparest for Thy Majesty an everlasting habitation of living and elect stones; assist Thy people, humbly entreating Thee, that this Church may be profitable unto us, not only for bodily convenience, but for spiritual benefits. Through.

Te Deum.

CONSECRATION OF A CEMETERY.

The Bishop, with the Ministers, Clerks, and people, shall make the circuit of the Cemetery, singing,

Ant. Thou shalt purge me with hyssop, and I shall be clean.

Ps. 51. Have mercy, &c.

Ant. Thou shalt purge me with hyssop, and I shall be clean : Thou shalt wash me, and I shall be whiter than snow.

If the circuit of the Cemetery occupy more time, others of the Penitential Psalms may be added. Then the Bishop, kneeling down at a faldstool placed in the centre of the Cemetery, and facing east, shall sing the Litany, with the following suffrage (said standing), after that for the Church Universal.

That it may please Thee to bl+ess, hal+low, and con+secrate this Cemetery ;

Ans. We beseech Thee, &c.

The Litany may be concluded at this point; the Bishop continuing as follows :

LORD, have mercy, &c.
CHRIST, have mercy, &c.
LORD, have mercy, &c.

Let us pray.

657. O GOD, Creator of the world, Redeemer of mankind, absolute Ruler of all creatures visible and invisible ; we humbly and devoutly beseech Thee that Thou wouldst vouchsafe to purify, hallow, and bless this Cemetery, wherein the bodies of Thy servants and handmaidens are to rest after the brief course of this life, and as Thou hast granted of Thy great mercy remission of all their sins to them who put their trust in Thee, bestow likewise perpetual consolation on their bodies which rest in this Cemetery, and await the trump of the Archangel. Through.

Ant. The LORD hath said, I will bring My people again, as I did from Basan.

Ps. 68. Let GOD arise, &c.

Ant. The LORD hath said, I will bring My people again, as I did from Basan : Mine own will I bring again, as I did some time from the deep of the sea.

LORD, have mercy, &c.
CHRIST, have mercy, &c.
LORD, have mercy, &c.

Then the Bishop, turning to the west, shall say,

Let us pray.

658. O LORD, Holy FATHER, Triune Majesty and one Godhead, FATHER, SON, and HOLY GHOST, Author of Righteousness, Bestower of pardon, Giver of good things, Fount of holiness, Distributor of graces ; Who dost lovingly welcome all who come unto Thee ; mercifully grant that this Cemetery, set apart in Thine honour [and in the name of Thy Saint *N.*], may be blessed and sanctified, as Thou didst bless the ground purchased for a burial place from the children of Heth, by Thy servant blessed Abraham the Patriarch ; and as Thou gavest the land of promise unto Thy people Israel, so of Thy gracious bounty grant a quiet abode and safety from all attack of evil spirits to the bodies of Thy servants and handmaidens, which come into this Cemetery, that after the resurrection of their souls and bodies they may obtain everlasting blessedness, of Thy bounty. Who livest.

Ant. He shall defend thee under His wings.

Ps. 91. Whoso dwelleth, &c.

Ant. He shall defend thee under His wings, and thou shalt be safe under His feathers.

LORD, have mercy, &c.
CHRIST, have mercy, &c.
LORD, have mercy, &c.

Then the Bishop, turning to the south, shall say,

Let us pray.

659. O LORD GOD, Shepherd of everlasting Glory, Light and Honour of wisdom, Guardian and Might of prudence, Help of the sick, Power of the strong, Comfort of the sad, Boast of the lowly; we humbly beseech Thee to bl+ess this Cemetery of Thy servants, and to guard and purify it from all defilement and craft of evil spirits, and grant that the bodies which are brought into this place may remain undisturbed; that whoso have received the Sacraments, have persevered in the Catholic faith, and at the end of this life have been laid to rest in this Cemetery, may have here of Thy bounty a peaceful habitation for their bodies, till on the day of judgment, at the Angelic summons, Thou biddest their souls and bodies together rise from the dust, and join the Saints on Thy right hand. Through.

Ant. Thou art my Hope and my portion.

Ps. 142. I cried unto the LORD, &c.

Ant. Thou art my Hope and my portion in the land of the living.

LORD, have mercy, &c.
CHRIST, have mercy, &c.
LORD, have mercy, &c.

Then the Bishop, turning to the north, shall say,

660. Almighty GOD, Who art the Keeper of the bodies and souls of Thy faithful; mercifully look upon our humble service, that at our coming in, this Cemetery may be puri+fied, bless+ed, hal+lowed, and con+secrated, so that the bodies of men which rest here in Thee may, after the troubles of this life, attain unto the joys of life everlasting. Through.

℣. The LORD, &c. ℟. And with, &c. ℣. Lift up your hearts. ℟. We lift them up unto the LORD. ℣. Let us give thanks unto our LORD GOD. ℟. It is meet and right so to do.

Bishop. It is very meet, right, and our bounden duty, that we should at all times, and in all places, give thanks unto Thee, O LORD, Holy FATHER, Almighty, Everlasting GOD, through CHRIST our LORD, Who is the Everlasting, unwaning Day, the Eternal Glory, Who commanded His followers so to walk that they may escape the darkness of everlasting night, and come happily to the land of brightness, Who, in the Manhood which He took upon Him, wept over Lazarus, and by the power of His Godhead restored him to life, and Who brought to salvation mankind, which had been crushed under the fourfold weight of sin : through Whom we humbly beseech Thee, O LORD, that they who are buried in this Cemetery may at the last day, when the trump of the Angels shall sound, be loosed from the chains of their sins, be restored to everlasting bliss, be numbered in the assembly of the Saints, may find Thee, Who art the Everlasting Life, gracious and merciful, and joyfully praise Thee with all Thine Elect for evermore. Who livest.

Ant. Let my prayer be set forth in Thy sight.

Ps. 141. LORD, I call upon Thee, &c.

Ant. Let my prayer be set forth in Thy sight as the incense.

℣. The Lord, &c. ℟. And with, &c. ℣. Let us pray.

661. Assist us, we beseech Thee, O Lord God, in our office and ministry as we visit this place, and as Thou didst bless the land of burial by the hands of our fathers, Abraham, Isaac, and Jacob; and afterwards, betrayed for our salvation, scourged and crucified, Thou didst Thyself hallow the earthly sepulchre which Joseph made ready for Thee; so now vouchsafe to bl+ess, hal+low, and con+secrate this Cemetery, and defend it from the snares of our unseen enemies, that all they whose bodies rest here after the toils of life may obtain the reward of everlasting blessedness, of Thy mercy, O Saviour of the world. Who.

662. O Lord Jesu Christ, Who hadst compassion on the widow of Nain, and saidst unto her, Weep not, and Who, by Thine Apostle, didst bid us not to be sorry as men without hope for those that sleep in Thee; visit, we pray Thee, with Thy compassion all who mourn here, and wipe away all tears from their eyes. Who livest.

The Bishop shall then give the Blessing, and with the Choir return to the Church, singing Psalm 130, *Out of the deep, &c.*

REOPENING OF A CHURCH.

The parts in [ ] shall be used when the Church has been desecrated.

The Bishop, Clergy, and Choir, after vesting in the Parsonage or other convenient place, shall go in procession to the Church, singing Ps. 48 with the following Antiphon:

Ant. Lord, I have loved the habitation of Thine House.

Ps. 48. Great is the Lord, &c.

Ant. Lord, I have loved the habitation of Thine House, and the place where Thine honour dwelleth.

On arriving at the Church door the Bishop shall say,

Peace be to this House, and to all that dwell therein; peace be to them that come in, and to them that go out. Alleluia.

Let us pray.

Almighty and merciful God, Who hast granted such grace unto Thy Priests that whatever they do fitly in Thy Name is held as done by Thee; we entreat Thy great goodness that Thou wouldst visit whatsoever we shall visit, and bless whatsoever we shall bless, and grant that, as we enter this place in lowliness of heart, the evil spirits may be put to flight, and the angel of Peace enter in. Through.

[Take away from us, O Lord, we beseech Thee, our iniquities, that we may with pure minds enter into Thy House to purify and reconcile it. Through.]

As the procession passes up the Church, Psalm 51 *shall be sung.*

Ant. Thou shalt purge me with hyssop, and I shall be clean.

Ps. 51. Have mercy upon me, &c.

Ant. Thou shalt purge me with hyssop, and I shall be clean, Thou shalt wash me, and I shall be whiter than snow.

The Bishop shall then kneel at a faldstool placed outside the screen, while the Litany is said or sung. After the suffrage for the Church universal the Bishop shall rise, and holding his pastoral staff with his left hand, and making the sign of the Cross with his right, shall say,

That it may please Thee to accept this our service and offering in the restoration and adornment of Thy House;
[That it may please Thee to purify, recon+cile, hal+low, and con+secrate this Church and Altar;]
Ans. We beseech Thee, &c.

*The Precentor may omit the remainder of the suffrages, continuing the Litany at "*O Son of God,*" &c.*
Before the Prayer of S. Chrysostom the following prayer may be inserted.

663. O God, Whose goodness hath neither beginning nor end, Whose property is to purify that which is defiled, to restore that which hath been neglected, and to rebuild that which is decayed; vouchsafe to hear our prayers, that Thou wouldst graciously receive this Church, and hallow by the outpouring of Thy heavenly grace, whatsoever in it has been defiled by the craft of our adversary the devil, and keep it pure from all stain, by Thine unspeakable loving-kindness for evermore.   Through.

At the conclusion of the Litany the Procession shall again be formed, and the Bishop, Clergy, and Choir, passing round the aisles of the Church, shall sing as follows :

Ant. Though ye have lien among the pots, yet shall ye be as the wings of a dove.
Ps. 68. Let God arise, &c.
Ant. Though ye have lien among the pots, yet shall ye be as the wings of a dove, that is covered with silver wings, and her feathers like gold.

When the Clergy and Choir have returned to their former position, the Bishop, standing at the fald-stool, the rest kneeling, shall say,

℣. The Lord, &c. ℟. And with, &c.   ℣. Let us pray.

664. O God, Who didst create man in Thine own Image, and, through the coming of our Lord Jesus Christ in the Flesh, didst restore that Image when defaced by the sin of our first parents; look graciously, we beseech Thee, on this Thy holy place, which we have re-edified and adorned anew to the glory of Thy Name.   Remember us, O our God, concerning this, and wipe not out our good deeds that we have done for Thy House and for the Offices thereof. Through.

[*If the Church have been used by schismatics, the following may be added.*

665. O Almighty God, Who in chastisement for our sins and for the more trial of our faith dost suffer heresies and schisms to rise up amongst us, whereby the peace of Thy Household hath been sorely disturbed; grant that this place, wherein heretofore some have walked disorderly, and not after the tradition which they have received from the fathers, may be henceforth preserved for the purity of Thy service, and that they who worship herein, keeping the unity of the Spirit in the bond of peace, may by Thy Presence be hidden from the provoking of all men, and be kept in Thy Tabernacle from the strife of tongues.   Through.]

[*If blood hath been shed in the Church, either by accident or otherwise, the following prayer shall be used.*

666. O God, Who hast permitted this Thy holy place to be defiled with blood, as Thou didst suffer Thy temple of old to be polluted by the death of Zacharias, son of Barachias, slain between the porch and the altar ; mercifully grant that by the merits and bloodshedding of our LORD JESUS CHRIST upon the Cross, it may be cleansed from all stain, and abide pure henceforward for ever. Through.]

667. O LORD JESU CHRIST, Who hast said that Thy House should be called a House of Prayer, and Who didst Thyself with a scourge of small cords purge Thy temple from all defilement; mercifully grant that Thy Presence abiding herein may keep this holy place void of offence, and purify the bodies and souls of the worshippers therein, that they may be preserved as fitting temples for Thee and Thy HOLY SPIRIT. Of Thy mercy.

℣. The LORD, &c. ℟. And with, &c. ℣. Stablish the thing, O GOD, which Thou hast wrought in us. ℟. For Thy temple's sake at Jerusalem.

[If there be no Celebration of the Holy Eucharist, here shall follow the Te Deum.]

Benediction. Almighty GOD keep far from you and from this Church all adverse things, and graciously pour upon you the gifts of His blessing; He inspire the hearts of you who have come together for this service with holy teaching, that ye may be filled with everlasting blessings, and that understanding what the will of GOD is, and accomplishing that which ye understand, ye may be purified amidst the troubles of the world from all stain of sin, may attain salvation, and become coheirs with the blessed spirits in the Kingdom of Heaven.

Then shall follow the Celebration of the Holy Eucharist.

———

Introit. I will return, and will build again the tabernacle of David, which is fallen down: and I will build again the ruins thereof, and I will set it up. Alleluia.

Ps. xxvi. 8. LORD, I have loved the habitation of Thine house: and the place where Thine honour dwelleth. Glory, &c. As it was, &c.

Collect.

668. O LORD, Who of Thy great goodness didst cause this Church to be dedicated to Thy Name, as a dwelling for Thine honour; and hast since, for our many sins, suffered it to fall into decay [*or*, to be defiled]; mercifully hearken now unto the prayers of Thy faithful servants, purify and hallow it anew with the visitation of Thy HOLY SPIRIT, and cleanse us, who seek Thee with our whole heart, from all defilement of body and soul, that we may be builded together for an habitation of GOD through the SPIRIT. And this we ask for JESUS CHRIST'S sake, our LORD. Who.

Epistle. Isa. lx. 10—19.

And the sons of strangers shall build up thy walls, and their kings shall minister unto thee: for in My wrath I smote thee, but in My favour have I had mercy on thee. Therefore thy gates shall be open continually; they shall not be shut day nor night; that men may bring unto thee the forces of the Gentiles, and that their kings may be brought. For the nation and kingdom that will not serve thee shall perish; yea, those nations shall be utterly wasted. The glory of Lebanon shall come unto thee, the fir tree, the pine tree, and the box together, to beautify the place of My sanctuary; and I will make the place of My feet glorious. The sons also of them that afflicted thee shall come bending unto thee; and all they that despised thee shall bow themselves down at the soles of thy feet; and they shall call thee, The city of the LORD, the Zion of the Holy One of Israel. Whereas thou hast been forsaken and hated, so that no man went through thee, I will make thee an eternal excellency, a joy of many generations. Thou shalt also suck the milk of the Gentiles, and shalt suck the breast of kings: and thou shalt know that I the LORD am thy SAVIOUR and thy Redeemer, the mighty One of Jacob. For brass I will bring gold, and for iron I will bring silver, and for wood brass, and for stones iron: I will also make thy officers peace, and thine exactors righteousness. Violence shall no more be heard in thy land, wasting nor destruction within thy borders: but thou shalt call thy walls Salvation, and thy gates Praise. The sun shall be no more thy light by day; neither for brightness shall the moon give light unto thee: but the LORD shall be unto thee an everlasting light, and thy GOD thy glory.

Gradual. Ps. cxxvi.

When the LORD turned again the captivity of Zion: then were we like unto them that dream. Then was our mouth filled with laughter: and our tongue with joy.

℣. Then said they among the heathen: The LORD hath done great things for them. Yea, the LORD hath done great things for us already: whereof we rejoice. Alleluia.

Sequence. (*People's Hymnal*, 460.)
"Awake, awake, O Sion."

Gospel. S. Joh

And the Jews'
hand, and JESUS
salem, and found
those that sold oxe
doves, and the ch
sitting: and when
scourge of small
them all out of the
sheep, and the ox
out the changers'
threw the tables;
them that sold d
things hence; ma
THER's house an h
dise. And His
bered that it was
of Thine house h
Then answered th
unto Him, What si
unto us, seeing t
these things? JES
said unto them, I
ple, and in three
it up. Then said
and six years wa
building, and wilt
in three days?
the temple of H
therefore He was
dead, His discip
that He had said
and they believed
and the word whic

The Offertory, &
be used h

CONSECRATION OF A PORTABLE A

The Portable Altar shall be laid upon the High Altar in Church, and the Bishop shall say,

In the Name, &c.
Our FATHER, &c.

℣. Our help, &c. ℟. Who hath made, &c. ℣. Glory, &c. ℟. As it was, &c.

Ant. Thou sha
hyssop, and I sha

Ps. 51. Have m

Ant. Thou sha
hyssop, and I sha
shalt wash me, an
than snow.

Then shall follow,

Dearly beloved, &c. (*see p.* 314).

℣. The LORD, &c. ℟. And with, &c. ℣. Lift up your hearts. ℟. We lift them up unto the LORD. ℣. Let us give thanks, &c. ℟. It is meet and right, &c.

669. It is very meet, right, and our bounden duty, that we should at all times and in all places give thanks unto Thee, O LORD, Holy FATHER, Almighty, everlasting GOD, Who after the first man's sinful fall didst ordain that propitiatory oblations should be offered unto Thee ; and that the sin which had been caused by pride might in time to come be expiated by gifts wherewith Thine altar and temple should be honoured. Let then Thine unspeakable lovingkindness and mercy be with us. Pour down the riches of Thy blessing upon this Altar-slab, that, of Thy bounty, whosoever shall thereat make his prayer unto Thee may obtain his desire, through Him Who willed that He should be named the Corner Stone and the Stone hewn without hands, our LORD JESUS CHRIST, Thy SON. Who.

O LORD, Holy FATHER, &c.
O GOD, Who, to hallow, &c.
Almighty GOD, &c. (*see p.* 315).

670. O GOD, Who didst rain Manna round the camp of the Israelites during their journey through the wilderness, and gavest them to drink of that Rock which followed them, which Rock was CHRIST ; grant that the power and grace of Thy Holy Sacrament may follow those who are at a distance from Thy House of Prayer, that they may be fed from this Altar with that Bread from Heaven, and be refreshed with that Spiritual Drink, even with the Body and Blood of our LORD JESUS CHRIST, Who with Thee and the HOLY GHOST, liveth.

671. Almighty and merciful GOD, Who sentest Thine angel to feed Thy prophet Elijah with the cake and cruse, to strengthen him for his journey through the wilderness ; graciously vouchsafe that Thy servants who are departing from this world may be so fed from this Altar with the Body and Blood of Thy SON our LORD, that they may go in the strength of that Meat through the unknown land, until at length they reach the mount of GOD, the heavenly Jerusalem, and there be united to the Church of the firstborn. Through JESUS the Mediator of the New Covenant. Who.

℣. The LORD, &c. ℟. And with, &c. ℣. Stablish the thing, O LORD, which Thou hast wrought in us. ℟. For Thy temple's sake at Jerusalem.

Benediction. The Bless✠ing of GOD Almighty, the FATHER, the SON, and the HOLY GHOST, descend and rest upon this Altar, and upon you all, now and for evermore. ℟. Amen.

BENEDICTION OF A CHURCH BELL.

The Bell being suspended at a convenient height, the Bishop, standing on its east side, begins :

In the Name, &c.
Our FATHER, &c.

℣. Sing we merrily unto GOD our strength. ℟. Make a cheerful noise unto the GOD of Jacob. ℣. O GOD, make speed to save us. ℟. O LORD, make haste to help us. ℣. Glory, &c. ℟. As it was, &c. ℣. Alleluia.

Ant. Praise Him upon the well tuned cymbals.

Ps. 29. Bring unto the LORD, &c.

150. O praise GOD, &c.

Ant. Praise Him upon the well tuned cymbals: praise Him upon the loud cymbals.

℣. Praise the LORD upon the harp. ℟. Sing to the harp with a psalm of thanksgiving. ℣. With trumpets also and shawms. ℟. O show yourselves joyful before the LORD the King.

Then shall the Bishop bless the Bell as follows :

℣. Our help is in the Name of the LORD. ℟. Who hath made heaven and earth. ℣. Blessed be the Name of the LORD. ℟. From this time forth for evermore. ℣. The LORD, &c. ℟. And with, &c.

Let us pray.

672. Almighty GOD, Who by the mouth of Thy servant Moses didst command to make two silver trumpets for the convocation of solemn assemblies, be pleased to accept our offering of this the work of our hands ; bl+ess, hal+low, and sanc+tify it with Thy heavenly benediction, and grant that through this generation, and through those that are to come, it may continually call together Thy faithful people, to praise and worship Thy Holy Name, through JESUS CHRIST our LORD. Amen.

673. Grant, O LORD, that whosoever shall be called by the sound of *this bell* to Thine house of prayer, may enter into Thy gates with thanksgiving, and into Thy courts with praise ; and finally may have a portion in the new song, and among the harpers, harping with their harps in Thine house not made with hands, eternal in the heavens, through JESUS CHRIST our LORD. Amen.

674. Grant, O LORD, that whosoever shall by reason of sickness or any other necessity, be so let and hindered that he cannot come into the house of the LORD, may in heart and mind thither ascend, and have his share in the communion of Thy Saints, through JESUS CHRIST our LORD. Amen.

675. Grant, O LORD, that they who with their outward ears shall hear the sound of *this bell*, may be aroused inwardly in their spirits, and draw nigh unto Thee, the GOD of their salvation, through JESUS CHRIST our LORD. Amen.

676. Grant, O LORD, that all they, for whose passing away from this world, the bell shall sound, may be received into the paradise of Thine elect, and find grace, light, and everlasting rest, through JESUS CHRIST our LORD, to Whom with Thee, and the HOLY GHOST, be all honour and glory for ever and ever. Amen.

677. Grant, O LORD, that all they who shall minister to Thy service by ringing *this bell*, may be fulfilled with all reverence and godly fear, and mindful of the sacredness of Thy House, may put away from them all idle thoughts and light behaviour in the discharge of their service, and so continue in holiness of life, that they may be counted to stand with them who praise Thee evermore in the heavenly Jerusalem. Through.

Then shall they ring one short peal, after which this Hymn may be sung.

Lift it gently to the steeple,
   Let our bell be set on high :
There fulfil its daily mission,
   Midway 'twixt the earth and sky.

As the birds sing early matins
   To the GOD of nature's praise ;
This its nobler daily music
   To the GOD of grace shall raise.

And when evening shadows soften
   Chancel cross, and tower and aisle ;

It shall blend its vesper summons
　With the day's departing smile.

Christian men shall hear at distance,
　In their toil or in their rest;
Joying that in one communion
　Of one Church they too are blest.

They that on the sick bed languish,
　Full of weariness and woe,
Shall remember that, for them too,
　Holy Church is gathering so.

Year by year the steeple music
　O'er the tender graves shall pour;
Where the dust of Saints is garnered,
　Till the Master comes once more.

Till the day of sheaves in-gathering,
　Till the harvest of the earth;

Till the Saints rise in their order,
　Glorious in their second birth.

Till Jerusalem, beholding
　That His glory in the east,
Shall, at the Archangel trumpet,
　Enter in to keep the feast.

Lift it gently to the steeple,
　Let our bell be set on high;
There fulfil its daily mission,
　Midway 'twixt the earth and sky.

Christ, to Thee, the world's salvation,
　Father, Spirit, unto Thee
Low we bend in adoration,
　Ever blessed One and Three.　Amen.

*Then the Bishop shall bless the
people.*

OFFICE FOR THE BENEDICTION OF AN ORGAN.

In the Name of the Father, and of the Son, and of the Holy Ghost.

R̷. Amen.

Our Father, &c.

℣. O sing unto the Lord a new song.

R̷. Let the congregation of saints praise Him.

Ant. O sing unto the Lord, for it is a good thing to sing praises unto our God.

Ps. 150. O praise God, &c.

Ant. O sing unto the Lord, for it is a good thing to sing praises unto our God: yea, a joyful and pleasant thing it is to be thankful.

The Chapter. 2 Chron. xxix. 25—28.

And he set the Levites in the house of the Lord with cymbals, with psalteries, and with harps, according to the commandment of David, and of Gad the king's seer, and Nathan the prophet: for so was the commandment of the Lord by His prophets. And the Levites stood with the instruments of David, and the priests with the trumpets. And Hezekiah commanded to offer the burnt-offering upon the altar. And when the burnt-offering began, the song of the Lord began also with the trumpets, and with the instruments ordained by David king of Israel. And all the congregation worshipped, and the singers sang, and the trumpeters sounded: and all this continued until the burnt-offering was finished.

R̷. Thanks be to God.

Let us pray.

678. O God, before Whose throne in heaven the Saints, standing on the sea of glass, sing the Song of Moses and the Lamb; grant us so to sing Thy praises here with the spirit and with the understanding also, that we may be counted worthy to learn the new song, which none can learn save those that shall be redeemed from the earth. Through Jesus Christ our Lord.

R̷. Amen.

Let us pray.

679. Sanctify, O LORD, we beseech Thee, this instrument of music of the LORD, made to praise Thee, because Thy mercy endureth for ever, and let it be bless+ed and hal+lowed in the Name of the FA-THER, and of the SON, and of the HOLY GHOST.

R︢. Amen.

Benediction. When the minstrel playeth, the hand of the LORD come upon you, and bless you, and strengthen you for evermore.

R︢. Amen.

THE CONSECRATION OF CHRISM AND HOLY OILS.

On Maundy Thursday of each year the Bishop shall consecrate the Chrism and Oils for his diocese after this form.

He shall celebrate the Holy Eucharist, and after the oblation of the Bread and Wine, at the end of the Church Militant Prayer, the Archdeacon or Chaplain shall present to him the vessel containing the Oil for the sick, (which shall be brought from the Sacristy by one of the assistant Ministers, attended by two servers), saying, Reverend Father in GOD, the Oil for the Sick.

The Bishop, placing the vessel at the Epistle corner of the Altar, shall say,

℣. The LORD, &c. R︢. And with, &c. ℣. Let us pray.

680. Send, O LORD, we beseech Thee, Thy HOLY GHOST the Comforter from heaven upon this fatness of the olive, which Thou hast vouchsafed to bring forth from the green tree, for the refreshment of body and soul ; that as Thou didst anoint Thy Priests, Kings, Prophets, and Martyrs, so this oil may, by Thy bless+ing, be to every one anointed therewith, a heavenly medicine and remedy, to banish all pain, weakness, and suffering of body and soul, and that Thy perfect anointing and blessing may abide within us for evermore. In the Name of our LORD JESUS CHRIST. Who.

Let us pray.

681. O LORD JESU CHRIST, Whose Name is as ointment poured forth in grace, purifying the world, bl+ess and sanc+tify this holy oil, the sign of Thy mercy, and impart it unto Thy servants for salvation and deliverance from sickness ; wash and cleanse the defilements of their souls, purge them from their manifold offences, assuage their sorrows, drive away their troubles, and scatter their afflictions. Through Thy mercy.

Then shall the Bishop deliver the Oil for the Sick to the Archdeacon, who shall cause it to be carried into the Sacristy.

Then shall the Oil for Catechumens be brought in like manner to the Bishop, who shall say,

℣. The LORD, &c. R︢. And with, &c. ℣. Let us pray.

682. O GOD, Bestower of all spiritual increase and progress, Who by the might of Thy HOLY SPIRIT confirmest the first efforts of feeble souls ; we pray Thee, O LORD, that Thou wouldst vouchsafe to send Thy bless+ing upon this oil, and grant through its anointing cleansing of body and soul to them who shall come to the laver of blessed regeneration ; that if any stains of their spiritual enemies have clung to them, they may depart at the touch of this hallowed oil. Let there remain in them no room for ghostly wickedness, no abode for the rebel powers, no lurking-place for secret sins ; but as Thy servants come to the true faith, and to be cleansed by the operation of Thy HOLY SPIRIT, let this unction be profitable for that salvation which they are to obtain through the birth of heavenly regeneration in the Sacrament of Baptism. Through.

Then shall the Oil of Catechumens be carried to the Sacristy, and the Celebration shall proceed to the end of the Preface and Sanctus.

The balsam and oil for the Chrism shall then be carried in two separate vessels by two Priests to the Archdeacon, while a third Priest bears the vessel in which they are to be mingled. While this is being done, the Choir sings:

O Redeemer, take the tribute of the song
  we raise to Thee,
Hearken, Judge of souls departed, Hope
  of frail mortality,
Hear us, as that gift we offer, once the
  pledge of peace to be.

Trees, which kindly light made fruitful,
  bore this oil from Thee designed,
And Thy suppliant people bring it to the
  SAVIOUR of mankind.
    O Redeemer, &c.

Lo, Thy Pontiff at the Altar vested stands
  in lowly prayer,
That the Chrism be duly hallowed which
  Thou trustest to his care.
    O Redeemer, &c.

Deign Thyself to bless and hallow, King
  of Thine eternal Land,
This oil-olive, living token 'gainst our
  ghostly foemen's band.
    O Redeemer, &c.

With this chrism let man and woman
  through anointing be renewed,
And our glory, which lies wounded, healing gain, with this bedewed.
    O Redeemer, &c.

When the font hath washed the spirit,
  guilt and evil flee apace,
When the brow receives anointing, in-
  wards flow the streams of grace.
    O Redeemer, &c.

Of the FATHER's Heart Begotten, Offspring of the Virgin's womb,
Grant Thy light to all anointed, save them
  from eternal doom.
    O Redeemer, &c.

Then the Bishop shall say as follows for the blessing of the Balsam.

℣. The LORD, &c. ℟. And with, &c. ℣. Let us pray.

683. O GOD, Who ordainest heavenly mysteries and powers ; hearken, we beseech Thee, to our prayers, and vouchsafe that this balsam, the sweet produce flowing from the bark of a fertile tree, which enriches us with priestly anointing, may be acceptable for Thy service, and be hal+lowed with Thy blessing. Through.

Let us pray.

684. O LORD, Maker of all creatures, Who by Thy servant Moses didst command holy ointment to be compounded of principal spices ; we humbly beseech Thy mercy that Thou wouldst bestow spiritual grace on this ointment, the fruit of a tree, and pour upon it the fulness of Thy hal+lowing. Let it be compounded for us, O LORD, with the gladness of faith, let it be the lasting Chrism of priestly anointing, let it be fitted for impressing the sign of the heavenly banner, that whoso are anointed therewith after being born again in holy Baptism, may obtain the fullest blessing of body and soul, and ever increase in the gift of that blessed faith which they have acquired. Through.

He shall then proceed to bless the Chrismal Oil, as follows:

685. Be present, O FATHER Most Highest, and hearken to the prayers of us miserable sinners who call upon Thee. Send us, O LORD, that HOLY SPIRIT wherewith Thou didst anoint Thy SON above His fellows, that Thou mayest hal+low with the savour of Thine ointments this Chrism here made ready, and fulfil it with Thy sevenfold spiritual grace. So vouchsafe to shine on them whom Thou redeemest by spiritual washing, that this holy anointing may be to them the Chrism of blessing, the wedding-garment, the bestowal of steadfastness, the remission of sins, the adoption of children, the increase of holy might, and the full perfection of spiritual grace; that whoso shall be signed with this holy anointing, and receive the Sacrament of the Body and Blood of Thy dear SON, may feel Thy protection, and obtain everlasting life. Through the same.

Then mingling the Balsam and Oil together, the Bishop shall say,

In the Name of the FATHER, and of the SON, + and of the HOLY GHOST, let this mingling be unto all anointed therewith for a propitiation and spiritual safeguard for ever and ever. Amen.

Let us pray.

686. O GOD, Who amongst other gifts of Thy bounty and lovingkindness hast given the wholesome fruit of the olive for the use of man, and for the making of holy Chrism; Who didst typify by that olive-leaf which the dove brought back to the Ark when the waters abated, the remission of sins in holy Baptism and the purifying unction of oil; Who didst command Thy servant Moses that his brother Aaron should be anointed therewith for the priesthood of the Old Testament; Who didst bestow on it yet greater honour, when Thy SON JESUS CHRIST our LORD caused Himself to be baptized by John in the waters of Jordan, and Thou didst send the HOLY GHOST upon Him in the form of a Dove, declaring Him to be Thine Only-Begotten, in Whom Thou art well pleased, and showing thereby that Thou hadst anointed Him with the oil of gladness above His fellows, as David Thy Prophet testified; we pray Thee, O LORD, our heavenly FATHER, Almighty, everlasting GOD, through the same Thy SON our LORD JESUS CHRIST, that Thou wouldst hal+low this matter of holy oil and fragrant balsam, sancti+fying it with the power of Thine Anointed. And we humbly beseech Thee, O LORD, that Thou wouldst enrich this fatness with the might of the HOLY GHOST, and make it abound with the sweetness of Divine love, and stablish it with all bless+ing. Let it be a holy unction and a sweet savour unto Thee, a sign of certain victory to those who are born again of water and the HOLY GHOST, a joyful anointing, a hope of blessedness, a cleansing from sin, a medicine of life, and a help on their way to the heavenly country; that being sanctified in soul and body, they may be acknowledged by Angels and Archangels and all the heavenly powers, be feared by all evil and unclean spirits, and become a chosen generation, a royal priesthood, an holy nation, sealed with Thy divine mystery, bearing Thy CHRIST in their hearts, made a meet dwelling for Thee, O GOD the FATHER, through the grace of Thy HOLY SPIRIT, Who livest and reignest in the TRINITY of co-eternal majesty, One GOD Almighty, world without end. Amen.

Then shall the Chrism be reverently carried to the Sacristy, and the Bishop shall proceed with the Holy Eucharist in the usual manner, ending with the Blessing.

BENEDICTION OF LITTLE CHILDREN.

℣. Our help is in the Name of the LORD. ℟. Who hath made heaven and earth. ℣. The LORD, &c. ℟. And with, &c. ℣. Let us pray.

687. O LORD JESU CHRIST, Who didst take into Thine arms little children presented and coming unto Thee, and laying Thine hands upon them (*here the Bishop shall lay his hands upon the child's head*) didst bless them, saying, Suffer the little children to come unto Me, and forbid them not, for of such is the kingdom of heaven, and their angels do ever behold the face of My FATHER; have regard, we beseech Thee, unto the innocence of *this* present infant, and the devotion of *his* parents, and mercifully bl+ess *him* by my ministry, that *he* ever advancing by Thy grace and mercy, may know Thee, love Thee, and fear Thee, may keep Thy commandments and those of *his* parents and happily attain everlasting life Through Thy mercy.

The Blessing of GOD the FA+THER Almighty, of the SO+N, and of the HOLY+GHOST, descend upon you, keep you, govern you, and abide with you evermore. ℟. Amen.

PRIVATE PRAYERS FOR BISHOPS.

For Wisdom in ruling.

688. O LORD JESU CHRIST, Shepherd and Bishop of souls, grant me to take the oversight of the flock committed to my charge, not as lording it over GOD'S heritage, but in the spirit of wisdom and justice, of love and gentleness, that guiding Thy sheep with Thy staff and rod, I may at length enter with them into Thine everlasting pastures. Through Thy mercy.

For wise Choice of Candidates for Holy Orders.

689. O GOD, Who didst guide the lot which fell upon Thy servant Matthias; grant me the gift of spiritual insight and discernment, that I may lay hands suddenly on no man, but choose for the ministry of Thine Altar and the preaching of Thy Word faithful men, who shall be an ensample to the flock in all godliness, and that no wolf may, by reason of my error or blindness enter in to ravin and destroy the sheep which Thou hast purchased with the Blood of Thy dear SON Through the same.

For Simplicity of Life.

690. O LORD JESU CHRIST King of kings, Whose earthly crown was of thorns, Whose sceptre was a reed; give me grace to shun all worldly pomp and luxury, and so to endure hardship as Thy good soldier, that I may at length attain the spiritual riches of Thine eternal Kingdom. Through Thy mercy.

For right exercise of Patronage.

691. Grant, O LORD, that I may bestow the offices which Thou hast intrusted to my stewardship, on fit and worthy persons, choosing in all purity and simplicity of heart not by favour or for my private advantage, lest I fall into condemnation for wasting Thy goods, but solely for Thy glory and the good of Thy people. Through.

Against Nepotism.

692. O GOD, Who sentest Thy judgments upon Eli, and tookest the High Priesthood from his house by reason of his guilt in passing over the wickedness of his sons; preserve me, in Thy mercy, from falling into the like sin, and grant that I may never prefer the advantage of my kindred to the claims of justice or the good of Thy flock. Through.

Before beginning any Action against a Clerk.

693. Take from me, O LORD, I beseech Thee, the spirit of anger and strife, grant me the spirit of peace and righteousness, that I may not enter upon this action with any thought of malice or revenge, nor rend thereby Thy seamless robe, but solely that just cause of scandal may be taken away from before Thy people, and that the godly discipline of Thy Church may be enforced. Through.

For Moral Courage.

694. Make me, O LORD, I pray Thee, as a defenced city and an iron pillar on behalf of Thy truth against the whole land, that I swerve not, like Pilate, from the right in order to content the people, but that righteousness may be the girdle of my loins, and faithfulness the girdle of my reins. Through.

For Zeal in Reforms.

695. O LORD JESU CHRIST, Who didst confirm the covenant of peace and the High Priesthood to Thy servant Phinehas, because he was zealous for his GOD, and Who didst Thyself drive out from Thy temple with a scourge of cords them who defiled it; fill me with such zeal for Thine house that, fearing no man, and jealous for Thine honour only, I may labour to cleanse and purge Thy sanctuary from all offence, and so to purify Thy priests and Levites as gold and silver, that they may offer to the LORD an offering in righteousness.   Who.

For a supply of Candidates for Holy Orders.

696. O GOD, Who hast taught us in the Gospel to pray unto the LORD of the harvest to send faithful labourers into His harvest, since the harvest is great and the labourers but few; we humbly beseech Thee to send forth in Thy Church such preachers of the Word as, enlightened by the Spirit of Wisdom, will steadfastly seek after Thy glory, not their own honour, the salvation of souls, not their own advantage, and will be stewards of Thy Word and of all that agreeth therewith, in its true, salutary, and Apostolic sense and meaning.   Through.

For the Clergy.

697. Hear our prayers, O LORD, and send the spirit of Thy blessing upon Thy servants the priests of this diocese, that, enriched with heavenly gifts, they may both acquire Thy Divine grace, and present to others an example of a godly life. Through.

For the Metropolitan.

698. O GOD, Shepherd and Ruler of all the faithful, mercifully look upon Thy servant N., whom Thou hast willed to govern Thy Church; grant him, we beseech Thee, to be profitable in precept and example to those set under him, that he may, together with the flock entrusted to him, attain everlasting life. Through.

For Peace in the Church.

699. O GOD, bestower of peace, and lover of charity, grant Thy servants true harmony with Thy will, that we may be delivered from all temptations which beset us. Through.

Against Persecutors of the Church.

700. Almighty, everlasting GOD, show forth again the wonderful works of Thine arm, as in old time, for the protection of the faithful, that our enemies may be subdued by Thy power, and we may serve Thee with Catholic faith and Christian devotion. Through.

701. O GOD, lover and keeper of peace and charity, grant to all our enemies true peace and charity, vouchsafe them remission of all their sins, and mightily deliver us from all their snares. Through.

For True Faith and Holiness.

702. O Heavenly FATHER, Almighty, everlasting, and merciful GOD, I beseech Thee to bestow on me true, sound, and Christian faith, sincere and incorrupt, neither entangled in the meshes of error, nor spotted with the stain of self-will.

Grant that my actions may so agree and correspond with my faith, that it may not be defiled by any evil doings, lest I should seem to deny Thee by an unholy life Whom I confess with a true faith.

Vouchsafe, O merciful FATHER, that I may serve Thee with good resolution and ready will, that I may fulfil the works of righteousness, love mercy and truth, shun all falsehood, think and speak no vain nor lying things, but fear, love, and worship Thee only, and keep Thy commandments.

Grant me this grace also, that I may follow after and acknowledge none other things than those which Thy holy Church, strengthened by

the Spirit of Truth, teacheth and confesseth, until such time as I come unto Thee in Thy kingdom. Through.

For Grace to rule well.

703. Almighty, everlasting GOD, behold and see by what awful perils I am beset on every side, by reason of the office which I discharge. I know that it is for me no lordship, but a service and duty. I know that it is not irrational creatures Thou hast committed to my charge, but Thy most chosen sons, united to Thee by so close a bond of love that for them Thou didst not hesitate to give Thyself unto death. Who am I, O my GOD, to fulfil such a task? A weak and feeble man, prone to err and to be deceived. The people is very great, and how can I be at hand in every place? Wherefore, O LORD, I humbly beseech Thee, give me wisdom that sitteth by Thy throne, send her out of Thy holy heavens, and from the throne of Thy glory, that being present she may labour with me, that I may know what is pleasing unto Thee, lest I should do aught through favour or hatred of any one, but may rather give my voice according to truth and righteousness. Through.

For Diocesan Schools.

704. Grant, O LORD, that we may not only ourselves abide in Thy Word and doctrine, but bring up our children also for the glory of Thy Name, in godly fear and discipline, in virtue and obedience, that they may grow in purity of life and piety of faith, so that we may rejoice according to Thy good pleasure, and praise Thee throughout our life. Through.

QUESTIONS FOR SELF-EXAMINATION, BEARING ON EPISCOPAL LIFE AND DUTIES.

Have I duly estimated the great responsibilities of my office, remembering that the Episcopate is a burden formidable even to the shoulders of an Angel?

Do I repent me of having yielded to the promptings of ambition at the time of my nomination?

Do I humble myself in secret, in view of the outward dignity and pomp which my office demands of me?

Do I maintain that dignity as a part of my episcopal duty, and not to gratify personal pride?

Do I bear in mind that the Episcopate is one form of the call to perfection, and that I must live accordingly?

Do I strive to acquire a personal knowledge of all my clergy, mindful that a good shepherd calleth his sheep by name?

Am I patient and forbearing in times of trouble and difficulty, so as not to begin nor foster strife in my diocese?

Do I strive against vacillation of purpose, when the path of strict duty is clear?

Do I remember that the greatest prelate is not he who holds the highest worldly station, but he who is most nearly conformed to the life of CHRIST in poverty, humility, and zeal for souls?

Have I taken care that the services over which I have direct control, such as those in my own chapel, shall be orderly, reverent, and a model for the diocese?

Have I laboured for the multiplication of occasions of public worship in my diocese, and for the increase of the beauty and order of the services?

Have I been frugal and modest in personal expenditure, and yet careful to observe due liberality and stateliness in the discharge of public functions?

Have I checked in my household all luxury, display, ostentation, and rivalry of secular persons?

Have I striven to make my household, by its order, moderation, and devotion, a model for the clergy of my diocese?

Have I suffered members of my household to assume any authority or position in the diocese to which they are not officially entitled?

Have I been given to hospitality, not so much by entertaining wealthy secular persons, as by welcoming my clergy, especially the poorer among them, to my house?

Have I shown readiness to support the diocesan charities by precept and example?

Have I borne in mind that the revenues of the See are but a trust in my hands for GOD and His poor, and that I have no right to amass wealth for my family out of them?

Have I kept all Ordination and Visitation fees, with other charges which press on the clergy, to the least possible sum?

Have I been careful myself to observe the Ember seasons as times of special fasting and prayer, after the example of the Apostles, and to urge the same on all candidates for Holy Orders?

Have I made sedulous inquiry into the history and moral character of candidates for Holy Orders, as well as into their theological and literary acquirements?

Have I maintained a high standard in examining for Holy Orders, so as to keep out illiterate candidates?

Have I ever admitted any one, otherwise unfit, to Holy Orders, as a matter of personal favour, or to oblige some influential person?

Have I ever given letters dimissory to an unfit Candidate in order to shift the responsibility of his Ordination from my own shoulders on those of another Bishop who is ignorant of the circumstances of the case?

Have I kept a written record of the condition of my diocese, and a watchful eye on the clergy, noting those who labour diligently and rule well, that I may promote them, or recommend them for promotion?

Have I set my clergy an example of diligence and activity in the discharge of duty?

Have I endeavoured to encourage learning amongst them, and shown personal zeal in study?

Have I striven to raise the standard of clerical efficiency in my diocese, by encouraging progress, and rebuking sloth and shortcomings?

Have I stimulated all agencies for promoting diocesan life and organization?

Have I made my Visitations realities, and searchingly inquired into defects and abuses, with a view to their removal?

Have I constructed my Charges with a real view to the actual needs of my Diocese, and not merely as pamphlets intended for the general public?

Have I ever attempted to make my private opinions and likings an iron rule for the diocese?

Have I remembered that the "erroneous and strange doctrines" which I have promised to drive away, do not necessarily mean opinions and practices which I personally dislike, but those which are contrary to the consent of the Church Universal?

Have I ever rebuked a clergyman for obeying a plain law of the Church, because it happened to be unpopular, or because I did not obey it myself?

Have I ever allowed a clergyman to go on wilfully breaking a plain law of the Church, because public opinion happened to connive at it? Have I ever done this myself?

Have I carefully discouraged my clergy from taking part with schismatics in religious services or meetings, and set a strict example in this respect?

Have I ever yielded to popular clamour, by condemning, or even by failing to support openly, things which in my conscience I knew to be right and lawful?

Have I ever treated an unbeneficed priest with harshness and severity which I should not have ventured on with a beneficed one?

Have I remembered always to rule with justice and courtesy, not lording it over GOD's heritage, but entreating the elder clergy as fathers, and the younger as brothers in the LORD?

Have I taken care to see and inquire personally into all things of moment, and not trusted to the reports of a clique?

Have I been careful not to surround myself with a clique of flatterers and parasites?

Have I allowed all my clergy free access to me at all reasonable times, and not kept them aloof by the means of a staff of chaplains?

Have I ever proceeded to the condemnation of a clerk without the knowledge and assent of the Diocesan Synod?

Have I ever broken the Apostolic rule by receiving an accusation against a priest from anonymous sources, or from mere public rumour?

Have I always looked on the patronage in my hands as a trust for GOD and the Church, and not a a means of obliging my private friends?

Have I imported strangers into the diocese unnecessarily, to the prejudice of the just claims of the clergy already in it?

Have I ever conferred a benefice on a relative or private friend when I knew of any one better fitted to discharge its duties?

Have I exacted a pledge from every one whom I have promoted that he will not allow any diminution in the standard of parochial efficiency maintained by his predecessor, but will rather raise it?

Have I ever hampered persons promoted by me with unfair or untenable restrictions before giving them institution?

Have I ever bargained with another Bishop or patron to promote his relatives and friends on condition of his promoting mine?

Have I ever connived at the wrong-doing of another Bishop, and thus sacrificed truth and justice to class-feeling?

Have I allowed private grudges to affect my teaching and practice?

Have I ever refused to discharge some duty in a parish (as, for instance, to hold a confirmation) by reason of a quarrel with the Incumbent?

Have I ever refused to license Curates, against whom no objection lay, in order to inconvenience and annoy an Incumbent I dislike?

Have I ever refused to countersign testimonials out of private grudge?

Have I ever issued illegal or ungodly monitions (such as attempts to diminish the services or beauty of GOD's House) out of pique or vindictiveness?

Have I been bold in rebuking offenders, without respect of persons, or regard to their position and influence?

Have I held Confirmations with sufficient frequency and variety of place to allow of all diocesan candidates coming to that Sacrament?

Have I ever repelled a child from Confirmation by reason of tender age, when it could say the Creed, the Our FATHER, and the Decalogue, as enjoined in the Rubric?

Have I been regular and fervent in intercessory prayer on behalf of the diocese?

Have I ever intrigued in order to obtain translation to another See?

Have I ever intruded into another diocese against the consent of its Ordinary?

Have I always borne in mind that I am Bishop of the whole diocese, and not of one school or party in it, and therefore shown wise tolerance and checked factiousness?

SCHEME OF ARTICLES OF EPISCOPAL VISITATION.

A. THE PARISH.

1. State the name, area, and population of your parish.

2. Who presented to the living at the last vacancy, and who is the present patron?

3. Is it urban or rural, and what is the chief industrial employment?

4. What proportion of the population are members of the Anglican Church, and how may the others be classified?

5. Is the Church in your parish gaining or losing ground in comparison with other religious bodies?

6. What number of places of worship does your parish contain?
   (a) Anglican.
   (b) Roman Catholic.
   (c) Protestant.

7. Have any of these, and if so, how many, been erected during your incumbency?

8. What is the greatest distance from any point in the parish to the nearest Anglican Church?

B. FABRIC AND ORNAMENTS OF THE CHURCH.

1. How many Churches and Chapels in your parish are under your

own control? what are their names? have they been consecrated or licensed? if so, give the dates. Are these all insured? and, if so, for what sums?

2. How many worshippers will these severally accommodate?

3. What is the distance of each Chapel from the Mother Church?

4. Are Baptisms, Marriages, Burials performed in the Chapels (if any) respectively?

5. Is there any want of further Church accommodation in your parish? if so, in what manner do you think it desirable that this want should be supplied?

6. Are any seats rented? and if so, how many, and what sum do they produce?

7. Is this collection of seat-rents a matter of custom only, or of legal right?

8. How many free and unappropriated seats remain?

9. Have the occupants of free seats equal advantages with the occupants of rented ones for seeing and hearing what goes on in Divine Service?

10. Are the rented seats thrown open to all comers if unoccupied up to a certain time in the service?

11. Are there any services held at which all the sittings are free?

12. What is the date of the erection of the Church or Chapels? Is each in thorough and substantial repair? Is there any debt on them? What means are taken to pay it off?

(*a*) Is the ground about the Church properly levelled and drained, so as to prevent injury to the foundations?

(*b*) Are the walls substantial and in good repair?

(*c*) Of what material is the roof composed, and is it weather-tight?

(*d*) Are the windows fully glazed, and are they protected from injury from without by wirework, or other fencing?

(*e*) Are the doors solid, properly hinged, and provided with sufficient locks?

(*f*) Of what material is the flooring of the Church, and in what condition is it?

(*g*) Of what dimensions is the chancel, and is it constructional, or only a quasi-chancel? How high is it above the level of the nave? Who is liable for its repair?

(*h*) Are there any side-chapels, and to what use are they put?

(*i*) Are the external drains and gutters in sufficient quantity, and in good working order?

(*j*) Is there a proper lightning conductor attached to the outside of the Church?

(*k*) What method of warming the Church is employed? what precaution is taken against fire, and how is the Church lighted at night?

(*l*) Are there any galleries in your Church, and how many sittings do they contain?

(*m*) Are they reserved for any special class of worshippers?

(*n*) How many bells are there, and in what condition?

(*o*) Are the ropes, pulleys, and woodwork in good order?

(*p*) Are there convenient means of access to the belfry for the purpose of repair?

(*q*) Do you retain in your own hands the key and consequent custody of the belfry?

(*r*) What means are taken to prevent misconduct on the part of the ringers?

13. (*a*) Is there a proper elevation for the altar, of not less than three steps, at the end of the chancel?

(*b*) Of what material is the altar composed, wood or stone, and is it at least 3 ft. 3 in. high, 7 ft. long, and 2 ft. wide?

(*c*) Is it, as the chief article of furniture in the House of GOD, of as solid construction and handsome design as the chief article of furniture in a wealthy man's private house would be?

(*d*) Is care taken not to allow anything to stand at any time on the Altar, save such things as are subsidiary to the Holy Eucharist?

(*e*) Is there any shelf or retable behind the Altar?

(*f*) Are there at the least two altar candlesticks, and a standard crucifix or cross to rest on this shelf, or else one carved on the reredos?

(*g*) Is there a book-rest or desk for the use of the Celebrant?

(*h*) Is there a credence table or shelf upon which to place the elements until the time of Oblation, according to the rubric?

(*i*) Is there a convenient piscina or drain for the ablutions?

(*j*) Are there sedilia against the south wall of the sanctuary for the Celebrant, Gospeller, and Epistoler?

(*k*) Is there any rail in the sanctuary for the convenience of infirm communicants?

(*l*) Is there a convenient stall on the south side of the chancel for the priest in charge? and are there any additional stalls for other clergy, and for choristers?

(*m*) Do any lay persons, not members of the choir, sit in the chancel, and, if so, on what is their claim based?

(*n*) Is there a screen of any kind between the nave and chancel? and if so, describe its condition.

(*o*) Are there any mats, carpets, hassocks, or rugs in the chancel, and, if so, in what condition are they?

(*p*) Is there a convenient pulpit for the preacher? Is it of moderate height, and disconnected from the priest's stall and the lectern?

(*q*) Is the pulpit so placed as not to conceal nor overtop the Altar?

(*r*) Is there a lectern for the Bible? of what material is it made, and where is it placed?

(*s*) Are the seats for the people pews, benches, or chairs? State their height, material, and present condition.

(*t*) What is the average width of each seat? can the occupants kneel conveniently? and what space is there in the passages of the nave and aisles?

(*u*) What mats or other conveniences are there in the seats to encourage the people to kneel?

(*v*) Is there a separate Baptistery? If so, does it contain a tank for adult baptism by immersion? Is the font of natural stone, and what are its dimensions? Is it in good repair, and duly provided with a drain? Is there any cover or canopy over it? Is it placed where it should be, near the entrance to the Church? If not, where else? Is the font itself regularly in use, or is any vessel substituted for it? Is care taken that it is kept scrupulously clean, and nothing put in it but the water at the time of Baptism?

(*w*) Are there one or more almschests provided with strong locks and keys, and set in convenient places?

(*x*) Is there an organ or other musical instrument, and is it in good repair?

(*y*) Are there any stained glass windows, carvings, mosaics, pictures, or monuments? if so, describe them, and state whether any of the monuments from their size or position obstruct the celebration of Divine service.

(*z*) What provision is made for the convenience of those coming to Confession, and where are Confessions heard?

C. The Sacristy: commonly called the Vestry.

14. (*a*) What are the dimensions and present condition of the Sacristy?

(*b*) Is it used in common by the clergy and the choir, or are there separate chambers?

(*c*) Is there a fireproof safe in it for the custody of parish books and other valuables?

(*d*) Are there convenient cupboards and pegs to contain the books and vestments belonging to the Church and choir?

(*e*) Is there a suitable lavatory in the Sacristy, duly furnished?

(*f*) What stock of books belonging to the Church is there under the following heads? (1) Bibles. (2) Lectionaries. (3) Prayer Books. (4) Celebrant's Altar Book. (5) Book of the Gospels. (6) Book of the Epistles. (7) Psalters. (8) Hymnal. (9) Music Books. (10) Do the Bibles contain the Apocrypha?

(*g*) Specify the articles of altar-plate belonging to the Church, mentioning their metal and condition. (1) Chalices. (2) Patens. (3) Flagons. (4) Ciboriums. (5) Cruets, (6) Spoons.

(*h*) How many altar-carpets are there? mention their colour, material, and value.

(*i*) What is the number and condition of the fair linen cloths, corporals, palls, and purificators?

(*j*) What is the number, material, and colour of the veils and burses?

(*k*) Is there a convenient box for keeping the Altar-breads?

(*l*) State the supply of Eucharistic vestments under the following heads, mentioning condition, colour, and material: (1) Amices. (2) Albs. (3) Linen girdles. (4) Stoles. (5) Maniples. (6) Tunicles. (7) Dalmatics. (8) Chasubles.

(*m*) Mention number, condition, material, and colour of copes.

(*n*) How many priests' surplices are there, how many choristers' cassocks, surplices, and caps, and in what condition are they?

(*o*) Enumerate and describe the processional crosses and banners, specifying their condition.

(*p*) What censers and incense boats are there?

(*q*) How many flower-vases for the Altar are there, and what is their material?

(*r*) Is there a bier? and what palls for adults and children are there? describe their size, material, and colour?

(*s*) What register-books have you? How have they been kept, and in whose custody are they?

(*t*) Is there a Church Kalendar in the sacristy?

(*u*) Is there a table of prohibited degrees in marriage?

15. Has anything in the Church been added, altered, taken away, or sold since the last Visitation? If so, by whom, and by what authority?

D. DIVINE SERVICE.

16. (*a*) Is the Holy Eucharist celebrated every Sunday, greater Holyday, and Saints' Day in your Church?

(*b*) At what other times is it celebrated besides these?

(*c*) If it be celebrated less frequently, state how often?

(*d*) What excuse have you to offer for celebrating it less frequently than is indicated in question D, 16 (*a*)?

(*e*) At what hours are the Celebrations in your Church, and are they ever separate services?

(*f*) Have you ever practised or sanctioned evening Communions in your Church?

(*g*) In what vestments do you celebrate the Holy Eucharist?

(*h*) Are you careful to place the Bread and Wine on the Altar at the offertory, in compliance with the rubric, and not before?

(*i*) Do you stand in front of the Altar during the Consecration Prayer?

(*j*) Do you say the words of administration separately to each Communicant?

(*k*) In what order do you communicate the people?

(*l*) How do you deal with the consecrated species of Bread and Wine which remain at the close of the Service?

(*m*) If you call up any communicants to consume them, in what position do they place themselves?

(*n*) How, when, and where does the celebrant cleanse the sacred vessels after the service?

(*o*) Is the Holy Eucharist ever celebrated chorally in your Church?

(*p*) Do you keep a record of the Communions made in your Church?

(*q*) If so, state,

(I.) How many Communions have been made during the past year?

(II.) What increase or decrease does this exhibit as compared with the three previous years?

(III.) The number of Communions made during the three last Easter-tides respectively.

(IV.) The proportion which the two sexes amongst the communicants bear to one another.

(V.) What proportion of the Churchgoers are habitual non-communicants?

(*r*) Do you encourage your whole congregation to remain during the Eucharistic office in order to join in the prayers, and that the uninstructed may become better acquainted with the ordinance?

(*s*) Have you repelled any persons from Communion since the last Visitation, and if so, why?

(*t*) Has the number of Celebrations increased or decreased since the last incumbency, and in what ratio?

(*u*) State what description of Bread and Wine you use for the Holy Eucharist. Is the Wine valid matter, i.e. *fermented* grape-juice?

(*v*) Are you very careful that the vessels, linen, &c., used in the Celebration are scrupulously clean?

17. (*a*) Is your Church open at any time in the day for private prayer; and if so, for how long a time?

(*b*) Is the daily morning and evening service duly performed in your Church; if not, is the neglect occasioned by sickness, or other equally urgent cause?

(*c*) Has morning or evening service been omitted on any Sunday since the last Visitation? If so, how often, and for what reasons?

(*d*) Has morning or evening service been performed in any other building than the Church? If so, for what reasons?

(*e*) Has your Church any special endowment for the maintenance of daily service? and if so, how is it expended?

(*f*) What Sunday services have you in addition to Matins, Evensong, and the Holy Eucharist? what are they, and at what hours?

(*g*) Which of the services is best attended?

(*h*) By what class are these services severally attended?

(*i*) Are the hours of service such as best to suit the convenience of the bulk of the parishioners?

(*j*) Have you increased or diminished the number of services maintained by your predecessor, and if so, how?

(*k*) Has any application been made to you for additional services, and how have you answered it?

(*l*) Is there a regular choir? If so, is it voluntary or paid, and of whom is it composed?

(*m*) What portions of the service are rendered chorally?

(*n*) Is there a paid organist, and how is his salary supplied?

(*o*) What Psalter and Hymnal are in use in your Church?

(*p*) What is the average attendance, morning, afternoon, and evening, on (1) Sundays, (2) weekdays?

(*q*) Does this exhibit an increase or decrease compared with former returns?

(*r*) Does the congregation take its proper share in Divine Service, by joining audibly in the Responses, Psalms, Hymns, &c.?

(*s*) Is there any invidious distinction made between rich and poor in the allotment, actual or virtual, of seats?

(*t*) Is the division of sexes practised in your Church?

(*u*) Are the children kept apart by themselves, or allowed to sit with their parents and friends?

(*v*) Is free ingress and egress during Divine service (without interference from vergers, &c.) permitted to both children and adults who behave decorously?

(*w*) How often during the week are Sermons preached as parts of the service?

(*x*) Are any additional services held under your direction in the parish?—if so, what are they, and distinguish them under the following heads:

(I.) Advent, Lent, and Passiontide services in Church.

(II.) Schoolroom and children's services.

(III.) Cottage lectures.

(IV.) Open-air services.

(V.) Occasional missions.

(VI.) Sermons and catechizings.

What results have been attained by these several agencies?

(*y*) Have there been any secessions from the Church in your parish since the last Visitation? If so, how many, and what Communion have the seceders joined?

(*z*) Have there been any conversions to the Church during the same time? If so, how many, and from what sects?

E. Occasional Offices.

18. *Baptism.*

(*a*) How many stated times in the month is Baptism publicly administered, and what are they?

(*b*) Do these Baptisms take place after the Second Lesson, or when?

(*c*) Are facilities afforded to parents of bringing their children at other times, should these not be convenient to them?

(*d*) Is especial care taken that this Sacrament is administered with the proper form of words, and by the actual contact of water with the person of the candidate?

(*e*) Do you in Public Baptism ever omit any portion of the service, and if so, what portion, and why?

(*f*) Are you prompt in attending to calls for the private Baptism of sick persons?

(*g*) Do you in such cases take with you surplice, stole, and a fitting

vessel, that the
reverently mini

(*h*) Do you
Baptism where
danger in brir
Church?

(*i*) Do you re
public receptior
vately baptized

(*j*) Are you
the Register-B
those privately

(*k*) Are any fe
or received for
tration, and if
text?

(*l*) What nu
has taken plac
year, (1) adults,

(*m*) What nu
persons still r
Church families

(*n*) What men
ing for bringing

19. C

(*a*) At what
each week do th
hear confessions

(*b*) Is distinc
the parishioners
places?

(*c*) Is care ta
ing the privacy
not to throw ur
around the proc

(*d*) What n
have made their
(and your assis
past year?

(*e*) Is the p
private confessi
in your parish?

(*f*) Have yo
hear a confessior

20. M

(*a*) When ca
any couple, are
quire whether

(1) Both pers

(2) They are
forbidden by th

(3) Either of
vorced, whose pa

(4) In case of those under age the parents' consent has been obtained?

(5) If the answers to these questions be unsatisfactory, do you refuse to celebrate the marriage?

(b) Have any marriages been celebrated in your Church between persons neither of whom is resident in your parish?

(c) Do you ever omit any portion of the marriage service,—if so, which portion, and why?

(d) Do you give to a newly married couple the opportunity of communicating, if they so desire it?

(e) What is the scale of marriage fees at your Church?

(f) Is this higher or lower than the charges made at the Registrar's office?

(g) Do you make any abatement in these charges in the case of poor persons?

(h) What number of marriages has taken place in your parish during the last twelve months?

(i) Do you know of any unmarried persons living together in your parish, and have you adopted any means to dissuade them from so continuing?

(j) Are you careful to teach your people by Sermons, or otherwise, that Christian marriage is a Divine institution, dissoluble only by death, and not by any human law?

21. *Visitation of Sick.*

(a) What system of parochial visitation do you employ?

(b) What share of this do you take on yourself?

(c) Are you careful to attend with promptness to sick calls?

(d) Do you ascertain whether the sick person has been baptized?

(e) Are you diligent in moving sick persons to confession, as the Prayer Book orders?

(f) Do you earnestly encourage sick persons to receive Holy Communion?

(g) In what attire, and with what vessels and other ornaments do you celebrate the Communion of the Sick?

(h) How many clinical Communions have you administered during the past year?

(i) Have you ever refrained from visiting any sick persons in your parish through fear of contagion?

(j) Has any fever or serious epidemic prevailed in your parish during the past three years?

(k) If so, what means did you adopt for meeting the additional spiritual needs of your parish at such a time?

(l) Do you make any difficulty about communicating sick persons when there are no other communicants?

22. *Burial of the Dead.*

(a) Have you had occasion to refuse burial to any one during the past year? If so, state the circumstances.

(b) What is the scale of burial fees in your parish?

23. *Churching of Women.*

(a) At what part of the Church, and at what point in the service do you perform Churchings? Where does the woman kneel?

(b) Do you ever church unmarried women after childbirth?

(c) What are the "accustomed offerings" at this service?

F. THE CLERICAL STAFF.

(a) What is the name of the Incumbent? State also his

(1) Place of education.

(2) University degree, with its date.

(3) University distinctions.

(4) Publications.

(5) Date of admission to Priest's Orders, with the name of the diocese and the Bishop ordaining.

(6) Date of institution and licence.

(7) Former charges held.

(b) Mention the names of the assistant Curates, if any, with the other details, as above. State the kind of work for which the members of the staff severally exhibit special aptitude.

(c) Has any Clergyman been assisting in the parish for more than two consecutive Sundays without licence? If so, state his name, and the Bishop by whom his testimonials are signed.

(d) Does the Incumbent hold any other benefice or Preferment, or Lectureship, or any other cure? and if so, what?

(e) Do the Curates perform any other duty, as Incumbent, Curate, Lecturer, Chaplain, Master, or Assistant in any school, and where?

(f) What are the sources and gross amount of the endowment of the benefice?

(g) Mention the necessary outgoings and the net remainder.

(h) What are the stipends severally paid to the Assistant Curates, and whence are they derived?

(i) Are these stipends fully paid in money, without any deduction or subsequent repayment?

(j) If not, how much is so deducted or repaid, and for what consideration?

G. Parsonage, Glebe, Graveyard, &c.

(a) Is there a parsonage or clergy-house attached to the Church? If so, when was it built, and in what condition is it now? Is it insured, and for what sum?

(b) Is it rented or freehold?

(c) Is the building free from debt?

(d) If there be any glebe, state its extent and annual value.

(e) How much of it does the Incumbent hold in his own hands, and how much does he let?

(f) Does the Incumbent actually reside in the glebe house? If not, why not, and at what distance from the Church does he live?

(g) What do you understand by the term "residence?"

(h) How many days during the past year has the Incumbent actually resided in his parish?

(i) If the Incumbent be not resident, state the reason of absence, and whether he holds a licence for non-residence?

(j) At what distance is the parsonage from the Church?

(k) Where do the Assistant Curates reside, and at what distance severally from the Church, or Chapel in outlying portions?

(l) Is there a churchyard attached to the Church, and are burials still performed in it? If not, state where the parishioners are buried.

(m) Is the churchyard well fenced and kept?

(n) Is it overcrowded, and if so, what steps have you taken to get it enlarged?

(o) Have there been any encroachments on it, or any door made into it, or any way through it, without permission of the Ordinary?

(p) Are the graves dug at a proper distance, at least six feet, from the foundation of the Church?

(q) Are the necessary paths through the churchyard kept clean and in good order?

(r) Have any trees in it been either planted or cut down since the last Visitation?

(s) Are you careful not to allow any pagan or otherwise unfit monuments, inscriptions, or emblems to be erected in the graveyard?

H. Schools.

(a) What is the number of children in your parish of an age to attend school?

(b) What is the total amount of school accommodation?

(c) What is the actual number of children on the school books?

(d) Distinguish the number of schools in your parish under the following heads: (1) Anglican, (2) Roman Catholic, (3) Sectarian, (4) Secular. How many children (so far as you can tell) attend these schools respectively?

(*e*) How many buildings for schools under your superintendence are there in the parish?

(*f*) When were the schools built, and at what cost?

(*g*) What number were they built to accommodate?

(*h*) Are they large enough for your present requirements?

(*i*) Is there sufficient playground attached to the schools?

(*j*) Are there convenient lavatories and closets attached to the schools, and are these well drained, and in good order?

(*k*) Are there suitable places outside the schoolrooms for hats, bonnets, cloaks, &c.?

(*l*) Are the schoolrooms well lighted and ventilated?

(*m*) When full, how many cubic feet of air are allowed for each child?

(*n*) Are the schools mixed, or are there separate rooms or buildings for boys, girls, and infants?

(*o*) When were the present desks, benches, and other fittings supplied, and in what condition are they? Are they sufficient in quantity?

(*p*) Are the benches supplied, as is desirable, with backs?

(*q*) Is the rest of the school apparatus in sufficient quantity, and in good order?

(*r*) How are the schools severally supported, distinguishing the following sources: (1) Endowments, (2) State aid, (3) Private benefaction, (4) Children's pence?

(*s*) Is there any special fund for repairs?

Pupils.

(*a*) At what age do the children generally come to school, and at what age do they leave?

(*b*) State the school hours, and also what holydays are given.

(*c*) Are there evening and adult schools, and what is their success?

(*d*) Is there a separate choir school?

(*e*) Is there any system of rewards in the schools for regular attendance, and proficiency in learning?

(*f*) What method do you adopt for discouraging irregularity of attendance?

(*g*) What religious instruction is there during the week, and who gives it?

(*h*) Are there any middle and higher schools in your parish, either public or private? In whose hands are they?

(*i*) Do any of the pupils in these establishments attend the parochial services?

(*j*) Have the parochial clergy access to these schools for the purpose of conveying religious instruction?

Teachers.

(*a*) What salaried teachers are in charge of your schools? Do they hold any diploma or certificate?

(*b*) What is the amount of their several salaries? whence is it provided?

(*c*) Are their residences provided for them? If so, in what state of repair are they?

(*d*) Have they any pupil teachers or volunteers to assist them?

(*e*) How often do the clergy visit the schools?

(*f*) Are the schools under any external inspection? If so, state what it is; and give a summary of the last report.

Sunday School.

(*a*) What Sunday schools have you? where are they held? and at what hours?

(*b*) How are they attended?

(*c*) What means are employed to make them attractive and not fatiguing to the children?

(*d*) What proportion of the day scholars attend the Sunday schools?

(*e*) What proportion of the Sunday scholars do not attend the day schools?

(*f*) Is the instruction given in

the Sunday school exclusively religious or partially secular?

(*g*) What services in the Church are the Sunday scholars expected to attend?

(*h*) What number of the children has been presented for Confirmation during the past three years?

(*i*) What proportion of former scholars continue to attend Church, and are communicants?

(*j*) Do any children of other than Church parents attend the Sunday school? If so, how many?

I. Parochial Organization.

(*a*) Is the parish subdivided amongst the clergy into districts?

(*b*) For what part of the active parish work is the Incumbent solely responsible, and how is the rest apportioned?

(*c*) Is there a rota of duty in the Church, to fix the services for which the members of the clerical staff are severally responsible?

(*d*) How often in the month has each priest an opportunity of celebrating the Holy Eucharist?

(*e*) What organizations are there in connexion with the parish? Answer under the following heads: (1) Brotherhoods, (2) Sisterhoods, (3) Guilds, (4) Confraternities, (5) District Visitors, (6) Sunday school Teachers, (7) Scripture Readers, (8) Mission Women, &c., (9) Committees, (10) Working Men's Club or Institute. Give the average number of members, and state under what management each section is.

(*f*) What classes for instruction other than in school are held in your parish? (1) Choir, (2) Bible Classes, (3) Confirmation, (4) Communicant, (5) Sunday school Teachers, (6) Mothers' Meeting.

(*g*) Is there a Parochial Lending Library? Of how many volumes does it consist, and in what condition are they?

(*h*) Is there in your parish any branch association in aid of the great Church Societies? State what is the amount collected for each.

(*i*) Are meetings held in aid of missions to the heathen among your parishioners? or what other means do you take to recommend such objects to their attention?

(*j*) What charitable organizations are there? (1) Benefit Clubs, (2) Penny Bank, (3) Clothing Club, (4) Coal and Blanket Fund, (5) Maternity Fund, (6) Soup Kitchen, &c.

(*k*) Are there any non-parochial religious or charitable institutions within your parish? If so, have you access to them, or any share in their control?

(*l*) What sums have you raised during the past three years for religious or charitable purposes by (1) The General Offertory, (2) Charity Sermons, (3) Collections at Meetings, (4) Subscription Lists, (5) Miscellaneous Donations, (6) Seat-rents (if any)?

(*m*) How often is the Offertory collected, and is it on the increase or otherwise?

(*n*) In case of any special Offertory, is care taken to apprise the congregation as to its object?

(*o*) Is a statement of the sums collected posted in the Church at least monthly, for the satisfaction of the congregation?

(*p*) Are the accounts audited at least annually by qualified and disinterested persons?

(*q*) Is an annual balance-sheet printed and supplied to members of the congregation?

(*r*) What portion of the sums collected is applied to religious and charitable uses external to the parish? What were these uses last year?

(*s*) With whom does the disposal of the alms rest, and in what way are they supplied?

(*t*) What steps are taken to prevent the alms being an encouragement to mendicancy and pauperism?

(*u*) In cases of real need, is help ever refused because of the religious opinions of the applicant?

(*v*) What annual parish festivals are observed? and can you mention any improvement which has recently taken place in their observance?

(*w*) Have you established anything of this kind? and with what object?

K. THE CHURCHWARDENS.

(*a*) At what time of the year and how are the Churchwardens elected, and who are the present holders of that office?

(*b*) Have the last wardens duly rendered their accounts to the Incumbent and parishioners, and made over to their successors the moneys and goods belonging to the Church or parish which were in their hands?

(*c*) What subordinate officials, such as parish clerks, vergers, beadles, sextons, &c., are employed? Are they persons of good character, and competent for their several offices? What salaries are they paid, and from what sources?

(*d*) Do the wardens themselves attend the services in Church?

(*e*) Do they fulfil their duty in preserving order and decorum in Church?

(*f*) Do they take an active part in the Church work of the parish?

———

To the Churchwardens.

(*a*) Are the Clergymen of your parish persons of sober and exemplary life?

(*b*) Are they physically competent to discharge the duties of their office?

(*c*) Are they regular, punctual, and diligent in the performance of Divine Service?

(*d*) Do they perform Divine Service audibly and reverently?

(*e*) Are they ready and careful to visit the sick, and to perform their other duties?

(*f*) Have you any charge of neglect, &c., to bring against them?

(*g*) Have any of them, to your knowledge, taken part in the public worship of sectaries, or allowed them to officiate in the Church or schoolrooms?

(*h*) Do you take care that the names of strange officiants are duly entered in a book, with the name of the Bishop who ordained them?

(*i*) Have such repairs and improvements as were ordered at the last Visitation been undertaken or completed?

(*j*) Have any alterations or additions been made in the fixtures, furniture, or services of the Church since the last Visitation, and if so, what?

(*k*) Have you any suggestions to make for the furthering of Church work in the parish?

A. B. Incumbent.

C. D.
E. F. } Assistant Curates.
G. H.

I. K. } Churchwardens.
L. M.

N.B. It is desirable that this paper, when duly filled up by the Incumbent and Churchwardens, should be signed as indicated above, in order to guard against ex parte statements.

BIBLIOTHECA SACERDOTALIS.

CONTENTS.

ABBREVIATIONS.

A. Anglican.
C. Calvinist.
E. Eastern Church.
J. Jewish.
L. Lutheran.
O. C. Old Catholic.
P. Puritan.
R. Roman Catholic.
U. Unitarian.
W. Wesleyan.

* Denotes works of primary importance to those who can procure only a few books.
† Denotes that the book must be read with much caution.

I. DICTIONARIES AND BIBLIOGRAPHY.

(R) †Addis and Arnold, Catholic Dict.
Allibone, Dict. of English Liter.
(R) Assemani, Bibliotheca Orientalis.
(R) Backer, Bibl. des Ecrivains S. J.
(R) Bellarmine, De Scriptoribus Ecclesiasticis.
(R) Bergier, Dictionnaire de Théologie.
(R) Biel, Thesaurus in LXX.
(A) Brande and Cox, Dict. of Literature, Science, and Art.
(A) Blunt, Dictionary of Doctrinal and Historical Theology.
(A) Blunt, Dict. of Sects and Heresies.
(L) Bretschneider, Lexicon of N. T.
(R) Brunet, Manuel du Libraire. (Last edition.)
(C) Buxtorf, Lexicon Chald. et Rabbin.
(R) Calmet, Dictionary of the Bible.
(A) Cave, Historia Litteraria.
(R) Ceillier, Auteurs Sacrés.
(L) Cremer, Biblisch-theologisches Wörterbuch der N. T. Græcität. (Also Trans. Clark's F. T. L.)
(A) Darling, Cyclop. Bibliograph.
De Morgan, Book of Almanacs.
(A) Dictionary of Proper Names of O. and N. T. (Williams and Norgate.)
(A) *Dowling on the Study of Eccles. History.
(A) Dowling, Notitia Scriptorum SS. Patrum.
(R) Ducange, Gloss. Med. et Inf. Græc.
(R) Ducange, Gloss. Med. et Inf. Lat. (or abridged by D'Arnis.)
(R) Du Pin, Biblioth. des Auteurs Ecclesiastiques.
(C) Eadie, Bible Cyclopædia.
(L) Fabricius, Biblioth. Ecclesiastica.
(L) Fabricius, Biblioth. Græca.
(C) Fairbairn, Dict. of Bible.

(A) Fosbroke, Cyclop. of Antiquities.
(L) Gesenius, Thesaur. Heb. et Chald.
(R) *Glaire, Dict. Ecclesiastique.
(R) Goschler, Dict. Encyc. Théol. Cath. (Trans. of Wetzer and Welte.)
(L) Graesse, Orbis Latinus, (Eccles. Geogr.)
(R) Herbelot, Biblioth. Oriental.
(L) Herzog, Real-Encyclopädie.
(L) Hofman, Lexicon Universale.
(A) Hook, Church Dictionary.
Imperial Dict. of English Lang.
(L) Ittigius, De Bibliothecis Patrum.
(A) Jones, Proper Names of O. T.
(C) *Kitto, Cyclop. of Bibl. Literature.
(R) Le Long, Biblioth. Sacra. 1778-90.
Lewis and Short, Latin Dict.
(A) Lowndes, Engl. Bibliogr. Manual.
(R) Macri, Hierolexicon.
(R) Migne, Encyclopédie Théologique.
(R) Moreri, Dictionnaire Historique. 10 vols. 1759.
(R) Moroni, Dizionario Storico-Eccles. 103 vols.
(R) Oudin, Comm. de Script. Eccl. Ant.
(R) Potthast, Biblioth. Hist. Med. Ævi.
(R) *Richard et Giraud, Bibliothèque Sacrée.
(C) *Robinson, Lexicon of N. T.
(A) Roget, Thesaurus of Engl. Words and Phrases. (Ed. J. L. Roget.)
(C) Schenkel, Bibel-Lexicon.
(L) Schleusner, Lexicon V. et N. T.
(A) Shipley, Glossary of Ecclesiastical Terms.
*Smith, Dictionary of the Bible, (or the "Concise" Edition.)
Smith and Cheetham, Dictionary of Christian Antiquities.
Smith and Wace, Dict. of Christian Biography.
(C) Spurgeon, Commenting and Commentaries.
(A) Stormonth, Etymological English Dict. (Good for Scientific terms.)
(C) Suicer, Thesaurus Ecclesiasticus.
(R) Theologische Bibliothek. (Freiburg in Breisgau.)
Ure, Dict. of Arts and Manufact.
(L) Wahl, Clavis N. T.
(L) Walch, Bibliothecæ Theologica et Patristica.
(A) Walcott, Sacred Archæology.
(R) Weitenauer, Lex. Biblicum Vulg.
(R) Wetzer u. Welte, Kirchenlexicon.
(A) Whitaker, Reference Catalogue of Current Literature.
(L) Winer, Biblisches Real-Wörterbuch.

(A) Woodward and Cates, Encyc. of Chronology.
(A) Wright, Bible Word-Book.
(L) Zedler, Universal Lexicon.

II. Holy Scripture.

†"Bible" in Encyc. Brit. 9th ed.
(C) Bruce, Chief End of Revelation.
(R) Butler (Charles), Horæ Biblicæ.
†"Canon" in Encyc. Brit. 9th ed.
(L) Carpzov, Critica Sacra.
(R) Concordantia Max. in Bibl. Vulg.
Conder, Handbook to Bible.
(A) Cosin, Scholastical Hist. of Canon.
Critici Sacri.
(C) Cruden, Concordance.
(A) *Davison on Prophecy.
(L) Delitzsch, Biblical Psychology.
(R) Didacus a S. Antonio, Enchiridion Scripturarum.
(R) Dutripon, Concordantiæ Vulgatæ.
(C) Eadie on the English Bible.
(C) Fairbairn on Prophecy.
(C) Fairbairn, Typology of Holy Scripture.
(C) Gerard, Institutes of Biblical Criticism.
(A) Geikie, Hours with the Bible.
(R) Glaire, Abrégé d'Introd. A. et N. Test.
(A) Hannah, Bampton Lectures.
(L) Hertwig, Tabellen zur Einleitung ins A. u. N. T.
(A) Hody, De Bibliorum Textibus et Versionibus.
(A) *Horne, Introd. to O. and N. T. 12th ed. 4 v. Also abridged ed.
(A) Bp. Jebb, Sacred Literature.
(C) Keach, Tropologia.
Kilber, Analysis Biblica.
(A) Lee on Inspiration.
(A) Bp. Marsh, Lectures on Criticism and Interpretation.
Mombert, English Versions of the Bible.
(L) *Polyglotten-Bibel von Stier und Theile.
(P) Poole, Synopsis Criticorum.
(R) Possevinus, Apparatus Sacer.
(C) Reuss, Hist. du Canon.
(A) Row, Nature and Extent of Inspiration.
(R) Sabatier, Versio Itala.
(R) Schouppe, Cursus Script. Sacræ.
(C) Scripture Textbook and Treasury. (Dublin Tract Society.)
(A) Selwyn, Notæ Criticæ.
(R) Spanner, Polyanthea Sacra.
(A) Abp. Trench, Hulsean Lect. 1845.
(C) Turpie, Old Test. in the New.

(R) Vulgate. Ed. Vercellone.
(A) Wall, Grounds for Revision of English Bible.
(A) Walton, Apparatus Criticus. Ed. Wrangham.
(A) Walton, Polyglott.
(A) Westcott, The Bible in the Church.
(A) Westcott, History of English Bible.
(A) Wordsworth, Hulsean Lect. 1846.
(C) Young, Analytical Concordance.

III. COMMENTARIES ON THE WHOLE BIBLE.

(C) Annotated Paragraph Bible. (Rel. Tr. Soc.)
(L) Barth, Practical Commentary, or Bible Manual.
(R) Biblia Sacra cum Glossa Ordinaria. Antw. 1634.
(A) *Blunt, Annotated Bible.
(R) Calmet, Commentaire littéral. 9 vols. fol. 1724.
(L) Calovius, Biblia Illustrata. Cambridge Bible for Schools.
(W) Clarke (Adam), O. and N. T.
(R) *Cornelii à Lapide Comment. in Vet. et Nov. Test.
(R) De La Haye, Biblia Magna. 5 vols. fol. 1643.
(R) De Lyra, Postilla in SS.
(R) Dionysius Carthusianus in SS.
(A) Bp. Ellicott, Comm. on O. and N.T.
(R) Estius, In difficiliora loca SS. Annot.
(P) Gill, Exposition of O. and N. T.
(C) Gray, Biblical Museum.
(C) Henry (Matthew), Expos. O. and N. T.
(R) Hugo à S. Charo, Comm. in Biblia.
(C) Kitto, Pictorial Bible. Daily Bible Illustrations.
(L) Lange, Bibelwerk. (Clark's F.T.L.)
(A) Mayer, Commentary on O. and N. T. 1653.
(R) Menochius, Comment. in SS. Pulpit Commentary.
(C) Reuss, La Bible.
(L) Rosenmüller, Scholia in Vet. et Nov. Test.
(R) Sa (Emmanuel), Notationes in totam Scrip.
(R) Sacy, La Sainte Bible. 32 vols. 8vo. 1692.
(A) The Speaker's Commentary.
(A) S.P.C.K. Commentary on Bible.
(R) Tostatus, Opera Omnia.
(P) Trapp, Commentary.
*Variorum Teachers' Bible.
(A) Wordsworth, Bible.

IV. OLD TESTAMENT.

(A) Barry, Introd. to O. T.
(R) Becanus, Analogia. Bible in Workshop.
(J) Biblia Rabbinica Magna, v. 4.
(L) †Bleek, Introd. to Old Test. trans. by Venables.
(L) Carpzov, Introd. ad Libr. Canonic. V. T.
(A) Churton on the Septuagint.
(C) Cocceius, Comm. in Vet. Test. Dank, Historia Vet. Test.
(C) †Davidson, Text of O. T. †Davidson, Introd. to O. T.
(C) Davidson, Hebrew and Chaldee Concordance.
(L) Delitzsch, O. T. Hist. of Redemption. Eng. Trans.
(L) †De Wette, Introd. to Old Test.
(A) *Driver, On the Hebrew Verb.
(C) Drusius, Test. Vet. Interpret.
(A) Edersheim, Bible History.
(L) †Ewald, Dichter d. Alten Bundes.
(L) †Ewald, Propheten d. Alten Bundes.
(L) Ewald, Hebrew Syntax.
(R) Fernandez in Visiones Veteris Testamenti.
(A) Field, Hexapla of Origen.
(A) Field, Septuagint. Fürst, Concord. Heb. et Chald. Vet. Test.
(A) Girdlestone, Old Testament Synonyms.
(C) Godet, Biblical Studies on O. T. Grant, Bible Record of Creation.
(L) Hävernick, Handb. d. Einleitung in d. A. T.
(L) Hengstenberg, Christology of Old Test. (Clark's F. T. L.)
(A) Holmes and Parsons, LXX.
(A) Horsley, Biblical Criticism. Jager, Septuagint.
(L) Jahn, Introd. in Vet. Test.
(L) Keil, Lehrbuch d. Einleitung in d. A. T.
(L) Keil and Delitzsch on Old Test. (Clark's F. T. L.)
(C) †Kuenen, Religion of Israel.
(L) Kurtz, Sacrificial Worship of O. T. (Clark's F. T. L.)
(L) Kurtz, History of the Old Covenant. (Clark's F. T. L.)
(A) Bp. Lowth, Sacra Poesis Hebræorum.
(A) Lyall, Propædia Prophetica.
(A) Maclear, Class Book of Old Test. History.
(J) Maimonides, More Nevochim. Ed. Munk.
(L) †Maurer, Comment. in Vet. Test.

(L) †Maurer, Kurzgef. Handbuch z. A. T.
(A) Maurice, Patriarchs and Lawgivers of O. T.
(A) Maurice, Prophets and Kings of O. T.
(L) Oehler, Theology of the Old Testament. (Clark's F. T. L.)
Oxford Septuagint, 1817, with Carpzov. Proleg.
(A) Plumptre, Studies in Old Test.
(L) Riehm, Messianic Prophecy. (Clark's F. T. L.)
(C) Reusch, Einleitung in das A. T.
(C) †Robertson Smith, Old Testament in Jewish Church.
(C) Schultz, Alt-testamentliche Theologie.
(R) Simon, Hist. Critic. V. T.
(A) Spencer, de Legibus Hebræorum.
(A) Sir E. Strachey, Hebrew Politics.
Taylor (Isaac), Spirit of the Hebrew Poetry.
(L) Theile, Hebrew Bible.
(L) Tischendorf, Septuagint. Ed. 4.
(C) *Trommii Concord. in LXX.
(A) Wigram, Englishman's Heb. and Chald. Concordance.
(A) Willis, Worship of the Old Covenant.
(P) Ainsworth, Pentateuch, Psalms, and Song of Songs.
(L) Bahr, Symbolik d. Mos. Cultus.
(A) CHRIST in the Pentateuch.
(L) Ebers, Egypten und die Bücher Moses.
(W) Etheridge, Targums on Pentateuch.
(A) Bp. Goodwin, Essays on Pentateuch.
(A) Graves on the Pentateuch.
(L) Hävernick, Der Pentateuchus.
(L) Hengstenberg, Der Pentateuchus.
(L) Hengstenberg, Ægypten und Moses.
(L) Knobel, Pentateuch.
(C) Macdonald on Pentateuch.
(R) Smith (W.) on Pentateuch.
(A) Warburton, Divine Legation of Moses.
(C) †Calvin on Genesis.
(C) Candlish, Lectures on Genesis.
(L) Delitzsch, Die Genesis ausgelegt.
Hershon, Genesis with Talmudical Commentary.
(C) Jacobus, Notes on Genesis.
(A) Jukes, Types of Genesis.
(J) †Kalisch on Genesis, Exodus, Leviticus.
(C) Murphy, Commentary on Genesis.
(A) Williams, Beginning of Genesis.
(C) Murphy, Commentary on Exodus.

Bonar, Commentary on Leviticus.
Curtiss, The Levitical Priests.
(A) Jukes, Law of Offering in Leviticus.
(R) Lorinus in Lib. Numerorum.
(R) Naxera in Lib. Josue.
(L) Bertheau, Judges, Ruth, Chronicles, Ezra, Nehemiah, Esther.
(L) Raabe, Ruth und das Hohe Lied.
(A) Wright (C. H. H.), Book of Ruth.
(L) Thenius on Samuel.
(A) CHRIST in the Prophets.
(A) Chandler, Critical History of the Life of David.
(L) Keil on the Books of Kings. (Tr. by Martin.)
(R) Ancessi, Job et l'Egypte.
(C) Caryl on Job.
(C) Cox, Commentary on Job.
(L) Dillman, Hiob. (Job.)
S. Gregory, Morals on Job.
(C) Hutcheson, Exposition on Job.
(A) Mason Good on Job.
(R) Pineda in Jobum. (Usually ranges with Corn. à Lap.)
(A) Rodwell, Translation of Job.
(A) Bp. Alexander, Bampton Lect. on Psalms.
(A) Armfield, Gradual Psalms.
S. Augustine on Psalms. (Oxf. Lib. Fath.)
(R) Bellarmine in Psalmos.
(A) Boys, Exposition of the Proper Psalms.
(C) Bythner, Lyra Davidica.
(C) Calvinus in Psalmos.
(A) Concordance to the Prayer-Book Psalms.
(C) Cox, the Pilgrim Psalms.
(L) Delitzsch, Comm. ü. d. Psalter.
(A) Greswell, Gramm. Analysis of Psalms.
(A) Hammond, Paraphrase on the Psalms.
(L) Hengstenberg on the Psalms. (Clark's F. T. L.)
(A) Horne on the Psalms.
(L) Hupfeld, Die Psalmen.
(A) Jennings and Lowe on the Psalms.
(A) Kay, Psalms translated with Notes.
(R) Le Blanc in Psalmos.
(L) Liber Psalmorum Hieron. Edd. Tischendorf, Baer, et Delitzsch.
(R) Lorinus in Psalmos.
(A) Mason Good, Historical Outline of Psalms, and Book of Psalms.
(C) Murphy, Critical and Exegetical Commentary on the Psalms.
(A) Neale and Littledale on the Psalms.
(A) Perowne on the Psalms (large ed.)
(A) Phillips on Psalms.

(A) *Plain Commentary on Psalms.
(R) Quesnel, Pseaumes de David.
(A) Simpson, Plain Words on the Psalms.
(C) Spurgeon, Treasury of David.
(A) Thrupp on the Psalms.
(L) Venema in Psalmos.
(L) Bertheau on Proverbs.
(A) Bridges on Proverbs.
(L) Delitzsch on Proverbs. (Clark's F. T. L.)
(R) Jansenius in Proverbia.
(R) Maldonatus in Proverbia.
(A) Pearson, Counsels of the Wise King.
(R) Salazar in Proverbia.
(L) Ginsburg, Coheleth.
(L) Hengstenberg on Ecclesiastes.
(C) Macdonald on Ecclesiastes.
(A) Preston on Ecclesiastes.
(A) Wright (C. H. H.), Ecclesiastes.
(L) Delitzsch, Das Hohe Lied.
(A) Galton on the Song of Songs.
(P) Gill on Solomon's Song.
(L) †Ginsburg on the Song of Songs.
(A) Harmer, Outline of Commentary on Solomon's Song.
(L) Hengstenberg, Das Hohe Lied.
(A) Littledale on the Song of Songs.
(C) Moody Stuart on the Song of Songs.
(A) Thrupp on the Song of Songs.
(C) †Robertson Smith, Prophets of Israel.
(C) Alexander on Isaiah.
(A) Birks on Isaiah.
(A) *Cheyne on Isaiah.
(L) Delitzsch, Jesaia.
(A) †Gesenius, Der Prophet Jesaia.
(L) Hengstenberg, Jesaia.
(L) Knobel, Der Prophet Jesaia.
(A) Bp. Lowth on Isaiah.
(A) Payne Smith on Isaiah.
(C) Vitringa in Jesaiam.
(A) Blayney on Jeremiah and Lamentations.
(C) Henderson on Jeremiah.
(R) Maldonatus in Hieremiam.
(L) Nägelsbach, Jeremiah and Lamentations.
(L) Thenius on Lamentations.
(C) Fairbairn on Ezekiel.
(L) Hävernick, Comment. in d. Prophet Ezechiel.
(R) Maldonatus in Ezechielem.
(R) Pradus et Villalpandus in Ezechielem. 3 vols. fol.
(L) Auberlen on Daniel and Revelation.
(L) Hengstenberg, Genuineness of Daniel.
(L) Keil on Daniel. (Clark's F. T. L.)
(R) Maldonatus in Danielem.

(A) Pusey, Lectures on Daniel.
(C) Tregelles, Defence of Authenticity of Daniel.
(C) Hutcheson, Brief Exposition of the Twelve Prophets.
(L) Keil on the Minor Prophets.
(A) Pusey on Minor Prophets.
(C) Burrowes on Hosea.
(C) Fairbairn on Jonah.
(C) Martin (H.), The Prophet Jonah.
(C) Redford, Studies in the Book of Jonah.
(A) Wright (C. H. H.), Zechariah.
(A) Deane, Book of Wisdom.

V. NEW TESTAMENT.

(A) Alford, How to study N. T.
(A) †Alford, Greek Testament.
(A) Barrett, Companion to Greek New Testament.
(L) *Bengel, Gnomon Novi Test.
(A) Blackley and Hawes, Critical English Test.
(L) †Bleek, Einleitung in d. N. T. (Engl. Transl.)
Bruce, Training of the Twelve.
*Bruder, Concord. Græc. Nov. Test.
(A) Burgon, The Revision Revised.
(A) Burkitt, Commentary on N. T.
(L) Buttmann's N. T. Grammar.
(C) †Calvin's Comm. Ed. Tholuck.
Catena Aurea. (T. Aquinas.)
(A) Churton and Jones, New Test.
(A) Cowper, Codex Alexandrinus.
(R) Curci, Il Nuovo Testamento.
(R) Dehaut, L'Evangile Medité.
(L) De Wette, Handb. z. N. T.
(C) Godet, Etudes Bibliques, N. T.
(A) Green, Grammar of N. T. Dialect.
Grimm, Lexicon of N. T. Greek.
(A) Grinfield, Editio Hellenistica.
(A) Guillemard, Hebraisms in Greek Test.
(A) Hammond, Paraphrase on N. T.
(A) Hammond, Textual Criticism of N. T.
(L) Hesse, Das Muratorische Fragment.
(L) †Hilgenfeld, Einleitung in d. N.T.
(R) Hug, Introd. to New Test.
(C) Jones on the Canon of the N. T.
(L) Kirchhofer, Quellensammlung z. Geschichte d. N. T. Canons.
(R) Langen, Einleitung in das N. T.
(R) Langen, das Judenthum in Palästina zur Zeit Christi.
(A) †Lewin, Fasti Sacri.
(A) Lightfoot on Revision of N. T.
(A) Maclear, Class-book of New Test. History.
(A) McClellan, New Testament.

(R) Mai, Codex Vaticanus.
(A) Maitland, Apostolic School of Prophetic Interpretation.
(A) Malan, Plea for English New Test. against Alford.
(L) †Meyer, Commentary on New Testament.
(A) Middleton on Greek Article. (H. J. Rose.)
(A) Norris, Comm. on New Testament.
(L) Olshausen, Comm. ü. N. T.
(A) Parallel New Test. 1611 and 1881.
(R) Quesnel, Nouveau Testament.
(R) Reithmayer, Einleitung in d. N.T.
(C) Reuss, Geschichte d. Heilig. Schrift. N. T.
(C) R. T. S. Greek Grammar of N. T.
(R) Salmeron, Comm. in N. T.
(A) Salmon, Lectures on Canon of N.T.
(L) Schmid, Biblical Theology of N. T.
(L) Schöttgen, Horæ Hebraicæ in N. T.
(L) Schürer, Lehrbuch der N. T. Zeitgeschichte.
(A) Scrivener, Codex Augiensis.
(A) Scrivener, Codex Bezæ.
(A) Scrivener, Cambridge Greek Test.
(A) Scrivener, Introduction to Criticism of N. T. 3rd edit.
(A) Scrivener, Six Lectures on the Text of N. T.
(A) Scrivener, Collation of Tischendorf's Cod. Sinait.
(A) Sewell, Microscope of New Test.
(C) Smith (W.), Student's N. T. Hist. Student's Concordance to Revised N. T.
(R) Sylveira in N. T.
Tauchnitz, English N. T.
(L) Tischendorf, Codex Sinaiticus.
(L) Tischendorf, Greek Test. Ed. 8.
Thoms, Concordance to Revised Version of N. T.
(C) Tregelles, Critical Greek Test.
(C) Tregelles, Collation of Critical Texts of New Testament.
(A) Abp. Trench, N. T. Synonyms.
(A) *Westcott, Canon of N. T.
(A) Westcott and Hort, Greek Test.
(A) Wilkinson, Instructions on Parables.
Wilson, W., Illustrations of N. T.
(L) Winer, Grammar of N. T. Idiom. (Tr. by Prof. Moulton.)
(A) Wordsworth, Greek Test.
(A) Alexander (Natalis) in Evangelia.
(A) Bp. Alexander, Leading Ideas of Gospels.
(L) Anger, Synopsis Evangg. Matt. Marc. Luc.
(R) Barradius, Concord. et Hist. IV. Evang.

(A) Boys, Dominical Epistles and Gospels.
(C) Bruce, Parabolic Teaching of CHRIST.
(A) *Burgon, Plain Commentary on the Four Gospels.
(A) Cook, Revised Version of First Three Gospels.
(A) *Denton on Gospels for Sundays and Holy Days.
(A) *Dunwell, Commentary on Four Gospels.
(A) Ford, Illustrations of Gospels.
(A) Goulburn, Thoughts on the Liturgical Gospels.
(A) Greswell on Parables.
(A) Greswell, Harmony of Gospels.
(R) Hirsch, Betrachtungen über die Sonntäglichen Evangelien u. Epistolen. (Tübingen.)
(L) Holtzmann, Die Synoptischen Evangelien.
(A) Humphrey, Comm. on Revised Ver.
(A) Jukes, Characteristic Differences of the Gospels.
(P) Lightfoot, Horæ Hebraicæ in IV. Evang.
(R) Lucas Brugensis in Evangelia.
(R) Maldonatus in Evangelia.
(R) Piconius, Triplex Expositio in Evangelia.
(A) Pieritz, Gospels from Rabbinical Point of View.
(A) Sanday, The Gospels in the Second Century.
(R) Stapleton, Antidota Evangelica.
(L) *Tischendorf, Synopsis Evangelica.
(A) Townson, Harmony of Gospels.
(A) *Trench on the Miracles.
(A) *Trench on the Parables.
(A) Trench, Studies in the Gospels.
(A) Westcott, Introd. to Gospels.
(A) Whish, Clavis Syriaca in Evangelia.
(L) Wieseler, Synopsis of Four Gospels. (Tr. Venables.)
(A) Williams (Isaac), Study of Gosp. S. Augustine on the Sermon on the Mount. (Trench.)
(A) Bp. Harvey Goodwin on S. Matth.
(R) Gratry, Comm. sur S. Matthieu. S. Hilary, Canones in Evan. Matt.
(C) Morison, Practical Comm. on S. Matthew.
(A) Nicholson, Comm. on S. Matthew.
(R) Paulus de Palacio in Matthæum.
(A) Sadler, S. Matthew.
(L) Tholuck, Sermon on the Mount.
(A) Burgon, Last Twelve Verses of S. Mark.
(C) Morison, Practical Comm. on S. Mark.

(C) Godet on S. Luke. (Clark's F. T. L.)
(A) Bp. H. Goodwin, Commentary on S. Luke.
(A) Hobart, Medical Language of S. Luke.
(R) Stella in Lucam.
S. Augustine on S. John. (Oxf. Lib. Fath.)
(R) Deutinger in Evang. Johan.
(L) †Ewald, Die Johanneischen Schriften.
(R) Ferus, Enarrat. in Ev. Johannis.
(C) Godet on S. John.
(L) Hengstenberg on S. John.
(L) Lampe, Commentarius in Joannem.
(A) Lias, Doctrin. Syst. of S. John.
(L) Lücke on S. John.
(L) Luthardt, S. John the Author of the Fourth Gospel.
(C) Oosterzee, Apologetical Lectures on John's Gospel.
(A) Sadler on S. John.
(A) Sanday on the Fourth Gospel.
(L) Tholuck on S. John.
(A) Westcott on S. John.
(L) Baumgarten, Apostolic History.
(A) Cook on Acts.
(A) *Denton on the Acts.
(A) Farrar, Early Days of Christianity.
(A) Farrar, Life of S. Paul.
(A) Ford, Illustrations of the Acts.
(R) Fromondus in Acta Apost.
(C) Gloag on the Acts.
(C) †Kuenen on the Acts.
(A) Lightfoot, Comment. on the Acts.
(R) Lorinus in Acta Apostolorum.
(A) Norris, Key to the Acts.
(R) Alexander (Natalis) in Epistolas Pauli.
(A) Conybeare and Howson, S. Paul.
(A) *Denton on the Epistles for Sundays and Holydays.
(A) Ellicott on Pauline Epistles.
(R) Estius in Epist. S. Pauli.
(R) Faber Stapulensis in Epistolas Pauli.
(A) Fell on the Epistles.
(C) Gloag, Introduction to the Pauline Epistles.
(A) Heathen World, the, and S. Paul. (S. P. C. K.)
(A) Irons, Bampton Lectures on S. Paul.
(R) Justiniani in Epist. Pauli.
(A) Lewin, Life and Ep. of S. Paul.
(A) Paley, Horæ Paulinæ.
(R) Piconius in Epistolas Pauli.
(R) Stapleton, Antidota Apostolica.
(C) Beet, Commentary on Romans.
(A) Chamberlain on Romans.
(L) †Fritzsche on Romans.

(C) Godet on Ep. to the Romans.
(L) Tholuck on Romans.
(C) Van Hengel on Romans.
(C) Beet, Comment. on Corinthians.
(A) Stanley on the Corinthians.
(A) Lightfoot on Galatians.
(R) Reithmayer, Kommentar an die Galater.
(L) Schott on Galatians.
(C) Windischmann on Galatians.
(L) Winer on Galatians.
(C) Eadie on Ephesians.
(L) Harless on Ephesians.
(A) Lightfoot on Philippians.
(C) Van Hengel on Philippians.
(R) Velasquez in Ep. ad Philipp.
(A) Bp. Davenant on the Colossians.
(A) Lightfoot on Coloss. and Philem.
(C) Fairbairn on the Pastoral Epistles.
(L) Bleek on Hebrews.
(L) Carpzov, Sacræ Exercitatt. in Epist. ad Heb.
(L) Delitzsch on Hebrews.
(A) McCaul on Hebrews.
(C) Owen on Hebrews.
(A) Randall, Epistle to the Hebrews.
(R) Ribera in Hebræos.
(L) Stier, Der Brief an die Hebräer.
(L) Tholuck on Hebrews.
(R) Justiniani in Cathol. Epist.
(A) Leighton on S. Peter. Ed. West.
(P) Adams on 2 S. Peter.
(A) Westcott, Epistles of S. John.
(L) Haupt on 1 S. John. (Clark's F. T. L.)
(L) Neander on 1 S. John.
(L) †Bleek on Apocalypse.
(A) Galton, Lectures on the Apocalypse.
(L) Hengstenberg on the Apocalypse.
(A) Todd, Lectures on the Apocalypse.
(A) Trench, Epistles to the Seven Churches.
(A) Williams (Isaac) on the Apocalypse.

VI. CHRISTIAN DOGMATICS.

(R) Alagona, Compend. Summæ Theolog.
(R) Abelly, Medulla Theolog.
(R) *Aquinas, Summa Theologica.
(L) Bähr, Lehre der Kirche vom Tode JESU in ersten 3 Jahrhundert.
(R) Bailly, Theologia Dogmatica.
(A) Bp. Barry, Lectures on the Atonement.
(L) †Baur, Lehre von der Versöhnung.
(L) Baur, Dreieinigkeit.
(R) *†Bellarmine, Corpus Controversiarum.

(A) Blackmore, Harmony of Eastern and Anglican Doctrine.

(A) Blenkinsopp on Development.

(A) Brewer on Athanasian Creed.

(A) Bull, Defensio Fidei Nicœnæ.

(A) Bull on Justification.

(A) Bp. A. Campbell, Doctrine of Middle State.

(L) Caspari, Taufsymbol.

(R) Canus (Melchior), de Locis Theol.

(R) Catéchisme de Persévérance.

(R) *Catechismus Concilii Tridentini. (Also English Trans.)

(R) Compendium Theologiæ Universæ, Thomas de Charmes.

(R) Dens, Theolog. Moral. et Dogm.

(R) Dieringer, Lehrbuch der Kathol. Dogmatik.

(L) Dorner, Gesch. d. Protest. Theol. (Clark's F. T. L.)

(A) *Drake, Teaching of Church of First Three Cent. on Priesthood and Sacrifice.

(R) Canon Eccles on Justification.

(R) Estius in Sententias.

(A) Ewer, Operation of HOLY SPIRIT.

(A) †Farrar, Mercy and Judgment.

(A) Forbes à Corse, Instruct. Historico-Theologica.

(A) *Bp. Forbes on the Nicene Creed.

(R) Gaume, Traité du S. Esprit.

(L) Gass, Geschichte d. Protest. Dogmatik.

(L) Gass, Symbolik d. Griechischen Kirche.

(R) Gerberti Opera.

(E) *Guettée, Exposition de la Doctrine de l'Eglise Orthodoxe.

(L) Hagenbach, History of Doctrines. (Clark's F. T. L.)

(L) Hahn, Bibliothek der Symbole.

(A) Harvey on the Three Creeds.

(L) Hase, Handb. d. Prot. Polemik.

(L) Hase, Libri Symbolici Eccles. Evangelicæ.

(A) *Heurtley, de Fide et Symbolo.

(A) *Heurtley, Harmonia Symbolica.

(A) Heygate, Catholic Antidotes.

(A) Hey, Lectures in Divinity.

(A) Hort, Two Dissertations.

(A) *Houghton on Calvinism.

(A) Hutchings, Person and Work of the HOLY GHOST.

(A) Jackson (Dr. T.), Works.

(A) Jones of Nayland, Works.

(R) Jungmann, Inst. Theol. Dogm.

(L) Kimmel, Monumenta Fidei Eccles. Oriental.

(R) Klee, Katholische Dogmatik.

(R) Klee, Lehrbuch der Dogmen-Geschichte. (Also French Version.)

(A) Knox (Alex.), Remains.

(R) Kuhn, Einleitung in Katholische Dogmatik.

(R) Kuhn, Gotteslehre.

(R) Kuhn, Lehre von Göttl. Gnade.

(R) Kuhn, Trinitatslehre.

(R) Langen, Die Trinitatslehrdifferenz.

(A) Abp. Laurence, Bampton Lectures.

(L) Leibnitz, Systema Theologiæ. (Trans. by Russell.)

(A) Leslie, Works.

(R) Lessius, de Perfectionibus Divinis.

(R) Liebermann, Inst. Theol. Dogm.

(A) Luckock, After Death.

(A) Lumby, Hist. of the Creeds.

(R) Card. de Luzerne, Œuvres.

(E) Macaire, Théologie Orthodoxe.

(A) MacColl on Athanasian Creed.

(C) Macdonald on the Atonement.

(R) Malvenda, Tract. de Antichristo.

(R) Marcus a Bauduino, Paradisus Theologicus.

(R) Maréchal, Concordantia SS. Patr.

(L) *Martensen, Christian Dogmatics. (Clark's F. T. L.)

(C) Matheson, Aids to Study of German Theology.

(A) Mede, Works.

(A) *Moberly's Bampton Lectures. The Administration of the Spirit.

(R) *Möhler, Symbolik. (Eng. Tr. by Robertson.)

(A) Mozley, Augustinian Theory of Predestination.

(A) Mozley, Theological Lectures and Papers.

(L) Müller, Christian Doctrine of Sin. (Clark's F. T. L.)

(R) Neumayr, Opera.

(A) *Newman, Lect. on Justification.

(R) †Newman on Development.

(L) Niemeyer, Collectio Confessionum in Eccl. Reformatis.

(A) Norris, Rudiments of Theology.

(A) Ommanney, Early Hist. of Athanasian Creed.

(C) †Oosterzee, Christian Dogmatics.

(R) Opstraet, Theolog. Christianus.

(A) Outram, de Sacrificiis.

(A) Owen, Introduction to Study of Dogmatic Theology.

(A) Palmer, Dissertations on the Orthodox Communion.

(A) *Pearson on the Apostles' Creed.

(A) Pearson, Minor Works. Ed. Churton.

(R) Pereira, Tentativa Theologica.

(P) Perkins, Works.

(R) Perrone, Prælectiones Theol.

(R) Perrone, de Fide, Spe, et Caritate.

(R) Perrone, de Divinitate D. N. J. C.

(R) Petavius, de Theologicis Dogma-
tibus.
(L) Plitt, Evangelische Glaubens-
lehre.
(E) Potessaro, Orthodox Doctrine of
Eastern Church.
(C) †Pressensé, Heresy and Christian
Doctrine.
(A) Pusey, What is of Faith as to
Everlasting Punishment?
(C) Rainy, Delivery and Development
of Christian Doctrine.
(C) Reuss, Théologie Chrétienne. (Also
English Version.)
(L) Ritschl, Hist. of the Doctrine of
Justification.
(L) †Rothe, Theologisch. Ethik.
(A) *Sadler, Church Doctrine Bible
Truth.
(A) Sadler, Justification of Life.
(R) Schouppe, Elem. Theolog. Dogm.
(L) Schoeberlein, Princip und System
der Dogmatik.
(R) Schram, Compend. Theologiæ.
(C) Shedd, Hist. of Christian Doct.
(C) Soulier, Doctrine du Logos chez
Philon.
(A) Bp. Steere on the Attributes of
GOD.
(L) Streitwolf, Libr. Symbol. Eccl.
Cath.
(A) Swete, Early Hist. of Doctrine of
HOLY SPIRIT.
(A) Swete, Hist. of Doctrine of Pro-
cession of the HOLY SPIRIT.
(C) Taylor (Isaac), Physical Theory of
Another Life.
(R) Thomassinus, Dogm. Theol. et De
Deo.
(R) Tournely, Prælect. Theolog.
(A) Abp. Ussher on Prayers for the
Dead.
(R) *Veronii Regula Fidei Catholicæ.
(A) Waterland on the Athan. Creed.
(L) Weber, Vom Zorne Gottes.
(R) Werner, Gesch. d. Kathol. Theol.
(A) Westcott, The Historic Faith.

VII. PERSON AND WORK OF CHRIST.

(C) Andrews, Bible Student's Life of
our LORD.
(A) Bp. Barry, Manifold Witness to
CHRIST.
(R) Ben Ezra (i.e. Lacunza), Coming
of Messiah in Glory.
(A) Blyth, Holy Week and Forty Days.
(R) S. Bonaventura, Life of CHRIST.
(A) Bright, Sermons of S. Leo on In-
carnation.
Brown (John), Discourses and
Sayings of our LORD.

(L) †Caspari, Chr
ische Einl
JESU CHRI
(R) Coleridge,]
LORD.
(R) Coleridge, Vi
(C) Dale, Lecture
(C) Des Champs,
Antichristi
(R) Digest of S.
the Incarn
(L) Dorner on th
(Clark's F
(A) Drew, The S
(L) Ebrard, Gosp
(U) †Ecce Homo.
(A) Edersheim,
JESUS the
(A) Ellicott, His
the Life of
(L) †Ewald, Life
(C) Fairbairn, St
CHRIST.
(A) *Geikie, Li
CHRIST.
(R) Günther, Inc
(C) Hanna, Life
(A) Hutchings, M
tation.
(A) Jukes, The N
Life.
(L) †Keim, JESUS
(L) Krummacher,
(R) Kuhn, Leben
(L) Lange, Life o
(R) Landriot, Le
tion.
(A) *Liddon, Bam
(R) *Ludolfi de S
(C) †M'Leod Cam
(C) Macpherson
of CHRIST.
(A) Medd, Bampt
(A) The Messiah.
(C) *Milligan, Re
(A) Michell, Gosp
(A) Mill on the
anity.
(A) Mill, The '
LORD.
(L) Nägelsbach,]
(L) Neander, Life
(C) Oosterzee, Im
(A) *Ottley, Tho
(R) Oxenham, C
the Atonen
(R) Pabst, Der M
schichte.
(A) Payne Smith
ration for
(R) Petavius, de
(C) Pressensé, JE

(C) Pye Smith, Testimony to the Messiah.

†Renan, Vie de JESUS.

(A) Ricketts, Saved by His Life.

(A) Sadler, Emmanuel.

(L) †Schenkel, Life of CHRIST.

(L) Stier, Words of the LORD JESUS. (Clark's F. T. L.)

(L) Stier, Words of the Risen SAVIOUR. (Clark's F. T. L.)

(A) Taylor (Jeremy), Life of CHRIST.

(L) Thomasius, CHRISTI Person und Werk.

(R) Thomassin, de Incarn. Verbi Divini.

(A) Trench, Hulsean Lectures, 1846.

(C) Tulloch, The CHRIST of the Gospels.

(A) Westcott, Gospel of the Resurrection.

(C) Whitelaw, Divinity of JESUS in Gospels and Epistles.

(A) *Wilberforce on the Incarnation.

(A) *Williams, Devotional Commentary on the Gospel.

(A) Young, The CHRIST of History.

VIII. THE CHURCH.

(A) Ashwell, Lectures on Holy Catholic Church.

(A) Brett, Church Government.

(A) Brett, Independency of the Church.

(L) Cassander, Tradit. Ecclesiæ Defensio.

(A) Clark, The Church, the Ministry, and the Sacraments.

(A) Bp. Cotterill, Genesis of the Church.

(A) Drew, Divine Kingdom.

(A) Ecclesia DEI.

(A) Field, Of the Church.

(A) Gladstone, Church Principles.

(A) Goulburn on the Holy Catholic Church.

(L) Geffcken, Church and State.

(A) Hooker, Ecclesiastical Polity.

(A) Maurice, Kingdom of CHRIST.

(A) Mitchell, Church Government.

(A) Miller, Church in relation to the State.

(A) Palmer, Treatise on the Church of CHRIST.

(A) Potter, Church Government.

(A) Sage, Principles of the Cyprianic Age.

(R) Suarez, de Legibus.

(A) Thorndike's Treatises.

(R) Turrecremata, Summa de Ecclesia.

IX. SACRAMENTS IN GENERAL.

(A) *Blunt (J. H.) on Sacraments.

(R) Bossuet, L'Eucharistie.

(R) †Bridgett, History of Holy Eucharist in Great Britain.

(R) Catech. Sem. Mechlinensis.

(R) Franzelin, de Sacramentis in Genere.

(L) Hahn, Lehre v. d. Sakramentem.

(A) Jackson, History of Confirmation.

(R) Juenin, Comm. Hist. et Dogm. de Sacramentis.

(R) Launoy, de Sacramentis.

(R) Le Tourneaux, Instructions sur les Sacrements.

(A) †Marriott, Eirenica.

(R) Pabst, Adam und CHRISTUS.

(R) Probst, Sakramente und Sakramentalien in 3 ersten Jahrh.

(R) Rituale Romanum.

(R) Sirmondus, Antirrheticus Secundus adv. Petr. Aurelium.

(A) Thorndike, Epilogue.

(R) Trombelli, Tract. de Sacramentis.

(R) Francis de Victoria, Summa Sacramentorum.

HOLY BAPTISM.

(A) *Bethell on Baptismal Regeneration.

(R) Catechismus Seminarii Mechlinensis.

(A) Maskell on Holy Baptism.

(A) Pusey on Holy Baptism.

(A) Pereira on Baptism.

(A) *Sadler, Sacrament of Responsibility.

(A) *Sadler, Second Adam and New Birth.

(A) *Wall on Infant Baptism.

(A) Wallas, Thoughts on Holy Baptism.

(A) Wilberforce, Doctrine of Baptism.

(A) Wilberforce, Sermons on New Birth.

CONFIRMATION.

(R) Catechismus Sem. Mechlinensis.

(A) Creswell, Prep. for Confirm.

(C) †Dallæus, de Confirmatione.

(A) Frere, Doctrine of Imposition of Hands.

(A) Jackson, Hist. of Confirmation.

(R) Morinus, de Confirmationis Sacram.

(A) Newland, Confirmation and First Comm.

(A) Bp. Rattray on Confirmation.

(R) Sainte Beuve, de Sacr. Confirmationis.
(A) Young, Lessons on Confirmation.

HOLY EUCHARIST.

(R) Arnauld, De la freq. Communion.
(R) Arnauld, Perpetuité de la Foi.
(R) Benedict XIV. de Sacrificio Missæ.
(R) Boileau, de Adoratione Eucharistiæ.
(A) *Bp. of Brechin, Theological Defence.
(L) Callixtus, de Commun. sub utraque.
(A) Carter, Spiritual Instructions on the Holy Eucharist.
(R) Catechismus Sem. Mechlinensis.
(A) *Cheyne, Six Sermons on the Holy Eucharist.
(A) *Cobb, Kiss of Peace.
(R) Dalgairns on Holy Communion.
(L) Ebrard, Abendmahl.
(R) Faber, Blessed Sacrament.
(A) Lord Forbes on Eucharist.
(R) Franzelin, Tractatus de SS. Eucharistia.
(R) Garetius, Eccles. de Euch. Consensus.
(R) Gerbert, Theol. de Eucharistia.
(A) Hall, Fasting Reception of Sacrament.
(R) Hesselius, Tract. de Eucharistia.
(A) Heygate, Types of the Eucharist.
(A) †Johnson (John), Unbloody Sacrifice.
(A) Bishop Jolly on Eucharist.
(L) Kanaris, Abendmahl.
(A) *Keble, Eucharistic Adoration.
(R) Kreuser, de Sacrif. Missæ.
The LORD's Supper. A Clerical Symposium.
(R) Lugo, de Eucharistia.
(A) Neale, Sermons on Blessed Sacrament.
(R) Paschasius Radbertus.
(A) *Phillimore, Judgment in Sheppard v. Bennett.
(A) Pierce on Infant Communion.
(R) Probst, Eucharistie als Opfer, u. als Sacramente.
(A) Pusey on the Real Presence, 2 vols.
(R) Rochall, Die Realpräsenz.
(L) Rückert, Abendmahl.
(A) *Sadler, The One Offering.
(A) Saravia on the Eucharist. Ed. Denison.
(R) Specht, Die Wirkungen d. Eucharist Opfer.
(L) Sudendorf, Berengarius Turonensis.

(R) S. Thom. Aqu
(R) Viringas, de
(A) West, Short Eucharist.
(A) West, Parish Eucharist.
(A) *Wilberforce rist.
(R) †Wiseman, I

PENANCE AND

(R) *Besombes,
(R) Boileau, Hist ricularis.
(A) *Carter, Doct
(R) Casus Consci
(R) Catechismus
(A) *Cooke, Pow in Absolut
(R) De Lugo, de
(R) De Ségur, La
(A) Elwin, Confe in the Bibl
(R) Examens sur des diverse
(R) Fuchs, Syste Sittenlehre
(R) Gaume, Man
(A) Gresley, Ord sion.
(R) †Gousset, Th
(A) Gunning on]
(R) †Gury, Casus
(R) †Gury, Theol
(R) Habert, Prati
(A) Laurence on] tion.
(R) Le Prêtre Jug
(R) †Liguori, Ho
(R) "Liguori," in
(R) Loarte (Gasp fessariorum
(A) Marshall, Per
(A) Maskell on A
(R) Melia on Con
(R) Methodus Cor
(R) Morinus, de]
(R) Navarrius, Co
(R) Petavius, de
(R) Podesta, Exa
(R) Pontas, Dict.
(A) Priest in Abs
(R) Reiffenstühl,
(R) Reuter, Neo-
(A) Sanderson, d Whewell.
(R) †Scavini, The
(R) Segneri, Il C
(R) Segneri, Il P
(R) Simar, Lehrb theol.

(A) Taylor (Jeremy), Ductor Dubitantium.
(A) S. Theodori Cantuar. Pœnitentiale.
(R) *Van Neercassel, Amor Pœnitens.
(R) Zetl, Confessarius.

MATRIMONY.

(R) Dupanloup, Le Mariage Chrétien.
(A) Evans (H. Davey), Christian Law of Marriage. (N. Y. 1870.)
(A) Keble, Marriage Indissoluble.
(R) Ledesma (Pet.), Magn. Sacr. Matr.
(A) Lea, Christian Marriage in England.
(R) Luis de Leon, La Perfecta Casada.
(L) Museus, Theses de Conjugio.
(R) Perrone, de Matrimonio.
(A) Pusey, Marriage with a Deceased Wife's Sister.

UNCTION AND VISITATION OF SICK.

(A) Grueber, Anointing of the Sick.
(R) Launoy, de Sacr. Unct. Infirm.
(A) Shipley, Tracts for the Day.
Smee, House Surgeon.
(R) Stub, Prêtre auprès des malades et des mourants.

HOLY ORDER.

(A) *Carter, Doctrine of the Priesthood in the Church of England.
(A) Chillingworth, Episcopacy Apostolical.
S. Chrysostom on the Priesthood, (Tr. by Cowper.)
(A) Comber on the Ordinal.
(A) Grueber, Catechism on Holy Order.
(A) Bishop Hall, Episcopacy of Divine Right.
(R) Hallier, de Sacris Electionibus.
(A) Hickes, Two Treatises on the Priesthood.
(R) Morinus, de Ordinationibus.
(A) Percival, Apology for Apostolical Succession.
(R) Petavius, de Potestate Consecrandi, &c.; de Episc. dignitate; Eccles. Hierarchia.
(A) Rose (H. J.), Sermons on Commission and Duties of Clergy.
(A) Saravia, Different Degrees of the Priesthood.
(A) Walcott on the English Ordinal.
(A) Wordsworth, Outlines of Christian Ministry.

X. THE PASTORAL OFFICE.

S. Ambrosius, de Officiis Clericor.
(R) *Arvisenet, Memoriale Vitæ Sacerdotalis. (Also Eng. by Forbes.)

(R) Bartholomœus a Martyribus, de Offic. Episc. et Sacerdotis.
(R) Bartholomæus a Martyribus, Stimulus Patrum.
(C) Baxter, Reformed Pastor.
(A) Bellairs, School and Parish.
S. Bernardus, de Consideratione.
(C) Blaikie, Work of the Ministry.
(A) *Blunt (J. H.), Directorium Pastorale.
(A) Blunt (J. J.), Duties of the Parish Priest.
(R) *S. Caroli Borromæi Instructiones Pastorum.
(R) Boudon, Sanctité de l' Etat Ecclesiastique.
(R) Boudon, Science Sacr. des Pasteurs.
(A) Burnet, Pastoral Care.
(R) Catechismus ad Ordinandos.
S. Chrysostom, de Sacerdotio.
(R) Deharbe, Examen ad usum Cleri.
(R) Dirckink, Manuale Pastorum.
(R) *Dubois, Zèle Ecclesiastique.
(R) Dubois, Le Saint Prêtre.
(A) Evans, Bishopric of Souls.
(R) Fidelis Minister Christi.
(R) Frassinetti, Parish Priest's Manual. (Eng. Tr.)
S. Gregory the Great, de Cura Pastorali.
(A) Herbert (George), Country Parson.
(A) Heygate, Ember Hours.
(A) Heygate, Good Shepherd.
(A) Heygate, Probatio Clerica.
(A) How, Pastor in Parochia.
(A) How, Lectures on Pastoral Work.
(A) Huntington, Church's Work in Large Towns.
(R) Libellus Libellorum.
(A) Liddon, Priest in his inner life.
(R) Lohner, Instructio Pract. Sacerdot.
(R) Mach, Tesoro del Sacerdote.
(R) Massillon, Addresses to Clergy.
(R) Miroir du Clergé.
(A) Monro, Sermons on Ministry.
(A) Monro, Pastoral Work.
(A) Monro, Parochial Work.
(R) Opstraet, Pastor Bonus.
(A) The Parish and the Priest.
(R) Rey, Devoirs des Prêtres.
(R) Sacerdos Christianus.
(R) Schenkl, Theol. Pastoral. Systema.
(R) Schneider, Manuale Clericorum.
(R) Schneider, Manuale Sacerdotum.
(R) Scrutinium Sacerdotale.
(R) Segneri, Il Parocho Istruito.
(R) Soc. de S. Sulpice, Examen raisonné sur les devoirs des Prêtres.
(A) Spirit of the Church.

(C) Spurgeon, Addresses to my Students.

(R) Valuy, Guide des Prêtres.

(R) Vendrickx, Sacerdos devote celebrans.

(C) Vinct, Pastoral Theology.

(A) Wilberforce, Addresses to Candidates for Ordination.

(C) Wilson, Life Studies of the Christian Ministry.

XI. APOLOGETICS.

(C) Abbadie, Traité de la Rel. Chrétienne.

"Apologetics," in Encyc. Brit. 9th edition.

(C) Duke of Argyll, Reign of Law.

(A) Baring-Gould, Origin and Development of Religious Belief.

(A) Barry, Boyle Lectures.

(A) Belcher, Miracles of Healing.

(A) Bentley, Discourse of Freethinking.

(A) Blunt, Undesigned Coincidences.

(A) Blunt, Hulsean Lectures, 1832.

(R) Bougaud, Le Christianisme du temps present.

Bowne, Studies in Theism.

(C) †Bushnell, Nature and Supernatural.

(A) *Butler, Analogy and Sermons.

(C) Byles, Foundations of Religion.

Cairns, Unbelief of the Eighteenth Century.

(A) "Calvinism and Modern Doubt," in Christian Remembrancer, Jan. 1863.

(C) Campbell, Dissertation on Miracles.

(A) Chandler, Defence of Christianity.

(L) Christlieb, Modern Doubt and Christian Belief. (Clark's F. T. L.)

Christian Evidence Society's Lectures.

(A) Church, Influences of Christianity.

(A) Church, Vindication of Miraculous Power.

(A) Clarke (Samuel), Being and Attributes of GOD.

(C) Cooper (Thos.,) Christian Evidence Series.

(A) Bp. Cotterill, Does Science aid Faith?

(R) *Crot, Etudes sur l'Ordre Nat. et Surnat.

(R) De Broglie, Réponse à M. Jules Simon (Questions de Religion et de l'Histoire.)

(L) Delitzsch, Geschichte d. Christlichen Apologetik.

(A) Bp. Douglas, The Criterion.

(A) Drew, Reasons of Faith.

(A) Drummond, Natural Law in the Spiritual World.

(R) Dupanloup, L'Atheisme.

(L) Fabri, Briefe gegen den Materialismus.

(A) Farrar (A. S.), Critical History of Free Thought.

(A) Farrar, Witness of History to CHRIST.

(C) Flint, on Theism.

(A) Footman, Reasonable Apprehensions and Reassuring Hints.

(C) Gillespie, Necessary Existence o GOD.

(C) Godet, Defence of Christian Faith (Clark's F. T. L.)

(R) Gratry, Les Sophistes et la Philosophie. Philosophie du Credo,

(C) Guizot, Meditations on the Actual State of Christianity.

(A) Hardwick, CHRIST and other Masters.

(A) Hessey, Boyle Lectures on Moral Difficulties of the Bible. 3 series

(R) Hettinger, Apologie des Christenthums.

Hucking, Dialogues founded on Butler.

(A) Irons, Bible and its Interpreters.

(C) Janet, Du Materialisme Contemporain.

(C) Janet, Final Causes.

(A) Jellett, Moral Difficulties of O. T

(A) Jellett, Efficacy of Prayer.

(C) Keith on Prophecy.

(R) Lacordaire, Conférences.

(R) Laforet, Why men do not believe.

(A) *Lardner on Credibility of Gospel History.

(A) Law, Letters to Hoadly.

(A) Lear, Are Miracles Credible?

(A) Lee, Essay on Miracles.

(R) †Le Noir, Harmonies de la Raison et de la Foi.

(A) Leslie, Short Method with Deists

(A) Liddon, Some Elements of Religion.

(A) Lightfoot, Reply to "Supernatural Religion."

(L) Luthardt, Apologetic Discourses (Clark's F. T. L.)

(L) Luthardt, Fundamental Truth of Christianity. (Tr. by Taylor.)

(A) Maclear, Evidential Value of the Holy Eucharist.

(C) McCosh, Christianity and Positivism.

(C) McCosh, The Supernatural in relation to the Natural.

(A) March Phillipps, Cumulative Evidences of Divine Revelation.

(R) Maret, Essai sur le Panthéisme.

(A) Maurice, Religions of the World.

(R) Migne, Demonstr. Evangeliques, 19 vols.

(A) Mill, Mythical Interpretation of the Gospels.

(A) Miller, Bampton Lectures.

(A) "Miracles," in Christian Remembrancer, Oct., 1863, 1866.

(A) "Miracles," in Church Quarterly Review, April, 1876.

(A) *Mozley, Bampton Lectures.

(C) Murphy, The Scientific Bases of Faith.

(C) Naville, Heavenly Father.

(R) Newman on Miracles.

(A) Newton on Prophecy.

(R) Nicolas (A.), Etudes Philosophiques sur le Christianisme.

(A) *Paley, Evidences and Natural Theology.

(R) Pascal, Pensées. Ed. Faugère.

(R) Perrone, Traité de la Vraie Relig.

Ragg, Creation's Testimony.

(C) Rainy, Bible and Criticism.

(R) Reusch, Bibel und Natur.

(A) Reynolds, The Supernatural in Nature.

(A) Reynolds, The Mystery of Miracles.

(A) Romanes, Christian Prayer and General Laws.

(A) Row, The Jesus of the Evangelists.

(A) Row, The Supernat. in N. T.

(A) Sadler, The Lost Gospel.

(R) Saisset, Modern Pantheism.

(A) The Scholar Armed.

(A) Salmon, Non-Miraculous Christianity.

(A) Sherlock, Trial of the Witnesses.

Stewart and Tait, The Unseen Universe.

(L) Steinmeyer, Miracles of our Lord. (Clark's F. T. L.)

(C) Taylor (Is.), Restoration of Belief.

(A) Abp. Thomson, Word, Work, and Will.

(C) Tulloch on Theism.

(L) Ulrici, Gott und die Natur.

(C) Vinet, Etudes sur Pascal.

(R) Vosen, Das Christenthum und die Einsprüch seiner Gegner.

(A) Wace, Bampton Lectures.

(A) Wace, Christianity and Morality.

(A) Wace, The Gospel and its Witnesses.

(A) Warington, Week of Creation.

(A) Warington, Can we believe in Miracles?

(A) Waterland, Works against Clarke.

(A) Watson, Apologies for the Bible.

(A) Westcott, Gospel of the Resurrection.

(A) Whewell, Vestiges of the Creator.

(A) Wordsworth, Bampton Lectures, The One Religion.

XII. Patristic and Mediæval Literature.

Albertus Magnus. Ed. Jammy. Comment. in Psalmos, Prophetas, Evang. et Apocalypsin.

Alzog, Patrologie.

S. Ambrose. Ed. Benedictina.
Expositio in S. Lucam.
Enarrationes in Psalmos.

S. Anselm. Ed. Benedict. Cur Deus Homo?

The Ante-Nicene Christian Library.

The Apostolic Fathers. Edd. Coteler, Hefele, Jacobson, Dressel, Gebhardt and Harneck.

Apostolic Fathers, Holland on the.

Assemani, Acta Martyrum.

S. Athanasius. Ed. Benedictina.
Vita S. Antonii.
Apologia contra Arianos.
Apologia de Fugâ.
Historical Writings. Ed. Bright.
Oratio de Incarnatione.
*Orationes contra Arianos. Ed. Bright.

S. Athanasius, Newman's Treatises on.

S. Augustine. Ed. Benedictina.
Anti-Pelagian Treatises. Ed. Bright.
*Confessiones.
De Catechizandis Rudibus.
De Civitate Dei.
De Doctrina Christiana.
De Gratia et Libero Arbitrio.
De Natura et Gratia.
De Trinitate.
*Enarrationes in Psalmos.
Opuscula. Ed. Marriott.
Sermones.
*Tractatus in Evang. Johannis.

S. Augustine, Trench on, as an Interpreter.

*Ayguan in Psalmos.

Baring-Gould, Lost and Hostile Gospels.

S. Basilius Magnus. Ed. Benedictina.
De Spiritu Sancto.
Homiliæ.
In Esaiam.

S. Beda Venerabilis. Ed. anno 1688.
Commentaria in SS. Scripturas.
Historia Ecclesiastica. Ed. Moberly.

*S. Bernard. Ed. Benedict. Epistolæ et Sermones.
S. Bonaventura.
  De Septem Donis S. Spiritus.
  Diæta Salutis.
  Meditationes Vitæ CHRISTI.
  Soliloquium.
Blunt on the Early Fathers.
S. Bruno of Asti.
  Expositiones in SS. Scripturas.
  Homiliæ.
†Bunsen, Analecta Ante-Nicæna.
Canisii Thesaurus Lectionum Antiquarum.
S. Cassian, Collationes.
Cassiodorus. Comment. in Psalmos.
S. Chrysostom, Homiliæ.
Cicheri, Vet. Patr. Theol. Univers. 13 vols.
S. Clemens Alex. Ed. Potter. Pædagogus and Stromata.
S. Clemens Romanus. Ed. Lightfoot.
Constitutiones Apostolorum. Delagarde.
Conybeare, Bampton Lectures.
Cowper, Apocryphal Gospels.
Corpus Script. Eccl. Lat. (Vienne.)
S. Cyprian. Edd. Fell, Benedictina.
  De Exhortatione Martyrii.
  De Lapsis.
  *De Unitate Ecclesiæ.
S. Cyrillus Alex. Ed. Pusey.
S. Cyrillus Hierosol. Ed. Touttée.
  *Catecheses Mystagogicæ.
S. Damasi Opp.
S. Dionysii Areopagitæ Opp.
Dodd, Sayings ascribed to our LORD.
Donaldson, Christian Literature.
The Epistle to Diognetus.
S. Epiphanius. Ed. Petavius. Panarium adversus Hæreses.
Eusebius Pamphili.
  Evangelica Demonstratio. Ed. Gaisford.
  Evangelica Præparatio. Ed. Gaisford.
Fabricius, Codex Apocryphus V. et N.T.
The Fathers for English Readers, (S. P. C. K.)
*Gerhohus in Psalmos.
John Gerson. Ed. Du Pin.
  Alphabetum Divini Amoris.
  Collectorium super Magnificat.
  De Mystica Theologia.
  De Vita Spirituali Animæ.
Gillebert de Hoylandia. Serm. in Cant. Canticorum.
S. Greg. the Great. Ed. Benedictina.
  Expos. Psalm. Pœnitent.
  Homiliæ in Evangelium.
  Hom. in Ezechielem.
  *Moralia in Jobum.
  Epistolæ.

S. Greg. Nazianzen. Ed. Benedictina. Orationes.
S. Greg. Nyssen, Hom. in Beatitudines.
Harphii Opera.
Herveus Venerab. in Epist. S. Pauli.
S. Hilary. Ed. Benedictina.
  Comment. in Psalmos.
  *De Trinitate.
Hildebertus Venerabilis. Ed. Beaugendre. Sermones.
S. Hippolytus, Philosophumena. Edd. Lagarde, Miller.
Hrabanus Maurus, de Sacr. Ordinibus.
Hugo of S. Victor.
  *Annotationes in SS. Scripturas.
  Institutiones Monasticæ.
  Eruditiones Theologicæ.
S. Irenæus, Contra Hæreses. Edd. Massuet, Stieren, Harvey.
S. Isidore of Seville, Comment. in Lib. Hist. Vet. Test.
S. Jerome. Ed. Vallarsi.
  Adversus Helvidium et Jovinianum.
  Comment. in S. Matthæum.
  Comment. in Prophetas.
  Epistolæ.
†Jansenius, Augustinus.
S. Joannes Damascenus. Ed. Le Quien. De Fide Orthodoxâ.
Justin Martyr, Apologies. Edd. Otto, Stieren, Trollope.
Bp. Kaye on Clement of Alex.
Bp. Kaye on Justin Martyr.
Bp. Kaye on Tertullian.
Keble on Mysticism of Fathers. Tract 89.
Lactantius. Ed. Dufresnoy. De falsa Religione Deorum, De Morte Persecutorum.
S. Laurentii Justiniani Opp.
S. Leo Magnus. Ed. Quesnel. Sermones.
Lightfoot, Apostolic Fathers.
Lightfoot, Epistles of S. Clement.
Lumper, Hist. Theologico-Critica de SS. Patribus.
Marriott, Analecta Christiana.
Minucius Felix, Octavius.
Möhler, Patrologie.
Oehler, Corp. Hæresilogicum.
Optatus Milev. de Schismate Donat.
Oracula Sibyllina. Ed. Alexandre.
Origen. Edd. De la Rue, Lommatzsch. Homilies on Pentateuch, Joshua, Jeremiah, and Gospels.
Otto, Corpus Apologetarum Christianorum.
Oxford Library of Fathers.
S. Paciani Opp.
Paschasius Radbert in S. Matth.
Pearson, Vindiciæ Ignatianæ.

S. Petrus Chrysologus. Sermones.
S. Petrus Damiani. Ed. Cajetan.
Petrus Blesensis. Sermones.
Petrus Cellensis. Sermones. Liber de
  Panibus.
*Petrus Lombardus.
Philo Judæus. Ed. Mangey.
Photii Bibliotheca.
Photii Epistolæ. Ed. Valetta.
Pitra, Spicilegium Solesmense.
Prudentius. Ed. Dressel.
Radulphus Ardens, Hom. in Evang.
  et Epist.
Remigius Autissiodorensis. Comment.
  in SS. Scripturas.
Richard of S. Victor. Ed. Rouen, 1650.
  In Apocalypsin.
  In Cantica.
  De Contemplatione.
  De Eruditione Hominis.
  De Trinitate.
Routh, Script. Eccl. Opuscula.
Routh, Reliquiæ Sacræ.
*Rupert of Deutz.
  Comment. in SS. Scripturas.
  De Victoria Verbi Dei.
Rusbrochii Opera.
*Schram, Analysis Operum Patrum.
†Scotus Érigena.
Tauler (John), Sermons.
*Tertullian. Ed. Rigaltius. Apologia.
Theodoret. Edd. Sirmond, Schulze.
  Comment. in Scripturas.
  Contra Græc. Affect.
  Historia Ecclesiastica.
S. Theodorus Studita, Epistolæ.
Theophylact. Comm. in N. T.
Thilo, Codex Apocryphus N. T.
S. Thomas Aquinas. Ed. De Rubeis.
  Comment. in SS. Scripturas.
  *Summa Theologica.
S. Thomæ a Villanova Opera.
  De Vita et Passione CHRISTI.
Thomas à Kempis, Opera.
Thomas Hibernicus, Flores Doctorum.
Tischendorf, Evangelia Apocrypha.
Victorinus, Scholia in Ep. et Apocal.
Vincentius Lirinens. Commonitorium.

XIII. ECCLESIASTICAL HISTORY.

(A) Abbey and Overton, EnglishChurch
  in Eighteenth Century.
(R) Alexander (Natalis), Historia Ec-
  clesiastica.
(R) Alzog, Kirchengeschichte. (Also
  · English and French Trans.)
(W) Arthur, The Pope, the Kings, and
  the People (Vatican Council).
(P) Baird, Rise of the Huguenots.
(R) Baronius et Raynaldus, Annales
  Eccles. cum Suppl. Pagi.

(C) Basnage, Hist. des Juifs.
(L) Baur, Die Christliche Gnosis.
(U) Beard, Hibbert Lectures on the
  Reformation.
(A) Beda, Hist. Eccles. Gent. Angl.
(R) Beugnot, Hist. de la Destruction
  du Paganisme.
(A) *Blunt (J. H.), History of the Re-
  formation in England.
(A) Blunt (J. J.), Church of First Three
  Cent.
(A) Blunt (J. J.), Reformation in Eng-
  land.
(A) Bond, Handy Book for Verifying
  Dates.
(R) Bossuet, Variations des Eglises
  Protestantes.
(R) Brady, Episcop. Success. in Eng.,
  Scot., and Irel., 1400 to 1875.
(A) *Bright, History of the Church
  from 313 to 451.
(A) Bright, Early English Church Hist.
(A) *Bryce, Holy Roman Empire.
(A) Buckley, Hist. of the Council of
  Trent.
(A) †Burnet, Hist. of Reformation.
  Ed. Pocock.
(A) Burton, Lectures on Church Hist.
(L) Busse, Grundriss d. Christ. Li-
  teratur.
(R) Butler, Historical Memoirs.
(A) Cardwell, Synodalia.
(A) Cardwell, Documentary Annals.
(A) Cardwell, Conferences on B. C. P.
(C) Cartwright on Papal Conclaves.
(L) Casaubon, Exercitat. in Baronium.
(A) Cave, Lives of the Apostles.
(A) Cave, Lives of the Fathers.
(A) Cave, Primitive Christianity.
(R) Cecconi, Storia del Concilio Va-
  ticano.
(A) Churton, Early English Church.
(A) Collier, Eccl. Hist. of Great Brit.
(C) †Cooke, Scottish Reformation.
(A) Conversion of the West. (S.P.C.K.)
(A) Cotton, Fasti Eccl. Hibern.
(A) Covell, Greek Church.
(A) Crake, History of the Church
  under the Empire.
(A) Creighton, Papacy during the Re-
  formation.
(C) Cunningham, Church History of
  Scotland.
  Dale, Synod of Elvira.
(R) De Broglie, L'Eglise et l'Empire
  Romain.
(R) De Marca, Concordantia Eccl. et
  Imperii.
(A) De Soyres, Montanism.
(L) Dieckhoff, Waldensen in Mit-
  telalter.
(A) *Dixon, Hist. of Ch. of England.

(A) Dixon and Raine, Archbishops of York.
(R) Döllinger, Church Hist. (Tr. Cox.)
(R) *Döllinger, First Age of the Church. (Tr. Oxenham.)
(R) Döllinger. Hippolytus and Callistus. (Tr. Plummer.)
(R) Döllinger, Jew and Gentile. (Tr. Darnell.)
(R) *Döllinger, Reformation.
(R) Dodd, Church Hist. of England. Ed. Tierney.
(A) Dugdale, Monasticon. Edd. Ellis and Bandinel.
Dyer, Life of Calvin.
Early Chroniclers of Europe. (S. P. C. K.)
(A) English Diocesan Histories. (S. P. C. K.)
Eusebius, Hist. Eccl. Ed. Bright.
Evagrius, Hist. Eccl. Ed. Valesius.
(L) †Ewald, Geschichte d. Volkes Israels. (Tr. R. Martineau.)
(L) Fabricius, Lux Evang. Salutaris.
(R) Ffoulkes, Christendom's Divisions.
(A) *Ffoulkes, Manual of Eccl. Hist.
(R) Fleury, Histoire Ecclesiastique.
(R) Florez, Espana Sagrada.
(A) Bp. Forbes, Kalendar of Scottish Saints.
(A) Fortescue, Armenian Church.
(R) Friedrich, Tagebuch Vat. Conc.
(R) Friedrich, Documenta ad illustrand. Conc. Vatican.
(A) Fuller, Church History.
(R) Gallia Christiana.
(R) Gams, Series Episcop. Eccl. Cath.
(C) Gasparin, Innocent III.
(L) †Gieseler, Kirchengeschichte. (Clark's F. T. L.)
(A) Gordon, Eccl. Chron. for Scotland.
(A) Gordon, Roman Cath. Church iu Scotland.
(A) Gorham, Reformation Gleanings.
(A) Grant, Bampton Lectures on Missions.
(L) Gregorius, Geschichte der Stadt Rom im Mittelalter.
(A) Greenwood, Cathedra Petri.
(A) Grub, Church Hist. of Scotland.
(R) Guettée, Hist. de l'Eglise de France.
(A) Gwatkin, Studies in Arianism.
(A) Haddan's Remains.
(L) Hagenbach, Kirchengeschichte d. Mittelalters.
(L) Hahn, Ketzer in Mittelalter.
(A) Hardwick, History of the Church in the Middle Ages.
(A) Hardwick, Hist. of Reformation.
(R) Harpsfield, Narrat. of Divorce. (Camden Soc.)

(L) Hase, Kirchengeschichte.
(R) Hefele, Concilien-Geschichte. (Clark's F. T. L.)
(R) Helyot, Hist. des Ordres Relig.
(L) Heppe, Geschichte der Quietistischen Mystik.
(L) Herzog, Romanische Waldenser.
(A) Hook, Archbishops of Canterbury.
(A) Hore, Eighteen Centuries of Church in England.
(R) Hübner, Life of Sixtus V.
(R) Huc, Hist. du Christianisme en Chine.
(A) *Hussey, Rise of the Papal Power.
(R) *Jaffe, Regesta Pontificum.
(A) Jennings, Ecclesia Anglicana.
(A) *Jervis, Hist. of Church of France.
(A) Jervis, Gallican Church and the Revolution.
(A) "Jesuits," in Encyc. Brit. 9th ed.
(L) Jost, Geschichte d. Judenthums.
(A) Joyce, England's Sacred Synods.
(L) Kahnis, History of German Protestantism.
(A) Bp. Kaye, Council of Nicæa.
(A) Keith, Cat. of Scottish Bishops.
(L) Kellner, Hellenismus u. Christenthum.
(A) Kennet, Register.
(E) Khomiakoff, Eglise Latine et Protestante au point de vue de l'Eglise d'Orient.
(C) †Killen, Eccl. Hist. of Ireland.
(L) Kurtz, History of the Church.
(R) Labbe, Acta Conciliorum.
(A) *Landon, Manual of Councils.
(O.C.) Langen, Geschichte der Römischen Kirche.
(R) Lanigan, Eccles. Hist. of Ireland.
(A) Lathbury, Hist. of Nonjurors.
(A) Lathbury, Hist. of Convocation.
(A) Lathbury, Hist. of Episcopacy in England.
Lea, Hist. of Sacerdotal Celibacy.
(A) Lear, Revival of Priestly Life in France.
(A) Le Neve, Fasti Eccl. Angl. Ed. Hardy.
(L) Lechler, Wiclif and his Precursors. (Tr. Lorimer.)
(C) Lenfant, Hist. des Conc. de Pise, Basle et Constance.
(R) Leon Pagès, Hist. de la Relig. Chrét. en Japon.
(R) Le Plat, Monument. Conc. Trident.
(A) Leslie, Regale and Pontificate.
(R) Lettres Edifiantes.
(R) Lingard, Anglo-Saxon Church.
(R) Lingard, History of England.
(L) Lommel, Johannes Huss.
(A) Luckock, Studies in History of Book of Common Prayer.

(R) Mabillon, Act. et Ann. O. S. B.
(C) M'Crie, Lives of Knox and Melville.
(A) Maclear, Christian Missions in Middle Ages.
(A) Mahan, Church History.
(R) Mamachi, Costumi dei Primitivi Cristiani.
(A) Mansel, Gnostic Heresies.
(A) Maitland, Albigenses and Waldenses.
(A) Maitland, Dark Ages.
(A) Maitland, Essays on Reformation.
(A) Maitland on Foxe's Martyrology.
(A) Malan, Hist. of Georgian Church.
(A) Marshall, Eccl. Hist. of Scotland.
(A) Mason, Persecution of Diocletian.
(C) Matter, Hist. Crit. du Gnosticisme.
(A) Maurice, Lectures on Eccles. Hist.
(R) Mejer, Geschichte der Romisch-Deutschen Frage.
(R) Melia on the Waldenses.
(A) Merivale, Conversion of Northern Nations.
(A) Merivale, Conversion of Roman Empire.
(A) †Milman, History of Christianity.
(A) †Milman, History of the Jews.
(A) *Milman, Latin Christianity.
(A) "Monachism," in Encyc. Brit. 9th edit.
(R) Möhler, Kirchengeschichte.
(R) Monumenta Reformationis Lutheranæ.
(R) Montalembert, Moines d'Occident.
(L) †Mosheim, de Rebus Christianorum ante Constantinum.
(L) Mosheim, Inst. Hist. Eccl. *Ed. Stubbs.
(E) Mouravieff, Hist. of the Russian Church.
(C) †Neal, Hist. of the Puritans.
(A) Neale, History of the Church of Alexandria.
(A) Neale, History of the Patriarchate of Antioch.
(A) *Neale, Introduction to the Hist. of the Eastern Church.
(A) Neale, Jansenist Church of Holland.
(L) Neander, Church History.
(L) Neander, History of Planting of Christianity.
(L) Neander, Memorials of Christian Life.
(R) *Newman, Church of the Fathers.
(A) *Newman, History of Arians.
(R) Newman, Historical Sketches.
(P) Original Letters, 1537—1558. (Parker Soc.)
(R) Ozanam, History of Civilization.
(R) †Pallavicino, Hist. Conc. Trident.

Parkman, Jesuits in America.
(A) *Perry, Student's Hist. of Church of England.
(A) Pocock, Records of the Reformation.
(R) Pomponio Leto, Eight Months at Rome during the Vatican Council.
(R) *The Pope and the Council. By Janus.
(C) Potter, Mémoires de Scipion de Ricci.
(C) Pressensé, Early Years of Christianity. 4 vols.
(C) Pressensé, L'Eglise et la Revolution.
(A) Prideaux, Connexion of O. and N.T.
(A) Pryce, Ancient British Church.
(A) Pusey on the Councils.
(R) Quirinus, Letters from Rome on the Vatican Council.
(L) Ranke, History of the Popes.
(A) Reeves, Life of S. Columba.
(A) Rendall, Julian the Apostate.
(A) Reichel, See of Rome in the Middle Ages.
(R) Richerius, Hist. Conciliorum.
(L) Ritschl, Entstehung d. Altkatholische Kirche. 1857.
(A) Robertson, History of the Church.
(L) Rothe, Anfänge der Christliche Kirche.
(R) Ruinart, Acta Sincera Martyrum.
(R) Sanders, de Schismate Angliæ. (English trans.)
(R) †Sarpi, Hist. Conc. Trident.
(R) Sartorius, Compendium Baronii.
(L) Schaff, Hist. of Apostolic Church.
(R) Schulte, Stellung der Concilien.
(L) Seckendorf, Hist. Lutheranismi.
(C) Sherring, Hist. of Protestant Missions in India.
(A) Shirley on the Apostolic Age.
(A) Simcox, Early Church History.
(A) Skinner, Ch. Hist. of Scotland.
(A) Smedley, The Reformed Religion in France.
(A) Smith, Church in Roman Gaul. (S. P. C. K.)
(A) Soames, Anglo-Saxon Church.
(A) Soames, Elizabethan History.
Socrates, Hist. Eccl. Ed. Bright.
Sozomen, Hist. Eccl. Ed. Hussey.
(A) Spelman, History of Sacrilege.
(R) Spondani Annales.
(A) †Stanley, Lectures on Jewish Church.
(A) Stanley, Lectures on Eastern Church.
(C) †Stoughton, Eccl. Hist. of Engl.
(A) †Strype, Works.
(A) *Stubbs, Regist. Sacr. Anglicanum.

(C) Taylor (Isaac), Hist. of Enthu-
siasm, Fanaticism, Spiritual
Despotism.
(R) Theiner, Acta Concil. Tridentin.
Theodoret. Ed. Gaisford.
(A) Theodorus, Hist. of the New (Old
Cath.) Reformation.
(R) Thierry, Saint Jérome.
(R) Tillemont, Mémoires.
(R) Tillemont, Hist. des Empereurs.
(A) Todd, Life of S. Patrick.
(A) Trench, Abp., Lectures on Mediæ-
val Church History.
(A) Trevor, Two Convocations.
(A) Tucker, "Under His Banner."
(Eng. Col. Ch. Hist.)
(L) Turretinus, Nubes Testium.
(R) Tzschirner, Der Fall des Hei-
denthums.
(R) Ughelli, Italia Sacra.
(R) Wadding, Annales Minorum.
(A) Wake, State of the Church and
Clergy in England.
(L) †Weingarten, Zeit-tafeln zur Kir-
chengeschichte.
(A) Wharton, Anglia Sacra.
(A) Wilberforce, History of American
Church.
(A) William of Malmesbury de Gestis
Pontificum.
(L) Wiltsch, Geography and Statis-
tics of the Church.
(A) Wordsworth, Hippolytus and the
Church of Rome.
(A) Wordsworth, Hist. of the Church.
(P) Zurich Letters. (Parker Soc.)

XIV. RELIGIOUS BIOGRAPHY.

(R) Abelly, Vie de S. Vincent de Paul.
(R) Acta Sanctorum, Bollandus.
(R) Life of Angelique Arnauld.
*S. Augustine's Confessions.
(R) Baillet, Vie des Saints.
(A) Baines, Life of Laud.
(A) *Baring-Gould, Lives of the Saints.
(P) Baxter's Journal.
(R) Bouhours, Vie de S. François Xa-
vier.
(A) Bowden, Life of Gregory VII.
(A) Brooke, Life of F. W. Robertson.
(C) Bungener, Life of Calvin.
(A) Bush (R. W.), Life and Times of
S. Augustine.
(R) *Butler, Lives of the Saints.
(L) Butler (J. E.), Life of Oberlin.
(A) Cave, Chartophylax.
(R) Chocarne, Vie de Lacordaire.
(A) *Church, Life of S. Anselm.
(A) Classic Preachers of the English
Church.
(A) Coleridge, Life of Keble.

(R) Coleridge, Life of Xavier.
(R) De Natalibus, Catalog. Sanctorum.
(A) D'Oyly, Life of Sancroft.
(R) Dryden, Life of Xavier.
George Fox's Journal.
(A) Froude's (R. H.) Remains.
(R) Giussano, Vita di S. Carlo Borro-
meo.
(A) Gore, Life of Leo the Great.
(A) Life of Bp. Gray of Capetown.
(R) Memoir of Eugénie de Guérin.
(A) Farrar, Saintly Workers.
(R) Fialon, Saint Athanase.
(C) Autobiography of Dr. Guthrie.
(R) Hefele, Life of Cardinal Ximenes.
(A) Hoole, Life of S. Cyprian.
(A) Jones, Life of S. Jane Frances de
Chantal.
(A) Jones, Life of S. Vincent de Paul.
(A) Justorum Semita.
(R) Kavanagh, Women of Christi-
anity.
(A) Keble, Life of Bp. Wilson.
(A) Kingsley, Hermits.
(R) Lacordaire, Vie de S. Dominic.
(A) Memoir of Laud in Mozley's Es-
says.
(A) Lear, Dominican Artist.
(A) Lear, Bossuet and his Contemp.
(A) Lear, Fathers of the Church.
(A) Lear, Life of Lacordaire.
(A) Lear, Madame Louise of France.
(A) Lear, Henri Perreyve.
(A) Lear, S. Francis de Sales.
(A) Lear, Last Days of Père Gratry.
(A) Le Bas, Life of Abp. Laud.
(R) Les Petits Bollandistes.
(A) Liddon, Life of Bp. Hamilton.
(R) Lipomanus de Vitis Sanctorum.
(C) Life of Norman Macleod.
(A) Journal and Letters of Henry
Martyn.
(A) Masters in English Theology.
Michelet, Luther.
(R) Möhler, Athanasius der Grosse.
(Also in French Translation.)
(R) Monnin, Vie du Curé d'Ars.
(R) Montalembert, Vie de S. Elizabeth
de Hongrie.
Morison, Life of S. Bernard.
(A) Neale, Virgin Saints.
(A) Neale, Life and Times of Bp.
Torry.
(C) Oliphant, Life of Edward Irving.
(C) Oliphant, Life of Montalembert.
(C) Oliphant, Francis of Assisi.
(A) Overton, William Law.
(A) Owen, Sanctorale Catholicum.
(R) Life of Nicolas Pavillon.
(R) Rémusat, S. Anselme.
(A) Robertson, Life of S. Thomas
Becket.

(R) Roswcyd, Vitæ Patrum.
   †Sainte Beuve, Port Royal.
(C) *Schimmelpenninck, Select Memoirs of Port Royal.
   Seebohm, Oxford Reformers, Colet, Erasmus and More.
(A) *Southey, Life of Wesley.
(A) Smith, Life of Basil the Great.
(A) Stanley, Life of Arnold.
(A) Stephen, Essays in Eccl. Biog.
(A) Stephens, Life of Dean Hook.
(A) Stephens, Life of Chrysostom.
(R) Autobiography of S. Teresa.
(A) Trench, Life of S. Teresa.
(A) Trench, Life of Charles Lowder.
(A) Tucker, Life of Bp. Selwyn.
(W) Tyerman, Life of Wesley, 3 v.
(W) Tyerman, Life of Fletcher of Madeley.
(R) Villari, Vita di Savonarola.
(A) Walton's Lives.
(A) Life of Bishop Wilberforce.
(A) *Williams, Life of Suckling.
(A) Wilson, The Christian Brothers.
(A) Wilson, Life of S. Vincent de Paul.
(A) Yonge, Life of Bp. Patteson.
(A) Yonge, Pupils of S. John.
(A) Yonge, Pioneers and Founders.

XV. BIBLICAL AND CHRISTIAN ANTIQUITIES AND ART.

(R) Alteserra, Asceticôn.
(A) *Ancient History from the Monuments. (S. P. C. K.)
(R) Aringhi, Roma Subterranea.
(A) Armfield, Legend of Christian Art.
(L) Augusti, Denkwürdigkeiten aus der Christlichen Archäologie.
(A) Bates, Lectures on Christ. Antiq. Biblical Things not generally known.
(A) *Bingham, Antiquities of Christian Church.
(C) Bocharti Opera.
(R) Bock, Liturgische Gewänder.
(R) Bourassé, Dict. d'Archéologie Sacrée.
(A) Brand's Popular Antiquities. Ed. Hazlitt.
(A) Burder, Oriental Customs.
   Bush, Illustrations of the Holy Scriptures.
(C) Buxtorf, Synagoga Judaica.
(R) Cabassutius, Notitia Ecclesiastica.
(R) Casalius, de Veteribus Ritibus.
(R) Caumont, Abécédaire d'Archéol.
(R) Ciampini, Monumenta.
(A) Clay, Virgin Mary and Traditions of Painters.
   Conder, Tent-Work in Palestine.
   Conder, Handbook of Bible.

(R) D'Agincourt, Histoire de l'Art.
(A) Dansey, Horæ Decanicæ Rurales.
(R) De Fleury, Etudes Iconographiques et Archéologiques sur l' Evangile.
(R) De Linas, Anciens Vêtements Sacerdotaux.
(R) De Rossi, Roma Sotterranea.
(R) Didron, Iconographie.
(A) Drew, Scripture Lands.
(C) *Edersheim, The Temple and its Services.
(L) Eisenmenger, Entdecktes Judenthum.
(W) Etheridge, Introduction to Hebrew Literature.
(R) Félix (Clement), Hist. générale de la Musique Religieuse.
(A) Fosbroke, British Monachism.
(A) Gally Knight, Eccles. Architecture in Italy.
(R) Gerbert, de Cantu et Musica Sacr.
(L) *Guericke, Handbook of Christian Antiquities. (Tr. by Morrison.)
(R) Haneberg, Alterthümer d. Bibel.
(A) Hart, Ecclesiastical Records.
(A) Hemans, Ancient Christianity and Art.
(A) Hemans, Mediæval Christianity and Art.
(A) Hemans, Historic and Monumental Rome.
(L) Jahn, Archæologia Biblica.
(A) Jameson, Sacred and Legendary Art.
(A) Jameson, Legends of Madonna.
(A) Jameson, Legends of Monastic Orders.
(A) Jameson, Life of our LORD in Art.
(A) Jennings, Jewish Antiquities.
(J) Josephus.
(A) Bp. Kip on the Catacombs.
(R) Lacroix, Arts of Middle Ages.
(R) Lacroix, Religious and Military Life of Middle Ages.
(R) *Lenormant, Manual of Anc. Hist. of the East.
(C) Lightfoot, Temple Service.
(A) Lord Lindsay, Hist. of Christian Art.
(L) Lübke, Eccl. Art in Germany.
(R) Mabillon, de Studiis Monasticis.
(A) McCaul, Christian Epitaphs of the first six centuries.
(A) Marriott, Vestiarium Christianum.
(R) Martigny, Dictionnaire des Antiquités Chrétiennes.
(A) Micklethwaite, Modern Parish Churches.
(R) Montfaucon, Palæographia Græca.
(L) Otté, Handbuch der Kirchlichen Kunst-Archäologie.

(A) Owen, Art Schools of Mediæval Christendom.
(R) Ozanam, Œuvres.
Palestine Exploration Fund Reports.
(A) Parker, A. B. C. of Gothic Architecture.
(A) Parker, Glossary of Architecture.
(R) *Pelliccia, Polity of Christian Church. *Tr. Bellett.
(R) Pugin, Works.
(A) Rawlinson, Histor. Illustr. of O. T.
Records of the Past. (Soc. of Bibl. Archæol.)
(C) Reland, Antiquitates Sacræ.
(C) Reland, Palæstina.
(L) Rheinwald, Christliche Archäologie.
(R) Ribera, de Templo.
(A) *†Riddle, Manual of Christian Antiquities.
(R) Rio, L'Art Chrétien.
(C) Robinson, Biblical Researches in Palestine.
(R) Roma Sotterranea, by Northcote and Brownlow.
†Siegel, Christl.-Kirchl. Alterthümer.
(C) *Socin, Handbook for Syria and Palestine. (Bædeker.)
(A) Stanley, Sinai and Palestine.
(A) Street, Gothic Architecture in Spain.
(C) Surenhusius, Mishna.
(R) Thomassin, Sur les Jeûnes.
(C) Thomson, The Land and the Book.
(A) Tristram, Land of Israel.
(A) Tristram, Land of Moab.
(A) Tyrwhitt, Art Teaching of Primitive Church.
(R) Ugolini, Thesaurus Antiqq. Sacr. 34 vols. fol.
(C) Van Lennep, Bible Lands.
(R) Viollet-le-Duc, Architecture.
(L) Vitringa, Synagoga Vetus.
(R) Vogué, Temple de Jerusalem.
(L) Volbedung, Thesaurus Commentationum.
(A) Walcott, Church and Conventual Arrangement.
(A) Webb, Continental Ecclesiology.
(C) Whitney, Handbook of Bible Geography.
(A) Wilkinson, Ancient Egyptians.
Wilson, Sir E., Egypt of the Past.
Wilson, Lands of the Bible.
(A) Winston, History of Glass Painting.
(L) Zola, de Rebus Christianis ante Constantinum.
(J) Zunz, Synagogale-Poesie d. Mittelalters.

XVI. LITURGIOLOGY AND HYMNOLOGY.

(A) Adams, Commentary on Prayer Book.
(O. C.) Alt-Katholisches Rituale.
(R) Arevalus, Hymnodia Hispanica.
(R) Assemani, Codex Liturgicus.
(R) Azevedo, Exercitat. Liturg.
(A) Badger, Nestorians and their Rituals.
(A) Barry, Teachers' Prayer Book.
(A) Bailey, Rituale Anglo-Catholic.
(A) Bennett, Catechism of Devotion.
(R) Bickell, Messe und Pascha.
(R) Biel, Expositio Canonis Missæ.
(A) *Blunt, Annotated Prayer Book.
(R) Bona, Psalmodia Divina.
(R) Bona de Rebus Liturgicis. Ed. Sala.
(A) Brett on the Ancient Liturgies.
(R) Breviarium Ambrosianum.
(A) Breviarium Eborac. (Surtees Soc.)
(R) Breviarium Monasticum.
(R) Breviarium Mozarabicum.
(R) Breviarium Ord. Prædicat.
(R) Breviarium Parisiense.
(R) Breviarium Parisiense. Noailles, 1713.
(R) Breviarium Quignonianum.
(R) Breviarium Romanum.
(R) Breviarium Rotomagense.
(A) Breviarium ad Usum Sarum.
(A) Breviarium Sarisbur. (Camb. Univ. Press).
(R) *Bridgett, Ritual of N. T.
(A) *Bright and Medd, Latin Prayer Book.
(A) *Bulley, Variations of Communion and Baptismal Offices.
(R) Cæremoniale Episcoporum.
(L) Calvör, Rituale Ecclesiasticum.
(A) Cardwell, History of Conferences on Common Prayer.
(A) Cardwell, Two Books, 1549, 1552.
(R) Carpo, Compendiosa Bibliotheca Liturgica.
(L) Cassander, Liturgica.
(R) Catalani Opera.
(R) Cavalieri (J. M.) Opera.
(A) Chambers, Divine Worship in England.
Christ et Paranikas, Anthologia Græca Carminum Christianorum.
(A) Clay, Prayer Book Illustrated.
(R) Clichtoveus, Elucidatorium.
(R) Dale, Ceremonial of Roman Rite.
(L) *Daniel, Codex Liturgicus.
(L) *Daniel, Thesaurus Hymnologic.
(A) Daniel, The Prayer Book.
(A) Deer, The Book of
(R) De Moléon, Voyages Liturgiques.

(R) *Denzinger, Ritus Orientalium.
(R) De Vert, Cérémonies de l'Eglise.
(A) Directorium Anglicanum.
(R) Dozio, de Cærem. Ambrosiano.
(R) Drouven, de Re Sacramentali.
(R) Durandus, Rationale.
(R) Durantus, de Ritibus Ecclesiæ.
(A) Egbert's Pontifical. (Surtees Soc.)
(A) †Forbes (Geo.), Panoply.
(R) *Fornici, Institutiones Liturgicæ.
(A) Freeman, Principles of Divine Service.
(R) Gandolphy, Book of Common Prayer.
(R) Gavanti, Thesaurus Rituum, à Merati.
(R) Gerbert, Liturg. Alemannica.
(R) Goar, Euchologion Græcorum.
(A) Goulburn, The Collects.
(R) Grancolas, Commentarius Historicus in Brev. Rom.
(R) Grancolas, Traité de la Messe et de l'Office Divin.
(E) Greek Service Books.
 Euchologion.
 Horologion.
 Menæa. 12 vols.
 Octoechus.
 Paracletice.
 Pentecostarion.
 Triodion.
 S. Gregory, Sacramentary.
(R) Guéranger, Institutions Liturg.
(R) Guyetus, Heortologia.
(R) Habert, Archieraticon Græcum.
(A) Hall, Fragmenta Liturgica.
(A) Hall, Reliquiæ Liturgicæ.
(A) *Hammond, Liturgies Eastern and Western.
(A) Hierurgia Anglicana.
(R) Hittorpius, de Offic. Eccl.
(A) Howard, Christians of S. Thomas and their Liturgies.
(J) Isaacs, Jewish Ceremonies.
(A) Bishop Jacobson, Fragm. Illustr. of Hist. of Common Prayer.
(A) Jebb on Choral Service.
(A) Julian, Dictionary of Hymnology.
(A) Karslake, Litany of Eng. Church.
(A) Keeling, Liturgiæ Britannicæ.
(A) Kehrein, Lateinische Sequenzen.
(A) King, Rites of Greek Church in Russia.
(R) Krazer, de Liturgiis Eccles. Occident.
(A) Lathbury, History of Prayer Bk.
(R) Le Brun, Explication de la Messe.
(A) Leofric Missal. Ed. Warren.
(A) L'Estrange, Alliance of Divine Offices.
(R) Le Vavasseur, Cérémonial Romain.

(R) Lienhard, de Antiquis Liturgiis.
(A) Littledale, Offices of the Eastern Church.
(R) Liturgia Armena in Italiano.
(R) Liturgical Discourse on H. Sacrifice of the Mass, by A. F. 1670.
(A) Liturgies of Edward VI. (Parker Society.)
(A) Liturgical Services of Queen Elizabeth. (Parker Society.)
(R) Lüft, Liturgik.
(R) Mabillon, Liturgia Gallicana.
(R) Mabillon, Iter Italicum.
(A) Malan, Coptic Documents.
(A) Malan, Armenian Offices.
(A) Manuale Eboracense. (Surtees Society.)
(R) *Martene, de Antiquis Ecclesiæ Ritibus.
(A) Maskell, Ancient Liturgy of the Church of England. (2nd ed. 1846.)
(A) *Maskell, Monumenta Ritualia Eccl. Angl.
(C) Miller, Singers and Songs of the Church.
(R) Missale Ambrosianum.
(A) Missale de Arbuthnot.
 Missale Drummondiense.
(A) Missale Eboracense. Ed. Henderson.
(A) Missale Herefordense. Ed. Henderson.
(R) Missale Mozarabicum.
(R) Missale Parisiense. Gondy, 1654.
(R) Missale Parisiense. Vintimille.
(R) Missale Romanum.
(A) Missale Sarisburiense. (Also English Translation.)
 Missale Vetus Hibernic. (Warren).
(R) Mone, Hymni Latini.
(R) Mone, Lateinische u. Griechische Messen.
(R) Muratori, Liturg. Rom.
(A) Myroure of Oure Ladye.
(A) Neale, Essays in Liturgiology.
(A) *Neale, Primitive Liturgies, and Translation.
(A) Neale, Sequentiæ e Missalibus.
(A) Neale, Tetralogia Liturgica.
(A) Neale and Forbes, Gallican Liturgies.
(A) Notes on Ceremonial.
(A) *Palmer, Origines Liturgicæ.
(R) Pamelius, Liturgica Latinorum.
(A) *Parker, Introduction to Books of Common Prayer.
(A) Parker, First Prayer Book of Edward VI.
(J) Pedahzur, Prayers of the Jews.
(A) Pickering's Prayer Books of 1549, 1552, 1559, 1603, and 1662.

(R) Pimont, Les Hymnes du Brev. Rom.
(R) Pitra, Hymnographie de l'Eglise Grecque.
(A) Pontificale Exoniense.
(R) Pontificale Romanum.
(A) *Prayer Book Interleaved.
(A) Prayer Book with Commentary. (S. P. C. K.)
(A) Priest to the Altar.
(A) Private Prayers, Queen Elizabeth. (Parker Soc.)
(R) Probst, Brevier u. Breviergebet.
(R) Probst, Liturgie in 3 ersten Jahrh.
(A) Processionale ad Usum Sarum.
(A) *Procter, Hist. of Book of Common Prayer.
(A) Bp. Rattray, Comparison of Ancient Liturgies.
(A) Rattray, Liturgy of S. James.
(R) Raulin, Liturgia Malabarica.
(R) *Renaudot, Coll. Liturg. Orient.
(A) *Ritual Conformity.
(A) Ritual Reason Why. 2nd edit.
(R) Rock, Church of our Fathers.
(R) Rock, Hierurgia.
(R) Rodwell, Ethiopic Liturgies.
(E) Romanoff, Rites and Customs of Græco-Russian Church.
(R) Schmidt, Manuale Liturgicum.
(A) *Scudamore, Notitia Eucharistica. 2nd ed.
(A) Sharp on the Rubric.
(A) Shipley, Ritual of the Altar.'
(R) Sicardi Mitrale. (Migne.)
(A) Simmons, Lay Folks' Mass Book.
(A) Sparrow, Liturgical Tracts.
(A) Sparrow, Rationale.
(A) Spark, Scintilla Altaris.
(C) Sprott, Scottish Liturgies of James VI.
(A) Stephens (A.J.), Irish Prayer Book.
(R) Thiers, Traité de l'Exposition du S. Sacrement.
(R) Card. Thomasii Opera.
(A) Three Primers of Henry VIII.
(A) Trollope, Greek Liturgy of S. James.
(L) Wackernagel, Deutsche Kirchenlied.
(A) Walton and Medd, Book of 1549.
(A) Warren, Liturgy and Ritual of Celtic Church.
(A) Wheatly on Book of Common Prayer. Ed. Corrie.
(A) Bp. Wilson on the LORD's Supper. Ed. Dr. Wright.
(A) Wirgman, Prayer Book with Scripture Proofs.
(A) York Manual. Ed. Henderson.
(A) York Pontifical. Ed. Henderson.
(R) Zaccaria, Bibliotheca Ritualis.

XVII. ECCLESIASTICAL AND CANON LAW.

(R) André, Dictionnaire de Droit Canon. (Ed. Migne.)
(A) Ayliffe, Parergon Juris Anglici.
(E) Balsamon, Comm. in Can. Apost.
(R) *Benedict. XIV. de Synodo Diocesana.
(A) Beveridge, Codex Canonum Eccl. Primitivæ.
(A) Beveridge, Pandecta Canonum.
(A) *Blunt, Book of Church Law.
(L) Böhmer, Jus Ecclesiasticum.
(R) Bouix, Princip. Jur. Can.
(A) Bright, Notes on Canons of First Four General Councils.
(A) Brooke, Churchwarden's Guide.
(L) *Bruns, Canones Apost. et Concc.
(A) Burn, Ecclesiastical Law. Ed. Phillimore.
(R) Carranza, Summa Conciliorum.
(R) Corpus Juris Canonici. Ed. Friedberg.
(R) Craisson, Communautés Religieuses à Vœux Simples.
(A) Cripps, Laws which affect the Clergy.
(A) Dale, Clergyman's Legal Handbook.
(R) Dictionnaire Eccles. et Canonique Portatif.
(A) Digest of Canons of the American Church.
(R) Denzinger, Eucheiridion.
(R) Dupin, de Antiq. Eccl. Disciplina.
(R) Ferraris, Prompta Bibliotheca Canonica.
(R) Fleury, Institution au Droit Ecclesiastique.
(A) Fulton, Index Canonum.
(A) Gibson, Codex Juris Eccl. Angl.
(A) Godolphin, Repertorium Juris.
(R) Gratiani Decretale, comm. Turrecremata.
(R) †Guyot, Somme des Conciles.
(A) Haddan and Stubbs, Councils and Documents, Gr. Brit. and Irel.
(A) Hammond, Definitions and Canons of Six General Councils.
(R) Hermant, Clavis Eccl. Disciplinæ.
(A) Hodgson, Instruct. for Clergy.
(A) Howard, Canons of Nicæa, Ancyra, &c.
(A) Johnson, English Canons.
(A) Joyce, Sword and Keys.
(R) Justellus, Bibliotheca Jur. Canon.
(A) Lambert, Codex Canonum Eccl. Universæ.
(A) *Landon, Manual of Councils.
(R) *Lequeux, Manuale Jur. Canon.
(R) Lupus, Synodorum Decreta.

(R) Luzerne, Droits et Devoirs des Evêques et des Prêtres.
(R) Lyndewode, Provinciale. Ed. 1679.
(R) Mansi, Concilia.
(A) Oughton, Ordo Judiciorum.
(A) *Phillimore, Ecclesiastical Law.
(A) Phillimore, Eccl. Judgments.
(A) Prideaux, Churchwarden's Guide.
(A) Reformatio Legum.
(R) Reiffenstühl, Jus Canon. Universum.
(R) Richard, Analysis Conciliorum.
(R) Schulte, Geschichte der Quellen u. Literatur d. Canon. Rechts.
(R) Schulte, Lehrbuch des Kath. Kirchenrechts.
(A) Smith, Summary of Law and Practice of Eccl. Courts.
(R) Soglia, Institut. Juris Canonici.
(A) Spelman, Concilia.
(A) Stephen's Ecclesiastical Statutes.
(A) Stopford, Handbook of Eccl. Law.
(R) Thomassin, Vetus et Nova Eccl. Disciplina.
(A) Urlin, Legal Guide for Clergy.
(R) *Van Espen, Jus Ecclesiasticum. Ed. 1781.
(A) Walcott, Canons of the Church of England.
(R) *Walter, Lehrbuch d. Kanon. Rechts. (Also French Trans. by Du Roquemont.)
(A) Wilkins, Concilia.

XVIII. Position and Principles of the Church of England.

(A) *Allies, Church of England cleared from Schism. 2nd ed.
(A) Andrewes, Answer to Bellarmine.
(A) Andrewes, Answer to Card. Perrone.
(A) Bailey, Defensio Ordinum Eccl. Angl.
(A) Bailey, Jurisdiction and Mission.
(A) Baker, Lectures on Church of Eng.
(A) Barrow on Papal Supremacy.
(A) Bennett, Church's Broken Unity.
(R) Bossuet, Defensio Cleri Gallicani.
(A) Bramhall, Works.
(A) Brewer, Endowments of Church of England.
(A) Bp. Browne on XXXIX. Articles.
(A) Bp. Bull, Vindication of Ch. of Eng.
(A) Church and World. 3 vols.
(A) Churton, Defence of English Ordinal.
(R) Courayer, Defence of Anglican Orders.
(A) Cox (Homersham), Is the Church of England Protestant?

(A) Curteis, Bampton Lectures on Dissent.
(A) Edwards, Babel of the Sects.
(A) Englishman's Brief on behalf of his National Church.
(A) Bp. of Exeter, Letters to Butler.
(A) *Farrar, The Christian Ministry.
(A) Bp. Forbes, Considerationes Modestæ.
(A) Forbes (Bp. of Brechin) on Thirty-nine Articles.
(A) *Freeman, Disestablishment and Disendowment.
(A) Fuller, Court of Final Appeal.
(A) Garnier, Church and Dissent.
(A) Gladstone, Rome and Newest Fashions in Religion.
(A) Gladstone, Church Principles in their Results.
(A) Gladstone, Gleanings, Vols. V. and VI.
(R) Gratry, Lettres à Mgr. Dechamps. (Also English Trans.)
(E) Guettée, Papauté Schismatique.
(A) Haddan, Apostolical Succession in Church of England.
(A) Hardwick, Hist. of Articles.
(A) Hook, Church and its Ordinances.
(A) *Hooker, Eccl. Polity. Ed. Keble.
(A) Hope, Worship in Church of England.
(A) Hope, Worship and Order.
(A) Hussey, Papal Supremacy.
(A) Irons, Dr. Newman and English Orders.
(A) Irons on Eccl. Jurisdiction.
(A) Jenkins, Privilege of Peter.
(A) Laud, Conference with Fisher.
(A) *Lee, Validity of Holy Orders in Church of England.
(A) Leslie, Case stated.
(A) Lord Lindsay, Œcumenicity of Church of England.
(A) Lord Lindsay, Scepticism and the Church of England.
(A) *Littledale, Plain Reasons against Joining the Church of Rome.
(A) MacColl, Lawlessness, Sacerdotalism, Ritualism. (3rd edition.)
(A) Mahan, Exercise of Faith.
(A) Manning, Rule of Faith.
(A) Manning, Unity of the Church.
(A) Mason, Vindiciæ Eccl. Anglicanæ.
(A) Mines, Presbyterian Clergyman looking for the Church.
(A) Moberly, Law of Love.
(A) Mozley, Theory of Development.
(A) *Newman, Romanism and Popular Protestantism.
(A) *Newman, Tract XC., with Preface by Pusey.
(A) Palmer on Development.

(A) Palmer, Letters to Wiseman.
(A) Palmer, Results of Gladstone's Expostulation.
(A) Papal Claims considered in Light of Scripture and History.
(A) Preface to Tertullian. (Oxf. Lib. Fathers.)
(A) Preface to S. Cyprian. (Lib. of Fathers.)
(A) *Pusey, Eirenicon.
(R) Renouf, Case of Pope Honorius.
(A) Robertson, Growth of Papal Power. ·
(A) Ross-Lewin, Continuity of Church of England.
(A) Russell (J. F.), Judgment of. Ch. of Eng. on Sufficiency of Scripture.
(R) Sancta Clara on XXXIX. Articles.
(A) Scudamore, England and Rome.
(A) Scudamore, Letters to a Seceder.
(A) Swete, England v. Rome.
(R) Tabarand, Institution Canonique des Evêques.
(A) Thorndike, Works.
(A) Tracts for the Times.
(A) Twysden, Histor. Vindicat. of Ch. of Eng.
(A) Ussher, Answer to a Jesuit.
(A) Wordsworth, Theophilus Anglicanus.

XIX. Ascetic and Devotional Books.

(R) Alvarez de Paz, de Virtutum Adeptione. Vita Religiosa.
(A) *Andrewes, Preces Privatæ.
(R) Androtius, Considerat. de Frequenti Communione.
(R) *S. Anselmi Meditationes.
(R) Arias, Tractatus Spiritualis.
(R) *Austin, Devotions.
(R) Avancini, Vita et Doctrina Jesu Christi.
(R) Avrillon, L'Année Affective. Guides for Advent and Lent. (English by Pusey.)
(R) *Baker (Augustin), Sancta Sophia.
(R) Baudrand, L'Ame sur le Calvaire.
(P) Baxter, Saint's Everlasting Rest.
(R) Bellarminus, de Ascensione Mentis in Deum.
(R) *Bellarminus, de Septem Verbis in Cruce prolatis. (Also Eng. Vers.)
(A) Benson, Spiritual Readings—Advent.
(R) Beuvelet, Méditations.
(R) Bibliotheca Ascetica. (Heberle.)
(R) Bibliotheca Ascetica. (Pez.)
(R) Blosii Opera.
(R) *Bona, Tract. Ascet. de Sacrif. Missæ, et Opuscula.

(R) S. Bonaventura, Stimulus Divini Amoris.
(R) Boppert, Scutum Fidei.
(R) Boudon, Vie Cachée de J.-C.
(A) Brett, Churchman's Guide.
(A) Bright, Ancient Collects.
(A) Brown (Lundin), Life of Peace.
(R) Camus, Esprit de S. François de Sales.
(A) Carter, Meditations on the Public Life of our Lord.
(R) Castanitza, Spiritual Conflict.
(R) Challoner, Meditations.
(A) Chandler, Horæ Sacræ.
(R) Cœleste Palmetum.
(A) Cresswell, Aids to Meditation.
(R) De Ponte, Christiani Hominis Perfectio.
(R) De Ponte, Meditations.
(R) Dirckink, Semita Perfectionis.
(R) Drexelii Opera.
(R) Duguet, Traité de la Croix de J.-C.
(R) Duquesne, L'Evangile Medité.
(R) Faber, Growth in Holiness.
(R) Faber, All for Jesus; Bethlehem.
(A) Bp. Forbes, Deepening of the Spiritual Life.
(R) *S. Francis de Sales, Devout Life.
(R) S. Francis de Sales, Love of God.
(A) Furse, Helps to Holiness.
(R) Gaudier, de Perfectione.
(R) Gautrelet, Traité de l'Etat Religieux.
(R) Gay, De la Vie et des Vertus Chrétiennes. 2 v.
(L) Gerhardt, Meditationes Sacræ.
(A) Goulburn, Pursuit of Holiness.
(A) Goulburn, Thoughts on Personal Religion.
(R) Gracian, Sanctuary Meditations.
(R) Grou, Intérieur de Jesus.
(R) Grou, Manuel des Ames Intérieures.
(R) Grou, Maximes Spirituelles.
(R) Grou, Science Pratique du Crucifix.
(R) Guéranger, The Liturgical Year.
(R) Guevara, Mysteries of Mount Calvary.
(R) Guevara, Oratorio de los Religiosos.
(R) Guilloré, Conférences.
(R) Hilton, Scale of Perfection. Ed. Guy.
(R) Hours at the Altar.
(A) Keble, Letters of Spiritual Counsel.
(A) Ken, Practice of Divine Love.
(R) Kroust, Meditationes.
(R) Lancisius, Opera.
(A) Law, Christian Perfection.

(A) Law, Spirit of Prayer.
(A) Law, Serious Call.
(A) Lear, Light of the Conscience.
(R) Lessius, de Nominibus Dei.
(R) Libellus Libellorum.
(R) Liguori, Love of CHRIST reduced to Practice.
(R) Liguori, Preparation for Death.
(R) Ludovicus Granatensis, Paradisus Precum.
(R) Luis de Granada, Opuscula. ·
(R) Luis de Granada, Christian Life.
(R) *Luis de Granada, Sinner's Guide.
(R) Luis de Granada, de Perfectione Amoris.
    S. Macarius, Christian Perfection.
(R) Manna Quotidianum.
(R) Manuale Ordinandorum.
(A) Marriott, Hints on Private Devotion.
(A) Medd, Hours of the Passion.
(R) Medulla Asceseos.
(R) Memoriale Vitæ Christianæ.
(R) *Merlo-Horstius. Paradisus Animæ Christianæ. (Engl. Trans.)
(A) *Milman, Love of the Atonement.
(C) Monod (Adolphe), Adieux.
(R) Nepveu, Œuvres.
(R) *Neudecker, Schola Religiosa.
(R) Neumayer, Triduana Exercitia.
(R) Nieremberg, Opera.
(R) Nouet, Life of JESUS CHRIST in Glory.
(R) Nouet, Œuvres.
(R) Ochoa, Tesoro de las Obras Misticas Espanoles.
(R) Palma, Hist. of Passion. (Tr. Coleridge.)
(R) *Pascal, Pensées.
(R) Perreyve, Journée du Malade.
(R) Pinamonti, Opera.
(R) Pinart, Les Flammes de l'Amour de JESUS. (Tr. Forbes, Meditations on the Life of CHRIST.)
(R) Pinart, Nourriture de l'Ame Chrétienne. (Also Tr. Forbes.)
(A) Pollock, Resting Places.
(R) Possinus, Thesaurus Asceticus.
(A) Pusey, Addresses to Companions of the Love of JESUS.
(R) Reflections and Prayers on Holy Communion.
(A) The Reformed Monastery.
(R) *Rodriguez on Spiritual and Religious Perfection. 3 vols.
(A) Rossetti, Annus Domini.
(R) Saint-Jure, Connaissance et Amour de Dieu.
(R) Saint-Jure, Homme Spirituel.
(R) Saint-Jure, Livre des Élus.

(R) Saint-Jure, L'Homme Religieux.
(R) Scaramelli, Directorium Asceticum.
(R) Schram, Institutiones Theologiæ Mysticæ.
(R) Scientia Sanctorum.
(R) Scotti, Meditations for Clergy.
(A) Scougal, Life of GOD in the Soul.
(R) *Scupoli, Spiritual Combat.
(A) Sherlock, Practical Christian.
(R) Sibthorp, Daily Bread.
(A) Skinner, Compendium of Moral and Ascetical Theology.
(R) *Spiritual Exercises of S. Ignatius.
(R) Stella, de Amore Dei.
(R) Stella, Contemptus Mundi Vanitatum.
(R) Stub, Méditations Ecclesiastiques.
(A) Sutton, Disce Vivere, and Disce Mori.
(A) *Taylor, Holy Living and Dying.
(R) *Thomas à Kempis, de Imitatione CHRISTI, et Opuscula.
(R) *Fra Thomé, Sufferings of JESUS.
(A) Treasury of Devotion.
(R) Tronson, Examen de Conscience.
(R) Tronson, Forma Cleri.
(A) Vaux, CHRIST on the Cross.
(R) Verrepæus, Enchiridion Precum Piarum.
(R) Via Vitæ Æternæ, Anton. Sucquet.
(A) Virgin's Lamp.
(R) Vitis Mystica. (Tr. Brownlow.)
(A) *Wilberforce (William), Practical View.
(A) Bishop Wilson, Maxims.
(A) *Wilson, Sacra Privata.
(A) Young (Peter), Daily Readings.

XX. SERMONS AND SERMON MATERIALS.

(A) Bp. Abraham, Sermons.
(P) Adams (Thomas), Sermons.
(A) Allestree, Sermons.
(A) Andrewes, Ninety-six Sermons.
(R) Arias, Thesaurus Bonorum Christi.
(A) Arnold, Sermons to Boys.
(A) Ashley, Promptuary for Preachers.
(A) Ashley, Year with Great Preachers.
(R) Bail, Théologie Affective.
(C) Baldwin Brown, Sermons on the Higher Life.
(A) Baring-Gould, Post-Mediæval Preachers.
(A) Baring-Gould, Preacher's Pocket.
(A) Baring-Gould, Sermons for Children.
(A) Baring-Gould, Sketches of Sermons.

(A) Baring-Gould, Village Conferences on Creed.
(A) Baring-Gould, Village Preaching.
(A) Baring-Gould, Village Pulpit.
(A) Barrow, Sermons. Ed. Napier.
(R) Barzia, Sermones Missionales.
(R) Bautain, Extempore Preaching.
(A) Benham, Companion to Lectionary.
(C) Bersier, Sermons.
(R) Billot, Prônes.
(L) Binchius, Mellificium Theolog.
(A) Prof. Blunt, Sermons.
(C) Boase, Tithes and Offerings.
(R) Bossuet.
(R) Bouillerie, Symbolisme de la Nature. 2 vols.
(R) Bourdaloue.
(L) Brandmüller, Conciones Funebres.
(A) Bright, Faith and Life.
(A) †Brooke (Stopford), Sermons.
(A) Brooks, Lectures on Preaching.
(R) Brydaine.
(A) Bull, Sermons.
Burgess on Art of Preaching.
(A) Butler (Archer), Sermons.
(A) Carter, Lenten Lectures.
(A) Carter, Sermons.
(U) †Channing, Works.
(C) Cheever, Moral and Relig. Anecd.
(A) Church, Sermons at Oxford.
(R) Combefis, Bibl. Patr. Conciona-toria.
(A) Cotton, Marlborough Sermons to Boys.
(A) Cowley-Brown, Daily Lessons on Life of our LORD.
(C) Dale, Lectures on Preaching.
(R) De Fonseca, Quadragesimale.
(R) De Kerckhoove, Manuale Missio-num.
(R) De la Rue, Sermons.
(R) De Ponte, Meditations on Myste-ries of the Faith.
(R) De Roquefort, Dict. des Predica-teurs.
(R) De Thoulouse, Sermons pour les Missions.
(C) Dictionary of Illustrations. (Dick-enson, publisher.)
(R) *Diez, Conciones.
(R) Digby (Kenelm), Compitum.
(R) Dirrhaimer, Sermones de Sanctis.
(A) Donne, Sermons.
(C) Du Bosc, Sermons.
(R) Dupanloup, La Prédication popu-laire.
(R) Duquesne, L'Evangile Medité.
(C) Eadie, Classified Bible.
(A) Ellicott, Destiny of the Creature.
(A) Erskine, Sermons.
(R) Faber, Notes on Doctrinal and Spiritual Subjects.

(R) Faber, Spiritual Conferences; Creator and Creature.
(A) Farindon's Sermons.
(R) Félix, Conférences.
(R) Fénelon.
(R) Fléchier.
(A) Bp. Forbes, Sermons.
(A) Frank, Sermons.
(A) Freeman, Advent Sermons.
(A) Fuller, Works.
(R) Gabriel, Le Christ et le Monde.
(R) Gesta Romanorum.
(R) Gother, Sermons.
(A) Gray and Pearse, Short Allegorical Sermons.
(A) Bishop Hacket, Works.
(A) *Bp. Hall, Contemplations.
(C) Hall (Robert), Works.
(A) Hancock, CHRIST and the People.
(A) Hare, Alton Sermons.
(A) Hare, Guesses at Truth.
(A) Hare (A.W.), Sermons on LORD's Prayer.
(R) Hartung, Sermones.
(A) Hole, Hints to Preachers.
(A) Holland, Logic and Life.
(C) Hood (E. P.), World of Religious Anecdote.
(A) Hook, University Sermons.
(A) Bp. Horsley, Sermons.
(R) Houdry, Bibliotheca Conciona-toria.
(A) Housman, Sermon Stories (for Children).
(C) Howe, Works.
(A) Hutchings, Person and Work of the HOLY GHOST.
(A) Hutchings, Aspects of the Cross.
(A) Hutchings, Mystery of Tempta-tion.
(I) †Irving (Edward), Works.
(A) Jacox, Secular Annot. on Scripture Texts.
(A) Jacox, Scripture Proverbs.
(A) Jacox, Bible Music.
(A) S. James's, Piccadilly, Lectures on Devout Life.
(A) Jelf (G. E.), Sermons.
(R) Justiniani (Laurentii) Sermones.
(A) Keble, Academical Sermons.
(A) Keble, Sermons for Christian Year.
(A) Keble, Outlines for Instruction and Meditation.
(A) Keble College Sermons.
(A) Kingsley, Sermons.
(R) Labata, Thesaurus Moralis.
(R) Lacordaire, Conférences.
(R) Lambert, L'Année Evangelique.
(R) Bp. Landriot, Œuvres.
(R) Landriot, The Valiant Woman.
(R) Landriot, Sins of the Tongue.

(A) Lee, Advent Sermons.
(A) Leighton, Works. Ed. West.
(R) Lejeune, Sermons.
(A) Liddon, University Sermons.
(R) Liguori, Sermons.
(R) Lohner, Biblioth. Manual. Concionatoria.
(R) Loriot, Prônes.
(R) Luis de Granada, Sermones.
(L) Luthardt, Moral Truths of Christianity.
(C) Macmillan, Bible Teachings in Nature.
(C) Macmillan, The True Vine.
(C) Macmillan, The Garden and the City.
(C) Macmillan, Sabbath of the Fields.
(A) Mahan, Works.
(A) Archdeacon Manning, Sermons.
(R) Mansi, Bibliotheca Moralis.
(R) Marchantius, Hortus Pastorum.
(L) Martensen, Christian Ethics.
(R) Martin, Panorama des Prédicateurs.
(R) Martin, Dictionnaire de la Prédication.
(U) Martineau, Endeavours after Christian Life.
(R) Massillon.
(R) Matthias Faber, Opus Tripartitum.
(A) Maurice, Lectures on Conscience.
(A) Melvill, Sermons.
(R) Migne, Orateurs Sacrés.
(A) Mill, University Sermons.
(A) Bp. Moberly, Sermons.
(A) Monro, Sermons.
(R) Moral Concordances of S. Antony of Padua.
(A) Mortimer, Notes for Meditation.
(A) Mozley, Parochial Sermons.
(A) *Mozley, University Sermons.
(R) Abbé Mullois, Clergy and Pulpit.
(R) Mullois, Eloquence Sacrée Populaire.
(R) Nampon, Manuel du Missionnaire.
(A) Neale, Lectures on Church Difficulties.
(A) Neale, Mediæval Preachers.
(A) Neale, Sermons in a Religious House.
(A) Neale, Sermons on the Song of Songs.
(A) *Neale, Sackville College Sermons.
(A) *Newman, Parochial and Plain Sermons.
(R) *Nicole, Instruct. Theolog. et Moral.
(C) Oosterzee, Year of Salvation.
(R) Osorii Sermones.
Outlines of Sermons on O. and N. T. (Hodder and Stoughton, pub.)

(A) Papers on Preaching, by a Wykehamist.
(A) Plain Sermons by Editors of "Tracts for the Times."
(A) Pollock, Gospel Words.
(R) Potter, Extempore Preaching.
(R) Potter, Sacred Eloquence.
(R) Potter, The Pastor and his People.
(A) Prynne, Parochial Sermons.
(A) Pusey, Parochial Sermons.
(A) Pusey, University Sermons.
(R) Ravignan, Conférences.
(R) Robert, Aurifodina Universalis.
(A) †Robertson (F. W.), Sermons.
(R) Rossi (Quirico) Sermons. (Tr. by Ashley.)
(L) †Rothe, Nachgelassene Predigten.
(R) Savonarola, Opere.
(R) *Schouppe, Adjumenta Oratoris Sacri.
(R) *Schouppe in Evangelia.
(R) Schouppe, Cursus Script. Sacr.
(R) Segneri, Homo Christianus.
(R) Segneri, Manna Animæ.
(R) Segneri, Quaresimale. (A partial Translation by Ford.)
(R) Ségur, Instructions.
(R) Sermons à l'usage des Missions.
(R) Sermons by the Paulists.
(A) Singleton, Sermons to Boys.
(A) South, Sermons.
(C) Spencer and Cowdray, Storehouse of Similes.
(R) Stapleton, Promptuarium.
(C) †Talmage, Sermons.
(R) Tauler, Sermons.
(A) Taylor (Jeremy), Sermons.
(R) Tharin, Atlas des Prédicateurs.
(R) S. Thomas Aquinas, Homilies. (Tr. by Ashley.)
(R) Traité de la Prédication. Par M. le Curé de S. Sulpice.
(A) Abp. Trench, Sermons.
(C) Vaughan, Children's Sermons.
(A) Vaux, Preaching—How to Preach and What to Preach.
(A) Vaux, Preacher's Storehouse.
(A) Vaux, Sermon Notes.
(R) Ventura, Sermons.
(R) Vieyra, Sermoes.
(C) Vinet, Discours.
(A) Wilkinson, Mission Sermons.
(A) Williams (Isaac), Characters of Holy Scripture.
(A) *Williams (Isaac), Sermons on the Catechism.
(A) Bp. Wilberforce, Sermons, Essays, and Mission Speeches.
(A) Woodford, Sermons.
(A) Wroth, Mystical Sermons.
(A) Young (Peter), Sermons for a Year.

XXI. CATECHETICALS.

(A) Adams, Comment. on Prayer Book.
(A) Andrewes, Catech. Doctrine.
(A) Arden, Aids to Catechising.
Bagster's 4000 Scripture Questions and Answers.
(A) Barry, Notes on Catechism.
(A) Bather, Hints on Catechising.
(A) Beaven, Aids to Catechising.
(A) Benham, How to Teach the Old Testament.
(A) Boyce, Catech. Hints and Helps.
(R) Canisius, Opus Catechisticum.
(A) Carter, Simple Lessons.
(A) *Catechism of Theology.
(R) *Catéchisme de Montpellier.
(R) Catéchismes Philosophiques. Migne.
(A) The Catechist's Manual.
(R) *Catechismus Conc. Tridentini.
(R) Cossart, Science Pratique du Catéchiste.
(R) Dupanloup, Entretiens sur le Catéchisme.
(R) Dupanloup, Méthode du Catéchisme.
(R) Dupanloup, L'Enfant.
(A) Ewer, Grammar of Theology.
(A) Fitch, Art of Teaching.
(R) Gaume, Catéchisme de Persévérance.
(A) Gibson, Catechism made Easy.
(C) Gray, Sunday School Guide.
(C) Gray, Topics for Teachers.
(A) *Grueber, Catechism on Church.
(R) Guillois, Catéchiste en Chaire.
(R) Guillois, Explication du Catéchisme.
(A) Hammond, Practical Catechism.
(A) Harper, Church Teaching for Children.
(A) Heathcote, Notes for Bible Teaching.
(A) Holy Teachings.
(R) Hornihold, Explan. of the Commandments and Sacraments.
(A) Jackson, Stories on Collects.
(A) Jackson, Stories on Catechism.
(A) Lear, Cousin Eustace.
(R) Martin, Cours supérieur d'Instruct. Relig.
(A) Menet, Practical Hints on Teaching.
(A) Mercier, Our Mother Church.
(A) Mill, Lectures on Catechism.
(A) *Monthly Paper of Sunday Teaching.
(A) Neale, Catechetical Notes.
(A) Northcote, Lesson Notes on Life of CHRIST.

(R) Nouveaux Plans d'Instruction, par un Curé de Liége.
(A) Pagan, Principles of Religion.
(A) Paget, Outlines of Church Teaching.
(A) Pash, Introductory Class-Book.
(R) Piété enseignée aux Enfans.
(R) *Poor Man's Catechism.
(A) Proby, Lessons on the Kingdom.
(A) *Sadler, ChurchTeacher's Manual.
(R) Schmid et Belet, Catéchisme Hist.
(R) Schmid et Belet, Repertoire du Catéchiste.
(R) Schmitt, Le Petit Catéchisme Expliqué.
(A) Stock, Lessons on the Acts.
(A) *Stock, Lessons on the Life of our LORD.
(A) Stretton, Catechism Explained.
(C) The Sunday School World.
(R) Tombret, Abrégé du Catéchisme.
(A) Wirgman, Prayer Book with Scripture Proofs.
(A) Bp. C. Wordsworth, Catechesis.
(A) Yonge, Conversations on Catechism.
(A) Yonge, Conversations on the Creed.
(A) Yonge, How to Teach the New Testament.

XXII. ETHNIC RELIGIONS.

BRAHMANISM.

Arnold, Book of Good Counsels.
Banerjea, Dialogues on Hindu Philos.
"Brahmanism," Encyc. Brit. 9th ed.
Burnouf, Bhâgavata Purâna, Histoire de Krishna.
Colebrooke, Essays on Relig. and Philosophy of Hindus. Ed. Cowell.
Elphinstone, Hist. of India. Ed. Cowell.
Haug, Aitareya Brahmana.
Julien, Les Avadânas, Contes et Apologues Indiens.
Langlois, Rig-Veda.
Manning, Ancient and Mediæval India.
Moor, Hindoo Pantheon.
Muir, Sanskrit Texts.
Max Müller, Hymns of the Rig-Veda.
Max Müller, Sacred Hymns of the Brahmins.
Max Müller, History of Ancient Sanskrit Literature.
Williams (Monier), Indian Wisdom.
Williams (M.), Hinduism. (S.P.C.K.)
Wilson (H. H.), Essays and Lectures.

BUDDHISM.

Alabaster, Wheel of the Law.
Arnold, Light of Asia.

Beal, Catena of Buddhist Scriptures.
Beal, Romantic Legend of Sakya Buddha.
Burnouf, Introd. à l'Hist. du Buddhisme Indien.
Burnouf, Saddharma Pundarîka, le Lotus de la bonne Loi.
Cunningham, Ladák.
Eidel, Lectures on Buddhism.
Hardy, Eastern Monachism.
Hardy, Manual of Buddhism.
Koeppen, Religion des Buddha.
Lillie, Popular Life of Buddha.
Max Müller, Buddhism and Buddhist Pilgrims.
Rhys Davids, Indian Buddhism.
St. Hilaire, Le Bouddha.
Schlagentweit, Buddhism in Tibet.
Schott, Buddhaismus in Hochasien.
Swamy, Sutta Nipáta, Dialogues of Gotama Buddha.
Wassiljew, Der Buddhismus. (Also French Trans.)

CONFUCIANISM, &c.

Callery, Li-ki, ou Mémorial des Rites.
Chalmers, Speculations of Lau-tsze.
De Guignes, Chou-King.
Douglas, Confucianism and Taouism.
Faber, Lehrbegriff des Confucius.
Faber, Quellen zu Confucius.
Gutzlaff, Chinese History.
Huc, Le Christianisme en Chine.
Julien (Stanislaus), Laou-tsze, Livre des Recompenses et des Peines; Laou-tseu Tao-te-king.
Julien, Voyages des Pélerins Bouddhistes.
Kesson, The Cross and the Dragon.
Legge, Chinese Classics.
Legge, Religions of China.
McClatchie, Chinese Theology. (Jour. As. Soc. 1856, xvi.)
McClatchie, Yih-King.
Malan, Who is GOD in China?
Marshman, Works of Confucius.
Medhurst, Shoo-King.
Medhurst, Theology of the Chinese.
Medhurst, Inquiry into the Word GOD in Chinese.
Neumann, Natur- und Religionsphilosophic der Chinesen. (Illgen's Zeitschrift, 1837.)
Pauthier, La Chine Moderne.
Pauthier, Confucius et Mencius.
Pauthier, Le Ta-kio.
Pauthier, Le Tao-te-king.
Pauthier, Livres Sacrés de l'Orient.
Schott, Confucius.

MOHAMMEDANISM.

Caussin de Perceval, Essai sur l'histoire des Arabes.
Döllinger, Muhammed's Religion.
Dugat, Histoire des Philosophes et des Theologiens Musulmanes.
Geiger, Was hat Mohammed aus den Judenthum genommen?
Gerock, Christologie des Koran.
Hughes, Notes on Mohammedanism.
Lane, Selections from Kur'án.
"Mohammedanism," Encyc. Brit. 8th edit.
Möhler, Verhältniss des Islams zum Evangelium.
Muir, Life of Mohammed.
Muir, The Koran. (S. P. C. K.)
Nöldeke, Geschichte d. Qorans.
Osborn, Islam under the Arabs.
Rodwell, Koran. 2nd edition.
Sale, Koran.
Smith (Bosworth), Mohammed and Mohammedanism. 2nd edit.
Sprenger, Leben und Lehre des Mohammed.
Stephens, Christianity and Islam.
Syed Ahmed Khan Bahadoor, Essays on Mohammed.
Syed Ameer Ali Moulvi, Life and Teachings of Mohammed.
Weil, Biblische Legenden der Muselmänner.
Weil, Einleitung in den Koran.
Weil, Mohammed der Prophet.

PARSEEISM.

†Hovelacque, D'Avesta.
Hyde, de Veteri Persarum Religione.
Wilson, The Parsi Religion.
Zendavesta, by Spiegel and Bleek.

POLYTHEISM, &c.

Bancroft, Native Races of the Pacific States, vol. iii.
Birch, Egyptian Ritual of the Dead.
Callaway, Religious System of the Amazulu.
Castren, Finnische Mythologie.
Champollion, Panthéon Egyptien.
Crantz, History of Greenland.
Faiths of the World. Lectures in Edinburgh.
Fergusson, Tree and Serpent Worship.
Gill, Myths and Songs of South Pacific.
Grey, Polynesian Mythology.
Lyde, Asian Mystery.
Lyde, The Ansyreeh.
Müller, Geschichte d. Amerikanischen Urreligion.

Le Maout and Decaisne, System of Botany. (Tr. Hooker.)
†Lewes, Biograph. Hist. of Philosophy.
Lewes, Physiology of Common Life.
Lindley, Treasury of Botany.
Longman's Text-books of Science.
Lubbock, Ants, Bees, and Wasps.
Lubbock, Chapters in Popular Natural History.
†Lyell, Antiquity of Man.
Lyell, Elements of Geology.
Lyell, Principles of Geology.
Macalister, Animal Morphology.
McCosh, Scottish Philosophy.
Macmillan's Science Primers.
Maine de Biran, Œuvres.
Malebranche, Œuvres.
†Mansel, Bampton Lectures.
Martensen, Christian Ethics. (Clark's F. T. L.)
†Martineau, Essays.
†Maudsley, Responsibility in Mental Disease.
Maurice, Moral and Metaphysical Philosophy.
Maury, Physical Geography of Sea.
†Mill, Political Economy.
†Mill, Logic.
Miller, Testimony of the Rocks.
Miller, Old Red Sandstone.
Mivart, Elementary Lessons in Anatomy.
Mivart, Genesis of Species.
Mivart, Lessons from Nature.
Mivart, Men and Apes.
Mivart, Nature and Thought.
More (Henry), Philosophical Works.
Max Müller, Lectures on Science of Language.
†Max Müller, Introduction to the Science of Religion.
Newman, Grammar of Assent.
Nicholson, Introduction to Biology.
Nicholson, Manuals of Zoology and Palæontology.
Owen, Comparative Anatomy.
Page, Text-books of Geology.
Parkes, Manual of Practical Hygeine.
Porter, The Human Intellect.
Prantl and Vines, Elementary Text-book of Botany.
Prichard, Natural History of Man.
Prichard, Researches into Phys. Hist. of Mankind.

Procter, Essays in Astronomy.
Quain, Dictionary of Medicine.
Reid, Works.
Rhind, Hist. of Vegetable Kingdom.
Ribot, Contemporary English Psychology.
Rollestone, Forms of Animal Life.
Roscoe, Elementary Chemistry.
Roscoe, Spectrum Analysis.
Sachs, Text-book of Botany.
Sayce, Principles of Comparative Philology.
†Schmidt, Doctrine of Descent and Darwinism.
Schwegler, Hist. of Philosophy, by Stirling.
Sewell, Christian Morals.
Sewell, Christian Politics.
*Smith (Adam), Wealth of Nations. Ed. McCulloch.
S. P. C. K. Manuals of Science.
†Spencer, Study of Sociology.
†Spinoza, Opera.
Stirling, Secret of Hegel.
Stewart (Balfour), Conservation of Energy.
Stewart (Dugald), Works.
Storz, Die Philosophie des H. Augustinus.
Abp. Thomson, Outlines of Laws of Thought.
Tylor, Anthropology.
Tylor, Early History of Mankind.
Tylor, Primitive Culture.
Tyndall, Lectures on Sound and Light.
Tyndall, Fragments of Science.
Ueberweg, System of Logic.
Ueberweg, History of Philosophy.
Vossii (G. J.) Opera.
Wallace, Contributions to Theory of Natural Selection.
Wallace, Geographical Distribution of Animals.
Whewell, Elements of Morality.
Whewell, Philosophy of Inductive Sciences.
Williamson, Chemistry.
Windischmann, Der Philosophie im Fortgang der Weltgeschichte.
Winn on Materialism.
Wyld, Physics and Philos. of the Senses.
Zeller, Greek Philosophical Schools.

INDEX TO COLLECTS.

(The figures denote pages.)

J. MASTERS AND CO., PRINTERS, ALBION BUILDINGS, BARTHOLOMEW CLOSE.